The Arcana of the Grail Angel

The Spiritual Science of the Holy Blood and of the Holy Grail
A study, developed out of the work of Rudolf Steiner, of the underground streams of Esoteric Christianity which flowed from the Brotherhood of the Holy Grail to the Order of the Knights Templars, and the true Rosicrucian Order.

by John Barnwell

"It is quite hard to realize that every soul possesses an organ better worth saving than a thousand eyes, because it is our only means of seeing the truth, and that when its light is dimmed or extinguished by other interests, these studies will purify the hearth and rekindle the sacred fire." Plato, *Republic*

Text & Diagrams

Foreword by Douglas J. Gabriel

Verticordia Press
Bloomfield Hills
1999

First published in the United States of America in 1999 by

Verticordia Press
726 E. Fox Hills
Bloomfield Hills, MI
48304-1361

Copyright © John Barnwell, 1999

All Rights Reserved.
No part of this publication may be reproduced,
stored in a retrieval system, or transmitted in
any form or by any means, electronic, mechanical
photocopying, recording or otherwise without
the prior permission of the publisher.
Reviewers may quote brief passages.

ISBN 0-9671503-0-2 (pbk.)

Table of Contents

Table of Contents 3
Foreword by Douglas J. Gabriel 9
Dedication 17
Initiation: An Introduction 23
Prologue 29
Lady Adventure 45

Part 1

The Major Arcana

0.   The Fool - Alchemical Sulfur 55
      Parzival - the "Noble Traveler"

I.   The Magician - Mercury 85
      Archangel Raphael
      Healing - 6 Petaled Lotus

II.   The High Priestess - Moon 101
      Archangel Gabriel
      Birth - 4 Petaled Lotus

III.   The Empress - Venus 121
      Archangel Anael
      Love - 10 Petaled Lotus

IV.   The Emperor - Aries 145
      Christ - the "King of Kings" - the "Lamb of God"
      the Son - the 2nd Logos - the "Word"

V.   The Hierophant - Taurus 165
      the Holy Spirit - the 3rd Logos - the Gift of Tongues
      St. Luke - the Doctor - the Initiate of Feeling

VI.   The Lovers - Gemini 187
      Seraphim - Spirits of Love

VII.   The Chariot - Cancer 203
      Cherubim - Spirits of Harmony

VIII.	Strength - Leo	217
	Thrones - Spirits of Will	
	St. Mark - the Lawyer - the Initiate of Will and Social Order	
IX.	The Hermit - Virgo	227
	Kyriotetes - Spirits of Wisdom	
	Spirit-Man	
	Isis-Sophia	
X.	The Wheel of Fortune - Jupiter	239
	Archangel Zachariel	
	Thought - 2 Petaled Lotus	
XI.	Justice - Libra	247
	Dynamis - Spirits of Movement	
	Life-Spirit	
XII.	The Hanged Man - Alchemical Mercury	261
	Christophorus	
XIII.	Death - Scorpio	273
	Exusiai - Spirits of Form	
	Spirit-Self	
	St. John - the Philosopher - the Initiate of the Thought Mysteries	
XIV.	Temperance - Sagittarius	297
	Archai - Spirits of Personality	
	Ego	
XV.	The Devil - Capricorn	303
	Archangeloi - Spirits of Fire	
	Astral Body	
XVI.	The Tower - Mars	321
	Archangel Samael	
	Speech - 16 Petaled Lotus	
XVII.	The Star - Aquarius	337
	Angeloi - Sons of Life	
	Etheric Body	
	St. Matthew - the Priest - the Initiate of Thought, Feeling, and Will	

XVIII.	The Moon - Pisces	349
	Humanity - Spirits of Freedom and Love	
	Physical Body	
XIX.	The Sun - Sun	367
	Archangel Michael	
	Waking Consciousness - 12 Petaled Lotus	
XX.	Judgement - Alchemical Salt	381
	the Raven (carbon) is Transformed into the	
	Philosophers' Stone (diamond) or Resurrection Body	
XXI.	The World - Saturn	387
	Archangel Oriphiel	
	Memory - 8 Petaled Lotus	

Part 2

The Archangelic Periods 409

I.	The Archangelic Period of Oriphiel: 200 B.C. - 150 A.D.	413
	Saturn - The World	
II.	The Archangelic Period of Anael: 150 - 500 A.D.	421
	Venus - The Empress	
III.	The Archangelic Period of Zachariel: 500 - 850 A.D.	431
	Jupiter - The Wheel of Fortune	
IV.	The Archangelic Period of Raphael: 850 - 1190 A.D.	453
	Mercury - The Magician	
V.	The Archangelic Period of Samael: 1190 - 1510 A.D.	475
	Mars - The Tower	
VI.	The Archangelic Period of Gabriel: 1510 - 1879 A.D.	501
	Moon - The High Priestess	
VII.	The Archangelic Period of Michael: 1879 - 2229 A.D.	509
	Sun - The Sun	

Part 3		
	The Seven Post-Atlantean Cultural Epochs	527
Part 4		
	Bibliography	533
Part 5		
	Grail Diagrams	579

I.	The Major Arcana and the Macrocosm and Microcosm
II.	The Rosicrucian Symbols of the Quintessence and the Four Elements, and the Corresponding Ethers
III.	The Venus Pentagram
IV.	The Seven Globes and the Law of Seven
V.	The Spiritual Beings and the Spheres of the Planets and Zodiac
VI.	The Ancient Chaldean Names for the Planets
VII.	The Planetary Spheres, the Kabbalistic Sefirot, and the Esoteric Christian Angelical Hierarchies
VIII.	The Two Sophias and the Seven Sacred Planets of Gnosticism
IX.	The Zodiac of the Lamb of God
X.	The Zodiacal Cosmic Crosses of the Holy Trinity
XI.	The Macrocosmic Cross of the Father
XII.	The Macrocosmic Cross of the Son
XIII.	The Macrocosmic Cross of the Holy Spirit

XIV.	The Order of the Four Gospel Initiations
XV.	The Seven Metals and the Seven Planets Geometrically Arranged According to their Atomic Weights
XVI.	The Seven Planets and the Seven Organs
XVII.	The Seven Planetary Spheres and the Physiological Motions
XVIII.	The Seven Planetary Spheres and the Seven Soul Moods
XIX.	The Seven Planets and the Seven Liberal Arts
XX.	The Three-Fold Soul Forces as they are Related to the Planets during Sleep and in the Waking State
XXI.	The Zodiacal Order of the 12 Senses and the 12 Philosophic Viewpoints
XXII.	The Aristotelian Categories and the Zodiacal Order of the 12 Senses and the 12 Philosophic Viewpoints
XXIII.	Another Perspective on the Zodiacal Order of the 12 Senses and the 12 Philosophic Viewpoints
XXIV.	The Temple of Man and the Seven Cultural Epochs
XXV.	The Sun Mystery and the Seven Cultural Epochs
XXVI.	The Spiritual Hierarchies and the Seven Cultural Epochs

Part 6

Appendix 635

From the History Lecture of the Rose-Croix Degree 637

"Thus I have delivered to thee the Key to unlock many Secret Gates, and have opened the door to the inmost adyta of Nature. But if anyone hath placed those things in another order, I shall not contend with him, inasmuch as all systems tend to the one truth." *Æsch Mezareph*

Foreword

by Douglas J. Gabriel

Seldom in modern esoteric Christian scholarship do we find an author with the breadth of understanding to encompass the Eastern, Central and Western Grail traditions. John Barnwell, in *The Arcana of the Grail Angel* synthesizes and illuminates the Grail tradition in the light of modern Spiritual Science, or Anthroposophy and the works of its founder Dr. Rudolf Steiner. Rudolf Steiner's Western esoteric stream of Christianity creates a backdrop of historical, philosophical, and religious archetypes that encompass the most comprehensive esoteric Christian Cosmology available. Add to this an extensive panoramic view of the historical, allegorical, and spiritual nature of the Grail, and together we find this refreshing work by John Barnwell - and immediately recognize a "must read" Anthroposophical classic like the works of Guenther Wachsmuth or Sergei O. Prokofieff. This is a book that has been long awaited, like the empty chair at the Round Table known as the "siege perilous", or the desolate kingdom crying for a king to renew the land, or the wounded and aging Grail King Amfortas who awaits the "fool" Parzival to arise to his true stature as a man and take over the Grail kingship.

Rudolf Steiner, the famous inspirer of many practical aspects of esoteric Christianity, once said to the effect that the Eastern, Central and Western esoteric streams would each have a special task, within the overall scheme of human culture, that they would need to develop to meet the future in a healthy way. The task of the Western stream, and in particular America, would be to develop an esoteric Christian Cosmology that would help place the modern spiritual aspirant in a healthy relationship to the past, the present, and the future as it is related to the living Being of Christ. This Cosmology would help the individual understand their place in the scheme of space and time, through the wisdom of the Sophia. And that they might cultivate, through this cosmological understanding, a more conscious relationship to their Guardian Angel and to the Spiritual Hierarchies; thereby, building a bridge to fulfill their connection to the intentions of Christ's Divine Plan.

The Guardian Angel is the spiritual "bridesmaid" that directs the individual's purging and soul-preparation, as a "bride" preparing for the heavenly, alchemical wedding of soul to spirit. No one view of this spirit-being, who in past history has had so many names, can ever afford the viewer a clear and comprehensive perspective. But when we live into the power of each chapter of *The Arcana of the Grail Angel*, each "letter of the soul" in the "ABC's" of the alchemical marriage of the soul to spirit, we drink anew from a fountain that never ends and brings the exact nourishment needed to quench the thirst of the aspirant. This wellspring does not run dry either in its historical depth nor in its cosmological scope, as the author spells out the esoteric correspondences that unveil the mystery and illuminate one's path to their Guardian Angel.

These cosmological correspondences are examined and thoroughly illuminated in *The Arcana of the Grail Angel*; and thereby, the wondrous experience of the connectedness of all things is drawn together like the threads of a giant tapestry. The many original diagrams of spiritual correspondences bring into focus an overview of the workings of all nature, and the spiritual history of humanity and of the Cosmos. With this book, the reader can find their place within space and time, history and consciousness as the author objectively spans the events and purposes of cosmic and human evolution.

The true meaning of life is found through knowing our relationship to "the big picture" and to the intentions of creation; and thereby, finding fulfillment within our unique destinies through giving the gift that only we can give to humanity by taking up the challenge of our individual sovereignty and becoming, within our own "domains", Grail King's and Queen's. Without this pervasive and objective view of oneself within space and time, the soul is empty and the spirit unfulfilled. Rudolf Steiner was right - we need a Cosmology to find our way within the stream of time - otherwise, we are lost and floundering without much needed celestial guidance, or a star by which to guide the "barque of the soul" to its spiritual homeland.

To fulfill this spiritual quest, we each need to be a Grail King or Queen and find meaning within our thinking that develops a sense of purpose for our actions; and thereby find peace within our feelings. Once we have accomplished this, we can hopefully one day become a vessel or "Grail" that glows with a halo of radiant spirit-light, and resonates to the singing of the Angelical Hosts - the heavenly "Music of the Spheres." For only then can we resound the harmonious note that is distinctly our own, and join in the conscious praise of creation, destruction, and re-creation that we see all around us and is the mystery of the Grail that lives within our very own heart's blood. Then will be revealed the great many Beings who, through incomprehensible sacrifice, have so wisely helped to create us and our world with so much love, harmony, and patience; and we shall know and converse with these Beings who are the righteous inhabitants of the living spiritual Cosmos. These are real Beings, whose influence has always been present whether or not we happened to notice. For these hierarchical Beings have all helped to create us and have maintained the universe in which we "live and move and have our being" according to the Divine Plan of the Holy Trinity.

The Arcana of the Grail Angel is a wonderful exposition of Christian Cosmology that can help one gain the spiritual insights that are so important for developing a conscious relationship to their own personal Guardian Angel. This "catechism of the soul" is a guidebook on the path of self-development that leads to the preparation and tempering of the Soul into a Grail that can hold the light of the Spirit which radiates from the core of one's True Self; and is, so to speak, held in waiting by one's Guardian Angel until one achieves the necessary maturity for its wholesome unfoldment. This spiritual light illuminates the path toward the supersensible perception of the ranks of angelic hosts that comprise the "Company of Heaven", and the "Grail Experience" of the elucidation of the Christ Mystery through the awakened Sophia forces.

Anthroposophy is not for the casual reader; for, to truly embrace a method of thought of such far-reaching significance necessarily requires a considerable amount of serious study. For those who do not have the time, a thoroughly versed commentator of Rudolf Steiner's works can be very helpful in approaching a synthesis of the various complex esoteric themes that are to be found within the teachings of Anthroposophy. John Barnwell is a representative of a new breed of anthroposophical commentators that strive to speak out of the context of Spiritual Science with extreme precision regarding the supersensible workings of the Spiritual Hierarchies that unfold within the stream of time. This level of spiritual insight and detail is far in advance of what many modern philosophies can encompass. And yet, Barnwell takes the indications of Anthroposophy and applies them in areas seldom discussed within the circles of Rudolf Steiner's followers.

The "heart of the matter" that is presented within *The Arcana of the Grail Angel* is addressed from the perspective of the author's personal understanding of the multifaceted ramifications of the Holy Grail within the realms of history, religion, science and philosophy. Subsequently, we experience a view into the hidden side of the Grail, that is examined utilizing the cosmological Angelology of Anthroposophy in such a way that it brings new insights - which in some instances are even beyond the indications of Rudolf Steiner. The author deftly does this through a method of interdisciplinary synthesis that attempts to take the indications of Rudolf Steiner and expand on them with insights gleaned from other author's and fields of study that includes: Ancient and Modern History, Astronomy, Physiology, Egyptology, Hermetics, Alchemy and Kabbalah, to name a few.

At the center of the cosmological matrix that joins it all together, is a spiritual perspective of the heart, and its occult physiology, that develops an understanding of the heart's central role within human evolution for the development of the forces of conscience and morality. This theme pervades Barnwell's insights into all the areas of study that are encompassed within this remarkable work of synthesis.

Barnwell has used the 22 major arcana of the tarot as an alphabet of archetypal approaches to the spiritual nature of the individual. When approached again and again from the 22 different archetypal vantage-points, the veils that obscure our personal communion with our Guardian Angel are gently lifted as we move into the future. In keeping with the tradition of presenting the various aspects of Initiation in a "memory theater", Barnwell presents the "Alphabet of the Archetypal Human Being" through the 22 major arcana of the tarot, or we could say the 22 letters of the Hebrew alphabet. Spelling out the "letters of the soul", so that each archetypal direction and context is expressed, is a methodology that has been used throughout history by esotericists as a vehicle for orchestrating the different aspects of the Mysteries, and as a tool for maintaining one's equilibrium through the various processes of Initiation. This method of living into a subject through 22 different fundamental perspectives is a balanced and healthy way of approaching a subject. As we again and again approach the subject from its various facets it begins to shine ever more brightly. These facets of the spirit are all aspects of the path that the "pure Fool" must travel on his journey of fulfillment.

The "12 labors of Hercules" are an archetypal image of what the modern aspirant for Initiation must accomplish. This is achieved by proceeding through the Zodiac consciously without battling with the animality represented by each of the 12 constellations. Instead, one brings into being new impulses through their individual nature that redeem the animal forces of each of the 12 directions of space. In this manner, one strives toward achieving a perfectly balanced angelically human perspective which encompasses and transcends them all.

Rudolf Steiner has said many times, in his over 6,000 lectures that are included within his over 400 volumes of profound esoteric Christian teachings, that to study the indications given out of Anthroposophical Spiritual Science enhances and develops the capacity to perceive the spirit and soul forces that work into the physical world. Through studying a work like *The Arcana of the Grail Angel*, the reader can begin to see through the many veils that hide the mysterious workings of the spirit and the manner in which they have helped shape the destiny of humanity.

Our Guardian Angels hold the personal, spiritual imprint that each of us has impressed upon the skein of time. Our efforts toward purifying our desires and perfecting our capacities of will are of great importance to the Beings who, in the service of the Divine, work unceasingly to bring our purpose of will and moral strivings into harmonious connection with others. We all desperately need to know, understand, and communicate to the "Higher Beings" who interpenetrate all the workings of our lives.

The need for books like *The Arcana of the Grail Angel* is paramount in these times of often shallow, pseudo-spirituality that can be found on the bulletin boards of every health food store or within local "psychic" magazines. "Spiritual" teachers of every imaginable size and shape are there for a price; but the "Pearl of Great Price" cannot be found except through the "law of necessity." No one can walk the path to your Guardian Angel for you; it is a road that must be walked alone, just as we walk through the gates of sleep and death. Others can speak of the signposts and point the way, but the journey is one's own individual path that leads to the perception of "Higher Beings." For those "who have eyes to see and ears to hear", this "travel guide of the soul" that leads toward the spirit can point the way and help the weary traveler reflect upon what they have seen and heard upon their journey toward the one life. What the individual gains on this journey becomes, as it were, fruits that are garnered from the "Tree of Knowledge of Good and Evil" - "And by their fruits shall they be known."

Many truly great thinkers, philosophers, artists and poets have had a profound experience of a supersensible "Higher Being" who became the inspiration for much of their work. Dante had his Beatrice, Novalis his Sophie, Socrates his Daemon, Christians their Guardian Angels, Gnostics their Sophia, and in today's vernacular - the soul has its spirit. Almost every spiritual author was inspired by a "Higher Being" or vision of the Divine Epiphany, that often manifests with the appearance of the opposite sex. Why is this? Barnwell points out that the next higher body of elementary forces above the physical body is ethereal in its composition, and that Rudolf Steiner has indicated that the etheric body of warmth, light, sound, and life manifests the opposite polarity of the sexual nature of the physical body of the individual. Is this any wonder? Since the great author's have had the experience of objectively meeting their Guardian Angel on the same plane of being as the etheric body; and in most cases, the being was experienced in a gender that was the opposite of the author's outer religious beliefs in God the Father. In addition to this, the intimate forces of nature are often depicted as female in the minds and experience of those who wrote about their experience of "Higher Beings." For Angels are by nature asexual even though they are frequently represented in the female form; and likewise, the divine attributes of God the Father are often seen as feminine; i.e., Prudence, Grace, Beauty, and so on.

Seeing with the heart's eye, and hearing with the heart's ear are all a part of a new seeing and listening to the forces that strive to nourish our spiritual growth. This new spiritual awakening, when the higher senses come alive like a blind man healed, is the Quest of the Grail - and it often begins with the meeting of your Guardian Angel. As you study this topology of the soul, you will begin to find the Grail anew and claim your royal nature as King or Queen of the Grail. Your heart will begin its transformation from a wounded, wondering soul into a shining, sounding, fountain of immortality. Our "little" selves, that are so often burdened by the present, will find that the past and the future know us as royal, divine participants in the dance of time. This mystery, this magical and spiritual perspective can be attained by understanding the multifaceted perspectives that are presented within *The Arcana of the Grail Angel*; and this writer is confident that the soul can "grow by degrees from dullness to blessedness" through its study.

It is with great honor that I have had some small part in helping *The Arcana of the Grail Angel* come to publication and to the public eye. For I truly believe, that like the Grail chalice or the "Cauldron of Plenty", *The Arcana of the Grail Angel* will be a source of continuing inspiration from the spirit that will nourish the soul of the reader. The well-seasoned esoteric student of Anthroposophy will find a wealth of wisdom gleaned from the works of Rudolf Steiner, and from many of the esoteric traditions of antiquity. While the new student of Rudolf Steiner's works will find a clear approach to the principle cosmological ideas that will stand the test of time. I would like to express my heartfelt gratitude and appreciation to John Barnwell for sharing with us his profound research, scholarship, and experience in these sacred matters - "Study to show thyself approved unto God . . ."

Douglas J. Gabriel, Berkley 1999

Dedication

The writing of a work of this nature rests on the able shoulders of a great many people, to whom I must confess my unending gratitude. First and foremost I must acknowledge the many patient, devoted, and loving contributions of my dearest Barbara Bols without whose continual encouragement and support this work would have surely never seen the light of day, there are no words to compensate so many willing sacrifices, except to say that I lovingly dedicate this work to her - for she has made it possible.

Secondly, I wish to thank Robert and Erika Eckerman who have both been unending sources of support, generosity and encouragement; to them I cannot even begin to express my appreciation, but can only say how much I cherish their warm and stimulating companionship, and sincerely heartfelt friendship.

I also wish to express my warmest gratitude to Douglas Gabriel who helped in so many ways; beginning from our earliest conversations on the work of Rudolf Steiner, through many years of friendship, all the way to writing a foreword to this book (which I hope to some day live up to); and also, for the many editorial comments, and assisting in the proof-reading which helped bring this work from a scattered assembly of my notes to a form which hopefully resembles an actual book. Thank you, I could not ask for a better and more understanding friend, for you truly "know what I think." This is not without extending my warmest appreciation to his loving wife Lori and his precious son Julian, who both gave up quality time with him so that he might help me with my thorny task.

Thanks are also extended to Rick Knutson who suffered through the reading of a couple early drafts of this work, and whose unsparing comments were taken to heart even though I did not always act on them. You are truly a special person that I am honored to count among my spiritual inner-circle of friends. This dedication would be incomplete without showing my appreciation to some of the other members of my spiritual inner-circle: Bobby Hankins, Brian Lynch, Robert Thibodeau, Howard Weingarden, and Chris Fessler; as many of the ideas herein were stimulated by questions that arose over the years through conversation with these special friends. Even though time and circumstance does not allow us to be together as often as we might wish, we are all (more or less) together in spirit - as much as can be expected from such a gathering of rag-tag individualists.

I must also recognize the tireless work of Ralph Marinelli which has laid a foundation for understanding that "the heart is not a pump"; for, it was his research that caused me to see the need for a book that attempted to approach the mysteries of the heart from the perspective of Rudolf Steiner's Anthroposophical Cosmology - and that if mankind is ever to rise to their rightful spiritual estate, they must come to understand that one's spiritual development is measured by the degree to which their heart expresses itself an organ of forgiveness.

I also want to thank Jim Nani for being there through the difficult early "gestation period" of this work; for, more than he realizes, his questions helped me to see how these thoughts might be shared to a larger circle of people.

Thanks are also extended to Greg Filipowicz and Laurence Ostrow, as it was through them that I first came to the work of Rudolf Steiner.

Beyond this I have to mention some of the people that I have had the good fortune to know, and who have helped to shape the thoughts in this book: Werner Glas - for his brilliant lectures and the many stimulating conversations about Rudolf Steiner and Walter J. Stein we had over late-night dinners; Hans Gebert - for his able handling of some of the more difficult aspects of Rudolf Steiner's work, and his encouragement of my lecturing; Charles Jayne - who was the first to insist I put my esoteric musings into print; Paul Swain - who always emphasized the three-fold nature of man; Sherwood Vickers - whose life was a model of service to the Rose Cross; Walter C. P. Johnson - who served as a bridge to the Magian stream; Bob Tandy - a heartfelt Christian if there ever was one; Fred Parsons - who connected me to numerous American esoteric byways; Mark "Singh" Vosko - who showed me so many of my limitations; Sharon Penland-Mace - we shared so many adventures; Cheryl Swanson - who showed me a great many things about Astrology; Marjorie Fisher and her daughter Dr. Marjorie M. Fisher - who are both fine examples of open-mindedness and generosity through their making possible a deepening of my knowledge of ancient Egypt and Mesopotamia, even though my ideas may be so very different from their own; Janet McGavin - for her spiritual-scientific understanding of the Pythagorean mysteries; Carlo Pietzner - who provided hints pregnant with meaning; William Bento - who has been a valued friend that has given certain key helpful suggestions, and will no doubt be confronted with the task of elaborating on this work to others; Jim Whetmore - in memory of all of the obscure esoteric byways we explored together; Ron Voelker - for believing in me; Ben Manistow - for the astro-economic research we did together; Helen

Weingarden - for keeping Howard together; Michael Dobson - for seeing the value of this work; All the folks at the Detroit Lodge of the Theosophical Society - who provided a forum for me to lecture over the years; Chrystyne M. Jackson and Serena DuBois - who were both sources of encouragement through publishing some of my early materials in their journals: Explore! - For the Professional, and Explore More!; Patrick Burns - who introduced me to the Tarot as a contemplative tool; Les Collins - a "noble traveler"; David Spangler - who serves as a continuing reminder of a genuine mood of openness; Milenko Mitanovich and Kathy Lightstone - two wonderful beings of clarity and purpose; and also, Gelek Rinpoche - although we may walk down different paths, I feel we are walking in the same direction.

I also must express my gratitude to many whose works have enabled me to write this book, which includes: Rudolf Steiner - who has, in many ways, affected my life more than any other human being; Marie Steiner - who ensured the preservation of Rudolf Steiner's works for posterity; Ita Wegman and Elizabeth Vreede - whose spirits live on to inspire all sincere Grail-Seekers; Walter Johannes Stein - whose studies on the Grail are incomparable; Ehrenfried Pfeiffer - whose notes were the foundation for the diagrams in this book, and whose *Heart Lectures* helped make clear to me the central significance of the heart in human evolution; Guenther Wachsmuth - who was the first to attempt to systematically present the teachings of Anthroposophy; Bernard C. J. Lievegoed - whose works helped to crystallize many important themes in this book; Friedrich Rittelmeyer and Emil Bock - whose spirits have penetrated to the very marrow of the Christian Mystery; Sergei O. Prokofieff - who through his synthesis of the works of Rudolf Steiner has done an invaluable service to humanity and the being Anthroposophia; Isabel Wyatt - whose work on the Grail continued on in the spirit of Walter Johannes Stein; Owen Barfield - a master of deft subtlety in his numerous expositions; Willi O. Sucher - who laid the foundations for Astrosophy, as a truly Anthroposophical Star-Wisdom; Robert Powell who helped develop Astrosophy from indications to methods; T. H. Meyer - who is accomplishing a great service by bringing the biographies of the early Anthroposophist's to light; and lastly, to H. P. Blavatsky - that indefatigable pioneer who managed to open a door that Rudolf Steiner walked through, although unfortunately she was not able to truly penetrate the esoteric Christian mysteries until after her death.

And finally, I must lovingly remember my dear Mother (who understood that, although I was quite social by nature I also had a deep love of solitude) and my dear Father (who has given me a certain tenacity of will) and his wife Pauline (for taking such good care of him); and also, my brothers Dick, Mike, David, and Tim and their families.

Beyond all of this, I must credit myself with all the numerous shortcomings of this work, and hope that the reader can find meaning amidst these many imperfections.

The Hermitage
Detroit
Easter, 1999

John Barnwell

A Note on the Structure of this Book

I have written this book so that each of the chapters could stand on their own; thereby facilitating the reading of each chapter as if it were a separate essay. This unusual manner of presentation has required a certain amount of repetition of key ideas within the individual chapters, which should be helpful to the beginner. As listed in the Table of Contents, there are 26 cosmological Grail Diagrams included in the back of the book; these are referred to in the text by a **bold** Roman numeral within brackets, as follows: (**XXVI**). I have also dispensed with footnotes and have dealt with the author and titles of the works cited within the text; and, I have italicized and indented most longer quotations so as to make it clear when I am quoting another author (although in the few instances when I did not italicize I used quotation marks). Editorial additions within quotations have been enclosed in square brackets [like so]. I have also revised the translation of a few passages in the quotations of Rudolf Steiner so as to hopefully make them more clear to the reader by bringing the language into a more contemporary American-English idiom.

Furthermore, in reference to my choice of language, while I am sensitive to the use of gender and the connotations often derived from the peculiarities of the English language (i.e., the masculine-gender also often serving for the neutral-gender - as in the case of the word *man*), I find that the use of a truly neutral-gender terminology often sounds awkward or strained; so, needless to say, the principles in this book are meant for both women *and* men; and when I say *man* I do not mean male, but rather, *man* in its etymological sense of thinker (Sanskrit, manas = thinking principle).

It should also be noted that Rudolf Steiner frequently made reference to the transition to the Consciousness-Soul epoch occurring in the year 1413 A.D., while I have given this date as 1414 A.D. In the course of his lectures Rudolf Steiner was in the habit of using the old dating system of Italy, and so he called this year 1413; when, in fact, by modern reckoning it should be 1414 A.D.

"Only for you, sons [and daughters] of doctrine and wisdom, have we written this work. Study this book, ponder that which we have intentionally scattered and arranged in a few places; what we have hidden in one place we have manifested in another, in order that it could be understood from your wisdom."

De Occulta Philosophia, Heinrich Cornelius Agrippa von Nettesheim, 1533 A.D.

Initiation: An Introduction

Standing on the threshold of the next millennium, mankind finds itself faced with questions that are increasingly difficult to answer. These questions are of such a nature that more and more people are searching in other lands, cultures, and times to find spiritual fulfillment. That they are searching down paths perhaps unknown to their ancestors shows that the traditions of their ancestors may have fallen short of bringing the fulfillment that they strive for, due to the manner in which they were presented. And yet, the traditions of the West are more than capable of meeting these needs, but perhaps not in the form that it has been presented to them. It is in response to this quest that I have written this book. Not that I have all the answers, but rather as a humble attempt to explore certain key questions. For it is by improving our questions that we will empower ourselves to meet the future on its own terms, and hopefully to someday live into the answer.

Under the name of the "Perennial Philosophy" is frequently described the spiritual heritage of all times, peoples and lands. This term, "Philosophia Perennis" was suggested by Augustino Steuco in the year 1540 to describe the universal sacred tradition. Rightly understood, this "Perennial Philosophy" is humanity's greatest treasure. On the surface one might think that, on account of certain similarities, the various traditional teachings are all the same. This is due in part to certain truths that are shared amongst all genuine traditions. In actuality it is through their differences that the various traditions have acquired their unique value to mankind, for these traditions were each given in a form that was appropriate for a particular group of people, to meet the needs of the time and place in which they lived.

If it is spiritual fulfillment that we strive for, then this fulfillment must be included in our vision of the future and of ourselves. One thing held in common to all the ancient cultures was the idea that an individual could, through initiation, come to a deeper relationship with the world and themselves. Some form of initiation has been available in all ages and lands; for by its nature, initiation must change to meet the needs of the time and place. Contrary to what some might say, humanity is evolving and so must the path of initiation evolve. That consciousness evolves is one of the central teachings of all true esoteric-spiritual streams. Part of the difficulty in finding a path of initiation, that is appropriate for modern humanity, is the fact that the nature of initiation has changed throughout history in order to meet the changing nature of human consciousness. Furthermore, initiation has not always been available to everyone as it is today. For in ancient times, people were selected for initiation and had to meet very strict conditions to achieve their initiation.

The strict limitation on gaining access to initiatic teachings has changed in the present day. For the methods of initiation are available in the spiritual scientific works of Dr. Rudolf Steiner to all who have a healthy capacity of perseverance and understanding; and furthermore, spiritual science does not require that you "believe" in the insights shared; but rather - that one only suspends their "disbelief." In these spiritual scientific works are revealed what Rudolf Steiner chose to call Anthroposophy, which means "human wisdom" (anthropos = human, sophia = wisdom). Anthroposophy is unique because, in addition to his scientific training, Rudolf Steiner was also a very highly developed clairvoyant and an Initiate, and he was able to combine clairvoyance and science into a true spiritual science.

Due to the nature of the higher worlds there exists what is known in occultism as the Akashic Record, where the actions of all of evolution are contained as permanent impressions within the cosmic memory. The Akashic Record can be perceived by those initiates who are sufficiently clairvoyant to experience time as spatial. Literally speaking, the mysteries of time are revealed spatially to the clairvoyant gaze of an Initiate. Rudolf Steiner has given mankind a great treasure by sharing so much of the content of this permanent record of the history of the Cosmos and mankind. As he once stated in his closing remarks of a lecture series given in Vienna, in August of 1909, that was published under the title, *East in the Light of the West*: "We have reached a point in civilization now where the elementary teachings of initiation are beginning to be disclosed." Also in this same work, Rudolf Steiner gives an aspect of the significance of the Akashic Record:

What is here stated need not necessarily be acquired from historical tradition. Suppose for example that the initiate wisdom of ancient and venerable India, of the Persian sages, of the Egyptian initiations, or of the Greek Mysteries had all been lost; suppose no external documents of any kind whatever were left to tell us of the pristine teaching concerning the spiritual foundations of our Earth evolution. Even then the possibility of developing supersensible consciousness would not be lost; everything that is said here can be discovered by means of supersensible investigation without the aid of any historical document. We have to do with something which at the present time can be studied at its source; even mathematics may also be learnt from original sources.

Rudolf Steiner further described the objective nature of his scientific, clairvoyant observations that are presented in Anthroposophy in a letter which he wrote to Eliza von Moltke on the 12th of August, 1904:

. . . In matters like this I am merely an instrument of Higher Beings whom I revere in complete humility. Nothing is my merit, nothing is dependent on me. The only thing I can claim for myself is the strict training I have undergone which protects me from any fantasy or illusion. This has been my first rule. What I experience spiritually is therefore free from any [ordinary] imagination, any deception, any superstition. . .

In the works of Rudolf Steiner are to be found the fruits of his investigations of the Spiritual World and of the Akashic Record - which portray, in the spiritual-scientific language of Anthroposophy, how mankind has been gradually evolving throughout human history, towards becoming a more perfect expression of the Spirit. This gradual path of spiritual-becoming, or Initiation, is -*"The Science of the Holy Grail."*

Time is inner space - space is outer time.   Novalis (1772-1801)

A Ƥ Ω

The Symbol for Tarok

"Those who were initiated into the Egyptian Mysteries [of the Graeco-Roman epoch] knew how to interpret this sign. They knew too, how to read the Book of Thoth, consisting of 78 leaves on which were inscribed all happenings in the world from the beginning to the end, from Alpha to Omega . . .

. . . and which could be read if the signs were rightly put together. These pictures gave expression to the life that dies and then springs again to new life. Whoever could combine the right numbers with the right pictures, were able to read the Book. This wisdom of numbers and of pictures had been taught from time immemorial. In the Middle Ages it was still in the foreground although little of it survives today."

Rudolf Steiner 3/17/1906

"The knowledge that man has to include himself in the construction of the great world temple has become increasingly forgotten. A person can be born and die today with out having any inkling of the fact that laws are working themselves out in us, and that everything we do is governed by the laws of the universe. The whole present-day life is wasted, because people do not know that they have to live according to laws. Therefore the priestly sages of ancient times devised means of rescuing, for the new culture, something of the great laws of the spiritual world. It was, so to speak, a stratagem of the great sages, to have hidden this order and harmony in many branches of life - yes even so far as in the games which men use for their recreation at the end of the day. In playing cards [and tarot cards], in the figures of chess, in the sense of rule by which one plays, we find a hint, if only a faint one, of the order and harmony which I have described. When you sit down with someone to a game of cards, it will not do if you do not know the rules, the manner of playing. And this really conveys a hint of the great laws of the universe. What is known as the Sefirot of the Kabbalah, what we know as the seven principles in their various forms, that is recognized again in the way in which the cards are laid down, one after the other, in the course of the game. Even in the allurements of playing, the adepts have known how to introduce the great cosmic laws, so that, even in play, people have at least a bit of wisdom. At least for those who can play cards, their present incarnation is not quite wasted. These are secrets, how the great Adepts intervene in the wheel of existence. If one told people to be guided by the great cosmic laws, they would not do so. However, if the laws are introduced unnoticed into things, it is often possible to inject a drop of this attitude into them. If you have this attitude, then you will have a notion of what it is which is symbolized in the mighty allegory of the lost temple."

Rudolf Steiner 5/15/1909

"The truth underlying the casting of a horoscope is that those who know these things can read the forces which determine a person's physical existence. A certain horoscope is allotted to a person because, within it, those forces find expression which have led him into being. If, for example, in the horoscope Mars stands over Aries (the Ram), this signifies that certain of the Aries forces are not allowed to pass through Mars, and are weakened. Thus is a man put into his place within physical existence, and it is in accordance with his horoscope that he guides himself before entering upon earthly existence. This subject, which in our times seems so much a thing of chance, should not be touched upon without out attention being called to the fact that nearly everything practiced in this connection today is simply dilettantism. It is pure superstition, and for the external world the true science of these matters has been, for the most part, completely lost. Consequently, the principles expressed here are not to be judged according to that which nowadays frequently leads a questionable existence under the name Astrology."

Rudolf Steiner in: *The Spiritual Guidance of Man*

"The heathen Flegetanis could tell us how all the stars set and rise again and how long each one revolves before it reaches its starting point once more. To the circling course of the stars man's affairs and destiny are linked. Flegetanis the heathen saw with his own eyes in the constellations things he was shy to talk about, hidden mysteries. He said there was a thing called the Grail whose name he had read clearly in the constellations. 'A host of angels left it on the earth and then flew away up over the stars. Was it their innocence that drew them away? Since then baptized men have had the task of guarding it, and with such chaste discipline that those who are called to the service of the Grail are always noble men.' Thus wrote Flegetanis of these things."

Parzival , Book IX: 454, Wolfram von Eschenbach, c. 1198 A.D.

Prologue

The Arcana of the Grail Angel, is a study of the mysteries which surround that elusive legendary "thing" known as the Holy Grail, as presented in the spiritual-scientific works of Rudolf Steiner. A great many books have been written about the history of the Holy Grail, and also upon its significance as a symbol of the spiritual life. From the perspective of Rudolf Steiner's Anthroposophy, or Spiritual Science, a most valuable study on the Holy Grail is the pioneering work by his student Walter Johannes Stein entitled, *The Ninth Century - World History in the Light of the Holy Grail.* Within this work is contained a solid foundation for understanding the historical milieu in which the Grail Mysteries were developed in the 8th and 9th centuries, as presented from the clairvoyant karma research of Rudolf Steiner. In addition to this, *The Ninth Century* includes a study of Wolfram von Eschenbach's *Parzival,* as viewed from its rightful perspective as a spiritual drama that is based on the themes of Grail Initiation - themes which are of continuing relevance to the pursuit of the spiritual quest in modern life. In light of all this, Walter Johannes Stein's masterful presentation has made it unnecessary for me to expand on certain themes in my humble continuation of this work, and I can only say that if one wishes later to deepen their appreciation of the matters which are presented in *The Arcana of the Grail Angel* I must wholeheartedly recommend that remarkable work - *The Ninth Century*.

In *The Arcana of the Grail Angel* I have utilized the esoteric cosmology of Rudolf Steiner's Anthroposophy as a foundation for understanding certain aspects of the path of Grail Initiation. Likewise, I have used the angelology of Rudolf Steiner as a means for deciphering the grand historical themes that surround the Holy Grail. In approaching the Holy Grail in this way, I hope to have presented a broader picture for the reader to enjoy; and thereby, to have created a context that lends itself toward deepening one's connection to this living path of renewal. In doing this, I will have succeeded if the reader develops an understanding of the Holy Grail as a multifaceted "spiritual leaven" that has been nurtured by the Angels for the unfoldment of the human soul, and which has been quietly working its way, within the course of human history, into the hearts of mankind.

In this book, I have tried to show how "the shining symbol of the Holy Grail" represents an actual, historical, underground stream of esoteric Christianity that is known as the Brotherhood of the Holy Grail. The esoteric content of the Brotherhood of the Holy Grail, in turn, was passed on to the Order of the Knights Templars, and from there to the original Rosicrucian Brotherhood. The once secret mysteries of this esoteric Grail stream would eventually be revealed around the turn of the century - for the benefit of all humanity - through the clairvoyant researches of Rudolf Steiner. This has provided mankind with the rare opportunity to study the mysteries of the Holy Grail directly from one of its greatest Initiates.

According to Rudolf Steiner, the Brotherhood of the Holy Grail has its pre-Christian beginnings in the Egyptian Sun Mysteries, and the Mysteries of Isis and Osiris. Furthermore, Rudolf Steiner indicated that the spiritual successors of this Egyptian mystery stream would later, in combination with certain other pre-Christian Christ Mysteries, establish the Brotherhood of the Holy Grail in the 8th and 9th centuries A.D. For, these pre-Christian Christ Mysteries had all been founded in ancient times by the great Initiates of the "Mother Lodge of Humanity", in preparation for the incarnation of Christ the "Great Sun-Being."

It is said that the 18th century Christian Initiate, known to posterity as the Comte St. Germain, always kept a copy of Giulio Camillo del Minio's book entitled *L'idea del Theatro* (1550) on his nightstand. In this book on the Ars Memoriae (the Art of Memory), the various departments of life are arranged in a Renaissance "memory theater", according to the categories of the planets in combination with the mythological symbolism of the Graeco-Roman pantheon.

The organizing of the various facets of life, according to their heavenly counterparts, is a method of esoteric study with a history that extends back to the Hermetic Mysteries of ancient Egypt. This method of study can bring one to a profound understanding of the interrelationships between the Macrocosm and the Microcosm; that is, between the Cosmos or the "great world" and the human being - the "little world."

In presenting these Grail studies I have elected to use the 22 Major Arcana of the Tarot as a system for the classification of ideas. For the Tarot shares in a cosmological tradition which adheres to the idea that there are 22 fundamental aspects of Creation; and likewise, that there are 22 fundamental aspects to Initiation.

I have chosen the Tarot, not because any of the images that are to be found on the existing Tarot cards are necessarily suited for representing modern Spiritual Science, or Anthroposophy (for the reader will note that, except for in a few places where, in order to demonstrate the methods of esoteric symbolism, I have referred to the images that are found on the widely known Rider-Waite Tarot deck, I have refrained from using any particular deck for purposes of illustration); but rather, I show that the 22 fundamental archetypes, or Arcana of the Tarot can be harmonized with the teachings of Anthroposophy. For, within the symbolism of the Tarot is to be found a remnant of the archaic occult wisdom that has been encoded for posterity. And furthermore, since the Tarot is so widely studied, it may provide a point of entry for some into the works of Rudolf Steiner.

For many years, Moses was the high priest of the Sun Mysteries in the Egyptian city of Heliopolis, the "City of the Sun" (the biblical On). As the Egyptian Mysteries had entered into a stage of decline, it was ordained by the divine-spiritual powers, which guide mankind, that there would be a change in the course of human evolution. Consequently, a divine mandate was given to Moses that he should lead the Hebrew people out of Egypt. When Moses finally lead the Exodus out of Egypt, the "Great Sun Being" that had inspired the Egyptian Mysteries of Osiris also departed.

While leading the Exodus out of Egypt, it was revealed to Moses on Mount Sinai how the Adam Kadmon, the primordial human being, was created by the Divine Word through the agency of the formative processes of the 22 letters of the Hebrew alphabet. This idea is expressed in the anonymous Hebrew text *Sefer ha-Temunah*, which I quote from the third chapter of the book by Elliot R. Wolfson entitled, *Circle in the Square - Studies in the Use of Gender in Kabbalistic Symbolism*.

> *These twenty-two letters with which the Torah was written . . . are specified in a great and hidden secret, and it is without doubt the true image (ha-temunah ha-`amitit), as it is written, 'he beholds the image of the Lord' (Num. 12:8), and this is the secret of the names of the Holy One, blessed be He, and the power of his actions. Permission has not been given to explain but some of them. They are the secret of the sefirot [the ten divine emanations of God] and the attributes (middot) and the secret of the angel and the secret of God. . . The secret of the sefirot [is that they] are in the image and form of an anthropos [human being].*

According to an esoteric tradition, after receiving this Holy Wisdom, which was encoded upon the original tablets that he brought down from Mount Sinai, Moses returned to his people - only to find them transgressing the law and worshiping the Golden Calf. This moved Moses to cast the tablets down and thereby shatter them to pieces; for Moses realized that the Hebrew people, in their present state, were unworthy to receive this Holy Wisdom as an *inner-law*. Consequently, Moses recognized that the Hebrew people were only capable of receiving an *outer-law*; and so, he caused a new pair of tablets to be carved which contained the Ten Commandments, that proscribed the ten transgressions against the ten sefirot - without revealing their holy mysteries.

This was done in order to prepare the Hebrews to be worthy of receiving in their midst a Messiah. This Messianic mission of the Hebrew people came to be fulfilled around 1,200 years later in the person of Jesus of Nazareth; in whom would fully incarnate for a period of around three years, for the one and only time in Earth evolution - Christ the "Great Sun Being."

Through this divine act of redemption, mankind was to receive the "new" higher, *inner-law* of love - the "Golden Rule" - that would proceed directly from the mouth of the "New Adam", "the Word made flesh." This is expressed by St. Paul in "Galatians" (5:14); "For all the law is fulfilled in one word, even in this; Thou shalt love thy neighbor as thyself."

This Holy Wisdom, which was encoded in the original Mosaic tablets, subsequently became secretly preserved in an oral tradition which was committed to memory by those who were deemed worthy to receive these great mysteries. In later periods, parts of this oral tradition came to be written down and transmitted to a select few through the body of esoteric teachings that came to be known as the Kabbalah (which means "to receive", or "tradition").

During his long career as the high priest of Heliopolis, Moses both received and conducted initiations into the Sun Mysteries and other mysteries of the ancient Egyptians. Like the esoteric training that was required for penetrating the mysteries of the Kabbalah, the preparation for initiation into the Egyptian Mysteries required years of study and dedication in order to fulfill the task of memorizing the fundamental images and ideas that are related to the path of Initiation. In ancient Egypt, these images and ideas were presented in the temple artwork, and in the sacred hieroglyphic language. The preliminary training began with the study of the language. After many years of study, if one was deemed qualified, they would be selected to study the secret scrolls that were kept in the scriptorium that was part of the temple complex, and was known as the Per Ankh, or House of Life.

The House of Life had a central place in the cultivation of the ancient Egyptian sacerdotal culture, and was conceived to be a means whereby the principle of Isfet (evil or chaos) was overcome through the principle of Ma`at (order). As a training center and repository of the ancient sacred texts, the House of Life was a means of maintaining continuity with the past; for the fundamental guiding principles, that were received through inspiration from the beings of the spiritual world, had been left to posterity in hoary antiquity by great initiates like Imhotep, the founder of a Sun Mystery center in Upper Egypt known as the Temple of Horus at Edfu, in the reign of the 3rd dynasty Pharaoh Zoser (Djoser, c. 2630-2611 B.C.).

The Egyptian temple itself was considered to be a sacred sanctuary that maintained harmony with the cosmic order, or Ma`at, through the transmission and guidance of the ritual activities that were performed within the sacred precincts of the temple itself. For these rites, which were centered around complex ritual formulae that were performed before an array of sacred images, served to maintain the connection of earthly life to the supersensible realms and the beings that dwelt therein. Furthermore, this sacred Ma`at-life, that was being generated through daily ritual activities, was given a wider dissemination beyond the sacred precincts of the temple through numerous yearly festivals; which included certain festivals during which the images of the gods (neters) were carried in processions outside of the temple, so that the common people could share more completely in the benefits of this generated Ma`at-life - that was conceived to be the very life-blood of Egyptian culture.

In ancient Egypt, several forms of language were taught: first, the hieratic script that was primarily used for mundane affairs, and second, the hieroglyphic picture language that was reserved for sacred and official use. There was also a cursive form of hieroglyphics that was learned first, before one learned the pictorial form of the sacred, monumental hieroglyphic script. (For the sake of being thorough on the subject of Egyptian language, I should mention that there was also another later written language called Demotic which was developed for daily use, in the 7th century B.C. out of the spoken language, and after that the Coptic language was developed through Greek influence in the 4th century A.D.)

The acquisition of a certain degree of mastery of the sacred language was considered vital by the ancient Egyptians for receiving Initiation, so that one would be in possession of a means for understanding the profound, supersensible experiences which resulted from the various Initiations. The understanding of the sacerdotal language was also deemed vital because it was believed to be necessary to know the sacred formulas which would allow safe passage through the different levels of the supersensible worlds - sacred formulas which were based on the names of the beings that would be encountered. Furthermore, the sacred training received would also serve as a vehicle for retaining the memory of these transformational Initiation experiences afterwords, in one's daily life.

These Initiations were acquired in ancient Egypt by traveling to the temples that were located in the sacred domains, or nomes, that were each dedicated to different deities. There were 22 nomes in Upper Egypt, and 20 nomes in Lower Egypt; and on one level, all 42 nomes together can be thought of as forming the body of 42 attributes that are judged in the afterworld, and are perfected by becoming one with Osiris. These 42 attributes of judgment are referred to in the *Pyramid Texts*: "I know the names of the 42 gods who are with you within the Hall of Two Truths."

This allusion to the "Hall of Two Truths" is, in a dualistic way, connected to the symbol of the scales of judgment. These scales represent Ma`at, the Egyptian goddess of truth and cosmic order, whose attributes connect her occultly with the goddess referred to by H. P. Blavatsky as "Karma-Nemesis", or by others as the "Great Goddess." The appearance of Ma`at, in association with the scales of judgment, is a demonstration of the dualistic nature of the assessment by the 42 gods, in the eyes of the ancient Egyptians. This was considered to be a process whereby the 42 gods would evaluate the testimony of the heart; or in others words, they would assess the karma of the individual so that "their names might be written in the book of life" by the divine scribe Thoth, or as he is referred to in the Hermetic writings, Hermes-Mercury the "Shepherd of Souls."

This ancient Egyptian idea of an assessment by 42 gods is paralleled, in the oriental teachings, by the beings referred to as Lipikas by H. P. Blavatsky in her book, *The Secret Doctrine* (volume 1, page 129):

> *The esoteric meaning . . . is, that those who have been called Lipikas, the Recorders of the Karmic ledger, make an impassible barrier between the personal Ego and the impersonal Self, the Noumenon and Parent-Source of the former. Hence the allegory. They circumscribe the manifested world within the Ring "Pass-Not."*

The esoteric significance of the number 42 is further deepened by the early Christian writer Clement of Alexandria (c. 150-215 A.D.) who stated that the complete corpus of Hermetic writings consisted of 42 sacred books that were bequeathed to the ancient Egyptians by Hermes Trismegistus, and were concerned with the 42 aspects of sacred knowledge. The number 42 is also mentioned in the kabbalistic text the *Zohar* (II, 234a), where it says, in reference to the first 42 letters of the opening verses of "Genesis": "The World was etched and established with 42 letters, all of them a crown of the Holy Name." Furthermore, the world was not only created via the number 42, but also received its redemption through the agency of the number 42 - through its connection to the 42 generations between Abraham and Christ Jesus as given in "The Gospel of St. Matthew"(1:17).

> *So all the generations from Abraham unto David are fourteen generations; and from David unto the carrying away to Babylon fourteen generations; and from the carrying away to Babylon unto the Christ fourteen generations.*

These 42 generations integrated cosmic processes into the hereditary stream through 42 stages, consisting of three groups of 14 stages. These three groups were each concerned, respectively, with three different aspects of the perfected humanity of Christ Jesus (the Physical-Body, Etheric-Body, and Astral-Body). This integration of cosmic processes into the humanity of Christ Jesus had to come about in preparation for His becoming the "new Lord of Karma"; and thereby, entering directly into the cosmic evaluation processes of the earthly human realm. For the cosmic evaluation process of the akashic time-content of the individual is, so to speak, coordinated by one's Guardian Angel and comes about through angelic beings (Lipikas) that are under the direction of the Elohim, or Spirits of Form; and so, are working with the cosmic forces of the 7th zodiacal constellation - the Scales of Libra - a process that, in the past, took place under the *inspiration* of the Solar Logos, the "Great Sun-Being" El-Elion ("the most High God" that was spoken of by Melchizedek to Abraham) - working with forces of the opposite constellation - the Ram of Aries. In the ancient Egyptian Mysteries, this was experienced through the workings of the *solar* Elohim, under the *inspiration* of the Solar Logos.

In the time of Moses, the nature of this karmic process underwent a profound change - in order to bring about a further unfoldment of the Divine Plan. For the Solar Logos had ceased to participate in what had become the decadent Egyptian Mysteries - and by a change from working through the agency of the *solar* Spirits of Form to the *lunar* Spirit of Form, Jehovah-Elohim - the Solar Logos led Moses out of Egypt. For, while Moses had previously presided over the Sun Mysteries at Heliopolis, the "Great Sun Being" that had been experienced in the ancient Egyptian Mysteries as Osiris, departed and continued to work directly with Moses through the *lunar* Spirit of Form, Jehovah-Elohim. These events had to take place in preparation for the incarnation of Christ, and culminated in Christ becoming the "new Lord of Karma" by entering directly into Earth evolution at the Grail Mystery which took place through the Crucifixion upon the hill of Golgotha.

Many other profound levels of meaning can be found in the myth of Osiris; for example, Osiris had been slain by his brother Set (Ahriman) and dismembered into 14 pieces that were strewn throughout the length of Egypt. This can be seen as representing, on one level, the seven dual aspects of Initiation (7+7=14), and by permutation the 49 fires of creation (7x7=49). In her *Theosophical Glossary*, H. P. Blavatsky provides us with further insights into these Mysteries of Osiris.

> *Of the many supreme gods, this Egyptian conception [of Osiris] is the most suggestive and the grandest, as it embraces the whole range of physical and metaphysical thought. As a solar deity he had twelve minor gods under him - the twelve signs of the Zodiac. Though his name is the 'Ineffable', his forty-two attributes bore each one of his names, and his seven dual*

aspects completed the fourty-nine, or 7 x 7: the former symbolized by the fourteen members of his body, or twice seven. Thus the god is blended in man, and the man is deified into a god.

As it is in harmony with these ancient traditions, I have elected to use the 22 Major Arcana of the Tarot as a "trestleboard" to symbolize the 22 facets of the *modern* Grail path of Initiation; which, in the progress of human evolution, has necessarily changed to meet the vastly different consciousness of modern humanity.

As can be seen in Grail Diagram number I (see: Part 4), the sequence of the 22 Arcana is composed of the numbers 3, 7, and 12 (3+7+12=22). These three numbers relate respectively to the 3 alchemical elements of Sulfur (fire), Mercury (fluidity), and Salt (solidity); the 7 planetary spheres (in the ancient sense, which includes the realms that are circumscribed by Sun and Moon and the five planets: Mercury, Venus, Mars, Jupiter and Saturn); and lastly, the 12 constellations of the Zodiac.

(Note: the references in this book refer to the 12 constellations of fixed stars which are referred to as the Sidereal Zodiac; as distinguished from the 12 "signs" of the Tropical Zodiac of common Astrology, which are the 12 divisions of the four seasons.)

This fundamental series of 22 ideas can be approached from a three-fold point-of-view. The three-fold point-of-view is a central element of all genuine occult teachings, and is also present within the less esoteric commentaries. For example, the three-fold point-of-view is discussed within the philosophical commentaries on the Torah known as the *Yemenite Midrash*. Within this collection, from medieval Yemen, of traditional commentaries on the *Pentateuch*, or "five books of Moses" is contained a work entitled, *Midrash ha-Hefes*. In this text is contained a discourse on the three-fold nature of reality, that is based on the line from "Genesis" (12:7), which says in reference to Abraham: ". . . and there builded he an altar unto the Lord."

Within the *Midrash ha-Hefes*. the commentary speaks of the building of three altars by Abraham as representing the three fundamental aspects of existence: the first (which he built upon hearing the Lord's promise of land for him) relates to the world of bodies, the second (which he built upon taking possession of this Promised Land) is the soul-world, and the third (because he was rescued from Ur Kasdim) relates to the intellectual or spiritual world. The first world being indicated by the senses; the second by the motion of bodies; and the third by the desire of the souls to understand. In keeping with this three-fold view of the world, the author of the *Midrash ha-Hefes* affirms that it is because the world is three-fold that the angels chant a "thrice-holy hymn." This reference to a "thrice-holy hymn" is an allusion to the sacred prayer of the Seraphim which can be found in "Isaiah" (6:1-3) where it says:

> *In the year that King Uzziah died I saw also the Lord sitting upon a throne, high and lifted up, and his train filled the temple.*
> *Above it stood the Seraphims - each one had six wings; with two he covered his face, and with two he covered his feet, and with two did he fly.*
> *And one cried to another, and said; 'Holy, holy, holy, is the Lord of Hosts - the whole Earth is full of his glory.'*

Another "thrice-holy hymn", that acknowledges the three-fold nature of sacred wisdom, is the well-known Christian hymn, *Holy, holy, holy,* which proclaims: "Holy, holy, holy, Lord God almighty, God in three persons, blessed Trinity." This three-fold nature of the divine Holy Trinity is, in turn, reflected in the three times three, or nine orders of Angelical Hierarchies; and, in another manner, is also reflected in the three-fold nature of the human being; which consists of spirit, soul, and body.

It is perhaps appropriate at this point to say that it is not without some hesitation that I have pursued the writing of a book which is concerned with such sacred matters. In light of this, I am reminded of the words of Johann Wolfgang von Goethe:

> *People act as if that incomprehensible and highest Being, Who is far beyond the reach of thought, were only their equal. Otherwise they could not say 'the Lord God, the dear God, the good God.' This saying becomes to them, especially to the clergy who have it on their lips every day, only an expression, a empty name, to which no thought whatsoever is connected. If His greatness had impressed them so much they would be speechless, and out of reverence, unwilling to say His name.*

It was due to his mastery of the sacred knowledge of the "three parts of wisdom of the whole world" that Hermes, the great Initiate of ancient Egypt, was called "Trismegistus", or "Thrice Greatest." Likewise, through the gradual mastery of the faculties of thinking, feeling, and willing we can increasingly participate in the "three parts of wisdom of the whole world." This wisdom, in turn, is manifested within the three realms of Spirit, Soul, and Body; and is inspired by the Angelical Hierarchies within the cycles of the seven planets, which circumscribe the seven planetary spheres, and are surrounded by the cosmic workings of the twelve regions of space known as the Zodiac.

If the Grail legends speak of anything, they speak in a veiled language of the secret initiation doctrines of Christian Occultism. For, it was the medieval Christian Initiates of central Europe who inspired the encoding of the esoteric principles of initiation-knowledge into the original Grail legends. In order to secretly convey this mystery knowledge, which had been received from higher Initiates, the early Grail writers Chretien de Troyes and Wolfram von Eschenbach utilized a symbolical language so as to veil the hidden truths from the uninitiated; and, through this imaginative symbolical form of writing, managed to avoid the censure of the church authorities. This was necessary because the Brotherhood of the Holy Grail, and later the original Rosicrucian Brotherhood, were bearers of a form of Esoteric Christian "occult" teachings that, in order to maintain its purity and avoid persecution, had to exist in secret - independent of the Church, or of any other earthly authority. Although, to this we must add, that for a brief period of around two-hundred years (c.1119-1312), these inner teachings found a safe-haven in the Order of the Knights Templars.

This Christian Occultism has nourished those souls who, with the utmost sincerity throughout the centuries, have strived to attain a stage of consciousness which would lead to a direct experience of Christ, like the experience of St. Paul on the road to Damascus. In this quest for the living experience of Christ, which is fulfilled through the inspiration of the Holy Spirit, the "catena aurea" or "golden chain" of Grail Initiates have quietly unlocked the deeper mysteries of the world and of humankind.

The modern successor to this "golden chain" of Grail Initiates is Rudolf Steiner. In basing the teachings of Anthroposophy upon the *scientific* method applied to his highly developed clairvoyant abilities and vast personal experience in the realms of initiation, Rudolf Steiner has taken the next step in the spiritual evolution of mankind - by creating the means for "any unbiased individual with a healthy capacity for understanding" to develop, through patient study, a Christ-centered scientific knowledge of the Spiritual World, a Christian Occultism.

By the word Occultism I mean: an esoteric path of knowledge which is derived from the direct experience of the supersensible realms that are normally hidden or concealed from perception (Latin, occulere = conceal). This direct experience of the supersensible realms comes about through clairvoyant perception, which can occur either through grace or initiation.

Due to the many misunderstandings that exist regarding such matters, the word "occult" is frequently associated inappropriately with the word "cult" (Latin, cultus = care) and all of its possible media-driven, negative connotations. This is not to deny the existence of certain "cults" with their unwholesome "occult" practices, which out of ignorance are clearly serving either the realm of "the shadow of death", or the realm of "false light", or some unhealthy combination of both.

In fact, the imbalanced paths of the "shadow" and of the "false light" are both represented by Wolfram von Eschenbach as temptations confronting Parzival on his quest to find the Holy Grail - temptations that, in their subtle way, confront each and every human being within the course of daily life. Although, in the manner they are woven together by Wolfram von Eschenbach in his epic poem *Parzival*, the distinctions between these two challenges to equilibrium are not so clearly defined - for neither are they in life. Nonetheless, we can make a basic distinction as a point of departure; for, the challenge of the realm of "the shadow of death" is the heartless, unlawful power that is embodied in the black magician Klingsor, the anti-hero who delighted in exerting his control over others. On the other hand, the challenge of the realm of the "false light" is the thoughtless, misdirected passion that is portrayed by Wolfram in the character of Kundry, "the temptress."

It is in its stark contrast to these two imbalanced paths of errors that we will recognize the purity of the occultism of the Grail, which is humbly presented to the reading public in this book. The true Grail Mysteries, which have been revealed to mankind through the works of Rudolf Steiner, are more accurately a form of "anti-cult" which strives for the wholesome unfoldment of the truly-free individual toward a sharing of universally human values. Furthermore, if the path of the Grail is pursued in a balanced manner, it can serve as a healthy antidote to the wide-spread lower-egotism that is so pervasive in modern life; and which finds expression in what Rudolf Steiner prophetically described as the "cult of personality" that would become a source of problems toward the end of the twentieth century.

If one is to come to an understanding of the Grail Mysteries, it is most helpful if one acquires the language and concepts that will enable one to have thoughts which are capable of serving as a, so to speak, Grail to receive this understanding. For, without the proper language or concepts how can one think the thoughts? It is this development of one's thinking, through the acquisition of the language of the Grail and the resulting living concepts - as if one were preparing to travel to a distant shore - that is the initial preparation of the Grail-seeker. In the initial stages, acquiring a spiritual vocabulary may appear to be a most difficult task; and yet, it is because of its difficulty that it is of value. For it is through the struggle to understand (and remember) the supersensible Grail teachings of Anthroposophy, or Spiritual Science, that inner development begins to unfold. The higher significance of this fact of Spiritual Science is made clear by Rudolf Steiner in the first lecture of the lecture cycle entitled, *Cosmic and Human Metamorphoses*.

The Kingdom of Christ Jesus is not of this world, but it must work in this world and the human souls must be instruments of the Kingdom that is not of this world. From this point of view we must consider the fact of how few today have asked themselves the question which, as regards individual acts, as well as events, must be put to the Christ. Humanity must, however, learn to ask of Him. How is that to come about? It can only be possible if we learn His language. Anyone who comprehends the deeper purpose of our Spiritual Science, realizes that it not only gives out a theoretical knowledge about different problems of humanity, the principles of human nature, reincarnation and karma, but that it contains a quite special language, that it has a particular way of expressing itself about spiritual things. The fact that through Spiritual Science we learn to hold inner converse with the spiritual world in thought, is much more important that the mere acquiring of theoretical thoughts. For Christ is with us always, even to the end of the Earth-epochs. And we must learn His language. By means of the language - no matter how abstract it may seem - in which we hear of Saturn, Sun, Moon, and Earth and of the different periods and ages of the Earth, and of the many other secrets of evolution - we teach ourselves a language in which we can frame out the questions we put to

> *the spiritual world. When we really learn inwardly to speak the language of this spiritual life, the result will be that Christ will stand by us and give us the answers Himself. This is the attitude that our work in Spiritual Science should bring about in us, as a sentiment, a feeling. Why do we occupy ourselves with Spiritual Science? It is as though we were learning the vocabulary of the language through which we approach the Christ. If we take the trouble to learn to think the thoughts of Spiritual Science, and make the mental effort necessary for an understanding of the Cosmic secrets taught by Spiritual Science - then, out of the dim, dark foundations of the Cosmic mysteries, will come forth the figure of Christ Jesus, which will draw near to us and give us the strength and force in which we shall then live. The Christ will guide us, standing by us as a brother, so that our hearts and souls may be strong enough to grow up to the necessary level of the tasks awaiting humanity in its further development.*

At no point in human history has mankind been without the presence of Initiates who, through their experience as "citizens of the Spiritual World", were able to share with mankind the fruits of their spiritual wisdom. It has only been in more recent history that the higher Initiates, or Adepts have not been given a central role in the guidance of civilization. For, according to the indications of Rudolf Steiner, Charles IV (1316-1378) the king of Bohemia who became the Holy Roman Emperor from 1346 to 1378, was "the last Initiate on the throne of the emperors." Up until this time, which just preceded the beginning of our present Consciousness-Soul age in 1414, the direct guidance of mankind by Initiates was becoming more and more infrequent. This was due to the decline of the old atavistic clairvoyance, which was being replaced by the intellect as a result of the unfolding individuation of the Ego.

In ancient times, the average individual was possessed of a natural clairvoyant ability which, since the the end of the Atlantean period, had been gradually declining as history approached the incarnation of Christ around 2,000 years ago. With the decline of the natural clairvoyant abilities of mankind, the opportunity for the cultivation of a relationship to the supersensible realms was to be sought through Initiation at the ancient Mystery Centers. But as mankind approached the incarnation of Christ, even the Mystery Centers had entered into a period of decadence and all but a very few had become but mere shadows of their former glory. It was in this period of decline that it became necessary for the content of the Ancient Mysteries to, so to speak, "go to seed." For this mystery wisdom had to "go to seed" so that it might blossom forth from within the hearts of mankind in a new way, after having undergone a metamorphosis through the Christ impulse - once mankind had evolved to the point where they would ask in perfect freedom, the healing Grail question: "Brother, what ails you?".

It is this challenge of the development of one's spiritual strivings as a free individual that confronts the modern Grail-seeker - on their path to the castle of the Grail. Yet, before them stands the Dragon of materialism that can only be slain by taking up the sword of Michael - the sword of the "knights of the Word" that is forged in the fires of spiritual wisdom, formed on the anvil of experience, and tempered in the blood of the heart.

In the city of Arnheim, on July 19th 1924, Rudolf Steiner spoke regarding the inability of some of "the most enlightened minds of the present age" to come to terms with the content of Anthroposophy.

> Such examples indicate how the most enlightened minds of the present age receive what must be established as the Michael Epoch in the world and what has to be done in order that the Cosmic Intelligence, which in accordance with the World Order fell away from Michael in the 8th century A.D., may again be found within earthly humanity. The whole Michael tradition must be renewed. Michael with his feet upon the Dragon - it is right to contemplate this picture which portrays Michael the Warrior, defending the Cosmic Spirit against the Ahrimanic Powers under his feet.
>
> This battle, more that any other, is laid in the human heart. There, within the hearts of men, it is and has been waged since the last third of the nineteenth century. Decisive indeed will be what human hearts do with this Michael Impulse in the world, in the course of the twentieth century. And in the course of the twentieth century, when the first century after the end of Kaliyuga has elapsed, humanity will either stand at the grave of all civilization - or at the beginning of that Age when in the souls of men who in their hearts ally Intelligence with Spirituality, Michael's battle will be fought out to victory.

Lady Adventure

"Open!"
"To whom? Who can it be?"
"I wish to come to you - into your heart."
"Then you wish for far too little space."
"How does it matter, if in such little space
  you have not felt the least bit crowded?
  For I wish now to tell you of marvelous things."
"Oh! Could it be you, Lady Adventure?"

Parzival, by Wolfram von Eschenbach

The Grail tradition can be thought of as a Golden Chain, the links of which were forged in pre-Christian times and joined together by Christ at the Mystery of Golgotha. This Golden Chain continues from the archaic periods on into modern times, working towards the future evolution of mankind. The links of this Golden Chain are the various pre-Christian Mystery streams and their initiates who were all, in their unique ways, contributing towards the development of humanity by working with the spiritual beings that were in service to the Christ.

The possession of a doctrine concerning the connection of the souls of Earth to the manifold spiritual beings that serve the Christ is a characteristic of the true esoteric Christian teachings. The traditional esoteric view of this connectedness, which is an important element of the reality of the multitude, or choir of beings, is referred to as the Pleroma and is characterized by the first Christian known by scholar's to have studied the esoteric tradition of the Hebrew Kabbalah, Ramon Llull "Doctor Illuminatus" (1235-1315), the author of *Ars Magna*.

> *A chain of concordances extends from the highest to the lowest. For there is a kind of universal affection among all things, in which they all share. It is a connection which many people, such as Homer, call the golden chain, or the cincture of Venus, a chain of nature, or a token which things have towards one another.*

Likewise, this doctrine of connectedness between all living beings is fundamental to the understanding of *all true esoteric teachings*. That this is so, is made clear by H. P. Blavatsky in volume 1 of her principle work, *The Secret Doctrine* (page 604).

> *From Gods to men, from Worlds to atoms, from a star to a rush-light, from the Sun to the vital heat of the meanest organic being - the world of Form and Existence is an immense chain, whose links are all connected. The law of Analogy is the first key to the world-problem, and these links have to be studied coordinately in their occult relation to each other.*

When the Holy Spirit as a dove winged down over Jesus of Nazareth at the baptism by John the Baptist in the river Jordan, "the Great Sun-Being" Christ - the creator and leader of the whole chain of Spiritual Hierarchies - entered directly into human evolution. This, one and only, incarnation of Christ into a human being led to the anointing of the Earth with - the Holy Blood of Christ - at the crucifixion upon the hill of Golgotha. Through the occult reality of the spilling of the blood of Christ, the spiritual Sun-Being of Christ entered the atmosphere of the Earth, thereby redeeming the evolution of mankind.

Christ was crucified upon the hill that legend says was the burial place of the skull of Adam, hence the name Golgotha, which means "place of the skull" (Aramaic, golgolta), this meaning is also represented in its other name, Calvary which is derived from the Latin word Calvarium, and means skull. From the Mystery of Golgotha onwards, the Christ-being has been present within the atmosphere of the Earth, as Christ once said; "I shall be with you always."

The servants of the Grail are those that serve the "sang-real", the "blood-royal" that is the blood of Christ, the "King of Kings." Numerous streams of the Ancient Mysteries converged in the Grail tradition, and survive in the images of the Grail stories. The Initiates of certain ancient pre-Christian mysteries would, through their initiations, have the experience of the Christ as a cosmic being approaching the Earth from higher worlds. The modern Grail server can find the Christ in the world of life, the etheric world nearest the physical, through uniting their own etherized blood with the etheric-blood of Christ. This etherized blood is generated out of the subtle nature of the spirit acting upon the blood vapor that is within the hollow space which is formed by the vortexing blood within the upright human heart. This occult fact of the etherization of the blood is discussed by Bernard C. J. Lievegoed in his book entitled, *Mystery Streams in Europe and the New Mysteries*.

> The Spirit-Self is the Astral Body purified and spiritualized by the ego (the Golden Fleece of the Greeks). This Astral Body, purified and spiritualized by the Christ, through which the turbid red blood, carrier of the passions, became the 'rose colored blood' of the chalice, was carried by the Christ in the hearts of men from East to West. And it was carried in the hearts of the first Christians from Asia Minor to Gaul and England.
>
> This was the strength of primal Christianity, that filled the hearts of men who took in the Christ.
>
> In the lectures on the etherization of the blood, Rudolf Steiner described how, by divine grace, the etheric stream goes through the human being from the heart to the pineal [gland], there irradiating the brain as spiritual etheric light. Only thus can we have spiritual thoughts; otherwise, we would be able only to have thoughts that connect with sense impressions.

This is the microcosmic Grail in us. The golden light of the etheric blood that irradiates the head was observed clairvoyantly as a lustre of gold around the head, when it united with the stream of the Christ etheric forces. In still later times, it appeared as a halo in the paintings of the medieval painters and became the traditional 'token' of holiness. The halo was the last memory of the working of the Grail.

The Ego can only fully manifest through the vertical blood-flow which comes about through the upright stature of a human being. The horizontal animal kingdom does not share in this uprightness, for the animals do not possess individual Egos; they have instead, group-souls that overshadow each of the various species from outside.

It is through our uprightness that we become individuals in possession of an "I Am", what St. Paul called "the Christ in you." It is through the realization of the "I Am" that one comes to find that we are all corpuscles in the body of Christ, and thereby links in the Golden Chain. The ancient mysteries of India, Persia, Egypt, Greece, and Europe among others, have prepared important links in this Golden Chain, though frequently exoteric Christians fail to understand the connection and materialists fail to see the point. The primordial nature of the Christian mystery is emphasized by St. Augustine of Hippo (354-430 A.D.).

That which is called the Christian Religion existed among the ancients, and never did it not exist, from the beginning of the human race until Christ came in the flesh, at which time the true religion which already existed began to be called Christianity.

The term "Judaeo-Christian tradition" has led historically to a very narrow understanding of the mission of Christ, as representing an exclusive manifestation within a single cultural stream; but "Christ came for all men." There were many initiates of the different Ancient Mysteries around the world that were awaiting the Christ out of their own prophetic initiatory traditions. The mission of the Messiah is not the exclusive property of the Hebrew tradition, even though the Hebrew people did have a singular role in preparing appropriate astral, etheric, and physical bodies to receive the Christ.

The teachings regarding the Christ impulse that were present in the Ancient Mysteries were given in the language of their respective peoples and times, and so, the pre-Christian Mysteries that led to the Christ Mystery are found to have different names in different lands and epochs; whether, Krishna or Vishvakarman in India, Ahura Mazdao in Persia, Osiris or Re' in Egypt, Apollo in Greece, Baldur in Northern Europe and, Hu the Mighty, or Cernunnos the "King of the Elements" in the groves of the Celtic-Druid Mysteries in the West of Europe.

Due to the failure of mankind to understand this connection between Christianity and the Ancient Mysteries, many people from other traditions that might have found the Christ - have not. This, in part, is the result of the inability of the exoteric Christians to make connections with other traditions; for, due to cultural and language barriers they often disrespect and disregard other traditions which have many valuable contributions and insights. This cultural disharmony, on the other hand, has primarily been the result of the failure of individuals to recognize the Christ "in all his glory" within their own hearts; from whatever tradition they might adhere, whether Christian or not. Those that call themselves Christians should keep their minds open to the Christ's working through all peoples and lands, even those who don't know any of his names; for Christ himself told the disciples how they shall be able to recognize the true Christians; "Ye shall know them by their deeds."

If mankind could only attune themselves to the inner promptings of a Christ filled heart, then perhaps they might - by the working of the spirit - discover that Christ's legacy to mankind is more profound than they ever dreamed. The universality of Christ's mission and some of the attendant challenges were commented on by Rudolf Steiner in a lecture he gave in Munich on the 15th of March 1910 entitled, *The Sermon on the Mount - The Land Shamballa*.

> *We are . . . approaching an age in which man will feel himself surrounded not only by a physical, sensible world but also, according to the measure of his knowledge, by a spiritual kingdom. The leader in this new kingdom of the spirit will be the Etheric Christ. No matter what religious community or faith to which people belong, once they have experienced these facts in themselves they will acknowledge and accept the Christ event. Those Christians who actually have the exper-*

ience of the Etheric Christ are perhaps in a more difficult situation than adherents to other religions, yet they should endeavor to accept this Christ event in just as neutral a way as the others. It will, in fact, be man's task to develop, especially through Christianity, an understanding for the possibility of entering the spiritual world independently of any religious denomination but simply through the power of good will.

"Except ye be as little children, ye shall not enter the Kingdom of Heaven." When Christ Jesus made this statement he did not explain its meaning; but nonetheless, it brings to mind an image of purity, clarity and innocence. The "little children" are by nature very close to Christ and his angels, they have not yet lost a certain heavenly quality of trust, and the vitality that the vibrant forces of life bring. Through the path of Esoteric Christianity one can reawaken these inner qualities and living forces, for as Christ said; "Let the dead bury the dead."

It is crucial at this stage of evolution that mankind enter into the clarity of living-thinking and breathe life into the dead bones of reason. For it is through our thinking that we are free, and it is by our thinking that we bring about our transformation. In order to make change we must first have the thought of change. Within Anthroposophy, the spiritual scientific teachings of Rudolf Steiner, the path of Grail, or Esoteric Christianity is presented in a manner that is suitable for a modern humanity that lives very strongly in their thinking.

In the Grail legend, Parzival had to cross the wasteland to reach the castle of the Grail, the image is clear; you must make the journey in order to reach the goal. Yes, Christ has said; "I shall be with you always", and if mankind were to truly act out of this understanding, the Earth would be transformed. But the path of the Christ impulse is slow and gradual, He wishes for mankind to evolve through free ideas - a heart capable of love, and a will with the fortitude to act from love's inspiration - as it says in "The Gospel of St. John"; "God is love." The Christ has said; "I have come to give you more life, and that abundantly", this life is the secret of the Grail; for, as Moses said ("Leviticus" 17:11):

For the life of the flesh is in the blood: and I have given it to you upon the altar to make an atonement for your souls: for it is the blood that maketh an atonement for the soul.

Natura

On the reward of the soul who has refused to be content
with anything short of infinity . . .

Wrapt in warmth of feeling,
the inner light has met the outer light.
The Goddess Natura enrobed in true shadows,
reflects all colors,
informing the vessels of her perception
with forms, gestures and riddles,
revealing their true natures.
The inwardness of the Sun-Being, enlivens and quickens
all humankind with the true light of Self.
Expressing itself in deeds true, in as much as they speak
the language of that unity of unities, called love.
The Courts of Love
speak the Language of the Birds,
inspiring our future being
with a tongue as ancient as the Heart-Sun;
dispelling the false light,
and its child of false darkness,
by harmonizing all melodies.
Father Time, rests on the other side of his song,
listening to the chorus of hearts,
giving birth,
ever so slowly,
to future Suns . . .

Part 1

The Major Arcana

"The Sages have been taught by God that this natural world is only an image and material copy of a heavenly and spiritual pattern; and that the very existence of this world is based upon the reality of its celestial archetype."

Michael Sendivogius, 1566-1646

0

The Fool

Alchemical Sulfur - Parzival - the "Noble Traveler"

In the 9th century, it was the Grail initiate Parzival, who - out of his own forces - was able to manifest the "I Am" or Ego that is carried in the warmth of the blood, and pierce "through the valley of the shadow of death" (Parzival = pierce the valley), passing from "dullness through doubt to 'saelde' or blessedness." This is the path of every aspirant to spiritual fulfillment through the Grail. In order to accomplish the goal one must choose a path, even more - one must become the path for "the king and the land are one." It is the spiritual embodiment of radiant macrocosmic-spiritual forces within the microcosmic-spiritual human being that is the receiving of the Holy Grail (**I**). As it is written in "The Gospel of St. Matthew" (13:43); ". . . then shall the righteous shine forth as the sun in the kingdom of their Father."

In the imagery of the Fool arcanum you see an innocent youth holding the white rose of purity with a small white dog that is attempting to stand upright as if in excited imitation of his master. In the innocence is shown the Fool's inexperience, in the white rose is symbolized the purity of the life of the Etheric-Body of formative-forces that is the highest expression in the plant kingdom; while the pouch, which is behind the Fool, represents memory - another aspect of the function of the Etheric-Body. The white dog, on the other hand, represents the Astral-Body, or desire body, which is the highest expression in the animal kingdom. The little dog's white color denotes that it has been tamed somewhat of its animality, although it can only rise partially upright for a short period of time. Uprightness is a quality of the Ego that separates humanity from the horizontal-astral animal world. An example of this from life is when a child begins to speak and say "I" after it has already begun walking upright; for uprightness, thinking, and speaking are expressions of the incarnating Ego of the child. An image that relates to this theme of uprightness was frequently carved upon the graves of knights in the Middle Ages, which show a knight standing cross-legged on a small dog with his hands over his heart in the position of prayer, representing a conquering of animality by the forces of the Spirit. It is interesting to note that in the story of *Parzival* his father Gahmuret's comrade in arms is named Schionatulander, which as Walter Johannes Stein points out means: in French; *li joenet u l'alant*, in German; *der Jungling mit dem Hunde* = the young man with the dog.

Schionatulander was the grandson of Gurnemanz, the teacher of Parzival. In the epic Grail poem *Titurel*, written in Germany by Albrecht von Scharfenberg in the second half of the thirteenth century, it tells of the great love between Schionatulander and the maid Sigune, though he meets a tragic end in Wolfram von Eschenbach's *Parzival*. (Wolfram's epic Grail poem *Parzival* was written around 1197 or 1198, which is one cycle of the Venus pentagram into the Christian era, a cycle that I explain in the chapter on the Magician arcanum.)

In the story of *Parzival*, Schionatulander is cradled in the arms of Sigune after having been slain by Orilus, who meant to slay Parzival in his jealousy over his wife Jeschute. All of this depicts the tragedy of the unredeemed astral-desire forces. The sight of Sigune with the body of her dead lover Schionatulander who has died in his place is a powerful awakening for Parzival; which is made even more painful to Parzival by the fact that Schionatulander had also fought to defend Parzival's land from Orilus' attempt to capture it following the death of Gamuret, Parzival's father. All of these images portray the complexity of human relationships within the world of desires. Ultimately, after further adventures, what this leads Parzival to realize is that the uprightness of the "I" (Ego) can rise above the turmoil of the astral-desire nature and achieve clarity in human relationships, by passing from dullness to doubt and then to "saelde", or blessedness.

In returning to the image of the Fool arcanum, the Fool holds a staff (yet another symbol of the uprightness of the "I" as manifested in the spinal column) but instead of being held upright as in the Hermit arcanum, the staff is thrown casually over his shoulder as if he were unaware of its significance. The staff is being used to hold on to a little pouch that represents memory, which is an aspect of the Etheric-Body. The staff and the white rose in his hand are pointed at the Sun, the image of spiritual light and life, which is behind his back, but the Fool doesn't appear to notice, for he is intoxicated by the world of the senses. The Fool's outfit is decorated with the alchemical symbol of the spirit, repeated many times over, but he doesn't seem to notice this either. For the Fool has not yet reached the maturity of the Hermit who is the developed upright individual, and who, by the power of the spirit, has developed sufficient soul-light to be not only "a lamp unto himself" - but to others as well.

The mission of the "I Am" is to be a child of God and develop to its most complete wholesome capacity, which is represented by the image of the Fool who is about to begin the journey - for with maturity one evolves. This spiritual maturity is portrayed by the Hermit arcanum, representing the constellation of Virgo and the unfoldment of the Sophia forces which manifest as cosmic wisdom that is born through human experience. These Sophia forces, which become active in the spiritual-human as soul forces, are carried by the Guardian Angel and held in waiting until the free individual has developed the necessary moral-aptitude to become a responsible spiritual-human (**XII**). The Hermetic author Arthur Versluis characterizes this relationship to the Sophia principle in his book entitled, *TheoSophia*.

> *In theosophy, Sophia represents inwardly an ambience in which the Logos can be born; she is the 'substance' or 'presence' through which Christ manifests within, but she is also the transcendent form or 'Virgin of Light' toward whom we move inwardly on our spiritual journey to realization of our transcendent spiritual center. Thus she is Mercy itself, as the divine 'element' within whom Christ is conceived through the Holy Spirit; but she is also revealed through spiritual discipline.*
>
> *Sophia is the 'pure element' in which the spiritual revelation of the Logos, or Spiritual Sun, takes place; she is therefore also the divine Presence as manifested in the cosmos. This is why Boehme wrote that Sophia is like a prism, through which the pure light of the Godhead is refracted into being; and also why he wrote that one must necessarily approach the Trinity via Sophia: Sophia is not a member of the Trinity - despite various attempts to make her so - but rather is the 'medium' or element through which we as created beings approach the Father, the Logos, and the Holy Spirit. This approach, which takes place in the spirituality of our visionaries only in an inward visionary realm, must be an approach to a 'Virgin of Light' that is, in an ultimate sense, our own true center.*

This approach to our own true center, which corresponds to the path that the Fool must take on the quest of initiation, is the process of the incarnation and development of the spiritual-human, or as I like to call it the "Ancient Child", as portrayed in my poem *The Ancient Child*.

The Ancient Child

The advancing Goddesses of the starry shore,
manifesting shapes beyond earth's threshold,
spin through their mutable destinies
beyond time's closed door,
awaiting the Child of Old . . .
The Child of my heart
arises within the stillness of the new morning,
breathing life into the dead bones of reason,
and sealing the casket of unfulfilled hopes and promises
with the touch of her hand.
She calls out to the night,
to await its turn,
to be exalted at the birth of a new day.
The Star-eyed Goddess
of limitless love and truth
holds the empty cup of meaning,
awaiting the wine of life,
to be distilled from the innocence of youth,
by the slow sure steps
of an Ancient Child . . .

It is this process of the growth and development of the "Ancient Child" that is represented by the Fool arcanum. The "Ancient Child", or "I Am", is taking the journey of individuation, and is carried in the alchemical warmth of the blood as it meets the principle of uprightness.

Rudolf Steiner explains this relationship of the Ego to the experience of uprightness in the lecture given in Berlin on October 26th, 1909 entitled, "Higher Senses, Inner Force Currents and Creative Laws in the Human Organism" which is published in the lecture cycle entitled, *The Wisdom of Man, of the Soul, and of the Spirit - Anthroposophy, Psychosophy, Pneumatosophy*.

The ego, then, acts downward from above; so how would its physical organ have to lie? The physical organ of the ego is the circulating blood; and the ego could not function downward from above without an organ running in the same direction in the human body. Where the main direction of the blood-stream is horizontal, not vertical, there can be no ego, as in men. The main direction of the blood-stream had to raise itself in man to the vertical in order to enable the ego to lay hold on the blood. No ego can intervene where the main blood-stream runs horizontally instead of vertically. The group ego of animals can find no organ in them, because the main blood-line runs horizontally. Through the erection of this line to the vertical in man, the group ego became an individual ego.

This difference between men and the animals shows how erroneous it is to set up a relationship inferred from purely external phenomena. That act of rising from the horizontal to the vertical is an historic incident, but it could no more have taken place without an underlying will, without the cooperation of spirit, than the raising of the hammer could have done. Only when a will, a spiritual force, courses through the blood can the horizontal line pass over into the vertical, can the upright position come about and the group soul rise to become the individual soul. It would be illogical to recognize the spiritual force in one case, that of the hammer, and not in the other, in man.

As regards to the past of our Cosmos, and the actions of the spiritual hierarchies, I would like to briefly mention a few aspects of cosmic evolution that are explained in detail by Rudolf Steiner in, *An Outline of Occult Science*: Out of the region of the constellation of Leo, the Lion, the longing of the Thrones, or Spirits of Will, brought about the donation of primal warmth that was the first manifestation of our creation, the seed of the Physical-Body, in the first condition of human evolution; which is called the Old Saturn incarnation of the Earth (**IV**). This first vortex of warmth is the prototype of what would become the organ of warmth - the Sun in man - the human heart. The region of Leo will also be the direction of space which will be the focal-point of the seventh condition of human evolution, the Vulcan incarnation of the Earth, which is the last condition in the chain of seven evolutionary stages; when mankind will have evolved three stages beyond the human stage of our present Earth, which is the middle, or, fourth condition in the chain of seven planetary incarnations; which are seven different conditions of life, consciousness, and form. Between each planetary incarnation, or period of activity or manifestation, is a condition of rest or Pralaya, an *unmanifested* state of being, for all the beings below the level of the Elohim, also known as the Exusiai, or Spirits of Form (**V**).

The Sophia forces are connected with the mystery of the Holy Spirit, which has a particular relationship to the region of the constellation of Taurus, the Bull (**X**). The cosmic wisdom of Sophia that works within the evolution of mankind was developed by the Kyriotetes, or Spirits of Wisdom, who donated the seed of the Etheric Body in the Old Sun incarnation of the Earth (**IV**). The Kyriotetes work out of the region of Virgo and have as their lowest member a vehicle that corresponds to the Atma, or Spirit-Man (**IX**); which is the highest principle in a human being and is the spiritual counterpart of the Physical-Body. The Kyriotetes can be seen as the bearers of the primal Sophia-Wisdom forces that will enable mankind, out of wisdom, to recognize the Christ love (**XIV**).

The Kyriotetes, along with the other hierarchies, performed the "great sacrifice" of bringing mankind and our Cosmos into being as the "Cosmos of Wisdom", to prepare it for the "Turning Point of Time", when out of the region of the Lamb, or Aries, would arise the sacrifice of the "Lamb of God." By this deed of sacrifice, which took place on the hill of Golgotha less than 2,000 years ago, Christ began the transformation of the "Cosmos of Wisdom" into the "Cosmos of Love."

Since this transformation began, we have gradually entered upon the path towards becoming co-creators with the nine Spiritual Hierarchies as the "Tenth Hierarchy", the "Spirits of Freedom and Love." In the actions of a Spirit of Freedom and Love are found deeds that express the plan of the Logos, the Christ, which must at this point be seen as a goal - as humanity is, as a whole, at the early stages of this process.

We are presently within the epoch of the Consciousness-Soul, the fifth post-Atlantean cultural epoch of Pisces, or the Fishes (see: Part 3), and therefore only in the next epoch after Golgotha and the Grail mystery of the Crucifixion, which took place in the fourth post-Atlantean cultural epoch of Aries, the Ram, which was the epoch of the Intellectual-Soul. The mission of our present epoch of the Consciousness-Soul consists, in part, in bringing individual clarity to human thinking, feeling and willing, out of a mood of trust in our karma and openness to others. All of this is but preparation for the Spirit-Self and its birth out of its relationship to the Guardian Angel in the next epoch, the sixth, the epoch of the Water Carrier, Aquarius. Rudolf Steiner discusses this mystery in reference to the Knights Templar Order in the lecture given in Berlin on May 22nd, 1905 entitled, "The Lost Temple and its Restoration", which is contained in the lecture cycle entitled, *The Temple Legend.*

> *Later in the Middle Ages, the idea of Solomon's Temple was revived again in the Knights Templars, who sought to introduce the Temple thinking in the West. But the Knights Templars were misunderstood at that time [which eventually led to the the torture, trial, and burning at the stake of Jacques de Molay, the Grand Master of the Knights Templar Order, along with many other Templars]. If we wish to understand the Templars, we must look deeply into human history. What the Templars were reproached with in their trial rests entirely on a major misunderstanding. The Knights Templars said at that time: 'Everything we have experienced so far is a preparation for what the Redeemer has wished for.' 'For', they continued, 'Christianity has a future, a new task. And we have the task of preparing the various sects of the Middle Ages, and humanity in general, for a future in which Christianity will emerge into a new clarity, as the Redeemer actually intended that it should. We saw Christianity rise in the fourth cultural epoch [the Graeco-Roman epoch, the epoch of the Intellectual-Soul]; it will develop further in the fifth [the Consciousness-Soul epoch], but only in the sixth [the epoch of the Spirit-Self] is it to celebrate the Glory of its resurrection. We have to prepare for that. We must guide human souls in such a way that a genuine, true and pure Christianity may come to expression, in which the Name of the Most High may find its dwelling place.'*
>
> *Jerusalem was to be the center and from there the secret concerning the relationship of man to the Christ should stream out all over the world. What was represented symbolically by the temple should become a living reality. It was said of the Templars, and this was a reproach to them, that they had instituted a kind of star-worship, or, similarly, a sun-worship. However, a great mystery lies behind this. The sacrifice of the*

> *Mass was originally nothing else but a great mystery. Mass fell into two parts; the so-called Minor Mass, in which all were allowed to take part; and, when that had ended, and the main body [of the congregation] had gone away, there followed the High Mass, which was intended only for those who wished to undergo occult training, to embark on the 'Path.' In this High Mass the reciting of the Apostolic Creed took place first; then was expounded the development of Christianity throughout the world, and how it was connected with the great march of world evolution.*

Later in the same lecture Rudolf Steiner gives further clarification regarding the esoteric mysteries of the Knights Templars:

> *We have traced the time from the first to the fourth cultural epoch. The sun proceeds through the heavens, and now we enter the sign of the Fishes [in our present epoch which is determined by the relationship of the Sun to the backdrop of fixed stars at sunrise during the spring equinox], where we are ourselves at a critical point. Then [in the future], in the time of the sixth epoch, the time will arrive when man will have become so inwardly purified that he himself becomes a temple for the divine. At that time the sun will enter the sign of the Water Carrier [Aquarius, the epoch of the Spirit-Self]. Thus the sun, which is really only the external expression of our spiritual life, progresses in heavenly space. When the sun enters the sign of the Water Carrier at the spring equinox, it will then be understood completely clearly for the first time.*
>
> *Thus proceeded the High Mass, from which all the uninitiated were excluded. It was made clear to those who remained that Christianity, which began as a seed, would in the future bear something quite different as fruit, and that by the name Water Carrier was meant John [the Baptist] who scatters Christianity as a seed, as if with a grain of mustard seed. Aquarius or the Water Carrier means the same person as John who baptized with water in order to prepare mankind to receive the Christian baptism of fire. The coming of a 'John/Aquarius' who would first confirm the old John and*

announce a Christ who would renew the Temple, once the great point of time should have arrived when Christ will again speak to humanity - this was taught in the depths of the Templar Mysteries, so that the event should be understood.

The Macrocosmic Temple of the Microcosmic Human Form

The image of the "Temple of Man" is a central theme of the esoteric Christian Mysteries. This idea of a Temple that expresses the mysteries of the human form can be traced back to the initiate-builders of the ancient Egyptian temples (**XXIV**). The ancient Greeks immortalized the ancient Egyptian builder they called Asklepios, the son of Hephaestos, his Egyptian name was Imhotep (which translates; "he who comes in peace"), son of Ptah ("the Opener").

The ancient Greeks considered Ptah to be equivalent to their god Hephaestos who was the divine blacksmith, the god of artisans who - like the "sons of Cain" in *The Book of Enoch*, or in the Rosicrucian *Temple Legend* - taught men the arts. Ptah was the patron god of builders and the chief god of the ancient city of Memphis. In the Memphite theology, it was Ptah who was said to have formed the "primal egg of creation."

The name of Imhotep's actual father is known to be Ka Nofer (who was also an architect although his works are unknown), his mothers name was Khreduankh. Imhotep is thought by some Egyptologists to possibly be the historical figure referred to as Hermes in the Hermetic writings. The initiate Imhotep flourished during the reign of the third dynasty Pharaoh Djoser (Zoser) who is considered to have ruled Egypt from around 2630 B.C. to 2611 B.C. Imhotep is the earliest architect whose works are known, he is also the earliest known physician, and he was deified by later Egyptians and Greeks as the divine patron of both of these arts. In addition to medicine and the building arts, Imhotep was also distinguished as a vizier in charge of administration, a royal seal-bearer, a prince of the palace, the high priest of Heliopolis, and as a chief kheri-heb, or lector priest who recited and directed the "Liturgy of Funerary Offerings", and the "Opening of the Mouth" rituals. Imhotep was also an astronomer, a sage, scribe, and magician. It is difficult to appreciate the exalted stature of this great initiate in the minds of the ancient world. Imhotep "the chief of all the works of the king" is considered to be the builder of the famous Step Pyramid of Sakkarah; which is considered by archaeologists to be the earliest large hewn stone structure known. He was also the builder of the first temple of Edfu near Memphis, which was said by the Egyptians to be "built upon a plan dropped from heaven."

From ancient Egypt, the knowledge of the mysteries of the Temple of Man continued from Imhotep to Moses about 1,400 years later; who, as the *Bible* tells us, was also the "high priest of On" (Heliopolis), a title which in ancient Egypt referred to the "chief of the astronomers." Heliopolis the "city of the Sun" is the ancient Egyptian city of On (Iunu), which is located at Tell Hisn in what is now a suburb of present day Cairo.

The mysteries of the Temple of Man later resurfaced in the teachings of the Adam Kadmon in the Kabbalah. The Kabbalah, which means "tradition", is the Hebrew esoteric teaching which is said by the Kabbalists to be an ancient oral tradition extending back to Moses, and is the fruit of Moses' experience on Mount Sinai, after his preparation in the Egyptian Mysteries, and through receiving the teachings of Jethro the Midian.

The mysteries of the Temple of Man were also expressed within the design of the Temple of Solomon that was built by Hiram Abiff. It is said that, although King Solomon could conceive of the Temple he lacked the necessary skills needed to build it; and so, Solomon brought Hiram Abiff, the Phoenician master-builder, to Jerusalem to build it for him.

The legend of the master-builder Hiram Abiff is celebrated in the mysteries and rites of Freemasonry; which, according to tradition, are said to have derived their pedigree from the builders of the great Gothic cathedrals of the Middle Ages, and they, in turn, from the initiates in the Holy Land who inspired the founding of the Knights Templars during the Crusades. This Freemasonic tradition is supported by the fact that the Gothic cathedrals were built within the same 200 year period of the Middle Ages that saw the founding and subsequent demise of the Order of the Knights Templars.

The continuation of the ancient mystery wisdom that was embodied in the Temple of Solomon, concerning the human being as a Microcosm, or reflection of the Cosmos, was the secret behind the design of the great Gothic cathedrals. The influence of the tradition of the Macrocosm and the Microcosm can also be seen in the writings of the great teachers of the school of Chartres Cathedral in the Middle Ages.

In reference to the traditions surrounding the Knights Templar Order, Isabel Cooper-Oakley in the chapter entitled "The Traditions of the Templars Revived in Freemasonry", which is to be found in her book entitled, *Masonry and Medieval Mysticism - Traces of a Hidden Tradition*, quotes the Masonic authority Roessler (whom I consider to be reliable source except that he made the mistake frequently made by scholar's who misunderstand the testimony that was extracted from the Knights Templars through torture; namely, that the Templars denied the divinity of Christ). In the following, is an excerpt from Roessler's account of the Knights Templars in Sweden:

> The Brother Templars were, according to their statutes as Hospital Brothers divided into three classes: 1. Into the class of the serving who, without distinction, nursed sick pilgrims and Knights Templars; 2. Into that of the spiritual Brothers destined for the service of Pilgrims; 3. Into that of Knights who went to war.
> We find in the Instructions of the Chevalier d'Orient, where are celebrated the foundation of the Knights Templars and the spread of their teachings in Europe the following declaration on the matter is given:
>
>> 'Eighty-one Masons ("These Masons are always in the figurative sense Knights of the Cross who had been admitted to the Mysteries of the working in the mystic Temple, and to the religion of the Children of the Widow") under the leadership of Garimonts, the Patriarch of Jerusalem, went in the year 1150, to Europe and betook themselves to the Bishop of Upsala who received them in very friendly fashion and was consequently initiated into the mysteries of the Copts which the Masons had brought with them; later he was entrusted with the deposit of the collection of those teachings, rites and mysteries. The Bishop took pains to enclose and conceal them in the subterranean vault of the tower of the "Four Crowns" which at that time, was the crown treasure chamber of the King of Sweden. Nine of these Masons, amongst them Hugo de Paganis [Payens], founded in Europe the Order of the Knights Templars; later on they received from the Bishop the dogmas, mysteries and teachings of the Coptic Priests, confided to him.
>> Thus in a short time the Knights Templars became the receivers and depositors of the

> *mysteries, rites and ceremonies which had been brought over by the Masons from the East - the Levites of the 'true Light.'*
>
> *The Knights Templars, devoted entirely to the sciences and to the dogmas brought from the Thebaid [Egypt], wished, in the course of time to preserve this doctrine in solemn fashion by a token. The Scotch Templars served as pattern in the matter, they having founded the three degrees of St. Andreas of Scotland, and adapted them to the allegorical legend to be found in the instructions referred to.*
>
> *Scotch Templars were occupied in excavating a place at Jerusalem in order to build a temple there, and precisely on the spot where the temple of Solomon - or at least that part of it called the Holy of Holies - had stood. During their work they found three stones which were the corner stones of the Solomon temple itself. The monumental form of these excited their attention; this excitement became all the more intense when they found the name Jehovah engraved in the elliptical spaces of the last of these stones - this which was also a type of the mysteries of the Copt - the sacred word which, by the murder of the Master Builder, had been lost, and which, according to the legend of the first degree, Hiram had engraved on the foundation stone of Solomon's temple. After such a discovery the Scotch Knights took this costly memorial with them, and, in order eternally to preserve their esteem for it, they employed these as the corner stones of their first temple at Edinburgh.'*

As a point of interest, this temple at Edinburgh was near the site of Rosslyn chapel, the westernmost place of pilgrimage on the routes of St. James, and the seat of the hereditary Grand Masters of Scottish Masonry, the lairds of Sinclair; about whom much information has come forth in recent years, some of which I discuss in later chapters. The quotation from Isabel Cooper-Oakley continues:

(The legend of these three stones has a striking resemblance to that of the three mysterious stones which the Nymphs found and brought to Minerva - the Goddess of Wisdom.) Our author further tells us that:

> 'The works began on St. Andreas' day: and so the Templars who had knowledge of this fact, of the secret of the three stones, and of the rediscovered word, called themselves Knights of St. Andreas; they appointed degrees of merit in order to attain, and these are preserved in the apprentice, companion, and master degrees known under the name of the Little Master-Builder, the Great Master-Builder, and the Scotch Master.
>
> By the instruction common to all Knightly Orders, the Crusaders were under obligation to make many journeys and pilgrimages where, as is said, they had to see themselves surrounded by dangers. Therefore they founded those degrees in order to recognize each other and to assist each other in need. For these journeys they took signs, words and particular touches or grips, and imparted to all Brothers a principle sign in order to find help in case of a surprise.
>
> In order to imitate the Christians of the East and the Coptic priests, these Knights preserved among themselves the verbal law which was never written down, and took care that it should remain concealed to the initiated of the lower degrees. All this is preserved with exactitude in the philosophic rite of our days, although this rite does not precisely seek to derive its origin from the Knights Templars.'

The continuation of the ancient Egyptian mystery wisdom was transmitted to the Templars by the esoteric Coptic Christians of the Egyptian Church, once known as the Alexandrian Church, which included Jerusalem in its bishoprics. The Egyptian Church was founded by the apostle St. Mark; and, according to Rosicrucian traditions, the inner-esoteric teachings were given by his student Ormus (who is a figure that is apparently unknown to orthodox scholars, although the Gnostic scholar Dr. April de Conick did remind me that a secret Christian school is alluded to by the existence of a Gnostic text entitled, *The Secret Gospel of St. Mark*). The tradition of the school of Ormus is commented on by the Freemasonic author John A. Weisse, M.D. in his book entitled, *The Obelisk and Freemasonry*.

> *The Rosicrucians have been traced to Ormus, who, about A.D. 46, founded an order that wore a red cross and were thence styled Rosicrucians. Ormus has been considered as a convert of St. Mark, the Evangelist. We are told they were joined by the learned order of the Essenes. The Knights Templars seem to have borrowed the red cross from the Eastern and Western Rosicrucians, so that this badge dates from A.D. 46 to our day.*

The Templars were also initiated into the remnants of the Gnostic mystery wisdom of Mani, the "son of the widow" (216-276 A.D.). Mani's followers came to be known as the greatly misunderstood Manichaeans. The Manichaean teachers showed a genius for adapting the revealed teachings to the various symbolical systems and languages of different cultures. After suffering violent persecution the Manichaean "Sons of the Widow" subsequently found a place in the symbolic rites of Freemasonry.

As spiritual successors to the Knights of the Holy Grail, the Templar Order was officially founded as "The Order of the Poor Knights of Christ and the Temple of Solomon" at Jerusalem in 1118. Two hundred years later the Templars, who had achieved great wealth as an order within the Catholic Church, fell victim to the greedy French king, Philippe "le Bel" ("the Fair"), and his "puppet Pope" Clement V, climaxing on March 18, 1314, with the burning at the stake of Jacques de Molay, the grand master of the Templars, with his companion Geoffroi de Charney, the "treasurer and visitor of the Temple" in France. (It is thought by some that he may be of the same de Charney family who are believed to have had possession of the famous Shroud of Turin at one time.)

In chapter one, of the fourth part, of his book *The Knights Templars*, C. G. Addison summarizes the mysterious events surrounding the fiery death of Jacques de Molay, the 22nd Grand Master of The Order of the Poor Knights of Christ and the Temple of Solomon:

In so important a matter as this, it is well to accumulate testimony. Thus speaks another writer: 'The Cardinal Alba read the eighty-eighty articles of accusation, followed by the so-called confessions of the prisoners, and then turning to them, called upon them to renew, in the hearing of the people, the avowals of guilt which, he said, they had admitted the Order to have incurred. Two, who seemed somewhat overcome and too languid to avow or deny, simply assented to whatever was required of them; but Jacques de Molay, the Grand Master, stepping to the front of the scaffold and raising his hands bound with chains towards heaven, first repeated the Lord's Prayer in a loud voice, and then exclaimed: 'To say that which is untrue is a crime both in the sight of God and man. Not one of us has betrayed his God or his country. I do confess my guilt, which consists in having, to my shame and dishonor, suffered myself, through the pain of torture and the fear of death, to give utterance to falsehoods imputing scandalous sins and iniquities to an illustrious Order which hath nobly served the cause of Christianity. I disdain to seek a wretched and disgraceful existence by engrafting another lie upon the original falsehood.' Guy, brother of the Prince of Dauphiny, echoed these assertions; but before he could proceed very far the Cardinals and commissioners, astounded at this exhibition of firmness and courage, hurried the Knights back to prison and immediately waited on the King to acquaint him with the occurrence. Enraged beyond measure at this unexpected declaration, King Philip the Fair, without consulting the puppet Pope Clement V, or any other spiritual person, summoned his counselors and decreed the two noble Knights should be burned to death. A pile was erected on the island in the Seine where the statue now stands - or lately stood - of Henry Quatre, and here on the same evening they were led forth to execution before a crowd greatly outnumbering that of earlier assemblages, and the Grand Master addressed the citizens thus: 'France remembers our last moments. We die innocent. The decree which condemns us is an unjust decree, but in heaven there is an august tribunal to which the weak never appeal in vain. To that tribunal within forty days I summon the Roman Pontiff.' A violent shudder ran through the crowd, but the Grand Master continued, 'Oh, Philip, my master, my King! I *pardon thee in vain, for thy life is condemned. At the tribunal of God, within a year, I await thee.'"*

The fate of the persecutors of the Order is not unworthy of notice. [On April 20th, thirty-three days] . . . after the above horrible execution, the Pope, Clement V, was attacked by a dysentery, and speedily hurried to his grave. His dead body was transported to Carpentras, where the court of Rome then resided. It was placed at night in a church which caught fire, and the mortal remains of the holy Pontiff were almost entirely consumed. His relations quarreled over the immense treasures he left behind him, and a vast sum of money, which had been deposited for safety in a church at Lucca, was stolen by a daring band of German and Italian freebooters. Before the close of the same year [on November 29], King Philip IV died of a lingering disease which had baffled all the art of his medical attendants, and the condemned criminal, upon the strength of whose information the Templars were originally arrested, was hanged for fresh crimes. 'History attests,' says Raynouard, 'that all those who were foremost in the persecution of the Templars came to an untimely and miserable death. The last days of Philip IV were embittered by misfortune. His nobles and clergy leagued against him to resist his exactions. The wives of his three sons were accused of adultery, and two of them were publicly convicted of that crime.'

The fulfillment of Jacques de Molay's appeal to the "tribunal of God" did not stop with these events; for the royal bloodline of Philip IV, the Capetian dynasty which had ruled France for around three and a quarter centuries, drew to an end in fourteen years as each of the three sons of the infamous Philip became king and died; and subsequently were branded by history as the "Accursed Kings."

Following the judgments pronounced on the Order, the Templar lands were seized; although mysteriously not a single ship of the Templar fleet, which was the largest in the world, was ever captured. Equally puzzling is the fact that after these events, the anonymous builders of the cathedrals no longer built in the gothic style. The Templar spiritual stream continued underground resurfacing later in the Rosicrucian Order. For, the Rosicrucian Order continued the initiatory esoteric Christian mysteries of the Macrocosm and the Microcosm, the image of the spiritual-human, as shown in the tradition of the Rosicrucian *Temple Legend*.

The architectural principles of the Master Builders were of such a nature so as to have a profound effect upon the spiritual development of the people. In the lecture he gave in Berlin on December 9th, 1904 entitled, "The Essence and Task of Freemasonry from the Point of View of Spiritual Science", and published in the lecture cycle, *The Temple Legend*, Rudolf Steiner gives clear indications regarding some of the architectural principles of the true Master Builders and the effect that their works had on the consciousness of mankind.

> . . . *The first true mason was Adam, the first man, who had an extraordinary [intuitive] knowledge of geometry at the time of his expulsion from Paradise. He was recognized as the first mason because, being the first man, he was a direct descendant of the Light. The true, deeper origin of Freemasonry, however, pre-dates humanity entirely. It resides in Light itself which existed before mankind.*
>
> *This is most profound and reveals, for those who can understand it, what theosophical wisdom has again made public through its description of the formation of the Earth through the first two Root Races [Polarian and Hyperborean] and into the third [Lemurian]. Whoever can apprehend this through Freemasonry has received into himself something of tremendous importance. But that takes place in only the rarest cases because Freemasonry is, as it were, degenerate today. This has come about because, since the sixteenth century, man has had little understanding of the true meaning of Freemasonry, namely that a temple has to be built in such a way that its proportions are a reflection of the great cosmic proportions, that a cathedral has to be built in such a way that its acoustics reproduce something of the harmony of the spheres, which is the source of all acoustics in the outer world.*
>
> *A knowledge of this original insight was gradually lost. Thus it came about that when Desaguliers [John Theophilus Desaguliers (1683-1744) From 1719 he was the Grand Master of the first English Grand Lodge. Desaguliers passes for the strongest personality of the so-called 'Revival' movement in Freemasonry. As a renowned scientist (pupil of Isaac Newton) he is numbered among those who prepared the way for the*

founding of the theory of electricity (note 13, page 369)] reunited Freemasonry in England during the first half of the eighteenth century, no one had any proper understanding of the fact that the word Freemasonry had to be taken literally; that it really did concern the work of the practicing mason, and that the mason was one who built churches and temples and other great buildings according to cosmic laws and incorporated into them heavenly and not earthly proportions.

This original insight and its reflection in Freemasonry was lost; there was no longer any conscious appreciation of the transformation wrought by a proper use of acoustics in a building where the speaker's words are thrown back and are thereby changed in their effect. Those who built the great cathedrals of medieval times were the great Freemasons. They were aware of the importance of the fact that what was spoken by the priest should be reflected back from the individual walls and the whole congregation immersed in a sea of sound, breathing and fluctuating in significant vibration which would exercise still greater effect on the astral body than on the physical ear. That has all been lost and it was inevitable that this should be so in the new age. That is what I meant when I told you that what is left of Freemasonry is only the husk of what it was in former times.

The Masonic tradition of the reflection of the macrocosmic laws in the microcosmic-human, as it is expressed in the laws of architecture - as the true Temple of Man - entered a new phase earlier this century with the building by Rudolf Steiner of a modern mystery temple which fulfilled this acoustic initiatory characteristic that is referred to in this lecture. In fact, this property was present to such a great degree, that in addition to the enhancement of the effect of the acoustics on the upliftment of the spoken word, the opposite was also true, that is, words spoken *without* the proper impulses behind them would reveal to the listener the lack of integration of the speaker within the realm of feeling (which is the realm of light). Rudolf Steiner was at first going to call this modern mystery temple the Johannes-Bau, the House of John; but instead, in acknowledgment of the principles of metamorphosis embodied in its structure, he called it the Goetheanum after the multi-faceted genius Johann Wolfgang von Goethe. The Architects of the time considered Rudolf Steiner to be a Master-Builder of the highest order. This building alone, even if it were his only achievement, was sufficient testimony that Rudolf Steiner was a world historic figure. This architectural masterpiece had a double cupola domed roof that was balanced on pillars, which was the largest domed roof in the world - larger still than the dome of St. Peter's cathedral in Rome. Even the noted American architect, Frank Lloyd Wright made the journey to Dornach Switzerland to see this building that required an unsurpassed knowledge of geometry, materials, and building techniques. The Goetheanum was built entirely out of wood with extensive carvings, paintings, and an original method of creating stained glass that artistically expressed the principles of metamorphoses that work within human evolution.

The Goetheanum was tragically burned down on New Years Eve 1922. All Rudolf Steiner could say at the time was; "Ten years of work." Later he was to say, to the effect, that this was especially unfortunate for Americans who stood to gain so much from experiencing the principles of metamorphoses embodied in its structure. The first Goetheanum was replaced by the second Goetheanum with its entirely new design, and which still stands as one of the great architectural wonders of Europe. It was the largest building made out of reinforced poured concrete in the world at that time (in 1924), utilizing a new method that Rudolf Steiner invented for the task.

The Chakras

> "The king travels through six towns in the heavenly firmament, but in the seventh he holds his court."
> "The First Key of Basilius Valentinius", Daniel Stolcius, 1624

When we refer to the microcosmic human being of Spirit-Soul-Body we must consider the seven chakras or lotus flowers, which are the seven primary astral centers that are visible to a clairvoyant and relate to the seven planetary spheres. There are many ways of looking at these relationships, depending on what aspect of their nature you are describing.

These seven supersensible centers are the "seven pillars of wisdom" that support the "Temple of Man", as it says in "Proverbs" (9:1-6); "Wisdom hath builded her house, she has hewn out her seven pillars." These "seven pillars" are fashioned through the workings of the Spiritual

Beings that are the builders which enact the Divine Plan of Christ - "The Great Architect of the Universe." This is accomplished through a divine co-mingling and donation of being, to use the words of St. Paul;

> . . . *for ye are the temple of the living God; as God hath said, I will dwell in them; and I will be their God, and they shall be my people.*

The harmonious development of these astral centers depends on the spiritual student fulfilling the conditions of initiation such as are described by Rudolf Steiner in his books, *Knowledge of Higher Worlds and its Attainment,* and, *An Outline of Occult Science,* and elsewhere. The fundamental relationships as given by Rudolf Steiner are as follows:

Saturn - Crown Chakra - 8 petaled:

The crown chakra relates to memory, it crowns the head. This center is sometimes called the thousand-petaled lotus due to its scintillating character. The yogic teachings describe how the total of the petals of the six chakras below the crown or sahasrara chakra equals fifty, and that there are twenty groups of fifty streams that converge at the crown of the head; 20 x 50 = 1000. The condition of consciousness that centers in the crown chakra corresponds to a state of trance consciousness that is deeper than deep, dreamless sleep.

Jupiter - Brow Chakra - 2 petaled:

The brow chakra relates to thought, it is centered at the brow and is the chakra that pertains to dreamless sleep. The two Uraeus Serpents on the crowns of the Egyptian pharaohs are an image of the brow chakra with its two petals. This chakra also brings to mind the brow markings of the Eastern religions, and in the West - the Welsh bard Taliesin whose name means "Radiant Brow." In chapter two of the book entitled, *Initiation and Its Results,* Rudolf Steiner describes the fruits of the development of the brow chakra.

It is pictures, then, that the student meets on his way up to the higher worlds, for the realities which are expressed by these pictures are really in himself. He must soon become sufficiently mature to prevent himself from desiring, at this first stage, veritable realities, but to allow of his regarding these pictures as appropriate. But inwardly he soon learns something completely new from his observation of this picture-world. His lower self only exists for him as mirrored pictures, yet in the midst of these reflections appears the true reality that is his higher self. Out of the pictures of the lower personality the form of the spiritual ego becomes visible. Then from the latter threads are spun to other and higher spiritual realities.

This is the moment when the two-petalled lotus in the region of the eyes is required. If this now begins to stir, the individual attains the power of setting his higher ego in connection with spiritual superhuman entities. The currents which flow from this lotus move so toward these higher entities that the movements here spoken of are fully apparent to the individual. Just as the light makes physical objects visible to the eyes, these currents reveal the spiritual things of the higher worlds. Through sinking himself into certain ideas which the teacher imparts to the pupil in personal intercourse, the latter learns to set in motion, and then direct the currents proceeding from the lotus-flower of the eyes.

At this stage of development especially, what is meant by a really sound capacity for judgment and a clear, logical training is manifested. One has only to consider that here the higher self, which had hitherto slumbered unconscious and like a seed, is born into conscious existence.

Mars - Throat Chakra - 16 petaled:

The throat chakra relates to speech, it is centered at the larynx and its corresponding state of consciousness is the dream state. In chapter one of the aforementioned book, *Initiation and Its Results,* Rudolf Steiner tells us that the development of the throat chakra, ". . . allows one to perceive clairvoyantly the thoughts of another person, and also brings a deeper insight into the true laws of natural phenomena."

Sun - Heart Chakra- 12 petaled:

The heart chakra is the focal point of the "I Am", or "True-Ego, and is the astral center that relates to waking consciousness, it centers in the heart as a reflection of the twelve sectors of the Zodiac. In addition to this, Rudolf Steiner says (ibid) that the development of the heart chakra through the methods of Rosicrucian training, ". . . permits of a clairvoyant knowledge concerning the sentiments of another person. He who has developed it can also observe certain of the deeper powers in animals and plants."

In chapter 10 of his book entitled, *Hermetic Astrology - Towards a New Wisdom of the Stars, vol. 1 Astrology and Reincarnation*, Robert Powell further describes the context of the heart chakra:

> *On the microcosmic level, where the seven lotus flowers correspond to the seven planets, this hermetic teaching signifies that the lotus flowers became disfigured through the Fall, each becoming capable of a particular aberration. For example, the 12-petalled lotus flower (the heart center, the organ of love, corresponding to the Sun, the fourth planetary sphere), instead of being an instrument of pure love, became capable - as a consequence of the Fall - of << domineering arrogance >> . . . In its essential nature the 12-petalled lotus flower is in the likeness of the Sun and radiates love - as the Sun radiates light and warmth. However, since the Fall the heart of the hermetic man - the likeness - has become subject to egotistical impulses that can result in the << domineering arrogance >> . . . In other words, after the Fall the 12-petalled lotus flower no longer radiated love selflessly but became a vehicle for selfish impulses, and so lost its divine likeness.*
>
> *The restoration of the likeness to its divine origin . . . is accomplished through taking up the Christ Impulse. Christ came to overcome the effects of the Fall. The Christ impulse, when taken up by the human being, begins to heal the disfigured lotus flowers. It brings them to radiate << like the Sun >> by infusing new spiritual light and warmth into them - as occurred at the transfiguration on Mt. Tabor, when Jesus Christ << shone like the Sun, and his garments became white as light >> (Matthew xvii, 2).*

Rudolf Steiner once spoke about the development of the heart chakra in Paris in May of 1906, which can be found in the 11th lecture of the lecture cycle entitled, *An Esoteric Cosmology*:

> *Nature is governed by one sovereign law, which is that rhythm must enter into all manifestation. When the twelve-petalled lotus-flower which constitutes man's organ of astral-spiritual perception has developed, he can begin to work upon his body and imbue it with a new rhythm whereby its fatigue is healed. Thanks to this rhythm and the restoration of harmony it is no longer necessary for the astral body to perform the restorative work on the sleeping physical body which alone prevents it from falling into ruin.*
>
> *The whole of waking life is a process destructive of the physical body. Illnesses are caused by excessive activity of the astral body. Eating to excess affords a stimulus to the astral body which reacts in a disturbing way on the physical body. That is why fasting is laid down in certain religions. The effect of fasting is that the astral body, having greater quiet and less to do, partially detaches itself from the physical body. Its vibrations are modulated and communicate a regular rhythm to the etheric body. Rhythm is thus set going in the etheric body by means of fasting. Harmony is brought into life (etheric body) and form (physical body). In other words, harmony reigns between the universe and man.*

Venus Sphere (the Planet Mercury) - Abdominal Chakra - 10 petaled:

This chakra, which is near the navel, relates to the Astral-Body. Certain aspects of the function of the Venus chakra are described by Rudolf Steiner in, *Initiation and Its Results*, as follows:

> *By means of the organ that lies in the pit of the stomach one acquires knowledge of the capacities and talents of a person: by this, too, one is enabled to see what parts in the household of nature are played by animals, plants, stones, metals, atmospheric phenomena, and so on.*

Mercury Sphere (the Planet Venus) - Pelvic Chakra - 6 petaled:

This chakra relates to the Etheric-Body, and is centered in the pelvis. Rudolf Steiner indicated the following concerning this chakra (ibid):

> *He who has evolved the six-petalled lotus can communicate with beings who are native to the higher worlds, though even then only if their presence is manifested in the astral or soul-world. In an occult school, however, no instructions concerning the development of this lotus-flower would be imparted before the student had trodden far enough on the upward path to permit of his spirit mounting into a yet higher world. The formation of these lotus-flowers must always be accompanied by entrance into this really spiritual sphere. Otherwise the student would fall into error and uncertainty. He would undoubtedly be able to see, but he would remain incapable of estimating rightly the phenomena there seen. Now there already exists in him who has learned to evolve the six-petalled lotus, a security from error and giddiness, for no one who has acquired complete equilibrium of sense (or body), passion (or soul), and thought (or spirit) will be easily led into mistakes. Nothing is more essential than this security when, by the development of the six-petalled lotus, beings possessed of life and independence, and belonging to a world so completely hidden from his physical senses, are revealed before the spirit of the student.*

Moon Sphere - Root Chakra - 4 petaled:

The root chakra is located a few inches above the base of the spine. It relates to the Physical-Body as an expression of the four elements of: fire (warmth ether), air (light ether), water (sound or number ether) and earth (life ether). As the lowest of the seven primary chakras, the four-petalled chakra is the center that regulates forces which involve the Physical-Body. The development of this chakra is concerned with the control of the will as it affects the Physical-Body via the activity of the four ethers of warmth, sound, light and life.

The Vital-Pole of the East
versus
The Consciousness-Pole of the West

In the yogic teachings of ancient India, the supersensible forces which are seated in the vicinity of the root chakra are collectively called the kundalini. Kundalini is a Sanskrit term which is variously translated to mean; "the coiled hair of the beloved", or the "serpent power." Certain occult schools attempt to arouse the kundalini utilizing Eastern techniques that relate to the Vital-Pole, accomplishing what in Yogic philosophy is called "transforming bindu to ojas"; that is, transforming the sexual forces into forces of higher consciousness through raising the released forces up the spine. These ancient methods are a remnant of the Old Indian Period, when mankind was at a very different stage of development. The modern spiritual-scientific methods of Esoteric Christianity, on the other hand, are concerned with the Consciousness-Pole rather than the Vital-Pole. Spiritual Science teaches that the three lower chakras are related to the earlier development of mankind. At the present stage in the evolution of Western humanity these lower chakras should not be worked on directly. By working on the higher centers, the lower centers will unfold in a healthy manner without the dangerous arousal of the kundalini, or "serpent power."

The path of Esoteric Christianity concerns itself with that which descends from above as - the "descent of the dove" at the Baptism, or the "tongues of flame" at Pentecost - rather than that which rises from below as, the "serpent power." Esoteric Christianity, rather than working directly on the three lower chakras, as in the Eastern occult schools, works on the development of the chakras from the heart up, preparing oneself to be a, so to speak, "Grail" to receive that which descends from above as Spirit (XIV). On the other hand, the Eastern yogic techniques of the *Vital-Pole* bring one to *a seven-fold revelation of the past Cosmos of Wisdom* by entering into a more intimate relationship with the body. The yogic practitioner strives to awaken supersensible forces through breathing techniques, this brings about a form of consciousness that is akin to what one was in the *past*, of what one was within the realm inhabited before birth. The Esoteric Christian techniques of the mastery of the *Consciousness-Pole* lead to a very different goal, which is *a twelve-fold revelation of the future Cosmos of Love*, with the experience of Christ as the Lord of Karma. For Christ, through His sacrifice as the "Lamb of God", saved us from ourselves by entering into a new relationship with the future development of mankind, within the sphere of the Earth - a new relationship that will last the whole of Earth evolution, and beyond.

From "Pure Fool" to "Noble Traveler"

The chakras, or astral centers, have experienced the fall into matter. The consequence of this is that our consciousness has become, as it were, opaque or sense-bound. This drama is portrayed by the "fall" of the angels which resulted in mankind being cast out of the paradise of the "Garden of Eden." This "fall" led humanity into physical forms that otherwise would have been no more dense than the fragrance of a flower. But as a result of the "fall", mankind gained the possibility of freedom.

The Physical-Body itself can be seen as a type of grail, or vessel that receives the influx of the spiritual world; a focal point where all the different levels of being come together. In the *Bible* it tells us that we are "living stones", it also speaks of "the stone the builders rejected." The image in the Grail legends of, "the Stone that was struck from the crown of Lucifer" that became the Holy Grail, symbolizes that which out of the past "Cosmos of Wisdom" was worthy to be a bearer of the Christ within the future "Cosmos of Love." Those that "serve the Grail" are chosen to be participants in the creation of the new "Cosmos of Love"; but that requires crossing the "wasteland" which leads to the Grail castle. In order to overcome this "dark night of the soul", the chakras need to be harmonized with the activities of the angelical hierarchies that are in service to the Trinity of the Father, the Son and the Holy Spirit. Through our striving, with the modern methods of Anthroposophical Spiritual Science, we regain the spiritual world in a new way with a clarity of wakefulness that was not possible in the past evolution of the human soul, we become, in the words of the alchemystical tradition, "Noble Travelers."

The three-fold being of man, of body, soul and spirit has evolved through stages of development that have come into being gradually (Grail = gradalis, which means gradually) throughout the cycles of human history and evolution. In order for humanity to pierce "the valley of the shadow of death", it is necessary that we acquire the spiritual qualities that will illuminate the undeveloped petals of the chakras, thereby bringing light into realms of being in which we are presently "in the dark." The path of this awakening is called "Initiation" whereby we accomplish "the work of the Chariot" (vehicle = chariot = merkabah, the kabbalistic Hebrew term for the supersensible development of a "vehicle with radiant wheels" with, the equivalent term in Sanskrit being, vahan = vehicle), and develop suitable supersensible vehicles to receive the influx of the worlds of spiritual light within the Grail of our souls and thereby become "a lamp unto ourselves" so as to be of service to others. For the spiritual worlds will remain in the dark until we acquire sufficient light of soul to illuminate our way. This is the work of the "slow burning fire" of the heart that is symbolized in the Rosicrucian formula; I.N.R.I. - Igne Natura Renovatur Integra - "In nature all things are renewed by fire." H. P. Blavatsky in, *The Secret Doctrine, volume 1,* (page 87), states:

> . . . *'The Lord is a consuming Fire' (Deuteronomy iv. 24); 'The Lord (Christos) shall be revealed with his mighty angels in flaming fire' (2 Thessalonians. i. 7, 8). The Holy Ghost descended on the Apostles like 'cloven tongues of fire,' (Acts ii. v. 3); [according to Hinduism] Vishnu will return on Kalki, the White Horse, as the last Avatar amid fire and flames; and [the Persian Zoroastrian Avatar] Sosiosh will be brought down equally on a White Horse in a 'tornado of fire.' 'And I saw heaven open and behold a white horse, and he that sat upon him . . . is called the Word of God', (Rev. xix. 13) amid flaming Fire. Fire is aether in its purest form, and hence is not regarded as matter, but it is the unity of aether - the second manifested deity - in its universality. But there are two 'Fires' and a distinction is made between them in the Occult teachings. The first, or the purely Formless and invisible Fire concealed in the Central Spiritual Sun, is spoken of as 'triple' (metaphysically); while the fire of the manifested Kosmos is Septenary, throughout both the universe and our Solar System. 'The fire or knowledge burns up all action [Karma] on the plan of illusion', says the commentary. 'Therefore, those who have acquired it and are emancipated, are called 'Fires'* . . .

The mystery of the alchemystical fire is elaborated on by the alchemical writer Oswaldus Crollius (1580-1609):

> *Nature is that medium which by an harmonicall consent joyneth the lowest things to the highest, and sometimes is*

called Animall, sometimes Vegetable, sometimes Minerall, according to the diversity of the subject or receptacle. Those who diligently seek out the Hermetick Phylosophy and the marvelous works of God, know that that same Spirit and Minerall Nature which produceth Gold in the bowells of the earth, is also in Man. That Spirit in Gold is the same generating fire, that Spirit in all creatures, and is the same and only generative Nature diffused through all things. This living spiritual Gold, this meer Fire, hath now assumed a naturall body; It is that which first moveth and ruleth Nature in all Naturall things, it preserveth all things, and all inferior things by a kind of harmonicall consent are governed by it . . .

The path of the spiritual transformation of the "Fool" is a perfecting of the vehicles through "trial by fire." Through this process, the spiritual seeker becomes purified and harmonized with the Divine Plan in such a way that their soul becomes aligned with the Divine Idea of a human being which radiates from the Spiritual Sun, and in doing so - becomes radiant like "Joseph's coat of many colors" in the *Old Testament*, or the "Woman Clothed with the Sun" in "The Revelation of St. John the Divine." In an undeveloped soul this light appears as more of a cloudy undefined mass in the region of the heart, because of "dullness." This is depicted in the story of Parzival who came to the court of King Arthur dressed as a bumpkin.

This development cannot take place in those who serve the dark forces, as it requires the cooperation of the spiritual world to bring it about, and the spiritual world is in the service of light and love. Those individuals who serve falsehood suffer from the ignorance of darkness, and don't realize that they are "chopping off the branch on which they are sitting", by drawing their inspiration from other unwholesome beings and forces that will retard their future development.

This fire is the fire of conscience that is awakened by the experience of the fruits of our deeds reflecting on the heart, which leads to a recognition of our spiritual destiny, and to the soul metamorphosis that is spiritual development. It is not that we are judged, but that we see and feel the results of our actions, become intensely aware of our shortcomings, and experience painful shame and remorse in the presence of Christ. Those who feel that they can transcend good and evil, make the mistake of Nietzsche's "superman" - who thinks he is beyond good and evil, when in fact he is not - with the end result being an atrophy of the heart forces of love. If one wishes to participate in the higher evolution of humanity then love has to become the central theme of one's existence; for as it says in chapter 4 of "The First Epistle of John":

> *Beloved, let us love one another: for love is of God; and every one that loveth is born of God, and knoweth God. He that loveth not knoweth not God; for God is love. . . If we love one another, God dwelleth in us, and His love is perfected in us. Hereby know we that we dwell in Him, and He in us, because He hath given us of His Spirit.*

The Christ said; "Know ye not that it is written: 'ye are Gods?' " For this to be fulfilled, it would necessitate an evolution of mankind beyond its present state, toward what St. Paul was referring to when he said; "Ye shall be as the Angels." We are gods in the becoming - but we are not there yet. We are like the caterpillar who can't even imagine the butterfly - for it has yet to become a chrysalis and undergo metamorphoses; and thereafter, take flight as a butterfly. As a result of our metamorphoses we shall hopefully, after many lifetimes, arrive at the "New Jerusalem" spoken of in "The Revelation of St. John the Divine." For Mankind will not return to the "Eden" of Moses, as the Edenic state represents an earlier stage of the evolution of mankind - in which mankind descended from the Higher Worlds, into the earthly realm, and began a process of evolution from *below* upward. On the other hand, the objective image of the "New Jerusalem" represents the future goal of the evolution of mankind - which will result from their moving forward with the fruits of their sojourn within the world of matter - into the "Celestial City" that will descend from *above*, from the Higher Worlds, like a dove anointing the awakened humanity.

We are all "Noble Travelers" and "Pure Fools." Even the lowest of the low will eventually find the light, if not in this life or cycle, then in some distant time; for it is the nature of the indestructible part of man to seek and find its source. Through lifetime after lifetime we journey on thinking that we are seeking a multitude of things - and we are. But if we look to the source of this abundance we find that all this came into being through the sacrifices made by multitudes of beings in the service of the one life. And so, in all humility, we must not forget to ask the question: "Whom does the Grail serve?" - when we arrive at the "Castle of the Grail."

I

The Magician

Mercury - Archangel Raphael - Healing - 6 Petaled Lotus

The Archangel Raphael is the archangel of healing (**XIV**). The healing forces of Raphael are deeply rooted in the processes of breathing; for the health is maintained by the harmonious rhythm of heart and lung. Pythagoras said; "All illness is a musical problem." It is the breath's musical, rhythmic cadence, moving in concord with the blood and heart that maintains the harmony between the different vehicles. The astral forces stream in through the breath, and are conditioned in their relationship to the Physical-Body by the four ethers: life ether, chemical ether, light ether and warmth ether. These four ethers are related to the four states of being in nature which are often referred to as the four elements of earth, water, air and fire. Many authors combine the four ethers and the four states of being in nature into one category and refer to the four ethers as the four elements, but this does not give one as detailed of an understanding of their nature as is presented by Rudolf Steiner.

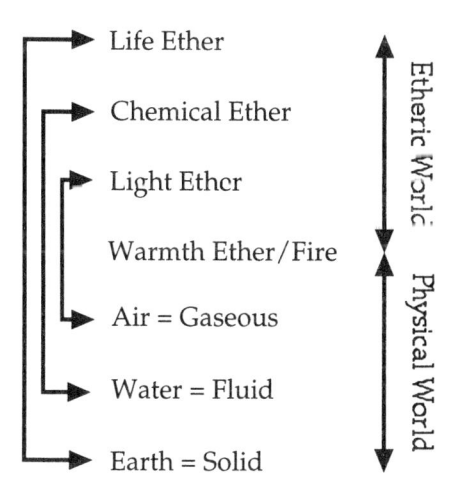

```
        ┌──► Life Ether                    ▲
        │                                  │   Etheric World
        ├──► Chemical Ether                │
        │                                  │
        ├──► Light Ether                   ▼
        │                                  ▲
             Warmth Ether/Fire             │
        │                                  │
        ├──► Air = Gaseous                 │   Physical World
        │                                  │
        ├──► Water = Fluid                 │
        │                                  │
        └──► Earth = Solid                 ▼
```

From the preceding diagram it can be seen that the warmth ether is the only ether that actually manifests somewhat in the physical world, while the other ethers exist within the etheric world. It is important to realize that the ethers are not to be thought of as increasingly refined states of matter; but rather, they should be thought of as existing in a state of being which is described by Rudolf Steiner as, "emptier that empty."

The ethers are extraphysical forces of the etheric world which act upon matter in such a manner so as to impart to substances their relative state of being, whether it be solid, fluid, or gaseous. This state of being can be modified through the action of the warmth ether. For example, depending on its temperature, water can manifest as either solid ice, fluid water, or gaseous vapor. In addition to their activity in the mineral world, the ethers also work as formative forces within the life-processes of the vegetable, animal, and human kingdoms.

Above the four ethers is a fifth ether, which is referred to as the "quintessence" by Paracelsus, and is called akasha (universal space) by the yogis (II). The teachings of Yoga do not assign any attributes to the akasha except sound, which is its primary manifestation within the world of time. Above the akasha ether are two more ethers which dwell beyond the realm of time within the world of duration, which are called in Sanskrit: adi tattva (primordial universal force), and anupapadaka tattva (the first differentiation on the plane of being). This brings the total number of ethers to seven, which is a fundamental number of creation in all true occult teachings.

The five ethers, during the course of the day, starting from sunrise, pass through cycles of about two hours each. The cycle of two hour periods begins with akasha, and then passes sequentially to the warmth ether, the light ether, the chemical ether, and lastly to the life ether. From there the cycle starts again, beginning with akasha, repeating the series which continues throughout the course of the day.

The understanding of the cycle of the ethers is the foundation of the Chinese system of acupuncture; wherein it is taught that to achieve the best results, one should apply therapies to the various bodily systems at different times of the day. The basis of this approach lies in the fact that the flow of chi (life-force) in the meridians is governed by the cycle of the five elements, with the different meridians, corresponding to the specific bodily systems, being most responsive to therapy at specific times of the day according to the cycles of the five elements (ethers).

The understanding of the cycle of the five ethers is also the basis of ayurvedic medicine as practiced in India, and a similar system that is practiced in Tibet. One case which I recall is from a documentary on Tibetan medicine which I saw many years ago. The producers of the film visited a woman who practiced Tibetan medicine and observed her methods of treatment. They did not realize how effective her approach was until the camera man told her that he had suffered from frequent and intense migraine headaches for many years, and that one was just beginning. The healer noted what time of day it was, and looked into her tables which gave the cycles of the ethers and the planets. She then instructed him to sit down facing a particular direction which she had determined from her tables; and then inserted a needle, much like a large acupuncture needle, into the top of his head and stuck a ball of herbs on top of it. Then, lighting the ball of herbs which slowly burned producing an aromatic smoke much like incense (a form of therapy commonly known as moxibustion), she chanted a series of healing mantrams. After a few minutes, the headache went away. At the time of the final release of the documentary film, many months later, the headaches had not returned.

Modern conventional, Western medicine is beginning to make some progress in this direction. For they are now developing therapies that take the element of time into consideration. This approach is based upon research that has shown certain medicines to be effective in smaller doses, if given at specific times of the day. Although Western medicine, at this point, does not appear to be very open to acknowledging the reality and significance of the ethers, I think this is slowly changing in the minds of growing numbers of people. This is due to the importance attributed to the understanding of the ethers by forms of medicine that are considered to be unconventional by mainstream, medical science, and yet consistently achieve undeniably positive results from their therapeutic approaches. Ironically, the great stumbling-block for Western conventional medicine is its theoretical foundation, which does not include the possibility of supersensible influences. They cannot detect the ethers directly with technology, and so, they do not consider them to have a scientific basis. Since the ethers themselves are "emptier that empty" they do not lend themselves to conventional forms of testing. If science wishes to "discover" the ethers, then they must look for the "footprints" of the ethers in the natural world. For, at this point, there are no technological devices for observing the ethers directly, but only for observing their effects. One such "technological device" is a simple, hand-held mirror.

It is possible to determine which of the five ethers is dominant at a particular time by holding a mirror under your nose and observing the shapes formed on the mirror by the vapor that is produced from your breath. In this way, it can be seen that each one of the ethers, through its influence on the breath process during its respective time period, will produce a specific geometric shape on the mirror. The warmth ether will produce a triangular shape, the light ether will produce a circle, the chemical ether will produce a crescent or half moon, the life ether will produce a right angle or squared shape, and the fifth element, akasha, will produce a cloudy formless shape. In addition to this, the form of the lungs is five-fold, the right lung having three lobes and the left lung only two. This asymmetry of the structure of the lungs is reminiscent of the five-fold cycle of the ethers.

In addition to bringing about a variation in the dominance of the ethers, the two hour breath cycle brings about an alternation between the right (Sun) nostril and the left (Moon) nostril. It is these subtle variations of the breath that condition the formative forces; which, in turn, regulate the bodily processes and thereby determine the state of consciousness and health. It is the workings of the ethers in the breath which act as a link between the Ego, Astral, Etheric and Physical Bodies. Furthermore, the ethers serve to connect the Macrocosm to the Microcosm as regards to the manifestation of life, form, and consciousness within the human being. The activities of the ethers in mankind are under the direction of higher spiritual beings; with the ether's functioning, so to speak, as the thread that weaves the web of life, form, and consciousness. And so, it is understandable that the functions of the ethers are not to be tampered with recklessly - such as with breathing exercises that are not guided by an experienced teacher.

It is from within the breath that the astral streams imprint the Etheric-Body in a fundamental way, which can only take place at this point within the human body. It is also the breath which becomes animated through speech, bearing the warmth of the Ego. Furthermore, it is the breath that carries the karmic signature of the individual which is combined in the exhaled breath with deadly carbonic gases. For only the exhaled breath of a resurrected human being expresses life-giving forces. This is achieved through their taking upon themselves a quality that can only be called plant-like in its purity. This purity of being redeems the carbon processes in the breath through changes that take place naturally within the rhythm of the breath. This enables the Initiate to internally complete the cycle of the breathing process - which normally depends on the plant kingdom for its completion. As a result, the Initiate no longer exhales unredeemed carbonic gases, but rather life-giving forces. This is why the breath of the higher Initiates has been described as having the subtle fragrance of flowers.

For ordinary humanity, at the present time, the exhaled breath of mankind is only life-giving for the plant kingdom, which then transforms the carbon dioxide through photosynthesis into oxygen that, in turn, is life-giving for men and animals. The primary remainder of our actions is the karmic imprint upon the Akashic Record, which occurs in the "ash" of the exhaled breath; and also, most importantly, in the akashic imprint upon the astral-etheric heart.

In the teachings of the Pythagorean and Platonic traditions, the five ethers also have an occult relationship to the Platonic Solids of geometry.

The Ethers and the Platonic Solids of Geometry

1. Earth - Cube

2. Water - Icosahedron

3. Air - Octahedron

4. Fire - Tetrahedron

5. Quintessence - Pentagonal Dodecahedron

The Macrocosmic Cycle of the Venus Pentagram

The microcosmic five-fold cycle of the ethers in the breath finds its macrocosmic reflection in what is called the Venus pentagram (III) The Venus pentagram is a cycle of 1,199 years, which can be determined by either the superior or inferior conjunctions of Venus to the Sun which occur when the planet Venus passes either between the Earth and Sun (the inferior conjunction), or crosses the line of alignment of the Earth and Sun on the far side of the Sun (the superior conjunction). These types of conjunctions or alignments both happen in sequences that occur 1/5th, or 72 degrees of the 360 degree zodiacal circle away from the previous conjunction in its series, (whether figured from the superior or inferior conjunction). After almost precisely eight years, the fifth conjunction brings the series to completion. The fifth conjunction, which completes the pentagram, returns to within around 2.4 degrees of the starting point of the series of five conjunctions. The gradual difference of 2.4 degrees of sidereal longitude is an astronomical point, within the circle of the Zodiac, that is slowly moving backwards in its relative position to the backdrop of the fixed stars. This can be visualized as a pentagram rotating slowly backwards in a cycle of 1,199 years, which according to Rudolf Steiner is the time lag of the commencement of a cultural epoch after the astronomical age has begun. This Venus cycle is commented on by Robert Powell in chapter three of his book entitled, *Hermetic Astrology - Towards a New Wisdom of the Stars, vol. 1 Astrology and Reincarnation.*

Why should the astronomical rhythm of 1,199 years of the planet Venus determine the time-lag between the start of an astrological age and the commencement of the corresponding cultural age [epoch]? What does this astronomical rhythm have to do with the process of transformation of a new zodiacal impulse to become a cultural impulse?

. . . the period of the rotation of the Venus pentagram around the sidereal zodiac is 1,199 years. Like the motion of the vernal point (the precession of the equinox), the rotation of the Venus pentagram is backwards; i.e., it regresses through the sidereal zodiac. But whereas the vernal point takes 25,920 years (12 x 2,160) to regress through the twelve signs of the zodiac, the Venus pentagram retrogrades through the entire zodiac in 1,199 years.

In the length of time that it takes for a complete cycle of the precession of the equinox through the sidereal zodiac (25,920 years), the Venus pentagram makes some 21 1/2 rotations (21 1/2 x 1,199 = 25,778 1/2 years). The ratio of the cycle of the Venus pentagram (1,199) to that of the precession of the equinoxes (25,920) is a little less than the ratio of one to twenty-four, which is the ratio of one hour to one day. In other words, if the complete precession cycle is likened to a "world day", then the rotation of the Venus pentagram is like the passage of a "world hour."

When a new astrological age starts, signified by the entrance of the vernal point into a new sign of the zodiac, a "world hour" still elapses before the new zodiacal impulse begins to register as a cultural phenomenon, and this lapse of time is measured by the rotation of the Venus pentagram. A new impulse starts to work on a spiritual level as soon as the vernal point enters a new zodiacal sign, but it has to filter through from cosmic realms, and the rotation of the Venus pentagram serves to indicate the mediation of cosmic forces from the realm of the zodiac. The Venus pentagram acts as a kind of cosmic transformer, stepping down the zodiacal impulse, which operates on a very high level, a religious level, to become a social impulse, which works on a more human level.

This cycle of the planet Venus is related to mankind from its orbit which is two planetary spheres above the Earth (the first is the sphere inscribed by the Moon, the second is the sphere inscribed by Venus). The second planetary sphere is, occultly speaking, the sphere of Mercury rather than Venus (**V**). This is the case because the occult significance of the names of Mercury and Venus were switched from their original esoteric Babylonian-Ptolemaic Greek designations, as an occult blind. The Egyptian system was not affected, for it was the Babylonian-Greek Ptolemaic system that was used by the astronomers of Europe. As a result, in the Western esoteric tradition, the planet Mercury is "occult Venus" and the planet Venus is "occult Mercury." This provides quite a challenge to modern interpretation, because you must know whether the planetary sphere or the planet is intended, when you hear the names Mercury or Venus.

The Seven Planetary Spheres and the Physiological Motions

Sphere of Saturn - Upright Motion
Sphere of Jupiter - Liver Activity
Sphere of Mars - Speech
Sphere of the Sun - Blood Motion
Sphere of Venus - Breathing Motion
Sphere of Mercury - Glandular Motion
Sphere of the Moon - Reproduction

The Seven Planets and the Seven Organs

Saturn - Spleen
Jupiter - Liver
Mars - Gall Bladder
Sun - Heart
Venus - Kidneys
Mercury - Lungs
Moon - Brain

It can be seen from the preceding diagrams, that there are seven physiological motions which relate to the seven planetary spheres (**XVII**). And, on the other hand, there are seven organs which relate to the seven planets (**XVI**). It should be noted that in the case of the planet Mercury, it relates to the lungs; while the planetary sphere of Mercury relates to glandular motion. The planet Venus, on the other hand, relates to the kidneys, and the Venus sphere to the breathing motion.

Lungs = Planet Mercury - Sphere of Venus = Breathing Motion
Kidneys = Planet Venus - Sphere of Mercury = Glandular Motion

The above relationships have a further significance, which was indicated by Rudolf Steiner, as regards to the purpose of the kidneys. For, in addition to the kidneys universally acknowledged function in dealing with fluids, the kidneys as an organ are related to the element of air. What this means, in occult physiology, is that the kidneys also serve as a kind of metabolic brain which regulates the amount of oxygen we take in. For healing purposes, this oxygen-regulation process of the kidneys can be modified with a substance that is produced from vegetable carbon and is called *carbo vegetabilis* (which points toward the oxygen-carbon cycle mentioned earlier).

The understanding of the exchange of Venus and Mercury, provides a key to many Hermetic-Rosicrucian esoteric teachings. Certain systems refer to the planets as we now call them, while other systems refer to the planetary spheres. For example, in the tradition of the Hermetic Kabbalah they have what are called magic squares, which are grids of numbers which are associated with the planets through the kabbalistic value of the numbers of rows that compose the grid. Examples of these can be found in the Hebrew kabbalistic work entitled the *Aesch Metzreph* (*The Purifying Fire*). If you wish to apply these magic squares to the planets then you must reverse Mercury and Venus, with the planet Mercury relating to the seven by seven magic square, and the planet Venus relating to the eight by eight magic square.

The reversal of Mercury and Venus resolves a discrepancy which is also present in the Tree of Life of the Hebrew Kabbalah (**VII**). For the eighth sefirah, or sphere of Hod actually relates to the planet Venus. While the seventh sefirah, or sphere of Netzach actually relates to the planet Mercury.

The true significance of the kabbalistic series is revealed if one looks at the numbers assigned to the sefirot or spheres of the Tree of Life. From the following diagram it can be seen that the sequence of the number series implies stages of manifestation as they are seen geocentrically; that is, from the point-of-view of a person on the Earth.

The Kabbalistic Tree of Life

1. Kether - the Crown - the Primium Mobile

2. Chochmah - the Sphere of the Fixed Stars

3. Binah - Understanding - Saturn Sphere

4. Chesed - Wisdom - Jupiter Sphere

5. Geburah - Strength - Mars Sphere

6. Tiphereth - Beauty - Sun Sphere

7. Netzach - Victory - Venus Sphere (the Planet Mercury)

8. Hod - Splendor - Mercury Sphere (the Planet Venus)

9. Yesod - Foundation - Moon Sphere

10. Malkuth - the Kingdom - Shekhinah - the Divine Presence - Earth

The doctrine of the planetary spheres, or sefirot, relates to the planes, or multiple levels of being which refer to the planetary orbits in the order that one encounters them by their relative distances from the Earth. The planetary spheres are fields of space that are circumscribed by the apparent movement of the planets around the Earth, in which are manifested levels of being that are the spheres of activity of specific angelic beings. This is an objective spiritual reality that is central to the traditions of both East and West. And therefore, the sefirot in turn relate to the planetary spheres in their ascending sequence as viewed from the Earth, and not to the planets as they are named in modern astronomy.

The way in which some authors attempt to explain why, in the Kabbalah, the sefirah Hod is assigned to Mercury, is that the orbit of Mercury is of a shorter period than that of Venus; but it is of primary importance to realize that the early Initiates of the Kabbalah and its tradition were working with a system that developed its conception of the Cosmos in harmony with the Greek and Babylonian star wisdom, and with the teachings of Zaratas and the Chaldean *Book of Numbers* (*Sepher Sefirot*) (**VI**). As it is the Graeco-Babylonian system that is the basis of modern astronomy (in which Mercury and Venus were exchanged), this affected a change in the related systems and names.

I am of the opinion that the various traditions that share in this exchange of Mercury and Venus developed out of a common milieu. Therefore, it is very likely that this fact points to the influence, upon the development of the Kabbalah, of the eclectic Neoplatonic and Gnostic teachings that developed out of the traditions of the Aristotelian, esoteric schools which were established by Alexander the Great in the 4th century B.C. as repositories of the Aristotelian wisdom that was striving for a synthesis of world culture.

The fundamental teachings on the ten sefirot of the Kabbalah are presented in the anonymous treatise on the Tree of Life known as the *Sefer Yetzirah* (*The Book of Formation*, c. 4th century A.D.) The ten sefirot are not only paralleled by the ten categories of Aristotle (**XXII**), but were probably influenced by them as a literary development; for apparently, the Kabbalah had first appeared as an established tradition among the Tanaim of Jerusalem, in the beginning of the 3rd century B.C. In support of this view, it is a well known fact that many Jews of the Graeco-Roman period spoke Greek as a primary language, and so are referred to as Hellenistic Jews. The influence of Graeco-Roman esotericism on the development of kabbalistic doctrines is commented on by the noted Hebrew scholar Joseph Dan in the book entitled, *The Early Kabbalah*.

> . . . Heikhalot [The Divine Palaces] and Merkavah [Chariot] literature has been described by scholars as belonging - at least to some extent - to the great and variegated family of Gnostic phenomena. G. Scholem once characterized this 'palace room' and 'chariot' literature as expressing a specifically Jewish-Gnostic world view. This thesis has been severely criticized in recent years, due largely to parallel investigation into contemporary Christian Gnosticism. Furthermore, much of the later Jewish esoteric systems lack most of what is regarded as classical and characteristic Gnostic symbolism. But early Kabbalah (and, somewhat surprisingly, sixteenth-century Kabbalah) abounds in Gnostic ideas and symbols. . .
>
> In the Kabbalah, the sephirot are a series of divine emanations, spreading forth from the Godhead and comprising the divine world, which separates the created worlds - the world of angels, celestial bodies and earth - from the hidden Godhead. This hidden Godhead does not take part in any change or activity, thus resembling to some extent the Aristotelian concept of the Prime Mover or First Cause, or the Plotinian One.
>
> As described by the early Kabbalists, the sefirot contain many elements derived directly from Neoplatonic theologies and cosmologies. . .

One early example of a thoroughly Hellenized Jew is Philo Judaeus of Alexandria (c. 30 B.C. to 45 A.D.), who was influenced by the Greek philosophers in his interpretations of the *Old Testament*. Furthermore, it is known that, after their dispersion, the Jews assimilated the languages and cultures of the countries in which they lived, and consequently the Hebrew language gradually fell into disuse.

The modern Hebrew language which is spoken today is actually not a continuation of an unbroken tradition; but rather, it was developed through the efforts of the Hebrew scholars of more recent times. In fact, it is uncertain to this day how the ancient Hebrew language was spoken, this is a problem which is further complicated by the absence of vowels in the written language. This absence of vowels was remedied by the Masoretes, who were scholars of the 8th and 9th centuries A.D. that added a series of dots, called masoretic points, in order to indicate the placement of vowels (although it is uncertain if this was the original vowel placement).

Albertus Magnus on the Planets and the Days of the Week

Sunday - Sun
Monday - Moon
Tuesday - Mars
Wednesday - Mercury
Thursday - Jupiter
Friday - Venus
Saturday - Saturn

The great teacher of St. Thomas Aquinas was Albertus Magnus "Doctor Universalis" (1193-1280), of the line of the Bavarian counts of Bollstadt. Albertus Magnus held one of the chairs of Theology for the Dominican order at the University of Paris, and was later was promoted to Bishop of Ratisbon. Subsequently, he resigned and returned to teaching, his true path, at Cologne. He was primarily concerned with applying Aristotelian and Neo-Platonic ideas to Christian teachings, and was also the author of the rules for the stone masons at Cologne Cathedral. Eventually Albertus Magnus was canonized as a Doctor of the Church in 1931.

In the preceding diagram which is based on his work entitled, *De Virtutibus Animalium*, Albertus Magnus gives the occult relationships between the planets and the days of the week, a relationship usually referred to as the "planetary rulership" of the days of the week.

The current names of the days were originally derived from the names of the planets and the ancient Germanic gods, and were put into a sequence that is very fundamental to occult teachings, as can be seen in the following diagram.

The Planets, the Days of the Week and the Germanic Gods

Saturday - Saturn day
Sunday - Sun day
Monday - Moon day
Tuesday - Mars day (from the Germanic god of war Tiu)
Wednesday - Mercury day (from the Germanic god Woden or Odin)
Thursday - Jupiter day (from the Germanic god Thor)
Friday - Venus day (from the Germanic goddess Frig)

The Planetary Conditions

1st condition - Old Saturn Period - Primal Warmth
2nd condition - Old Sun Period - Etheric
3rd condition - Old Moon Period - Astral
1st half of the 4th condition, or Earth evolution - Mars Period
The Mystery of Golgotha - "The Turning-Point of Time"
2nd half of the 4th condition, or Earth evolution - Mercury Period
5th condition - Jupiter Period
6th condition - Venus Period
7th condition - Vulcan Period

In *An Outline of Occult Science*, Rudolf Steiner describes the stages of the planetary evolutionary chain, which are given the names of the planets, with the addition of Vulcan, as can be seen in the preceding diagram. In this scheme, the 7th condition is the Vulcan Period; as the 4th condition, or Earth evolution, is divided into a Mars half and a Mercury half, with the Mystery of Golgotha planting the seed for the transition from the Mars Period to the Mercury Period (**IV**).

This transformative mystery of Mercury, which provides a glimpse of the future development of the consciousness of mankind into the Macrocosm, is hinted at in the, *Tabula Smaragdina*, or *Emerald Tablet* of Hermes Trismegistus which, a legend says, was discovered in a cave by the great initiate Apollonius of Tyana, in the 1st century A.D. The earliest extant example of this text dates from the 9th century A.D. The *Emerald Tablet* is traditionally considered to be a central key to understanding the Hermetic Mysteries, for it is the clearest exposition of the mystery of the Macrocosm, or the "Great Universe", and the Microcosm, or the "Little Universe" which is the human being.

The *Emerald Tablet* has been, and continues to be, a central guiding light of the development of the Hermetic tradition in the West. It serves as a riddle to bring about an awakening to the mysteries of the Macrocosm and the Microcosm; and so, its doctrines are fundamental to the understanding of the Rosicrucian and Alchemical traditions. Furthermore, it is a statement which is based on such pure spiritual truths, that it will continue to be true to the end of the Earth and beyond. It is a wonderful meditation, and more than worth the time that one might spend reflecting on its ever deepening mysteries.

The Emerald Tablet

I. It is true and without error, in complete certainty it is true.
II. That which is below is like that which is above, and that which is above is like that which is below; in order to bring about the Miracle of the one thing.
III. And just as all things that exist have come into being from the One, so all things have been born from this one thing through adaptation.
IV. The Father is the Sun, and the Mother is the Moon. The wind has carried it in its womb, and the Earth is its nursemaid.
V. The Father of all works of wonder throughout the whole World is here.
VI. It manifests its power perfectly, if it be transformed into Earth.
VII. Gently and with great wisdom, separate the Earth from the Fire, and the Subtle from the Gross.
VIII. For it ascends from the Earth to Heaven, and again it descends into the Earth; receiving its power from the forces of things above and below. Through this means thou shalt possess the glory of all the world; and by it, all ignorance will fly far from thee.
IX. This is the greatest of all powers, the force of all forces; for it will overcome every subtle thing and penetrate every solid substance.
X. Thus the world was created.
XI. Hence there will be marvelous transformations achieved, through this manner of working.
XII. For this reason I am called Hermes Trismegistus, because I possess the three parts of the wisdom of the whole world.
XIII. What I wish to say about the operation of the Sun is accomplished and perfected.

II

The High Priestess

Moon - Archangel Gabriel - Birth - 4 Petaled Lotus

As the Archangel of the Moon, Gabriel is the guardian of the mysteries of birth, this is shown in the Annunciation of the birth of Jesus by the Archangel Gabriel to the Virgin Mary, in "The Gospel of St. Luke." The Virgin Mary is later depicted Resurrected in chapter twelve of "The Revelation of St. John the Divine", not only with the Moon but with the Sun, and a zodiacal crown of twelve stars:

> And there appeared a great wonder in heaven; a woman clothed with the Sun, and the Moon under her feet, and upon her head a crown of twelve stars.

The Mother Mary, described in "The Gospel of St. Matthew", received the being of the Heavenly Eve-Kadmon at the Baptism; and afterwards, passed through a further anointing by the Holy Spirit at Pentecost to become the true embodiment of the Virgin-Sophia, the wisdom (Sophia = wisdom) which had not suffered the consequences of the "fall" from heaven, or paradise, and was henceforth virgin.

Macrocosmically, the Sophia is connected with the forces that work out of the zodiacal constellation of the Virgin (**IX**), which is under the regency of the Kyrioteles, or Spirits of Wisdom, who have as their lowest principle the Spirit-Man, or Atma which in man is the highest principle, and is, so to speak, reflected by the Physical-Body.

In the distant past, the essence of our vehicles were donated by the beings of the spiritual world. In the distant future, as we develop toward our angelic destiny, the Ego will work into these vehicles to such an extent that the individuating Christ forces of the higher being of man will bring about a change of the carbonic nature of the Physical-Body. As a result of this process, which begins through the etherization of the blood within the hollow of the heart, the carbonic nature of the Physical-Body will undergo a transformation into the Phantom-Physical, or Resurrection Body. The Resurrection Body will arise like a phoenix out of the Physical-Body as a shining, transparent, fluid-diamond "the stone that fell from heaven" - a radiant Grail fashioned from the Sophianic substance of wisdom to be a Christophorus, a bearer of "the Christ in you."

The convergence of the Cosmic-Sophia forces with the primordial substance of the Father has prepared humanity to be a Grail to receive the Christ principle of the "I Am." This is one of the deepest mysteries of Christianity. From one viewpoint, this can be seen as a coming together of the leading Sun spirit among the Kyriotetes, the Spirits of Wisdom, with Jehovah-Elohim, who dwells in the sphere of the Moon, and is the leader of the other Spirits of Form, the Elohim, or Exusiai, who dwell in the sphere of the Sun. This coming together resulted in the development of the human form as a true image of the Spirit-Man. In the future, the human form will undergo further metamorphoses by the "Alchemical Wedding" of the Spirit-Self to the Spirit-Man which will give birth to the Life-Spirit.

The accomplishment of this lofty goal is being hindered by the retarded Luciferic beings that have been relentlessly striving against the Divine Plan since ancient times, and trying to find a means of unlawfully working into the unfolding human forces. For, as the necessary conditions for the development of the Elohim or Spirits of Form were no longer to be found on Earth, they left the Earth when it separated from the Sun. In departing from the Earth, the Elohim now inhabited the realm of the Sun and continued to work upon the development of humanity from outside. This threatened to leave mankind wholly under the influence of these retarded Luciferic beings. And so, to protect "infant humanity", the leader of the Elohim, rather than leaving the Earth, stayed behind as a sacrifice to counteract these unwholesome, retarded, Luciferic beings.

Jehovah-Elohim is how one would refer to the combined activity of the leader of the Spirits of Form with the other six Spirits of Form. For the name Elohim is plural, and refers to all seven Spirits of Form. On the other hand, when one refers to the Spirits of Form as individual beings they are referred to as Eloah, which is their name in the singular form. Although they reside in the Sun sphere directing the activity of the planetary spheres, the six Elohim as a group are all working through the mediation of the Eloah-Jehovah from within the Moon sphere, this is why Jehovah is referred to in the plural form of Jehovah-Elohim. This occult fact has been the case since Jehovah made the great sacrifice to work in the sphere of the Moon, which resulted in the Moon separating from the Earth in the ancient Lemurian period. This deed of Jehovah-Elohim brought into being the sexes, which is portrayed in the Garden of Eden story.

In order to come to a deeper understanding of the significance of the Cosmic Sophia in human evolution it is important to consider Rudolf Steiner's indications as to how the Zodiac relates to the seven principles of the Sophia and of the human being, and also to the nine Spiritual Hierarchies and the Holy Trinity. This scheme of interrelationships is referred to by Rudolf Steiner as the "Zodiac of the Lamb of God" and is the fundamental system of correspondences that I have used in the writing of this book (**IX**). For further study, the relationship of the "Zodiac of the Lamb of God" to the esoteric symbolism of the first Goetheanum that was built by Rudolf Steiner, and subsequently destroyed by fire in 1922, has been thoughtfully examined by Sergei O. Prokofieff in his book: *The Twelve Holy Nights and the Spiritual Hierarchies*.

The chart below gives us a picture of the workings of the spiritual beings as they relate to the spiraling ladder of manifestation. It would be easy to misunderstand this scheme as merely an abstract means of classifying the spiritual beings into a symbolical order; but this would be a mistake, as the continued study of Spiritual Science will reveal the objective reality of these relationships as they are connected to human history and evolution.

The Cosmic Sophia and the Hierarchies as Revealed in Man

Virgo
7th principle - the Spirit-Man
Kyriotetes - the Spirits of Wisdom

Libra
6th principle - the Life-Spirit
Dynamis - the Spirits of Movement

Scorpio
5th principle - the Spirit-Self
Exusiai - the Spirits of Form

Sagittarius
4th principle - the Ego
Archai - the Spirits of Personality

Capricorn
3rd principle - the Astral-Body
Archangeloi - the Spirits of Fire

Aquarius
2nd principle - the Etheric-Body
Angeloi - the Spirits of Life

Pisces
1st principle - the Physical-Body
Humanity - the Spirits of Freedom and Love

All of the preceding principles shown above, numbered from below upwards, together form the embodiment of the Cosmic Sophia; and likewise, these principles will become manifested through the future evolution of the spiritual human being.

The following members, on the other hand, are beyond our human principles, and consist of the planes of manifestation of the highest principles of the spiritual beings that are beyond mankind; the Angels, Archangels, Archai, and so on, throughout the ranks of the Spiritual Hierarchies.

Here follows the extra-human levels of the "Zodiac of the Lamb of God" that spiral up the "ladder" of the higher planes of manifestation:

The Zodiac of the Lamb of God - Beyond the Human Realm

Beyond the Zodiac
"the Father ground of being"
1st member of the Trinity - 1st Logos
"Our Father Who art in Heaven, hallowed be thy Name."
7th Principle of the Kyriotetes

Aries
"Behold My Son; in Whom I am well pleased"
2nd member of the Trinity - 2nd Logos
The Christ "... the Lamb of God who takes away the sins of the world."
7th Principle of the Dynamis

Taurus
Holy Spirit
3rd member of the Trinity - 3rd Logos
"And they were all filled with the Holy Spirit,
and began to speak with other tongues,
as the Spirit gave them utterance."
7th Principle of the Exusiai

Gemini
Seraphim - Spirits of Universal Love
7th Principle of the Archai

Cancer
Cherubim - Spirits of Harmony
7th Principle of the Archangeloi

Leo
Thrones - Spirits of Will
7th Principle of the Angeloi

Another aspect of this work of evolution is called in the Hermetic writings, "the Virgin of the World." In numerous places, Rudolf Steiner points to the occult fact that mankind is being nurtured in their evolution by the Sophia forces arising from the region of the constellation of Virgo, which relates to the Kyriotetes, or Spirits of Wisdom. The Virgin Sophia, who works out of the region of the Virgin (Virgo), in another manner corresponds to the Atma, or Spirit-Man in the "Zodiac of the Lamb of God."

Sophia means wisdom, and refers to that great being that the ancient Egyptians called Isis. The ancient Egyptians also related Isis to the star Sirius-Sothis, the brightest star in the sky, which is in the vicinity of the constellation of Gemini, and is ruled by the hierarchy of the Seraphim, the Spirits of Universal Love, the highest of the nine Celestial Hierarchies beneath the Trinity (XII). According to Ehrenfried Pfeiffer, the Sirian system is where the Exusiai, or Spirits of Form experienced their human state before the beginning of our evolution in the Old Saturn incarnation of the Earth. In addition to this, Ehrenfried Pfeiffer says that the Sirian system is presently experiencing an angelic or, Jupiter evolution.

The star Sirius can be seen rising in the night sky during the fall season, around twenty degrees after the rising of the three stars in the belt of Orion, (Orion is in the region of the Bull, the sign of the Holy Spirit, in the "Zodiac of the Lamb of God", **IX**). The belt of Orion is perhaps the easiest stellar configuration to find in the night sky, with its three bright stars that are almost in a row. Once you have located the belt of Orion, extend your arm straight towards it, then extend your thumb and little finger beneath the belt at a tilt of about two o'clock and you will find the star Sirius, near the tip of your little finger. The helical rising of Sirius was used to determine the yearly flooding of the Nile river, and was the basis of the Egyptian agricultural calendar. The Sirius-Sothis aspect of the Isis-Sophia forces relates to the mystery of *cosmic-time*, while the Virgo aspect relates to the mystery of *cosmic-space*.

The great wisdom that is found expressed in the physical body, through the miracle of birth, can be referred to as the Madonna Mystery; that is, the cosmic wisdom that works in the womb, in the creation of a human being as a true reflection of the Spirit-Man. This is the Sophia at work microcosmically in the realm of Earth-Moon, expressing the macrocosmic Sophia who manifests the combined working of the pleroma of beings leading all the way up to the the realm of the Kyriotetes, or Spirits of Wisdom, mediating forces from the zodiacal constellation of the Virgin to Jehovah-Elohim who mediates the forces of the constellation of Scorpio from within the sphere of the Moon. This combined working of the hierarchies brings about the development of mankind as a true reflection of the Spirit-Man, according to the Divine Plan of the Trinity.

In Mary-Sophia we find a meeting of that which works from within human development below - the Bodhisattva human realm - with that which works as divine intervention from above - the Avatar divine realm - combining the cosmic and earthly realms. Mary-Sophia, as the purest manifestation of the Paraclete, is the divine-human guardian of the mystery of the forces that manifest the human form through the *imagination* of the Holy Spirit that works through the Spirits of Form in the Moon-Sphere, under the direct *inspiration* of the "Word" of Christ as the Lamb of God, Who from the region of Aries, the Ram of Abraham, manifests the will of the Father (*intuition*).

The mysteries of the Ram of Abraham point to the *lunar* Abel mysteries of the shepherds; the mysteries of animal husbandry and birth, which led to religion and philosophy. In the *solar* mysteries, which led to art and science, we find the Cain mysteries of agriculture and death, which are later portrayed in the sacrament of the bread and wine that was given to Abraham by Melchizedek. The seed for the reconciliation of these two streams of Cain and Abel came about through the sacred deeds of the Last Supper and the crucifixion of the "Lamb of God" at Golgotha. In the "Woman Clothed with the Sun" with the crescent Moon beneath her feet, we find the future fulfillment of the reconciliation of these two streams that will come about through the "elucidation" of the twelve-fold harmony of the heavens. In a lecture given on February 3, 1913, entitled, *The Being of Anthroposophy*, Rudolf Steiner spoke of the significance of the Sophia for modern mankind:

> *Man has learnt to relate to the Sophia through his Consciousness-Soul, to associate her directly with human beings. This happened during the Consciousness-Soul age. The Sophia has therefore become the Being that 'elucidates' man. Once having entered into humanity, she has to take up this human nature and set it objectively before mankind. She detaches herself again but takes with her what man is and places herself outside him, no longer merely as Sophia but as AnthropoSophia, as that Sophia who has passed through the soul of man, through man's being, and henceforth bears this being of man within herself.*

Regarding the Sophia, Emil Bock explains some of the mystery of her embodiment in Mary as portrayed in "The Gospel of St. Luke":

> *In her Being and her countenance there is reflected, in the most radiant purity and perfection, a divine archetypal picture which hovers over mankind in the spiritual world. Just as in the Child that she is to bear there is mirrored and embodied the archetypal image of the child and of childhood (a focus of all that is childlike upon Earth), so is the Luke Mary an Earth-translated archetypal picture of all virginal womanhood, the manifestation of the 'Eternal Feminine', the woman of all women. Although outwardly insignificant, here was a human soul wholly overshone and imbued by the World-Soul, and hence by that pure Being of Cosmic Light who in antiquity was called Isis-Sophia and in Christendom the 'Holy Spirit' [or Paraclete].*

The Mother Mary of "The Gospel of St. Matthew" through her embodiment of the Cosmic Sophia, which came about at the Baptism of Jesus, was capable of being a recipient of the deepest inner teachings of Christ Jesus as explained by Rudolf Steiner in his lecture cycle entitled, *The Fifth Gospel*. She shared this spiritual transmission with St. John the Beloved "the disciple whom Jesus loved", in the Holy Land, and later at Ephesus and on the island of Patmos, in the years following the Mystery of Golgotha which preceded the writing of "The Book of Revelations." In "The Gospel of St. John" (19:26-30), it says:

When Jesus therefore saw his mother, and the disciple standing by whom he loved [St. John], he saith unto his mother, Woman behold thy son! Then he said to the disciple, Behold thy mother! And from that hour that disciple took her unto his own home. After this, Jesus knowing that all things were now accomplished, that the scripture might be fulfilled . . . gave up the ghost . . .

Rudolf Steiner spoke of the deep mystery of Mary-Sophia in the lecture given on December 24, 1920, which is published in the lecture cycle entitled, *The Search for the New Isis, the Divine Sophia*:

It is not on account of something happening by itself from without that Christ will be able to appear again in His spiritual form in the course of the twentieth century but rather through human beings finding the force represented by the Holy Sophia. The tendency in recent times has been to lose precisely this Isis force, this Mary force, which has become stamped out through that which has arisen within the modern consciousness of humanity. And the more recent Confessions have partially obliterated the perspective concerning Mary. To a certain extent this is the mystery of modern mankind, that basically Mary-Isis has been killed, and that she must be sought again, sought in the widespread heavenly realms with the power which Christ is able to kindle within us when we devote ourselves to him in the right way.

In the Middle Ages, the way to the Holy Sophia was taught at the Platonic school at Chartres Cathedral, which was built upon an ancient site dedicated to the Black Virgin. The Anthroposophical author Rene Querido, who was a student of Walter Johannes Stein, tells us of these ancient Druid mysteries and how they flowed into the spiritual life of the Middle Ages in chapter one of his book, *The Golden Age of Chartres*.

> *An essential part of the Celtic mysteries at Chartres was the cult of the Black Madonna. Because the statue of the Madonna used in the ritual of this cult was kept in Chartres Cathedral until the French Revolution, when it was destroyed, we know from documentation something about the statue and the ritual. Hewn out of pear wood, the life-sized statue was of a seated female figure holding in her lap a standing male child. Referred to as the Virgo paritura because it represented the prophecy of a virgin destined to bear a child, the statue was also called the Black Madonna, for its wood had been darkened by fire.*
>
> *In the ancient Druidic ritual enacted at Chartres, each autumn when the might of the sun began to wane, the Black Madonna was taken in procession into the underground grotto of the promontory, where she was venerated by the light of torches. When the renewing power of the sun returned in spring, the Black Madonna was carried out into the light amid celebrations of joy and renewed hope. All that had weighted down the soul during the dark, heavy months of winter now blossomed into the upward surging forces of the sun's light. Nature, or the being Natura, was reborn and the promise of the birth of the child fulfilled. During the summer months, the statue remained above ground, possibly in an open shrine, and was worshipped in the light of day. Then, as the cycle of the year ran its course, the statue was again taken into the depths after the fruits of the harvest had been gathered, in a ritual that enacted the powerful polarity of darkness and light, midwinter and midsummer.*

The Gothic cathedrals, specifically the series of cathedrals that are dedicated to the Blessed Virgin (the "Notre Dame") play a significant role in the transition from the mysteries of the ancient world to the world of the Middle Ages. These "bibles in stone" gave the people exalted images, in the carvings and stained glass, which kept the world of the spirit in the forefront of their consciousness. One of the most curious mysteries concerning the cathedrals and their builders, is the magnificent red and blue glass of Notre Dame de Chartres Cathedral. This glass, and that of a few other cathedrals, is tinted in such a way that no pigmentation is revealed through chemical analysis; this is mentioned by R. A. Schwaller de Lubicz and also in a guidebook of the Cathedral. R. A. Schwaller de Lubicz tells us that this is due to an alchemical process which was also known in ancient Egypt. R. A. Schwaller de Lubicz, who in addition to being a scholar of medieval alchemical texts, was an Egyptologist whose major work is a three volume set on the Temple of Luxor. Schwaller de Lubicz tells us that he found examples of this kind of colored glass (without traceable pigmentation) dating to the early Pharaonic period. Eventually he was able by alchemical means to produce this glass with the help of the noted alchemist Fulcanelli. The unusual way in which this glass radiates, as if with its own light, causes one's Ego to, so to speak, reach out towards it, as opposed to other stained glass which bathes one in colored light and does not have the same effect of drawing one out toward the light.

In addition to its mysterious stained glass, Chartres cathedral also reveals a Sun mystery when the noon-day Sun enters through a special opening on the longest day of the year and strikes a particular tile that is different from any other in the whole building. The mystery of the cathedrals is compounded further by the subtle presence of a profound star-wisdom possessed by the builders of the cathedrals dedicated to the Notre Dame.

The ancient Egyptians, and other ancient cultures, often positioned their temples and other sacred buildings according to specific astronomical alignments, which were thought to bring heavenly influences to Earth (**XII**). The existence of this star-wisdom is demonstrated by Louis Charpentier in chapter two of his book entitled, *The Mystery of Chartres Cathedral*:

> There exists in what was Belgian Gaul, in the old provinces of Champagne, Picardy, Ile-de-France and Neustrie, a certain number of XIIth and XIIIth century cathedrals, bearing the name of Notre-Dame, which reproduce, taken together, on Earth the constellation of the Virgin as seen in the

sky. If one relates the stars with the towns in which these cathedrals stand, *l'Epi de la Vierge* would be Reims: Gamma, Chartres: Zeta, Amiens: Epsilon, Bayeux. Among the smaller stars we find Evreux, Etampes, Laon, all of these having a Notre-Dame of the best period. One even finds, in the place of the smaller stars, near *l'Epi*, a Notre-Dame de l'Epine, which was built much later, but its building opens a mystery.

Maurice Leblanc had already noted, before others, that the Benedictine Abbeys of the Caux country trace on Earth the form of the Great Bear. It has recently been discovered that the fields which surround Glastonbury, in Somerset (where the Isle of Avalon is traditionally said to have been, with the Druidic well of the Grail: Chalice Well and Arthur's Tomb) befigure the twelve signs of the Zodiac . . .

"On Earth as it is in Heaven"

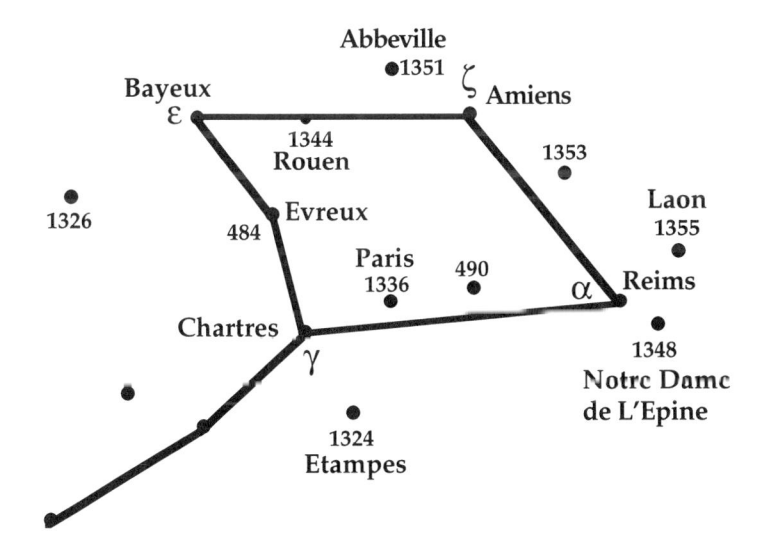

The Path to One's Guardian Angel

The sphere of the Moon corresponds to the sphere of the Angels who have as their lowest vehicle an Etheric-Body, so that Angels are essentially ethereal beings. There are many different types of Angels that perform various functions from within the etheric world. One specific type of Angel is the Guardian Angel. Each individual person has a Guardian Angel that is united with them in the most intimate way, so that it may act as a sort of spiritual midwife, birthing the soul through the agency of the Spirit-Self, by observing the individual's life and serving as a guardian over the individual's personal Akashic Record.

Although the Guardian Angels maintain a very close relationship with their individuals in the early years, they step back a bit at the Saturn return, which happens at the end of the fourth seven-year cycle, around the age of twenty-eight, when the planet Saturn returns to the original position it was in the birth horoscope. Later in life, after six complete seven-year cycles, the Guardian Angels, so to speak (for they never really leave), re-approach their individuals in a different way.

Around the age of forty-two one has completed the six seven-year cycles of human development that are necessary for the complete development of the Consciousness-Soul - which enables a more complete differentiation to occur between thinking, feeling, and willing.

With the end of the Consciousness-Soul period, at age forty-two, begins the period of the Spirit-Self. In the cycle of the Spirit-Self, the Guardian Angel is still in a waiting mood of soul, not wishing to interfere in our destiny, patiently waiting for free-will to arise within the human soul in a harmonious manner which is capable of serving as a, so to speak, Grail, or crescent moon, to receive the rays of the Spiritual-Sun of Christ.

According to the laws of the cycles of unfoldment, the seventh seven-year cycle begins at forty-two, and if the individual is perceptive they will sense the Guardian Angel's presence more readily than earlier in life if they have developed in the proper way - a more sensitive and permeable consciousness through the overcoming of the astral-desire nature.

The Guardian Angel is guarding our personal Akashic Record, which carries the memory of our whole life, and of all of our previous lives. What infinite patience and willingness to serve Christ they must have, to go through the sacrifice of remembering our so often uninteresting lives filled with so many errors and shortcomings. Contemplating these thoughts makes one not want to disappoint their Guardian Angel. In the lecture "Self Knowledge and Experiencing the Christ in Oneself" that was given in Dornach on February 2nd, 1923 and was published in the lecture cycle entitled, *Earthly Knowledge and Heavenly Wisdom*, Rudolf Steiner spoke of the challenge of our humanity:

> . . . now we have the noble task of becoming aware of our humanity. Our task on earth is to represent the true human essence as fully as possible. We, too, are faced with the challenge to know ourselves. Because of our intellectual consciousness, we can take hold of the inner force of pure thinking and the inner soul condition of freedom in the process of self-knowledge. We can behold the human being with our soul's eye, so to speak. However, being able to know ourselves to a certain extent should not make us arrogant. We have to be aware at every moment that we have to struggle for our true freedom. We have to be aware that in our passions and emotions, in our feelings and sentiments, we are dependent on the subhuman.

The High Priestess arcanum, represents the Blessed Virgin Mary standing on the crescent Moon, who through her embodiment of the purest Isis-Sophia forces is a representative of the potential purity of the human soul. Likewise, the High Priestess arcanum represents the pleroma of beings behind the veil of the senses, known as the Heavenly Isis-Sophia. In the ancient Egyptian mysteries it was said: "I am what was, what is and what will be. I am Isis - no mortal hath lifted my veil." For in order to lift this veil, one has to be an immortal soul, rendered immortal through one's connection to the imperishable Spirit. In ancient India they called this connection the antaskarana, the "rainbow bridge", it is referred to in the Hermetic tradition as "the knowledge and conversation of the Holy Guardian Angel", which is the fruit of the development of a more *permeable* state of consciousness. H. P. Blavatsky in her pioneering reference work entitled, *Theosophical Glossary*, attempts to define the ancient Indian Sanskrit term Antaskarana:

> The term has various meanings, which differ with every school of philosophy and sect. Thus Sankaracharya renders the word as 'understanding'; others, as 'the internal instrument, the

Soul, formed by the thinking principle and egoism'; whereas the Occultists explain it as the path or bridge between the Higher and the Lower Manas, the divine Ego, and the personal Soul of man. It serves as a medium of communication between the two, and conveys from the Lower to the Higher Ego all those personal impressions and thoughts of men which can, by their nature, be assimilated and stored by the undying Entity, and be thus made immortal with it, these being the only elements of the evanescent Personality that survive death and time. It thus stands to reason that only that which is noble, spiritual and divine in man can testify in Eternity to his having lived.

To "build" the "rainbow bridge", and hear the "still small voice" of your Higher Self, you must cultivate a profound centered-stillness; which, in turn, leads to a more permeable consciousness. In addition to this receptivity, or penetrability, one needs wakefulness in order to achieve the realms of Spirit in a proper manner for our time - so as to be able to act with clarity of intent and achieve a wholesome result.

The time for approaching the Spiritual World in a dreamy soul-mood has become a part of the past evolution of consciousness. Now we have to strive to gradually bring awareness of the dream-world into our day-time waking state - and wakefulness into the dream-world at night. Eventually this permeability leads to a continuity of consciousness between waking and sleep, and the memory of past lives. Some relevant aspects of this modern path of Initiation are characterized by Walter J. Stein in chapter seven of the book by Johannes Tautz entitled, *W. J. Stein - A Biography*:

Through continual exerting of one's thinking changes are brought about in one's spiritual make-up which spiritual science describes as a freeing and making independent of the etheric from the physical body. Thinking is enhanced until it becomes experience which includes feeling and willing. In this way an ability of the perception of spiritual beings and events is attained, an active perception of the spirit which is an intuitive thought experience 'In intuitively experienced thinking man is carried into the spiritual world also as perceiver' is how Rudolf Steiner expresses it in his Philosophy of Freedom.

The story of the "prodigal son" is a story of the return of the lost son with the fruits of worldly experience. After the son separates from the mother he becomes the father through the wisdom of experience. The medieval monastic vows of poverty, chastity, and obedience were methods that were appropriate for the cultural epoch of the Intellectual-Soul; for this type of discipline of the thinking (poverty), feeling (chastity), and willing (obedience) was an effective method of development for the Intellectual-Soul, which is dependent on paternalistic, external authority.

In the Middle Ages, the Intellectual-Soul was to bear fruit in the Scholastic school of philosophy. The most comprehensive and perhaps highest example of Scholasticism is St. Thomas Aquinas (1225-1274), who is considered to be the authoritative scholastic philosopher by the Catholic Church. This is especially so since the papal decree of 1869 regarding "papal infallibility", the encyclical *Aeterni Patris*, which curiously is exactly 1,000 years after the Oecumenical Council of 869 A.D. when the Catholic Church said that a human being was only a being of body and soul, and that the soul could have spiritual qualities but that a human being did not possess an individual spirit. This 1869 papal decree shows an effort by the Catholic Church to cultivate an environment suitable for the development of the Intellectual-Soul - for the methods of Scholasticism are especially suited for the Intellectual-Soul. But we are presently in the cultural epoch of the Consciousness-Soul which began in 1414 A.D.; and so, we must move beyond the development of the Intellectual-Soul, and those methods that were once suitable for its cultivation.

In the epoch of the Consciousness-Soul (1414-3574 A.D.) we find ourselves having to distinguish between our thinking, feeling, and willing out of our own individual forces, free of external authority. It therefore becomes critical that we bring about a harmonizing of this separation of thinking, feeling, and willing so that they may be united in a higher way in this life, and in our future incarnations as we move towards the cultural epoch of the Spirit-Self which will begin around 3574 A.D.

This incarnation can be seen as training for later incarnations when the Higher-Self will be more fully realized - and the "veil of Isis" will be lifted. Unless of course, one achieves it in this life through initiation, as in the path that is outlined in the works of Rudolf Steiner, specifically in his books: *Knowledge of Higher Worlds and its Attainment*, and *An Outline of Occult Science*. The task of the present epoch can also be seen as a stage of preparation for the future relieving of our Angel's burden; when, by taking over the responsibilities of our Guardian Angel, we liberate our Angel to continue on to yet higher tasks. Those that have achieved this in advance of mankind are the Initiates - the great "Leaders of Mankind." This is a central mystery of Grail Christianity, which is alluded to in the statement of St. Paul; "Ye shall be as the angels", and also in the saying of Christ; "Know ye not that it is written; 'Ye are gods?' "

In the first century after Christ, women had a more equal role amongst the early Christians and shared in the leadership of many Christian communities. But the Catholic Church soon became male dominated and the Divine Feminine was lost with the change in policy - for the Church had become an institution with centralized paternalistic policies. The cult of the Divine Feminine continued nonetheless in the Cult of the Virgin Mary, and became prominent in the Middle Ages within the schools of Chartres, Notre Dame of Paris, and in the Order of the Knights Templars. In the Catholic liturgy, the teachings of the Sophia were reserved for the High Mass which excluded those who were not initiated into the Order of the Knights Templars, and other select circles.

In the book, *Cosmographia*, by Bernardus Silvestris, the great teacher of the Platonic school of Chartres, Bernardus speaks of another heavenly goddess who he calls "Noys." He considered Noys to be a being of the order of the Thrones, who mediates the impulses of the Holy Spirit. By this we can perhaps understand him to mean the primal great Mother Goddess "Karma-Nemesis", who as a pleroma of beings includes all nine angelical hierarchies beneath the Holy Trinity.

In the angelical system of Dionysius the Areopagite, the Thrones are the third order of the first hierarchy, just below the Cherubim (V). In the teachings of the Hebrew Kabbalah, this would relate to the sphere of Binah, or Understanding (VII). For the mystical inner-word of Binah is "Aima", which means mother, and refers to the collective activity of the first hierarchy which works through the Thrones. By being a pleroma or multiplicity of beings, the "Great Mother" Aima is considered feminine, while the singular working of spiritual beings is considered masculine.

The High Priestess arcanum, as I have mentioned, relates to the Moon which is the *innermost* planetary sphere, the sub-lunar world, and the sphere of the Angels. The present planet Saturn (the sphere of the Thrones), on the other hand, formed at the periphery of the Old Saturn globe and is the gateway to the *outermost* limit between incarnations.

There is an occult significance to the way the Moon with its 28 day cycle reflects the 28 year cycle of Saturn. The Moon's cycle influences the development of the vertebrae within the womb (especially the lower 28 vertebrae); while the oldest member of the human being, the skeleton, is under the rulership of the present planet Saturn. The skeleton is a metamorphoses of the primal seed of the physical, of the primal warmth received from the Thrones during the Old Saturn incarnation of the Earth; which is three complete planetary conditions before our present Earth evolution and is the "ring-pass-not", or limit of our evolutionary chain. The planet Saturn is also related to the spleen, which along with the bone marrow is the birth place of blood cells for the bloodstream; which, in turn, is the carrier of the warmth of the blood and the Ego that dwells therein.

The Holy Trinity and the Three Hierarchies

The Holy Trinity
1. Father - First Logos 2. Son - Second Logos 3. Holy Spirit - Third Logos

1st Hierarchy - the Spirits of Strength
1. Seraphim 2. Cherubim 3. Thrones

2nd Hierarchy - the Spirits of Light
1. Kyriotetes 2. Dynamis 3. Exusiai

3rd Hierarchy - the Spirits of Soul
1. Archai 2. Archangeloi 3. Angels

Mankind - the Spirits of Freedom and Love
1. Willing 2. Feeling 3. Thinking

As seen above, the Thrones are the third order of the first hierarchy, while the Angels are the third order of the third hierarchy; which, in turn, relates to the third Logos or third aspect of the Holy Trinity, the Holy Spirit. These hierarchical manifestations find expression within the threefold human being in many ways, depending on what you are attempting to describe.

A further indication of the relationship between mankind and the beings of the spiritual world is given by Rudolf Steiner regarding the connection between thinking and the world of the Angels. Literally speaking, we think in the realm of the Angels, for the realm of the Angels is the etheric world, which is fundamental to the thinking process.

On the other hand, when we have feelings it is an activity that is related to the astral world, which is the realm of the Archangels, this is shown especially within the feelings that are revealed through speech.

By carrying this idea one stage further, we see that when we act we are expressing the will, which participates in the realm of the Archai, or Time Spirits (Zeitgeist). The corresponding human states of consciousness that are related to these spheres can be described as follows: we are awake in our thinking, dreaming in our feelings, and as regards to our will it is related to our conscious mind in a similar manner as is deep, dreamless sleep. These relationships are summarized in the following chart:

The Spirits of Soul and their Relationship to Mankind

1. Archai - Willing - Actions - Deep, Dreamless Sleep or Unconsciousness

2. Archangels - Feeling - Emotions - Dream Consciousness

3. Angels - Thinking - Concepts - Waking Consciousness

"The Woman Clothed with the Sun..."

The High Priestess arcanum encodes the great mystery of how that which is born in the heights is mirrored in the depths - this great mystery of the Macrocosm and the Microcosm is portrayed in "The Revelation of St. John the Divine" through the apocalyptic image of the "Woman clothed with the Sun" that I made reference to in the opening of this chapter.

That St. John chose to use an ordering consisting of twenty-two chapters, to unfold the Spiritual Imaginations that are so powerfully expressed within the "Book of Revelation", is a further level of encoding which is in keeping with the twenty-two arcana of our present exposition. For there are twenty-two keys to the mysteries of the Macrocosm and the Microcosm - twenty-two keys which unlock the mysteries of the heights and of the depths.

Furthermore, St. John was emphatic concerning this ordering of his prophetic arcana into twenty-two chapters. This is implied through the words of his closing admonition: "And if any man shall take away from the words of the book of this prophecy, God shall take away his part out of the Book of Life . . ." For any exposition of the mysteries of the Macrocosm and the Microcosm - whichever scheme of ordering one uses - must be complete in order to faithfully portray the wholeness of being.

It is through the contemplation of this ordering or numbering (Hebrew, sefirot = numbering) of the divine emanations of the "Book of Life" that, God willing, one may begin to receive the "twelve manner of fruits" of the "Tree of Life", and thereby lift the seven veils of the robe of wisdom of the Heavenly Sophia that both conceal and reveal "the throne of God and of the Lamb."

> *And he shewed me a pure river of water of life, clear as crystal proceeding out of the throne of God and of the Lamb.*
>
> *In the midst of the street of it, and on either side of the river, was there the tree of life, which bare twelve manner of fruits, and yielded her fruit every month: and the leaves of the tree were for the healing of the nations.*
>
> *And there shall be no more curse: but the throne of God and of the Lamb shall be in it; and his servants shall serve him:*
>
> *And they shall see his face; and his name shall be on their foreheads.*
>
> *And there shall be no night there; and they need no candle, neither light of the sun; for the Lord God giveth them light: and they shall reign for ever and ever.*
>
> "Revelation" (22:1-5)

III

The Empress

Venus - Archangel Anael - Love - 10 Petaled Lotus

In Plato's *Symposium,* when Socrates gave the speech which he attributed to his teacher, the woman Diotima, he revealed what was to become a fundamental view of love in the Graeco-Roman world, and later of the Western tradition in general. Socrates quotes Diotima as saying: "Men call it Eros, which means to wander about, but the gods call it Pteros, which means to grow wings." This image of love as a path of spiritual growth is at the heart of the Esoteric Christian teachings. For as Rudolf Steiner tells us, with the incarnation of Christ, our Earth evolution transformed from a "Cosmos of Wisdom", into a "Cosmos of Love."

In the Middle Ages, there developed the Courts of Love of Eleanor of Aquitaine, the Troubadours of Provence in the south of France in the area which was known as the Languedoc, the Trouveres in the north of France, the Bards in the British Isles, and the Minnesingers of Germany. All of these cultural impulses were living manifestations of the "path of love" as it was understood at that time, it was a seeking for the divine within the realm of feeling, outside of the control of the institution of the Church.

At the heart of these developments within the secular-cultural sphere, the Christ impulse was at work to a greater or lesser degree depending of course, upon the specific individual circumstances. But out of this secular literature, art, and music developed the life of the community. In their native languages, these minstrels and poets gave birth to forces that were an expression of the Archangelic Folk-Souls of the various nations. For it was primarily through the sharing of a common language that the different peoples expressed their national identities, each with their respective gifts to bring mankind. Rudolf Steiner characterizes this Grail mood in the lecture, "The Royal Art in a New Form", which is published in the lecture cycle entitled, *The Temple Legend.*

> *Does it further my knowledge if a corporate body, be they ever so great, proclaims mathematical truth through their*

official spokesmen? If I want to learn mathematics, I must occupy myself with it, and gain an understanding of it for myself. And of what use is it if a corporate body possesses the power of the Cross? If I want to make use of the power of the Cross, the control of what is living, then I must achieve this myself. No one else can tell it to me, or communicate it through words; at best they can show it to me in the symbol, give me the shining symbol of the Grail, but it cannot be told in an intellectual formula.

The first accomplishment of this medieval occultism would have been, consequently, what appeared in so many different movements in Europe: the striving for individuality in religion, the escape from the rigid uniformity of the organized church. You can barely grasp to what extent this tendency underlies Wolfram von Eschenbach's Parzival. What manifested itself for the first time in the Reformation was already inherent in the symbol of the Holy Grail. Whoever has a feeling for the great meaning of what can confront us in this symbolism, will understand its great and deep cultural value. The great things of the world are not born in noise and tumult, but in intimacy and stillness. Mankind is not brought forward in its development by the thunder of cannons, but through the strength of what is born in the intimacy of such secret brotherhoods, through the strength of what is expressed in such world-embracing symbols, which inspire mankind.

Since that time, through innumerable channels, the hearts of men have received as an inflow, what was conceived by those who were initiated into the mysteries of the Holy Grail in the middle of the twelfth century; who had to hide themselves from the world under pseudonyms, but who were really the leaven preparing the culture of the last four hundred years . . . the first dawn is already beginning, for the use of these living forces in the affairs of social life; that is the real secret surrounding the Grail.

In the sagas of chivalry you find the knight rescuing the damsel in distress. In the story of *Tristan and Iseult* they drink the magic love potion and from then on, their destinies are inextricably intertwined. Symbolic themes such as these are to be found in the fairy tales and legends that were told or sung around the fire at night. Within these simple stories and innocent images can be found a wealth of soul nourishment; but "sub rosa", or on another level of meaning, these stories speak - in imaginative picture language - of the path of spiritual fulfillment.

As much as one might think, from all of these romantic symbolical images, that the path is tinged with mere sentimentality; in fact, the truth of the matter is that the Grail teaches harmony of feeling through the path of wisdom gained by personal experience. On the other hand, there may be those who think that the path of Anthroposophical spiritual science is too intellectual. Rudolf Steiner speaks of the relationship of love to thinking in the first chapter of his book entitled, *The Philosophy of Spiritual Activity*:

> *It is not maintained that all our action springs only from the sober deliberations of our reason. Far be it from me to consider human in the highest sense only those actions which result from abstract judgments. But as soon as our conduct rises above the sphere of the satisfaction of purely animal desires, our motives are always permeated by thoughts. Love, pity, and patriotism are motivating forces for deeds which cannot be analyzed away into cold concepts of the intellect. It is said that here the heart and mood of the soul hold sway. No doubt. But the heart and the mood of the soul do not create the motives. They presuppose them and let them enter. Pity enters my heart when the representation of a person who arouses pity appears in my consciousness. The way to the heart is through the head. Love is no exception. Whenever it is not merely the expression of bare instinct, it depends on the representation we form of the loved one. And the more idealistic these representations are, just so much the more blessed is our love. Here too, thought is the father of feeling. It is said: Love makes us blind to the failings of the loved one. But this also holds good the other way around, and it can be said: Love opens the eyes just for the good qualities of the loved one. Many pass by these good qualities without noticing them. One, however, sees them, and just because he does, love awakens in his soul. He has done nothing other than form a representation of something, of which hundreds have none. They have no love because they lack the representation.*

The Spiritual Hierarchies and Their Relationship to Mankind

Sun Sphere - Exusiai, or Elohim - Spirits of Form - Spatial Relationship
Venus Sphere - Archai - Spirits of Time - Willing
Mercury Sphere - Archangels - Feeling
Moon Sphere - Angels - Thinking

On one level, the symbolism of the Empress-Venus archetype is related to the realm of the Archai, the Time Spirits, or Spirits of Personality. Within the ranks of the spiritual hierarchies, the Archai are three evolutionary stages beyond mankind, which relates to the third planetary sphere above mankind, the sphere of Venus (**V**). The soul is intimately connected to the qualities of time through the actions of the Archai. This is shown through the Archai's direction of the unfolding of the proper impulses within the twelve epochs of the precession of the equinox, the twelve cultural epochs of the "Platonic Great Year" of 25,920 years. The cycle of the precession of the equinox is reflected in the rhythm of the breath, so that we take around 25,920 breaths during the course of a day, with each day of our life being a reflection of the "Platonic Great Year." The complete cycles of the "Great Year" are presided over by the Exusiai (who are the regents of the complete planetary condition and lead us through the pralaya or rest between planetary incarnations). On the other hand, as mentioned above, the twelve epochs of a cycle of the precession are under the direction of the twelve-fold workings of the Archai. The Archai were also called by Rudolf Steiner, the Spirits of Personality, for their lowest vehicle is on the same plane of being as the Ego, which in an individual human being is carried in the warmth of the blood.

The breath rhythm is related to the sphere of Venus, while the heart rhythm is related to the sphere of the Sun (**XVII**). The rhythmic system, which includes the heart and lungs, is primarily the realm of feeling. Every sense impression and thought has an effect upon the rhythm of the heart and lungs. This is most obvious in the more extreme circumstances that evoke strong emotions, such as laughing and weeping. The breathing rhythm continues unconsciously unless we choose to effect it, such as the act of holding one's breath. The rhythm of the blood and heart, on the other hand, is not consciously determined, unless we choose to think of something that arouses an emotion, such as anger, and a change in the heart rate results. This rhythmic system continues independently of our conscious will throughout our lives, it connects us to the realm of time, which is the realm of the Time Spirits or Archai. This rhythmic relationship is reflected in the Earth-Sun precession cycle of 25,920 years.

The Human Being in Relationship to Space and Time

Thinking - Activity Beyond Space and Time
Breath and Heart Rhythm - Activity in Time
Movement of Limbs - Activity in Space

Rudolf Steiner described the relationship of the spiritual beings to the rhythmic nature of man in a lecture he gave to the Esoteric Section of the Theosophical Society in Berlin on October 7th, 1905, the notes of which were published in the lecture cycle entitled, *Foundations of Esotericism*.

> *He has, for instance, no influence on the circulation of the blood. Such things are developed by degrees. Here other beings co-operate, Deva beings [Deva is Sanskrit for Angel, literally "shining ones"], so that all creatures having a blood circulation are dependent on deva forces for its regulation. The astral body is permeated and worked upon by different Deva forces. The lowest work on the astral body. Higher forces work on the etheric body and still higher Devas on the physical body. The physical heart is indeed very clever; the stupid one is the astral body, that directs into the heart all kinds of poisons. The most perfect part of man is the physical body, less perfect is the etheric body and still less perfect is the astral body. What is only in its beginnings, the baby in man, is the ego organization. This is the four-fold man, which contains the ego as the temple contains the statue of a god.*
>
> *The whole development of human culture is nothing other than the working of the ego into the astral body. Man enters into life filled with desires, impulses and passions. In so far as he masters these . . . he is working his ego into the astral body. When the Sixth Root-race, the Sixth Period, has reached its conclusion, the ego will have completely worked into the astral body, until then the astral body will continue to be dependent on the support of the Deva. As long as the ego has*

not permeated the entire astral body, so long must the Deva forces support the work. The second stage of development, which follows that of the cultural, is the development of the esoteric pupil. He works the ego into the etheric body. Through this the Deva forces are gradually released by the work of his own ego. Then he also gradually begins to see into himself.

Verticordia and the True Nature of Heart Action

Any honest assessment of human consciousness must admit that we are deeply sleeping in our wills, even though we do perform deeds through choice, we are awake to it through our thinking, but in the actual act we are really sleeping in unconsciousness. This is especially obvious in involuntary bodily functions where we are not consciously involved, such as the metabolism, or the heart beat.

The heart is an example of an organ in transition, this can be seen in the way the heart muscles have a crisscross structure like *voluntary* muscles; for in the *involuntary* muscles the fibers run in one direction. According to Rudolf Steiner, this is an indication that in the future mankind will control the heart, once they have evolved to a sufficient degree to take over the heart's function from the spiritual beings that are responsible for maintaining the heart's activity. An example of this can be seen in certain Yogis who are able to affect the action of the heart voluntarily.

The ancient Romans revered a being that was considered by them to have a great influence on the heart forces. This being they referred to by the name Venus Verticordia (the "goddess who turns the heart", from the Latin: vertere = to turn, cor = heart), this is generally thought by scholars to have only moral implications, as an epithet referring to the goddess' ability to change hearts from lust to chastity. In retrospect, it can be seen as a perfect poetic description of the true heart function. For the turning movement of the heart was already described by Aristotle (384-322 B.C.). By this turning movement the heart functions as a vortex-momenta-booster, as proven by Ralph Marinelli.

The name Verticordia can be used to refer to the heart movement; and thereby, tie in a series of concepts that are meaningful on the many different levels of being that converge within the heart, and relate to the different vehicles of man that are described in Anthroposophy - for all the levels of the being of man converge in the heart. And so, the name Verticordia can accomplish this by reminding us of various concepts that are key to understanding the true nature of the heart and its meaning and function in man as an organ of cognition and moral forces.

There are numerous reasons why I consider Verticordia to be an ideal name for the true nature of the heart's turning movement, which is under the direction of numerous spiritual beings. The Verticordia (vortex-momenta-booster) concept frees us from the "heart as a pump" concept; which by its materialistic illusion prevents us from seeing the heart's connection to cosmic-spiritual processes; and thereby, prevents us from understanding the heart's significance as an organ of spiritual cognition. In the following points I will attempt to summarize some of the the compound ideas I have chosen to encompass with the name Verticordia.

1. The initial evolutionary will impulse for what became the rhythmic heart activity proceeded from the Thrones, the Spirits of Will, who could also be called the Spirits of Courage (cour = heart) working from the region of Leo the Lion (**XIV**). In the Old Saturn incarnation of the Earth the region of Leo was the point of orientation for the beginning and end of the rhythmic-cycle of rotation of the Old Saturn globe, which cycle is the initial formative impulse of what would, much later on Earth, bring about the rhythmic life of the heart (**IV**). This occult reality is elaborated by Rudolf Steiner in the lecture he gave in Dusseldorf on the evening of April 17th, 1909 which is published in the lecture cycle entitled, *The Spiritual Hierarchies and the Physical World*.

> . . . *The sages of primeval wisdom spoke of this moment as follows: The first foundation of the human physical body was formed on Old Saturn. This earliest foundation was formed only out of warmth, but within this warmth body all future organs were already present in seed form. At that point, where the initial movement again comes to rest, the seed is created for that organ in the human body, which, when the body is later set in motion, also ensures that all of the functions of the physical body may be brought to rest again - that is, the heart. Here - from the first impulse of movement - the germ of the heart appears, but it only comes into existence in its first manifestation so that the movement will again be brought to*

rest at this point. Thus the heart becomes that organ through which the entire physical body in all of its functions is brought to rest when the heart itself stops beating.

In ancient languages, each member of the human body was identified with a very precise name. The heart was called the 'Lion' in the body. Thus the primeval world wisdom asked, 'In which zodiacal direction must one point to find the region where the first seed of the human heart was planted?' They pointed upward, and designated the Thrones, Seraphim, and Cherubim who worked on the heart, the zone of the Lion. The human being projected elements of the body into the cosmos, and the region of the body one is used to identifying as the inner manifestation of the Lion was also identified outwardly as the region of the Lion in the Zodiac. This is how such matters relate to one another.

2. Early in human evolution, after the Exusiai, or Spirits of Form separated the Sun from the Earth, mankind began to develop toward an experience of themselves as somewhat individuated beings through their experience of inner warmth. This period of the development of the human being is described by Rudolf Steiner in chapter four of *An Outline of Occult Science*.

At this stage of evolution, man felt himself during his earth existence as an independent being. He felt the inner fire of his life body united with the external fire of the earth. He was able to feel the heat streaming through him as his own ego. In these currents of heat, interwoven with life, the first tendency to form a blood circulation is to be found. The human being did not, however, quite feel his own being in what streamed into him as air. In this air the forces of the already described higher beings [the Spirits of Form] were active. But that part of the effective forces within the air streaming through him, which belonged to him already by virtue of his previously created ether forces, had remained. He was ruler in one part of these air currents and to the degree that this was so, not only did the higher beings operate in fashioning him, but he himself also assisted in his own formation. According to the images of his

> astral body he fashioned the air portions. While air thus streamed into the human being from without, becoming the basis of his breathing, a part of the air he contained developed into an organism that was impressed into him; this became the foundation of the later nervous system. Thus man of that time was connected with the external world of the earth by warmth and air.

3. The verticordial blood and heart movement, at our present stage of development, is being maintained by spiritual beings. The fundamental ideas for understanding which Hierarchies are involved in the activity of the blood and heart system; and furthermore, how man is brought into being through the deeds of the Spiritual Hierarchies, are clarified by Rudolf Steiner in the first lecture of the lecture cycle entitled, *Supersensible Man*.

> . . .The human form is in truth no earthly creation. The Earth merely provides the substance for the embryo. The Archai, Archangels and Angels work in from the Cosmos, building up the human form. If we now advance further and come to perceive the confluence of the planetary movements, of which confluence the nervous system and the secreting glands are an after-copy, we find, interwoven with the movements of the planets, the Beings of the Second Hierarchy: Exusiai, Kyriotetes, Dynamis. Beings of the Second Hierarchy are active in the shaping of the cosmic archetype of the nervous and glandular systems in man. It is thus at a later period after death that is to say, some time after we have learned to understand the human form from its cosmic archetype - that we ascend to the world of the Second Hierarchy, and realize that the earthly human being to whom we now look back as a memory was fashioned and created in his nervous and glandular systems by the Exusiai, Kyriotetes and Dynamis. Then we no longer regard the human being as the product of forces of electricity, magnetism and the like; we receive knowledge of how he as physical man has been built up by the Beings of the Second Hierarchy.
> We go still further and ascend to the sphere of Cosmic

> Music - Cosmic Melody and Cosmic Rhythm, where we find yet another cosmic archetype of the being of man. This time we do not move onward in the Hierarchies. It is the same Beings - the Beings of the Second Hierarchy - who are at work here too, but they are engaged in a different kind of activity. It is difficult to express in words wherein their first work - upon the nervous system - differs from their work upon the rhythmic blood-system, but we may think of it in the following way. In their work upon the nervous system, the Beings of the Second Hierarchy are looking downwards, towards Earth. In their work upon the blood system they are looking upwards. Both the nervous system and the blood system (as well as the organs connected therewith) are created by the same Hierarchy.

Likewise, it is due to the activity of the beings of the Second Hierarchy that the unceasing movement of the blood and heart is maintained throughout our earthly lives. In the far future, through mankind's natural wholesome development into Spirits of Freedom and Love, the movement of the blood and heart eventually will be maintained by our own inner forces as a result of the development of consciousness within realms of which we are now unconscious, or at best only aware of in a dream-like manner.

4. At the present stage of evolution, from the point of view of the consciousness of mankind, the heart-beat is actually being maintained by a rhythmic activity that is beyond the reach of our normal waking consciousness; a rhythmic activity that finds its origin within the astral world, the realm where also dwell the Archangels. This aspect of the many faceted nature of the heart is touch upon by Rudolf Steiner in the lecture given in Berlin on March 6th, 1917 entitled, "The Human Soul and the Universe", which is included in the lecture cycle published as *Cosmic and Human Metamorphosis*:

> In speaking of the four-fold division of man, we begin at the top by speaking of his 'I', his ego. All that a man can call his own in the soul and spirit sense, in his physical life between birth and death, works through the instrument of the physical

body; and we can ask concerning each of the four principles of man: with which part of his body is each physically connected? A real and sufficiently penetrating spiritual observation shows us that what we call the ego of man - strange as it may seem, for the truth is often very different from what the superficial consciousness supposes - strange as it may seem, the ego of man is, between birth and death, physically connected with what we call the lower part of the body. For the ego, as I have often said, is really a baby as compared to the other parts of man's nature; the seed of the physical body was already laid down in the Old Saturn epoch, the seed of the etheric body during the Old Sun, and that of the astral body during the Old Moon; but the ego was only laid down in our earth-period - it is the youngest member of man's being. It will only attain the stage at which our physical body now stands, in the far distant era of Vulcan. The ego is attached to the lowest bodily part of man, and this part is really always asleep. It is not so organized that it can bring to consciousness what takes place within it; what takes place there is, even in the normal waking periods, ceaselessly asleep. We are just as little conscious of our ego as such, in its reality, in its true being, as we are of the processes of our digestion. The ego of which we are conscious is but a reflex conception, the image of what is reflected into our head. We never really see or realize our ego, whether in sleep, when in normal conditions we are quite without consciousness, or in our waking state; for the ego is then also asleep. The true ego does not itself enter our consciousness, nothing but the idea, the concept of the ego is reflected therein. On the other hand, between sleeping and waking, the ego really comes to itself; only a man in normal sleep knows nothing of it, being himself still unconscious in this his deep sleep during the earth-period. Thus the ego is in reality connected with the lowest bodily part of man; during the day, in the waking time, it is connected therewith from within; and during sleep from without.

If we now pass on to the second principle in man's nature, to what we call the astral body, we find that as regards to the instrument through which it works, it is, from a certain point of view, connected with the breast-part of man. Of all that goes on in this astral body working through the breast-

part, we can, in reality, only dream. As earth-men we can only know something of the ego when we are asleep, consciously we know nothing. Of all that the astral body works in us, we can only dream. This is really why we dream constantly of our feelings, of the sentiments that live within us. They actually live a sort of dream-life within us. The ego of man is actually outside the region which we as human beings, with our ordinary sense-consciousness, can grasp; for it is continuously asleep. The astral body is also in a certain respect outside that region too, for it can only dream. With respect to both of these we are, in reality, whether asleep or awake, within the spiritual world - we are really and truly within that world.

What we know as the etheric body is, however, as far as the body is concerned, connected with the head. Through the peculiar organization of the head, the etheric body is able to be constantly awake when in the human body, when connected with the physical head. We may therefore say: The ego is connected with the lowest parts of our body; and the astral body with our breast-part. The heart - as to the workings of which we have no full consciousness, nothing but a dream consciousness - beats and pulsates under the influence of the astral body. When the head thinks, it does so under the influence of the etheric body. We can then further differentiate our physical body, for in its entirety, it is connected with the whole external world.

We now see a remarkable connection: the ego is connected with the lowest parts of the body, the astral body with the heart, the etheric body with the head, the physical body is really during the waking condition in constant connection with the outer environment. Just as we, with our whole body are in relation to the outer environment, so is the etheric body to our head, the astral body to the heart and so on. This will show you how really mysterious are the connections in which man lives in the world. In reality things are generally just the opposite to what the superficial consciousness may lightly suppose.

The lowest parts of man's nature are at present the least perfected forms of his being; hence these parts of the body, as such, correspond to what we have called the baby - our ego. Innumerable secrets of human-life lie concealed in what I am here referring to, secrets without number. If you go thoroughly into this subject you will understand above all, that the whole man is formed out of spirit, but at different stages. The head of man is formed out of spirit, but is more fully moulded, it belongs to a later stage of formation than the breast, of which one might say, that it is just as much a metamorphoses of the head, as, in the sense of Goethe's theory of the metamorphoses of plants, the flower is a metamorphoses of the leaf. If we consider the rhythm between sleeping and waking from this point of view, we may say that the ego actually dwells during the waking time in all the activities of the human body, in all the lowest activities, which finally culminate in the formation of the blood. The ego is present in all these activities during the waking hours. These activities are those which are at the lowest stage of spirituality; for of course, everything connected with the body is spiritual. Now it must be carefully noted that while - during the waking hours - the ego stands at the lowest stage of spirituality; during the hours of sleep it stands with respect to man, at the highest stage.

5. The heart receives its impulse to beat from the pulsating blood, this heart-beat is in actuality the turning verticordial movement of the heart which boosts the living movement of the blood in a spiraling vortex.

6. By its vertical (vertere = to turn) or upright nature, the heart is the true organ of the Ego, and by development can express the higher Ego forces.

7. The upright, or vertical nature of the heart allows a hollow center to form in the vortexing blood, which is necessary for the formation of a true vortex. This hollow center in the vortexing blood in the heart is occultly significant; since, according to Rudolf Steiner, it is in the emptied out spaces in man that the most spiritual processes take place. It is in this hollow space within the vortexing blood that etherization can take place; whereby, the etheric nature of the blood is permeated with the forces of the Life-Spirit of Christ that work from within the etheric world.

8. The heart is the organ of moral forces. For the heart is the place in man where the "Christ in you" resides, that is referred to in the writings of St. Paul; furthermore, the heart is the door to Christ's love through the action of His Life-Spirit upon man. The heart (Sun) is the higher spiritual organ for the "still small voice" of conscience mentioned by St. John; which, according to Rudolf Steiner, is seated in the kidneys and is related to the planet Venus (**XVI**). For conscience is a process that takes place between the heart and kidneys, that is, in the relationship between the Sun and the planet Venus. Within the supersensible nature of the heart, is also to be found the center of akashic memory, where the individual karmic personal history is inscribed. Although the sensitivity to these spiritual facts is dulled by the self-interest of the undeveloped Astral-Body.

9. The Temple of Venus Verticordia was originally erected in ancient Rome to promote the purity of the heart forces of the Vestal Virgins. The Vestal Virgins were priestesses of Vesta, the goddess of the hearth (a word that is poetically reminiscent of the word heart, and which are both places of warmth). The Temple of Vesta was the place where the goddess Vesta (in Greek Hestia) was represented not by a statue but by the "eternal fire" burning on her altar. The Temple of Vesta was the most sacred shrine of ancient Rome. The "eternal fire" was said to have been originally brought from Troy by Aeneas. All of the household hearths were also considered to be shrines of Vesta, and which were ritually ignited with fire taken from the Temple of Vesta.

In mankind, the true "eternal fire" is the warmth of the heart, the true alchemical "slow burning fire" which is the purest remnant of the primal warmth that was donated by the Thrones, or Spirits of Will, from the region of the constellation of Leo in the Old Saturn incarnation of the Earth. It is this warmth in the blood that carries the Ego in the present, connects us to the most ancient past, and bears forces that are central to our distant future.

In the city of Rome, in the year 114 B.C., a Vestal Virgin was struck by lightning, which led to the trial of three Vestal Virgins for inchastity. We can interpret this to mean that the lightning bolt was seen by the Roman authorities as an omen sent by Jupiter indicating that the astral-desire realm was out of harmony with the will of the gods, and of the Archangel, or Folk-Soul, of the Roman people. The Roman people's lack of harmony with the gods was considered to be manifesting the corruption of the Vestal Virgins. Upon consulting in the books of the Sibylline Oracle for a remedy to this lack of harmony, the words of the Cumaean Sibyl led the Romans to erect a temple, orædes (a place where the god resides), for the statue of Venus Verticordia. The statue of Venus Verticordia itself predated the temple by about a century. This was the Roman way, through external ritual action, of trying to balance the heart forces that were being corrupted by the undeveloped Astral-Body. For the human soul in the Graeco-Roman cultural epoch was being confronted by the challenge of the arising Ego, and the development of the Intellectual-Soul; which in developing powers of reason, was losing the ancient powers of atavistic (blood) clairvoyance that in the past had been a source of moral order.

The only image we have of Venus Verticordia is a coin that was struck in 46 B.C. by one Cordius Rufus (Cordius = heart, Rufus = red) in commemoration of the erecting of the temple. This coin shows Venus Verticordia draped and standing holding a balance, or scale, in her lowered right hand while holding a long scepter in her left hand (which can be seen as symbolic of the Earth's axis, and likewise the axis of the heart). Cupid the servant of venusian love, is hovering and looking over her left shoulder.

In its higher expression, Venus Verticordia can be seen as a pre-Christian image of the virginal Sophia forces, acting out of the inspiration of the Holy Spirit in harmony with the Divine Plan - working through Venus and activating powers of conscience which are seated in the astral nature of the kidneys; which in turn, harmonizes the rhythm of the breath.

In the clockwise "Zodiac of the Lamb of God" (**IX**), Venus Verticordia is Virgo holding the scales of Libra (which is ruled by Venus), and the scepter of Leo (which is ruled by the Sun), gazing out upon the mystery of Christ, the "Lamb of God", the Macrocosmic Adam, written in the heavens. For through the incarnation of Christ a new evolutionary vortex has come into being. Now Verticordia does not face the center of the heart of man (as in the counterclockwise Graeco-Roman Zodiac), but rather she faces her new domain in the periphery of the heavens to *await* the Christ Impulse freely arising out of the hearts of humanity.

With the incarnation of Christ, the Ego forces of the "I Am" began a gradual transformation of the human soul. This is evident in the faces portrayed in pre-Christian artwork where one does not see an individual "I Am" looking out at you, but rather one sees a much more vacant or impersonal expression. In the *Bible*, it tells of how Moses meets the "I Am" outside of himself in the lightning and in the burning-bush. Likewise, in the Egyptian mysteries, the Initiate was only united with Osiris in trance or in the after-death state.

It is the task of the present age, for the "I Am" to manifest more completely in the waking state within the individuated Consciousness-Soul, which is in preparation for the future awakening of the Spirit-Self in the sixth cultural epoch. This will come about through the agency of the Guardian Angel, as a servant of the Christ Impulse, freely working from within the heart center of man, with the assistance of forces that proceed from the divine Heavenly-Sophia, the "Woman Clothed with the Sun", the purest embodiment of wisdom working from the periphery of the Cosmos.

In order to come to a more complete understanding of the significance of Venus Verticordia as she was related to the moral nature of the Intellectual-Soul of the ancient Romans, one must realize that the awakening of the Intellectual-Soul brought about a darkening of the old clairvoyant consciousness which was derived from the working of the atavistic, ancestral powers within the blood. With the darkening of the old powers of clairvoyance, doubts arose concerning the nature of the world, and with these doubts came a willingness to question the authority of the ruling powers of Rome. It was in light of this that the Romans strove to harmonize the intellect through impulses that were considered by them to proceed from Venus.

The Vestal Virgins were custodians of the old clairvoyance, who used celibacy as a way of keeping alive the more dreamy consciousness of the Sentient-Soul. The Vestal Virgins, along with the Sibylline and other oracles, were remnants of the ancient feminine, *lunar* mystery wisdom of the Sentient-Soul that had been gradually declining since the emergence of the Intellectual-Soul with its *solar* male dominated cultural forms.

"From dullness through doubt to Saelde or Blessedness"

To deepen our view of the occult significance of the heart, the kidneys, and the liver, we only need to refer to the traditional ideas of hermetism regarding the Macrocosm and the Microcosm. For Hermetics is the true foundation of western scientific understanding. Considered together as Astronomia, the "Mother of the Sciences", astrology and astronomy were always connected in the minds of the ancient world, an understanding which continued up to the more recent astronomers: Tycho de Brahe, Johannes Kepler, Isaac Newton, and Benjamin Franklin. It is only in recent times that astronomers have failed to grasp the significance of genuine astrology, which they choose to discredit as "superstition" without ever having investigated it. To carry our understanding of the heart, kidneys, and liver further we have the traditional views of Hermetic Astrology, which leads us back to the Aristotelian schools that were founded by Alexander; and also, more obviously, to the works of Ptolemy (Claudius Oleaginous Ptolemaeus, c. 139 A.D.) which are the foundation of all later astrology and astronomy (**XVI**).

The astrological teachings of Ptolemy associated the heart with the Sun and the sign of Leo the Lion, the liver with Jupiter (the ruling planet of Sagittarius and Pisces), and the kidneys with the planet Venus. Astrological doctrine associates the planet Venus, in turn, with the signs of Taurus the Bull, and Libra the Scales. In addition to this, Taurus the Bull "rules" the throat, and Libra the Scales "rules" the kidneys.

In the 1911 issue of *The Journal of the Manchester Oriental Society*, there appeared a group of articles attempting to interpret the significance of the heart and kidneys, or reins (Latin, renes = kidney) in the ancient Near East. The first article, by George Elliot Smith, is entitled, "'Heart and Reins' in Mummification", where he explores the customary ancient Egyptian practice in mummification of leaving the heart and kidneys intact while removing the other viscera, for either containment in canopic jars (the earlier practice), or wrapping and reinserting in the body cavity (the practice after the 21st dynasty). In this article he makes the connection between the heart as the seat of the life and mind, and the kidneys as the seat of the emotions, which is considered to be the traditional view of the ancient Egyptians.

In order to further our understanding of the "heart and reins", and why they were left intact in the mummies in preparation for judgment in the kingdom of Osiris, I refer to the scene in the ancient Egyptian *Book of Coming Forth by Day* where Thoth (who the Greeks and Romans equated with Hermes-Mercury) is weighing the heart on the scales of justice against the ostrich feather representing Ma'at, or truth and cosmic order. This scene takes on additional significance through considering the traditional astrological connection of the scales with Libra and the kidneys which are "ruled" by Venus, and of the heart which is "ruled" by the Sun and Leo. The heart is being weighed against the ostrich feather. The ostrich feather can be seen to represent the breathing system which in its formation is "ruled" by the planet Mercury, although the breathing rhythm itself relates to the sphere of Venus (**XVI-XVII**). For it is the rhythmic center of the heart and lungs which reflect the cosmic order of Ma'at. The details regarding this I have discussed earlier concerning the cycle of the 25,920 year precession of the equinox reflecting the rhythm of the 25,920 breaths in a day, and other related numbers; such as, the pulse rhythm of 72 beats per minute relating to the one degree precession of the equinox which takes place within a 72 year period.

The Oriental concept of karma can be seen as being related to the ancient Egyptian principle of Ma`at, or cosmic order, which was reckoned by Thoth (or to use the more ancient Egyptian name, Djehuti). Thoth was considered by the ancient Greeks and Romans to be Hermes-Mercury, and was the psychopomp, or "shepherd of souls." For Hermes as the "shepherd of souls", was thought to be the one who helped the deceased find their proper place in the after-world. The traditional view of Egyptologists is to see Thoth primarily as a Moon god. This is a source of misunderstanding, for I am of the opinion that Thoth refers to the Mercury beings that work with the recently deceased from within the Moon sphere. This, along with his attribute of plotting lunar cycles, explains the frequent iconography of Thoth depicting him with lunar symbolism. Furthermore, the Egyptologist's also consider the god Khonsu to be a lunar god of childbirth. In this I think they are correct in that Khonsu seems to relate to the lunar beings that are concerned with childbirth; whereas, Thoth does not seem to refer to lunar beings, but rather to beings that are *active* within the lunar sphere - judiciously observing the akashic "testimony" of the heart - and discerning how the heart and lung rhythm have harmonized with the polarity of the astral forces of the kidneys.

In the, *Journal of the Manchester Oriental Society*, referred to above, there is an article by Hope W. Hogg entitled, "'Heart and Reins' in the Ancient Literatures of the Nearer East", in which the author cites extensive biblical, and other more ancient, as well as later sources, that look upon the "heart and reins" as being - that in man which is under the scrutiny of the deity or deities. In the following, I cite some of the references he gives concerning the heart and reins, or kidneys.

Thus my heart was grieved, and I was pricked in the kidneys.
"Psalms" (73:21)

Whose heart would not be affected thereat, and whose reins would not be agitated at this word of judgment that is gone forth against them? "Enoch" (68:3)

He became filled with zeal and his reins trembled.
"Maccabees I" (2:24)

But, O Lord of hosts, that judgest righteously, that triest the reins and the heart . . .   "Jeremiah" (11:20)

I the Lord search the heart, I try the reins, even to give every man according to his ways, and according to the fruit of his doings.   "Jeremiah" (17:10)

. . . for the righteous God trieth the hearts and reins.
              "Psalms" (7:9)

Examine me, O Lord, and prove me; try my reins and heart.
              "Psalms" (26:2)

. . . I am he which searcheth the reins and hearts: and I will give unto every one of you according to your works.
              "Revelation" (2:23)

God is a witness of his reins, and a true inspector of his heart.
              "Wisdom" (1:6)

In the following, I quote some of H. W. Hogg's further indications:

Just as 'Psalms' chapter 16, verse 7 ['I will bless the Lord, who hath given me counsel: my reins also instruct me in night seasons.'] carries this a stage further, for there in the stillness of the night the kidneys teach him the Law. In the Talmud, however (Berakhoth, 61a), only one of the kidneys is a trustworthy guide; the other gives evil counsel . . . Gesenius ('Thesaurus') quotes Ibn Ezra as explaining k`layoth [Hebrew for kidneys] as the seat of desire, lust . . . in the much later Hebrew 'Testimony of Naphtali' (106) . . . it is said that with his heart a man thinks (yehsobh), with his liver he is angry (yikh`os), and from his kidneys he receives counsel (na`os) . . . The Syrian Father Ephraem, explains more fully (ii., 316 C): In the kidneys are seated reasonings (husabhe), and there dwells in them the faculty of discernment (pursana); they distinguish truth from falsehood, and judge what is base and what is noble.

In the lecture entitled, *Spiritual Relations in the Configuration of the Human Organism*, that was given at Dornach, Switzerland, on October 22, 1922, Rudolf Steiner addressed the nature of a particular aspect of the occult physiology of the kidneys as they were experienced later in the Grail Mysteries; during the time of the transition from the Intellectual-Soul to the Consciousness-Soul.

You see, around the turn of the 12th, 13th, and 14th centuries, an attitude comes about in Europe, which I have already characterized, in the Parzival legend, in all that has been written by the poets like Wolfram von Eschenbach, Hartman von der Aue, Gottfried von Strassburg, and so on. There the motifs emerge. In the Parzival epic, in the true Parzival epic one motif especially arises. It consists in the sudden desire, to now present how man has to develop himself towards something one called at that time 'Saelde.' It is the feeling of a certain inner sensation of happiness - 'Saelde' - related to what we would call 'bliss' but it is not the same. 'Saelde' means being penetrated by a certain feeling of happiness. This emerges and dominates the whole civilization of the 13th and 14th century. All poetic motifs, but in particular the Parzival motif, are permeated by it and everything strives towards it. One strives towards this 'Saelde', towards this inner feeling of bliss, which should not be irreligious, or perhaps a state of blissful comfort, but a state of being ensouled with the divine forces of the Creator.

Why does this arise? It arises because the transition from the kidney activity to the liver activity takes place. You will be able to understand this if you are aided by physiology. The earlier physiologists, of course, were better physiologists in many respects than the materialistic physiologists of today. Those, I mean, were the writers of the Old Testament, where one, for example, said, if one had bad dreams - I have already drawn attention to this - : 'the Lord has punished me this night through my kidneys.' The knowledge of certain connections of an abnormal kidney-activity with bad dreams continued, and in the 8th, 9th and 10th centuries, for example, one was still deeply permeated by the conviction, that one becomes heavy through the activity of the kidney. The activity of the kidney had developed into something like heaviness for man. Of course, one spoke outwardly only about something that became heavy for man. One couldn't quite get out of it. One was stuck to the earthly. And then one sensed that one became penetrated by the gall from the physical side - but in a way that was connected with being 'inwardly permeated by Saelde' - as a deliverance, an inner redemption, but it was an inner God-filled feeling of bliss, a striving away from the dullness of the kidney. It is so, that the kidney also develops an activity of thinking. The kidney develops the dull thought-activity in man via the detour of the ganglious system. This is then connected through induction with the system of the spinal cord and the system of the brain. It develops in particular that kind of thinking which also played a direct role in the Middle Ages. One called it at that time 'dullness' (Tumpheit). And this development from 'Tumpheit' to Illumination (Saelde), this was what became the motif of Parzival. Parzival develops from dullness to 'Saelde.' One must not look at this in an abstract manner, but one must also look at it with feeling and a sensitivity. In the beginning Parzival is as one arising out of a culture that has become heavy. One cannot quite get him in movement. Only later, after he has passed through his doubting, does Saelde permeate him. This doubt in him arises through being jolted by the heart-lung system. After he has gone through that, he finds the entry into Saelde.

The inward self-reliant quality, that is the hallmark of the potential development of the Consciousness-Soul, is revealed through the path of "saelde", or the "state of being ensouled with the divine forces of the Creator." In the biography by T. H. Meyer, *D. N. Dunlop - A Man of Our Time* (pages 95-96), this state of being is characterized by D. N. Dunlop, as a means whereby the esoteric pupil passes through "doubt to blessedness", overcoming the dullness of the realm of kama or desire through the independent self-awareness of the Consciousness-Soul:

And when there is a 'day of judgment' in a man's life every day, none will be necessary after death. When you are able to see yourself standing in the center as a thinker, you will attach a true, discriminating judgment to every act of the day. You will feel the vibration of immortality in your own being which nothing can shake. With practice you will be able to see that which was foolish and small and petty, and that which is pure and lovely and full of peace will also be clearly revealed. I have tried it a little and know I am talking of something which every being can realize for himself. This is the kind of life men and women want to begin to live; they want to enter into that calm, penetrating, peaceful state of the mind. When you begin to judge yourself that way, life is robbed of many of its fears. My friends, face it! Look life straight into the face! Only then will you understand what it is to live without fear, and to let the world crash around you. Only then will you see that the first result of penetrating into your own life by your own mind will be a joy which is unspeakable. To realize yourself as immortal, to realize that the passing things of the body have not stained that stainless self, is in itself a wonderful thing.

If people can only develop to the stage of the Intellectual-Soul - with its dependence on external authority - then they will not unfold the "ethical individualism" of the Consciousness-Soul. This tragedy will open the possibility of the future Spirit-Self descending into mankind from the realm of the Luciferic spirits, rather than from the Holy Spirit.

A major shortcoming of the Intellectual-Soul is its intolerance of nonconformity in the realm of ideas. In the book of poetry, compiled by Douglas Gabriel in celebration of the Sophia Mysteries, entitled, *Goddess Meditations - From Isis to Sophia*, is included a poem of mine, which I dedicate to the memory of Esclarmonde de Foix (esclaire-monde = "light of the world"), the protectress of the Cathars and patroness of Montsegur, the Cathar stronghold high in the Pyrenees mountains. Esclarmonde was the sister of the troubadour patron Count Raymond Roger of Foix, and was bitterly chastised for her defense of the Cathars. Esclarmonde further irritated the clergy through her eloquent participation in the debate with the Cathars that took place in Pamiers in 1207 under the supervision of St. Dominic, the founder of the Dominican Order. Her words in this debate prompted one of the associates of Dominic to state: "Madame, go wind your distaff! It is not fitting that you should argue matters of this kind." Later, in 1244, 200 or so Cathars were put to the flames of martyrdom at Montsegur due to the intolerance of the Catholic Church.

The Embrace of the Trees

Spoken as a gift . . .
As the wind ever renews its embrace of the trees,
for she did go unto the woods forever and ever;
and she did lie, east of the shadow of an' stately oak.
They knew not what brought her there, far from the affairs of men,
some say it was enchantment, while others love.
But far and far away she did go, to learn the language of the ebb and tide,
that was spoken by the undines while embracing the shores
of many a far-forgotten land.
They told her of the lives and sorrows of joy;
and spoke in riddles of the love between the moon
and the deep glassy seas.
At night she would sit and watch,
the most motionless dance of the willows in a western wind.
Waiting patient lest a solitary slyph surrender a serene gesture of truth,
or bring fair and glad tidings;
the kind sleeping fairies weave into gossamer tapestries
within a midsummer's dream.
And so it went, that she did go
deep into the stillness only mountains would know,
and kissed eternity with her immortal brow . . .

IV

The Emperor

Aries - Christ - the "King of Kings" - the "Lamb of God" the Son - the 2nd Logos - the "Word"

From the perspective of the esoteric Christian viewpoint, the Masonic tradition of the "Great Architect of the Universe" can be looked upon as an image of Christ as the divine author of creation. In certain medieval art works, Christ is represented holding a compass and circumscribing the periphery of the Earth. This portrayal represents the forming attribute of the divine creative idea of Christ, the "Word", working through the Elohim, or Exusiai, the Spirits of Form. This is symbolically revealed in the laws of creation as represented in the opening verses of "Genesis."

The Christ as the creative "Word" is depicted in the opening verses of "The Gospel of St. John." For, the Logos or "Word" is the primary source of creative manifestation. As it says in "The Gospel of St. John" (1:3); "All things were made through Him, and without Him was not anything made that was made." This concept is central to understanding the intentions of the master builders who attempted to reveal in stone the great mystery of the creative "Word" in the architecture of Chartres, and other Gothic cathedrals (**XXIV**).

The Gothic cathedrals are marvels of architecture that were constructed by master builders, whose names for the most part are now unknown to us, as a selfless contribution toward the understanding of the Divine Plan. These master builders left us a legacy of initiatic instruction in the artwork and in the principles of "harmonious form" that are expressed within these great buildings. The occult principles that were used by the master builders in the architecture and artwork of the cathedrals were intended to be a wholesome spiritualizing influence on all who experienced them, though the understanding of its deeper esoteric significance was limited to the few. The stained glass images in the cathedrals were like the tarot arcana, in that they each embodied, in symbolical picture language, a particular facet of the path of spiritual unfoldment.

In the Emperor arcanum, he is shown sitting regally upon a throne (Latin, cathedra = chair or throne) of granite with mountains in the background. The emphasis upon stone in the picture, combined with the ankh, the Egyptian "symbol of life" in his right hand and the globe in his left hand, connects the symbolism of the Emperor arcanum with the master builders. In the Masonic legend of the golden triangle, when the Queen of Sheba was introduced to the Phoenician master builder Hiram Abiff by King Solomon, Hiram called to order all of the builders of King Solomon's Temple by holding up a tau cross. (The tau cross is a T-shaped symbol and makes up the lower part of the ankh, which is a circle added to the top of a tau.) The geometric symbolism of the tau cross relates to the world of form, while the circle on top - which makes it an ankh - relates to the principle of spirit and the life that proceeds from it.

In "The Gospel of St. John" (1:4) it says; "In Him was life, and the life was the light of men." The mystery of the origin of life as a creative impulse that proceeded from the Logos or the "Living Word" is central to the doctrines of the master builders, who are sometimes referred to as the "Brothers of John." Always in nature, life precedes form and brings it into being. It was this arising of form out of life, according to the mathematical and geometrical principles of harmony, which is expressed in the structure of the Temple of Solomon and of the Gothic cathedrals; for these buildings were meant to represent the mysteries of the human body. The master builders viewed the human body as a microcosmic image of the heavens - the Macrocosm. These master builders were attempting to architecturally express in the cathedrals, as a seat (cathedra) or "house of the Word", the mysteries of the Macrocosm and the Microcosm. Through their "bibles in stone" the master builders revealed the mystery of the "Lamb of God" as inspired through the spiritual wisdom of Sophia. This tradition of the "house of the Word" was continued by Rudolf Steiner through the esoteric symbolic artwork and architectural principles that were embodied in the first Goetheanum. The tradition of the "Brothers of John" is commemorated through Rudolf Steiner's original intention to call this building the Johannes-Bau, which means the "house of John."

In the symbolism of the Emperor arcanum, Christ is represented as the "King of Kings", and His dominion is shown by the golden globe that is resting in his left hand. That the globe is made of gold represents its relationship to the Sun, while the cross that is shown on top relates to the Earth and is another symbol that utilizes the cross and the circle of the ankh; except that in this case, the cross is surmounting the circle or sphere - symbolizing the exaltation or resurrection of matter.

The golden crown upon the head of the Emperor symbolizes the mystery of the Zodiac as it "crowns" the dome of the head. For the head is itself a microcosmic dome of the heavens, and expresses the Zodiac in the twelve-fold structure of the cranial nerves. The golden (solar) crown upon the zodiacal dome of the head of the Emperor, also represents the redemption of the "fallen" nervous system that took place through Christ Jesus reasserting the "Sun-laws" that were established in the Old Sun incarnation of the Earth.

In the Emperor arcanum there are four ram's heads shown on the Emperor's granite throne. These represent the working of Christ, from the etheric world, upon the world of form through the four elements of fire, air, water and earth. This can be seen as a picture of Christ the "Great Sun-Spirit", through the aforementioned "Sun-laws", gradually transforming the Earth from within the etheric world into a future Spiritual-Sun. "On Earth as it is in Heaven" (**IV**). The four ram's heads on the Emperor's throne can also be seen to represent the working of Christ through the four directions of space, and through the four seasons of the year. This idea of the working of Christ through the four seasons is expressed in a Latin work that was in use in the Middle Ages entitled, *Hymnus in Vesperis Nativitatis*: "Christus, lumen et splendour Patris, mundi salus, currens per anni circulum." ("Christ, light and splendor of the Father, world salvation, proceeds through the annual circle.")

The region of the starry sky that corresponds to the constellation of the Lamb, or Ram is called Aries (**IX**). Christ came as the "Lamb of God" in the epoch of Aries to give us "more life, and that abundantly." The Mystery of the Lamb is clarified by Sergei O. Prokofieff in the second chapter of his book (which explores the esoteric significance of the first Goetheanum) entitled, *The Twelve Holy Nights and the Spiritual Hierarchies*:

> *This also sheds light upon the various names of Christ. When He enters the zodiac through the gate of the Ram, Christ is the Son, and on the Sun He is the "Great Sun-Spirit" (an expression very frequently used by Rudolf Steiner). The name, Christ (from the Greek, Χριστοσ, Christos, the Lord's Anointed), He receives only at that time when He extends His influence over the lunar surroundings of the Earth; while on the Earth He works as Christ-Jesus, as God-Man. And through all these stages, as though permeating them with a*

single stream, there radiates the idea of Christ as the Logos or Word. From the region beyond the zodiac ('In the beginning was the Word, and the Word was with God and the Word was God') it appears in the sphere of the zodiac, in the region of the Ram, as a new creative impulse ('All things were made through Him, and without Him was not anything made that was made.'), and there it sounds through all the descending ranks of the Hierarchies, becoming, on the Sun in its starry aspect, Life ('In Him was life'), and in its planetary aspect, Light ('and the life was the light . . .'), and then meeting and overcoming the dark forces in the sphere of the Moon ('And the Light shines in the darkness, but the darkness has not understood it') so as to become, on the Earth, the Incarnated Word, the God-Man, Christ-Jesus ('And the Word became flesh . . .'). Thus we may truly say, in Rudolf Steiner's words: 'Christ is, in His individual essence, not only to be thought of as dwelling for three years in the sheaths of Jesus of Nazareth but also as the Leader and Guide of all the beings of the higher Hierarchies.' "

The Stages of the Anointing of Humanity

Beyond the Zodiac - Extra-Cosmic
"In the beginning was the Word, and the Word was with God . . ."
Through the Zodiac - the "Lamb of God" - Aries
"All things were made through Him . . ."
From the Sun - the "Great Sun-Spirit"
"In Him was life . . ."
From the Planetary Realm - the "Light of the World"
"and the life was the light . . ."
From the Moon Sphere - the "Burning Bush" - *"I Am the I Am"*
"And the Light shines in the darkness . . ."
In Jesus at the Baptism - the "God-Man" - the "Son of God"
"And the Word became flesh . . ."
In the Atmosphere of the Earth
"I shall be with you always"
In the Human Heart - the "Man of God"
"the Christ in You"
In the Distant Future
"Ye shall be as the Angels"

On a macrocosmic-stellar level, the process of the development of the Spiritual-Human is connected with the beings and forces of the Zodiac under the regency of Christ. To begin with, the first stage of human evolution that is described by Rudolf Steiner is a condition of warmth, which was brought into being through the sacrifice of the Thrones, or Spirits of Will (and which Rudolf Steiner also referred to as the Spirits of Courage), working out of the region of the constellation of Leo, the Lion (**IV**). The present manifestation of this original sacrifice is the warmth of the blood which is centered in the heart; it is this warmth that bears the Ego in a human being. This courageous leonine sacrifice of the Thrones is mirrored within the heart-forces of courage (cour = heart) (**XIII**).

In the distant past, Christ directed the work of creation from outside - from "beyond" the Zodiac. Then, Christ as the "Lamb of God" (**IX**) entered into our Cosmos through the region of the constellation of Aries the Ram, or Lamb, passing from the transcendent region of the Father beyond the Zodiac (**V**), so as to direct cosmic evolution from within the region of the Sun. This can be seen as a movement in stages - from the periphery of the Zodiac to the center of the Sun.

This movement by Christ, from the periphery of the Cosmos, continued further until He entered into the very heart of Jesus of Nazareth. This movement points towards the mystery of "the periphery and the center", and took place first on a cosmic level within the solar system - through Christ's movement from the circumference of the Zodiac to the center of the Sun. Afterwards, this mystery of "the periphery and the center" was, in turn, unfolded within the human form of Jesus of Nazareth. This holiest of mysteries came about through the Logos - that once dwelt beyond His creation - finally entering into Jesus. For Christ began gradually moving closer to the Earth until, at the "Turning Point of Time", Christ entered into Jesus at the Baptism; and, in time, He gradually accomplished the indwelling of the human form and condition. After dwelling in Jesus for around three years, Christ brought about the redemption of Earth evolution through the "Mystery of the Holy Blood" which took place through the Crucifixion upon Golgotha (**XXV**).

The Cosmos is reflected in the human being, and likewise, those principles upon which the future evolution of mankind depends - will approach man from outside. For the higher principles, that are to be added to the supersensible being of man, will approach from the periphery as the donated substance of higher spiritual beings. These principles will be added to the continuing unfoldment of the macrocosmic reflection in the human microcosm, and will find their center within the heart.

In a lecture given at Pforzheim on the 7th of March, 1914 entitled, *The Pre-Earthly Deeds of Christ*, Rudolf Steiner described how during the Lemurian epoch, through the divine workings of the Holy Spirit, under the direction of Christ, ". . . the Spirits of Form poured the Ego into man out of their own substance. And the first manifestation of this inflowing of the 'I' was that inner force by means of which man raised himself into an upright position." Rudolf Steiner further adds that had this not taken place, "Lucifer and Ahriman would have been able to bring about disaster to the whole of humanity . . ." The next "deed of Christ" came about in the Atlantean period when through the direction of Christ (ibid):

> *The Spirits of Form poured themselves into man and permeated him, and thereby he became able to speak a language . . . If he had been abandoned entirely to the Earth, if cosmic-spiritual influences had not come down to Earth and poured into him, everything connected with his speech must have become debased through the Luciferic and Ahrimanic influences. If nothing had been brought about by Christ, man in the Atlantean epoch would so have developed his whole life-culture - all his bodily organs: larynx, tongue, throat, etc., and indeed even the organs lower down such as the heart in so far as they are connected with the former - that he would only have been capable of expressing his own selfish joy or pain, desire or bliss, in poor babbling sounds somewhat like the utterances of Sibyls or mediums. Certainly he would have been able to utter much more artistic or intelligent sounds than an animal can produce, but these sounds would only have been expressive of that which lived in him, of the bodily processes taking place in his organism. He would have found expressive interjections for these only; his speech would have consisted entirely of interjections. . . This disorder in the power of speech in so far as it would have affected man's inner being was averted; the second Christ-event prevented it from entering human evolution. . . The power of grasping the 'objective' was brought about through the second Christ-event.*

These two "deeds of Christ" were followed by a third "deed", which occurred toward the end of the Atlantean period. This "deed of Christ" succeeded in rescuing the power of human thought from the dominion of the Luciferic and Ahrimanic beings (ibid).

> *But the power of so describing outer things in words, in order that the words should rightly indicate them, was still in danger from the Luciferic and Ahrimanic influences right into the Atlantean epoch. Then came the third Christ event. For the third time that Being in the spiritual heights, later to be born as the Nathan-Jesus, united himself with the Christ Being and again poured the forces so received into the human power of speech. The force of this Christ-Jesus Being now permeated once more the organs of the human body in so far as those organs come to expression in the power of speech. In this way it was made possible for the power of speech to create, by means of words, actual signs representative of the external environment, thus enabling mankind to create language as a means of communication between the different inhabited regions.*

These three "deeds of Christ" are recapitulated in the early developmental stages of a small child. The child first learns to bring himself to an upright position, then follows the rudiments of speech which lay the foundation for the life of thought. It could be argued that there are animals that have an upright stature - but it must be remembered that they acquire this stature by nature from birth, only human beings raise themselves up from the horizontal to the vertical by the working of the forces of the Ego.

The significance of the upright stature for the development of speaking and thinking is illustrated by the case of a pair of Siamese twins who were joined together at the hip, and were the subject of a television documentary a few years ago. These Siamese twins were joined together in such a way so that only one of them could walk upright, while the other twin could only raise itself when standing to a position that was slightly more than horizontal. As these Siamese twins developed it was noticed that only the upright child was learning to speak, while the other horizontal child could only incoherently babble. The doctors, meanwhile, had determined that the Siamese twins could be surgically separated, and were waiting for them to get a little older so as to increase the chances of a successful operation. The retardation of the horizontal child continued to become more pronounced in comparison to the upright child which was speaking and developing its intelligence in a normal way. The surgery was successfully performed, and from that point on the retardation of the child that was once horizontal began to improve. It gradually developed speech and the ability to communicate ideas, soon catching up to the development of its sibling. This case demonstrates in a very dramatic way how the upright forces of the Ego take hold of the Physical-Body, through the continued working of the Christ principle, according to the path of evolution that was made manifest through the three "pre-earthly deeds of Christ."

The fruit of the third "deed of Christ" in the realm of thinking only gradually came about during the course of evolution in the post-Atlantean epochs. For thinking still was a process of picture formation until the fourth, or Graeco-Roman cultural epoch of Aries the Ram (ibid).

The fourth post-Atlantean civilization began in the eighth century before Christ. About three and a-half centuries later thought had ripened sufficiently to be expressed by the Greek philosophers with such clarity that it led to the Platonic Philosophy. Then the life of man was permeated with the Christ-Impulse.

This "ripening" of thinking in the Graeco-Roman cultural epoch laid the foundation for mankind's development of conceptual thinking, which is necessary in order to more fully understand the significance of the entry of Christ into human evolution. The seed for this understanding is expressed in the opening verses of "The Gospel of St. John." Below I give a contemplation of the opening verses of "The Gospel of St. John" in which I have attempted to explore their deeper meaning.

In the Primal Beginning of creation the Word was in existence. And the Word was in the company of God the Father. And a God was the Word in His absolute totality of being. This Word was at the Primal Beginning of creation in the company of God the Father. Through the intermediate agency of the Word all things came into being, and not even one thing came into being

> *without the Word. In the Word was the original existence of life. And this life was the light that is the essential core of a human being. And the light that dwells in the midst of darkness shines without ceasing. And the uncomprehending darkness cannot overwhelm the light, but rather will become illuminated by it through the limitless grace and truth which arises out of the unceasing love of Christ, the Living Word, for His creation.*

As a result of the gradually awakening Ego consciousness that came about through Christ's intervention in human evolution, mankind has the potential to become free and independent beings. The penultimate stage in this development took place when Christ brought the highest forces of the Holy Trinity into a completely new relationship to mankind by entering into the human realm.

The "Lamb of God" is the great mystery of the constellation of Aries the Lamb (**IX**). Part of this mystery is revealed by the fact that the Mystery of Golgotha took place during the epoch of Aries, around 2,000 years ago (**XXVI**). The sequence of Christ's relationship to human evolution can be seen as a gradual transition from the Macrocosm to the Microcosm. The Christ, Who had previously worked from outside of mankind, began to transform humanity from within the human heart; and the Sophia forces, which had in the past worked from within mankind were now to work from the periphery (**XII**).

Rudolf Steiner once characterized the effect of the incarnation of Christ, "the Word", upon the blood and nerves in a lecture he gave in Berlin on June 13th 1916, entitled, "Blood and Nerves", which is published in the lecture cycle entitled, *Toward Imagination*.

> *In Spiritual Science we consider all matter or substance to be a manifestation of the spiritual. But the essential question is always how a particular material phenomenon manifests the spiritual . . .*
>
> *There is a very ancient, yet ever new, saying to the effect that the human being is a microcosm. Human beings in the physical world are, in the first place, material phenomena. If we seriously believe that the human being is a microcosm, that our physical being contains the secrets of the whole Cosmos, then we will think it worthwhile to examine how our physical*

being reveals the spiritual. If you study the physical aspect of the human being and think about it . . . you will see that there are two totally different kinds of substance within our physical being. It only takes ordinary thinking and observation to see that there are two fundamentally different kinds of substance within us: the blood substance, or blood material, and the nerve substance.

Of course, you may say that at first glance there are all sorts of other substances too, muscle tissue, bone matter, and so on. But all these substances are actually built up from the blood, as you will see when you study them more closely. Thus, their existence does not contradict the fact that we have primarily two substances in us: blood substance, or blood material, and nerve substance.

One of the differences between these two substances can easily be observed; you need only consider that everything connected with the blood is involved, so to speak, from the inside, from within our metabolic processes. Although it is generated as a result of external influences, our blood is produced from within us; and it, in turn, generates what is necessary for physical existence.

On the other hand, the most important nerves show themselves to be extensions of our sense organs. For instance, in the eyes you find the optic nerves extending out from the back of the eyes and merging with the nerve substance of the brain. Similarly, all nerves are actually extensions of our sense organs. The processes that take place in them are, more or less, the result of outside influences, of everything working upon us from the outside. We can say that just as magnets have two poles, and just as we have positive and negative electricity, so too the blood and the nerve substances are the two poles of our physical being. And these two kinds of substance are inwardly very different from each other . . .

If you investigate both the blood substance and the nerve substance in the light of Spiritual Science, you will easily see the tremendous difference between the two. Our nerve substance is not of the Earth, but the blood substance is of the Earth. Nerve substance originated in processes that took place before the formation of the Earth. Our blood substance, and everything that streams and flows within it, finds its origin completely in earthly processes. Our nerve substance is absolutely extraterrestrial, so to speak, and is woven into us as something cosmic - it is related to the Cosmos.

Our nerve substance has been transferred into the earthly realm; it exists here upon the earth where we live as physical beings. Thus, we all bear something of an extraterrestrial origin within us that has been transplanted onto the Earth. This is a very important fact; for the nerve substance, as it rests in us - is actually dead. You only need to open any current anatomy or physiology textbook to see that in terms of substance, the nerve substance is the most durable in our body. It is the most resistant to change and, unlike the substance of the blood, it is least subject to direct, mechanical interference from the outside. For our nerve substance is affected by the influences of our sense perceptions; but it cannot be influenced directly and mechanically - because it was originally a living substance and it is now dead because we are carrying it within us as earth beings. We might say, if it were not paradoxical - though it is true in a spiritual sense regardless of any paradox - that if we could take our nerve substance and raise it to a sphere beyond the influence of the forces of the Earth, it would become a marvelous, living, vibrant being.

This nerve substance is, so to speak, designed for life in the heavens, within the extraterrestrial realms; but because it is in our organism and has thus entered into the earthly sphere, it has died. This is very strange, isn't it? We have this nerve substance within us that is alive in the realm of the Cosmos but dead in the realm of the Earth. If we were to take some of this nerve substance up beyond the reach of earthly influences, we would have a wonderful, living, and luminous substance. Although, of course, as soon as we returned it to our earthly sphere, it would revert again to the still, lifeless condition in which it now rests within us. Our nerve substance, then, is alive in the Cosmos and dead on Earth.

In fact, as far as its material composition is concerned, the nerve substance that we have in us is an extraterrestrial element. All of this can be very clearly expressed with a symbol . . . Usually people distinguish only five senses; but then, we counted twelve. Human beings actually have twelve senses, if everything that can really be called a sense is taken into *account. For ultimately, our senses are nothing more than points of departure whereby our nerves extend into us.*

So we really have twelve senses, and from these twelve senses the nerves extend into us like little trees. This is because the nervous system, that belongs to our outer senses, is an expression of the passage of the Sun through the twelve constellations of the Zodiac, and is symbolized by the relationship of our entire nervous system to each of the twelve senses. This shows that we carry within us, in the spatial relationship of our whole nervous system to the twelve senses, what really exists out there in the Cosmos as the Sun's passage through the constellations of the Zodiac [**XXI-XXIII**]. *When you look at that part of our nervous system which is located deeper inside of us, within the spinal cord, you will find that the nerve-fibers extend through the ring-like vertebrae of the spine. In fact, these rings correspond to the months, to the orbit of the Moon around the Earth. Thus, the passage of each of the nerve-fibers through these openings in the vertebrae of the spine corresponds to each day of the month - another cosmic relationship! The orbit of the Moon around the Earth is actually symbolized through this relationship of our inner nerves to the spinal cord.*

Our nerve substance is entirely built-up from out of the heavens, out of the Cosmos. Therefore, we can only really understand this marvelous organization of the nerve substance within us - when we see in its tree-like arrangement - an image of the whole starry firmament. And the forces that are flowing outside from star to star and expressing themselves in the movements of the heavenly bodies - these same forces are actually flowing within our nervous system; which is, however, dead within us. This connection between the organization of the Cosmos and the structure of our nervous system, like many other things, reveals that the entire Universe is manifested within us. And, insofar as our nervous system is built for the heavens, it is alive in the heavens, within the Cosmos - but it is dead within us - because it has entered into the earthly sphere.

Our blood substance is quite different because it belongs entirely to the Earth. Due to the inner composition of the blood, the processes that are taking place within it would really have to be completely earthly processes. The peculiar thing about them, however, is that they are not living processes. As you know, the mineral realm, the lifeless kingdom, was developed during evolution upon the Earth. And the nature of our blood corresponds completely to this lifeless kingdom. Although our blood lives as long as it is within us - it is not destined for life by its inner, earthly nature. Strangely enough, our blood is alive only because it is connected to the cosmic element in us. Our nervous system is actually destined for life in the Cosmos beyond the Earth - and yet, it is dead inside of us. Our blood, on the other hand, is meant to be dead within us and to receive its life from outside. In a sense, the nervous system yields its life to the blood; therefore, comparatively speaking, the nervous system is dead while the blood is alive. Our blood is, by its very nature, dead upon the Earth - and has only a borrowed life, a cosmic life forced upon it. Life itself, is not at all of our Earth. That is why the nervous system must take death upon itself in order to become earthly; and also, why the blood has to become living - so as to enable us, as beings of earthly substance, to turn to the world beyond the Earth.

This is the point where all that we have learned through Spiritual Science takes on a deeply serious character. For we have to realize that the nerve substance, which we have in us, is by its very nature destined for life - and yet it is dead. Why is that? It is dead because it has been transplanted onto the Earth. Death - as you can read in the cycle of lectures I gave in Munich [August 24th-26th, 1913 published as "The Secrets of the Threshold"] - is actually the kingdom of Ahriman. Thus, because our nervous system lost its life through its descent into the earthly sphere, we carry an Ahrimanic element within us. Also, because our blood is alive - though by its very nature it is destined for death, that is, for mere chemical and physical processes - we have a Luciferic element within us. Ahriman can exist in us because our nervous system is dead; and, because our blood is alive, Lucifer can live in us. Now you can see the significant differences between these two substances - for they are polar opposites, just as the North Pole is to the South Pole.

Let us now consider the realm beyond the Earth, but not by condensing Spiritual Science into an abstract theory; but rather, by keeping it alive so it can speak to our feelings. We look out into the Universe and realize that out there is the spirit that could live within our nervous system - if the latter had not descended to the Earth. We can sense the spirit out there, filling the Universe - the spirit that belongs to our nervous system. When we then turn our thoughts to the blood, we understand that by its very nature it is actually destined only for physical and chemical processes, only for the assimilation of oxygen such as is described within anatomy and physiology. However, because it lives in us, it participates in the life of the Cosmos. It has, nonetheless, a primarily Luciferic life.

And now think deeply, and with great sensitivity, of a recurrent common theme of our talks and remember all we have said about the descent of Christ from the Cosmos into our earthly sphere. Then we can connect what we remember with the thoughts we have just discussed. We ourselves originated in this Universe, in the Cosmos. Long ago, in the Lemurian epoch, or within the course of earthly evolution in general, we descended and have connected our evolution with the Earth. But by entrusting the development of our nervous system to the Earth, we have consigned it to death - and have left its life behind in the Cosmos. That life that we left behind later followed us - and descended in the Christ Being. In other words, the life of our nerves, which we have not been able to bear within us ever since the beginning of our earthly existence, followed us later in the Christ Being. And what did that life need to take hold of within earthly existence? It had to take hold of the blood! This is why we speak so often about the Mystery of the Blood.

Our nervous system had lost its cosmic life and our blood has received a cosmic life; that is, life became death and death became life. They live separately within us. And yet, a new connection between them was achieved when the life of our nervous system, which had been left behind, descended to us from the Cosmos, became human and entered the blood; that, in turn, united itself with the Earth, as I have explained before. And now we, as human beings, can reconcile the contrast between the blood system and the nervous system through our participation in the Christ Mystery.

This polarity that we carry within us manifests in various ways. For instance, there is the material science of the outer world. It has found the culmination of its goal, within the present-day natural science, that sees the world as being built-up out of atoms. However, these atoms are pure fantasy - they simply are not to be found out there. Then why do we talk about atoms? Because we have within us our nervous system which is built-up out of little globules, and we project this structure upon the outside world. The world of atoms out there is really nothing but a projection of our nervous system! We project ourselves into the world, and so, we think of it as consisting of atoms - from our nervous system being composed of many individual ganglion-globules. Science will always tend towards atomism - for it originates from within the nerve substance. By contrast, mysticism, religion, and so forth come from the blood; and so, they do not look for atoms but always for unity. These two opposites are in conflict with each other in the world [Cain = nerve, Abel = blood]. We do not understand their conflict unless we know it is really the struggle within us between the nerve substance and the blood substance. There would be no conflict between science and religion if there were none in us between the nerve and the blood substances.

Reconciliation is found if we unite ourselves in the right way with the Christ Being - that pulsates through the Earth since the Mystery of Golgotha. Every feeling and experience that we have in connection with the Mystery of Golgotha contributes towards this reconciliation. So far, we have not advanced very much in bringing about this reconciliation, but we must continue to strive for it.

Even in our circles, very often we see that the contrast I have described manifests in one way or another. There are many among us who listen to the teachings of Anthroposophy and accept them in the same way that they accept conventional science. And as a result, many people see no difference between Anthroposophy and ordinary science. But we understand Anthroposophy rightly only when we grasp it not just with the head, but allow every one of its utterances to enkindle our enthusiasm and to live in us so that it finds its way from the nervous system to the blood system. Only when we warmly take up the truths that are presented in Anthroposophy - do we truly understand it. As long as we only approach it abstractly and study it as we would study the multiplication *tables, an arithmetic book, instruction manuals, or a cookbook, we do not understand it at all! We cannot understand Anthroposophy if we only study it in the same manner that we would chemistry or botany. For, only when it generates warmth in us, and replenishes us with its own vibrant life, do we begin to really understand it.*

My talk began like a conventional scientific talk, perhaps one about anatomy or physiology, by looking at the substances within the human being, but now we find the transition to the loftiest knowledge we can have on Earth - to Christology. You cannot find this transition in any other science. Spiritual Science shows you that our nerve substance lost something by becoming earthly substance. But where is that which our nerve substance has lost? When Jesus of Nazareth was thirty years old, Christ entered into his body and went through the Mystery of Golgotha. Try to warm yourselves through and through with this thought. What is lacking within our nervous systems because we are living on Earth, what has been replaced with an ahrimanic element, is what we find in the Mystery of Golgotha.

It is our task as human beings to take this Mystery into our blood and to fill the luciferic element there with Christ, to enkindle our enthusiasm so that it can live in us. Our abstract thinking is connected to the nerve substance; while our feelings, our heart and soul, enthusiasm, or mood, are connected to the blood. The relationship between nerve substance and blood substance within our organism is the same as the relationship in our soul between abstract-cold thinking and the enthusiasm we can feel when things do not remain for us merely as cold thoughts, but instead, are warmed within us by the spirit. This warming that comes about through the spirit does not come naturally - we have to train ourselves to attain it.

Now you can see in spiritual and psychological terms, as it were, what the Mystery of Golgotha accomplished. What we had left behind in the Cosmos has followed us. It can now, once again, permeate our soul - because it did not permeate our body at the beginning of our Earth existence - for then we would have become automatons of the spirit. As it was, we went through a period of evolution upon the Earth before we were to be ensouled by what did not permeate our body right from the very beginning. This great and wonderful connection reveals the activity of the spiritual in matter.

We are not speaking here of the general, vague spiritual element . . . that pantheists speak of so glibly, but of the specific and definite spirit we see as having undergone the Mystery of Golgotha. That is what I meant when I said that the general truth - that all matter is a manifestation of the spiritual - really does not say very much. We know something only when we know in detail how a specific, physical being manifests the spiritual. The findings of conventional science are an abundance of facts and material just waiting to be permeated with spiritual understanding. For, spiritual understanding can penetrate them so deeply that even the most material science of all can be connected with Christology.

Here, Rudolf Steiner has given us a panoramic view of the various fruits that are to be garnered through the working within humanity of the Grail-deed of Christ - the "King of Kings." A sacred deed of sacrifice, which reversed the tide of Earth evolution - and brought about, for all time - through the expelling of mankind's forces of lower egotism with the excess blood shed on Golgotha - a transformation of the relationship between the nerves and blood; which thereby, redeemed the rift between the Cain (art and science) and Abel (religion and philosophy) streams.

In other places, Rudolf Steiner has described how the nervous system is an earthly counterpart to that which streams between the stars and the planets within the Cosmos; and that, during sleep we are united with this cosmic-astral realm - but we are unconscious of it; and so, upon waking we only have a vague sense for this realm of Cosmic Life, where we were united with Cosmic Beings. The earthly expression of this experience of being united with Cosmic Beings is love; while the opposite experience - that of feeling oneself as separate from the Cosmic Beings - manifests as the faculty of memory.

It must be said at this point that within these spiritual-scientific ideas, which are presented above, are contained the seeds for the development of a truly spiritual life - but only if it is grasped with one's whole being - so that it can become a true heart-wisdom, or what was called by the Rishis of the ancient East - harda-vidya (Sanskrit, harda = heart, vidya = knowledge, or wisdom). To grasp these ideas only with the head, as though one were learning any ordinary type of knowledge, is to deny oneself a true *participation* in what is being expressed. This fundamental spiritual truth is very difficult for modern man to grasp, as he likes to think that in acquiring the "facts" he has completed the learning process; for, in many instances, this is no doubt the case - when one is trying to learn ordinary things.

The development of heart-wisdom (and it can only be described this way for that is what it truly is) is a process that necessarily occurs over time and is nurtured through the repetition of the elements of spiritual wisdom; on the other hand, head-knowledge, which can be learned almost instantaneously, is of an entirely different character - and finds repetition monotonous. For the learning process of the head consists in the acquisition of facts; while developing heart-wisdom is an actual process of becoming - of unfoldment; whereby, one embraces the knowledge acquired with the wisdom gained through experience over time, in such a way, so that it generates warmth within one's being, and becomes a source of joy and radiance. This process of acquiring heart-wisdom, Rudolf Steiner tells us, generally takes "about three or four times as long" as the acquisition of head-knowledge - although we must bear in mind that he also said: "Sometimes the soul develops quietly in a very short time. One could say: It is not in any way a matter of time in development, but only deep inward peace."

Please, do not misunderstand me, for I am not de-emphasizing the importance of head-knowledge; in fact, heart-wisdom begins in the head, and can be seen as a "ripening" of one's head-knowledge. But if the spiritual knowledge that one acquires only remains as head-knowledge - although it may be very spiritual - it will not bring about a real spiritual transformation unless it is integrated with the feelings and the will - within the deep recess of one's very own blood and heart. If one does not approach spiritual knowledge in this way - with the feelings and the will - it can only exist within oneself in an abstract way as head-knowledge.

This distinction was recognized by the teachers of the ancient East, who felt that in order to bring the sacred wisdom, the Brahma-vidya (Sanskrit, Brahma = God, vidya = knowledge, or wisdom), into a deeper level of union or self-realization as heart-wisdom, or harda-vidya - one should introduce the rhythmic element into the spiritual practice. This was done through the methods of mantra-yoga (Sanskrit, mantra = instrument of thought, yoga = union); that is, through the extended chanting of mantrams (which consists of the rhythmic repetition of incantation formulas that were comprised of seed ideas, words, or divine names) - you could awaken the heart forces into a higher level of understanding.

Likewise, Rudolf Steiner used a method that was similar in his spiritual exercises, in that it included the element of rhythmic repetition; but this repetition did not extend so far that it became, so to speak, mechanical in nature. This was so, because the path of attaining spiritual knowledge and wisdom, for modern Western humanity, has changed from the methods that were appropriate for the past evolution of mankind. For it became necessary that mankind begin to free themselves, in their thinking, from a spiritual path that consists of a total immersion within the rhythmic nature of the blood, heart, and lungs. This rhythmic element is still present - but one should strive to stand before the heart forces as an independent "I", just as one should strive for a "once removed vantage-point" from the nerve-sense realm; and thereby endeavor to bring about a harmonization between the two realms of the head and the heart. This is not to say, of course, that the methods of the past are bad; but rather, that it is a matter of personal choice, and of individual karma, which path one decides to follow.

By pursuing this path of the harmonization of the head and the heart, as presented in modern Spiritual Science, we begin to cultivate a relationship to Christ - so that through our spiritual activities, which are enacted during the waking state, we carry over into the realm of sleep a potential to receive inner-teachings from Christ as to the true nature of the Zodiac. Rudolf Steiner tells us that, through this guidance by Christ, we can learn more than we could ever learn from all of the books in the world. If, on the other hand, one experiences the Zodiac in the realm of sleep - without the guidance of Christ - it is experienced as meaningless gibberish.

For only through Christ, the "Living-Word", can we develop the heart-language needed to penetrate these mysteries - as it is through the development of the heart as an organ of supersensible perception that we can receive this spiritual wisdom - the heart has to take up the redeemed life of the nerve-sense realm so as to become transformed into an organ of spiritual cognition. When this takes place, the memory of being united with the beings of the spiritual world arises as the experience of Cosmic Love. Then the heart begins to hear and speak a language of process and context that consists of only verbs - for the heart-language is the language of Cosmic Love and so must be a language of action, a language of deeds. It is like Christ has said; "Ye shall know them by their deeds."

V

The Hierophant

Taurus - the Holy Spirit - the 3rd Logos - the Gift of Tongues
St. Luke - the Doctor - the Initiate of Feeling

Hierophant is the title of the high priest of the Eleusinian Mysteries in ancient Greece, and means "revealer of sacred mysteries" (hiero = sacred, phantes = to reveal). In modern times, hierophant has come to mean any priest that presides over sacred mysteries. In ancient Egypt, the hierophants were considered to be both healers and magicians. This fact is commented on by Jamieson B. Hurry M.D. in his book entitled, *Imhotep - The Egyptian God of Medicine*.

> *Magic and medicine were closely allied in the time of the Pharaohs. Magic is generally regarded as the older of the two and never lost hold of her offspring. By magic actions are implied such actions as persons perform for their own or others benefit and which demand certain mysterious and miraculous powers for their performance. According to the Egyptian belief, wizardry could work all kinds of wonders which were not possible by simple means.*

In addition to being healers and magicians, the ancient Egyptian hierophants directed the Hermes initiation rites whereby the individual receiving the initiation would be brought into a state of trance consciousness, or temple-sleep. There were two basic types of temple-sleep practiced in the ancient mysteries, these were described by Rudolf Steiner as the microcosmic mysteries of the "Lower Gods" and the macrocosmic mysteries of the "Upper Gods." The first type of temple-sleep which led to the experience of the workings of the Lower Gods was an experience of the higher hierarchies working microcosmically within the human body. The second kind of temple-sleep brought about an experience of the Upper Gods and was an experience of the lower hierarchies that worked outside of man in the Cosmos. The mysteries of the Lower Gods, and of the human body, were primarily practiced in the southern regions such as ancient Egypt, while the mysteries of the Upper Gods and of the Macrocosm were more prevalent in the northern regions, such as were established by Zarathustra in ancient Persia, and by Scythianos in the North of Europe. Although each type of temple-sleep could be found in both the mysteries of the North and of the South.

The initiation into the mysteries of the macrocosmic Upper Gods and the microcosmic Lower Gods was also present in ancient Greece in a manner which was in keeping with their northern and southern character. For the macrocosmic mysteries of Apollo were said to have come from the far North of Europe, from Hyperborea, which means "the place beyond the North wind." While the microcosmic mysteries of Dionysus were said to have come into Greece from the South, from Egypt (**XIX**).

The theme of the macrocosmic Upper Gods and the microcosmic Lower Gods is alluded to in a passage from the late classical author Apuleius of Madauros (b. 125 A.D.) in the work entitled, *Metamorphoses* (commonly known as *The Golden Ass*) where he gives an account of the initiation into the Isis mysteries as they were practiced at that time.

> *I drew nigh to the confines of death, I trod the threshold of Proserpine, I was borne through all the elements and returned to earth again, I saw the sun gleaming with bright splendor at dead of night, I approached the Gods above and the Gods below and worshipped them face to face.*

In an effort to describe how these two types of temple-sleep were practiced by the Egyptian hierophants, I must go beyond the indications of Rudolf Steiner. For he said that both types of temple-sleep were practiced in the Egyptian Mysteries - but, to my knowledge, he did not provide many details surrounding this fact; and so, we must take what is known of ancient Egypt and see how it relates to his indications.

It is well known that Egyptologist's consider the Great Pyramid to be the tomb of the Pharaoh Cheops, although his mummy and funerary equipment have never been found. This has led Egyptologist's to consider that the Great Pyramid was plundered, and these items were removed. The tentative state of knowledge on this problem is addressed by Laszlo Kakosy in his article entitled "The Plundering of the Pyramid of Cheops."

In the present state of knowledge, from these scattered data the history and fate of the Pyramid of Cheops after the Old Kingdom [c. 2500-2100 B.C.] can be outlined as follows:

1. There is no way of proving that the Pyramid was opened before the Saite period [c. 720 B.C.].
2. Even after this period, we have reliable evidence only for the knowledge of the Lower Chamber and Descending Corridor.
3. On the other hand, Arabic accounts fail to provide sufficient grounds for deducing that Cheops' body and equipment were still in the Pyramid during Ma`mun's time [the son of Caliph Harun al-Rashid who forced open the Pyramid in the 9th century A.D.], so an earlier plundering operation must be assumed, the time of which was certainly after Herodotus' period [c. 480-425 B.C.], probably during the Second Persian Rule (343-332 B.C.). (Herodotus remarks that Cambyses [Persian ruler of Egypt 525-522 B.C.] had ancient tombs opened in Memphis [III. 37], but he makes no mention of Pyramids. This and other accounts by Herodotus, discussed above make it highly unlikely that the upper section of the Pyramid [containing the Grand Gallery, King's Chamber and Queen's Chamber] was penetrated during the first Persian Rule or at least during its first half.)

In other words there is absolutely no proof that the Great Pyramid was exclusively used as a tomb for Pharaoh Khufu; furthermore, there is no actual proof, beyond certain features of its structure and that of the surrounding complex, that it was ever used as a tomb at all. The description of the Pyramid as a tomb is only a widely accepted theory. Although he is not considered by scholars to be a reliable source, living as he does at a time when hieroglyphics could no longer be read (which was five or six hundred years later after Pharaoh Khufu than we are after him), the classical author Diodorus Siculus of the 1st century A.D. states (I. 64) that the 4th dynasty pyramid builders had themselves buried in an undisclosed secret location. A puzzling fact that adds to the mystery is that the giant granite sarcophagus in the King's Chamber is missing its large granite lid, which would have been far too large to remove through the only opening into the upper chambers that exists to this day; and therefore, its removal would have required the difficult task of breaking it up into smaller pieces. Why someone would go to all that trouble to retrieve broken fragments of granite is difficult to understand. On the other hand, if one considers the Great Pyramid to be an initiation temple constructed for the temple-sleep initiation rites, then perhaps there would have been no need for a sarcophagus lid; and yet, there is a lip provided for a lid on the inner rim of the sarcophagus.

The inner structure of the Great Pyramid consists of extensive corridors which end in three chambers: the first is an unfinished chamber which is carved deep into the bedrock underneath the pyramid, it is assumed by Egyptologist's to be abandoned; the second chamber is called the Queen's chamber, which is appropriately named since it has a channel carved which, as noted by Virginia Trimble, leads toward the surface at an angle that points to the star of Isis, the star Sirius-Sothis; the third chamber is called the King's chamber and is also appropriately named since it has a channel carved leading toward the surface, which in this case (as also noted by Virginia Trimble), is at an angle that points to the kingly stars of the constellation of Orion, which is called Sahu by the ancient Egyptians and is the constellation of Osiris whom they considered to be the king of the after-death realm.

Whether or not the Great Pyramid was a tomb, an initiation temple, or both, the apparent symbolism of these chambers remains the same; for the Queen's chamber has the appearance of a Ka chapel which would connect it to the mysteries of the etheric body, as the Ka is related to the attributes of form, nourishment and vitality, which are functions of the Etheric-Body. The King's chamber, on the other hand, has the appearance of a burial chamber where the "winged" form of the Ba or Astral-Body could journey into the Duat, or after-world and then return the Physical-Body; and also, where the Akh or spiritual form (the Atma-Budhi-Manas) would be transformed to meet its stellar or solar destiny. Viewed in this way the symbolical layout of the chambers in the Great Pyramid appear to meet the criteria for it being both a tomb and an initiation temple, or, at the very least, analogous to the two fundamental realms of initiation.

It is quite possible that the Queen's chamber was where the temple-sleep rite was performed which led to the experience of Isis and the inner mysteries of the human body that were revealed through the microcosmic mysteries of the "Lower Gods." The King's chamber, on the other hand, could possibly be where the temple-sleep rite was performed which led to the experience of Osiris and the macrocosmic mysteries of the "Upper Gods", the mysteries of the outer Cosmos.

In the Old Kingdom *Pyramid Texts* (c. 2300 B.C.), the stellar destiny of the after-death state of the deceased Pharaoh is sometimes described as a process whereby he unites his Akh, or eternal spirit, with a star in the constellation of Orion. Due to the nature of the mortuary texts that have come down to posterity from ancient Egypt, these texts are interpreted by Egyptologists as being only associated with funerary rites. Although we know from the indications given from the Akashic Records by Rudolf Steiner, that these texts are also representative of the initiation rites that were performed on the living. The macrocosmic-stellar character of the Osiris rite is evident in the following quotation from the *Pyramid Texts*, as translated by Raymond O. Faulkner, and gives one a sense of the renewal that was achieved through the initiation experience that brought about an expansion into the Macrocosm.

> *O king, you are this Great Star, the Companion of Orion, who traverses the sky with Orion, who navigates the Duat (Underworld) with Osiris; you ascend from the east of the sky, being renewed in your due season, and rejuvenated in your due time. The sky has born you with Orion . . .*

Although these mysteries of the Macrocosm and the Microcosm must not be considered to be entirely separate; but rather, as initiations into the relationship between what the ancient Egyptians represented as Osiris and Isis within the two different realms. By the goddess Isis, whose name is written with a *throne*, was understood to mean the Divine Feminine as as a representative of the pleroma of beings which brought into existence the Physical and Etheric Bodies, and thereby revealed the mysteries of Cosmic Time. Osiris, on the other hand, (whose name is written with an *eye* combined with the *throne* of Isis) is the being of the Cosmic Word approaching the Earth from cosmic realms, bringing the upright forces of the Cosmic "I" or Ego (which in the future, through the incarnation of Christ, would be revealed the mysteries of Cosmic Space). This Cosmic "I" or Ego aspect of Osiris was symbolized by the Djed pillar, which is the symbol of Osiris and represents the memory of the gift of uprightness which was given to mankind by Christ during the ancient Lemurian epoch that preceded Atlantis.

It should be said at this point that I am aware the Great Pyramid is considered to have been constructed in the 4th dynasty and that, other than the cartouche containing the name of Khufu, the Great Pyramid is devoid of any writings. I am also aware that the first textual references to Osiris were found carved on the walls of royal pyramids which were built a century or so later in the 5th dynasty. These carved hieroglyphics which are known as the *Pyramid Texts,* are the oldest discovered ancient Egyptian religious texts. Furthermore, it must be remembered that, due to their highly developed literary form, the *Pyramid Texts* are considered by many scholars to be based on more ancient texts that are as of yet undiscovered.

In light of this, and in consideration of the indications of Rudolf Steiner: the Mysteries of Isis and Osiris were a mystery wisdom that was introduced by Thoth-Hermes, and were the fruit of his receiving the donated Astral-Body of Zarathustra. These Mysteries were combined with the Sun Mysteries that streamed into Egypt in the beginning of the dynastic period from the central Asian home of the "Mother Lodge of Humanity" (**XXV**). These impulses, in turn, were developed further by Thoth-Hermes in his later incarnations in ancient Egypt.

In the "microcosmic" temple-sleep, after extensive training and preparations (which brought about a purification of the Astral-Body), the aspirant was brought into a trance by the hierophant who would then bring about a separation of the aspirant's Astral and Etheric-Bodies from the Ego and Physical-Body; which would allow the Astral-Body to more readily imprint the Etheric-Body with the impulses of the Spiritual World. After this sojourn of the Astral and Etheric-Bodies in the Spiritual World, separated from the Ego and Physical Body, they were reintegrated with them; thereby bringing to the Ego and Physical Body, the fruits of the immersion of the Etheric-Body in the currents of the purified Astral-Body. This, in turn, caused a change to come about in the rhythmic relationship between the breath and the heart-beat; and also, brought about a state of initiate consciousness which could be further cultivated by the performance of seasonal and other mystery rites.

The "macrocosmic" temple-sleep, on the other hand, consisted of the Ego and Astral-Body of the individual being separated from their Physical and Etheric-Bodies while in a trance and brought to an experience within the Spiritual World of the beings and forces of the Macrocosm, the realm of the Upper Gods - the realm of Osiris. This was done by the hierophant in such a way so that the individual would be able to retain a memory of the supersensible worlds which are normally only experienced in the after-death state, and unconsciously during sleep. This was made possible by the hierophant's ability to cause a partial separation of the Etheric-Body from the Physical-Body. Which means that when the Astral-Body and Ego returned from being out of the body for three days during the temple trance-sleep - due to the Etheric-Body's partial separation from the Physical-Body - the Etheric-Body would be able to receive, within the etheric "eye" that is located in the region of the heart, a more lasting impression of this experience; and thereby, convey in imaginative memory-pictures, these experiences to the person upon awakening.

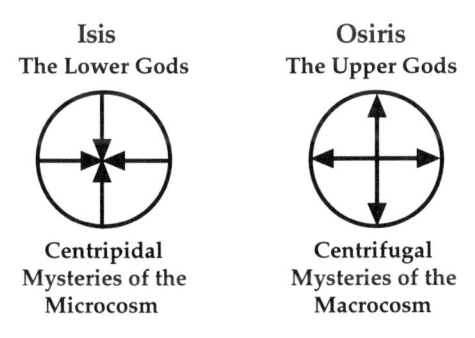

Isis	Osiris
The Lower Gods	The Upper Gods
Centripidal Mysteries of the Microcosm	Centrifugal Mysteries of the Macrocosm

The Hermes Initiation into the mysteries of Isis and Osiris is described from the Akashic Record by Rudolf Steiner in the lecture given in Berlin on February 5th, 1913, which was published in the lecture cycle entitled, *The Mysteries of the East and of Christianity*.

> *When the aspirant who was going through the Isis initiation had reached the furthest shore of existence and had gazed upon the beings who build up the physical body and the etheric body; when he had stood before the silent Goddess from whom Warmth and Light come forth for the innermost of the human soul, he said to himself: 'That is Isis. That is the mute and silent Goddess whose countenance can be unveiled to no-one who sees only with mortal eyes, but only to those who have worked themselves through to the shores which have been described, so that they can see with those eyes which go from incarnation to incarnation and are no longer mortal. For an impenetrable veil hides the form of Isis from mortal eyes.'*
> *When the aspirant had thus gazed upon Isis and had*

experienced in his soul the feeling described, he understood what had been described as the birth. What was this 'birth'? He understood that it can be designated as 'The resounding through all space of the Music of the Spheres,' and as the merging of the tones of this sphere-music with the creative Cosmic Word - the Word which permeates space and pours into the beings everything that has to be so poured into the physical and etheric body after passing through the life between death and a new birth. Everything that has to be thus poured out from the spiritual world into the physical world, so that what is poured out acquires the inward character of soul, is poured in from the Harmony of the Spheres resounding through space. The Harmony of the Spheres gradually assumes such a form that through the inner significance it expresses it can be understood as the Cosmic Word - the Word which ensouls the beings that are vitalized by the forces of Warmth and Light which pour into those bodies that arise from the divine forces and beings perceived with the vision already attained.

Thus did the aspirant look into the world of the Harmony of the Spheres, the world of the Cosmic Word; thus did he look into the world which is the veritable home of the human soul during the time between death and a new birth. That which is hidden deep in the physical earthly existence of man, but lives between death and a new birth in the splendor of the Light and Warmth; that which deeply veils itself in the physical world as the world of the Harmony of the Spheres and the Cosmic Word, was experienced in the Hermes-Initiation as coming to birth from Isis. There Isis stands before the aspirant, Isis herself on one side, and on the other side the being she has borne, whom one must speak of as Cosmic Tones and the Cosmic Word. The aspirant feels himself in the company of Isis and of the Cosmic Word born of her. And this 'Cosmic Word' is, in the first place, the appearing of Osiris. 'Isis in association with Osiris': thus do they appear before direct vision; for in the very oldest Egyptian Initiation it was said that Osiris was at the same time spouse and son of Isis. And in the older Egyptian Initiation the essential thing was that the aspirant, through this Initiation, experienced the mysteries of soul-life, which remain united with man during the period between death and a new birth. Through the union with Osiris it was possible to recognize oneself - in one's deeper significance - as human.

The Osiris initiation continued to be practiced throughout the Pharaonic period of Egyptian history, although the actual supersensible meeting and union with Osiris came to an end, around the beginning of the Archangelic Period of Samael (c. 1262 B.C.), in the 13th century B.C. during the Ramesside period of the 19th Dynasty, probably during the reign of the Pharaoh Ramesses II (c. 1290-1224 B.C.), or perhaps during the reign of his son Merneptah (c. 1224-1214 B.C.). For, as Rudolf Steiner tells us, the cosmic being of Osiris had departed from the Egyptian Mysteries with the High Priest of Heliopolis who led the Exodus of the Hebrew people out of Egypt. This priest was Moses, who had received the donated Etheric-Body of Zarathustra which culminated in Moses' experience of the "Great Sun Being" announcing Himself on Mount Sinai with the words "I Am the I Am." For this "Great Sun Being", that was once known as Osiris, had abandoned the Egyptian sanctuaries - leaving Isis as a "mourning widow" - and now began to work directly with the Hebrew people through Jehovah Elohim. All of this sequence of events was in preparation for the incarnation of Christ the "Great Sun Being" Who suffered through the Mystery of Golgotha for the redemption of Earth evolution.

In the fourth lecture of the previously mentioned lecture cycle, *The Mysteries of the East and of Christianity*, Rudolf Steiner revealed some of the deeper implications of this change that came about in the Mysteries of Osiris and how it is an antecedent to the Mysteries of the Holy Grail.

Let us enter into the tragic mood of one about to be initiated during the Egyptian epoch. We transpose ourselves into this mood and find that it originated from experiences that the aspirant could express only by saying to himself: 'Formerly, when I entered the spiritual worlds, I found Osiris permeating cosmic space with the Creative Word and its meaning, which represent the ground-forces of all being and development. Now the Word has become mute and silent. The God who was called Osiris has forsaken these realms. He is preparing to penetrate into other regions; He has descended into the Earth-region in order to enter into the souls of men.'

The Being who had been known spiritually to human

souls in earlier days first became manifest in physical life when Moses heard in the physical world the Voice that in earlier ages had been heard only in the spiritual worlds: 'Ejeh asher Ejeh' - 'I Am the I Am, Who was, and is, and will be.' And then this Being who, as the Creative Word, had gradually become lost to the experience of the candidate for Initiation, transferred His life into the Earth-region so that He could gradually come to life again in the souls of earthly men; and in this new life, rising to ever higher and higher glory, would consist the further development of the Earth, even to the end of Earth-evolution.

Let us try to transport ourselves as vividly as we can into the frame of mind of one of these candidates, and realize how in the spiritual regions to which he could first attain he felt the Creative Word disappearing, sinking down into the Earth-region and becoming lost to spiritual sight. Let us follow the evolution of the Earth, and we shall see that for spiritual sight this Creative Word now goes forward somewhat as a stream which has been on the surface and then disappears for a certain time below the Earth's surface, in order to reappear later at another place. And so there reappeared that which for the souls who were being initiated in the later Egyptian Mysteries had been sinking tragically out of sight. It reappeared, and could be looked upon by those in later times who were permitted to participate in the Mysteries. And they had to bring into the picture what they could see arising again, but arising now in such a way that henceforward it belonged to Earth-evolution.

How did That reappear which had become submerged in ancient Egypt? It reappeared in such a way that it became visible in the Holy Vessel which is spoken of as the 'Holy Grail', guarded by the Knights of the Holy Grail. In the rise of the Holy Grail can be found That which had sunk down in ancient Egypt, and in this arising of the Holy Grail there stands before us everything that went into the post-Christian renewal of the principle of the Ancient Mysteries. Fundamentally speaking, the phrase the 'Holy Grail', with all that belongs to it, involves a reappearing of the essence of the Eastern Mysteries.

The Symbolism of the Holy Trinity

In the 13th lecture of the cycle of lectures given in Paris between May 25 and June 14, 1906, which were published under the title, *An Esoteric Cosmology*, Rudolf Steiner characterized certain aspects of the Trinity:

> *The Ego or "I" principle of man is created by the third Logos. We should try to conceive the power of the higher Ego as being suffused through the whole universe as a life-begetting warmth and then we reach the conception of the second Logos by Whom macrocosmic life is quickened and Who is reflected in the creative activities of the human soul. The one primal source and center of manifestation is the first Logos - the unfathomable Godhead. In every age these three Divine principles have been represented in occultism by these three signs.*

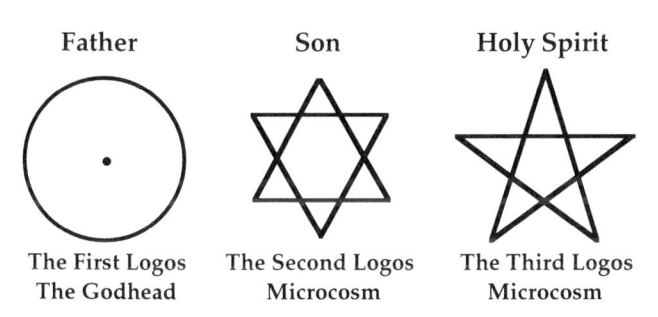

Father	Son	Holy Spirit
⊙	✡	☆
The First Logos	The Second Logos	The Third Logos
The Godhead	Microcosm	Microcosm

The Zodiacal Crosses of the Holy Trinity

Cross of the Father - the Cardinal Signs - Aries, Cancer, Libra, Capricorn
Cross of the Son - the Mutable Signs - Pisces, Gemini, Virgo, Sagittarius
Cross of the Holy Spirit - the Fixed Signs - Taurus, Leo, Scorpio, Aquarius

The ancient Egyptian culture took place during the cultural epoch of the Bull (see: Part 3), which relates in the "Zodiac of the Lamb of God" to the Third Logos, the Holy Spirit (**IX**). Viewed from another aspect, the constellation of the Bull is further related to the Holy Spirit, by it forming part of the Zodiacal Cross of the Holy Spirit as given by Rudolf Steiner (**X, XIII**). These Zodiacal Crosses relate to the workings of the Holy Trinity primarily in the stream of time-memory; while the "Zodiac of the Lamb of God" (**IX**), on the other hand, can be seen as revelatory more in terms of space-consciousness. The Cross of the Holy Spirit (**XIII**) coincides with Taurus and the fundamental Bull symbolism of ancient Egypt, Babylon and Assyria.

The Cross of the Father (**XI**) coincides with the constellation of Aries. And at the beginning of the *astronomical age* of Aries we find the ascension of the ancient Egyptian mysteries of the Ram god Amun; and likewise, at the beginning of the *cultural epoch* of Aries we find that it coincides with Abraham's sacrifice of the Ram. Although the central mystery of the *cultural epoch* of Aries is the sacrifice of Christ the "Lamb of God."

The Cross of the Son (**XII**) coincides with the constellation of Pisces the Fishes - which symbolizes with water the etheric world of life - and relates to our present Piscean cultural epoch. It is within this etheric world of life, Rudolf Steiner tells us, that the "Reappearance of Christ" has begun, starting from the first third of the 20th Century.

In the third Post-Atlantean cultural epoch of the Bull (**XXVI**), the Sentient-Soul forces of the Egyptians were configured in such a way, so as to be still in a stage of imaginative picture-consciousness; that is, a pre-intellectual form of thinking which depended on the forming of mental pictures rather than conceptual thinking, this characteristic is shown by their hieroglyphic picture-language. For the development of conceptual thinking did not come about until the next epoch, the Graeco-Roman epoch of the Intellectual-Soul, during the cultural epoch of Aries which began in the year 747 B.C.

The ancient Egyptians went to great lengths through their elaborate mummification rites in an effort to maintain their relationship to the physical world in the after-death state. This practice helped the Egyptian hierophants maintain a relationship to a particular class of Moon beings, that in the past, in the Old Indian cultural epoch (7227-5067 B.C.), was maintained through yogic breathing exercises. In the present day, these Moon beings inhabit the atmosphere that is created through rituals, such as are practiced in Churches and in Freemasonry. As we move towards the future, these Moon beings will assist in the spiritualizing of the Earth, as we move towards the Jupiter evolution, when that part of Earth that can move forward will be transformed into an ethereal globe.

In opposition to these *wholesome* Moon beings that were active in the ancient Egyptian period, are another class of *unwholesome* Moon beings that are a remnant of the decadent lunar impulses of the ancient Egypt mysteries; these beings foster materialism in all of its forms.

The mummification rites of the ancient Egyptians, which came about with the decline of the initial purity of the Egyptian Mysteries, were an attempt to remain connected clairvoyantly with the souls dwelling in the after-death realm. The earlier cultures did not need to go to such extreme ends, due to the fact that a state of initiate consciousness was easier to achieve before mankind had descended so far in their relationship to matter. As an added result, the ancient Egyptian mummification rites created an effect in the soul of the person, enabling the deceased to maintain a stronger relationship to the physical world after death. This, in turn, resulted in an enhanced relationship to the physical world in the later incarnations of the individuals who had undergone these mummification rites. For upon reincarnating in later periods, such as our present age, those who had undergone this process in the Egyptian period, brought with them, into the present life, an inherent capacity to understand the laws working in the physical world, and so are able to work very deeply into the mathematical sciences of mechanics, economics, and finance.

In light of this, we are presently in the epoch of Pisces and of the Consciousness-Soul, and are recapitulating the epoch of Taurus; which means that we are the same number of years *after* Christ as the epoch of Taurus was *before* Christ. This means that time-wise we are reflecting the Egyptian Period when figured from the historical time-axis of the Christ event (**XXV**). We are essentially at the opposite point from ancient Egypt in the cycle of Earth evolution, in terms of Incarnation and Resurrection - with Christ holding the middle-point between. In light of this, we have experienced a little less than 2,000 years of the working of the Christ impulse in Earth evolution since the mystery of Golgotha - while the Egyptian Initiates were in their prime around 2,000 years before the Mystery of Golgotha. To be more specific, we are reflecting the Middle Kingdom period which lasted from around 2040 to 1640 B.C. Now that we have passed the incarnation of Christ, at the "Turning Point of Time", we are on an ascending cycle rising out of matter, or rather etherizing matter. On the other hand, the ancient Egyptians were still in a descending incarnational cycle - moving deeper into matter. The present day forces of materialism are in a particular way the end result of the impulses of the ancient Egyptian Mysteries, with their tendency to work with very formal structured images in their thinking (**XXVI**). What is now needed, is a freeing up of thinking into a greater mobility of thought - a sense-free thinking that is not limited to sense impressions (**XXI-XXIII**).

The Pentecostal mystery of the Holy Spirit (**XIII-XIV**) is ultimately connected with the development of the Resurrection-Body, which is prefigured by the ancient Egyptian story of the resurrection of Osiris in the next world, the world of the after-death state. As mentioned above, the ancient Egyptian hierophants brought about the initiation trance-sleep where the individual being initiated into the Hermes Mysteries would have an experience, in the next-world, of Isis as a being of Comic Light and Warmth, after which they would experience Osiris, which was an experience of the Cosmic Word approaching the Earth from within the sphere of the Moon. The Cosmic Word was only to be experienced by the ancient Egyptians in the next world, for the Cosmic Word - Christ the "Great-Sun-Being" - had not yet incarnated into Jesus at the Baptism in the River Jordan. As a result of this occult fact, the ancient Egyptian hierophants taught the initiate that - after his death he would become one with Osiris, the Cosmic Word, and travel in the Boat, or Bark of Re' (the ancient Heliopolitan Sun god, whose cult rose to prominence in the 4th and 5th dynasties) (**XII**).

In the *Pyramid Texts,* that were inscribed on the inner walls of royal pyramids dating from the 5th and 6th dynasties (around the end of the Archangelic period of Oriphiel, the Archangel of Saturn, and the beginning of the Archangelic period of Anael, the Archangel of Venus c. 2300 B.C.), it tells of how the Pharaoh would become one with the imperishable stars around the pole, and also, how he would become a star in the constellation of Orion, which is in the region of Taurus the Bull (Hathor). This shows the profound connection of the ancient Egyptian culture to the forces of the Holy Spirit that proceeded from the region of the Bull, and which forms part of the aforementioned Cross of the Holy Spirit (**XIII**).

The two kinds of Egyptian hierophants, who actually performed the rites of Osiris, were called: the kheri-heb her tep, and, the sem priests. The funerary ritual was recited by the chief lector priest, or kheri-heb her tep, this is described by Jamison B. Hurry in his book, *Imhotep - the Egyptian God of Medicine*:

> *The Kheri-heb took an important part in ceremonies known as the 'Liturgy of the Funerary Offerings' dealing with the presentation of gifts to the dead, the formula which was pronounced over each element, being supposed to change it into a divine and spiritual food, which was partaken of by the*

souls of the departed. The material elements of the offerings were eaten by the priests and by relatives of the deceased, who were thus brought into communion with the blessed dead and with the gods. Although the formulas in the liturgy were recited by the Kheri-heb priest, who held in his hands a roll of papyrus and directed the assistant priests, most of the ceremonies were performed by the Sem-Priest, assisted by several ministrants.

In the other series of ceremonies known as 'The Opening of the Mouth', the object was to restore to the inert corpse the functions of which it had been deprived by death and embalmment. . .

The "Opening of the Mouth" ritual was performed by the sem-priest with an *adze*, which was a ritual tool frequently made from meteoric iron. Meteoric iron was the only iron available to the earlier ancient Egyptians, for the Iron Age had not yet begun with the introduction of iron mining. The adze in shape resembles our present constellations of Ursa Major and Ursa Minor, the Big and Little Dippers, that reside in the Northern region that the Egyptians called the "Imperishable Stars", the stars that never set in the course of the year because they surround the North Pole. Furthermore, the inclination of entrance to the Great Pyramid is oriented so as to point at the "Imperishable Stars" of the North Pole. In the ancient Egyptian Zodiac, the constellation at the North Pole is called the "Fore-Leg of Seth", or Meshtw, the "Thigh" which is a depiction of a Bull's front-leg. This becomes more interesting in light of the fact that according to the Ancient Egyptian legend, the skeleton of Seth (the adversary of Osiris, and later of Horus) was said to be formed of iron.

It is the impulses of Mars that are working in the metal iron, which relates to the incarnational "Mars-half" of earth evolution that led to the incarnation of Christ at the "Turning Point of Time", when the Mystery of Golgotha planted the seed for the change to the "Mercury-half" of Earth evolution (**IV**) that was to come in the year 333 A.D. (the actual mid-point of Earth evolution); but was delayed, until around 1414 A.D., through the workings of the Spirits of Hindrance. Furthermore, as Aries is the sign traditionally related to Mars, this incarnational Mars impulse was further supported through it being the ruling impulse in the cultural epoch of Aries (747- B.C.-1414 A.D.), the latter half of which coincided with the time period (333-1414 A.D.) in which these retarded impulses were proceeding from the aforementioned Spirits of Hindrance. And yet, these Mars forces were already being prepared in the Egyptian Mysteries before the Iron Age, during the Copper Age, the Age of Taurus, the Bull (2907-747 B.C.), which is traditionally related to Venus, and copper which is the metal of Venus (XV).

These Mars forces can be seen working very strongly in the Roman Empire; and after that, within the Roman Catholic Church, which is very much like ancient Rome with its Intellectual-Soul methodology. In fact, the title of the Roman Caesar, pontifex maximus (Latin, pontifex = "bridge builder" the high priest or hierophant, maximus = supreme), became the title of the leader of the church of Rome, the pontiff or pope. The Roman Catholic Church also carried over a certain remnant of the Sentient-Soul impulses of the Egyptian hierophants (and other ancient mysteries) in its sacerdotal rites. In addition to this, the Catholic Church also adopted from the Manichaean Church the ritualistic usage of bright colors and music.

The mortuary rites of ancient Egypt, in a sense, can be seen to have continued on in the modern habit of embalming, which is thought by some to be important so as to preserve the Physical-Body beyond death so it can await the Resurrection, (which is an overly materialistic interpretation of the mysteries of the Resurrection-Body). This is a good example of something working beyond its time, for now we need to free ourselves from the Physical-Body after death; cremation being the preferred practice in modern times for freeing the spirit of the departed. In modern times, our embalming practices are a decadent carry-over of something that once served a worthwhile purpose within the development of particular incarnational impulses for mankind. It is another instance of how something that was proper in one time period, is improper in another time period.

The ancient Egyptian mortuary-initiation text, *The Egyptian Book of the Dead*, which as pointed out by Thomas George Allen and others, should really be called, *The Book of Coming Forth By Day*, describes the experiences of the soul on the other side of the threshold of death, sleep, and initiation. The various recensions of *The Book of Coming Forth By Day*, date from the New Kingdom Period (c. 1550-1070 B.C.), which is based on formulas from the earlier Middle Kingdom *Coffin Texts* (c. 2040-1640 B.C.) and the even earlier *Pyramid Texts* (c. 2300 B.C.). The *Pyramid Texts*, in turn, are considered to be based on earlier undiscovered sources, which the ancient Egyptians attributed to Thoth-Hermes.

In *The Book of Coming Forth By Day*, is found a description in picture language of the transformation of the deceased into an Osiris. This transformation was believed by the ancient Egyptians to take place after the soul has undergone interrogation at each of the seven stages or "arits." At each of these stages there were three gods; a doorkeeper, a watchman, and a herald who conduct the interrogation. These seven stages can be seen as an imaginative picture of certain stages of the after-death state that are described by Rudolf Steiner in his book, *Theosophy*. Furthermore, an interesting study of the conception of the after-death stages in early Christian writings can be found in the book by April D. de Conick entitled, *Seek to See Him - Ascent and Vision Mysticism in the Gospel of Thomas*.

It was the goal of the ancient Egyptian death mysteries for the Pharaoh to be reborn into the realm of the dead as an Osiris, and to thereby achieve immortality just as the legendary king Osiris had in the primeval past. The ancient Egyptians ritualistically assimilated the mummy into identification with Osiris (Wsir) the "lord of the underworld", the ancient Egyptian god of resurrection who is connected, as I have said, with the constellation of Orion. Orion is in the same sector of the Zodiac as the constellation of Taurus the bull, the ruling constellation of the ancient Egyptian cultural epoch. The bull of Taurus corresponds to Hathor the Egyptian cow-goddess of love, which relates to Venus (furthermore, there is also a Mnevis bull which pertains to Osiris, and various other bulls that are included in the Egyptian pantheon.)

The ancient Egyptians called the constellation of Orion, Sahu. Sahu is a word which is phonetically *similar* to the Egyptian name for the mummy; nonetheless, due to a misprint in Alan Gardiner's *Egyptian Grammar* they have been thought to be the *same* by certain authors, but they are not, as pointed out by Jaromir Malek; although I might add that the ancient Egyptians believed that words having similar sounds have a related occult value, as is also the case in the Hebrew Kabbalah.

As I mentioned earlier, the forces that were working at that time in the Egyptian Mysteries led the ancient Egyptians into a more intimate connection with the forces of the material world. This is perhaps most obvious in the sphere of technology, which is a modern development that can be seen as a continued working of the deepened relationship to the material world that was cultivated by the mummification rites in the ancient Egyptian cultural epoch.

It was brought to my attention by my friend Brian Lynch, one of the deeper students of the esoteric that I have come to know, that the karmic beginning of modern technology can be found in Egyptian glass making.

Upon investigating this lead, I found that we can see the initial impulses of modern science manifesting in the Old Kingdom Period (c. 3000 B.C.), with the invention of a synthetic form of blue glass, that was used as a paint pigment for the beautiful blues that can be found in the Egyptian Temples. (Rudolf Steiner tells us that the perception of the color blue and the cool end of the spectrum of colors came into mankind with the developing intellect, which is indicative of why the ancient Greek poet Homer calls the sea wine-red; for there was a lack of words for the cool end of the spectrum in comparison to the warm end of the spectrum in ancient languages.)

The ancient Egyptian tinted glass is the first synthetic substance known to have been created by man, and is a precursor of the famous stained glass of Chartres Cathedral; which, according to R. A. Schwaller de Lubicz, was tinted by a secret alchemical process. For, although I have not been able to verify this statement (other that its mention in a Chartres tour guide), apparently - the substances used for pigment, in certain rare examples, are said to defy detection by standard scientific analysis.

The "accidental" discovery of this process of tinting glass, so it appears, was due to the slag of melted sand that was produced from the ancient method of smelting metals in a sand pit. The metals, and other minerals present, upon intermixing with the molten sand that was formed by the great heat in the pit, would tint the glass. While this "accidental" discovery theory sounds very logical, we must keep in mind that the ancient Egyptians stated that Thoth-Hermes taught them the arts and sciences, which is a view that is supported by the findings of Rudolf Steiner.

The "priests", or hierophants, of modern materialistic science are the scientists, who approach the unseen world in an abstract way through mathematics. Modern mathematics is a development that is a descendant of the beginnings of abstract-mathematical thought which came about in Egypt through Ptolemaic astronomy, and astrology, in the epoch of Aries, as pointed out by Rudolf Steiner in his *Astronomy Course*. For Ptolemaic astronomy, and astrology were developed out of the Aristotelian Greek influences that came into Egypt with Alexander the Great and mingled with the content of the earlier Egyptian, Babylonian, and Persian streams.

This abstract separation of thought from sense perception that came about through astronomy was carried further - within the realm of language - in the early Christian era by St. Augustine (Aurelius Augustinus, 354-430 A.D.). For in his strivings to understand Christ, St. Augustine developed a type of thinking that was not derived through observing the world, but through observing the interrelationship of concepts within the thought process.

Although the materialistic scientists might not consider it in this way, it really is the case that they develop theories regarding things they cannot see by the transposition of ideas that they have about things that they can see, as pointed out by Goethe. Many wonderful things have been developed through science and its methods, in spite of their frequent atheistic tendencies and their need to see the universe as an almost uninhabited mechanistic-chemical process, or a giant clock that is slowly winding down.

We must not hold science to blame for its errors; but rather, we must see these errors as resulting from the flaws of certain ideas of individual scientists, who transposed their understandings of the mineral kingdom upon the world of living things. But now mankind is moving toward a time when, first-hand knowledge of the supersensible worlds will increasingly become a human faculty; and it is very important to realize that the fruits of scientific thought, applied in the proper manner, will be the key to future spiritual understanding. Though in order for this to come about, a more *permeable* form of consciousness will be necessary.

Mankind is destined to take the fruits of the intellect, which have developed through the sense of feeling separated from the worlds of spirit, into the realms of spirit. If this is to happen in the right way, mankind must be able to achieve sense-free thinking. Eventually this leads to being able to maintain a wakeful consciousness when one is free of the Physical-Body within the world of sleep, and is also very helpful to the soul in the after-death state.

By the development of sense-free thinking, one can work out levels of karma that are usually accomplished in the after-death state; thereby freeing oneself to more easily pass through the lower states of existence in the afterlife and move on to the higher realms of the spiritual worlds, thus alleviating unnecessary suffering in the state of Kama-Loka, the "place of desire" (Sanskrit: kama – desire, loka – place).

The ancient Egyptian ideas of the after-life that can be found in their mortuary literature were an expression of things experienced in trance consciousness, and were an attempt to address this challenge. On the other hand, in the present age we must find a different *fully awake*, individual path to the Spiritual World, as a result of the continued working of the "deed" of Christ on Golgotha.

Rudolf Steiner speaks of this spiritual autonomy in reference to the Grail tradition in the lecture, "The Royal Art in a New Form", which is included in the lecture cycle entitled, *The Temple Legend*:

The medieval occultist expressed the symbol of the Grail (the symbol for awakening perfection in the living) in the form of a triangle. That does not need a communal church, entwining itself around the planet in a rigid organization - though this can well give something to the individual soul. But if all souls are to strike the same note, then the power of the Holy Grail must be awakened in each individual. Whoever wants to awaken the power of the Grail in himself will gain nothing by asking the powers of the official church whether they can perhaps tell him something; rather, he should awaken this power in himself, and should not question all that much. Man starts from dullness (of mind) and progresses through doubt to strength. This pilgrimage of the soul is expressed in the person of Parzival, who seeks the Holy Grail. This is one of the manifold deeper meanings of the figure of Parzival.

Through the "Second Coming of Christ" - within the etheric world of life - mankind will, gradually as we move into the future, begin to receive the gifts of the working of the Holy Spirit (**XIII-XIV**). This will quicken the soul forces of the Astral-Body and open the chakras or astral centers - like flowers that open to the rays of the Sun. This, in turn, will awaken the spiritual forces that are waiting dormant within the Astral-Body; which will become, through its transformation, the Spirit-Self or Manas. In this way, an individual may develop an independent relationship to the Spiritual World, and become a "true" hierophant - with no need for a priest as an intermediary between them and the manifold spiritual beings that are in service to the Divine Plan of the Holy Trinity.

VI

The Lovers

Gemini - Seraphim - Spirits of Love

Early in this century, Rudolf Steiner spoke of certain individuals that epitomized in their writings the true nature of the human soul as it was experienced in their lifetimes. These individuals were: King David - the author of the *Psalms*, Homer - the author of the epic poems, *The Iliad* and *The Odyssey*, which helped to shape the soul-life of the ancient Greeks, William Shakespeare - the author of the poems and plays that contributed so much to the formation of the English language by manifesting, without precedent, and seemingly out of nowhere, the greatest works of the English language, Dante - the author of *The Divine Comedy*, a poetical work that summarized the world veiw of the Middle Ages and gave the Italian language its highest expression, and Johann Wolfgang von Goethe - whose major work *Faust*, dramatized the challenges that confront the human soul in the modern age in which we live, and whose literary genius makes him the true father of the modern German language. Is it a coincidence, that all of these "masters of the human soul" mentioned by Rudolf Steiner were poets? I think not, for someone once said that, "poetry is the most concentrated form of language." It is the mission of poetry to give artistic expression to the highest sentiments of the human soul through the purest conceptual and imaginative language.

But whence comes this highest poetic inspiration? In the city of Zurich, Switzerland, in October of 1918, Rudolf Steiner gave a lecture now published as a booklet entitled, *The Work of the Angels in Man's Astral Body*. In this lecture he describes how the Angels as a group, and also our individual Guardian Angels, work toward the development of humanity by projecting pictures into the Astral-Bodies of mankind which serve the purpose of stimulating our spiritual evolution. Rudolf Steiner describes this occult fact:

> *It is then revealed that these Beings of the Hierarchy of the Angels - particularly through their concerted work,*

although in a certain sense each single Angel also has his task in connection with every individual human being - these Beings form pictures in man's astral body. Under the guidance of the Spirits of Form (Exusiai, or Elohim) the Angels form pictures. Unless we reach the level of Imaginative Cognition (beginning clairvoyance) we do not know that pictures are all the time being formed in our astral body. They arise and pass away, but without them there would be for mankind no evolution into the future in accordance with the intentions of the Spirits of Form. The Spirits of Form are obliged, to begin with, to unfold in pictures what they desire to achieve with us during Earth-evolution and beyond. And then, later on, the pictures become reality in a humanity transformed.

Through the Angels, the Spirits of Form are already now shaping these pictures in our astral body. The Angels form pictures in man's astral body and these pictures are accessible to thinking that has become clairvoyant. If we are able to scrutinize these pictures, it becomes evident that they are woven in accordance with quite definite impulses and principles. Forces for the future evolution of mankind are contained in them. If we watch the Angels carrying out this work of theirs - strange as it sounds, one has to express it in this way - it is clear that they have a very definite plan for the future configuration of social life on earth; their aim is to engender in the astral bodies of men such pictures as will bring about definite conditions in the social life of the future.

People may shy away from the notion that Angels want to call forth in them ideals for the future, but it is so all the same. And indeed in forming these pictures the Angels work on a definite principle, namely, that in the future no human being is to find peace in the enjoyment of happiness if others beside him are unhappy. An impulse of Brotherhood in the absolute sense, unification of the human race in Brotherhood rightly understood - this is to be the governing principle of the social conditions in physical existence.

That is the one principle in accordance with which the Angels form the pictures in man's astral body.

But there is a second impulse in the work of the Angels. The Angels have certain objectives in veiw, not only in connection with the outer social life but also with man's life of soul. Through the pictures they inculcate into the astral body their aim is that in future time every human being shall see in each and all of his fellow-men a hidden divinity.

Quite clearly, then, according to the intentions underlying the work of the Angels, things are to be very different in the future. Neither in theory nor in practice shall we look only at a man's physical qualities, regarding him as a more highly developed animal, but we must confront every human being with the full realization that in him something is revealing itself from the divine foundations of the world, revealing itself through flesh and blood. To conceive man as a picture revealed from the spiritual world, to conceive this with all the earnestness, all the strength and all the insight at our command - this is the impulse laid by the Angels into the pictures.

Once this is fulfilled, there will be a very definite consequence. The basis of all free religious feeling that will unfold in humanity in the future will be the acknowledgment, not merely in theory but in actual practice, that every human being is made in the likeness of the Godhead. When that time comes there will be no need for any religious coercion; for then every meeting between one man and another will of itself be in the nature of a religious rite, a sacrament, and nobody will need a special Church with institutions on the physical plane to sustain the religious life. If the Church understands itself truly, its one aim must be to render itself unnecessary on the physical plane, as the whole of life becomes the expression of the supersensible.

The bestowal on man of complete freedom in the religious life - this underlies the impulse at least, of the work of the angels.

And there is a third objective: To make it possible for men to reach the Spirit through thinking, to cross the abyss and through thinking to experience the reality of the Spirit.

Spiritual Science for the spirit, freedom of religious life for the soul, brotherhood for the bodily life - this resounds like cosmic music through the work wrought by the Angels in the astral bodies of men.

All that is necessary is to raise our consciousness to a different level and we shall feel ourselves transported to this *wonderful site of the work done by the Angels in the human astral body.*

The Forces of Healing which are a Result of the Musical Laws of Etheric Resonance

The way in which mathematics is used by mankind has great effect on the nature of the world in which we live, beyond even the technology that results from the mathematical sciences. Mathematics plays a central role in how we perceive the world within, as well as without, and also how we communicate our perceptions to others. There are healthy and unhealthy manifestations that result from mathematics, not only in the sphere of technology, but in the types of thinking that result from the way in which one relates to the mathematical world, and also in the types of supersensible beings that are accommodated through the nature of one's thoughts.

The understandings that arise from mathematical thinking can lead one to ideas that sound good, but are not true. A good example of this is all the work that has been done in trying to discover "higher dimensions", the so-called fourth, fifth, and beyond, dimensions. The source of this quest is due to misunderstandings based on the improper use of mathematism, which leads to illusory ideas regarding space and time. Regarding the problem of the illusion of fourth, fifth, and other dimensions, I refer you to the book by Olive Whicher entitled, *Sunspace - Science at a Threshold of Spiritual Understanding* that includes one of Rudolf Steiner's indications on this subject, which I quote from page 39:

> . . . *Rudolf Steiner then refers to the possibility in modern mathematics of extending algebraic calculations to postulate a fourth and even higher dimensions, thus conceiving of other spaces and other geometries well known today.*
>
> *'These operations are logical in the mathematical sense and quite correct, but anyone who knows the genesis of our idea of space, as I have described it, will detect something quite special here.' Referring to the to and fro movement of a pendulum, he says that just as it does not swing further and further out, but turns back, so too, in reality; 'one cannot pass*

> *on into an indefinite fourth dimension; one must turn back at a certain point and the fourth dimension becomes simply the third with a minus sign before it . . . Our perception of space must return into itself.'* In turning back through the third, second and first dimensions, we annihilate them one after another and reach to a point in 'negative space' . . . 'then space is filled with spirit, whereas three-dimensional space is filled with matter.'

By exposure to highly developed technology mankind has developed a confidence in scientific materialism well beyond the sphere of its moral expertise. Furthermore the mathematical approach of materialistic science has thus far, for the most part, been oblivious to the world of the living with its vital growing forces of levity, and is really only effective regarding the laws that work within the "dead" mineral realm. Rudolf Steiner speaks of this dilemma in a lecture entitled, "The Lost Temple and its Restoration" which is published in the lecture cycle, *The Temple Legend*.

> *There is another kingdom above that which man has immediately and physically around him. But to which kingdom does man in his physical nature belong? At the present stage of his evolution, he belongs with his physical nature to the mineral kingdom. Physical, chemical and mineral laws hold sway over man's physical body. Yet even as far as his spiritual nature is concerned, he belongs to the mineral kingdom, since he understands through his intellect only what is mineral; Life, as such, he is only gradually learning to comprehend. Precisely for this reason, official science disowns life, being still at that stage of development in which it can only grasp the dead, the mineral. It is in the process of learning to understand this in very intricate detail. Hence it understands the human body only in so far as it is a dead, mineral thing. It treats the human body basically as something dead which one works, as if with a substance in a chemical laboratory. Other substances are poured into a retort. Even when the doctor, who nowadays is brought up entirely on mineral science, sets about working on the human body, it is as though the latter were only an artificial product.*

> *Hence we are dealing with man's body at the stage of the mineral kingdom in two ways: man has acquired reality in the mineral kingdom through having a physical body, and with his intellect is only able to grasp facts relating to the mineral kingdom. This is a necessary transitional stage for man. However, when man no longer relies only on the intellect but also upon intuition and spiritual powers, we will then be aware we are moving into a future in which our dead mineral body will work towards becoming one that is alive. And our science must lead the way, must prepare for what has to happen with the bodily essence in the future. In the near future, it must itself develop into something which has life in itself, recognize the life inherent in the earth for what it is. For in a deeper sense it is true, it is the thoughts of man that prepare the future. As an old Indian aphorism rightly says: What you think today, that you will be tomorrow.*

From the understanding of the living nature of the etheric world, in the future, there will be developed new etheric technologies - from which will come new forces of a very different character. For these forces will be an expression of the dynamic activities of the supersensible beings that work behind the world of the senses. In the not too distant future, certain types of technology will radiate healthy forces through the way in which etheric technology expresses what can only be called, "the moral forces of the Divine-Spiritual Beings." The operation of this etheric technology will be a sacred act, which depends on the operator having developed the necessary moral forces to be able to cause the machine to function. When technology develops to this point, it will depend more on the interaction of the beings of the spiritual world, which will operate through the agency of elemental beings that are active within the etheric world.

The participation of the supersensible beings in the operation of this etheric technology will be an act of joy and harmony. This joy and harmony will radiate from the device, and also from the operator, as a healing force for both the whole Earth and to those nearby. This etheric technology will, through its musical nature, help to harmonize the unwholesome dissonant residue of unhealthy technologies and other inharmonic human activities.

This wholesome, resonant quality will even be present when the machine is turned off, due to its mathematically harmonious form. These etheric devices will function in harmony with the interplay between the spirits of the circling stars and the "heart of the Sun." They will also harmonically resonate with the "little sun" in the human heart that mirrors the macrocosmic processes of the Sun and stars.

The deeper issues underlying the quality of the effect of this etheric technology depend on the human heart and mind being in harmony with the moral impulses of the spiritual world. This point is clarified by Rudolf Steiner in the fifth lecture of the lecture cycle entitled, *Three Streams in the Evolution of Mankind*:

> *What then should we be looking for? Is there anything in nature itself to enlighten us? Yes, there is: for example, the rainbow - the rainbow is a true picture of a natural phenomenon. Just think - of course you know this - if you could get to where the rainbow is, you could quite comfortably pass through it: it is brought about simply by the interworking of certain processes. Just as spectrelike, just as ghostlike, are all the processes in nature, only this is not perceived; they are not what they appear to be to the eye, the ear, or the other senses; they are the combined outcome of other spiritual processes. We tread the earth, believing we have solid matter below us; in reality it is merely what we perceive as with the rainbow - and when we believe we are treading on firm ground it is Ahriman sending up the force from below.*
>
> *Directly we get free from what is merely spectrelike, ghostlike, in natural phenomena, we meet the spiritual. In other words, all searching for so-called solid matter is really rather nonsensical. [Even materialistic scientists admit that their concept of the atom in quantum physics is composed of over 99% of what appears to be empty space.] If man will only give up looking for anything coarsely material as the basis of nature - and this he will do before the fourth millennium - he will come to something quite different: he will discover rhythms, rhythmical orderings, everywhere in nature. These rhythmical orderings are there, but as a rule modern materialistic science makes fun of them. We have given artistic expression to them in our seven pillars, and so on, in the whole configuration or our building. This rhythmical order is there in the whole of nature. In the plants, one leaf follows another in*

rhythmical growth; the petals of the blossoms are ordered rhythmically, everything is rhythmically ordered. Fever takes a rhythmical course in sickness; the whole of life is rhythmical. The discerning of nature's rhythms - that will be true natural science.

By learning to understand the rhythms in nature we shall even come to a certain application of the rhythmical in technology. This would be the goal for future technics: harmoniously related vibrations would be set going; they would be small at first but would act upon each other so that they became larger and larger, and by this means, simply through their resonance, a tremendous amount of work could be done.

Now tomorrow I will show you in greater detail why it is so truly wise on the part of the Christian world-order - which in this sense is the wise divine world-order - to let mankind become ripe in the course of centuries for the knowledge of which I have just been speaking, whereas the Academy of Jundi Sabur [in what is now Iraq] (around the 9th century) wanted to force it upon men. For men must have something else as their aim if this knowledge is to come to them. These forms of knowledge may be bestowed upon mankind only if, simultaneously with a development towards them, there comes into being as widely as possible . . . an entirely selfless social order. No rhythmical technics can be introduced without causing harm to mankind, unless at the same time a selfless social order is striven after; to an egoistic society they would bring only hurt.

The fundamental condition for the achievement of an "entirely selfless social order" such as Rudolf Steiner is referring to, depends upon mankind realizing that the blood is living; and that, "the heart is not a pump", which as Rudolf Steiner indicated is evident from embryology. Through this understanding will arise the awakening of the heart as an organ of supersensible cognition, and the faculty of "Moral Imagination."

The scientific ground work for the understanding that "the heart is not a pump" has been achieved in recent years by Ralph Marinelli, as explained in the article: "The Heart is Not a Pump: A Refutation of the Pressure Propulsion Premise of Heart Function", by Ralph Marinelli,

Branko Furst, Hoyte van der Zee, Andrew McGinn, and William Marinelli, which can be found in the journal that is published by: The Center for Frontier Sciences at Temple University entitled: *Frontier Perspectives* (vol. 5, number 1, Fall/Winter, 1995).

In 1982, Ehrenfried Pfeiffer's *Heart Lectures* were published and in these lectures it was emphasized how critical Rudolf Steiner thought the overcoming of the "heart as a pump" concept was, towards overcoming science's overly materialistic-mechanistic views of man and nature. That this significance extended even into the social sphere is shown by Rudolf Steiner's statement that, "when science overcomes the 'heart is a pump' concept social conditions will improve."

The developments in true medical understanding, technology, and the social order, will help bring mankind into their rightful development as spiritual beings. This is the destiny of mankind as regards to their free, wholesome development. How this comes about depends on the efforts of individuals and their contribution to the overall scheme of things. Through the conscious, free cooperation of individual minds, hearts, and wills, we shall find the way to the true realization of, "peace on Earth to men of good will", which is the fruit of the active striving of what is described in the biblical "Song of Solomon" and in the legend of the Grail as "a love as strong as death."

Rudolf Steiner, once indicated that science will discover the workings of the Spirit through physiology. Certain key ideas that help one to come to a greater understanding of the importance of this concept were shared by Ehrenfried Pfeiffer in the *Heart Lectures,* which he gave in December of 1950.

> *The human heart and blood constitute one of the most far reaching of subjects. Dr. Steiner spoke of the etherization of the blood that takes place there, i.e. the transformation of matter into etheric forces. One can quote Dr. Steiner, but one would like to understand why and how he was able to speak about such things. Today the science of physiology has only very little evidence regarding the function of the heart. But occult groups other than the anthroposophical know these secrets of the heart, and some groups do not want them made known to others. So we feel it a kind of challenge. Also, Rudolf Steiner, in 'The Spiritual Guidance of Mankind', speaks of the need for a science which will be able to observe the working of*

Christ in Nature. This is something far in the future, but we cannot approach the future unless we begin to do so in the present. So as an anthroposophical scientist one feels that one wants to study the human heart as an organ where a bridge is being built between man's physical body and spiritual entity.

Sixteen years ago I met a leading occultist (he is not publicly known). He works in a realm which is not anthroposophical, nor is it a realm of black magic but rather gray, in between and nearer to the dark than the light forces. This man, a medical man by profession, told me a story: He said that Dr. Steiner's illness - according to the research of himself and his associates - was due to the fact that Dr. Steiner wanted to tell more regarding the spiritual function of the human heart, and other occultists did not want this known at present. So they brought to bear on Rudolf Steiner forces against which he was unable to defend himself, and he became ill [and as a result passed away in March of 1925].

This knowledge which Rudolf Steiner had concerns 'the fifth chamber of the heart.' The idea is that in our time there are certain changes taking place in the heart, by which gradually a fifth chamber will develop [that is connected to the higher functions of the peripheral, etheric center that is in the beginning stages of formation behind the head]. In this fifth chamber man will have a new organ which will allow him to control life forces in a different way than is possible at the moment.

It is known that there is a kind of endocrine action in the blood. There have been found traces of a sort of 'suprarenalin', like adrenalin, indicating that the heart has a kind of gland function. Rudolf Steiner was willing to tell more regarding etherization, and the heart as a dual purpose organ, both physical and spiritual. The heart is not a pressure pump, but an organ in which etheric space is created so that the blood is sucked to the heart rather than pumped. He said too that it was important to change the scientific concept from the idea of the heart as a pump to something else. It is difficult to bring evidence on this point, which can be presented. The matter needs more study; it is no help to quote Rudolf Steiner.

Is is encouraging to realize that overwhelming scientific evidence now exists to refute the "heart as a pump" concept; i.e., in the work of Ralph Marinelli et al., regarding the heart's turning, verticordial movement which acts as a vortex-momenta-booster assisting the natural living movement of the blood. This "open secret" is slowly working its way through the scientific community, which unbeknownst to them, is a sort of spiritual leaven for the spiritual development of mankind. Regarding the importance of understanding the true nature of the heart, Ehrenfried Pfeiffer further relates in the *Heart Lectures*:

> *Together with the wrong concept of the heart as a pump is connected the fact that we have a wrong social life today. A healthy social life can develop only if the old pump-concept is removed and is replaced by the proper one. So this is a subject that should interest the student of social problems. Rudolf Steiner said that a true cognition in this regard would also make it possible to build machines that are in accord and in harmony with the human being and not destructive to him. He said that only when people know that it is the invisible in man which moves the heart, will it be possible to construct proper machines and to solve the social problem.*

From this it is evident to the intuitive individual just how important it is for the wholesome spiritual development of mankind that this new understanding of the heart come about; for in actuality, the heart is a spiritual organ of moral cognition which is connected with spiritual processes that are not physically visible but can only be perceived through supersensible means.

Through the understanding of the supersensible being and destiny of man, we shall evolve beyond the materialistic conception of man as a biochemical machine, to the rightful idea of man as a three-fold being of body, soul, and spirit - with the spirit recognized as the primary core of a human being. In the same lecture series, Ehrenfried Pfeiffer provides us with a deepening of some of the concepts that can help illustrate this topic:

> *I have spoken in the past of Rudolf Steiner's exercise for learning imagination: You form the image of a sphere,*

metamorphose it to a central point, and from this center again out to a sphere. You can think of concentric circles getting smaller until they become a point and then enlarging again. One day you will try to apply this to the outermost Cosmos. Then you will feel it concentrate, with everything into the earth, and then the earth itself will contract finally into the central point of the sphere. Then you will experience the central point of your own heart as the central point of the sphere. This has to be experienced, just thinking about it has no value. If you have this as experience, you then expand again, and what expands is not the past Cosmos but it is you. Then if you are objective and strong enough, you find that you face yourself on the Threshold of the Spiritual World. And if the Guardian allows you to pass, you then see how small you are. This new sphere which expands is an incomplete and spotty cosmos, some parts of it more outlined, some less so. This is not depressing but is an objective experience. You see everything that is spiritual radiating out, you feel its radiating power; and you also experience other, dark spaces.

What you have done is to concentrate your entire God-made Cosmos to a center and from this center radiate outward what will some day be a new Cosmos. This is what makes the heart move, the motion which radiates out from the heart. This is what Rudolf Steiner was ready to give and what occultists opposed giving out. In fact, Rudolf Steiner has given it in a meditation.

The same occultists to whom I referred earlier said when we were wrestling about these things: 'We have discovered since the death of Dr. Steiner that unless this knowledge of the center of the heart is made known, there will be no salvation for the human race but only destruction.' One can call this sensational or one can say: 'How deep a secret that even the dark forces have to recognize it.'

The continuing progress of the spiritual evolution of mankind does not depend on the masses but on individuals, and then small groups of people, gradually making the transition to the next stage of development; with the masses later following the developmental path of these pioneer souls. The understanding of this fact has always been known to occultists.

Further details on the Christology of this heart mystery, and how it is connected to the spiritual development of the individual human being, are provided by Ehrenfried Pfeiffer in his aforementioned *Heart Lectures*:

> *With every pulse of the heart a certain amount of substance is absorbed, is taken away as physical pressure and added to the etheric substance. This then begins to radiate outward. Dr. Steiner said that a clairvoyant could see the amount of radiation that goes up from the heart to the brain, and that if a person knew this they would be ashamed to fall asleep at a lecture in the presence of a clairvoyant. The radiation from this etheric organ of the heart is actually developing into a spiritual sense organ. A new sense organ is developing in this etheric heart, and this is the only organ by which man is able to sense and to recognize the Etheric Christ.*
>
> *I can think: 'Not I but Christ in me.' Such a thought might stimulate us to healthy feelings, but in itself this is not enough. There has to be something which goes through our will, and since our will is combined with metabolism to produce etheric substance, so 'Not I but Christ in me' has to work through the etheric heart, transforming substance into pure ether, pure radiance.*
>
> *For us there is an experience of the heart similar to the way in which, in the old Mysteries, the Sun was experienced. We experience in every heart a Sun. The Sun shines on all people, it shines on the fields of the Earth, it shines on other planets. And all the time it is consuming its own energy. The Sun dissolves matter and transforms it into radiant energy. Its light can be seen everywhere in our earthly cosmos. The same power that dwells in the Sun wills to live in every human being.*
>
> *If you become aware of the heart as a spiritual organ, you begin to develop the power to see the Etheric Christ. You do this by realizing that the force in the heart is the same as the force in the Sun, physically as well as spiritually. If you take this as a reality, there will still be conflicts but there will also be the realization that your entire picture of the world changes. The force from the heart is a force which will be good . . . All that we can do is to be aware of the forces of the etheric heart. Because these will shine . . .*

What is needed for the further evolution of humanity is a true "heart thinking", that is - a living thinking that is centered in the light processes of Cosmic Feeling - which are found working in the spiritual center of the heart. This is the goal of the Grail path outlined in Rudolf Steiner's work. This is achieved, as Wolfram von Eschenbach tells us in *Parzival*, by passing "from dullness, through doubt, to saelde" (saelde = blessedness). Viewed from the understanding of the organ systems, as presented in Anthroposophical Spiritual Science, this saelde is achieved by moving from the dullness and fear of the Venus-kidney processes, to the confident and wakeful "saelde" of the Jupiter-liver process (which I have discussed in the chapter on the Empress arcanum) as a transition to the completion of the supersensible development of the Sun-Heart center, and to a free, fully-conscious spiritual-citizenship.

If mankind is to heal themselves and the Earth, they must first take responsibility for the type of thoughts that they choose to entertain - for all true healing proceeds from the therapeutic response of the soul forces which stimulate the healing forces of the body; with the resulting healing, occultly speaking, being a harmonization of the four members of the being of man.

The Four-Fold Human Being

Ego - the "I Am", or "Christ in you", which is the true manifestation of human individuality, and is carried in the warmth of the blood.

Astral-Body - the desire body which gives animation, or movement. The Astral-Body is the highest vehicle embodied within the animal kingdom.

Etheric-Body - the body of formative forces that is responsible for the capacities of growth and memory. The Etheric-Body is the highest vehicle embodied within the plant kingdom.

Physical-Body - is acted upon by the higher members of man, but upon death, it reverts to the chemical laws of the mineral kingdom to which it relates, and decomposes. The Physical-Body is at present the only vehicle acknowledged by orthodox science.

As shown above, if one looks at the nature of a human being in a four-fold manner, there are three parts of man beyond the Physical-Body. Through modern science going beyond the knowledge of the mineral kingdom and coming to an understanding of these higher members of the being of man (**II**), a true spiritual science of healing will result - the foundations for which already exist in the Anthroposophical medicine of Rudolf Steiner.

As Pythagoras said; "All illness is a musical problem." That is the challenge of the present epoch, that mankind begins to understand the higher spiritual laws, and as a result, gradually takes upon themselves - the joyous responsibility of manifesting harmony within the world. For as it is written; "Love hath healing on its wings."

VII

The Chariot

Cancer - Cherubim - Spirits of Harmony

The Chariot arcanum represents the constellation of the Crab, Cancer, which is symbolized by the double-vortex: 69 with a gap between, out of which can arise new impulses. The constellation of the Crab is associated, in the "Zodiac of the Lamb of God" (**IX**), with the second highest of the spiritual hierarchies mentioned by Dionysius the Areopagite, the Cherubim, or as they are called by Rudolf Steiner, the Spirits of Harmony (**V**). From these exalted Cherubim, at the beginning of the Old Saturn incarnation of the Earth (**IV**), proceeded the highest levels of harmony that manifested through their contemplation of the outpouring of love by the beings that are one stage beyond them, the Seraphim, or Spirits of Love. This outpouring of love by the Seraphim, in turn, came about through their contemplation of the plan of the Holy Trinity, which was the first impulse of creation. This harmonious response of the Cherubim moved the Thrones to offer up warmth from their very own being as a sacrifice, and resulted in the initial vortex which began creation; for all manifestation is brought about through the action of the vortex on all planes of being, as revealed by Rudolf Steiner in a lecture given on October 20th, 1906 entitled, *The Path of Knowledge and its Stages.*

> *In the higher worlds there is a process which appears also in the physical world: the rotation of a vortex. You can observe this phenomenon if you watch a starry nebula, for example that of Orion. There you see a spiral. That is on the physical plane. But you can observe it on all planes. You find that one spiral swirls into another.*

Not all of the Cherubim were moved to accept the offering of the Thrones, and thereby bring into being a vortex of a more simple harmony. As a consequence of these particular Cherubim refraining from action, the initial vortex was changed in such a way so that it affected all of the subsequent impulses of creation. This had the end result of setting the stage for mankind to descend deeper into manifestation - and become dense physical beings subjected to the laws of death - in the fourth incarnation of the Earth, which is our present physical Earth. Had this "spin" on the initial creative-vortex not happened, mankind would have had a less individuated evolution, with their human, or fourth evolutionary stage being "no more dense than the fragrance of a flower." But this was not to be. Nonetheless, great potential for good did ultimately come about as a result of this initial contrary impulse, which one might see as a sort of "rebellion in Heaven." Although this divergence between the actions of the Cherubim cannot be thought of as a true "rebellion", such as the "luciferic rebellion", for Rudolf Steiner made it clear that the actions of the highest beings were in purest conformity with the Divine Plan of the Holy Trinity.

Due to the introduction of contrary impulses within evolution, mankind has achieved the possibility of error, and so, the possibility of freedom. Had these contrary impulses not been introduced into the initial vortex of evolution, mankind would have been very pure and good, but with no sense of individuality or freedom. It is because these particular Cherubim rejected the sacrifice of the Thrones that a wider range of possibilities became available to the luciferic beings, which in turn, made their later rebellion possible. As a result of this chain of events, we now have the possibility of error, and likewise, the possibility of freedom. And also - as a result of this "spin" on the initial vortex of creation - we have mineral skeletons as the foundation of our dense physical bodies.

The densest "signatures" of the vortex in man are manifested in the skeletal formations of the spine and ribcage, and also the spiral-formed cochlea of the inner ear.

A crab has an exoskeleton shaped in a more ovoidal-domed form, like the top of the head, rather than an internal skeleton. In the human body, this external surrounding tendency can be seen in the ribcage which surrounds the rhythmic system of heart and lungs with twelve pairs of ribs. This "vortex" of twelve pairs of ribs, surrounding the heart and lungs, forms an image of the twelve-fold zodiac. When viewed from above, this curved shape of the ribcage can be seen as forming a lemniscate, or figure 8 when considered along with the vertebrae encircling the spinal cord. Together these formations constitute a skeletal lemniscate that enfolds both the nerve-sense and rhythmic systems.

The heart has a particular relationship to the Sun (**XVI-XVII**), and occultly speaking, can be thought of as the Sun in man. The lungs, on the other hand, are related to the planet Mercury (**XVI**) and the sphere of Venus (**XVII**). The Sun and the planets Mercury and Venus, when considered heliocentrically, appear to be located within the orbit of the Earth and Moon and so have an internalized nature in our solar system; while in man, the heart and lungs are also internalized within the rib cage. The constellation of Cancer is related to the Moon. Due to its movement around the Earth, the lunar cycles of the Moon appear to be forming spirals heliocentrically around the Sun, Mercury, and Venus; while geocentrically, that is from the vantage point of here on Earth, the Moon spirals around the heart and lungs, surrounding them in the course of the thirteen lunar cycles of the year which have a formative relationship to the development of the twelve pairs of ribs within the embryo.

As Rudolf Steiner has said, the symbol for the sign Cancer is actually a vortex, it is usually drawn as two swirls with a gap between them, it is out of this gap that new manifestations can arise. The gap is also related to the state of rest between manifestations, which is called in Sanskrit "pralaya", out of which new worlds come into being. The constellation of Cancer, with its glyph of two spirals with a gap between them (69) can be seen as the two sides of the enclosure of the ribcage that surrounds the rhythmic system. The form of the ribcage itself, with its enfolded cup-like shape, creates a hollow space for something new to come into being. Reminiscent of this is the way in which a cyclone, or any vortex, forms a sort of inner and outer "skin", a "ring pass not", limiting the substances that are part of the vortex itself. In addition, the overall curved form of the developing embryo can be seen as a further suggestion of this spiral-formed growth.

One must come to an understanding of the "Grail-Heart" as a "chalice" or vehicle, that is formed within the "tabernacle" of the ribcage; which, through its spiritual metamorphoses, develops the capacity to receive the living impulses of the Spiritual World. This leads us to the most obvious *spiral* activity to be found in the human body, which has passed virtually unnoticed to modern medical science and physiology - the spiral movement of the blood - which is most apparent in the heart itself. Scientists for 300 years have believed the theory that the "heart is a pressure-pump." In the 1920's Rudolf Steiner told a group of medical doctors that this *mistaken notion* that the "heart is a pump" could be disproven by observing the embryo. Ten years later, sufficient observations of the embryo had been made to confirm his statement, as noted by Ralph Marinelli, although these observations passed unnoticed.

Ralph Marinelli, by working on the indications of Rudolf Steiner which dispute the theory that the "heart is a pump", discovered what he calls the "vortex-momenta-booster" blood propulsion principle. This activity of the circulatory system arises initially in the embryo as vortisanguia (vortexing-blood); which later, after the formation of the heart, brings about verticordia (turning-heart). Simply stated, verticordia is a term that is suitable, as mentioned elsewhere, to describe the twisting or turning motion made by the heartbeat with its seven layered, spiraling muscles rapidly beating, with the transition between systole (contraction) and diastole (dilation) forming a small lemniscate, or figure 8 that can be detected by observing the apex or bottom of the heart. This verticordial movement of the heart ejects the blood in an enhanced vortex form of flow, or vortisanguia.

Returning to Rudolf Steiner's statement regarding the embryo being the key to understanding how "the heart is not a pump"; in the 1930's, as noted by Marinelli, only ten years after Rudolf Steiner's statement, sufficient scientific observations of the embryo were made to disprove the "heart as a pump" theory. The embryologists discovered that the blood moves on its own before the heart and blood vessels are even formed; in other words, the blood was found to have its own motive force. In addition to this, what might be unknown to some - the blood flow of the embryo is entirely separate from that of the mother, which is demonstrated by the fact that the mother and child frequently have different blood types.

In light of all of this it is most important to keep in mind that the movement of the blood and consequently the heart (which receives its cue through its ability to sense the blood's rhythmic activity) is maintained by the Beings of the Second Hierarchy (Kyriotetes = Spirits of Wisdom, Dynamis = Spirits of Movement, Exusiai = Spirits of Form) as a rhythmic pulsation and movement that is a reflection of the rhythmic nature of the circling stars; and more specifically, of the Sun as it is experienced from the Earth (V). For occultly speaking, the living movement of the blood has more in common with the forces which bring about planetary movement than to any sort of pump. And so we must resist the tendency to go too far in attributing the movement of the blood to sense perceptible processes, for it is through the Astral-Body rhythmically acting upon the Etheric-Body that the blood and heart rhythm arises. In the future, through further careful investigation of the blood movement in the embryo, science will ultimately realize that the "prime mover" of the blood cannot be perceived with the physical senses. If I may at this point make use of an analogy which was once used by Rudolf Steiner (which is only helpful as an example of the part that external processes play in an *entirely different* phenomena of movement): a compass is moved by forces outside of it, no scientist will dispute this fact; for they all agree that it is through the external magnetic forces and not a force originating from within the compass that causes it to move. In a similar way, the movement of the blood does not originate in the blood itself; but rather, originates from the supersensible activities of the Second Hierarchy, who are working *outside* of man from the surrounding Cosmos, and who are also working *inside* of man from within the astral-etheric nature of the blood.

I shall now attempt to paint an imaginative picture of this Divine-Spiritual process that takes place both within and without the human being: the blood movement and heart beat are the fruit of the relationship between the two realms of the Macrocosm and the Microcosm, as they are perceived by the beings of the Second Hierarchy (most immediately by the Exusiai or Spirits of Form, the biblical Elohim) as they, so to speak, look upwards towards the Cosmos from within the blood and heart of man. This perception of the cosmic order by the Second Hierarchy is mingled with the karmic essence of the earthly and cosmic processes that proceed from the individual human being; and thereby, the blood movement and heart beat arise through the striving of the Second Hierarchy for harmonization between the human being and the Cosmos.

I the Lord [Elohim] search the heart, I try the reins, even to give every man according to his ways, and according to the fruit of his doings. "Jeremiah" (17:10)

For the Elohim look into the being of man most clearly in the empty spaces, such as are found in the gaps that are present in the synapses of the nervous system when they look down; on the other hand, when the Elohim look outward from within the human being - from the emptied-out etheric space that is present within the vortexing blood in the heart (or, within the ducts of the reins or kidneys) - they perceive how it harmonizes with the "Music of the Spheres" arising from the Dynamis, or Spirits of Movement enacting the Divine Plan of the Cosmos as it is perceived by them through the inspiration of the Kyriotetes, or Spirits of Wisdom.

Rudolf Steiner makes frequent reference to the central significance of the heart in occult physiology. One of the places where he gives a more comprehensive description is in a lecture given in Dornach on May 26th, 1922 entitled, *The Human Heart*. In the following I give a summary that is modified with certain supporting ideas which I have derived from his other works. The complete lecture is included in the book by Douglas J. Gabriel entitled, *The Spirit of Childhood*.

The Human Heart

The process of the forming of a human being begins in one's pre-earthly life as one descends into incarnation. The incarnating spirit, as it is being drawn into the earthly realm by the incarnational forces of the Moon sphere, envelops itself with forces of the etheric world. These forces are woven into a sphere which is an image of the Cosmos at that moment in time, revealing the world of the stars at its periphery and within the image of the Earth, Sun, Moon, and Planets (**XI**). This cosmic image remains during the development of the embryo and beyond, up until the change of teeth around the age of seven, all the while gradually fading as its incorporation with the Physical-Body slowly comes into being. At the change of teeth the fading star-images of the periphery become rays that begin to draw together inwardly. Ever so slowly between the change of teeth and puberty this drawing together of these stellar etheric rays takes place. These rays find their center within the heart region forming a unique etheric counterpart to the physical heart.

This etheric heart is a microcosmic picture of the macrocosmic processes that transpired in the surrounding universe when the incarnating soul first united with the embryo (**XI**). Up until the complete formation of the individual's own etheric heart at puberty there is an etheric heart that arises out of the forces of the embryo. The embryonic etheric heart gradually fades as the individual's new etheric heart replaces it slowly up until the time of puberty. And so, at puberty what has come into being is our permanent etheric heart, to serve as the center of all of our etheric activities pertaining to life, form, and memory. In addition to the Physical and Etheric-Bodies you also have an Astral-Body and Ego (**II**). These also find their center in the heart by integrating *into the human being over time.*

It is the Etheric-Body of formative forces that orchestrates the development of the embryo and the resulting human form. The formation of the head is an image of the contraction of zodiacal forces with the twelve-fold processes of the Zodiac expressing in the twelve pairs of cranial nerves (**XXII**). *The Etheric-Body is a vehicle that we have in common with the plant kingdom, for the highest vehicle of the plant kingdom is etheric. (Except certain plants that incorporate the astral somewhat and so have movement, like the Venus flytrap, or the sensitive plant and others, that by having movement border the animal kingdom.)*

The Astral-Body, or as it is sometimes called the Desire-Body, relates to feelings of sympathy and antipathy and contains the astral centers, or chakras. We have an Astral-Body in common with the animal kingdom who have it as their highest principle. The Astral-Body is the vehicle of sentience and is the animating principle that makes movement possible.

Like the Etheric-Body, the Astral-Body gradually integrates with the human being. At birth, the Astral-Body is highly individualized and filled with many radiant forms that were brought into being from the experiences between the last death and the present birth. These radiant forms flow into the infant in the first few days of life. First, flowing into the brain and sense organs. Then, other forms flow into the lungs; still others flow into the heart and arteries. This first integration only takes place into the organs approximately above the diaphragm. The Astral-Body later integrates with the rest of the organism through the arteries. And so, the Astral-Body envelops the upper systems directly, then it streams into the lower systems via the arteries. The initial astral organ sheaths are like the initial Etheric-Body in that they are inherited and gradually replaced at around puberty by the permanent Astral-Body. The radiant forms of the incarnating Astral-Body are diffused as they integrate into the physical organs bringing the Astral-Body into more of a fog-like appearance; the early-life condition of the Astral-Body is very resilient in that the sense experiences of the child make very little lasting imprint. This more individuated karmic imprinting really only truly begins to be permanently inscribed from around puberty onwards. The impressions of the life before puberty do not make as clear and lasting effect, and are much more generalized in content. This shows the wisdom in the saying: "All good children go to heaven." For the karmic consequences of life before puberty are not as complete due to the resilience of the Astral-Body. It reflects the impressions off of itself, and they dissipate into the astral light. As the permanent astral integrates, the impressions made become more lasting until at around puberty; the astral heart has finished its initial forming where it becomes the repository of all our actions, and also of the actions that we've told others to do. So the impressions become more lasting as the child learns to speak and develop the memory of ideas, and these impressions find their center in the astral heart which is where the images of our deeds meet the image of the Cosmos within our etheric heart. This astral heart imparts rhythm to the etheric heart which imparts the rhythm to the physical blood, which in turn imparts rhythm to the blood vessels and heart, (which should be thought of as one organ together with the blood). The heart is the point in a human being where all the levels of the Spirit, Soul and Physical being of man come together. For the higher being of man; the Ego organization, enters with the first breath into the lungs. The Ego slowly flows to the heart, and from there takes possession of the rest of the organism through the periphery of the blood vessels. Merging gradually with the blood itself where it is carried in the warmth of the blood. The Ego has taken hold of the circulatory system and centered in the heart by around puberty. It then develops from that point in an individual way. The various levels of soul and spirit, all of which have found a common center in the heart, proceed in their integration with man from that time in approximately seven-year cycles of development. Just as the Sun is the center of the Solar system, so the heart is the center of the human being.

This co-creative weaving and integration of the different levels of the human being is brought about by the working together of the angelic hierarchies with the incarnating individual. It is a process of gradual development that leads from incarnation to incarnation, which hopefully in the future will bring about a "Grail Heart" capable of perceiving and expressing the Spirit - or, in the language of the Grail, " . . . and the dove descends upon the Holy Grail" (**XIV**). As Rudolf Steiner once said in the lecture, "The Cosmic Origin of the Human Form" which is published in the cycle of lectures entitled, *The Mystery of the Trinity and the Mission of the Spirit*: "For in its true essence our heart is something much more majestic, something vastly greater than any Sun."

The dove is a symbol of the third member of the Trinity, the Holy Spirit (**XIII**), and is related to the integration of the activity of the beings of the spiritual hierarchies as a group with the will of the first member of the Trinity, the Father (**XI**). This integration comes about, in response to the promptings of the third aspect of the Trinity, the Holy Spirit, according to the Divine Idea of the second member of the Trinity, the Son, which is the Christ-Logos (**XII**). The Father is the transcendent, "unmanifested ground of being"; while the Holy Spirit refers to that immanent aspect of the Trinity which can manifest in a particularly individuated way to the individual, created beings by acting from outside as the Paraclete. The Son is the Logos, or "Word", Who first brings about the symphony of manifestation, and then indwells His creation. Esoterically, you can carry this idea further by finding the microcosmic analogies in the human form.

The primal warmth of the Old Saturn incarnation of the Earth (**IV**) is the point of origin of what eventually became the Physical-Body, consequently the Physical-Body is the oldest vehicle and so, the most developed, and corresponds to what has been formed out of the "Father Ground of Being." The Physical-Body is a counterpart to the Spirit-Man, or Atma, as it is called in Eastern Sanskrit terminology, and where it is said; "Atma and Atman are one", or; "Atma and Brahma are one" meaning that "the drop and the ocean are one." The ocean is the Father, the drops are brought into being through the activity of the Holy Spirit, according to the promptings of the Son. Or explained another way; the Father relates to Cosmic Will - Divine Darkness, the Holy Spirit relates to Cosmic Feeling - Divine Light, the Son relates to Cosmic Thought which mediates between Cosmic Will and Cosmic Feeling.

The individuated monad as the microcosmic Atma relates to the Holy Spirit. The undifferentiated macrocosmic Atman, or Brahman, on the other hand, is the unified sea of Cosmic Will of the Father, the highest manifestation of the Godhead. Furthermore, the Atma is the Sophia principle in man through being of the nature of the lowest substance of the Spirits of Wisdom, the Kyriotetes; who have a most intimate relationship to the Holy Spirit (**IX**).

The most mature vehicle is the Physical-Body, with the skeleton being that which is akin to the mineral world; furthermore, the skull is the oldest member of the skeleton through its formative connection with the Old Saturn incarnation of the Earth (IV). For the skull reflects the starry dome of "our Father in Heaven" as it meets the starry script that is inscribed in the heart.

The highest principle of man, the Atma, or Spirit-Man, is expressed through the whole being of man (i.e.; the physical, etheric, astral, and all the soul and spirit manifestations within these vehicles); although the Atma's most developed reflection is the Physical-Body. While the Atma radiates through the whole being of man, it focuses its light within the "cave of the heart", and its reflection - in the Physical-Body - comes to a focus *in the consciousness of man* at the brow near the base of the nose.

The consciousness is crucified at Golgotha the "Place of the Skull", between the "murderer and the thief", Ahriman and Lucifer; between the experience of left and right, below and above. Our consciousness is a thin film, as it were, crucified between the two adversaries, traveling the path of the razor's edge; which is mentioned in the old Indian scripture, *The Katha Upanishad*. Likewise, this challenge is portrayed in the Old High German Grail story, of the thirteenth century, by Heinrich von dem Turlin entitled, *Diu Crone (The Crown)*, in which it is necessary for Gawain to cross a dark river on a steel bridge as wide as a hand, to reach the "revolving castle." Also, in the story of *Lancelot*, we find that Lancelot must cross a bridge "as thin as a sword blade" to reach the castle.

In *Parzival*, it says that: "Anyone who wants to win the Grail must clear his path towards this precious object with weapons in hand." It is obvious that what Wolfram is trying to say is that the Grail-seeker must have all of his principles under the dominion of his higher nature; for in seeking the Grail - one must conquer oneself so as to become a worthy vehicle, or "chariot" (Hebrew, merkavah = chariot) of the Spirit.

The Seven Principles

1. Physical-Body: the base of the nose
2. Etheric-Body (Prana): the liver
3. Kama Rupa (Astral-Body): the digestive system and stomach
4. Kama-Manas (Astral-Ego): the umbilical cord
5. Higher-Manas (Spirit-Self): the heart and blood circulation
6. Budhi (Life-Spirit): the larynx and gullet
7. Atma (Spirit-Man) the Akasha: the whole being of man

Although there are various ways of relating the principles within the being of man, one good scheme is seen above - which is useful for meditation on the human being as a vehicle, or "chariot" of the Spirit. It was given by Rudolf Steiner in lecture four of the lecture cycle entitled, *The Temple Legend*.

The Macrocosm and the Embryo

The workings of the Cosmos as it is revealed in the development of the human body is the true key to understanding the nature of the Cosmos itself, and is also the key to understand the activity of the beings of the spiritual world as they are related to the being and destiny of man. For the development of the human form gives us a true picture of the Macrocosm. This occult fact is often emphasized in Anthroposophical teachings, but is said most clearly in a quotation from Rudolf Steiner that can be found on page 53 of the book by Olive Whicher entitled, *Sunspace: Science at a Threshold of Spiritual Understanding*.

> *Embryology today makes the mistake of looking at the human ovum only as it develops in the mother's body. All the forces that form the human embryo are supposed to be therein. In reality, the whole cosmos works through the mother's body upon the configuration of the embryo. The plastic forces of the whole cosmos are there, just as the magnetic needle is directed by the forces of the earth.*

This formative relationship between the Cosmos and embryology was elaborated on by Dr. Karl Koenig in the six lectures that he gave on embryology during two week end seminars of the "Mitteleuropaisches Studienwerk in Freiburg im Breisgau", that were published in English with the title, *Embryology and World Evolution*.

> *. . . There are many ways of studying embryology, as with anything else. Rudolf Steiner, for instance, did on one occasion demand that embryology should be considered afresh in conjunction with astronomy. Well if one considers that on one*

occasion he did state quite definitely that from the moment of birth every human being bears the constellation of his birth inscribed upon the surface of the cerebrum, the cortex, so that one might say that we are always carrying our birth constellation with us. If one looks at the course of the planets out there and at the development of the organs within the growing embryo, then one does find some remarkable correspondences, from the moment when one uses not only the microscope but considers things as a whole and studies the coming into being, the formation and transformations of the brain, the budding of a liver, the descent of the kidneys. Then one will find that processes which apply in astronomy lie hidden in this, one only has to crack them open. One might be able to do this if one could get an astronomer interested, so that he would help one understand the concepts which apply in his field. And one could link embryology not only with astrology, but also for instance - and that would be illuminating - with the whole field of projective geometry. This I have attempted to do on various occasions in the past with my friend, the late Mr. George Adams, and we did find promising points of contact here and there, e.g. in the development of the eye, the development of the liver, the development of the kidney. That God geometrizes not only out there, but also right in the human embryo and in the human foetus. All this is extremely complicated and only a mathematician and geometrician of genius will be able to do something of this kind, in collaboration with some embryologists.

Further important details in this regard, concerning the form of the heart, are given in the first lecture of Rudolf Steiner's *Astronomy Course,* which was published in a translation by Rick Mansell under the title, *Eighteen Monographs by Rudolf Steiner on Astronomy.*

If we were able to apply to the structure of the human organism everything that has been thought out in non-Euclidian geometry, then we would be working with really important ideas instead of meandering in mere speculations. If the mathematician were trained in such a way as to interest himself in reality, for example in the appearance of the heart, he could form a certain concept of how, by means of a special mathematical process, he could turn the whole heart inside out. Furthermore, if he were properly trained, he would realize that out of that the whole human form would develop. If he were taught to use mathematics in actual life circumstances, then he would find himself working in the realm of reality.

On the one hand, we have astronomy tending to become more and more closed in by mathematical thought-forms. On the other hand, there is a branch of science which can be called the counterpole to astronomy, and it cannot be studied in its real nature without a knowledge of astronomy. Today it seems impossible to build a bridge from astronomy to embryology. If you want to really work with reality, you must study the starry skies, on the one hand, and, on the other, you must study the development of the human embryo.

VIII

Strength

Leo - Thrones - Spirits of Will
St. Mark - the Lawyer - the Initiate of Will and Social Order

In numerous places, I have referred to various aspects of Rudolf Steiner's description of the mystery of our evolution first arising, in the Old Saturn incarnation of the Earth, out of the donated warmth of the Thrones, or Spirits of Will (**IV**). This primal act of creation first began in relationship to the region of space we now call the constellation of Leo, the lion. The lion can been seen as an objective example of the rhythmic heart system manifesting within the animal kingdom, for a lion truly is a outer manifestation in nature of the heart forces. To be courageous like a lion relates to the heart forces; for the word courageous is derived from the word "cour" which means heart, like the fixed-star Cour Leonis which is the "heart of the lion" in the constellation of Leo (**XIII**). On the other hand, the ancient Egyptians considered Cour Leonis, or Regulus to be the paw of the lion, which can be seen as a reference to the will forces that come to a focus in the claws as an outward expression of leonine courage. The Thrones, Rudolf Steiner tells us, could also be called the "Spirits of Courage." In addition to all of this, by our own experience we all know that true courage is a heart-force.

Christ taught the path of love which is born within the heart in freedom. In the *Bible* we are told that Jesus was a "lion of the tribe of Judah." In the esoteric tradition the twelve tribes of Israel correspond to the twelve signs of the Zodiac, with Leo representing the tribe of Judah. This mystery of Judaism is supported by a large zodiacal mosaic that was discovered recently by archaeologists on the floor of a synagogue in the Holy Land dating from the Graeco-Roman period; which, incidentally, has caused considerable controversy within the world of biblical scholarship regarding the place of astrology in the traditions of Judaism and Christianity.

The "Teacher of Righteousness" mentioned in *The Dead Sea Scrolls* is the great Essene teacher Jeschu ben Pandira (ben Pandira means "son of the panther") - revealing another connection to Leo within the core of esoteric Christianity. This Initiate Jeschu ben Pandira has frequently been confused with Christ Jesus. In the Hebrew *Talmud*, Jeschu ben Pandira is said to have been stoned and hung from a tree in Egypt. There are those that confuse the two by their somewhat similar manner of death. In response to this question, according to Rudolf Steiner, the stream of esoteric Christianity is very connected with the karma and destiny of Jeshu ben Pandira, through whom the spirit of the successor to Gautama Buddha worked - that great being known in the East as the Maitreya Buddha.

In the future, the Maitreya Buddha will be one of the greatest messengers of Christ the "Great Sun Being", and will fulfill his mission as the "Teacher of Righteousness"; speaking words of moral force for which we do not even have a language capable of expressing at this time. The Maitreya Buddha is *not* the "Second Coming of Christ", but will be a future *human* development that has been made possible through the direct intervention of Christ in human evolution.

The Christ is the highest manifestation on Earth of the Supreme Godhead, for He is the 2nd Logos, or "Word", the second Being of the Trinity, that descended into the Holy Grail - the "Sangreal", the "Blood Royal" of Jesus of Nazareth, the "Lion of the tribe of Judah." The Christ is working from above downwards into Earth evolution as the Maha-Avatar, or highest Divine Incarnation; whereas, the Initiate Jeschu ben Pandira is one of the twelve Bodhisattvas (or embodiments of purity), who work from below upwards, from within the human realm - so as to receive the inspiration of the Christ-Logos.

Jeschu ben Pandira, as the "Teacher of Righteousness", was the custodian of the hereditary Birth Mysteries of the Essenes; which were concerned with preparing, through the Hebrew Mysteries, Physical, Etheric, and Astral Bodies that were suitable to receive the incarnation of Christ. The Essene mission was to bring about through the principles of heredity, a suitable vehicle, or "Grail" to receive the Christ - as instructed by the "Teacher of Righteousness", in his messianic prophecies that were discovered in the *Dead Sea Scrolls* regarding the "Priestly Messiah" and the "Kingly Messiah." The fulfillment of the prophecies concerning the "Priestly Messiah" can be found in "The Gospel of St. Luke." While the fulfillment of the prophecies concerning the "Kingly Messiah" can be found in "The Gospel of St. Matthew." This helps one to understand why the Essenes, who referred to themselves as the "Sons of Light", disappeared from history at the beginning of the Christian era; for they had completed their mission, within the messianic Birth Mysteries, through the incarnation of Christ.

Cosmic Midnight

It is from the direction of the constellation Leo the Lion that we experience the "Cosmic Midnight", or turning-point between earthly incarnations (XIII). After reaching beyond the sphere of Saturn to the Zodiac, to the "ring-pass-not" or outer-limit of the period between our incarnations, we make our descent into physical incarnation upon Earth - with the fruits of our sojourn in the Cosmos centered within the akashic center of the heart. Furthermore, there is yet another connection of the Birth Mysteries to the constellation of Leo, which is described by Rudolf Steiner in the lecture entitled, "The Cosmic Origin of the Human Form" which can be found in the lecture cycle that was published under the title, *Man's Life on Earth and in the Spiritual Worlds*:

> . . . there is a time between death and new birth when we go through the Sun while the Sun is in the sign of Leo. (It need not be at birth; it can be farther back in time.) . . . we unite with the interior of the Sun. What do you imagine the interior of the Sun to be? If you could enter there, you would find it altogether different from what our physicists naively and unwittingly suppose. The interior of the Sun is no mere ball of gas; it is in fact something less than space - a realm where space itself has been taken away. If you begin by imagining an extended space in which some pressure is prevailing, you must conceive the interior of the Sun rather as a realm of suction. It is a negative space - space that is emptier than empty. Few people have an adequate idea of what this means. Now when you go through there, again you have a definite spiritual experience which you are able to elaborate and work upon, and as you do so it becomes the form of the human heart . . . the heart form is fashioned from the Sun. But this is only possible when the Sun contains the forces which issue from it as from the constellation Leo.

The ancient Egyptians and Greeks, among others, saw the central significance of the heart, in fact, they considered the mind to be centered in the heart. In our own experience, we see that though we examine our lives with our thinking, we make our decisions ultimately through our feelings.

The ancient Egyptians communicated in hieroglyphics, which is a picture language that is more consistent with the picture-forming nature of the Sentient-Soul, which preceded the development of the Intellectual-Soul with its tendency to relate in concepts rather than pictures. In a scene that is often painted on examples of the ancient Egyptian text, *The Book of Coming Forth by Day*, the heart is shown being weighed upon a scale (Libra) against the ostrich feather of the goddess Ma'at, who represents truth and cosmic order. Standing to one side is Thoth the Egyptian equivalent of the Graeco-Roman, Hermes-Mercury. Thoth (or Djehuti to use the more ancient Egyptian name) is writing down the dictation of the heart while it is being weighed against the feather of Ma'at, representing truth and order. This is a perfect image of the central place of the heart in the ancient Egyptian's experience of what today is perceived inwardly as conscience, except that the ancient Egyptians saw Ma'at, or cosmic order, as something that was surrounding them from outside and streaming in as cosmic wisdom, due to the very different configuration of the Sentient-Soul forces at that time.

Later on, during the epoch of the Intellectual-Soul, the ancient Greeks still saw the ancient equivalent to what we now call conscience as an external drama, up to the time of the early part of the 5th century B.C. This is evident in Orestes' description of the assault of the Erinyes, (the avenging furies that approach the wrongdoer from outside). Yet only a few decades later, we find Euripides (c. 450 B.C.) referring to the hearing of an inner voice of conscience. Rudolf Steiner points this out in the lecture cycle *The East in the Light of the West,* as being the entry of conscience into human consciousness as a result of the approach of the Christ to the Earth realm. In the present epoch of the Consciousness-Soul, we speak of "pangs of conscience"; whereas, in the next cultural epoch, the epoch of the Spirit-Self, we shall be able to feel the suffering of others as a result of the development of the heart as an organ of karmic cognition through the forces of the Life-Spirit - which are centered in the heart - and which will unfold in mankind through the entry of Christ into Earth evolution.

Looking at the constellation of Leo from an even wider cosmic veiwpoint, we find that we shall experience the Vulcan incarnation of the Earth (which is the end of the seven-fold evolutionary chain, of which our whole human Earth evolution is but one seventh of the journey) oriented to the same point where we began; that is, in relationship to the constellation of Leo - which was our orientation at the beginning of the Old Saturn incarnation of the Earth. The exception being that our experience of the forces of Leo in the far distant Vulcan incarnation of the Earth shall be entirely different - for we will have achieved in the Vulcan period (the seventh) the rank of Archai, the stage of spiritual evolution that is called by Rudolf Steiner; the Spirits of Personality, or Time Spirits (**IV**).

In the second lecture of the lecture cycle published under the title *Karmic Relationships - Esoteric Studies, Volume V*, Rudolf Steiner vividly describes the central significance of the development of the heart, as it relates to our spiritual evolution, within an individual human life:

> *What we must realize in all its profound significance is that during his life in the Cosmos between death and a new birth, man himself fashions and shapes what he bears within him. In external life man perceives little, very little, of his own make-up and organization. An organ can only really be understood when there is knowledge of its cosmic origin. Think of the noblest organ of all - the human heart. Scientists today dissect the embryo, observe how the heart gradually takes shape and give no further thought to the matter. But this outer, plastic structure, the human heart, is in truth the product of what each individual, in co-operation with the Gods, has elaborated between death and a new birth. In the life between death and a new birth man must work, to begin with, in the direction leading from the Earth towards the zodiacal constellation of Leo. This stream which flows from the Earth towards the constellation of Leo teems with forces and it is along this direction that the human being must work in order that when the time comes he may project the germinal beginnings of the heart - a vessel in which cosmic forces are contained. Then, having passed through this region in the far spaces of the Universe, man comes to regions nearer the Earth; he passes into the Sun sphere. Here again forces are at work which bring the heart to a further stage of development. And then man enters the region where he is already in contact with what may be called the Earth-warmth. Out yonder in cosmic space there is no Earth-warmth, but something altogether different. In the region of the Earth-warmth the preparation of the human heart reaches the third stage. The forces streaming in the direction of Leo out of which the human heart is fashioned are purely moral and religious forces; in its initial*

stages of development the heart contains only moral and religious forces. To anyone who realizes this it seems outrageous that modern natural science should regard the stars merely as neutral, physical masses, ignoring the moral element altogether. When man is passing through the Sun-region, these moral forces are taken hold of by the etheric forces. And it is not until man comes still nearer to the Earth, to the warmth, that the forces which shape the physical seed for the being of soul-and-spirit who is descending, begin to be active.

Each organ is produced and shaped by cosmic forces. In very truth man bears the stars of heaven within him. He is connected with the forces of the whole Cosmos . . .

When we look from the Earth out into the Cosmos beyond the Earth, then, for the first time, part of the world is revealed. For after all it is only a part that becomes visibly manifest. The stars are not what they present to the physical eye - what the eye beholds is merely the sense-image - but to this extent they are, after all, visible. The whole world through which we pass between death and a new birth is invisible, supersensible. There are regions which lie above and beyond the world that is revealed to the senses. Man belongs to these realms of supersensible existence just as surely as he belongs to the world of sense. We can have no real knowledge of the being of man until we consider the life he has spent in the vast cosmic expanse. And then it dawns upon us that when, having passed through the gate of death into the Cosmos, we have returned to the Earth once again, the connections with this cosmic life are still alive within us. There is within us a being who once dwelt on the Earth, ascended into the Cosmos, passed through the cosmic realms and has again come down into a restricted existence on Earth. Gradually we learn to perceive what we were in an earlier existence on Earth; our gaze is carried away from the physical, transported into the spiritual. For when we look back into earlier lives the power inherent in initiation-science takes from us all desire for materialistic pictures.

In this connection, too, many strange things have happened. At one period there were certain theosophists who knew from oriental teachings that man passes through many *earthly lives, but they wanted a materialistic picture although they deceived themselves to the contrary. It was said at that time that the physical organism of man disintegrates at death but that an atom remains and passes over in some miraculous way to the next earthly life. It was called the "permanent atom." This was simply a way of providing a materialistic picture. But all inclination for materialistic thinking of this kind vanishes when one realizes that in very truth the human heart is woven and shaped by the Cosmos.*

The liver, on the other hand, forms in the near neighborhood of the Earth; the liver has only little direct connection with the cosmic expanse. The knowledge gradually acquired from initiation-science makes us realize that the heart could not exist at all if it had not been prepared and inwardly formed by the Cosmos. But an organ like the liver or the lungs only begins to form in the neighborhood of the Earth. Viewed from the Cosmos, man is akin to the Earth in respect of the lungs and liver; in respect of the heart he is a cosmic being. In man we begin to discern the whole Universe. According to spiritual anatomy, the lungs and certain other organs might be depicted by sketching the Earth; the forces contained in these organs operate in a realm near the Earth. But for the heart one would have to make a sketch of the whole Universe. The whole Universe is concentrated, compressed, in man. Man is in truth a Microcosm, a stupendous mystery. But knowledge of the Macrocosm into which man is transformed after death is free from every element of materiality. We now learn to recognize the true connections between the spiritual and the physical, between one quality of soul and another.

In *The Astronomy Course*, Rudolf Steiner indicated that through the proper application of mathematics, one can analyze the structure of the interior of the heart and find that it is in actuality a metamorphosis of the form of the human body; which arises as a microcosmic reflection of macrocosmic processes. And so, likewise, the heart is also a miniature expression of the Macrocosm - although in this case it is inside-out.

Throughout Anthroposophical Spiritual Science one finds the reoccurring theme of the relationship between the center and the periphery. The fundamental manifestations of this principle in the human body are the heart and the nervous system. The heart is the center of the being of man, like the Sun within the planetary system when viewed heliocentrically. The nervous system, on the other hand, is like the Zodiac (this is most evident in the twelve pairs of cranial nerves in the dome of the skull). Rudolf Steiner tells us that the nervous system is a manifestation of that which once streamed between the stars and planets, but has since fallen into materiality. On the other hand, the blood itself is of an earthly nature; but through the nerve-sense system acting upon it, the blood can receive something of Cosmic Life.

This unfoldment of Cosmic Life within humanity became possible through the Mystery of Golgotha. This is so because, through the shedding of His blood, Christ brought new life to humanity by transforming the bread and the wine (nerves and blood). For although the nerves conceal the mystery of Cosmic Life, the nerves had to take up something of the death processes. The nerves had, in a very real sense, to participate in death processes in order to manifest within the physical world. Because of this occult reality it was necessary that Christ Jesus perform the *Grail Deed* on Golgotha, for He was the first and only being from the realm of the "Upper Gods" to experience death, and through experiencing death was able to overcome death through the Resurrection (**XXVI**). And now He can act within the human heart, through the etherization of the blood, to resurrect that which had fallen into death processes, within the nerve-sense realm. For as Christ has said; "I have come to give you more life and that abundantly."

It is a great gift to mankind that the nature of the blood, which was originally derived from earthly mineral processes, was spiritually transformed through the Incarnation of Christ within Jesus of Nazareth at the Baptism in the River Jordan, so that the blood became capable of being the bearer of the human Ego as a living spiritual being.

And likewise, it is an immeasurable gift to mankind - a gift of tremendous courage which we are incapable of repaying - that through the Crucifixion and the Resurrection, by the action of the spiritual heart-forces that worked within His Holy Blood, Christ Jesus transformed that aspect of mankind which had succumbed to the world of death within the nerve-sense realm, so that gradually more and more, mankind through receiving the fruit of the Mystery of Golgotha, by the working of the Holy Spirit, could evolve into beings of Cosmic Life once again (**XIV**).

IX

The Hermit

Virgo - Kyriotetes - Spirits of Wisdom - Isis-Sophia - Spirit-Man

On the Hermit arcanum can be seen a robed ancient Initiate who has left his secret cave hermitage in order to assist mankind in their struggle to pass through "the valley of the shadow of death." He has climbed upon a mountain peak and is holding, in his right hand, a lantern that radiates light from a six-pointed star; and, in his left hand, he holds an upright staff - symbolizing the uprightness of the "I Am." He is looking down upon mankind below, illuminating their path up the mountain with his lantern. The six-pointed light in his lantern represents the spiritual light of the "Heart-Sun"; for, in the Kabbalah, the sixth sefirah represents the sphere of the Sun - which is on the *middle-path* of the "Tree of Life." Concerning the *middle-path* it is said that: "Equilibrium is the basis of the work"; and so, one must find the point-of-balance between the two "pillars" of Rigor and Mercy, in the Temple of Solomon, to find the "Sun behind the Sun."

The "Midnight Sun", or the "Sun behind the Sun" - is related to the experience of enlightenment; which is called in the Kabbalah - Kether the "Crown." When the enlightened ancient Egyptian Initiates spoke of their experience of a "Midnight Sun", it was in reference to their clairvoyant perception, through the Earth, of the *inner* spiritual radiance of the Sun. They symbolized this experience in the *outer* Cosmos as Kephra, the scarab who moves the bark of the Sun god Re' above the eastern horizon after its nightly journey in the under-world - through the body of the star-goddess Nut. Enlightenment, the *inner* counterpart to the "Midnight Sun", is none other than the radiance of the Atma, or Spirit-Man, experienced through the agency of the Spirit-Self as the light of the Holy Spirit.

The paradoxical relationship between the two different realms of light (that is, the spiritual *inner-light*, and the physical *outer-light*) is resolved by the realization that the spiritual *inner-light* is experienced through cognitional forces that are developed from out of the Cosmic Feeling realm; and that, ultimately, as far as the Physical-Body is concerned, the *inner light* is experienced through spiritual processes that occur between the pineal gland and the heart; for, the peripheral, spiritual light of the Holy Spirit meets the indwelling "Christ in you" within the heart, and forms spiritual organs in the head and the heart which begin to radiate and bring one to an experience of *inner-light*. On the other hand, physical light has also formed organs - the two eyes, to serve as its counterparts, and form a bridge to the "fallen" optic nerves.

It is through the Spirit-Man being a manifestation of the spiritual world, that it is of light; but through its descent into matter, the spiritual light became, as it were, polarized and encased in the darkness of the physical world. This is what is referred to in Gnosticism when they speak of Sophia Achamoth, the "fallen" Sophia, or "fallen" light of wisdom that has been exiled into the world of matter (**VIII**). The rescuing of the "fallen" Sophia forces is the challenge of the Grail path - the rescuing of the fair damsel from the dragon's lair. For Isis-Sophia has been "slain" by Lucifer and exiled into the world of the Zodiac.

The resurrection of Sophia (wisdom) is brought about through the living spiritual activity of a Christ-filled heart. In order for this to occur, one must have what is described in the Grail story as, "a love as strong as death." Sophia (the light of wisdom) must be reawakened through the equilibrium that is brought about by the activity of Cosmic Thinking mediating between Cosmic Feeling and Cosmic Willing. The Sophia (Cosmic Feeling) must be brought to her "Chymical Wedding" (**I**) with the Christ (Cosmic Thinking) within the cave of the heart (Cosmic Willing). "Salus per Naturam Sponsus Praesentandi Nuptiis" ("Rescue through Nature the Guest of the Bridegroom at the Wedding").

It says in the *Bible*; "God is Light." Jesus said; "If therefore thine eyes be single, thy body shall be filled with God's light." In the Vedas of ancient India, the light of God is described as "brighter than a thousand suns." This light is initially experienced at the focal point of the Ajna or brow center, and is the true origin of the term "enlightenment." The experience of the light is the experience of that which is eternal in man, the reincarnating monad; which is of the one light by its own nature - it is literally a part of the eternal light of God. For as the Hindu scriptures say; "Atma and Brahma are one." Likewise, the Kabbalah says; "Kether (the Light of the Crown) is in Malkuth (the Earthly Kingdom)" (**VII**).

To experience the light for the sake of liberating only oneself, is to join the Children of Lucifer (Phosphoros = the light bearer) and to deny the light is to fall prey to the minions of Ahriman (Satan = the spirit of the darkness of matter); but to radiate the light of Sophia in love to all beings is to become one of the Brothers and Sisters of Christ, a *Christophorus*, or bearer of the Christos. For as it is written; "My little children, of whom I travail in birth again until Christ be formed in you." ("Galatians", 4:6).

Although the Divine Light is first experienced at the point of equilibrium in the brow center (the two-petaled ajna chakra that relates to the sphere of Jupiter (**V**) and thereby to the Kyriotetes, the Spirits of Wisdom), the true "seat" of the "clear-light" of being is in the heart - the eternally living radiance of the Atma - or more appropriately of the Jivatma (Sanskrit: Jiva = individual soul as a part of the One Life, Atma = spirit; the spirit of life, or Atma-Budhi - the Life-Spirit in conjunction with the Atma or Spirit-Man; which according to the Advaita Vedanta or "non-dual" Vedanta of Gaudapada and Shankara is projected by the Atman, or "non-dual" universal consciousness, into a "dualistic-mayavic" state of manifestation, or relative state of existence as an individuated being). In "The Gospel of John" (1:4) it says; "In Him was life, and the life was the light of men." St. Paul after his blinding experience on the road to Damascus spoke of, "the Christ in you"; in "Galatians" (4:19), St. Paul says; "And because ye are sons, God hath sent forth the Spirit of his Son into your hearts, crying, Abba (Father)."

Rudolf Steiner tells us that humanity can seek the Christ in the etheric world of life, and receive the blessings of the Life-Spirit of Christ from (what is called in the East) the Budhic plane of being - which is the higher counterpart to the etheric world of life. In the East, this meeting of the universal life with the individual life - within the heart - is of central importance to the spiritual destiny of man.

H. P. Blavatsky in *The Secret Doctrine* (volume 1, page 132) refers to the journey of the liberated soul after death, according to the teachings of the Hindu Visishtadvaita ("qualified non-dualism") school of Ramanuja (c. 1050-1137 A.D.), which points out the central role of the life that dwells within "the cave of the heart."

> *After reaching Moksha (a state of bliss meaning 'release from Bandha' or bondage), bliss is enjoyed by it in a place called Paramapadha, which place is not material, but made of Suddasatwa . . . There, Mukhtas or Jivatamas (Monads) who have attained Moksha, are never again subject to the qualities of either matter or Karma. 'But if they choose, for the sake of doing good to the world, they may incarnate on Earth.' The way to Paramapadha, or the immaterial worlds, from this world, is called Devayana. When a person has attained Moksha and the body dies:*

> 'The Jiva (Soul) goes with Sukshma Sarira [the illusion body] from the heart of the body, to the Brahmarandra in the crown of the head, traversing Shushumna, a nerve [more precisely a spiritual-etheric channel that is a counterpart to the nerves that lead from the vicinity of the heart to the spine] connecting the heart with the Brahmarandra. The Jiva breaks through the Brahmarandra and goes to the region of the Sun (Suryamandala) through the solar rays. Then it goes through a dark spot in the Sun, to Paramapadha [the place where - according to the Visishtadwaita Vedantins - bliss is enjoyed by those who reach Moksha (bliss). This "place" is not material but made, says the Catechism of that sect, 'of Suddhasatwa, the essence of which the body of Iswara' (Divine Spirit), the Lord, "is made", says H. P. B. in the, "Theosophical Glossary"] The Jiva is directed on its way by the Supreme Wisdom acquired by Yoga. The Jiva thus proceeds to Paramapadha by the aid of Athivahikas (bearers in transit), known by the names of Archi-Ahas . . . Aditya, Prajapati, etc. The Archis here mentioned are certain pure souls, etc., etc.' (**Visishtadwaita Catechism,** by Pundit Bhashyacharya)

This mention of the guidance by "certain pure souls" is reminiscent of Dante's *Divine Comedy*, where he is guided first by Beatrice, and then later, as he passes to the highest levels of Heaven, his guide becomes St. Bernard of Clairvaux (which means, "the valley of light", clair = light vaux = valley), the Cistercian monk who was the author of the rules of the Order of the Knights Templars and a central figure of the Middle Ages.

In his essay, "The Ether in the Heart", the Traditionalist author Rene Guenon discusses the significance of the "Atma which dwells within the heart" within both Eastern and Western esoteric traditions. In this exposition, Guenon takes note of Dante's work *Vita Nuova* (2) where Dante speaks of the "spiritu della vita", or "spirit of life" that dwells within the heart, in the same cavity spoken of within the doctrines of Hinduism concerning the Jivatma; and that the expression "spiritu della vita" which Dante uses, ". . . is as literal a translation as possible of the

Sanskrit term Jivatma, though it is most unlikely that he should have had any means of knowing this." Rene Guenon goes on to make the point that; ". . . the 'Atma which dwells in the heart' is not simply the Jivatma, the individual and human soul, but is also the absolute and unconditioned Atma, the divine and universal Spirit . . ."

It is at this point that we arrive at one of the most subtle realms of esoteric doctrine; for it is here that we find many apparent contradictions concerning the manner in which the Atma is manifested within the human realm; therefore it would perhaps be useful to consult the early Hindu Theosophist, that Rudolf Steiner once referred to as "the very wise T. Subba Row", concerning the nature of the Atma or 1st principle as presented in his article entitled, "The Constitution of the Microcosm", that was published in *The Theosophist* (May, 1887):

> . . .*One fact about it is pretty nearly certain. It must be considered as the Logos, there being no other entity in the Cosmos which possesses the attributes assigned to it. It has been often declared, as far as my recollection goes, that the ancient occultists regarded this principle as something existing outside of the body and not in the body. It was once loosely stated that this principle should be considered as a principle running through the other principles [pg. 197, Five Years of Theosophy]. This might be true as regards its light or aura; but the Logos itself is never present in the microcosm except when it finally enters into a man before his final emancipation from the trammels of incarnate existence.*

It is these fine points, which are so concisely made by T. Subba Row, that are critical to the proper understanding of the nature of the Atma, or Spirit-Man; for, in the above, we are given concepts that are useful for understand the various indications by Rudolf Steiner concerning the "location" of the Atma - that could be interpreted as being contradictory; i.e., focused at a point between the eyes, centered within the heart, distributed throughout the "whole being of man"; and finally, like the Spirit-Self, it descends into man from outside. For, in the "higher sense", the totality of the human being is a, so to speak, "projection" of the Atma; and so, through being "projections" of the 1st principle or Atma, the other 6 principles should be considered as being "one" with the higher, or 1st principle; but this is a description from a "non-dual" absolutist-standpoint - that is from beyond the relative states of being. But when speaking in the context of evolution *within the realm of time* we must conceive of the Atma not only in terms of its transcendental nature as pure will (Voluntarism, XVIII) - but also in terms of its functionality *within the realm of space* as the radiance which, by its reflection, makes the independent being of man arise as a multiplicity of forms or principles unfolding in time.

The Holy Trinity and the Three-Fold Order of the Hierarchies

1st Logos - Father
2nd Logos - Son
3rd Logos - Holy Spirit

Father —
1st Hierarchy - Spirits of Strength
1 - Seraphim (Father)
2 - Cherubim (Son)
3 - Thrones (Holy Spirit)

Son —
2nd Hierarchy - Spirits of Light
1 - Kyriotetes (Father)
2 - Dynamis (Son)
3 - Exusiai (Holy Spirit)

Holy Spirit —
3rd Hierarchy - Spirits of Soul
1 - Archai (Father)
2 - Archangeloi (Son)
3 - Angeloi (Holy Spirit)

Through being the highest of the three Spirits of Light, the Kyriotetes are connected to the 1st Logos in a unique way. By their inclusion within the second hierarchy of the Spirits of Light, the Kyriotetes have a special role in relationship to the 2nd Logos. In addition to these relationships, the first principle of the Kyriotetes dwells on the first Logic plane (that of the

Father), while their second principle dwells on the second Logoic plane (that of the Son), and their third principle dwells on the third Logoic plane (that of the Holy Spirit).

This is not to say that the Kyriotetes are the Logos - but that, as regards to their relationship to mankind, the Kyriotetes are the purest embodiment of the Logoic wisdom, and have a very special mission in service to the Divine Plan concerning the life, form, and consciousness of mankind. In addition, this shows a very key group of relationships, that are very helpful toward understanding the central place of the Kyriotetes within the Sophia Mystery, and consequently of the archetype of the human being. Likewise, the manner in which the interrelationships of the other Spiritual Hierarchies are displayed in the preceding diagram is very helpful toward developing an understanding the nature of their being and work in the Cosmos (Gnosis, **XVIII**; Spiritism, **XXI**).

In developing the idea as to how the Atma or Spirit-Man came to be the pinnacle of the spiritual makeup of mankind, Rudolf Steiner describes the relationship of the Spiritual Hierarchies to the Zodiac and the principles in man. One way of looking at the relationship of the realm of the Zodiac to the Spiritual Hierarchies is that - on a macrocosmic level - the constellation of Virgo, or the Virgin, relates to the activity of the Kyriotetes, or Spirits of Wisdom (**IX**); which are the highest beings of the Spirits of Light - the second hierarchy within the three-fold schema of the spiritual hierarchies.

From another viewpoint that is - microcosmically - the constellation of Virgo relates to the Atma or "divine spark" that is focused within the core of the spiritual being of man. The Atma is the highest level of manifestation within the seven-fold human archetype; that, through its primary nature - is a mirror of the highest levels of divinity. This mystery is touched upon by Angelus Silesius: "Man, if thou wishest to see God, there or here on earth, thy heart must first become a pure mirror." This idea is reminiscent of the famous saying of Meister Eckhart: "The eye by which I see God is the same eye by which He sees me." This vision of God, as if in a mirror, is elaborated further by Meister Eckhart (**XVIII, XXI**):

> *When I saw into myself I saw God in me and everything God ever made in earth and heaven. Let me explain it better. As you know right well, anyone who faces God in the mirror of truth sees everything depicted in that mirror: all things, that is to say...*

The Seven Principles and the Hierarchies

Archai	Archangel	Angel	Human
1st Principle			
2nd Principle	1st Principle		
3rd Principle	2nd Principle	1st Principle	
4th Spirit-Man	3rd Spirit-Man	2nd Spirit-Man	1st Spirit-Man
5th Life-Spirit	4th Life-Spirit	3rd Life-Spirit	2nd Life-Spirit
6th Spirit-Self	5th Spirit-Self	4th Spirit-Self	3rd Spirit-Self
7th Ego	6th Ego	5th Ego	4th Ego
	7th Astral	6th Astral	5th Astral
		7th Etheric	6th Etheric
			7th Physical

It can be seen in the preceding chart, that the ascending ranks of the Spiritual Hierarchies manifest their seven-fold principles on ascending planes of being. The lowest principle of the Angels is the Etheric-Body; therefore, they have a first principle that is one stage higher than the Spirit-Man, or Atma, of a human being; so that, while our first principle, the Spirit-Man, is on the same plane of being as the lowest principle of the Kyriotetes, or Spirits of Wisdom (**IX**); the Angel's first principle, is one stage higher on the same plane of being as the lowest principle of the Thrones. The Archangels, who have as their lowest principle an Astral-Body, are one stage beyond the Angels. Thus the Archangels have a highest, or first principle, on the same plane of being as the lowest principle of the Cherubim, or Spirits of Harmony; which is one stage higher yet than the first principle of the Angels, so that the Archangel's third principle is on the same plane of being as the Spirit-Man of a human being, which is the same plane of being as the second principle of the Angels. The Archai, or Spirits of Personality, are one stage higher yet than the Archangels; and so, the first principle of the Archai is on the same plane of being as the lowest principle of the Seraphim, or Spirits of Love.

The lowest principle of the Archangels is two stages above the physical, within the astral world. The Archangel's densest manifestation can be seen clairvoyantly on the other side of sunlight; as in the Arthurian Mysteries, where they would observe the sunlight as it shone on the waves hitting the shore at the rocky cliffs of Tintagel. This natural event would provide a window, as it were, for the Arthurian initiates to experience the interplay between the Archangels and the Angels, as the Angel's densest potential manifestation is akin to water vapor. This watery aspect of the Angels is also recalled in the legendary healing spirits of the wells, such as Chalice Well on the island of Glastonbury, or the well at Chartres Cathedral. Likewise, in the *Bible*, you have the story of the angel that is "troubling the waters" at the pool of Bethesda.

"The Stone the Builder's Rejected . . ."

There is a very profound mystery revealed through the manner in which Christ descended from the constellation of Virgo the Virgin (Spirit-Man) and incarnated into the Physical-Body of Jesus of Nazareth on September 23rd, 29 A.D., at the time of the Sun's ingress into the constellation of Libra the Scales (Life-Spirit); for, as we know from Rudolf Steiner, the Physical-Body of a human being can be seen as a reflection of the Atma, or Spirit-Man; and furthermore, when Christ descended to Earth He left His Atma, or Spirit-Man behind - within the Sun realm.

This means that while the Sophia principle, or Spirit-Man centers its rays (which find their cosmic origin in the region of the Virgin) from the periphery into the "Sun in man" within the "cave of the heart" - the Spirit-Man of Christ, the "Great Sun Being", remained within the Sun realm. In leaving His Spirit-Man behind within the Sun realm, Christ's earthly manifestation in Jesus of Nazareth was able to become a, so to speak, "Grail" to receive the Sophia principle, or Spirit-Man of the pure Nathan-Jesus Being, the Adam Kadmon, in such a manner so that, as the "Representative of Mankind", He completely transformed the future outcome of human evolution, all the way down to the most physical levels of being, through reasserting the "Sun laws" - that were established by the Kyriotetes out of the region of the Virgin, during the Old Sun incarnation of the Earth - without the loss of human freedom.

This mystery has far reaching implications for the being and destiny of humanity during their sojourn through the Sun realm before birth, and in the effect that this has upon the subsequent development of life, form, and consciousness in human, earthly life; and likewise, this mystery also profoundly changes the nature of the after-death state - through Christ's intimate relationship to human evolution as the "new Lord of Karma."

Furthermore, this mystery can give one insights into the account of the Crucifixion by St. John; for, according to "The Gospel of St. John", not a bone was broken in the body of Christ Jesus at the Crucifixion. This was necessary so that the prophecy, "a bone of Him shall not be broken" would be fulfilled, and so that the true mirroring of the Spirit-Man by the Physical-Body could be accomplished through the integration of the "Mystic Lamb" with the human form and the Sophia principle, by the penetration of the Spirit of Christ, in the final stages of the Crucifixion, all the way into the most physical substance of the skeleton.

With the completion and fulfillment of the Mystery of Golgotha through the Resurrection, the "Great Architect of the Universe" had entered into the stream of human evolution. This can be seen as the highest manifestation of the redemptive stream that descends from above to below - the Avatar stream - with the incarnation of Christ in Jesus of Nazareth being the highest earthly manifestation of the Godhead that has ever, or will ever occur within Earth evolution (**XXVI**). The *Macrocosmic-Christ* had incarnated into the *Microcosmic-Jesus*; thereby establishing, through this Deed, an entirely new process of development for "infant humanity." This Deed brought about the fulfillment of the human archetypal being, the "Adam Kadmon" through the "Sun laws", and works as a spiritual "leaven" toward the redemption of mankind, all the way down to the most physical levels of being; and likewise, also transformed mankind's relationship to the highest principle - the Spirit-Man.

Working in concert with the Christ-impulse, that descended from the spiritual world above - from the realm of the "Upper Gods" down to mankind on the Earth below - you have that stream of Initiates that have worked from the earthly, human realm below developing upward toward the Spiritual World (**XXV**). These Initiates have been servants of Christ since ancient times, and are referred to in the East as Bodhisattvas.

If you think of Christ Jesus as being merely a human initiate, you cannot truly comprehend His mission regarding the evolution of mankind. Through Christ being the highest and most complete manifestation of the Godhead in Earth evolution, He is, what would be called in the Sanskrit language of ancient India, the Maha-Avatar of the whole scheme of human and angelical evolution - the most complete manifestation of the being that is beyond the nine Spiritual Hierarchies, which they called Vishvakarman (Sanskrit, "all-creating").

Vishvakarman is the Divine Being "beyond the gaze of the seven Rishis" that was known as the "Great Architect of the Universe"; and, as the Takshaka ("carpenter"), he was the Divine patron of architects. Vishvakarman's festival begins the month of Bhadrapada (Bhadrapada = "beautiful feet", August-September), and on that day no building tools are to be used. (It is a curious fact that Bhadrapada is also the "Great Square" in the constellation of Pegasus; which is near Pisces, and opposite Virgo;

and so, the *month* of Bhadrapada has not coincided by precession, with the *constellation* of Bhadrapada, since the epoch of Virgo, **XXV**). In the *Vedas*, Vishvakarman is the creative aspect of Brahma - who made a sacrifice of himself as a sacrifice for all creation; and therefore, all sacrifices were thought to help sustain the Cosmos through their relationship to this great, universal sacrifice. In the *Rig Veda*, Vishvakarman is depicted as binding together Heaven and Earth. Vishvakarman is equivalent, in the *Satapatha Brahmana*, to Prajapati ("Lord of creation") who is above the other 33 gods. Vishvakarman had an earlier, partial Avatar manifestation as Krishna (b. December 25th) who died during a multiple planetary conjunction that occurred on February 17th-18th, 3102 B.C. at the start of the lesser Kali Yuga (Iron Age), the 5,000 year cycle that ended in 1899 A.D.

The fundamental difference between Krishna and Christ Jesus is that Christ did not fully incarnate within the Physical-Body of Krishna as He did in Jesus of Nazareth. For the Christ-Being had only *overlighted* Krishna - through the Nathan-Being - in a way that was more intimate, but similar to, the manner in which the Christ had accomplished the three "Pre-Earthly Deeds" that brought to humanity the evolutionary gifts of uprightness, speaking, and thinking (concerning which, see the chapter on the Emperor arcanum). On the other hand, the incarnation process of Christ into Jesus of Nazareth began at the Baptism in the River Jordan, and proceeded all the way to His complete integration with the Spirit-Man of the Nathan-Being - which culminated with His incarnation into the mineral nature of the bones during the Crucifixion upon Golgotha.

In the Ancient Mysteries, before the Mystery of Golgotha, Christ was always perceived as being outside of mankind, gradually approaching the Earth - beginning from beyond the Zodiac, and then proceeding through the heart of the Sun. At the Mystery of Golgotha, through the shedding of His blood into the "Holy Grail" of the Earth, Christ entered directly, in a human way, into Earth evolution. As a result, mankind must find the Christ within, for He has entered into the hearts of mankind - "Not I, but Christ in me." This is not to say that He wishes for us to become automatons to the Christ Impulse that is working within us, but rather that we should freely develop upon the path of love, guided by His example and by His continuing presence within human evolution. For as Christ said; "I shall be with you always." The fruit of this intervention by Christ on behalf of mankind will gradually lead, towards the end of Earth evolution, to the transformation of the carbonic nature of the Physical-Body into the "Phantom" Physical-Body, the Atma-Physical - which is the "body of light" that is the true Resurrection-Body of the "New Jerusalem."

X

The Wheel of Fortune

Jupiter - Archangel Zachariel - Thought - 2 Petaled Lotus

Through spiritual disciplines, such as those outlined in Rudolf Steiner's book, *Knowledge of Higher Worlds and Its Attainment*, movement begins to take place in the astral centers, or chakras, transforming their colors from a muddy, cloudy hue of earthen tones, to the bright, radiant colors of the rainbow. The two-petaled ajna chakra is the initial focal point of this spiritual activity, which draws together at the point of equilibrium near the root of the nose. As a result of the development of the brow chakra one can eventually develop sufficient inner radiance to illuminate the world of dreamless sleep. This world is dark or unconscious until it becomes illuminated with the light of one's own inner being. The initial stage of preparation for this path of occult development is study. For, to begin our development - we must first have the thought to do so.

The Seven Stages of Rosicrucian Training

1. Study - Entering the Invisible College - Anthroposophia
The Raven
2. Imagination - Riding the Lion - Angeloi
The Peacock
3. Inspiration - Reading the Occult Script - Archangeloi
The Swan
4. Intuition - Preparation of the Philosopher's Stone - Archai
The Phoenix
5. Correspondence between the Macrocosm and Microcosm - Exusiai
The Adam Kadmon
6. Living into the Macrocosm - Dynamis
Entering the Palace of the King
7. Divine Bliss - Kyriotetes
The Chymical Wedding

The Rosicrucian training proceeds in seven stages "although not necessarily consecutive." The seven stages of Rosicrucian training shown above were given by Rudolf Steiner in the lecture cycle *Theosophy of the Rosicrucians*, and elsewhere. In the preceding chart I have also included the Spiritual Hierarchies and the alchemical images that are related to these seven stages of initiation.

The Rosicrucian initiation drama, *The Chymical Wedding of Christian Rosenkreutz* by Johann Valentin Andreae, culminates on the seventh day with the hero of the story Christian Rosenkreutz and his other associates, receiving the title "Eques Aurei Lapidis", which translated from the Latin is "Knights of the Golden Stone."

The "Golden Stone" is an image of the accomplishment of the alchemystical initiation of Christian Rosenkreutz that is being portrayed in this imaginative drama, it can also be thought of as a symbolic counterpart to the Holy Grail that is found in the initiation drama of *Parzival*. The "Golden Stone" can also be seen as an image of the complete series of 22 Major Arcana of the Tarot, and consequently, of the corresponding 22 fundamental aspects of initiation (**I**) when it is viewed imaginatively in the following manner.

A cube has 12 edges, which represent the 12 signs of the Zodiac. The 7 planets, on the other hand, are represented by the 7 axes of rotation that are formed by imagining lines that run through the center; 3 at right angles to the 6 sides, and 4 diagonally from the 8 opposite corners. This gives us 19 Arcana out of 22, for the remaining 3 Arcana we include the alchemical elements of sulphur, mercury and salt. To do this we only need to visualize a point in the center with lines radiating out to a sphere which surrounds the periphery; thereby representing the three-fold nature of the alchemical elements. To carry this further as a visualization, one must imagine the cube rotating on each of the 7 axes of rotation; first individually, and then combining the movements together one at a time.

In this Rosicrucian image of the "Golden Stone" we have an imaginative symbol to represent the "Sun laws" that were established in the Old Sun incarnation of the Earth (**IV**) through the relationship between the center and the periphery. These "Sun laws" came about through the working of the Kyriotetes from the center of Old Sun; which, in turn, inspired the Archangels to respond from the periphery by radiating light. It is the integration of these radiant "Sun laws" into the hearts and minds of humanity that will lead them to their angelic existence in the future Jupiter incarnation of the Earth.

If one works with symbols such as this only within the world of thought, it generates from the etheric world an activity that extends into the astral world. If we imbue this symbol with feelings of aspiration towards a higher spiritual goal, then we extend our activity into the lower levels of Heaven; which realm is known in occultism as Lower Devachan. If we allow these higher feelings of aspiration to inspire us to do good deeds, only then does our activity extend into the higher levels of Heaven, or Higher Devachan. This aspect of spiritual development is dealt with at length in the lecture given by Rudolf Steiner in Leipzig on November 4th, 1911, entitled, "Jeshu ben Pandira Who Prepared the Way for an Understanding of the Christ Impulse", which is included in the collection of lectures that were published under the title, *Esoteric Christianity and the Mission of Christian Rosenkreutz*.

> **Upper Devachan - Will: moral action**
> **Lower Devachan - Feelings: aesthetic ideals**
> **Astral World - Thought: etheric nature**
> **Physical World - Corporeality: physical-material nature**

The Rosicrucian's clothed in symbolic form the path of initiation into supersensible knowledge. This method of working with symbols rather than concepts enabled the esoteric teachings to avoid the censure of the Church. This symbolical path was transmitted to the Rosicrucians from the Knights Templars, who had received it in turn from the Grail Brotherhood - the true successors to the Initiates of Egypt and the Holy Land. Rudolf Steiner gives us a picture of this esoteric Christian mystery wisdom in lecture six of the lecture cycle, given at The Hague in March of 1913, entitled, *The Effects of Spiritual Development*.

> *Symbolized by the brain situated in the skull, terrestrial man appears like an enchanted being living in a castle. We see our human entity as a being living in a castle. We see our human entity as a being imprisoned behind castle walls. The symbol of this, the shrunken symbol as it were, is our skull. Externally it appears in the form of a diminutive skull. But when we look at the etheric forces which fashion the skull then terrestrial man appears to us in fact as a being who, within the skull, finds himself imprisoned in this castle. And then from the*

rest of the organism there stream upwards the forces which sustain this being who is imprisoned in the skull as in a fortified castle. The forces are directed upwards; first the force which comes from the instrument of the human astral body, an instrument which extends through the organism; everything that inspires man and lends him strength and energy streams through the nerve fibers. In terrestrial man all this is united and appears as the mighty sword which he has forged for himself on earth. Then the forces of the blood stream upwards; we gradually feel them, we come to recognize them, and they appear as that which in reality wounds the 'brain' man lying in the enchanted castle of the skull. The forces which, in the etheric body, stream upwards towards the terrestrial man lying in the enchanted castle of the brain are like the blood-stained lance. And then we realize that we are able to observe everything that is permitted to stream towards the noblest part of the brain. Until now we did not have the slightest suspicion of this.

[the skull --- the enchanted castle]
[astral body and nerves --- the mighty sword]
[etheric body and blood --- the blood-stained lance]

... No matter how much animal flesh a man may eat, it is of no value for a certain part of his brain, it is simply ballast. Other organs may be nourished by it, but the etheric body of the brain immediately rejects all that comes from the animal kingdom. Indeed, from one part of the brain, from one small, important part of the brain, the etheric body rejects all that comes from the plant kingdom and tolerates only the mineral extract; there, in the vital part of the brain, it unites this mineral extract with the purest radiations entering through the sense organs. The purest elements in light, sound, and warmth here come in contact with the most refined products of the mineral kingdom; the noblest part of the brain is nourished by this union of the most delicate sense impressions with the most refined mineral products. The etheric body selects from the noblest part of the human brain all that comes from the plant and animal kingdoms. All the substances that man absorbs as food are directed toward the brain. But the brain has also less noble *parts; these are nourished by everything that is carried up to the brain and which also provides sustenance for the whole organism. It is only the noblest part of the brain that must be nourished by the most perfect union of sensory perceptions and the finest mineral extract. We thus learn to recognize a wonderful cosmic relationship between man and the rest of the Cosmos. We here perceive, as it were, a region where we are shown how human thought, through the instrument of the nervous system in the service of the astral body, forges the sword which lends man strength on earth; there we become acquainted with all that is mingled with the blood and which, to a certain extent, contributes to the death of all that is most noble in the brain. And this noblest element in the brain is continually sustained by the union of the most delicate sense perceptions with the purest products of the mineral kingdom. And then, during sleep, when thought is not using the brain, there stream towards the brain the products which have been formed in the lower organs of man from the plant and animal kingdoms.*

Thus, when we penetrate into our own etheric body, it seems as if we have reached an abyss, and beyond it we can see what is going on in the etheric body; and all this appears in mighty pictures representing the process of the spiritual man during sleep. The Ego and astral body - the spiritual man - descend into the castle which is simply a symbolic representation of what takes place in the skull where, wounded by the luciferic forces in the blood, the human being lies asleep, he whose countenance betrays that his strength lies in thinking - that which must open itself to be nourished by everything that originates in the kingdoms of nature, that which in its noblest part must be served by all that is most refined which we have described before - all this represented symbolically was the origin of the Grail legend. And the legend of the Holy Grail tells us of that miraculous food, prepared from the finest activities of the mineral extracts, whose purpose is to nourish the noblest part of man throughout his life on earth; for all other nourishment would kill him. It is this celestial food which the vessel of the Holy Grail contains.

And what otherwise takes place, what thrusts its way up from the other kingdoms we find unobtrusively depicted in the original Grail legend where a meal is described at which a haunch of venison is first served up. This invasion of the brain where forever floats the Grail - the vessel destined for the noblest nourishment of the human, who here lies in the castle of the brain and who is killed by every other form of nourishment - all this is depicted. And the best account is not that of Wolfram, but the account where it is presented externally, exoterically - for almost everyone, when his attention is drawn to it, can recognize that the legend of the Grail is an occult experience which everyone can experience every evening. The best account, despite a certain profanation, is that of Chrestien de Troyes. And though he has given many indications of what we wished to convey, he has presented it in an exoteric form, for he refers to his teacher and friend who lived in Alsace and who supplied him with the esoteric teaching to which he gave an exoteric form. This took place in the epoch when it had become necessary to do this, on account of the transition of which I have spoken in my book 'The Spiritual Guidance of Man.' It was shortly before this period of transition that the Grail legend appeared in exoteric form - in the year 1180.

Through this purest Grail impulse acting within the higher centers in the head, we gradually begin to reclaim the blood from the hold of the "rebellious" Luciferic spirits, and claim it for the Christ impulse that dwells within the region of the heart; whereby, a minute portion of the blood becomes etherized through uniting with the activity of, what could be called, the "etheric blood" that streams from the Resurrected Christ within the etheric world of life. The wholesome development of this Resurrection process is connected, in turn, to the strivings of the "advanced beings" that inhabit the spiritual environment of the planet Jupiter, and are working toward the development of the future Jupiter incarnation of the Earth; beings that also played an important inspirational role in the Spiritual Council that occurred the 4th century, when Zarathustra, Scythianos, and the nirmanakaya (spiritual form) of the Buddha came together with Mani; in order to determine ways to meet the future tasks of human spiritual culture.

These future tasks are specifically connected to the proper cultivation, in mankind, of the Jupiter brow chakra; which comes about through achieving balance, with the forces of thinking, between the forces of Cosmic Feeling and Cosmic Willing; and thereby, through the further development of the warming process of heart-wisdom, the transformative occult process of the etherization of the blood is established; whereby, a stream of etheric warmth rises up from the heart and bathes the higher centers in the head - in the region of the pineal and pituitary glands.

Through meeting the conditions of discipleship, and developing a spiritual practice (such as, contemplating the revelations of Spiritual Science in such a way so that it becomes warmed through with heart forces, and is combined with the cultivation of "a deep inward peace" - that can be achieved through meditation) the chaotic emotions, which agitate the Astral-Body, become calmed and the pituitary gland begins to radiate a golden light; which brings about a re-orchestration of the Astral-Body into Manas, or Spirit-Self.

When these emanations, that are proceeding from the pituitary gland, become more developed they extend far enough so that they bathe the pineal gland within this golden spiritual-light; this, in turn, awakens the higher functions of the pineal gland (which have been made possible, in part, through the depositing of pyramidial calcium carbonate crystals on the outer surface of the pineal gland - a central aspect of "the most refined mineral products" referred to above by Rudolf Steiner). This awakening of the pineal gland, that occurs through the pituitary gland bathing the pineal gland - in its rays of golden spiritual-light, brings about a re-orchestration of the Etheric-Body into Budhi, or Life-Spirit.

After these occult processes have reached sufficient maturity - so that a harmonious re-orchestration of the Astral-Body and the Etheric-Body, into Spirit-Self and Life-Spirit has occurred - this culminates in the development of the "Golden Triangle" (that is, the higher triad of Atma-Budhi-Manas, or Spirit-Man, Life-Spirit, and Spirit-Self, II); this "Golden Triangle" is referred to in the arcane legend of Hiram Abiff (the builder of the Temple of King Solomon), known as the *Golden Legend*, which was circulated among Rosicrucians and Freemasons.

Through the gradual unfoldment of this "Golden Triangle" a frontal etheric-column is formed - as a "middle pillar" establishing a middle path (Cosmic Thought) between the two pillars of mercy (Cosmic Feeling), and rigor (Cosmic Willing) that silently stand before the "Temple" of the human body - which is the true "Temple not made with hands." This frontal etheric-column is the seed impulse of our future evolution - when mankind will begin to manifest the creative powers of light and life that proceed from the "Cosmic Word." This is the true "open secret" of the *Sang Real* - the "Blood Royal."

XI

Justice

Libra - Dynamis - Spirits of Movement - Life-Spirit

The image on the Justice arcanum shows a crowned goddess seated before the veil of the unseen, between the two pillars of strength and mercy in the "Temple of Wisdom." Her right (active - solar) foot is showing beneath her robe due to its forward position. In her right hand, she holds a sword upright representing the narrow path of the word of justice "Fiat Justicia" ("let justice be done"), in her lowered left (receptive - lunar) hand she holds the balancing scales of justice, and she is facing the heart of man, deliberating between strength and mercy with the laws of love, compassion, and forgiveness. For the depth of one's spirituality is measured by one's capacity for forgiveness, and by the moral forces of conscience that are revealed through one's deeds.

This image of the Justice arcanum is very reminiscent of the statue of the goddess Venus Verticordia, "the goddess who turns the heart"; a temple for which was erected in ancient Rome in 114 B.C., a subject which I discuss in the chapter on the Empress arcanum. Although in the Justice arcanum, the scales are in the opposite hand, and she holds a sword instead of a long scepter. Venus Verticordia can be seen as representing, on the one hand, the moral forces of Venus that are revealed through the astral nature of the kidneys; which, as Rudolf Steiner has indicated, are the seat of conscience. On the other hand, Venus Verticordia reminds one of the spiritual beings that are striving to maintain harmony with the "Music of the Spheres", and the sounding of the Cosmic Word through maintaining the heart and lung rhythm for mankind - which rhythm, in turn, is affected by every thought, feeling, and deed of an individual.

Venus Verticordia is shown holding a pair of balancing scales in her lowered right hand, and in her left hand is a long scepter (which is tilted like the axis of the Earth). Venus Verticordia herself is one manifestation of Virgo the Virgin. The scales represent Libra, and the scepter symbolizes Leo. This can be seen as a macrocosmic image of the Isis-Sophia in her starry aspect of Cosmic Space as it extends from Libra to the Life-Spirit, and from Virgo to the Spirit-Man, in orientation to the solar forces of Leo

247

- which is the region of the initial rhythmic impulses that are related to the formation of what became on Earth, the human heart - "the Sun in man."

The first condition of our existence, the Old Saturn incarnation of the Earth, began with the donation of warmth by the Thrones (**IV**). This warmth is the most ancient part of humanity, the primal physical being. It is this rhythmic, vortexing warmth that is the initial source of the being of humanity. In a present day human being, this rhythmic, vortexing warmth finds its initial manifestation in the pulsating blood that forms the heart and blood vessels, after it has established a dynamic flow within the early stages of the embryo. Once it is sufficiently formed, the heart participates in the dynamic living, vortexing movement of the blood through its verticordial (turning heart) movement. These activities within the human body are maintained by spiritual forces that proceed from the Exusiai, or Spirits of Form. This comes about through the harmonization by the Spirits of Form with the beings that are one stage beyond them, the Dynamis or Spirits of Movement (**V**). The Spirits of Movement, in turn, are inspired by the Kyriotetes or Spirits of Wisdom, which are the embodiment of the highest spiritual wisdom regarding the intentions of the Holy Trinity. This is so because the three highest principles of the Spirits of Wisdom are manifestations of the spiritual substance of the first, second and third Logoic planes, which are the planes of being where dwell the Holy Trinity (**IX**).

The forces which maintain the rhythmic life of the blood proceed from the divine beings that dwell within the Sun Sphere; the Exusiai, or Elohim. These forces proceeding from the Exusiai, which maintain the movement that is life, are also being continually harmonized by the Exusiai with all of the Angelical Hierarchies. The Exusiai thereby establish further concord and harmony with the "Music of the Spheres", which is the sounding of the inspiration of the Spirits of Movement in service to the Divine Plan of the Holy Trinity as perceived by the Spirits of Wisdom. The resulting delicate rhythmic balance of the beating heart and the breathing lungs is our central human experience of the dance of living movement which connects us with the one life of all lives of the Holy Trinity - as meant in the saying of Christ; "I am . . . the Way, the Truth and the Life."

Consider more closely the statue of Venus Verticordia (Virgo) I mentioned above; it shows her standing with her right hand lowered, holding the scales (Libra), while with her left hand she is steadying a long scepter that symbolizes the fire sign of Leo. In the symbolism of the Tarot, a scepter relates to the suit of wands, and is traditionally associated with the element of fire and points toward "the slow-burning fire" of the heart.

If you picture the right-left orientation of Venus Verticordia within the traditional counter-clockwise Zodiac, this would show her gazing at the Sun (which is occultly related to the heart) from the periphery of the Zodiac, between Libra and Leo, in the constellation of Virgo. The scales of Libra in her right hand, show her judiciously mediating the forces of cosmic compassion - the order that arises out of love - which is of the nature of the Budhic principle, the Life-Spirit, which is the "Christ in you."

The association of Venus Verticordia to the constellation of Virgo points to a deep mystery of our human evolution, for the constellation of Virgo relates to the Kyriotetes, the Spirits of Wisdom who in the Old Sun incarnation of the Earth donated the essence of the Etheric-Body (**IV**), and whose activity at that stage brought into being the fundamental nature of the macrocosmic Heavenly Sophia, the cosmic representative of the company of Angelical Hierarchies that together contribute to the body of light of Sophia which embodies the "Sun laws" that were established by the Kyriotetes during the Old Sun incarnation of the Earth. This body of light of the Heavenly Sophia includes in its purest archetypal form all of the principles that would be incorporated into future humanity from the lowest principle, the Physical-Body, on up to the highest principle, the Spirit-Man or Atma (**IX**).

Libra is ruled by Venus, which tells us that Libra is connected with the Budhic principle. This venusian principle of higher love is called in the Bible "agape", and can only manifest through our relationship to others. On the other hand, in its lower manifestation Venus relates to fear (which can be seen as the absence of love). For, Venus relates to the after-death realm of Kama-Loka, known in the Christian tradition as Purgatory, the astral realm, where the dead are purified of their unredeemed earthly natures. This purification is necessary to the extent that we have not embraced the law of love - Christ's "Golden Rule" - which is the expression of the purest Budhi, or Life-Spirit of Christ.

The constellation of Libra (the Scales), corresponds *macrocosmically* in the "Zodiac of the Lamb of God" to the Dynamis, or Spirits of Movement (**IX**). In mankind, *microcosmically* the constellation of Libra corresponds to the second principle - the Budhic principle or Life-Spirit - the "Christ in you", which is the vehicle (or Grail) of the first principle - the Atma or Spirit-Man - "the divine spark" which is - the "Sophianic substance of Wisdom." The Life-Spirit is the higher counterpart of the Etheric-Body, and embodies the "Sun laws" that came about through the light that was radiated by the Archangels in response to the working of the Kyriotetes in the Old Sun incarnation of the Earth (**IV**).

Rudolf Steiner tells us that the Life-Spirit of Christ, which was working within the atmosphere of the Earth, was experienced in the Hibernian Mysteries of ancient Ireland, and was the original spiritual stream that led to the foundation of Celtic Christianity. With this Hibernian stream is especially connected the Arthurian Mysteries, where the courageous knights of the Round Table used the power of the sword to overcome the decadent, lawless, lower astral forces represented in the legends by ogres and dragons. For the Arthurian initiates could perceive the workings of the Life-Spirit of Christ in living nature which had come about through the Mystery of Golgotha; whereby, the Life-Spirit of Christ had transformed nature from within the realm of the etheric world (which is the fundamental realm of the plant kingdom). Likewise, with their developed etheric clairvoyance, the Hibernian Initiates had also observed the changes in nature that came about through the Mystery of Golgotha.

According to Rudolf Steiner, the "Second Coming of Christ", from within the etheric world of life, began in the first third of the 20th Century, and has a particular significance in our present age for the development of the Life-Spirit in mankind due to the harmonic relationship between the Etheric-Body and the Life-Spirit. Rudolf Steiner tells us that the Life-Spirit is manifested in an individual to the extent that they have undergone a transformation of the Etheric-Body - which results from the integration of the Ego with the Etheric-Body, and the divine "Sun laws" of the Cosmic Word. That is, the Life-Spirit is *not* something new that is added, but is actually the Etheric-Body re-orchestrated through the divine-forces of the Cosmic Word. Likewise, the Spirit-Self is formed through the Astral-Body becoming spiritualized by the Ego's integration with the forces of Cosmic Feeling - which are the forces of Cosmic Light and Warmth. And in addition to this, the Spirit-Man is manifested through the spiritualization of the Physical-Body as a result of the Ego's integration with the forces of Cosmic Will.

The natural result of the working of Christ within the Etheric-Body (and consequently the Life-Spirit) is a subtle *inward* harmonization of the rhythm of blood and breath with the moral forces of the Cosmos; what the ancient Egyptians would call Ma'at, or "divine order." In the ancient Egyptian text *The Book of Coming Forth by Day*, the scales are shown balancing the heart against the ostrich feather of Ma'at, thus showing an image of how this initiatic principle of harmony was represented by the ancient Egyptians, through the picture-forming nature of the Sentient-Soul. For, the ancient Egyptians believed that mankind was subjected to the laws of Ma'at; which, occultly speaking, we can understand to mean the pleroma of beings that maintain the moral order through acting upon mankind from *outside*.

To the ancient Egyptians, the goddess Ma'at represented the pristine state of the first period after creation. The descent of Ma'at into creation is discussed by Laszlo Kakosy in his article entitled, "Ideas About the Fallen State of the World in Egyptian Religion: Decline of the Golden Age."

> *Egyptian mythology like that of other peoples, regarded the first period after creation as the happiest era of human history. . .*
>
>> *'Law was established in their time, Justice (Maat) came down from heaven to earth in their age and united herself with those on the earth. There was an abundance on the earth; stomachs were full, and their was no lean year in the Two Lands [Egypt]. Wall did not collapse, thorn did not prick in the time of the primeval gods.'*
>> (*Urkunden VIII*, 76, 90 sq.)
>
>> *'There was plenty of food in the bellies of the people; there was no sin on the earth; the crocodile did not seize prey, the serpent did not bite in the age of the primeval gods.'*
>> (*Urkunden VIII*, 81, 93 sq.)
>
> *It was thus in primeval times that Justice, Maat, who played the role of the law of the world in Egyptian philosophy, descended upon the earth. The concept of Maat has a remarkable comprehensiveness; it includes absolute peace reigning on earth and the perfect harmony of nature, resulting, according to the myth, from the state of innocence. Miseries, the painful struggle of nature and man, famines and poverty are opposed to the idea of Maat.*

The ancient Egyptians are well known for the profound teachings regarding the after-death state that are depicted in their tombs. The Egyptian temples, on the other hand, did not present the mysteries of death and resurrection. The temples, in distinction from the tombs and mortuary temples, were there in an effort by the ancient Egyptians to maintain harmony with the moral forces of the cosmic order that were represented by Ma'at, through the performance of rituals to the various deities. This dynamic polarization between the mysteries of life and the mysteries of death is also shown in the geographical layout of Egypt itself, with the mortuary temples primarily located West of the Nile; while the temples that were concerned with the needs of the living were usually located East of the Nile. Although it must be stressed that to the ancient Egyptians there was a continuity between earthly life and the after-life, with both conditions being mutually supportive through the larger context of life. The significance of the "land of the dead" being located in the West is discussed, along with the solar destiny in the after-life, by the Egyptologist Jaroslav Cerny in chapter three of his book entitled, *Ancient Egyptian Religion*.

The sun rises in the morning, shines all day and disappears in the evening on the western horizon. But this disappearance is only apparent and temporary, for the sun has not ceased to 'live', the best proof being that it reappears the next morning after having spent the night in an invisible world. The Egyptians formed the conviction that human life is a close parallel to the course of the sun: man is born like the sun in the morning, lives his earthly life and dies, like the sun, which emits its life-giving rays the whole day and sets in the evening; but the analogy requires that his death should not be final, and that in a certain sense it does not take place at all. Man continues to live after the so-called death in a world outside his perception, and as a logical corollary, will at some time be born again in a new life. Thus the West, where both sun and men disappear, is called 'onkh' 'life' [ankh]; both sun and men go there in order to 'have a rest in life.' Expressions like 'wahm onkh' 'who reiterates life' or, in late times, 'ankh hotep' 'who lives and rests', are appended to the name of the deceased. The coffin, too, is called 'neb onkh' 'lord of life.' The question as to when exactly and under what conditions the new or renewed life will take place is left undecided by the sun-religion, but these details did not matter very much. The deceased - like the king - took part in the nightly course of the sun as a spectator in the company of the sun-god. From the analogy between the sun and man, however, only a small step was needed to a complete identification of the two, where man, after physical death, was supposed to form part of the sun-god's substance, becoming 'excellent spirit of Re' ('ikh oker en Re').

Furthermore, according to ancient Egyptian teachings, the central guiding spiritual-impulses were thought to originate within the heart. This point is emphasized by Jaroslav Cerny earlier in the same chapter:

What we call conscience was, according to the Egyptian, seated in the 'heart' ('yeb') which was also the seat of reason and desires. The voice of the heart was 'the voice of God' and 'he whom it had led to a good course of action was happy.'

Likewise, the ancient Egyptians thought, this was not only true in life but also in death - for the final word on whether one had been a successful member of the moral order (Ma'at), was "spoken" by one's heart in testimony during the after-death state. This is an occultly accurate picture of how the content of the personal Akashic Record, the individual "cosmic memory" that is inscribed in the astral-etheric heart, is communicated to the beings of the Cosmos. It is this content of the heart that is pictorially represented as being "weighed" against the ostrich feather of Ma'at, the goddess of truth and order, or karma. This image of Ma'at is akin to the oriental goddess referred to by H. P. Blavatsky as "Karma-Nemesis", about whom one can envision a collective choir of beings that embodies all of the nine Spiritual Hierarchies up to the Seraphim (**V**), and is also referred to in ancient times as the "Great Goddess." With the transition to Christ becoming the "new Lord of Karma" the relationship of the akashic center of the heart to the laws of Karma-Nemesis has been entirely changed. This change has come about through the compassionate Life-Spirit of Christ, so that the karma of mankind will not prevent Earth evolution from reaching its goal within the "New Jerusalem" (**XIV**).

As I have mentioned before in the chapter on the Empress arcanum, Venus Verticordia can be seen as a pre-Christian, Roman image of the Virgin Sophia working through Venus and acting out of the inspiration of the Holy Spirit, in harmony with the Divine Plan of the Holy Trinity.

Viewed from the perspective of the clockwise "Zodiac of the Lamb of God" (**IX**), Venus Verticordia is Virgo holding the scales of Libra (which is ruled by Venus) in her right hand; and in her left hand, the scepter of Leo (which is ruled by the Sun) gazing out upon the mystery of Isis-Sophia written in the heavens. Through the coming of Christ a new evolutionary vortex has come into being. Now, Verticordia does not face towards the center of the heart the "Sun in man"; but rather, she faces to the periphery of the heavens to await the "Cosmos of Love" that is freely arising through the Christ Impulse working within the hearts of mankind. This positioning of right and left gives us an image of the change in the relationship of the Zodiac to mankind through the incarnation of Christ.

I have used this image of Verticordia to illuminate the activity of the pure wisdom forces of Isis-Sophia, that have shifted from working within the hearts of mankind - to streaming in from the periphery of the Cosmos. This shift is also depicted in the zodiacal diagrams in this book where the Zodiac is shown in the reverse order; that is, in a clockwise sequence which represents the arising of a new creative vortex of manifestation as a result of the Mystery of Golgotha at the "Turning Point of Time" - the point of balance (Scales) for Earth evolution. Zodiacally speaking, the "Lamb of God" is represented by Aries the Ram (the historical epoch of the Mystery of Golgotha), and is opposite the Scales of Libra; that are held by both Venus Verticordia and by the goddess on the Justice arcanum. This can been seen as representing the occult fact that the polarity of *center* and *periphery* has shifted between the Christ and Sophia. Christ, who once worked from the periphery of the Zodiac, now works from within the center of man - within the "cave of the heart." Likewise, the Sophia wisdom forces that once worked within the center of man, now have shifted to streaming in from the periphery of the Zodiac.

The wisdom forces of Sophia are that which must be redeemed from the hold of Lucifer; for, as Rudolf Steiner said; "Lucifer has slain Sophia." This can be understood to mean that, throughout human history, the luciferic beings have striven to prevent the Christened Sophia forces from working within the center of man. This has been fruitful for mankind in that we have come to experience ourselves as separate individuals with the possibility of freedom through our being "cast out of the garden of Eden." Now we must strive toward the "New Jerusalem" by taking up the Christ forces within our hearts, and perceive the workings of the wisdom of Sophia within the new "Cosmos of Love." For thereby, mankind shall redeem the "luciferic rebellion" - through the luciferic spirits perceiving the anointed Christ forces radiating from within the hearts of mankind (**XII**).

Isabel Wyatt characterizes this redemption in chapter seven of her book, *From Round Table to Grail Castle*:

> . . . on the cross of the repentant thief on Golgotha, the great rebellious spirit, Lucifer, had been in prototype redeemed. This was known to the Early Church Fathers. St. Gregory of Nyassa, for example, says:
> 'Through the Crucifixion, good was done, not only for all lost creatures, but also for the Author of our perdition.'
> But the corona of Luciferic spirits have their own free-will. Dr. Steiner tells us that they had till the year 869 A.D. to be redeemed - the year in which the Arthur Christianity met the Grail Christianity, the year in which the Cosmic Christ met the Christ in the hearts of men. [Now, the possible future redemption of the Luciferic spirits, who did not find redemption before 869 A.D., depends upon the Luciferic spirits perceiving the Christ forces radiating from the hearts of mankind.]
> Steiner speaks of Christ and Lucifer as in a certain respect changing places, in that Christ becomes *inner* and Lucifer *outer*. Those unredeemed Luciferic impulses which still work 'in' man, should, if and when redeemed, be working from the periphery of universal thinking, bringing enlightening thought. (We glimpse here something of the mystery of the connection of Lucifer with the Holy Spirit). [In a general sense; Lucifer can be seen as the opponent of the Holy Spirit, Ahriman as the opponent of the Son, and the Asuras as the opponent of the Father.] If one may think of that meeting of the two streams as the moment of Christ becoming inward, we can see why the year 869 A.D. is the point at which the Luciferic spirits have finally to decide whether to follow the way of evolution - i.e. by becoming outward, or whether to continue working, now wrongfully, 'within' man.

If we consider once again the Justice arcanum in its relationship to the "Zodiac of the Lamb of God" (**IX**), it depicts the activities of the Dynamis, or Spirits of Movement presiding over the planetary movements that orchestrate karma within space and time with infinite justice, under the direction of the Christ as the "new Lord of Karma" - replacing the Father principle of "bones and law", or retribution, with the Son principle of "blood and love", and forgiveness; and likewise, redeeming Karma-Nemesis through the Pentecostal imagination of "the Woman Clothed with the Sun." For unlike the statue of blind Justice (representing the inexorable law of Karma-Nemesis), the Justice arcanum is not blindfolded, and so can perceive the light of Cosmic Feeling working from within the hearts of mankind.

The Seven Stages of the Initiation of Gautama Buddha

1. Earth Initiation

2. Water Initiation

3. Air Initiation

4. Fire Initiation

5. Moon Sphere Initiation

6. Mercury Sphere Initiation (the planet Venus)

7. Venus Sphere Initiation (the planet Mercury)

According to Rudolf Steiner, through achieving his enlightenment, Gautama Buddha had - out of his own forces - attained a level of consciousness whereby he was able to directly experience the inspiration of the Spirits of Movement associated with the planet Mercury (V). By looking at the initiation of Gautama Buddha in a seven-fold manner, it can be seen what Rudolf Steiner meant concerning how far the consciousness of the Buddha could reach out of his own forces (this is not to say of course, that the Buddha could not - through the grace of higher beings - experience higher realms). Through the inspiration of the Spirits of Movement, the Buddha achieved the direct experience of Cosmic Budhi (IX), which enabled him to manifest in the spiritual world as a nirmanakaya (Sanskrit for a "transformed spiritual body"); and thereby, act as an exalted helper of mankind. This nirmanakaya was seen accompanying the Angels by the shepherds at the birth of Jesus, as seen in the Akashic Records by Rudolf Steiner. He speaks of this in the lecture he gave in Neuchatel on December 18th, 1912 which is included in the collection of lectures that were published with the title, *Esoteric Christianity and the Mission of Christian Rosenkreutz*:

> *The occultists of the East rightly believe - for they know it to be the truth - that the Buddha who in his twenty-ninth year rose from the rank of Bodhisattva to that of Buddha, had incarnated then for the last time in a physical body. It is absolutely true that when the individuality of a Bodhisattva becomes a Buddha he no longer appears on the earth in physical incarnation. But this does not mean that he ceases to be active in the affairs of the earth. The Buddha continues to work for the earth, although he is never again present in a physical body but sends down his influence from the spiritual world. The 'Gloria' heard by the shepherds in the fields intimated from the spiritual world that the forces of Buddha were streaming into the astral body of the child Jesus described in the St. Luke Gospel. The words of the Gloria came from Buddha who was working on the astral body of the child Jesus. This wonderful message of peace and love is an integral part of Buddha's contribution to Christianity. But later on too, Buddha influences the deeds of men - not physically but from the spiritual world - and he has co-operated in measures that have been necessary for the sake of progress in the evolution of humanity.*

Through his "Venus Sphere" (**V**) initiation, the Buddha had conquered Kama Loka "the place of desire", which is the after-death state that is called Purgatory in the Christian tradition. This attainment of the Buddha enabled him to rise above the earthbound aspects of human nature and to achieve Nirvana, or Enlightenment. It was the attainment of Nirvana which liberated the Buddha from the necessity of earthly incarnation. Rudolf Steiner tells us that this liberation from earthly incarnation was also attained by the Buddha's spiritual pupil, St. Francis of Assisi, who has had only one incarnation on Earth (where he died in childhood) since his incarnation as St. Francis; and as a nirmanakaya, or

Spiritual Being, has been of the greatest benefit to mankind. This fact of Spiritual Science shows how intimately intertwined the streams of esoteric Christianity and esoteric Buddhism really are, as are connected the higher initiates of these and other streams to the "Mother Lodge of Humanity" (**XXV**).

Rudolf Steiner further indicated how the Buddha (who through the eight-fold path had perfected the sixteen-petaled lotus of the throat chakra that relates to Mars) went to the Mars realm, the realm of strife, as a sacrifice for mankind at the request of Christian Rosenkreutz. The presence of the Buddha in the Mars sphere (which is one of the states of being experienced between incarnations) "is like an island of peace amidst a sea of strife." The influence of this peaceful being can be very beneficial to one within the realm of sleep, in the after-death state, and can also help deepen one's meditations. For the Buddha is one of the greatest servants of Christ, one of the "Masters of Wisdom, and of the Harmony of Sensations and Feelings" of the "Mother Lodge of Humanity", that are working toward the wholesome evolution of humanity with infinite patience, compassion, and forgiveness.

In regard to the esoteric, Christian, spiritual scientific view-point, it is perhaps important at this point to emphasize that when we speak of the macrocosmic image of the Spiritual Hierarchies and how they relate to the microcosmic spiritual-human (**IX**), we are not merely speaking in abstract concepts that relate to lifeless energy fields, but we are speaking in living concepts that refer to living beings. The lifeless representation of spiritual-initiation as being merely concerned with "energy states", which is often presented by certain occult schools, misses the point of the living Universe. The Universe is in essence the sum total of the beings that inhabit it and their activity, however different the nature and form of consciousness of these beings may be. Therefore, I must emphasize the importance of realizing that we are dealing with actual beings, when we speak of the Guardian Angel and the other beings, including the nine-fold Spiritual Hierarchies. These spiritual beings are not merely "the symbolical archetypes of the collective unconscious" as they are described by the student of Sigmund Freud, the Swiss psychoanalyst Carl G. Jung. By thinking in terms of the "unconscious" one can easily make the mistake of thinking that because you are unconscious of it - it is unconscious of itself. In fact, it is the spiritual world that is the most significant realm of which we are unconscious. I might add, that there are numerous indications that Jung himself was well aware of the living nature of the unseen realms, but that he chose to treat them in symbolical terms only, refraining from direct reference to spiritual beings. Although it is known that on occasion Carl Jung did have certain experiences of a supersensible nature, it is evident that he was not an Initiate.

Instead of presenting initiation knowledge on its own terms, Carl Jung developed his own system of psychological processes and used the symbols of the esoteric tradition for communicating his own ideas about the human psyche. This manner of working with the symbols, while not without value, does not penetrate the esoteric veil of their true meaning; but rather, substitutes another more exoteric psychological significance to them that, occultly speaking, can create a form of thought-barrier that is very difficult to penetrate, and leaves the reader thinking that he has fully revealed the esoteric meaning; when in fact, he has acquired yet another conceptual "veil" that is based on the world of sense impressions. For, to use the words of the Buddha, we must have "right thinking" to penetrate the worlds of Spirit.

XII

The Hanged Man

Alchemical Mercury - Christophorus

From a hermetic perspective, the Hanged Man arcanum can be seen as an image of the Alchemical Mercury carrying the "Philosophic Gold." Through the impulses of the Alchemical Mercury (**I**) within the unfolding consciousness, the "earthly" gold is awakened to its living Sun-nature as "Philosophic Gold." This "Philosophic Gold" can be seen as representing the living manifestation of the "Sun laws" that were established in the Old Sun incarnation of the Earth (**IV**). These "Sun laws" manifest in the human being through the spiritualizing process that is described by Rudolf Steiner as the "etherization of the blood", this spiritualizing process, in turn, brings about a golden radiance in the aura of the Grail seeker.

This process is portrayed in the Hanged Man arcanum which shows a man suspended by his foot upside-down (which reminds one of St. Peter who was crucified upside-down); he is seen with a radiant golden halo surrounding his head, his arms are clasped behind his back forming an upward pointing triangle, representing spirit, surmounted by the cross of matter formed by his crossed legs (which are reminiscent of the cross-legged tomb effigies of the Knights Templars, and because of this the Templars were sometimes referred to as the "cross-legged knights"). His right (or Solar) leg, by which he hangs, is suspended by a cable-tow from a Tau cross (**T**) with living foliage.

This reversed position on the Hanged Man arcanum can be seen as representing the shift in the consciousness of humanity from earthbound consciousness to a higher consciousness that responds to the promptings of the spiritual world. This shift is the result of the overcoming of animality (represented by the horizontal-astral principle), that in the future will lead to a more passionless plant-like existence (represented by the vertical-etheric principle). The further understanding of this is seen in the fact that the plants are formed as an upside-down reflection of the human kingdom, with the root relating to the head, the leaves to the lungs, and the flowers to the procreative organs. From this it can be seen that the Hanged Man is, in a sense, symbolic of the Etheric-Body, which is that which is without passion or plant-like in man; and from which, in the future, will flower forth through the transformed larynx - the creative "Word" of the christened Life-Spirit.

The reversed position of the Hanged Man can also be seen as symbolic of the shift to the Mercury half of Earth evolution (**IV**), the new evolutionary vortex that is gradually coming into being as a result of the spiritual "leaven" of Golgotha; that is, the Incarnation and Resurrection of Christ at the "Turning-Point of Time." By the occult process of the etherization of the blood, Christ is evolving mankind out of the earlier incarnational Mars half of Earth evolution, to the spiritualizing Mercury half of Earth evolution, with a shift from material sense-bound soul activities to spiritual-soul activities, which leads to higher faculties of judgment that are in a conscious relationship to the Divine Plan of the Holy Trinity (**XIV**). This relates to the observation of the Neo-Hermetic, Catholic author Valentin Tomberg, in regard to meaning of the Hanged Man arcanum, which he sees as a symbolical image of the biblical saying "Not my will but thy will be done" - although he mistakenly suggests that this is only possible by conforming to the external authority of the Church.

The mysterious alchemist Fulcanelli in his book *Le Mystere des Cathedrales*, which developed out of his hermetic relationship with R. A. Schwaller de Lubicz, gives an alchemical interpretation of the symbolism of the most famous Cathedral in Paris that is dedicated to the "Notre Dame", or "Blessed Virgin." In chapter nine, Fulcanelli relates the Alchemical Mercury to the mystery surrounding two of the St. Christopher statues that were removed from the Notre Dame Cathedral in the mid-18th century:

> *The space in front of the cathedral was once bordered on one side by the imposing basilica itself and on the other by a picturesque conglomeration of little buildings, decorated with spires, spikes and weathercocks, these were interspersed with painted shops, having carved beams and cosmic signs. At the corners of the buildings were niches, ornamented with madonnas or saints, flanked with turrets, pepper-pot towers and bastions. In the middle of this space stood a tall, narrow stone statue, holding a book in one hand and a snake in the other. This statue was part of a monumental fountain, on which was written this couplet:*

> *'Qui sitis, huc tendas: desunt si forte liquores,*
> *Pergredere, aeternas diva paravit aquas.'*

> *'You, who are thirsty, come hither:*
> *if, by chance the fountain fails*
> *The goddess has, by degrees,*
> *prepared the everlasting waters.'*

The people used to call it sometimes Monsieur Legris (Mr. Grey), sometimes the Dealer in Grey, the Great Fasting Man or the Fasting Man of Notre Dame.

Many interpretations have been given of these strange expressions applied by the common people to an image, which the archaeologists have not been able to identify. The best explanation is the one given by Amedee of Ponthieu, which seems to me all the more interesting since the author, who was not a hermeticist, judges without prejudice and without any preconceived idea.

'In front of this temple,' he tells us, 'stood a sacred monolith, which time had rendered shapeless. The ancients called it Phoebigenus (Engendered by the sun or by gold), the son of Apollo. Later the people called it Maitre Pierre, meaning master stone, stone of power. It was also called Messire Legris (Mr. Grey), since grey signified fire and particularly feu grisou (fire damp), will-o-the-wisp . . .

According to some, these unformed features resembled Esculapius, Mercury, or the god Terminus (the busts of Terminus were busts of Hermes-Mercury). According to others they were the features of Archambaud, Mayor of the Palace under Clovis II, who had donated the ground on which the Hotel-Dieu was built. Others saw the features of Guillaume de Paris, who had built it at the same time as the portal of Notre Dame. The Abbe Leboeuf saw the face of Christ; others St. Genevieve, patron saint of Paris.

This stone was removed in 1748, when the square of the Parvis-de-Notre-Dame was enlarged.'

At about the same time, the chapter of Notre Dame received the order to suppress the statue of St. Christopher. This collossus, painted in grey, stood back to the first pillar on the right, as you enter the nave. It had been erected in 1413 [the *year before the transition from the epoch of the Intellectual-Soul to the epoch of the Consciousness-Soul] by Antoine des Essarts, Chamberlain to King Charles VI. Its removal was suggested in 1772, but Christopher de Beaumont, Archbishop of Paris at that time, opposed this formally. It was only at his death in 1781 that it was dragged away and broken up. Notre Dame of Amiens still has a good Christian giant carrying the Child Jesus, but it must have escaped destruction only because it forms part of a wall. It is a sculpture in bas-relief. Seville Cathedral has also preserved a collossal St. Christopher, in the form of a fresco. The St. Christopher in the church of St. Jacques-la-Boucherie was destroyed by order in 1768, only a few years before the one in Paris.*

Behind such acts there must obviously have been powerful motives. Although they do not appear to me to be justified, we can, however, find their cause in the symbolical expression drawn from the legend condensed - doubtless all too clearly - by the image. St. Christopher, whose primitive name Offerus, is revealed to us by Jacques de Voragine, signifies to the masses: he, who carries Christ (from the Greek Χριστοφορζ); but the phonetic cabala discloses another meaning, which is adequate and in conformity with the hermetic doctrine. Christopher stands for Chrysopher: he, who carries gold (Greek Χρυσοφορος). From this one can better understand the extreme importance of the symbol of St. Christopher. It is the hieroglyph of the solar sulphur (Jesus), of the nascent gold, raised on the mercurial waters and then carried, by the proper energy of this Mercury, to the degree of power possessed by the Elixir. According to Aristotle, the emblematic colour of Mercury is grey or violet, which explains why the statues of St. Christopher were given a coating of that colour. A certain number of old engravings of the collossus, kept at the Cabinet des Estampes in the Bibliotheque Nationale, are executed in simple outline in bistre. the oldest dates from 1418.

This description by Fulcanelli of the Hermetic interpretation of this image, and of the secret of the Alchemical Mercury, is further clarified by the way in which a miner pans for gold. A miner would fill his pan with gravel from the river-bed, and then rotate the pan to pour off the water, so that all that was left was the fine gravel and the particles of gold, which are heavy and settle to the bottom of the pan. The miner then pours in a small amount of mercury which absorbs and suspends the gold particles. After draining off the remaining water, the residue that remains is poured into a cloth and squeezed; only the mercury that is suspending the gold passes through the cloth. Then the miner burns off the mercury, which leaves only the gold remaining. Here you have a thought provoking image in a chemical process of St. Christopher as a bearer of the Christ impulse.

The Bodhisattvas and the Mission of Cosmic Intelligence

In *Parzival*, Wolfram von Eschenbach's epic poem, Parzival's family coat of arms is a panther - which W. J. Stein points out is also one of the three animals present at the beginning of Dante's *Divine Comedy*. The panther is also mentioned in the Zarathustra legend. Another initiate associated with the panther is Jeshu ben-Pandira (the "son of the panther", ben = son, pandira = panther), the Essene "Teacher of Righteousness" mentioned in the *Dead Sea Scrolls*. Jeshu ben-Pandira was stoned and hung from a tree in Egypt around 100 B.C. by the Jews; and consequently, he is frequently confused with Jesus of Nazareth. Rudolf Steiner relates that Jeshu ben-Pandira reincarnated in the first century as the Neo-Pythagorean initiate Apollonius of Tyana, who after many years of traveling throughout the known world established a school at Ephesus (the city of the great Temple of Artemis - one of the seven wonders of the ancient world). As St. John was also in Ephesus at this time, they may have known each other. In this great initiate, Jeshu ben-Pandira, worked that great being who is called in the East the Maitreya Bodhisattva and is said to be the embodiment of compassion. In the far future (around 4000 A.D.), the Maitreya Bodhisattva will become the next Buddha. As the Maitreya Buddha he will speak words imbued with such powerful moral forces that, at the present time, we do not even have a language that is capable of expressing such exalted content.

The Maitreya Bodhisattva incarnates approximately every century, according to Rudolf Steiner, and works behind the scenes in the service of Christ. He is one of the twelve Bodhisattvas, or "embodiments of purity." He is of the rank of Bodhisattva, which means that he has not yet achieved the rank of Buddha. The Maitreya Bodhisattva is a leading initiate, a bearer of the Christ impulse - a Christophorus. One should not confuse this being, and his mission, with the "Second-Coming of Christ." For, the

Christ is the super-individuated being of the Logos, the Son of God, who is one with the Father in Heaven. While on the other hand, Bodhisattvas are incarnations within the human realm of beings who, though they are far in advance of ordinary humanity - are, nonetheless, but lowly servants of Christ. The nature of the exalted spiritual attainment of a Bodhisattva was described by Rudolf Steiner in the lecture he gave in Berlin on the 1st of October, 1905, which is published in the lecture cycle entitled, *Foundations of Esotericism*:

> ... Once man was perfect and he will become so again. But there is a great difference between what he was and what he will become. What is around him in the outer world will later become his spiritual possession. What he has won for himself on the Earth will later become the faculty of being creatively active. This will then have become his innermost being. One who has absorbed all earthly experiences, so that he knows how to make use of every single thing and has thus become a creator, is called a Bodhisattva, which means a man who has taken into himself to a sufficient degree the Bodhi, the Budhi of the Earth. Then he is advanced enough to work creatively out of his innermost impulses. The wise men of the Earth are not yet Bodhisattvas. Even for such a one there always remains things to which he is still unable to orientate himself. Only when one has absorbed into oneself the entire knowledge of the Earth, in order to be able to create, only then is one a Bodhisattva; Buddha, Zarathustra, for example, were Bodhisattvas.

As regards to Gautama Buddha, Rudolf Steiner indicated that his advanced development was due to his inhabiting the pre-human colonies of beings that existed on the planet Venus (occult Mercury) before the Earth had separated from the Sun. This fact of Spiritual Science enables one to understand the statements by H. P. Blavatsky in *The Secret Doctrine* where she equates Buddha with Mercury; for, as a result of the exchange of the names of Mercury and Venus, this in actuality refers to the planet Venus. Which means that the Gautama Buddha, along with other Bodhisattvas, evolved in the spiritual realm of the planet Venus before the Earth was formed (**V**).

The Bodhisattvas have worked for mankind throughout human

history, preparing mankind to receive the Christ impulse. The Bodhisattvas can be thought of as Spiritual Elders of mankind who have overcome the consequences of the "Fall", and who are bearers of the Christ impulse that assist in nurturing the spiritual development of "infant humanity."

Through their overcoming the consequences of the "Fall" in their life, form, and consciousness, the work of the Bodhisattvas is occultly related to one of the greatest servants of Christ, the Archangel Uriel whose name means "fire of God", and who manifests within the spiritual world the "unfallen" nature of Venus. The work of the Archangel Uriel is also occultly related to the beings which are collectively known in the East as the Kumaras "the seven sons of Brahma." According to occult teachings, the Kumaras or "mind-born sons" inhabited the spiritual sphere of the planet Mercury (occult Venus) before the Earth had separated from the Sun, and are connected with the donation of the Manasic principle (Spirit-Self) to mankind.

Although the Archangel Uriel is infrequently mentioned by Rudolf Steiner, his significance should not be under-emphasized. The Archangel Uriel is discussed by Rudolf Steiner in the lecture cycle entitled *The Four Seasons and the Archangels*, where he describes the influences that proceed from the working together of the "four Archangels of the Presence" within the cycle of the four seasons: Michael (Michaelmas = Fall), Gabriel (Christmas = Mid-Winter), Raphael (Easter = Spring) and Uriel (St. John's Tide = Mid-Summer) (**XI, XIV**). In lecture four, Rudolf Steiner gives an imagination of the stern countenance of Uriel as a guardian of Cosmic Intelligence:

> . . . *whose own intelligence arises fundamentally from the working together of the (seven-fold) planetary forces of our planetary system, supported by the working of the fixed stars of the (twelve-fold) Zodiac.*

This image of Uriel is in keeping with the tradition derived from *The Book of Enoch*, where Uriel is attributed with being the original teacher of star-wisdom to mankind. There is also a tradition that states that it was Uriel who revealed the Holy Kabbalah to Moses. Likewise, we can consider Uriel as a guardian of that aspect of the Grail mystery which is described by Wolfram von Eschenbach in *Parzival* as "learning to read the starry-script." The Archangel Uriel looks down upon mankind and sees the imperfections of mankind in stark contrast to the manner in which the "Music of the Spheres" is so perfectly reflected in the growth of the crystals within the mineral kingdom.

The Hermetically Sealed Inner Tradition of Esoteric Christianity

In the Christian tradition there has always been an inner occult, or hidden teaching that is, as it were, hermetically sealed with seven seals. This is made clear in "The Gospel of St. Mark" (4:11):

> *And He said unto them, 'Unto you it is given, to know the mystery of the kingdom of God: but unto them that are without, all these things are done in parables . . .'*

This message is also given in "The Gospel of St. Luke" (8:10):

> *And He said, 'Unto you it is given to know the mysteries of the kingdom of God: but to others in parables; that seeing they might not see, and hearing they might not understand.'*

Mankind has reached a point in its spiritual evolution, where the opportunity is available for anyone to begin to understand the deeper occult, or hidden teachings of the esoteric Christian mysteries. But these mysteries cannot bear fruit unless they are nurtured in the proper way, which takes the greatest patience. This deeper esoteric message is pointed at in "The Gospel of St. Matthew" (13:33-35):

> *Another parable spake He unto them; The kingdom of Heaven is like unto leaven [Atma, Budhi and Manas], which a woman took, and hid in three measures of meal [the three-fold human of spirit, soul and body], till the whole was leavened. All these things spake Jesus unto the multitude in parables, and without a parable spake He not unto them: That it might be fulfilled*

which was spoken by the prophet, saying, I will open my mouth in parables; I will utter things which have been kept secret from the foundation of the world.

Christ entered into a new relationship with Earth evolution by incarnating into Jesus at age thirty, thereby replacing the Ego of Jesus at the Baptism in the River Jordan by John the Baptist (**XXVI**). This incarnation in Jesus of Nazareth is the *only* physical incarnation of Christ that will take place in the whole of Earth evolution. On the other hand, the "Second-Coming of Christ" must not be understood to be a physical incarnation, for this would mean that the first incarnation was a failure, which of course it was not. The meaning of the expression "the Second-Coming of Christ" is very different, for it refers to the appearance of Christ in the etheric world of life that has begun in our era. In His ethereal form, Christ will be perceived by more and more people as we move into the future.

We are all, from the most humble infant to the highest initiate, "corpuscles in the body of Christ", but no man or woman can be "The Christ" - for He has come already and as He has said; "I shall be with you always." The reappearance of Christ in the etheric world - the level of being nearest the physical - is spoken of by St. Paul as; "Christ coming in the clouds and the air." This "Second-Coming of Christ" in the etheric is like the experience of St. Paul on the road to Damascus. This experience of the Christ will be vouchsafed to those individuals to whom the Christ wishes to reveal Himself; and furthermore, in future stages of the evolution of mankind, Christ will reveal himself in progressively higher spheres.

The "Christ in you" of St. Paul is the "I Am" or spiritual "leaven" which is the fruit of the incarnation of Christ in Jesus of Nazareth at the "Turning-Point of Time", beginning the *new spiral* of the Mercury half of Earth evolution (**IV**). In response to this *new spiral*, mankind begins through this "alchemical" Mercury impulse working from within the blood - to shift its consciousness from the gravity of Earth to the etheric levity of a future Sun. For through their conscious and free participation in the Divine Plan, humanity will be spiritually transformed by the activity of the etheric blood of Christ. This provides an important key to understanding the mystery of the thirteenth, for thirteen is the number of the "I Am", or Spiritual-Ego that has overcome the lower animality of the twelve-fold forces of the Zodiac (zoo = animal), so as to be able to function freely and without compulsion; and thereby - become an agent of transformation within the world through the Christ Impulse. This occult reality is shared by Robert Powell in chapter ten of his book entitled, *Hermetic Astrology - Towards a New Wisdom of the Stars, Volume 1*:

> *Moreover, by way of the restoration of the likeness through the transfiguring Christ Impulse, the work of redemption of the whole of nature - including man's corporeality - is set in motion. When this is carried further - towards the goal of the Resurrection - the influence of the Fall and the working of heredity will gradually be overcome. Through the Christ Impulse the human body itself will become transformed in the course of time, eventually to become resurrected, like the Resurrection Body of Christ. The Resurrection Body is truly in the image of God. It is the new zodiacal man, a body cleansed of the blemishes of the Fall, in which, correspondingly, the personality of the human being is raised up to become an expression of the divine image. This stage of evolution was attained and lived out in advance for the rest of mankind by the 'Son of man', Jesus Christ, who appeared to St. John on the island of Patmos; 'His face was like the Sun shining in full strength' (Revelation, 1:16). The face which begins to shine 'like the sun' denotes the power of resurrection at work in redeeming the fallen physical body and correspondingly raising up the personality to manifest the divine image . . .*

With the realization of the occult facts of Esoteric Christianity, we are confronted with a challenge to overcome ourselves and begin to work towards becoming a Christophorus; that is, to develop our three-fold nature of thinking, feeling, and willing within the seven seals of embodiment (the seven chakras) through the alchemystical process of the twelve labors of Hercules (the zodiacal twelve - which is composed of seven light signs and five dark signs). This leads to our fulfillment as spiritual beings amongst other higher spiritual beings, and with this comes a mood of wonder, awe, and reverence. This mood is enigmatically expressed by the Comte St. Germain (the Prince Rakoczy) in an alchemical poem (I have translated from the French) concerning the "Philosophic Gold" that is concealed within the depths of the "Double Mercury."

An Alchemical Poem by the Comte St. Germain

Curious scrutator of the whole of nature,
I have known the great All, its principle and its end,
I have seen gold in its power deep within the mine.
I have seized its material, and surprised its leaven.

I explain by what art, the soul within the Mother's womb,
makes its home, carries it out, and as a grape-seed
placed against a grain of wheat, under the humid earth;
the one plant and the other vine, are the bread and wine.

Nothing was, God willed, and nothing became something.
In my doubting, I sought out that on which the universe is poised.
Nothing appeared to sustain the equilibrium,
or to serve as a support!

Finally, with the weights of praise and of blame,
I weighed the eternal, it called my soul,
I died, I adored, I knew nothing more.

XIII

Death

Scorpio - Exusiai - Spirits of Form - Spirit-Self
St. John - the Philosopher - the Initiate of the Thought Mysteries

In the symbolism of the constellation of Scorpio, the Scorpion is related to the sphere of the angelic hierarchy that are called, in the Greek of Dionysius the Areopagite - the Exusiai (**IX**). In the Hebrew of the *Old Testament* they are called Elohim (in the plural form), and Eloah (in the singular form). Rudolf Steiner called the Exusiai, the Spirits of Form, and related that when the Sun was separating from the Earth, the conditions that were compatible with the stage of development of the Spirits of Form, at that time, were to be found in connection with the departing Sun. But one of the seven Elohim, Jehovah-Eloah - called in the *Old Testament* Jehovah-Elohim since He directed the activities of all seven Elohim in Earth evolution - as a sacrifice, remained connected with the Earth.

Jehovah-Elohim made this sacrifice in order to counteract the activity of the "fallen" Luciferic spirits by working out of the sphere of the Moon; thereby directing the separation of our present satellite, the Moon, from the region near the Indian Ocean during the Lemurian period. With the separation of the Moon, Jehovah-Elohim brought about the creation of the sexes, as imaginatively represented in the Biblical story of Adam and Eve being cast out of the Garden of Eden. As a result of the "fall" from the edenic state, humanity evolved first into fluid, and then into solid bodies. The resulting male and female mortal physical bodies became subject to the laws of death as portrayed in the story of Cain and Abel.

Toward the end of the edenic state, mankind had become overly permeated by the light ether, which had led to an increase in their consciousness of the environment, but was a disruption in the harmony of the working of the four ethers within the human form (**II**). At this time, occurred the "temptation" of mankind by the "fallen" Luciferic beings, who had themselves been striving for the development of an inner life that could only be achieved through denying their own nature, which was only possible by embracing falsehood; literally - in order to develop an inner life they had to become "Spirits of Falsehood." These Luciferic beings were of seven basic types, and are reminiscent of the seven devils driven out of Mary Magdalene by Christ. Rudolf Steiner mentions this challenge of the seven types of Luciferic beings.

> *Backward Luciferic beings of seven different kinds remained behind upon the Moon and worked upon the human astral body. We know that if our evolution is not carried out aright, it is owing to the power of these seven different kinds of Luciferic beings.*

These "fallen" Luciferic spirits permeated mankind with their influence - while humanity experienced a "fall" from the edenic state with a separation of the sexes, and also a separation as to the nature of the working of the four ethers within the human form. Two of the ethers remained in the conscious realm (warmth ether and light ether) while the other two (the chemical or fluid ether, and the life ether or earth ether) passed into the realm of unconscious activity.

The overcoming of this estrangement from Paradise at the end of Earth evolution is represented in the description of the New Jerusalem in "The Revelation of St. John the Divine." The fundamental ideas which lead to an understanding of this vision of St. John are given in the first fourteen verses of "The Gospel of St. John"; which, as Rudolf Steiner tells us, was a daily meditation verse of the original Rosicrucians.

St. John can be thought of as the Initiate of the Thought-Mysteries (the Manas or Spirit-Self) - the Philosopher (**XIV**). The ability to think is the result of the freeing-up of etheric life forces which bring about growth; this, in turn, leads to a sort of death-process within the nervous system. Literally speaking, we can think because the nervous system has taken upon itself something of the realm of death; for it has "fallen", and has been transformed from the "Tree of Life" into the "Tree of Knowledge."

The separation between the *conscious* realm of the light and warmth ethers, and the *unconscious* realm of the chemical and life ethers is mirrored in the human form. One way of looking at it is - the nerve-sense system expresses the *unconscious* working of the life ether in its manifest form; which is much like a tree with its branches, while it expresses the *conscious* working of the light ether in its sense activity. On the other hand, the blood expresses the *unconscious* working of the chemical ether in its fluid nature, and in its metabolic chemical activities. In addition to this, the blood carries the warmth of which we are *conscious* primarily through the perception of our relationship to other temperatures through the sense of warmth.

We are also *conscious* of the workings of the warmth ether through its relationship to the feeling realm; for we can become cold with fear, or hot with anger. But although the feelings are actually a manifestation of realm of Cosmic Light, we are only *conscious* of their workings in a dream-like manner.

Furthermore, the general activity of all four ethers within the body is regulated by the breath, which normally works *unconsciously* - under the direction of the beings of the Second Hierarchy - but can be affected *consciously*.

As a consequence of the "fall" from the Garden of Eden, the Cosmic Life that is represented by the Tree of Life, "fell" to the earthly realm and became the Tree of Knowledge of Good and Evil, or the nerve-sense system. Now, the most vital and living part of a person is the blood, which was in its origin composed of the "dead" mineral-earthly nature that entered mankind early in Earth evolution in order to become a vehicle for the living warmth - the living warmth, which is a remnant of the Old Saturn incarnation of the Earth, and is the most ancient part of our being.

Out of the mineral realm, the blood carries the incarnational Mars impulse as iron; a certain amount of which is lost by women during menstruation. In addition, higher amounts of copper, which relates to Venus, are present in women. This is related to the occult fact that women retain something of the "unfallen" edenic human nature.

The nerve-sense system, that was once the Tree of Life dwelling in the realm of Cosmic Life, succumbed to the "sting of death" and "fell" to Earth to become the Tree of Knowledge. Consequently, for redemption to come about for mankind it was necessary for the blood, coming originally from the "dead" mineral-metal realm, to be lifted up to a higher existence through the bearing of the earthly-life in preparation for the reception of the workings of the Cosmic Life of the Life Spirit of Christ.

Through the Mystery of Golgotha the Christ Impulse entered into human evolution. This began a gradual transformation of the nature of the blood so that it may eventually become the seat of Cosmic Love; thereby, redeeming the Tree of Knowledge and freeing the earthbound spirit. Which is to say that, through the Christ-force of Resurrection mankind will, in the future, be transformed into beings of light (**IV**). For, in the words of Rudolf Steiner; "Every substance upon the earth is condensed light."

> *Neither can they die anymore: for they are equal unto the angels; and are the children of God, being the children of the Resurrection.*
>
> "The Gospel of St. Luke" (20:36)

Christ Jesus, the "Lamb of God", through the shedding of the living blood at the Mystery of Golgotha as the "Representative of Mankind", manifested the unfallen nature of the primal human being - the Adam Kadmon - bringing about a resurrection of the fallen life and chemical ethers and thereby of the total human being, so that in the future mankind could also attain the Resurrection.

In a lecture which Rudolf Steiner gave in Berlin on September 30th, 1905, that was published in the lecture cycle entitled, *Foundations of Esotericism*, he pointed out some of the deeper aspects of the occult physiology involved in the Resurrection process which come about through the transformation, by the Christ impulse, of the workings of warmth and light within the human being.

> *. . . Man's activity is to be sought in what streams from him as inner warmth. Out of what proceeds from warmth: passions, impulses, instincts, desires, wishes and so on, karma arises. Just as the parallel organ to the ear is the organ of speech, so the parallel organ to the warmth of the heart is the pituitary gland, the hypophysis. The heart takes up the warmth from outside, as the ear does sound; thereby it perceives world warmth. The corresponding organ which we must have, in order to be able to produce warmth consciously, is the pituitary gland [Saturn] in the head, which at the present time is only at the beginning of its development. Just as one perceives with the ear and produces with the larynx, so one takes up the warmth of the world in the heart and lets it stream forth again through the pituitary gland in the brain. Once this capacity has been achieved, the heart will have become the organ it was intended to be. There is a reference to this in the words from 'Light on the Path' [by Mabel Collins]: 'Before the soul can stand in the presence of the Masters, its feet must be washed in the blood of the heart.' Then our heart's blood streams out as today our words stream out into the world. In the future,*

warmth of soul will flood over mankind.

Somewhat deeper in evolution than the warmth organ stands the organ of sight. In the course of evolution the organs of hearing, warmth and sight, follow in sequence; the organ of sight is only at the stage of receiving, but the ear already perceives, for instance in the sound of a bell, its innermost being. Warmth must flow from the being itself. The eye has only an image, the ear has the perception of innermost reality. The perception of warmth is the receiving of something that rays outwards. There is an organ which will also become the active organ of vision. This is today germinally present in the pineal gland [Jupiter], the epiphysis, the organ which will give reality to the images which today are produced by the eye. These two organs, the pineal gland and the pituitary gland as active organs, must develop into the organ of vision (eye) and the organ of warmth (heart). Today fantasy is the preliminary stage leading to a later power of creation. Now man has at most imagination. Later he will have magical power. This is the Kriyashakti power. It develops in proportion to the physical development of the pineal gland. . .

Warmth has its life on the Shushupti plane [the Budhic plane of the Life-Spirit]. To make conscious use of this is possible for one who understands and controls the life of warmth, as in a certain sense man today controls the life of the air. In his development man must now approach the forces of the Shushupti plane [through the development of Budhi-Manas]. The Fifth Sub-Race [or, Fifth post-Atlantean cultural epoch] has mainly the task of developing Kama-Manas [Consciousness-Soul]. One finds Manas in everything which is placed in the service of the human spirit. Our age has placed its highest powers at the service of these needs, whereas the animal is satisfied without such achievements.

Now however Budhi-Manas must also begin its development. Man must learn something beyond speech. Another force must be united with speech, such as we find in the writings of Tolstoy. It is not a matter of what he says, but that behind what he says stands an elemental force that has something of Budhi-Manas, which must now enter civilization. Tolstoy's writings work so powerfully because they are consciously opposed to West European culture and contain something new and elemental. A certain barbarism which is still contained in them will later be brought into balance. Tolstoy is just a small instrument of a higher spiritual power which also stood behind the Gothic initiate Ulfilas. This spiritual power uses Tolstoy as its instrument.

"Lapis exillis is its name."

The nerves and the blood vessels run parallel throughout the human body and consciousness takes place in the gap between them. The nerves are continually inscribing the Ego, dwelling within the warmth of the blood, with the content of the senses. Through the methods of imaginative inner concentration upon symbols, such as the black cross surrounded by seven red roses, one is able to withdraw the nerve activity from the blood, which enables the forces of the the Higher Self, the Spirit-Self, to be perceived. This comes about through overcoming the astral forces of kama, or desire, in the blood, which lowers the consciousness. The Spirit-Self, in turn, is a bridge to the perception of the Life-Spirit, the "Christ in you", the True Self which manifests through love without kama, or desire, and is a manifestation of the redeemed Etheric-Body. To express it imaginatively, the black cross surrounded by red roses is transformed into a green cross surrounded by magenta (or peach blossom) roses, which in turn is transformed into a silver cross surrounded by golden roses.

The transmutation of the Astral-Body into Manas, or Spirit-Self is pictured in the alchemical writings as the "Riding of the Lion", the rhythmic system, which awakens Imagination. In the *Bible* there is the story of Daniel in the lion's den. This is an image of the conquering of the Astral-Body through courage within the feeling realm, which is centered in the rhythmic system of the heart (the Lion) and lungs (the Twins).

This rhythmic heart warmth leads us back to the primal warmth of the Old Saturn incarnation of the Earth, which began in relationship to the constellation of Leo, the Lion (**IV**). In addition to Leo being the constellation that relates to the beginning of cosmic evolution, Leo is also the constellation that relates to the completion of the seven-fold evolutionary chain, the Vulcan Period where humanity will have achieved the stage of Archai with a fully developed Spirit-Man or Atma, our present seventh and highest principle. This mystery of the primal warmth is alluded to in the manuscript from the Hermetic Order of the Golden Dawn entitled, "The Book T", which is the source material for most of the books that have been written on the Tarot in the last century. In "The Book T", they relate the arcana of the Tarot to a sidereal Zodiac with the cusps of the constellations calculated from the star Regulus, or Cor Leonis "the heart of the Lion", in the constellation of Leo (**XIII**).

The "Riding of the Lion", or the conquering of the astral is a necessary preparation for overcoming the death processes of the body, an experience represented as the attainment of the "noble stone." This stage of initiation requires tremendous heart-forces of courage, and is a stage in the Grail-path which is described by Wolfram von Eschenbach in chapter IX of *Parzival*. This subject is dealt with by Walter Johannes Stein in chapter five of *The Ninth Century - World History in the Light of the Holy Grail*. Below I quote at length, beginning from where Walter Stein describes the meeting between Parzival and the hermit Trevrezent.

> The hermit wishes to say to Parzival that there is no sense in seeking for the Grail. The only sense is in fulfilling with enthusiasm the demands of the Grail - to work upon oneself and to serve the world. Whether one comes to the Grail or not, that one must leave in the hands of God, that is a grace. He gives to what he says a still greater force, by mentioning that he has himself seen the Grail. Parzival asks him - were you there? The hermit says that he was. Then Parzival was silent. He could not find the courage to claim that he too had been there. And so he only asked about the Grail. He says: 'At Monsalvasch there is a castle where the Grail is cared for by the Knights Templars. These knights have gone through many adventures. The purpose of all their journeys is to fulfill the demands of destiny. All these valiant knights live by the power of a stone. It must be a noble kind of stone. What is it called?'
>
> 'Lapis exillis is its name.' (Chapter IX: line 630)
>
> The word is obviously derived from lapis exilii. Du Cange, 'Glossarium mediae et infimae latinitatis' defines the word exililum as 1) dissipatio, destructio, 2) Peregrinatio [a state of exile, a foreigner or pilgrim. reminiscent of the Biblical image of "the stone the builders rejected."]. Lapis exilii must therefore be translated 'stone of destruction', or, 'stone of

death.' Basil Valentine speaks of the stone, produced from fire, in the fourth of his 'Twelve Keys.'

> 'When ashes and sand are thoroughly baked for just the right amount of time, the master makes a glass out of them which henceforth will always resist the fire and resembles in colour a transparent stone and can no longer be recognized as ash. To the ignorant that is a great mysterious art, but not to the wise, for by knowledge and repeated experience it becomes a handicraft . . . At the Last Judgement the world will be judged by fire - fire that has been created by the Master out of nothing - the world must again become ashes through fire; out of these ashes will the Phoenix at last bring forth her young. For in such ashes is verily concealed the true Tartarus, which must be dissolved, and from a solution of which the solid castle of the kingly dwelling can be revealed.'

That means, man then comes to body-free, pure soul-spiritual experience.

The next lines that the poet gives us have to do with the experience of death. When the human being becomes free of his body and passes out of his body, a remarkable experience confronts his inner gaze. Human capacity for feeling is such that it penetrates the flesh but not the bones. When through becoming free of the body the capacity for feeling is released from its dependence upon the body; or, to express this in anthroposophical terms, when the astral body leaves the physical body, and the human being in imaginative experience is confronted by his astral body, then the space that the bones had occupied appears as a hollow space, as unoccupied space. That means that the human being has in imagination the skeleton in front of him. The picture is brought about just as a negative on a photographic plate. Rudolf Steiner explained this experience to me in the following way:

If the capacity for feeling the astral body presses against the bones, the inner part of the bones, which otherwise would have remained unconscious, becomes conscious. The fine cancellous tissue within the bones is perceived, and in the moment when this is experienced, no other word can be found for the experience than ashes. Because the experience appears with especial strength in the region of the teeth, one speaks of the ashes the dead have in their mouths. The next stage of this experience is that not only the bony structure is experienced but the blood in process of formation in the marrow of the bones is experienced too. As soon as this occurs, the bones begin to shine. The poet now describes this:

> '. . . by its magic the wondrous bird,
> the Phoenix, becometh ashes,
>   and yet doth such virtue flow
> from the stone, that afresh it riseth
>   renewed from the ashes glow,
> and the plumes that erewhile it moulted
>   spring forth
>   yet more fair and bright.'
>   (Chapter IX: lines 630-633)

So the poet describes the stepping out of the body, the becoming free of the body, the passing of the living body through the Gate of Death, the entrance into the spiritual world. But it is not actual death, it is the experience of death which is vouchsafed to successful inner schooling on the way into the spiritual world. Hence the poet emphasizes that this illness is not unto death, but to the glorifying of the divine in man.

> 'Yet he dies not that same day
>   that his eyes behold the Grail,
> nor yet in the week to come,
>   and his features stay unchanged.'

As they certainly would not do were he really to die.

> 'His colour fadeth not,
>   if he daily sees the Grail,
> but remaineth pure and bright
>   as in youth or maidenhood.'

He who has this experience notices that he has lived through it before in childhood as if in prevision. But then he could not understand it. The explanation of this experience too I owe to Rudolf Steiner. The poet refers to this fact:

> 'His hair would not turn grey,
>   tho' he gazed two hundred years,
> such strength it gives to man,
>   that both his flesh and bones
>   are quickened to new life:
> this stone is called the Grail.'

When the human being experiences the approach of body-free consciousness, when he experiences the stepping-out of his supersensible organization, the weakness of death overtakes him, but he does not die, he is led to the point of looking at the birth of the light-forces out of the skeleton man, the Light of the World illuminates death. If he has this experience, his bodily organization becomes penetrated with new force. What then is the Grail? It consists of the vessel and of the substance within it. The vessel is the skeleton and the substance is the blood penetrated marrow within it.

> *'This stone is called the Grail.'*

That is the microcosmic aspect of the Grail, experienced for the whole man. The experience can also be made in the head, as Rudolf Steiner has often described. There are in fact many ways of encountering the Grail.

Scorpio - "The Sting of Death"

In the Fall season of Scorpio, we see the approaching death forces of nature bringing about the falling of the leaves from the trees and the plants going to seed. It is in this time of year that we can experience a deepening of the powers of thought, as we move from the externalized sense processes of summer, to the inward reflective mood of winter. It is this transition that is symbolized by the scorpion who stings himself with his own powers of death; though Scorpio has a higher symbol in the eagle, who soars on the wings of thought; and above this, Scorpio has an even higher symbol in the phoenix, who rises out of its own ashes and is resurrected (**XIII**).

These symbols, which are left as clues by the ancients, point toward a higher path for mankind - the path of initiation. Through the principles of initiation, the scorpion becomes the eagle as death (the scorpion) becomes life (the winged eagle) leading to resurrection (the phoenix) which is the eternal life that can be described as - "panaeonic immortality", or existence without cessation of consciousness - that is, without sleep or death.

The completion of the stage of the phoenix is the point where the initiate has developed the ability to complete the natural cycle of the breath within his own being and thereby ceases to exhale unredeemed death-forces through his breath. By attaining this stage, the initiate redeems the cycle of oxygen and carbon dioxide, a process on which we are normally dependent on the plant kingdom to complete outside in nature. What this means is that the initiate has developed the ability to maintain these bodily processes and complete the carbon cycle within his own being. Through achieving this stage of inner development, the initiate liberates the exalted spiritual beings that were involved in maintaining this carbon cycle for him up to that point.

The eagle is the symbol of St. John, with a tradition going back to Polycarp, the direct disciple of St. John (**XIV**). The traditional account of the martyrdom of Polycarp tells of how he was pierced while being burnt at the stake, and that his blood flowed so powerfully that it extinguished the flames. This can be seen as an image of the Christ forces working so strongly in the blood of Polycarp - that it caused the blood to powerfully flow from his wound, due to the super-abundant life radiating from the Christ forces that were manifested within the blood of Polycarp.

The System Bible Study, which is a traditional bible study that was compiled by a team of scholars and published in 1927, speaks of St. John, "the eagle that soars upon the wings of spiritual thought", in the following words:

> *He writes long after the other gospels, and assumes what they have, as a rule, and adds incidents and conversations and discourses that reveal the true deity and humanity of Jesus. Mark wrote for the Romans [and Egyptians]; Matthew for the Jews; Luke for the Greeks and other Gentiles; John for the spiritually minded of all lands and ages, as with eagle eye he seized the central facts in the life and teaching of Jesus Christ the Son of God. Both Matthew and Luke have sections that resemble the teachings in John's Gospel, but he has preserved the intimate teaching of Jesus concerning his own person and mission, such as we find in Chapters 3-17 . . . It is the greatest book of all time in its simple grandeur and power. Chapters 14-17 give us the very heart of Christ.*

It is the Eagle - St. John, "the disciple whom Jesus loved", who most completely gives us the key to understanding the spiritual nature of man within the realm of the mind. The region of the Eagle of Scorpio relates to the Manas, or Spirit-Self in man (IX), the Higher-Self that finds expression in the "still small voice" of conscience (that is mentioned by St. John), when acting out of the promptings of the Budhi, or Life-Spirit.

The Manas is manifested through the spiritualized higher thought processes that result from the overcoming of the lower instinctive impulses of the astral, this leads to what H. P. Blavatsky described as a "permeable consciousness"; that is, a mind that is rendered permeable so as to receive the inspiration of the Spirit, rather than being imprisoned in the opaque realm of the senses, the realm of "death."

Occultly speaking, physical light is spiritual darkness, while spiritual light is physical darkness, and so in the Fall when we move towards winter, the physically dark time of the year, we are moving towards the time of spiritual light; midwinter, the time of the "Sun that shines at midnight", the Spiritual Sun of the Christmas season (XI).

The poet Goethe once said: "It takes a temperate climate to produce a philosopher." What he was intuitively getting at is an occult reality of our present existence. In the Summer when the forces of nature awaken, the soul of the Earth is actually sleeping in the realm of manifested life. In the Winter, when the forces of nature are withdrawn from the realm of plant growth, the soul of the Earth awakens from its sleep.

Likewise in sleep we find this mystery expressed; for, during sleep we enter the Spiritual World, although we may only remember the experience as the unconscious darkness of sleep, we were actually within the realm of spiritual light (**XX**). This mystery is also true as regards death - where we also enter into the realm of spiritual light - although it may seem to be a realm of the darkness of death to the unawakened consciousness. One must pierce the veil of darkness, the "veil of Isis", to perceive the "Sun that shines at midnight" - which the ancient Egyptians refer to in the story of Osiris being transported nightly, across the body of Nut (the starry sky), in the bark of Re' (the Sun) that arises daily out of the underworld as Kephra, the scarab beetle, rolls the Sun above the Eastern horizon (**XII**).

In ancient Egypt, it took 70 days to prepare the Pharaoh for burial - to begin his nightly journey as Osiris, in the Midnight-Sun, this was equated with the 70 day absence, from the night sky, of the inundation star Sirius-Sothis. According to Ehrenfried Pfeiffer, the "Sun that shines at midnight", is occultly related to Sirius-Sothis, and is the evolutionary system where the Exusiai, or Spirits of Form, of our present Earth evolution went through their fourth, or human stage of development; and so, would provide a key as to how "God created man in His own image."

Because our souls have not been illuminated with sufficient spiritual light - we do not see into the soul and spiritual worlds. The light of the sense-world drowns out the experience of spiritual light. It could be said that, one must die to the realm of the senses to be born again in the realm of spiritual light - that is not to say that you should reject the world - but rather, that through this awakening participate in its redemption. For, in order to find the world of light, one may through the principles of initiation become "a lamp unto oneself" (**XIV**).

Christ said; "Let the dead bury the dead." By entering into the realm of spiritual life - through an awakened thinking - we see the sleeping thinking for what it really is, a shadowy death-process. By gradually awakening this living-thinking, we create a center in the head that moves down to the throat center; until later, after the necessary development of the astral petals of the chakras, it finds its center within the heart - *the true spiritual center of man*. This process *within* the center of man is connected to a process that takes place at the *periphery* of man. Starting from behind the back of the head, a spiritual web, as it were, is formed that surrounds the individual in spiritual light - which is the halo that is shown in religious iconography. This halo is the fruit of becoming a *true human being*.

The word "human" is derived from the Latin word humanus. Hu is like hue which refers to color, or light; while the word "man" relates to the Sanskrit term Manas, the thinking-principle, or mind - so that the word human can be understood to mean the "light of thinking." Through the spiritualizing processes that manifest through the participation in Cosmic Thought one may also awaken the realm of Cosmic Feeling, which is the realm of Cosmic Light. The word "man" is also related to the Sanskrit word for "jewel", Mani. From this perspective, the word "human" could refer to "the jewel of light", the *stone* that is the Grail.

The alchemists called this struggle of the inner-work - "the method of the rectification of the one substance." Through alignment with the Christ Impulse, the warmth of the heart rises up as an etheric stream to bathe the centers in the head, while the "ash" descends to earth inscribed with the akashic imprint of the present moment.

The present moment is also imprinted in the akashic center within the heart. This is the crux of the matter: "to accomplish the miracle of the one substance" through the creation of the "Philosophers' Stone" - the transformed carbon of the "phantom" Physical-Body; which comes about through the transformation of the breath and blood rhythm; and, as a result of this process, the exhalation of this transformed breath becomes life-giving as we move towards a more plant-like existence, and no longer exhale the unredeemed carbonic gases - that carry forces of death.

While there is a Divine Plan, within the context of freedom the future of the Earth is undetermined as of yet - according to degree. To the extent that mankind diverges too far to the right or to the left, or too high or low, there is the experience of unnecessary suffering. Michael is the leader of this impulse of freedom and he can only help us to the extent that we help ourselves. Michael has already conquered the Ahriman, "the dragon of materialism" - on all levels of being. If it does not seem to be so - it is the failing of mankind and not of Michael.

For those who develop in advance of humanity - through the principles of initiation - beyond the Consciousness-Soul to the Spirit-Self, it is vital that Spirit-Self, or Manas, is tinged with the Life-Spirit, or Budhi, *without the loss of the experience of individuality*. The Spirit-Self must become a Grail or receptacle for the influx of the Christ impulses of the Life-Spirit, ". . . upon this rock I will build my church, and the gates of hell shall not prevail against it . . .", or there is a danger of the Spirit-Self descending upon mankind from the realm of the Luciferic spirits.

On the other hand, if mankind falls prey to the overly materialistic impulses of Ahriman, and does not develop the "permeable consciousness" of the Spirit-Self, then the development of mankind will be stunted at the level of the Consciousness-Soul; thereby, increasingly separating off from the Divine Plan as we move toward our future evolutionary stages of unfoldment.

With the transition from the ancient world, mankind experienced a darkening of consciousness. This was due to the loss of the powers of atavistic clairvoyance that resulted from the development of the Intellectual-Soul. This darkening of consciousness had to come about in order for mankind to experience themselves as individual beings.

Rudolf Steiner describes how, through the decline of the Sentient-Soul there was a further "fall" for mankind which gradually darkened that level of the being of man which perceived the stars as colonies of beings, and that within this part - that was gradually being cut off from the supersensible - the Intellectual-Soul would begin to develop a longing for the sense of individuality that would later come about more fully, within the realm of thought, in the Consciousness-Soul epoch, which began around 1414 A.D. In the collection entitled, *Anthroposophical Leading Thoughts,* Rudolf Steiner gives a more complete picture of this transition toward individuated-freedom in ancient Greece.

> *The ancient Greek did not form thoughts for himself and then look out upon the world with them as his own creations, but when he thought he felt that a life was being kindled within him - a life which also pulsated in the objects and events outside him.*
>
> *Then for the first time there arose in man the longing for the freedom of his own actions - not yet true freedom, but the longing for it.*
>
> *Man, who felt the life and activity of Nature asserting itself in him, could develop the longing to detach his own activity from the activity which he perceived outside him and around him. But after all, this outer activity was still perceived as the final result of the active spirit-world, which is of like nature with man himself.*
>
> *Only when thoughts were imprinted in the physical body and when the consciousness extended only to this imprint - then only did the possibility of freedom arise. This condition came with the fifteenth century A.D.*

In light of this "fall" in thinking, one of the difficulties in *New Testament* interpretation is that, in the Greek language, words frequently have numerous meanings; consequently, when scripture is translated "word for word", they must choose one word out of several possible words which can greatly affect the depth of interpretation. This difficulty is evident in the use of the word "repent" to translate the saying of John the Baptist "metanoia" (Greek, μετανοεω, meta = beyond, higher, over, or after; noia = nous = mind). This can be seen by comparing the King James translation with the Kenneth S. Wuest translation entitled, *The New Testament - An Expanded Translation*. In his translation, Wuest attempts to express the numerous meanings of the Greek words, hence it is an "expanded translation." To make the true depth of meaning more evident, I will compare the relevant passages from these two translations, although I must admit that stylistically the "expanded translation" tends to detract from the poetic beauty of the text. In the following, I quote the King James translation of, "The Gospel of St. Matthew" (3:1-2):

> *In those days came John the Baptist, preaching in the wilderness of Judea, and saying, 'Repent ye: for the kingdom of heaven is at hand.'*

And now compare Kenneth S. Wuest's translation of the same passages:

> *Now, in those days there makes his public appearance John the Baptizer, making a public proclamation with that formality, gravity, and authority which must be listened to and obeyed, in the uninhabited region of Judea, saying; 'Be having a change of mind which issues in regret and a change of conduct, for there has come near and is imminent the kingdom of heaven.'*

These passages become more meaningful when one considers the occult significance of what John the Baptist is saying. That is, that "metanoia" means to: change your way of thinking - to a thinking that is sensitive to the spiritual world - and that will necessarily bring about an experience of remorse due the personal shortcomings that become so evident in the presence of the higher reality of the spiritual world. This is an experience so profound in its effect - that one cannot help but be moved to change their way of acting. John the Baptist is proclaiming with the word "metanoia", that people should awaken to their higher (meta) mind (noia) - which is, at present, unawakened. This initiatory concept of bringing about spiritual transformation through the awakening of the higher mind is referred to by St. Paul in "The Epistle to the Romans" (12:2); "... μεταηορφονοσθε τη αυακαιυωσει του νοος ...", which translates; "... let yourselves be transformed by the renewing of your minds ..."

The "Lamb of God" Zodiac and the Higher Principles of Man

The Three-Fold Ego or Self

Ego - the Ordinary Self - Sagittarius - Archai
Spirit-Self, Manas - the Higher Self - Scorpio - Exusiai
Life-Spirit, Budhi - the True Self, the "Christ in you" - Libra - Dynamis

Above the Ego is:

Spirit-Man, Atma - the "Divine Spark", the Sophia - Virgo - Kyriotetes

Beyond the Spirit-Man is:

Thrones - Leo
Cherubim - Cancer
Seraphim - Gemini

Who receive the purest inspirations of the Trinity

Third Logos - The Holy Spirit - Taurus - "the Beautiful"
"And there appeared a great wonder in Heaven;
a woman clothed with the Sun, and the Moon under her feet,
and upon her head a crown of twelve stars."

Second Logos - The "Lamb of God" - Aries - "the True"
"I am the Way, the Truth, and the Life."

First Logos - "Our Father who art in Heaven ..." - Beyond the Zodiac
"Only My Father in Heaven is Good."

The Trial and Death of the Templars

The Neoplatonic philosopher Plotinus (205-270 A.D.) in his work entitled the *Ennead*, used three words, "the Good, the True, and the Beautiful", to refer to the triune nature of the unity of the Godhead - which he called "the One." Plotinus' trinitarian ideas have been very influential on Christian philosopher's attempts to understand the nature of the Holy Trinity since the Middle Ages. According to the teachings of Plotinus, evil was considered to be a state of lack, or privation - that is, a non-participation in the Good, the True, and the Beautiful. It is from this idea, that we can perhaps come to a greater understanding of the trial, torture, and death of the Knights Templars.

On numerous occasions during the trials of the Templars, testimony was given under torture that they had "denied the cross" and "venerated a head." This testimony was used against them by the Catholic Church to dissolve the order, and put many of its members to death. Furthermore, this testimony has led to all manner of confusion amongst historians as to the nature and purpose of the Templar order.

In occult teachings it is known that in order to achieve a higher state of being, this state is naturally preceded by a period of separation or isolation - a state of "peregrination"; this is what is shown in the Biblical story of the Garden of Eden and the subsequent "fall" from the state of grace. In alchemy, this principle is expressed by the formula, "solve et coagula" (solve = to separate, coagula = to unite), which means that in order to achieve the higher unity of the "transmutation" there must first be a state of "exile" - as in Wolfram's *Parzival*, where it says regarding the Grail, "Lapis exillis is its name" (chapter IX: line 630); which, as mentioned earlier, is the "stone [lapis] the builders rejected." This principle is vividly portrayed in, "The Gospel of St. Matthew", (16:13-23), in relation to another "stone" that is rejected - Peter (Latin, Petra = rock).

> When Jesus came into the coasts of Caesarea Philippi, He asked his disciples, saying; 'Whom do men say that I the Son of man am?'
>
> And they said; 'Some say that thou art John the Baptist: some, Elias; and others, Jeremias, or one of the prophets.'
>
> He saith unto them; 'But whom say ye that I am?'

> *And Simon Peter answered and said; 'Thou art the Christ, the Son of the living God.'*
>
> *And Jesus answered and said unto him; 'Blessed art thou, Simon Bar-jo'na - for flesh and blood hath not revealed it unto thee, but my Father which is in Heaven.*
> *And I say also unto thee, that thou art Peter, and upon this rock I will build my church; and the gates of hell shall not prevail against it.*
> *And I will give unto thee the keys of the kingdom of heaven; and whosoever thou shalt bind on earth shall be bound in heaven.'*
> *Then charged He his disciples that they should tell no man that He was Jesus the Christ.*
> *From that time forth began Jesus to shew unto his disciples, how that He must go unto Jerusalem, and suffer many things of the elders and chief priests and scribes, and be killed, and be raised again the third day.*
> *Then Peter took him, saying; 'Be it far from thee, Lord: this shall not be unto thee.'*
> *But He turned, and said unto Peter; 'Get thee behind me, Satan - thou art an offense unto me; for thou savourest not the things that be of God, but those of men.'*

These contradictory reactions of Christ to Peter, show that Peter had not completed his transformation, and so, could not yet consistently act out of his higher judgment (Manas). This represents Peter's "exile" from "the things that be of God" to "those that be of men." This state that is "of men" is called "doubt" in Wolfram's *Parzival*. When Christ spoke these words, Peter was yet in a state of "tumpheit" or dullness, which leads to doubt. As I have mentioned before, Rudolf Steiner has pointed out that the path of the Grail passes from "dullness through doubt to 'saelde' or blessedness"; although one must first pass through the the stage of doubt - "the dark night of the soul." The future doubt and denial of Christ by Peter is predicted by Christ in "The Gospel of St. John" (13:37-38).

> *Peter said unto him; 'Lord, why cannot I follow thee now? I will lay down my life for thy sake.'*

> *Jesus answered him; 'Wilt thou lay down thy life for my sake? Verily, verily, I say unto thee. The cock shall not crow, till thou hast denied me thrice.'*

As a result of his dullness and subsequent doubt, Peter was later to fulfill the prophetic words of Christ, and deny Him three times before the cock crowed at dawn.

Christ said; "Thou art Peter, and upon this rock I will build my church . . ." when Peter was speaking out his Higher-Self, or Manas, which is a state of consciousness that is *permeable* to the influence of the higher worlds, ". . . for flesh and blood hath not revealed it unto thee, but my Father which is in Heaven." On the other hand, when Peter was speaking out of his *impermeable* Ordinary-Ego, Christ said; "Get thee behind me, Satan - thou art an offense unto me; for thou savourest not the things that be of God, but those of men."

In the second of two lectures, "Concerning the Lost Temple and How it is to Be Restored", which are included in the lecture cycle entitled *The Temple Legend,* Rudolf Steiner gives further indications regarding the significance of St. Peter as related to the secret initiation rites of the Order of the Knights Templars.

> *Moreover, the Templars said: Today we live at a point in time when men are not yet ripe for understanding the great teachings; we still have to prepare them for the Baptist, John who baptizes with water. The cross was held up before the would-be Templar and he was told: You must deny the cross now, so as to understand it later; first become a Peter the Rock who denied the Lord. That was imparted to the aspirant Templar as a preliminary training . . .*

Rudolf Steiner gives the following further indications in the same lecture.

> *This struggle to raise oneself up to a proper understanding of Christ, first passing through the stage of Peter [of doubt and denial] - none of the Templars found it possible under torture, to make clear to the judges.*

At the outset, the Templars put themselves in a position, as if they had abjured the Cross. After all of this had been made clear to the Templar, he was shown a symbolical figure of the Divine Being in the form of a venerable man with a long beard (symbolizing the Father). When men have developed themselves, and have come to receive in the Master a leader from amongst themselves, when those are there who are able to lead humanity, then, as the Word of the guiding Father, there will stand before men the Master who leads men to the comprehension of Christ.

And then it was said to the Templars: When you have understood all this, you will be ripe for joining in building the great Temple of the Earth; you must so co-operate, so arrange everything, that this great building becomes a dwelling place for our true deeper selves, for our inner Ark of the Covenant.

If we survey all this, we find images having great significance. And he in whose soul these images come alive, will become more and more fit to become a disciple of those great Masters who are preparing the building of the Temple of Mankind. For such great concepts work powerfully in our souls, so that we thereby undergo purification, so that we are led to abounding life in the spirit.

We find this same medieval tendency as manifested in the Knights Templars, in two round tables as well, that of King Arthur, and that of the Holy Grail. In King Arthur's Round Table can be found the ancient universality, whereas the spirituality proper to the Christian knighthood had to be prepared in those who guarded the Mystery of the Holy Grail. It is remarkable how calmly and tranquilly medieval people contemplated the developing power (fruit) and outward form of Christianity.

When you follow the teachings of the Templars, there at the heart of it is a kind of reverence for something of a feminine nature. This femininity was known as the Divine Sophia, the Heavenly Wisdom. Manas is the fifth principle, the spiritual self of man [the Spirit-Self, or Higher Self = Scorpio], that must be developed, for which a temple must be built. And just as the pentagon at the entrance to Solomon's Temple characterizes the fivefold human being, this female principle similarly typifies the wisdom of the Middle Ages. This wisdom is exactly what Dante sought to personify in his Beatrice. Only from this viewpoint can Dante's 'Divine Comedy' be understood. Hence you find Dante, too, using the same symbols as those which find expression in the Templars, the Christian knights, the Knights of the Grail, and so on. Everything which is hidden [concerning the future evolution of mankind] was indeed long since prepared for by the great initiates, who foretell future events, in the same way as the 'Apocalypse', so that souls will be prepared for these events.

According to legend, we have two different currents when humanity came to the Earth: the children of Cain, whom one of the Elohim begat through Eve, the children of the Earth, in whom we find the great arts and external sciences. That is one of the currents; it was banished, but is however to be sanctified by Christianity, when the fifth principle comes into the world. The other current is that of the children of God, who have led man towards an understanding of the fifth principle. They are the ones that Adam created. Now the sons of Cain were called upon to create an outer sheath, to contain what the sons of God, the Abel-Seth children created.

In the Ark of the Covenant lies concealed the Holy Name of Yahveh. However, what is needed to transform the world, to create the sheath for the Holy of Holies, must be accomplished again through the sons of Cain. God created man's physical body, into which man's ego works, at first destroying this temple. Man can only rescue himself if he first builds the house to carry him across the waters of the emotions, if he builds Noah's Ark for himself. This house must set man on his feet again. Now those who came into the world as the children of Cain are building the outward part, and what the children of God have given is building the inner part.

These two streams were already current when our race began . . .

Throughout history mankind has been confronted with the struggle between the two streams of Cain and Abel, of science and religion. If mankind is ever to resolve this struggle, it must be taken within and resolved internally inside the individual consciousness of man. This comes about through the harmonizing of the "waters of the emotions" and leads to the development of the fifth principle of Manas, or the Spirit-Self (**IX**). For what is this struggle? It is none other than the struggle between the head (Cain) and the heart (Abel) - between the nerves and the blood. And until we resolve this struggle within, why should we expect it to be resolved outside of us in the world? The seed for this reconciliation was planted two thousand years ago upon Golgotha - the place of the skull - through the spilling of Christ's Holy Blood. And now it is up to mankind, acting in complete freedom, to find the path of harmony through the Christ impulse by consciously embracing tolerance and forgiveness through the power of spiritual love. As Christ said; "Forgive them for they know not what they do."

XIV

Temperance

Sagittarius - Archai - Spirits of Personality - the Ego

The constellation of the Archer, Sagittarius, is related to the beings that are three stages beyond humanity - the Archai, or, as they are called by Rudolf Steiner, Spirits of Time (Zeitgeist), or Spirits of Personality (IX). How the Ego perceives the nature of the impulses of the Time-Spirits is directly related to the quality and level of consciousness the Ego is manifesting at the time; whether the Ego is lagging behind the times, in tune with the times, or developing in advance of mankind, through the principles of Initiation, future forms of consciousness.

Under the guidance of the Time-Spirits (who, in turn, are under the guidance of the Exusiai, the Spirits of Form), human consciousness is continually undergoing metamorphoses. Due to the nature of this metamorphoses, in our current age, it is necessary that the spiritual aspirant develop a truly living-thinking that can adapt to the changing times through cultivating a sense for truth.

The teachings of Spiritual-Science were meant by Rudolf Steiner to be a path of the Spirit that is suitable for a modern thinking person. Due to the clarity, precision, depth and scope of Rudolf Steiner's spiritual-scientific work within Anthroposophy, it is sometimes difficult for a person who is accustomed to thinking in an ordinary materialistic-scientific way to approach Spiritual-Science at first; but, if one is patient and applies oneself, the organs of understanding are formed through the act of thinking about what is given in the literature of Anthroposophy.

Thinking is primarily supersensible in its own nature, and so finds itself quite at home in the spiritual world - from which it derives its substance. Rudolf Steiner emphasizes this fact in chapter iv of, *An Outline of Occult Science*:

> . . . *We must also consider the fact that anyone who finds their way purely through thinking into what supersensible cognition has to impart is not at all in the same position as someone who*

listens to the description of a physical process that he himself is unable to observe, since pure thinking is itself a supersensible activity. Thinking as a sensory activity, cannot of itself lead to supersensible occurrences. If, however, this thinking be applied to the supersensible occurrences described by supersensible perception, it then grows through itself into the spiritual world. In fact, one of the best ways of acquiring one's own perception in the supersensible realm is to grow into the higher world by thinking about the communications of supersensible cognition; for, entrance into the higher realms in this way is accompanied by the greatest clarity of perception. For this reason a certain school of spiritual-scientific investigation considers this thinking the most excellent first stage of all spiritual-scientific training. It should be quite comprehensible that in this book the way in which the supersensible finds its verification in the outer world is not described in all the details of earth evolution as it is perceived in spirit. That is not what was meant when it was said that the hidden is everywhere demonstrable by its visible effects. The idea is, rather, that whatever is encountered can become entirely clear and comprehensible to man, if the manifest processes are placed into the light afforded by spiritual science.

It is the effort that one puts toward achieving clarity in their understanding of the findings of Spiritual Science that becomes a bridge to the spiritual world. Once when some friends and I were conversing with the Dalai Lama, he stated; "More important than being smart is *being clear.*" It is the striving for clarity that is the key to manifesting harmony in one's thoughts, words, and deeds; and thereby, finding the middle path of balance that is the fruit of the Christ impulse.

Lucifer and Ahriman are the supersensible beings that tempt mankind into following inappropriate impulses in the present moment. Lucifer wishes for mankind to act out of the impulses that were proper in the past history of mankind. This activity of Lucifer is evident in the current tendency of people to pursue spiritual paths with the thought that "the more ancient the tradition the better"; thereby, they completely disregard the needs of our current Consciousness-Soul epoch. Ahriman, on the other hand, wishes to bring about future impulses in an unwholesome way, due to mankind's inability to utilize these impulses with the proper spiritual maturity; and so, the fruits of these impulses become, so to speak, the property of Ahriman. A good example is atomic energy. Mankind as a whole is far too immature to possess such tremendous power, and while we have been able to avoid extensive use of the atomic bomb thus far (other than the tragedy of Hiroshima and Nagasaki, and countless tests), we suffer under the contamination of improperly utilized and stored atomic waste, which is to a large extent due to human greed and the wish to dominate others.

Rudolf Steiner characterized certain aspects of the challenge of the adversaries in a lecture he gave in Dornach on October 4th, 1918, which is published in the lecture cycle entitled, *Three Streams in the Evolution of Mankind*:

> *Where historical life is concerned it is always Luciferic forces that lead us to hatch out far-reaching world-dreams which fail to reckon with the nature of man. In the course of human thought what a vast number of ideas have been devised for making the world happy! And in the firm opinion of those who devise them, the world can become happy only through these particular ideas. This is because such Luciferic thinking is of an airy kind, soaring aloft and taking no account of all that is swarming around below, and believing that the world can be organized on the lines of these airy notions. Such ideas of how to make the world happy, resting always upon a defective knowledge of man, are of a Luciferic nature; dreams of world power derived from particular realms of human activity are of an Ahrimanic kind. For these dreams are developed out of the subconscious. It is Ahrimanic to take a certain realm of human activity and to wish to bring the whole world under its aegis. All that is connected with man's lust for ruling over his fellows, all that is in opposition to healthy social impulses, is of an Ahrimanic nature. The man of whom it could be said - not in a superstitious way but in our own sense - that he is possessed by Lucifer, loses interest in his fellow men. The man possessed by Ahriman would like to have as many men as possible in his power and then to proceed - if he is clever - to make use of human frailty in order to rule over men. It is Ahrimanic to seek the sub-earthly, in the subconscious, for human weakness as a means of ruling men.*

One must come to understand that the nature of the Luciferic and Ahrimanic beings is such that they are what Rudolf Steiner described as retarded spirits; that is, beings who have departed from the normal stream of evolution, and bring about influences that are the result of their working in spheres of activity that are not their normal spheres of activity. Certain aspects of this mystery are made clear by Rudolf Steiner, in the lecture mentioned above:

> . . . *Luciferic Beings, who really belong to the ranks of Spirits of Wisdom [from the realm beyond time - the realm of duration], but because they work in time they do so in the character of Spirits of Form. And that which would otherwise work timelessly in man's soul during life is brought into time by these Spirits. Hence it comes about that certain things which could always be in existence for us were we allowed to take our course, according only to the realm of duration, succumb to time. For instance, we may forget them, or remember them either more or less well, and so on, and this remembrance depends only upon our bodily-soul nature, not upon our soul-spiritual nature.*
>
> *Spirits of Duration, therefore, who act as Spirits of Time - they are Luciferic powers . . .*

And Rudolf Steiner says further regarding the Ahrimanic Spirits:

> *If therefore as men we were subject only to the Spirits of Form proper to us, we should in every way place ourselves into space, bring the spaceless into realization in space, for the Spirits of Form do not live in space. Anyone who seeks the Divine in space will not find it . . . that goes without saying. Anything which arises as form in space is a realization of the spaceless.*
>
> *Those Beings who are Spirits of Form but act as Archai, as Primal Forces, should really, according to their essential nature, belong to the spaceless. But they enter space, they work in space. And this is characteristic of the Ahrimanic - that spiritual Beings who in their true nature are intended to be*

> *spaceless have preferred to work in space. This enables forms to arise in space that do not ray directly out of the spaceless. Thus the spatial is portrayed in the spatial, so that one spatial form reflects another.*
>
> *Perhaps I may take a concrete case. We men are all different from one another because we are placed here out of the spaceless. Our archetypes are in the spaceless. Everything is different from everything else . . . We resemble one another because there are spiritual Beings who form the spatial according to the spatial, not merely the spatial according to the spaceless. We resemble each other because we are permeated by Ahrimanic forces. This must be recognized, or we shall merely inveigh against Ahrimanic and Luciferic forces without any wish to understand them.*

In keeping with the path of equilibrium that is represented by the Temperance arcanum - the challenge that has been set before mankind by the divine spiritual powers is to find a place of balance, of *temperance,* amidst the struggle of the retarded beings that are trying to influence the souls of humanity - and thereby achieve their own ends. The way to meet this challenge is not to utterly eliminate the opposing forces; but rather, to harmonize the realm of Luciferic *immateriality* with the realm of Ahrimanic *materiality* - through the Christ impulse. By embracing the Christ impulse, one presses back the unlawful activities of Lucifer and Ahriman to their rightful domains outside of the soul of man. One must keep them at bay from within one's own personal sphere with the Christ force of the "I Am." For to utterly eliminate them from one's personal sphere is to cause an even greater burden to fall on others who would be subjected to their temptations in addition to the temptations of their own personal adversaries. And so, in closing, I quote a statement by Rudolf Steiner (ibid):

> *A fact connected with many of the secrets of existence is that there is truly nothing in life which, if carried to an extreme conclusion, does not turn into something bad or unfortunate.*

XV

The Devil

Capricorn - Archangeloi - Spirits of Fire - Astral Body

The true path of occult development requires the taming of one's animal nature - so as to become a free spiritual-human. In the Grail story, we find Parzival encountering the temptress Kundry, who is from the court of the castle of Klingsor - the evil black magician of the anti-Grail stream. The Klingsor character that is described by Wolfram von Eschenbach (as reported by Eugen Kolisko) represents an actual historical figure of the 9th century, Landulf of Capua of Sicily (whom, as history ironically tells us, is an ancestor of St. Thomas Aquinas; and which shows us how, even in that early period, a great soul could overcome the forces of the blood). The graphic image of Kundry, as seen in Wolfram von Eschenbach's *Parzival*, is described by Walter Johannes Stein in chapter five of his book, *The Ninth Century - World History in the Light of the Holy Grail*:

> *How strange a being is man, that he complains of a painful blow of destiny which he encounters, even when it is sent to him for his highest good. So it happens with Parzival. He ought to have recognized that his good angel approaches - and what does he see? . . . She wore a blue cloak and a hat of peacock's feathers. Over her hat she slung her plait, black and thick, about as soft as the hair on a hog's back Her nose resembled that of a dog. Two tusk's projected a hand's length out of her mouth. The eyebrows terminated in thick tresses. Her ears were shaped like the ears of bears. The harshness of her face did not exactly invite tender yearnings. She carried a scourge with knotted cords. Its handle was made of ruby. Her skin was the colour of a monkey's skin, and instead of nails she had a lion's claws. One can scarcely consider the maiden beautiful, and yet, she is only the counterpart of what the human being bears in himself when he is still full of desire. And yet this being is the messenger of the Grail. Only he will be*

astonished at this who is not yet clear how beautiful the ugly becomes when it is transmuted. The most detestable lust needs only to be transformed into its counterpart to show itself as a glorious force. This Parzival does not yet know. He is obliged still to experience what this being says as a curse.

Had Parzival not encountered Kundry in her shadow aspect, he would have joined the Knights of the Round Table; and so, Parzival never would have become the Grail King, which was his true, higher calling. The Kundry image is like a mirror for Parzival which reveals to him the state of his vehicle of desire, the Astral-Body. It is Kundry who admonishes Parzival for his failure at the Grail castle to ask the healing question (ibid):

. . . the strict rule of the Grail; 'If thou wilt approach the Grail, thou mayest not come alone, thou must bring with thee thy brother man. Thou mayest not seek only thine own development, thou must seek it for the sake of other men. And thou must bring with thee not only those who themselves have the capacity to see the Grail, who already wear the white robe, but thou must also lead to the Grail those who appear still black and white, in whom heaven and hell have part. They cannot see the Grail, but they can see the Grail bearer, they cannot see the spiritual world, but they can perceive how he who does see it behaves in practical life.' So Parzival is warned that the important thing is to acknowledge the Grail in the conduct of one's life.

The path to the Grail is not a smooth road, for the undeveloped human nature is rough (like the "rough ashlar" of Masonic lore). It is the refinement of the soul which leads to the experience of the Grail, for the world receives its redemption from within the human soul through the ennobling of human relationships. This is the path of the overcoming of the astral-desire nature, which is very clearly described by Rudolf Steiner in the lecture given in Dornach on February 2nd, 1923 entitled, "Self-Knowledge and Experiencing the Christ in Oneself" which is included in the lecture cycle that was published with the title, *Earthly Knowledge and Heavenly Wisdom.*

> . . . *now we have the noble task of becoming aware of our humanity. Our task on earth is to represent the true human essence as fully as possible. We, too, are faced with the challenge to know ourselves. Because of our intellectual consciousness, we can take hold of the inner force of pure thinking and the inner soul condition of freedom in the process of self-knowledge. We can behold the human being with our souls eye, so to speak. However, being able to know ourselves to a certain extent should not make us arrogant. We have to be aware at every moment that we have to struggle for our true freedom. We have to be aware that in our passions and emotions, in our feelings and sentiments, we are dependent on the subhuman.*

The key to attaining self-knowledge is to respond to the moral forces of the spiritual world in one's thinking, feeling, and willing. But these forces are not merely inanimate forces, as a materialist might think of them; these forces proceed from the activities of actual beings of the world of spirit. If one wishes to attain rightful entry into this world of spirit, one must recognize that its pure moral content is a living reality; and, to the extent of one's ability, strive to harmonize with these higher impulses with the utmost clarity. Regarding this challenge, in the tenth lecture of the lecture cycle, *The Effects of Spiritual Development,* Rudolf Steiner says that:

> . . . *a person influences his occult development by the degree of his moral development. A man who is still the victim of his personal emotions and passions, who acts under the influence, one might say, of human instincts, is still living entirely in his Sentient-Soul: he does not moderate his instincts at the behest of reason, nor by the development of his consciousness.*

In this statement, Rudolf Steiner provides a key as to how the three fundamental manifestations of soul play into the challenge. For the Sentient-Soul is pre-intellectual in nature and so it is not using reason as a soul function; for reason is a characteristic of the Intellectual-Soul. As to the Consciousness-Soul (or as it is sometimes called, the Spiritual-Soul), we find a level of soul function that transcends the powers of reason, and is capable of maintaining a separate and independent relationship between the thinking, feeling and willing (although one should strive to maintain harmonious integration between these attributes in the waking state, **XX**). Rudolf Steiner speaks of these three soul levels in the second lecture of the lecture cycle entitled, *Macrocosm and Microcosm*:

> *What are the differences between Sentient-Soul, Intellectual or Mind-Soul, and Consciousness-Soul? The Sentient-Soul operates when we are merely gazing at the things of the external world. If we withdraw our attention for a time from the impressions of this outer world and work them over inwardly, then we are given over to the Mind-Soul. But if we now take what has been worked over in thought, turn again to the outer world and relate ourselves to it by passing over to deeds, then we are given over to the Consciousness-Soul.*

    The nature of the Consciousness-Soul, gives the individual Ego the possibility of approaching the challenges upon the spiritual path from a higher level of synthesis - through its capacity of will - it can overcome the sense-bound thinking and instinctual habits that put one to sleep as regards the things of the spirit. Even Albert Einstein once said to the effect that the problems that mankind has were created at a level of consciousness incapable of solving them. If mankind is to ever overcome the temptations of unbalanced self-interest, it will be through overcoming the kama, or desire nature which strives to dominate the human heart.

    This challenge of overcoming oneself, is the challenge of the Astral-Body that confronts every aspirant to spiritual knowledge. In lecture seven of the aforementioned lecture cycle *The Effects of Spiritual Development*, Rudolf Steiner elaborates on the challenge of the Astral-Body, as it is represented in the Grail story:

> *While the Paradise legend is given, so to speak, for the benefit of terrestrial humanity in so far as they contemplate the origin, the starting point of earth evolution; while the Paradise legend is therefore given in order to enlarge man's horizon so as to embrace the whole of mankind - the Grail legend is given*

in order that it may penetrate into the innermost depths of the astral body, into the fundamental interest of the astral body; because, if left to itself, it becomes an egoist and takes into consideration only its egoistic interests.

When it is a question of the interests of the astral body one can err in two directions only, that of Amfortas; and, before Amfortas is fully redeemed, that of Parzival. The true development of man lies between these two in so far as his astral body is concerned.

This astral body tries to develop within itself the forces of egoism. But if it introduces personal interests into this egoism - it is undermined; for, while it ought to extend its interests to embrace the whole earth these interests become limited to the single, isolated personality. But that must not be, for if this happens, then through the influence of the personality whose Ego is expressed in the blood, the whole human personality becomes wounded - we fall into the error of Amfortas.

The fundamental error of Amfortas is to have introduced the personal wishes and desires, that may still persist in man, into the sphere where the astral body should have acquired the right to be an egoist. The moment we introduce personal interests into the sphere where the astral body ought to overcome personal interests, it is fatal, we become the wounded Amfortas.

But this other error may also lead to disaster - which can only be avoided if the being who is exposed to this misfortune is spotless like Parzival. Parzival sees the Grail pass repeatedly before him. To a certain extent he makes a mistake. Every time the Grail is carried past, it is on the tip of his tongue to ask for whom this food is really intended; but the question dies on his lips, and finally the meal ends without him having asked the question. That is why he has to withdraw after the meal - without having had the opportunity to correct his omission.

It is as if a man, not yet fully mature, were to become clairvoyant for a moment during the night, as if he had been separated by an abyss from what is contained in the citadel of the body and were to contemplate it briefly - without having acquired the necessary knowledge, that is without having asked the appropriate question - as if everything were again withdrawn from his gaze; even if he were then to awaken, he

307

would not be able to enter into the citadel again. What did Parzival really fail to do?

We have heard what the Holy Grail contains. It contains that by which the physical instrument of man on earth must be nourished; that is, the pure mineral extract that is derived from all the foods - which unites in the purest part of the human brain with the finest sense impressions. To whom shall this food be served? As we discover when from the exoteric description we then turn to the esoteric presentation given in the mysteries - it is destined for the human being, who has acquired an understanding of what makes man sufficiently mature, to gradually raise himself consciously to the vision of the Holy Grail. How does one attain the capacity to lift oneself consciously to the Holy Grail?

In the poem it is clearly indicated for whom the Holy Grail is destined. When we turn to the presentation of the legend of the Grail in the mysteries, then it is abundantly evident. In the original legend, the lord of the castle is the Fisher King, a king who ruled over a fisher folk.

There was another who also dwelt amongst the fisher folk and who did not wish to be king over them, but desired a different relationship to these fishermen. He refused to rule over them as a king; he brought them something other than the reigning king - and this was Christ Jesus.

An indication is thus given that the error of the Fisher King - who is Amfortas in the original legend - is the error which inclines him in the one direction. He is not wholly worthy to receive healing through the Grail because he wishes to rule over his fisher folk by force. He does not permit the spirit alone to rule amongst this fisher folk.

At first Parzival is not sufficiently inwardly awake to ask in full self-consciousness the question: What is the purpose of the Grail? What does it demand? It demands of the Fisher King that he should eradicate his personal interest and enlarge his interest to embrace the interest of all mankind after the fashion of Christ Jesus. In the case of Parzival, it is necessary that he should raise his interest above that of a mere innocent spectator of things to the inner understanding of what is common to all men, of what is everyone's due - the gift of the Holy Grail. Thus, in a wonderful way, the ideal of the Mystery *of Golgotha manifests itself between Parzival and Amfortas, the original Fisher King. At the decisive place in the legend there is a delicate hint that, on the one hand, the Fisher King has introduced too much personality into the spheres of the astral body; and that, on the other hand, Parzival has shown too little interest in the general affairs of the world - he is still too naive, too unresponsive to world affairs.*

The immense pedagogical value of the Grail legend is that it could so influence the souls of the disciples of the Holy Grail so that one perceived a kind of balance; on the one hand, by what Amfortas represented; on the other hand, by what Parzival represented. And they knew that a state of balance had to be achieved. For, if the astral body follows its innate, original interest it will raise itself to the ideal of universal humanity which is attained when these words become truth; 'For where two or three are gathered together in my name, there am I in the midst of them' - no matter where these two may be found in the course of terrestrial evolution.

At this point, I beg you not to mistake a part for the whole, but to take today's lecture and that of tomorrow together; for, taken by itself, a single lecture may cause misunderstanding.

It is absolutely necessary that at this point the astral body of man should in its development be raised to the plane of humanity in a very special way so that the interests common to all mankind can become its interests - so that it feels hurt, affronted, and sad at heart when mankind is offended in any way. Furthermore, when through his esoteric development man has gradually succeeded in making his astral body free and independent of the other members of human nature, it is necessary that he should arm and protect himself first of all against the possible influences of other astral bodies. For when the astral body becomes free, it is no longer protected by the physical and etheric bodies which are a strong citadel for the astral body. It is free, it becomes permeable and the forces in the other astral bodies could easily work into it. Astral bodies stronger than itself can gain influence over it, unless it can arm itself with its own forces. It would be disastrous if someone were to be able to freely dispose of his astral body; and yet, in relation to the condition of his astral body, were to remain as innocent as Parzival was initially. That will not do, for then all sorts of influences proceeding from other astral bodies might have a corresponding effect upon his astral body.

... You see how necessary it is that occultism, wherever it is to be cultivated, must be accompanied by morality - for clearly occultism cannot be cultivated unless we strive, at the same time, to emancipate the astral body from the other vehicles. The most disastrous thing in the field of occultism is when stronger personalities are animated by a thirst for power at all costs in order to further their personal interests, their personal aims and intentions.

Only those persons who renounce completely all personal influence are really entitled to work in the field of occultism. The supreme ideal of the occultist, who is to achieve anything legitimate, is to sacrifice everything that is connected with his personality; and to eliminate, as far as possible, his personal sympathies or antipathies from anything he wishes to achieve. He who has sympathies or antipathies for one thing or another and wishes to work as an occultist - must carefully restrict his sympathies and antipathies to his private affairs and tolerate them only in this sphere. In any case, he may not foster or cherish these sympathies and antipathies in a domain where it is intended that an occult movement should develop.

And, paradoxical as it may seem, we can say that to the occult master his teaching is a matter of little consequence; of least consequence is this teaching - which after all is circumscribed by the limitations of his talents and temperament. It will only be of consequence if nothing of a personal nature enters in, but solely what can be of help to the human soul. Therefore, an occult teacher will never impose upon his age any aspect of his knowledge if he knows that it is unsuitable for this age and might be suitable only for another age. We must bear these things in mind when we speak of the peculiar nature of the astral body under the influence of occult development.

In lecture ten of the same lecture cycle, Rudolf Steiner further clarifies the challenges of Initiation:

Therefore, the case may arise where a person has developed only as far as the Sentient-Soul; that is to say, he is dominated entirely by his appetites and impulses. Let us assume that his progress had been accelerated through occult development. The consequence of this would be that he would have transformed his Sentient-Soul into the Intuition-Soul and so he would experience certain Intuitions; but these Intuitions, however, would represent simply the transformation of his own personal impulses, appetites, and instincts.

A person who, in his moral development, has arrived at the Intellectual-Soul (i.e., who has acquired clear-cut, more universal ideas; and, whose mind embraces the general interests of the world), such a person will at least be able to transform his Intellectual or Mind-Soul into the Inspiration-Soul. And so, he is able to arrive at certain Inspirations - although his clairvoyant vision has still not become completely unclouded.

It is only when a person has penetrated with his Ego as far as the Consciousness-Soul that he is able to transform his Consciousness-Soul into the Imagination-Soul - the rest follows as a matter of course because he has already passed through the other stages.

In our epoch, therefore, the purpose of a clairvoyance that is appropriate to this epoch must be, to set man the task of cultivating his moral development; so that, first of all, he divests his impulses and desires of the personal element - and raises them to the level where his personal interests become world interests. Then he must endeavor to really understand himself as an Ego - but as an Ego in the Consciousness-Soul. For, then the Sentient-Soul, the Intellectual-Soul and the Consciousness-Soul can safely be transformed into the Intuition-Soul, the Inspiration-Soul and the Imagination-Soul.

Consciousness-Soul --- Imagination-Soul
Intellectual-Soul --- Inspiration-Soul
Sentient-Soul --- Intuition-Soul
Astral-Body --- Spirit-Self
Etheric-Body --- Life-Spirit
Physical-Body --- Spirit-Man

Rudolf Steiner discusses the nature of the three-fold soul later in the same lecture:

> *On the physical plane, the provisionally transformed Astral-Body is the Sentient-Soul; the provisionally transformed Etheric-Body is the Intellectual or Mind-Soul, and the provisionally transformed Physical-Body is the Consciousness-Soul.*
>
> Astral-Body --- Sentient-Soul --- Intuition-Soul
> Etheric-Body --- Intellectual-Soul --- Inspiration-Soul
> Physical-Body --- Consciousness-Soul --- Imagination-Soul

Rudolf Steiner described the results of this soul-development in the lecture given on the 6th of September, 1921 that was published in the lecture cycle entitled, *The Fruits of Anthroposophy*:

> When the results of Imagination are revealed, man's soul perceives . . . everything encompassed within his life from the time of birth as one cohesive stream. The ego grows beyond the here and now, sensing and experiencing itself within the whole river of life, from the time of birth. As man advances to Inspiration, the world in which he lived before birth, or before conception, opens up before him - and this is also the world he will live in when he has gone through the gate of death. In this way, the immortal element that is part of man's life becomes the object of his perception. Finally, through the development of Intuition, the possibility opens up for one to achieve the perception of past earthly lives.
>
> Therefore, the things anthroposophical spiritual science speaks of may be defined as being of such a nature that the individual steps needed to achieve these results are stated in every case. Furthermore, that the results are verifiable, as I have said - because they have to be expressed in thought forms that are accessible to everyone.
>
> Initially, therefore, man is presented with the discoveries made in anthroposophical spiritual science that relate purely to

human nature. As we begin to find ourselves, as we learn to express in summary form what we experience in our spirit, in our ego, we arrive at the whole of our self opened out and spread out - the self that encompasses both temporality and eternity. We are able to do so by making the findings of spiritual science our own. That is how man finds himself, and it is for the time being the most significant outcome within quite general human terms. At the same time, however, the whole of man's consciousness is expanded.

The findings that have been made in spiritual science have arisen from thought processes that have been enlivened and re-formed; and because of this, they also have an enlivening effect upon human souls when taken into those souls and tested for their truth. As a result, human consciousness gains a new kind of insight into the world.

As mentioned before, Rudolf Steiner has often indicated that the influences that hold mankind back from finding the Christ are basically two-fold, they are the Luciferic and Ahrimanic beings. The simplest view of these two groups of beings is that: the Luciferic beings wish to draw in mankind to the view that matter is only an illusion; while, on the other hand, the Ahrimanic beings want to hold back mankind into thinking that all that exists is matter and that the spirit is an illusion.

In the sixth lecture of the lecture cycle entitled, *Initiation Eternity and the Passing Moment*, Rudolf Steiner has given us some very helpful indications regarding the challenges that result from the temptations of Lucifer working from above, and Ahriman working from below. Through developing the awareness of this polarity of beings one can find the path of balance whereby God willing, one may find the way to Christ.

Can we then say that Lucifer is evil, or can we say that Lucifer is good? One can only say that if a man maintains that Lucifer is evil, and that we must flee from him, then it must also be said that we must avoid fire, because in certain circumstances it destroys life. On the path of initiation we find that the words good and evil cannot be used in this way for the description of any being of the supersensible world order. Fire is good when it acts in good conditions, evil when it works in evil ones - in itself it is neither the one nor the other.

So it is with Lucifer. He exercises a good influence on man's soul when he becomes the instigator of man's sacrifice on the altar of human evolution of all that is most individual in his soul. Lucifer becomes an evil being - rather, what he does becomes evil - when he arouses impulses leading only to self-gratification in the human soul. Thus, once our attention has been drawn to these beings, we have to follow up the effect that their deeds have in the world. The acts of supersensible beings can be described as good or bad - the beings themselves, never!

Just imagine that somewhere, on some island or other, there was a group of people who were of the opinion that, in all circumstances, one must protect oneself from Lucifer and that he has to be kept at the greatest possible distance. That would not prove that the men of this island had better knowledge of Lucifer than anyone else; but simply, by virtue of their particular nature that these men were only capable of converting into evil what Lucifer could give them. The views about Lucifer that are held by the people of this island would only be characteristic of the people - not of Lucifer. I will not say whether or not this island actually exists. You can look for it yourselves in the evolution of the world.

We must seek for the actual attributes of Lucifer in the being of Lucifer himself - whom we meet in the supersensible world. The true manner of his working has to be sought in how his powers take on a different character when, for instance, they work on such an island and their effects ray out on such an island.

And the Ahrimanic? What is that? When we meet Ahriman in the supersensible world, we find that his particular attributes are quite different from Lucifer. To come into a proper relation with Lucifer in the supersensible world, we really only need to purify and cleanse ourselves from all the dross of faulty egohood and the egotism of sensory existence. For then, Lucifer will be a good guide within the actual supersensible world - and we shall not easily become his prey. But with Ahriman it is very different; for he has another task in world evolution. While Lucifer reveals all that is hidden, Ahriman's task for the world of the senses can be described by *saying that - where our world of the senses is, wherever it becomes visible, there is Ahriman, but he permeates it invisibly, supersensibly.*

How does Ahriman help us? He helps us considerably in the physical world - he helps every soul. Indeed, he helps every soul carry into the higher worlds as much as possible from the world of the senses, of what can be enacted out only there; because the world of the senses exists for a purpose and is not merely maya (illusion). It exists as the stage for events that beings may experience - and what is thereby enacted and experienced must be carried up into the supersensible worlds. The power to carry into eternity what is of value in sensory existence is the power that belongs to Ahriman. To give the passing moment back to eternity, that is in Ahriman's power.

However, for the relationship of the individual soul to Ahriman, something quite different comes into consideration. What men experience, which is primarily in the realm of the senses, is of infinite value to them. And I hardly think I shall meet with much opposition if I say that the enthusiasm and the inclination to carefully preserve what we experience in the realm of the senses, and to save it up as far as possible for eternity, is generally much greater than the other tendency; namely, to bring down into the realm of the senses all that we can from the hidden spiritual worlds.

Man quite naturally and understandably loves the world of the senses, and would like to take as much as possible of it with him into spiritual existence. Certain religious faiths, in order to comfort their adherents, tell them that they can quite well take with them into spiritual life all that is in sensory existence. No doubt they say it because they unconsciously realize how much man loves what is his in physical existence. This is what Ahriman's power strives to bring about - that all that we have here can be carried on with us into spiritual worlds.

This inclination and desire to carry up the physical into the superphysical is both strong and forceful in the soul. It is not at all easy to get rid of it when, through death or initiation, you rise from the world of the senses into higher worlds. Therefore, you still have it in you when you become a being of the higher worlds. If you meet Ahriman there - this is just

315

where he becomes dangerous - because he willingly helps you carry into these supersensible worlds all you have gained and experienced in the realm of the senses.

There can be no more cherished companion than Ahriman for those who wish to preserve each passing moment for eternity. Many men, as soon as they have passed the gateway into the supersensible worlds, find Ahriman to be a most accommodating companion; for, he is always seeking to make what takes place on earth play its part in the higher worlds - and to claim it there for himself and for those who work with him. But even that is not the worst, because you do not enter the supersensible world without having in a certain respect cast off your selfhood. If you gained entrance there with merely your ordinary, normal impelling force, you would soon take hold of Ahriman and feel him to be a very easy-going companion. But you cannot enter in that state of being. Upon entering the higher worlds, you already have the faculty for recognizing him as partaking of the divine nature - since, with overwhelming tragedy, he permeates earth evolution from within sensory existence and is forever at pains to so transform it so that it will become a spiritual life.

This is Ahriman's deep tragedy! He would like to change everything that has ever appeared within the physical into the spiritual; and so, within the world order, he battles for the purification and cleansing, in cleansing fires, of everything physical. In this sense it is good, but it would be evil in the sense of the Divine-Spiritual Beings if Ahriman - who is their opponent in the world order - could achieve all of his goals . . .

Rudolf Steiner elaborates further in the same lecture:

So once more we see how what emanates from Ahriman cannot, in itself, be called either good or bad; but rather, becomes good or bad according to how men decide to position themselves before it, and thereby, enter into a relationship with it. Through this we can realize how easy it is for descriptions to be superficial when answering questions that show so little real thought; such as, 'What is Ahriman like?' or, 'What is

Lucifer like?' In the higher worlds, where descriptions of these beings are only possible, there really are no such statements, and no such questions. Thereby, man is drawn into the labyrinth of life. Both Lucifer and Ahriman are working in this labyrinth, and man needs to discover how to have the proper attitude toward them.

This necessity - to strive to find our right relationship to the beings of supersensible worlds - is what gives us the power for self-development. The connections to the supersensible worlds are not maintained through striving for a knowledge that is based on the realm of the senses; but rather, by creating a proper relationship to the spiritual beings in the way we have just described. For this reason, men must proceed into the darkness of life - in which beings work who can just as well be good as evil; and, who can become good or evil through the effects of what they do - which depends on the way in which we relate ourselves to them. This is what brings about the darkness of life.

And so, the light of life, spiritual light, can only shine into the darkness of life by our acquiring the proper relation to, and by getting to know, the various powers of the supersensible worlds who influence our physical world. And also that, when we wish to speak of supersensible worlds, we change our ideas and concepts. . .

These indications of Rudolf Steiner give us a vivid portrayal of the challenge of equilibrium that is embodied in the true meaning of "sin." For, according to Kenneth S. Wuest, the noted scholar of biblical Greek, there are several different words in the Bible which are traditionally translated from the Greek as "sin", one of these words means "to miss the mark." This concept provides a clear picture as to how the Christ Impulse is manifested through "hitting the mark", by being neither too high nor too low, neither to the right nor to the left, but at the point of perfect equilibrium where dwells the "I Am" - the "Christ in you."

At the "Turning Point of Time", Christ was crucified on Golgotha between the thief and the murderer (which represent respectively the Luciferic and Ahrimanic adversaries). Through this deed, Christ made it possible for mankind to come to the point of balance between these two extremes; and, through a change of mind (metanoia) be able to say with

Christ; "Get thee behind me Satan [Ahriman]." (Luke 4:8); and likewise, to return Lucifer to his proper realm outside of the soul of man. For through this mankind will achieve its rightful place as the tenth hierarchy - the "Spirits of Freedom and Love."

XVI

The Tower

Mars - Archangel Samael - Speech - 16 Petaled Lotus

The sixteen-petaled lotus of the throat chakra relates to the sphere of Mars. According to Rudolf Steiner, the throat chakra is a center of speech for expressing the "Word." Furthermore, the sword is a symbol of the "Word" in the Grail legends; such as in this scene from Wolfram von Eschenbach's, *Parzival*:

> *The sword will withstand the first blow,*
> *at the next it will break in twain,*
> *An thou to these waters bring it,*
> *from their flow 'twil be whole again.*
> *Yet where at its source the streamlet*
> *flows forth from its rocky bed,*
> *Shalt thou seek those healing waters*
> *ere the sun stand high o'erhead.*

Regarding this passage Rudolf Steiner says:

> *The Grail Sword breaks when it has grown old; therefore, that of which only the fragments have been handed down must be brought back to its source. What is old must be renewed at the living spiritual source. There the Grail Sword will become whole again . . . Above the well was a globe, and on this sat a dragon. The dragon that sits above the well from which the spring bubbles out, points to the savagery of the men at that time. Parzival must conquer this savagery, the savagery of the forces of the blood.*

This theme is introduced by Walter Johannes Stein in the first chapter of his book entitled, *The Ninth Century - World History in the Light of the Holy Grail*. Later, in chapter five, he provides a key to the symbolism of the martial issues which can be related to the Tower arcanum, as well as to the sixteen-petaled lotus-flower of the throat chakra. For in *Parzival*, Wolfram tells the story of the siege of Patelamunt, the city of sixteen gates, which is being fought over by two armies. The first army is, "proud Friedebrand's Scottish army" who are dressed in white, and guard the city while it is being besieged by an army wearing black that is avenging the death of Eisenhart, the suitor of Belakane.

The name Belakane means pelican, which is a traditional medieval symbol of Christ. According to legend, the pelican fed its young with the flesh of its own breast, symbolizing the sacrifice of Christ upon the hill of Golgotha. The symbol of the pelican is also present in the symbolism of the Rosicrucian tradition, and was also later adopted as a symbol of the Rosicrucian degree of Freemasonry. The bleeding breast of the Pelican is a picture of the mystery of the sacrifice of the Holy Blood. In the first of "The Twelve Keys of Basilius Valentinius" (who is one of the greatest of the alchemical adepts) it says:

> . . . Then the king will come forth; without a blemish, clean, he will stand before you. He can decorate you with his blood, and renovate you.

Belakane, although a pagan, through the purity of her own heart forces is a servant of Christ, and is the mother of Parzival's half-brother Feirefis - whom Wolfram describes as being both black and white. Upon achieving the Grail, Parzival is instructed to bring one other with him to serve the Grail; and so, Parzival chooses Feirefis. Wolfram von Eschenbach has given us a further picture of Feirefis, for he is the father of Prester John - the great Christian "king" in the East. It was this story of Prester John that inspired the Age of Exploration later in the fifteen century; for the European explorers were actually trying to find this legendary kingdom of Prester John in the East.

The kingdoms of Europe in the West, on the other hand, experienced the influences of Parzival as the "king" in the West with his "son" Lohengrin the "Swan Knight", and his "descendants." This Parzival stream in the West, along with the Prester John stream in the East, symbolized the custodians of the esoteric teachings of the Holy Grail, the "Knights of the Word."

To be a "Knight, or Lady of the Word" requires a spiritual connection between thinking and the higher heart forces - as it is by the wakefulness of the heart chakra that one approaches the castle of the Grail; which is an image of the skull enclosing the brain and the pineal and pituitary glands. For it is within this "castle" of the skull that the pineal and pituitary glands receive the mingling of the "earthly and cosmic nutrition streams."

Readiness is the key to all spiritual development, and it is this challenge that Parzival fails to meet when he first arrives at the Grail castle. It is because Parzival fails to ask: "What ails you?" (which would have been the right question to ask of the wounded Grail King Amfortas), that Parzival is at first denied the full attainment of the Grail. As a result of this failure of his "quest", Parzival only has a brief glimpse of the Grail. Amfortas, we are told, is found lying down and has been wounded through desire with "a wound that will not heal." This symbolizes the occult fact that the unchecked astral-desire nature traps the consciousness in a lower state of being within the horizontal-astral principle; which means that the upright forces of the "I Am" must conquer the Mars forces of the throat chakra through the clarity of the awakened, upright Higher-Ego. Because of Parzival's "dullness" he fails at first, only to achieve the "thing" later. For once he has attained the necessary wakefulness he finally achieves "saelde", or blessedness, and becomes the Grail King. What this occultly means is that Parzival overcame - through the power of wakefulness - the selfishness of the Lower-Ego and the astral forces, by putting the welfare of others before his own.

The principle of selfless secrecy that worked within the Brotherhood of the Holy Grail and in other genuine, wholesome occult streams, is described by Rudolf Steiner in the lecture "Evolution and Involution as they are Interpreted by Occult Societies - The Atom as Congealed Electricity", given in Berlin, on December 23rd 1904. This lecture is contained in the lecture cycle entitled, *The Temple Legend*:

> *One cannot attain to what is usually known as immortality unless one is to some extent familiar with the occult sciences. The fruits of occult science do, of course, find their way out into the world along many different channels. A great deal of occult knowledge exists in the various religions, and all those who participate deeply and sincerely in the life of a*

religious community have some share in this knowledge and are preparing themselves for the attainment of immortality in the real sense. But it is still something different, to subsist on the knowledge of this immortality and the feeling of belonging in the spiritual world in concrete experience and with full awareness.

All of you have lived many times; but not all of you are conscious that you have lived through these many lives. However, you will gradually attain this consciousness, and without it, man's life is lived through with incomplete consciousness. It has never been the aim of occult science to inculcate into man a dim feeling of survival, but to impart a clear, fully conscious knowledge of onflowing life within the spiritual world. And there is a certain great law which governs the progressive development of consciousness in all future stages of life. Namely, it is what man works at to help others attain such consciousness which contributes the most to its development. It is an apparently paradoxical proposition: everything a being works at without aiming at developing its own consciousness, helps to maintain that being's consciousness. . . Whatever men do in business merely for the sake of their own livelihood, to the extent that their own business only serves that end, just so much is lost in the way of spiritual gain. On the other hand, everything that is introduced into the work for an objective end, everything that is connected with the interests of another, helps to conserve our consciousness for future evolution. So this is quite clear.

Now think of the Freemasons. In the original arrangement, they gave this injunction to their members: Build such buildings as make no contribution at all to, nor have anything to do with, your own subsistence. All that has survived of the good old Freemasonry, are certain charitable institutions. And although the lodges have lost their living roots in the ancient wisdom and the occult knowledge that was once within their possession, these charitable institutions are evidence of a humanitarianism which, while it is empty [of esoteric substance] it still persists and is cultivated as a tradition. Selfless activity is something that belongs to Freemasonry. For, Freemasonry did originally urge its members to work in the service of humanity, and to build in the objective world.

. . . When you make a machine, you have introduced your spirit into that machine. The actual machine does, of course, perish and become dust; it will be broken up. Not a trace of it will survive. But what it has done does not vanish without a trace, but passes into the very atoms. Every atom bears a trace of your spirit and will carry this trace with it. It is not a matter of indifference whether or not an atom has at some time been a machine, and this change you have wrought in the atom will never again be lost to it. Moreover, through your having changed the atom, through you having united your spirit with the mineral world, a permanent stamp has been made upon the general consciousness. Just so much will be taken from us into the other world.

It is a fact that all [genuine] occult science consists of knowing how a man can act selflessly in order to attain the greatest enhancement of his own consciousness. Consider how certain men who have known this very clearly, have been so selfless that they have taken steps to prevent their names from going down to posterity . . .

In the Middle Ages, no one could say who had built many of the cathedrals or painted many of the pictures. It is only in our epoch that people have begun to attach such value to an individual human name. In earlier epochs, more spiritual than our own, the individual name had less importance. Spirituality in those days was directed at reality; whereas our epoch adheres to the delusion that what is merely transient should be preserved.

I have said this only in order to indicate to you the principle on which these secret societies depended. It mattered to them to efface themselves altogether as personalities, and to allow what they did to live only in its effects. And this brings us to the heart of the secrets. The fact that some particular thing is kept secret is of less importance than keeping one's own share in the work secret. Everyone who keeps his own part secret thereby secures immortality for himself. The rule is therefore clear and unambiguous: As much as you yourself put into the world, that much consciousness the world will give you back. This is connected to the greatest universal laws.

The Siege of the Sixteen Gates of Patelamunt

The frequency of the number sixteen in the Grail stories points to the importance of conquering the challenges of the sixteen-petaled throat chakra (eight of the petals of which were developed in the past evolution of mankind, and are related to the old atavistic dreamy clairvoyance, while the remaining eight petals are connected with the issues that are mentioned in the Buddha's "eight-fold path", and are concerned with the conscious development toward mankind's future evolution).

The common father of Parzival and Feirefis is Gamuret, who has sixteen squires; there are also sixteen chapters in Wolfram von Eschenbach's *Parzival*. If you subtract the prologue, Chretien de Troyes' version of the Grail, *Percival*, also has sixteen chapters. In the game of chess, which is said to have originated in ancient Persia, there are sixteen men in each army: twice sixteen is thirty-two, which equals the twenty-two paths and the ten spheres, or sefirot, on the kabbalistic "Tree of Life." Twice thirty-two equals the sixty-four squares on the chessboard; which is the eight-by-eight magic square of the sphere of Mercury-Budha, and symbolically relates it to the healing forces and compassion of the Buddha who has conquered the Mars sphere with Mercury forces. (To this we can add the sixty-four hexagrams of the Chinese oracle, the *I-Ching*, which is based on the sixty-four permutations of binary-hexadecimal mathematics, which is also the foundation of computer language.) And now, according to Spiritual Science, the Buddha works with Mercury forces from the Mars sphere striving to overcome the ahrimanic-materialistic influences of the retarded Mars spirits that are trying to undermine the human spirit through promoting selfish, sense-bound ideas.

Iron is the metal that traditionally relates to Mars and speech (**XVII**). In the ancient Egyptian mysteries, they performed the "Opening of the Mouth" ritual with a tool called an adze - which was frequently made from meteoric iron. The Grail initiate must bring together the broken sword of the "Word" and conquer the dragon of the lower nature, like the image of the Archangel Michael subduing the dragon with a sword of iron.

In Wolfram's *Parzival,* the story of the death of Eisenhart and the resulting martial warfare, is an image of the chaotic forces of the untamed astral nature, and the battleground of the senses. In the East, the "eight-fold path" of the Buddha strives to overcome the unredeemed astral forces by pointing out the sources of suffering. This was an appropriate way to meet these forces in the pre-Christian era. In lecture eight of the lecture cycle entitled, *Rosicrucian Esotericism,* Rudolf Steiner states:

> *In the lofty heights of the spheres of the Spiritual Hierarchies there is no question of Buddhism opposing Christianity, or vice versa. There the Buddha stretches out his hand to Christ, and Christ reaches out to the Buddha.*

Rudolf Steiner, spoke on many occasions, of the change in the path of supersensible knowledge that came into being through the Incarnation of Christ. As a result of the "Mystery of Golgotha", and the Resurrection of Christ Jesus, humanity has undergone a gradual transformation which has changed the nature of the path of spiritual development for all time. In lecture nine of the same lecture cycle, Rudolf Steiner gives a further indication regarding the relationship between the Buddha and Christ:

> *Now think of the Buddha's teaching. Through observing old age, illness, death, and so forth, the great truth concerning suffering dawned in him. He now taught of the cessation of suffering, of release from suffering through elimination of the desire for birth, for physical incarnation. Now think of humanity six hundred years later. What do you find? Humanity reveres a corpse. Men gaze at Christ on the cross, Christ who dies and through his death brought life. Life has vanquished death.*
>
> *1. To be born is suffering? No, for Christ entered into our earth and henceforward for me, a Christian, to be born is no longer suffering.*
>
> *2. Illness is suffering? But the great medicine will exist, which is, the power of the soul that has been kindled by the Christ impulse. For in uniting himself with the Christ impulse, man spiritualizes his life.*
>
> *3. Old age is suffering? But whereas man's body becomes frail and infirm, in his real self he grows ever stronger and more powerful.*
>
> *4. Death is suffering? But through Christ the corpse has become the symbol of the fact that death, physical death, has been vanquished by life, by the spirit - death has finally been overcome by life.*
>
> *5. To be separated from the being that one loves is suffering? But the man who has understood Christ is never*

separated from the one he loves, for Christ has brought light to the world that stretches between death and a new birth; and so, a man remains united with the object of his love.

6. Not to receive that for which one craves is suffering? He who lives with Christ will no longer crave for what does not come to him, or is not given to him.

7. To be united with what one does not love is suffering? But the man who has recognized Christ kindles in himself that universal love that envelops every being, every object according to its value.

8. To be separated from what one loves is no longer suffering; for in Christ there is no more separation.

Thus, for the illness of suffering, which Buddha proclaimed and recognized, the remedy has been given through Christ. This turning of humanity to Christ, and to the dead body on the cross, is the greatest transformation that has ever come to pass in evolution.

The close tie between Christian Rosenkreutz and the Buddha is one of the inner mysteries of the Rosicrucians. In the inner Rosicrucian teachings, they referred to three Masters in particular - in addition to Christian Rosenkreutz - who are sources of Rosicrucian inspiration: Buddha, Skythianos and Zaratas. These three great initiates have worked together within the Rosicrucian stream in the most intimate ways. Above these great initiates, guiding their efforts, is one of the very highest initiates, Mani; who, as Rudolf Steiner tells us, was incarnated as an historical figure of the 9th century, and who worked behind the scenes bringing spiritual impulses into the social life of Europe leading into the Middle Ages. This great initiate came to be known in the legends of the Middle Ages as Parzival. Furthermore, the original impulse behind Freemasonry also leads to Mani, although it came to be guided by Christian Rosenkreutz. Mani is concerned with an even higher mystery than those of Freemasonry, or Rosicrucianism - the future Manichaean mystery of overcoming evil through selfless-goodness that will arise in the 6th epoch, the epoch of the Spirit-Self, the Aquarian Age (**X, XIV-XXV**).

The Buddha is traditionally associated with the Mercury-Wotan impulse, for Budhi is the equivalent of Mercury in the Hindu and Buddhist teachings; and furthermore, according to Rudolf Steiner, Gautama Buddha was related in an earlier incarnation to the Odin (or Wotan)

Mercury Mysteries of the Teutonic people of Northern Europe.

Odin is the name that represents the Archangel who renounced his own evolution to the rank of Archai in order to bring to the Teutonic people the gift of language; for Odin was "the lord of the runes." In Teutonic mythology it says that Odin gave up his eye when drinking at the well of Mimir. The well of Mimir represents the wisdom of seeing that expresses in speech, and Odin sacrificed his eye there - which was able to see all knowledge and wisdom. This symbolizes the loss of the old atavistic clairvoyance of the third or pineal eye, which resulted in a more awake and individuated form of consciousness. But these are images that are concerned with the past evolution of man. That which points to the future in the Teutonic mysteries is the silent Vidar (pronounced Veedar), whose mission within the Teutonic Mysteries was essentially Michaelic in character.

Rudolf Steiner describes how the nirmanakaya, or spiritual form of the Buddha, had inspired a Scythian mystery-center in the region of the Black Sea, which had been originally founded by the Master Skythianos. It was here that the spirit incarnated who in the future would incarnate as St. Francis of Assisi. Later in the Middle Ages, St. Francis taught a path of overcoming the astral that resembles the teachings of the Buddha more closely than any other Christian teaching. Rudolf Steiner also tells us that in addition to receiving the inspiration of the nirmanakaya of the Buddha, St. Francis was in possession of a Christened Astral-Body, that had been transformed by the Christ, and so became free of all lower forms of desire.

Other than one brief incarnation that ended in childhood, St. Francis, like the Buddha before him, has not had any physical incarnations since reaching his spiritual awakening. He continues to be a powerful source of spiritual-healing forces from his present existence as a nirmanakaya, or spiritual being. The Buddha and St. Francis continue in their spiritual bodies to work together for mankind from within the sphere of Mars, ever working towards the overcoming of materialism. The Buddha's inspirations are working in the astral world that is experienced between incarnations and during sleep. But, although he is working within the sphere of Mars, which is the sphere of the Dynamis or Spirits of Movement, his inspiration derives from the realm of the Spirits of Movement who are associated with the *planet* Mercury (occult Venus - the sphere of the Archai, **V**). The Buddha's inspirations to mankind are powerful healing forces that, in addition to the above mentioned activities, "ray" down upon mankind from the *sphere* of Mercury, which is the sphere of the Archangels. These healing influences are intimately related to the Archangel of Mercury, the Archangel Raphael. This is evident in the festival of the Buddha in early May which is called Wesak, and occurs in the spring season which is associated by Rudolf Steiner with the healing impulses of the Archangel Raphael (**XIV**).

Here we have an image of Mercury - through the clarity of stillness - acting upon Mars and bringing healing to the wounding that is brought about by the unchecked astral-desire nature. The Tibetan Buddhist's have a saying; "If there is a lake, the swans will come." This can be seen as an image of the spiritually evocative power of the inner calm that can arise through the mercurial forces of meditation. The theme of Mercury acting upon Mars is a central theme of Earth evolution as described by Rudolf Steiner (**IV**). For the Earth has made the transition from the Mars half of evolution to the Mercury half of evolution. The first half of Earth evolution is called by Rudolf Steiner the Mars half. The second half of Earth evolution is called the Mercury half. During the Mars half of evolution we were descending into matter; whereas, in the Mercury half of evolution we are resurrecting matter. The transition point is the "Mystery of Golgotha", the Crucifixion and Resurrection of Christ. This transition can be seen as leading from the incarnational Mars half, to the healing "etherization" stream of Mercury that began at Golgotha through the entry of Christ into Earth evolution.

On the other hand, the Mars impulse has led to the grasping of the material world and the subsequent freedom it can bring through the development of the individual Ego. But the downside of this Mars impulse is that it has fostered the development of excessive materialism - which has led to the loss of the awareness of the spirit working both in nature, and within the human realm. A higher aspect of the Mars sphere that can potentially manifest in human consciousness (after it has been through the "etherization" process that is bought about through the Mercury forces working within the thinking) is the experience of Inspiration, which can be described as *inner hearing*. This begins with the growing harmonious movement of the throat chakra, which happens due to the development of the remaining eight petals of the chakra. For as the chakras develop, they begin moving like rotating flowers or wheels, and gradually start to participate in their higher nature.

We have what are called the eustachian tubes which connect the ears to the throat; this shows how the throat center is connected to hearing as a part of the sphere of speech. The eustachian tubes serve as a connection for the sensing and expression of feelings within the throat, and on a higher level they provide hollow spaces for the participation of Spiritual

Beings in human existence - that can be perceived through the experience of Inspiration.

In the story of *Parzival*, it is told how he defeats the Red Knight, and as a result wins the red armor. Parzival then removes his fool's outfit, and puts on the red armor. Parzival's wearing of the red armor signifies his initiation into the sphere of Mars, which is occultly related to the color red. This is an image of the overcoming of the Lower-Ego's astral-desire forces that are working in the blood. For the blood is the bearer of the passionate forces of animality that have to be conquered by the Spiritual-Ego. This is portrayed in alchemical symbolism as the "riding of the Red Lion."

The Alchemical path of overcoming these lower forces relates to the understanding of the metals (**XV, XIX**). The mysteries of the metals are summarized by Marie Steiner in her digest of the cycle of lectures entitled *Initiate Consciousness - Truth and Error in Spiritual Research,* which was given by Rudolf Steiner in August of 1924 at Torquay, on the South-West coast of England. I have extracted parts of this digest in order to give a picture of how the metals relate to mankind. Although we are concerned with Mars and iron in the Tower arcanum, often things are rendered meaningful through their relationship to other things; and so, I have included Rudolf Steiner's indications about all seven planetary metals.

> *Before attaining this knowledge, we feel a renewed anxiety in regard to certain forms. In this there mingles a moral element: one feels all the sins of which one might even be capable, as a weight which would cast one down into the abyss. The permeability of the crystallized mineral becomes a terrible admonisher. But if one lays hold of the center of gravity of one's being in the divinity of one's own inner life, one gains the courage to go further. One learns to know the metallity of the minerals, not only their form but also that which permeates them as substance; one learns how one is sustained in the universe by certain representative basic metals. In the heart lies the center of gravity . . . If one forces a way through to the substantiality, to the metallity, one comes to the feeling: at the point where the physical muscles of the heart lie, there is forced together everything that gives one a firm hold. That which sustains one in the waking earth-consciousness is the element which works upon no other organ with such directness as upon the heart - gold. Its force sustains our heart, maintains our*

consciousness. If now we concentrate upon iron, we feel as if our consciousness were mounting up from the heart to the larynx. Through this means one enters into the soul-world; the Earth disappears, one lifts oneself up to the planetary spheres. Still further outward lives the consciousness which one may develop through concentration upon tin. This slips still further out of the body into the region of the eyes. One feels oneself to be in the wide expanses of the universe, yet still within the stars. The Earth begins to become visible as a remote star. Tin reaches as far as Jupiter; iron as far as Mars; gold is upon the Earth. If one comes to the concentration for lead, the initiate then passes completely out of himself; consciousness reaches all the way to Saturn . . .

Through concentration upon the metallity of copper, one comes, not to a feeling of swooning, but instead the feeling that one is filled with something. Copper fills one. It radiates into the entire body from the middle point beneath the heart. One feels oneself inwardly pressed by a second man. He is for a moment separable from the body. With him one can follow the dead. Now one is not faint, but more compact in consciousness. One has passed out of space and entered into time. . .

In spiritual science all that is metallically fluid is called mercurial. In the state of Nature that we know, only quicksilver is of this character, and is therefore a representative of the mercurial. Its effect upon the human being is to eliminate from him everything that he experiences by way of influences from the physical world and also from the elemental world. In subtle dissemination mercury is everywhere in the world. The moment that a human being takes into himself somewhat more of mercury than this normal quantity, his organism tends at once to eliminate the functioning of all those organs which are derived from the physical world (such as the brain, the glands) and also from the elemental world (such as the senses). The astral body claims possession of those organs which have been built up out of the stars. The human being now becomes filled with a third man, with a soul-organism far more compact and inward. The circulation of the juices now lays hold of the man. Everything within him becomes activity and movement, and relates itself also with the activity without. The human being has now left behind him the world of the Earth and the elements with their airy movement. Persephoneia has reversed her position and turned her face towards the stars. The stars are round about us, and they are colonies of spiritual beings. We are now in the world in which we pass our life as a human being between death and a new birth. It is mercury which carries us there through its effect upon the circulation of our bodily juices, in whose inner activity we come to know our own inner temperament, which is formed between death and a new birth. But along with the temperament is admixed the karma, the testing of fate. The mystery of quicksilver lies in the fact that it is capable of bringing together that which is spiritual in the human being and those organs which derive their formation out of the life between death and a new birth . . .

If man intensifies his relationship to silver, he brings himself into touch with a still deeper organization within him. He brings himself into contact with what comes over as a force out of previous earth-lives. By means of mercury he brought himself through the vascular organization into connection with the spiritual circulation in the entire Cosmos; now, by means of concentration upon silver, he draws together within himself those forces which are connected with the fact that warmth circulates through the course of the blood: this warmth, with the spirituality of the blood which permeates it, has active within itself that which works over out of earlier earth-lives. The direction of the circulation of the blood comes from the world of the stars; in that which pulsates in the blood as warmth, there is effective what comes over as a force out of earlier earth-lives. Silver is the external divine symbol for the course of human life on Earth. It is for this reason that the mystery of silver is bound up with all those things which have to do with reproduction; since through reproduction the being of man is united with his previous earth lives. The mystery of the warmth of the blood is the mystery of silver. Let us turn from the normal to the pathological course of the blood. Fever, in a spiritual sense, is the tearing loose of the human organization from its normal connection with the forward-working previous earth-lives. If such a state comes about, the physician must use silver in his therapy. In all forms of disease which are in any way to be traced back to a karmic connection, silver proves to be a wonderful means of healing.

The Mystery of the Metals

Saturn - Lead - trance consciousness - the crown of the head:
"... the feeling that one has in the presence of the crystallized *mineral* world ... that at any moment one might faint away and dissolve into the Universe."

Jupiter - Tin - deep-dreamless sleep - the brow-point between the eyes:
"... in the region of the eyes is the consciousness of the *plant* forms; down below are their mirrored images."

Mars - Iron - the dream state - the larynx:
"... in the larynx the consciousness develops which I have described to you as that extending into the realm of the animals, to the *animal* kingdom, to those higher forms lying at the basis of the animal kingdom."

Sun - Gold - the waking state - the Ego - the heart:
"It is in the heart primarily that the center of gravity lies which will not permit one to sink, to fly away in space, which presses neither toward the right nor toward the left, but holds one fast. If one maintains the courage ... *one then comes to find oneself held fast within the Universe.*"

Venus - Copper - the Astral-Body - near the navel:
"... leads to the possibility of following the experiences of *the dead*, the so-called dead, beyond that point of time when they pass through the portal of death."

Mercury - Mercury - the Etheric-Body - the pelvic region:
"Mercury takes possession of a certain part of our human being, lifts it up out of the rest of our being, bears this part of the human being into that spiritual world of which *the world of the stars* is an external manifestation."

Moon - Silver - the Physical-Body - near the tip of the spine:
"We may say here that the secret of *the warmth of the blood* is the secret, the mystery, of silver."

XVII

The Star

Aquarius - Angeloi - Sons of Life - Etheric Body
St. Matthew - the Priest - the Initiate of Thought, Feeling & Will

In the "Zodiac of the Lamb of God" (IX), the constellation of Aquarius (the Water-Bearer) relates to the hierarchy of the Angels, the Angeloi, or Sons of Life, and to the Etheric-Body. The densest vehicle of the Angels is the Etheric Body, just as the Archangels lowest vehicle is the Astral-Body, and so on, up the ascending states of being where dwell the Spiritual Hierarchies.

By counting clockwise around the Zodiac starting from Pisces, one sees the relationship between the seven-fold being of man and the Spiritual Hierarchies. This is as seen from the periphery in terms of Cosmic Space.

The Seven-fold Human Being and the Spiritual Hierarchies

Virgo - Kyriotetes, Spirits of Wisdom - Spirit-Man - Sophia

Libra - Dynamis, Spirits of Movement - Life-Spirit - True Self

Scorpio - Exusiai, Spirits of Form - Spirit-Self - Higher Self

Sagittarius - Archai, Spirits of Personality - Ego

Capricorn - Archangels, Spirits of Fire - Astral-Body

Aquarius - Angels, Sons of Life - Etheric-Body

Pisces - Mankind, Spirits of Freedom and Love - Physical-Body

On the other hand, when viewed in terms of Cosmic Time, the Star arcanum relates in the cycle of the "Platonic Great Year" of 25,920 years to the sixth cultural epoch, or Aquarian cultural epoch (**XXIV-XXVI**).

The Seven Post-Atlantean Cultural Epochs

1st Cultural Epoch - Cancer - 7227 B.C.
2nd Cultural Epoch - Gemini - 5067 B.C.
3rd Cultural Epoch - Taurus - 2907 B.C.
4th Cultural Epoch - Aries - 747 B.C.
5th Cultural Epoch - Pisces - 1414 A.D.
6th Cultural Epoch - Aquarius - 3574 A.D.
7th Cultural Epoch - Capricorn - 5734 A.D.

As I have explained in the chapter on the Magician arcanum, the cultural epochs occur 1,199 years later than the astronomical ages, due to the cyclic rotation of the Venus pentagram (**III**). The astronomical ages can be seen as a seeding of a new impulse in the evolution of humanity which will become the dominant spiritual-cultural impulse by the beginning of the cultural age 1,199 years later. According to this principle of the rotation of the Venus pentagram, the Aquarian *astronomical age* begins in 2375 A.D., while the Aquarian *cultural epoch* begins in 3574 A.D. (see: **Part 3**).

An image of the path towards realizing the challenges represented in the region of Cosmic Space described by the ancient initiates as Aquarius (the Water Bearer), is given in the story of the Three Magi carrying their gifts of gold, frankincense, and myrrh in "The Gospel of St. Matthew." This is a picture of the three-fold being of man: thinking, feeling, and willing, and of the three-fold: spirit, soul, and body. It is fitting that this is portrayed by St. Matthew, who represents the "Initiate of thought, feeling and will" (**XIV**); for, according to Rudolf Steiner, St. Matthew is of the lineage of Mathai, who was a student of the great Essene "Teacher of Righteousness" Jeshu ben Pandira; and therefore, the content of the "The Gospel of St. Matthew" is an expression of this particular pre-Christian Essene esoteric stream.

The symbol for St. Matthew, according to Polycarp the disciple of St. John, is the Angel. In the Zodiac it is the Angel carrying water. The etheric world is the realm of the Angels, the "Sons of Life", who have an Etheric-Body as their lowest vehicle; and also, if an Angel were to manifest itself most completely, it would appear as if composed of water vapor. For water is a substance that has a natural affinity to the etheric world, the world of life that participates in all living things. It is water that brings forth, from the etheric, the life of a seed.

Rudolf Steiner once described how in the Arthurian Mysteries of Tintagel, the initiates of the Round Table observed the way the sunlight played upon the ocean waves breaking upon the rocky coast of Cornwall in western Britain. This enabled them to experience the cosmic working of Christ in the etheric world as the "King of the Elements." This way of relating to the natural world was due to the working of the Life-Spirit of Christ in the etheric atmosphere of the Earth. For, since the Mystery of Golgotha, this manner of relating to Christ had set them apart from other Christian streams, as they were inspired directly by the working of the forces of Christ as experienced in nature, and not by the developing historical Christianity that was spreading from the Holy Land.

The Mysteries of the Four Directions

Wotan Mysteries
Blood Warmth
Ego
North

Arthurian Mysteries   **Grail Mysteries**
Etheric-Body   Astral-Body
Life-Spirit   Spirit-Self
West ◄─────────────────────► East

South
Spirit-Man
Physical-Body
Egyptian Mysteries

The mysteries of the East-West axis can be seen as a polarity between the Spirit-Self in the East, and the Life-Spirit in the West. On the other hand, the mysteries of the North-South axis can be seen as a polarity between the Ego in the North and the Spirit-Man in the South. This view of the polarization of the ancient mysteries is developed by Bernard C. J. Lievegoed in his book entitled, *Mystery Streams in Europe and the New Mysteries*.

The Arthurian Mysteries represent a stage in the metamorphoses of the working of the Christ impulse as a zodiacal macrocosmic mystery that is revealed within the world of nature. It is this *macrocosmic* mystery that is the key to understanding the affinity between the Arthurian Mysteries and the Magian Star Wisdom of Persia; for both were mysteries that were performed outside in the open air. The Egyptian Mysteries, on the other hand, primarily took place within temples; for they were essentially *microcosmic* mysteries of the human body, and so, were necessarily more inward in character.

The Egyptian Mysteries, which took place in the age of the Sentient-Soul, can be seen as an expression of the Spirit-Man as it was experienced through the forces of the Sentient-Soul. The ancient Egyptians were greatly concerned with the inner wisdom of the Physical-Body, which is a reflection of the world of the Atma, or Spirit-Man. In light of this, the Egyptian Mysteries of Isis and Osiris were mysteries of death and resurrection; and were, in a sense, prophetic regarding the Resurrection of Christ Jesus at Easter through His manifestation of the Atma-Physical.

In Northern Europe, the Mercury Mysteries of Odin, or Wotan, were concerned with developing courage from out of the impulses of the individual Ego. This concept explains the wildness of the Viking warriors who fought independently rather than in organized fighting units; for the Ego is the youngest part of a human being through its having entered human evolution at a later stage than the Physical, Etheric, or Astral-Bodies. When the Scythian Prince Wotan brought the Mercury impulse from the region of the Black Sea mystery center that had been established by Skythianos, it was to cultivate the Ego within the Germanic tribes through the heart forces of courage. To test this courage, at the Externsteine mystery center in Germany, the warriors had to walk across a narrow rope-bridge that was strung up high between two giant stones.

This stream of the Ego impulses had to be developed in the North to harmonize with the Spirit-Man impulses of the South. Just as the Life-Spirit impulses in the West provided a polarity to the impulses of the Spirit-Self in the East. Although the Spirit-Self mysteries, that had been preparing in the East through the Persian Mysteries, were star-mysteries of the open air - they had a decidedly more inward character than the Celtic Cosmic-Christianity of the Arthurian Mysteries in the West.

The Arthurian Mysteries in the West observed the working of Christ in nature and were "Knights of the Sword" - that conquered the dragon *without*. On the other hand, in the Grail Mysteries from the East they experienced the working of Christ in the human heart as "Knights of the Word" - the stream of the "priest-kings" who conquered the serpent *within*. These Grail Mysteries, of the "Knights of the Word", provided the seed impulse out of which will develop the future working of the Spirit-Self in mankind during the Aquarian epoch.

The Aquarian path of the unfoldment of the Spirit-Self is symbolized by the Star arcanum, and is the path of the Magian priest-king who follows a star - representing those individuals who have developed the spirit and soul forces that are necessary in order to commune with their personal Guardian Angels, and to act in the light of that understanding as a sovereign "I Am" working through the Spirit-Self (which is the vehicle directly above the Consciousness-Soul, and which manifests its consciousness within the realm of the Angels).

The path of the Magian priest-king is represented in "The Gospel of St. Matthew" by the three Magi - Melchior (European), Balthazar (Asian), and Caspar (African), with their three gifts respectively of gold, frankincense, and myrrh, representing the three-fold mysteries of the spirit, soul, and body, and the mastery of the thinking, feeling, and will. According to the indications of Rudolf Steiner, the three Magi (one of which in another life was Pythagoras) had previously incarnated together, in Babylon during the 6th century B.C., as students of the teacher Zaratas - who was an incarnation of the original Zarathustra that had founded the Magian stream during the Old Persian epoch, and whose ". . . task was to find the connection between the physical and the spiritual world."

Of the three Magi, the aforementioned Caspar came from North Africa in the South with his gift of myrrh and was the bearer of the remnant of the resurrection mysteries of Osiris which streamed from ancient Egypt - and were the ancient mysteries that were most intimately concerned with the Physical-Body.

This Magi Caspar, with his gift of myrrh, could also be thought of as a successor to one of the greatest "Leaders of Mankind" - the Manu, who had previously incarnated as Senenmut, the aforementioned wise counselor to Queen Hatshepsut. This becomes even more meaningful when one considers that the costly incense myrrh, which is extracted from the tree *commiphora abessinica*, was imported into Egypt from a land to the South which the Egyptians called Punt, and is considered by modern scholars to have been probably located in either present-day Somalia or southern Arabia (also, according to the *Kebra Negast*, during the time of King Solomon, in this region was located the legendary domain of the Queen of Sheba). On the walls of the magnificent temple at Deir el-Bahri, that was built for Queen Hatshepsut by Senenmut, a trade expedition to Punt is depicted; in which, coincidentally, myrrh is shown being imported on ships from Punt to Egypt.

This great individual Caspar was previously incarnated as the "young man of Sais" (a city in Egypt) - who was put to death for attempting to prematurely reveal the Mysteries of Isis. This Magi Caspar, who was initiated into all the Egyptian, Persian, and Greek star-wisdom that was present at that time in Alexandria, died shortly after the birth of the Solomon Jesus and was soon reincarnated as the "youth of Nain" who was raised from the dead by Christ Jesus; thereby further deepening his relationship to the Resurrection Mysteries. This series of lives led up to his incarnation as Mani, and prepared him for his task in the 9th century as the Grail King Parzival - the bearer of the esoteric Magian star-wisdom of the Holy Grail; and furthermore, as the representative initiate of the Consciousness-Soul, and the prototype of our modern consciousness.

The "priest-king" Parzival was the link that connected the Grail stream of the Spirit-Self from the East, with the Arthurian stream of the Life-Spirit from the West (**XXIV**). This mingling of streams, which happened in the year 869 A.D., was an antidote to the change in the teachings of the church which no longer taught the doctrine of St. Paul; which is, that a trinity of spirit, soul, and body comprise the human being.

In the course of evolution, mankind is destined to separate out from nature as individual, free, spiritual beings. In order to bring this about, mankind must necessarily develop the intellect - which results in feeling a sense of separation or isolation; and so, one must "pass through the valley of the shadow of death" (Parzival = "pierce the valley") until one achieves true higher knowledge of the spiritual world. Parzival is the knight who found Christ all on his own and became the Initiate "Grail-King", without the intermediary of the church.

Parzival's "half-brother" Feirefiz, was able to find the Grail as a result of his relationship with Parzival; for Parzival was instructed that he must bring another with him to serve the Grail. According to Wolfram von Eschenbach, the "son" of Feirefiz was the "priest-king" in the East known in the Middle Ages as Prester John. The legends that developed around the name Prester John would later in the 15th century inspire the Age of Exploration. Prester John is a mystery name which represents one of the leading initiates of Grail Christianity, who in a later incarnation would come to be known as Christian Rosenkreutz. Regarding Prester John, Wolfram von Eschenbach says in chapter XVI, verses 587-592 of *Parzival*:

> *Then first in her distant journey*
> *did Repanse de Schoie find joy,*
> *And in India's realm hereafter*
> *did she bear to the king a boy;*
> *And Prester John they called him,*
> *and he won to himself such fame*
> *That henceforward all kings of his country*
> *were known by no other name.*
> *And Feirefiz sent a writing*
> *through the kingdoms*
> *whose crown he bore,*
> *And the Christian faith was honored*
> *as it never had been of yore.*

Later in the Middle Ages, the underground stream of the Cosmic Christianity of the Grail was to resurface in the Order of the Knights Templars. Curiously, even though the events in Wolfram's story *Parzival* took place according to him, eleven generations earlier - which would point to the 9th century - Wolfram, who was writing in the 12th century, makes the Knights Templars the guardians of the Grail, and yet the Order of the Knights Templars was not officially founded until 1118. It is clear that Wolfram (who was himself a member of the Order of Teutonic Knights) wants to make the connection between the Grail Brotherhood which was founded in 717 by Charibert von Laon, and the Templars which were founded in 1118. The star-wisdom of the Brothers of John (as this stream is sometimes referred to) was later carried by the Rosicrucians, after the demise of the Templars. Rudolf Steiner provides us with further details in the lecture entitled, *On the History of Christian Rosenkreutz*:

> *What happened later through the legend of the Holy Grail is also expressed in the saga [of Flor and Blanchflor] . . .*

Flor and Blanchflor are not a 'real' outer couple. In the lily is expressed the soul which finds its higher egohood. In this union of lily-soul and rose-soul was seen something which can find a relation to the Mystery of Golgotha. It was said that over and against that stream of European initiation which is brought about by Charlemagne, and through which is united exoteric and esoteric Christianity, over against this the purely esoteric Christianity is to be kept alive, is to be continued in purity.

In the circles of the Initiates it was said: The same soul which was in Flos or Flor [Charibert von Laon] and which is celebrated in the song of the saga, appeared again and reincarnated in the 13th and [again in the] 14th century in order to found a new Mystery School which is to cultivate in a new form, corresponding to modern times, the Christ Mystery. It appeared in the founder of Rosicrucianism [Christian Rosenkreutz]. Thus we meet with the secret of the rose in comparatively early times, for the saga really comes from the time before Charlemagne.

Thus it is that esoteric Christianity flows into Rosicrucianism. Since the 13th and 14th centuries Rosicrucianism has developed those initiates who are the successors of the ancient European Mysteries, the successors of the school of the Holy Grail.

This lecture in its entirety, is contained in the book entitled *A Christian Rosenkreutz Anthology*, which was compiled and edited by Paul M. Allen in collaboration with Carlo Pietzner. This is a valuable work that specifically studies the Rosicrucian Mysteries. Furthermore, Paul Allen also takes note (page 616) of another interesting possibility concerning Rosicrucian history where he mentions a certain Fr. Wittemans, who is a lawyer and member of the Belgian Senate:

An important communication has been made by H. Roegsen (should be Roesgen) von Floss (sic) of the Hague, who writes: 'according to a tradition which exists in the family von Roegsen (Roesgen) Germelshausen, its members were included among the initiates in the German Mysteries. Although swept away by the current and become Christian, this family remained faithful to the neo-Gnostics who appeared in the Order of the Albigenses. The latter made adherents, especially in France, and they also had branches in Germany. The assassination in 1208 of the Papal Legate, Pierre de Castelnau, furnished the Pope, Innocent III, with a pretext for accusing the Order of the Albigenses with it and having them exterminated. He confided this mission in Germany to the Dominican Order. The castle of Germelshausen was besieged, set on fire, and sacked. The whole family was exterminated in the most barbarous manner. But the youngest scion, Christian, escaped and fled, proceeding toward the East. Aided by co-religionists, he arrived finally in Turkey and Arabia where he was judged worthy of having revealed to him the secrets of the Order of the Rosy Cross, which [were a Christian synthesis of the ancient Egyptian rites, that were established in Memphis by a converted Serapian priest named Ormus in 46 A.D., and] had long been flourishing in those countries. Returning to Europe, Christian renounced his family name and took that of Christian Rosenkreutz.

This provides us with an intriguing picture of the joining of the Eastern, Southern and Northern streams in Rosicrucianism. About this story Paul Allen further notes:

If the data contained in the note above is accepted as factual, then it well may have been that the boy was placed in the monastery as a means of protecting his life, to begin with. - In addition, the well-known scholar, Dr. Johann Solomon Semler (1725-91), professor of Theology at Halle from 1752 until his death, and historian of Rosicrucianism, reports that this was the St. Agneten Monastery of the Augustinian Order near Zwolle, in the Netherlands. According to Semler's data, one of the fellow-brothers of Rosenkreutz was Thomas a Kempis (1380-1471), who wrote there a 'Hortulus Rosarium', and whose four books of the 'Imitation of Christ' Theophilus Schweighardt called the 'fons et origo', fount and origin of the Rosicrucian 'credo.'

This is very interesting in light of the fact that the book by Thomas a Kempis, *Imitatio Christi*, or *The Imitation of Christ* is probably the second most widely read Christian book in history next to the *Bible*. Thomas a Kempis, whose actual name is Thomas Hammerlein, was born near Cologne in the Dutch town of Kempen, from which is derived his pen name Thomas a Kempis (Thomas of Kempen). Before entering the Augustinian monastery at Mount St. Agnes near Zwolle, Thomas a Kempis studied, along with his older brother John, at the school in the nearby town of Deventer that was run by the Brethren of the Common Life; which was a pietist lay-group that was associated in that area with the Augustinian canons. The Brethren of the Common Life were successors to the group of German Christian mystics known as the Friends of God, an association that was founded by the followers of the teachings of the "Friend of God from the High County" (An important figure that I discuss more fully in the chapter on the Archangelic Period of Samael). It was out of this circle of the Friends of God that another classic of Christian mysticism, known as the *Theologia Germanica* (*German Theology*), was anonymously written, and which is very similar in tone to *The Imitation of Christ*. Paul Allen then provides further information from Semler's account:

> *Dr. Solomon Semler records that in the year 1393 the Bishop of Utrecht, Florentius Radewijns died. He had been engaged in alchemistic studies at the St. Agneten Monastery with the Deacon, Gerhard Groote (1340-84) [Geert Grote, an associate of the Brethren of the Common Life]. As their 'adjunct and collaborant' a boy served them, whom in jest they called 'Rosenkreutz', but whose real name was different. After the death of the Bishop, his patron and protector, the young 'Famulus' Rosenkreutz went on a journey to the Orient.*

Theophilus Schweighardt, who is mentioned in the earlier quotation, is one of the pseudonyms of a man named Alberti who was a friend of Johann Valentin Andreae, the author of *The Chymical Wedding of Christian Rosenkreutz*, and other principle Rosicrucian writings.

Further intriguing indications, concerning the Rosicrucian circle that Johann Valentin Andreae was associated with, are given in the book entitled *Archiv fur Freimaurer und Rosenkreuzer*, which was published in Berlin in 1783, where it says (ibid):

In the posthumous writings of M. C. Hirschen, pastor at Eissleben, it has been found that John Arnd informed him in confidence as a near friend and former colleague how he had been told by Johann Valentin Andreae - also subrosa - that he namely Andreae, with thirty others in Wurtemburg had first sent forth the 'Fama Fraternitatis' [one of the principle early Rosicrucian works], that under this screen they might learn the judgment of Europe therein, and also what lovers of true wisdom lay concealed here and there, and would then come forward.

Concerning the Rosicrucian Order and the mystery of the Temple of Solomon, Rudolf Steiner gives indications in a lecture about "The Legend of the True Cross" or "Golden Legend" entitled, "Concerning the Lost Temple and How it is to be Restored", which is to be found in the lecture cycle entitled, *The Temple Legend*.

So we shall only understand theosophy when we look upon it as a testament laying the ground for what the Temple of Solomon denotes, and for what the future holds in store. We have to prepare for the New Covenant, in place of the Old Covenant. The old one is the Covenant of the creating God, in which God is at work on the Temple of Mankind. The New Covenant is the one in which man himself surrounds the divine with the Temple of Wisdom, when he restores it, so that this 'I' will find a sanctuary on this earth when it is resurrected out of matter, and set free.

So profound are the symbols, and so was the instruction, that the Templars wanted to be allowed to confer upon mankind. The Rosicrucians are none other than the successors to the Order of the Templars, wanting nothing else than the Templars did, which is also what theosophy desires; they are all at work on the great Temple of Humanity.

XVIII

The Moon

Pisces - Humanity - Spirits of Freedom and Love - Physical Body

Humanity is the tenth hierarchy in the becoming, what Rudolf Steiner called the "Spirits of Freedom and Love." The spiritual human being is just beneath the Angels in the ranks of the Celestial Hierarchies, and has as its lowest vehicle the Physical-Body (**IX**). The spiritual destiny of humanity is to develop the spiritual faculties which are necessary to become a "citizen of the Cosmos", and not just of the physical world. This necessitates an overcoming of the animal nature, or astral-desire principle.

In the imagery of the Moon arcanum we see a crayfish at the edge of the water, as crayfish by nature walk backwards, we know that it is descending into the water. This implies the importance, on the path of Initiation, of the mirror image (water) of memory - for looking back on one's life - on "what has been." The path the "Fool" travels leads through the middle, which passes between a dog on the left and a wolf on the right. This reminds one of Christ, "the Representative of Mankind", crucified at Golgotha - between the thief (Lucifer) and the murderer (Ahriman).

The dog symbolizes Lucifer "the light bringer", who as Prometheus was the thief who stole fire from the Olympian gods in Greek mythology. The name Lucifer is usually esoterically assigned to the planet Venus, the bright "Morning Star." But in "The Revelations of St. John the Divine" (16:??), Christ says; "I am . . . the radiant morning star", about which Rudolf Steiner says; "we must speak of [the sphere of] Mercury as the Morning Star" (**V**). Lucifer wishes to set himself up as a substitute Savior with his self-contained, effulgent light. The Christ-Light is like the warm, radiant light of the Sun, while the planet Venus is merely a mirror reflecting the sunlight, it only appears to radiate light. Lucifer wishes to divert mankind to a lesser good through bypassing the principle of freedom and achieving automatic goodness through habit and external authority - for the dog can be put on a leash and made to obey.

The wolf on the other hand, symbolizes Satan, or as he is known by his Persian name, Ahriman "the murderer", who wishes to kill all knowledge of the spirit by keeping mankind concerned only with matter. Fenris the wolf, in Norse mythology, was chained to the earth by the gods; this is the destiny of the souls that fall prey to the snares of Ahriman, the "spirit of materialism."

The two towers in the background of the Moon arcanum represent the bondage that is the fruit of these two paths of error. The luciferic error leads to a sub-spiritual evolution that is beneath the goal of a Spirit of Freedom and Love, while Ahriman wishes to transform the Earth into an extremely clever mechanical world - devoid of spirit. In the *Bible*, when the term "Devil" is used it is in reference to Lucifer the "light-bringer", and when the name Satan is used it refers to Ahriman, the "Father of lies."

In the Grail legends it is told how the Grail is fashioned from a stone that fell from the crown of Lucifer. This picture relates to a great mystery regarding the Crucifixion of Christ between the thief and the murderer. For, the Mystery of Golgotha has provided a healing force even to the "fallen" spirits of Lucifer. On the cross of the repentant thief on Golgotha, the great rebellious spirit, Lucifer, had been given an opportunity for redemption. This was known to the Early Church Fathers, and is expressed in the words of St. Gregory of Nyassa:

Through the Crucifixion, good was done, not only for all lost creatures, but also for the author of our perdition.

By this deed of Christ at the Crucifixion, the Luciferic spirits were given an opportunity to align themselves with the Divine Plan if they so desired. The time frame set aside for the Luciferic spirits to accept their redemption extends from Golgotha, until the year 869 A.D.

This dedication to redeeming the "fallen" ones is shown by the example of the Order of the Knights Templars in the Middle Ages. For, if a man became excommunicated from the Catholic Church he could always find refuge by joining the Order of the Templars. It is this aspect of grace that is shown by Christ when He was asked why He was keeping the company of criminals and sinners He said, to the effect, that the saints didn't need his company to be good.

At the top of the Moon arcanum is the image of the Moon, inside is shown a crescent Moon; this can be seen as an image of the Grail chalice, which is tilted so that its contents can be shared with the Grail server. This sharing of the Spirit is shown by the "tongues of flame" that are beneath the Moon. These represent the "tongues of flame" that descended upon the heads of the disciples of Christ at the Mystery of Pentecost - which is a major festival of the Christian calendar. The festival of Pentecost occurs on the fifteenth day of Eastertide, and is often referred to as Whitsun, or Whitsunday, which means "White Sunday" and is a name derived from the Old English expression "Hwita Sunnandaeg."

The name of the Grail King, Parzival, is "written" on the dark part of the Moon that rests above the light crescent part like a host over a chalice; but Parzival must pass between the two adversaries and "pierce the valley" to realize his destiny as the Grail King. The thirty-two beams that surround the image of the Moon are the thirty-two paths of wisdom spoken of in the kabbalistic work the *Sefer Yetzirah*. The thirty-two paths of wisdom are composed of the combination of the ten sefirot (which are images of the planetary and stellar spheres of the Angelical Hierarchies (**VII**) and the twenty-two paths on the Tree of Life that are symbolized by the twenty-two major arcana of the Tarot (**I**).

A form of Christian alchemystical and kabbalistic symbolical teachings were utilized by the Rosicrucians, who were the esoteric successors to the Knights Templars. To use the words of Johann Valentin Andreae, the Rosicrucians were "founded upon the ruins of the Knights Templars." The Rosicrucian link to the Templars is further shown by the saying "In hoc signo vinces" ("In this sign conquer") which is present on the wedding invitation that is given by an Angel to Christian Rosenkreutz, in the Rosicrucian drama that is attributed to the hand of the aformentioned Andreae: *The Chymical Wedding of Christian Rosenkreutz.*

The symbolical engravings that are to be found in the Rosicrucian tradition serve as a means of expressing the mysteries of esoteric Christianity; and in addition, according to Rudolf Steiner, these symbolical engravings were helpful in neutralizing the untamed elemental forces that can be released within the soul upon the path of Initiation. The Christian kabbalistic teachings provided the Rosicrucian's with an effective "memory theater", to aid in remembering the system of planetary and stellar correspondences that relate to the mysteries of the Macrocosm and the Microcosm.

I remember many years ago, Douglas Gabriel and I had a private conversation with Carlo Pietzner where he spoke of how the Rosicrucian tradition had two basic streams of manifestation: the artistic, and the scientific. He also spoke of various highly, significant individuals who received Rosicrucian inspiration at different times within these two fundamental areas of endeavor.

To give some examples, in the artistic realm we find: Johann Valentin Andreae - the author of the seminal Rosicrucian writings, William Shakespeare - who needs no introduction, and Jacob Boehme - one of the greatest European mystics.

Among those inspired by Christian Rosenkreutz in the scientific realm were: Johannes Baptista van Helmont (who was identified as a true Rosicrucian by Rudolf Steiner). Van Helmont made important chemical discoveries, such as the discovery of carbonic gas which he called "gas sylvestre", he also wrote numerous medical works. Also we may include, Robert Fludd, who in addition to writing many works of astrological cosmology (that were illustrated with the wonderful engravings by Theodore de Bry), also wrote numerous medical works (which were influenced by Paracelsus), and was a pioneer in pulse diagnosis.

Concerning the history of Rosicrucianism that can be gleaned from published sources, the eminent scholar Dame Francis Yates gives quite a comprehensive view in her numerous works on the Hermetic-Rosicrucian tradition. She also investigates the Hermetic-Rosicrucian influence in the architecture of the Globe Theater, which is shown in its name and geometrical design. Shakespearean theater is a cosmic picture of life by a true master of the human soul, a "memory theater" of the world in miniature as portrayed by the characters in the play. For more in-depth historical information regarding the events surrounding Rosicrucianism (although she does not realize that Christian Rosenkreutz was an actual historical figure) see her books especially: *The Art of Memory*, and, *The Rosicrucian Enlightenment*.

The artistic works of the Rosicrucian tradition were concerned with the awakening of the human soul, while the scientific works were concerned with the workings of the spirit in nature, with an overlapping of these two streams of art and science in varying degrees by different authors. This has led to the tradition of looking for alchemical secrets in works of art, and also to looking for mystical revelations in alchemical works; for, art and science are intimately intertwined in Rosicrucianism.

Central to the Rosicrucian tradition is a form of Christian spiritual initiation which leads to higher knowledge. In order to understand this tradition, you must distinguish between the Rosicrucian brothers themselves, and those that received inspiration from a Rosicrucian impulse. The Rosicrucian Brotherhood, like the Order of the Knights Templars before them, and earlier still the Brotherhood of the Holy Grail - had an inner circle of twelve, and a larger outer circle, as well as those - who for varying times and for various reasons - were inspired by the impulses that proceeded from this branch of the "Mother Lodge of Humanity" (**XXV**).

Rudolf Steiner has shared from his clairvoyant investigations of the Akashic Records, numerous indications regarding the most fundamental circle of the twelve great "Spiritual Leaders of Mankind" that compose the inner circle of the "Mother Lodge of Humanity", and which "Lodge" of the servants of Christ is alluded to in the *Bible* with the reference to Jesus being a "Priest after the Order of Melchizedek." From this central source, numerous spiritual developments have occurred throughout history whereby members of this inner circle have sought to nurture the development of humanity towards the embodiment of the "I Am", "the Christ in you." Among these developments are included the Brotherhood of the Holy Grail and the original Rosicrucian Brotherhood.

The founder of the Rosicrucian Brotherhood in Europe is the actual historical figure of Christian Rosenkreutz, who in his incarnation as Charibert von Laon, founded the Brotherhood of the Holy Grail (**XXIV**); and is an incarnation of Lazarus who was raised from the dead by Christ Jesus and subsequently became known as John "the Disciple whom Jesus loved."

Throughout history Lazarus-John has had an intimate relationship to another individual who was the "son of the widow" raised from the dead by Christ Jesus, and who is referred to in the *Bible* as, "the youth of Nain." About the "youth of Nain" the *Bible* tells us very little, although we know from Rudolf Steiner, that he was later to incarnate as Mani the founder of Manichaeism. For a long time, the only source of information on Manichaeism was the writings of its opponents; over the last century, numerous Manichaean writings have been discovered in Egypt and Asia.

In the writings of his opponents there had first appeared a legend that Mani had received from a widow the writings of Skythianos; which, though it is probably not historically true in all of its details, nonetheless, it points toward the connection between Mani and the great initiate Skythianos; and also, connects Mani, once again, with the designation of the "widow's son."

In his writings, Mani describes his numerous clairvoyant experiences, the first of which he had when he was but twelve years old, of an Angelic being he referred to as his "twin", or "companion" (Arabic, el-Tawan; Syriac, Tom); who was a messenger from "the High God, the King of the Gardens of Light." Mani described this as an experience of "the Living Paraclete" in the Coptic text known as the *Kephalaia*; and, in the following, I quote a relevant passage which I have adapted from several translations of the text:

> *In the very year that Ardashir was to receive the crown (i.e., March 228-April 229), the Living Paraclete descended down to me and he spoke with me. He revealed to me the secret mystery which was hidden before the [creation of the] worlds and generations - the mystery of the Depths and of the Heights; he revealed to me the mystery of the Light and of the Darkness - the mystery of the struggle, fight and great war which the Darkness waged against the Light. After which he showed me how by mingling the Light had interpenetrated the Darkness, and how this world was founded . . . [He revealed to me] the mystery of the creation of Adam, the First Man, and the mystery of the Tree of Knowledge from which Adam ate - through which his eyes were made to see; also the mystery of the Messengers who are sent into the world to choose out the churches [i.e., to establish the religions] . . . Thus through the Paraclete was revealed to me everything that is and will be - all that the eye sees and ear hears, the mind thinks and the heart desires - I have learnt everything through him. Through him I saw the All, and I became One Body and One Spirit [therewith].*

And so Mani, as a result of his uniting in spirit with the "Paraclete", which can be thought of as a microcosmic, angelic emissary of the macrocosmic Heavenly Sophia, *the purest manifested servant* of the Holy Spirit - began his mission as a teacher at the young age of eighteen. Some years after this, Mani retreated to a cave for a year to pray, fast, and meditate. During this retreat, Mani had an experience of the spiritual being of Christ that paralleled St. Paul's experience on the road to Damascus, and which fully accomplished Mani's anointing as an emissary of the Risen Christ. Mani was led by the Risen Christ into the experience of the complete chain of evolution which extends from Old Saturn to Future Vulcan (**IV**). From these experiences Mani was then able to put into his own words, in symbolic picture-language, the content of his revelation cloaked in the language of Zoroastrian dualism combined with the influence of the *Old Testament* Enoch literature, and the Christian writings along with other influences. For these Zoroastrian influences were appropriate for one of his primary missions, as an Apostle to the Persians.

As a result of his attempts to bring the living understanding of Christ to the followers of Zarathustra, Mani was martyred. After his death, as a

"Grail Angel", Mani would continue working - from within the Spiritual World, as a leader of the "Mother Lodge of Humanity" - to inspire mankind's strivings toward a living experience of Christ.

In the 4th century, we know from Rudolf Steiner, Mani participated in a great spiritual council of leading representatives of the "Mother Lodge of Humanity" concerning the future spiritual path of humanity. This great spiritual council of the "Masters of Wisdom and of the Harmony of Feeling" included Mani, along with the current incarnations of Zarathustra, Skythianos ("the mysterious hidden one"), and the nirmanakaya, or spiritual form of the Buddha. In his next incarnation, after this momentous spiritual council, Mani incarnated as Parzival in the 9th century and took upon himself the task of finding the spirit in a new and purely individually, human way - from within the Consciousness-Soul - as a prototype for the future development of the Consciousness-Soul during the fifth cultural epoch, which would begin in 1414 A.D. This attainment by Parzival of a spiritualized consciousness, that was achieved from within the Consciousness-Soul, would insure the possibility of the future development of the spiritualized, "permeable consciousness" of the Spirit-Self (or Manas) in the sixth cultural epoch (after the development of the Consciousness-Soul in the fifth cultural epoch - which by its own nature only perceives the reflection of the sense perceptions upon the brain and nervous system). Upon achieving this attainment, which is described as the "kingship of the Holy Grail", Parzival then united the Brotherhood of the Holy Grail with the Knights of the Round Table as an earthly reflection of the "Mother Lodge of Humanity."

Prester John is said to be the mysterious "nephew" of Parzival who is represented by Wolfram von Eschenbach, and other medieval sources, as a great "king" with an empire in the East. According to Spiritual Science, the name Prester John alludes to an incarnation of Lazarus-John, who is the spiritual leader of an occult brotherhood disseminating impulses proceeding from the "Mother Lodge of Humanity", and who would later incarnate as Christian Rosenkreutz. This would mean that soon after his incarnation in the 8th century as Charibert von Laon, he would of incarnated in the 9th century as "Prester John", who is represented by Wolfram as the "son" of Feirefiz, the "half-brother" of Parzival.

Lazarus-John and the Youth of Nain were previously incarnated together in the 15th century B.C., along with perhaps the most complete grouping of the "Leaders of Mankind" and their representatives to be incarnated together at one time (**XXV**), in the court of the 18th Dynasty Egyptian Queen regnant Hatshepsut Ma`atkare' (reigned c. 1473-1458

B.C.). Although Hatshepsut was not the only woman to have ruled Egypt, for she was proceeded and followed by others, Hatshepsut was the only woman, in the approximately 3,000 year history of dynastic Egypt, to take on the full title of pharaoh. This uniting in Egypt of the key figures of the "Mother Lodge of Humanity", centered around Hatshepsut's counselor Senenmut (who, according to Ehrenfried Pfeiffer, was an incarnation of the Manu), and came about as an impulse to save the pure Sun Mystery impulse from the decadent impulses of the Moon Mysteries.

The indications of Rudolf Steiner regarding the emphasis of the Sun Mystery impulse in the reign of Hatshepsut is now finding support in the recent research of modern egyptology. These findings within egyptology have led to the writing of a scholarly work by the noted egyptologist Jan Assmann entitled, *Egyptian Solar Religion in the New Kingdom - Re, Amun and the Crisis of Polytheism*. This book is concerned with the increased solar emphasis of Egyptian religion in the 18th dynasty of the New Kingdom. In the following, I quote an instance from the aforementioned book where the author points to the development of new solar impulses during the reign of Hatshepsut:

> *The earliest solar hymns in Theban tombs date from the time of Hatshepsut and Tuthmosis III and are concerned with the establishment of solar chapels that had a regular cult both in the mortuary temple of Hatshepsut at Deir el Bahri and the temple complex of Amun-Re at Karnak.*

This development of the Sun Mysteries in the 18th dynasty had also been commented on earlier by the egyptologist H. M. Stewart in his important article entitled, "Some Pre-`Amarnah Sun-Hymns", (*Journal of Egyptian Archaeology, volume 46*, London 1960).

> *During the New Kingdom private individuals continued to some extent to entertain ideas of a hereafter in the bark of Re' [the boat of the sun-god Re'] - a democratization of the royal destiny of the Old Kingdom - and in some spells the deceased even claimed identification with the sun-god (among other deities). More normal, however, and more consistent with Osirian beliefs, was the modest wish to go forth from the*

Netherworld each morning to see the sun. With the establishment of the idea of Re''s night-journey through the Netherworld, men hoped on either theory to be perpetually in his following.

No doubt this wish was related to certain developments which occurred in private funerary architecture during the Eighteenth Dynasty, and which furnish our chief sources for the study of solar hymns. The typical tomb-chapel of the New Kingdom consisted of a number of chambers arranged on an axis, which was, in theory at any rate, oriented east and west, the entrance facing the rising sun. The outer parts of the chapel, including the pyramidal superstructure, formed what was virtually a solar complex, distinguished in its scheme of decoration from the inner or Osirian parts of the tomb. The thicknesses of the outer doorways during the early half of the Eighteenth Dynasty often showed the owner on both sides facing outwards and worshiping the sun-god . . .

The growing popularity of sun-hymns throughout the Eighteenth Dynasty is shown both in the increasing extent of their distribution in the tomb and in their greater length . . .

It is known that the construction of Djeser-djeseru ("Holiest of holies"), the great temple of Hatshepsut at Deir el-Bahri, was supervised by Senenmut; in fact, he even caused himself to be carved into the temple walls, a practice that is highly unusual within the history of Egypt, especially for one such as he who was not of noble birth. Furthermore, in addition to his central role in the building programs and numerous other administrative activities of Hatshepsut, Senenmut is known to have been in charge of the ambitious construction of Hatshepsut's giant obelisks (solar symbols) that were quarried out of single pieces of granite some 140 or so miles away at Aswan (a feat that is depicted upon the temple walls at Deir el-Bahri, and that would be exceedingly difficult even with todays technology). In addition to this, Senenmut was also in charge of the solar innovations at the temple complex of Amun-Re' at Karnak.

This Sun Mystery impulse leads back to the Pyramid Age of the 4th and 5th dynasties of the Old Kingdom, around 2,500 years B.C. But over time, the influence of over-materialized lunar impulses had threatened the existence of these pure Sun Mystery impulses. This led to the necessity of reasserting the solar impulses into Egyptian culture. This task, concerning the ascendancy of the pure solar mysteries over the decadent lunar mysteries in the New Kingdom, was not to proceed without opposition, for some 20 years after Hatshepsut's death there was a great campaign to erase her name from the monuments Hatshepsut had erected (a fate that also later fell to Akhenaten). In addition to this, because she was a woman, Hatshepsut's name was excluded from all later lists of pharaohs.

The impulse that proceeded from these great Initiates incarnating together in the court of Hatshepsut, is the historical seed from which the Grail Mysteries later developed. This 15th century B.C. impulse of the "Mother Lodge" in Egypt stands as an historical mirror-image in time, as it were, of the founding of the Rosicrucian Brotherhood in Europe in the 15th century A.D. The reign of Hatshepsut took place around 1,460 years B.C., while the initiation of Christian Rosenkreutz occurred on Easter eve, March 24, 1459 A.D. From this it can be seen that these two momentous events in the spiritual history of mankind are further united through their occurrence the same amount of time - before and after - the beginning of the Christian era (**XXV**).

The occult significance of this particular reflection in time, between the years 1460 B.C. and 1459 A.D. acquires even deeper significance when it is related to what is known as the Sothic Cycle. The Sothic Cycle is an approximately 1,460 year cycle of the helical rising in the East of the star of Isis-Sophia, the star Sirius the "Sun behind the Sun", which went in and out of phase with the Egyptian calendar year in a cycle given in the ancient sources as 1,460 years (and sometimes wrongly as 1,260, perhaps as an occult blind for the 2,160 year precessional epochs). The Sothic Cycle is explained by the egyptologist Richard A. Parker in his article "Sothic Dates and Calendar 'Adjustment' ", (*Revue d'Egyptologie, Tome 9*, Paris 1952):

> . . . I must formulate once more the relation between the heliacal rising of the star Sirius, or Sothis, and the civil calendar of twelve months of thirty days each with five additional, 'epagomenal' days. As there was never a leap year in this calendar it moved forward by one day every four years with respect to the natural year and eventually - unless arbitrarily adjusted - it made a complete circuit in 1,460 years (4 X 365). Any fixed event in the natural year such as the heliacal rising of Sothis would normally fall, in four year periods, on successive days of the civil calendar. (Since Sirius itself moves very slightly through the centuries this statement is not strictly

true, but the possible divergence is of no interest for the present discussion.) Therefore any two dates of the rising of Sothis would be separated in time by a number of years roughly equal to four times the difference between them in days. . .

According to M. F. Ingham in his article, "The Length of the Sothic Cycle", in the *Journal of Egyptian Archaeology* (volume 55, London 1969), the other astronomical variables, such as the effect of the precession of the equinox, would affect the precise length of the Sothic cycle to a mean length during the ancient Egyptian period of about 1,454.25 years to be more precise.

In addition to the ancient Egyptian texts, the Manichaean texts also refer to a cycle of 1,460 years - pointing to their knowledge of the initiatic significance of the star Sirius. For, as mentioned in the chapter on the High Priestess arcanum, the Sirian system is the star system in which our present Spirits of Form, the Exusiai, or Elohim went through their human or fourth stage of evolution. Furthermore, the lowest vehicle of the Spirits of Form is on the same plane of being as the human principle of the Spirit-Self. In light of this, we also know from Spiritual Science, that the Spirit-Self - is initially experienced by one undergoing initiation through the appearance of the Guardian Angel - who as a representative of the cosmic-wisdom of Isis-Sophia - nurtures us in our spiritual development.

The ancient Egyptians developed a profound initiation knowledge through their awareness of Isis-Sophia, who was experienced as a being of Cosmic Light and Warmth. This initiation knowledge was developed, in part, through the wisdom of Cosmic Time that they received through observing Sirius-Sothis, the star of Isis, rising in the East just after the constellation of her mate Osiris (the constellation of Orion) called in ancient Egypt - Sahu. Osiris is the image that embodies the Egyptian experience of the Cosmic Word - before the incarnation of Christ. This Isis wisdom also worked as Cosmic Space out of another region - the region of the Virgin - creating a "womb" of Cosmic Light and Warmth for the birthing of the infant Horus to arise as an earthly *representative* of the Cosmic-Word Osiris. This prefigures the infant Jesus who becomes the most complete earthly *embodiment* of the Cosmic Word, Christ the "Great Sun-Being" (**XII, XXVI**).

The shift to a solar focus, which occurred in the reign of Hatshepsut, set the stage for an even more profound focus upon the Sun Mysteries in the solar "monotheism" of Hatshepsut's descendant - the Pharaoh

Amenhotep IV Neferkheprure' wa`enre' (c. 1353-1335 B.C.); who has become famous under the name Akhenaten which he gave himself to proclaim his central place as pharaoh and supreme high-priest of the Sun to his people, as the earthly representative of the spirit of the Sun-disc (Akh-en-aten = Spirit of the Sun, Akh = Spirit, Aten = Sun-disc; according to the translation of Donald B. Redford, the name Akhenaten can also be thought to mean "Effective for the Sun-disk").

In the article entitled, "King Arthur and the Problem of East and West", which is included in the collection of essays by Walter Johannes Stein entitled *The Death of Merlin - Arthurian Myth and Alchemy*, W. J. Stein commented on the spiritual-scientific significance of Akhenaten within the evolution of mankind.

> *Now King Akhenaten was placed in a remarkable position. He knew that after a few centuries, with the returning Saros-period (and this connection is also a discovery of Rudolf Steiner), the power of the ancient clairvoyance must vanish. [Note: Saros is a Chaldean-Babylonian name for an eclipse cycle that completes within a 3,600 year period.] He knew that in no very distant future the worshipers of Ammon [Amun] would no longer be able to perceive the living divine revelations directly but would know of them by tradition. Rather than submit to the outward advance of this shadow, he took the splendid and courageous decision not to leave things to take their course with the inevitable silencing of the Word of Inspiration, but to change over, with complete consciousness of what he was doing, and with a clear spirit, to the worship of the world as it is revealed to the senses, and to the worship of its ruler, the disk of the sun, Aton [Aten].*
>
> *When one reads the hymns of Akhenaten, when one allows his magnificent rhapsodies to the sun to work upon one's feeling, one cannot but be stirred to the depths by this tremendous revolution taking place within a human soul, and one is profoundly moved by his really 'modern' words. Here there speaks to us a human being of our own times, one who belongs to our world, who has inclined himself towards the earth and towards a materialistic culture.*

In order to fulfill the continuation of this Sun Mystery impulse that came out of Egypt and culminated in the Mystery of Golgotha, the great "Leaders of Mankind" - Lazarus-John, and the Youth of Nain - came together again when Christian Rosenkreutz had received his initiation in 1459 A.D. from the current incarnation of Mani at that time.

In a letter to Edouard Schure, which is usually referred to as the "Barr Document", Rudolf Steiner gave certain indications regarding the nature of the mission of Christian Rosenkreutz and Rosicrucianism, and the unique tasks that were set before western mankind in preparation for a cosmopolitan world culture.

> *Christian Rosenkreutz went to the Orient in the first half of the 15th century in order to find the equilibrium between the initiation of the East and of the West. A consequence of this was the definite founding of the Rosicrucian orientation in the West after his return. In this form, Rosicrucianism was to be the strictly secret school of preparation for what would become the public task of esotericism at the turn of the 19th and 20th centuries, after natural science had achieved the preliminary solution of certain problems. Christian Rosenkreutz designated these problems as follows:*
>
> *1. The discovery of spectral analysis, whereby the material constitution of the cosmos saw the light of day.*
> *2. The introduction of material evolution into the science of the organic.*
> *3. The knowledge of the fact of a condition of consciousness differing from the usual one, through the recognition of hypnotism and suggestion.*

In addition to these scientific goals, we also see the Rosicrucian path of initiation artistically portrayed in Rosicrucian works. Rudolf Steiner in his article on the Rosicrucian story that was first published at Strasbourg, Germany in 1616 by Johann Valentin Andreae (1586-1654) entitled *The Chymical Wedding of Christian Rosenkreutz,* shows how this story is an initiation document which gives us an imaginative picture of the encounter by Christian Rosenkreutz with his Guardian Angel. This article by Rudolf

Steiner is also entitled, *The Chymical Wedding of Christian Rosenkreutz*, (*Die Chymische Hochzeit des Christian Rosenkreutz*) in which he says:

This experience of renewal comes to him on the eve of the Easter Festival, at a time of an exalted mood of soul. He feels as if a storm is raging around him. Thus it is made clear to him that he experiences a reality not dependent on perception by means of the physical body. He is lifted out of the condition of balance as regards to the world forces, into which man is placed through his physical body. His soul does not share in the life of the physical body, but feels united only with the (etheric) body of formative forces that interpenetrates the physical. However, his formative-forces body is not inserted within the balance of the world forces - but rather it is within the mobility of the supersensible world - which stands next to the physical and is first perceived by the individual when the gates of spirit vision open. It is only in the physical world that the forces rigidify into the state of balance demanded by definite form; in the spiritual world perpetual mobility rules. That he is caught up into this movement comes to the seeker's consciousness through the perception of a violent storm. Out of the indeterminate character of this perception is revealed the manifestation of a spiritual being. This revelation occurs through a definitely formed Imagination. The spirit-being appears in a blue mantle covered with stars, but this description must be kept free from all that the dilettante esotericist would so gladly 'explain' symbolically. We have to do with a non-physical experience which the one experiencing it expresses in a picture for himself and others. The blue, star-spangled mantle is indeed no more a symbol for the blue night-sky, or anything of the sort, than is the idea of a rose tree in ordinary consciousness a symbol for the sunset-glow.

In supersensible perception a much more animated and conscious activity of the soul is present than in that of the senses. In the case of the wanderer to the 'Chymical Wedding' this activity is exercised by the formative forces body, just as in physical sight the eyes are the mediators for the physical body. This activity of the formative-forces body may be compared with the stimulation of outstreaming light. Such light falls upon the spirit being, who is revealed, and is rayed back by the latter. Thereby, the seer perceives his own out-raying light, and beyond. And by virtue of its limits, he beholds the being who limits and reflects his own light. Through this connection of the spirit being with the spiritual light of the formative-forces body, 'blue' appears, the stars being that part of the spiritual light which is not rayed back but absorbed by the being.

The spirit being is an objective reality; the picture by which this being is revealed is a modification brought about by it through the raying-out of the formative-forces body. This Imagination must not be confused with a vision. The subjective experience of one having such an Imagination is something completely different from that of the visionary. The visionary lives in his vision through an inner compulsion; the one that is experiencing Imagination unites this to the spirit being referred to, or to a spiritual event, with the same conscious inner freedom with which a word or a sentence is used to express an object of the senses.

Anyone without knowledge of the nature of the spiritual world might suppose that it is completely unnecessary to clothe the pictureless experiences of this spiritual world in Imaginations that evoke the semblance of the visionary. To this it must be objected that in reality it is not the Imagination that is the essential thing in what is spiritually perceived; but rather, that this is the means through which what is essential must reveal itself within the soul. A sense color cannot be perceived without the definite activity of an eye; just as, one cannot experience something spiritual without meeting it from within by a definite Imagination. But this does not hinder the use of pure concepts, such as are customary in natural science or philosophy, for representing spiritual experiences attained through Imagination. The present article uses such concepts in describing the content of the Chymical Wedding. However, in the seventeenth century when J. V. Andreae wrote the book it was not yet customary to use such concepts to any great extent; instead, the direct Imagination, through which the super-sensible beings and events had been experienced, was represented. . .

In the same article, Rudolf Steiner also indicated that the Christ Impulse provided Christian Rosenkreutz with the central point of stability out of which this experience of initiation arises. This spiritual fact is confirmed to Christian Rosenkreutz by his experience, in the world of Imagination, of the words that point to the Christian path of the Knights Templars - "In hoc signo vinces" ("In this sign conquer").

The bearer of the experiences described in the Chymical Wedding is aware that on his path as an alchemist he needs a strengthened capacity for distinguishing between truth and illusion. According to the life-connections out of which he enters upon his alchemical path, he seeks to gain his support out of Christian truth. He knows what unites him with Christ has already brought to unfoldment, within his life in the sense world, a force in his soul leading to truth, which does not need the support of the senses and can therefore hold good when this support is no longer present. In this attitude his soul stands before the being in blue garments who shows him the way to the Chymical Wedding. To begin with, this being could just as well belong to the world of error and illusion as to that of truth. The pilgrim to the Chymical Wedding must distinguish. But his capacity for distinction would be lost, and error would overpower him if he could not, within the supersensible experience, remember what unites him with an inner-force to truth in the sense-world. Out of his own soul there arises what has happened within it through Christ; and, over and above his own light, the Christ-light also radiates from his body of formative-forces, toward this being who is revealed; and so, the right Imagination is formed. For, the letter which shows him the way to the Chymical Wedding contains the sign of Christ and the words: 'In hoc signo vinces.' Thereby, the pilgrim knows he is connected with the being who appears by a force which points to the truth . . .

XIX

The Sun

The Three-fold Sun - Archangel Michael
Waking Consciousness - 12 Petaled Lotus

The Sun is specifically associated with the twelve-petaled lotus of the heart chakra. It is the gradual awakening of the heart chakra, the abode of the "I", which leads to the free, waking-conscious, spiritual-citizenship of the Grail seeker. This is a process that requires not only the development of the chakras, or astral-centers, as organs of supersensible perception, but there must be a mastery and development of the forces of the Etheric-Body of formative-forces as well. For the awakening of the chakras works upon the Etheric-Body and brings about an actual restructuring of its nature.

This restructuring of the Astral and Etheric-Bodies is a process that proceeds through three stages of development which pass in succession from the head, to the throat, and then to the heart. Initially this process begins in the head with the formation of "a provisional center" or focal point at the "third eye" chakra, or two-petaled lotus-flower, Jupiter center, which is located near the center of the brow between the eyes. This process begins through the development of a rational clarity in one's thinking that has become free of the sense impressions of the physical world. One's thinking thereby becomes a more living-thinking, with greater mobility of thought that is capable of being brought completely into the control of one's powers of concentration. This focus of concentration brings about a harmonization of the Astral-Body with the streams of the Etheric-Body through the action of the Ego, which causes movements within the chakra that can be perceived clairvoyantly.

After establishing its supersensible activity within the brow center, as a result of one's further development, this focal point or provisional center begins to move down to the area of the sixteen-petaled, Mars lotus of the throat chakra. Once activity has been established in the throat chakra, it enables the spirit-pupil to control the forces of the Etheric-Body to a certain extent, and brings about a sheathing of the Etheric-Body in the periphery which differentiates it further from the etheric world as a whole.

In the next stage of supersensible development this focal point, or provisional center, moves down to the heart-sun center - where the "I Am", or "Christ in you" dwells. When activity has been established in the heart-sun center, it begins to radiate light within the auric sheath. Through the further development of this center, one will begin to see into the Akashic Record with the "eye" that is in the heart. This "seeing" with the heart was how the Christian stigmata Ann Catherine Emmerich described her experiences of clairvoyantly seeing the life of Christ. This stage of consciousness development ultimately leads to an expansion of the Etheric-Body beyond the surface of the Physical-Body, especially around the head where a new center is formed behind the back of the head that is a, so to speak, second "etheric-heart" which gradually surrounds the whole head with a radiant "halo." This supersensible process is the beginning of an inversion, or shift, from the focusing of etheric forces within the inner-core of the heart and blood system, to a radiation of etheric forces to the outer-periphery of the new "etheric-heart", and "etheric-circulatory-system" that now surrounds the Physical-Body.

This turning inside-out of the forces of the Etheric-Body, as an historical process within human evolution, began in the first quarter of the 18th century, and is the spiritual destiny of the wholesome development of mankind through the Christ impulse that is meant to be accomplished by the end of Earth evolution. This radiance of the transformed vehicles is depicted in paintings of Christ and Mary where they are surrounded by a radiant aura that encircles the whole body and not just the head as a halo. In yogic teachings this is called the brahmarandra chakra.

The supersensible vehicles that have been brought to perfection by Initiates (and I use the term perfection in the relative sense, for the true representative of the perfection of mankind is the Christ) are conserved in the "etheric-ring" around the earth (which can be thought of as the brahmarandra chakra of the Earth), where they serve as archetypes of perfection, and in certain cases, can be used by an individual to gain the experience and symmetry of the vehicle, either through actually incarnating a vehicle (a process which in Tibetan Buddhism is called "tulku", in reference to Incarnate Lamas), or by a perfected vehicle temporarily influencing an individual. This can happen either from a perfected vehicle working from outside as an overlighting, transformative radiance and source of inspiration; or, by coming into alignment with the vehicle of the individual and setting into motion a metamorphoses of its structure. Either of these two experiences could last for a short period of time, or for an extended period as the case may be.

The Christened vehicles of the Saint's are recipients of the highest healing Christ forces, whether it be a Christened Etheric-Body with its powers of memory and clarity of thought, as was the case with St. Augustine, or a Christened Astral-Body as possessed by St. Francis of Assisi - who overcame the astral realm of sympathy and antipathy through complete purity of heart.

The true Macrocosmic Temple of the Holy Grail is this living ring that surrounds the Earth, and is the real secret of the Holy Grail. This spiritual zone is called Shamballa in the East, and is watched over by Noah-Manu. The Manu was the leader of the Sun Mystery center of Atlantis, and led the migration into Central Asia at the end of the Atlantean period; later appearing as Melchizedek to Abraham (**XXV**). Manu is the 13th who guides the 12 principle Masters.

This concern for the Etheric and Astral Bodies is one reason why the ancient Egyptians went to such great lengths to preserve the relationship of these vehicles to the physical through their elaborate burial rites. The Egyptian Initiates, by ritual acts and offerings, made provision for the sustaining of the Etheric-Body, which they called the Ka; they also wished to keep the Soul, or the Astral-Body, or Sentient-Body, which they called the Ba returning to the Sahu, or mummified Physical-Body. The true goal was symbolically represented by the ancient Egyptians as - becoming an Osiris and riding in the "bark of the Sun", or having one's Akh, or Spirit (the higher triad of Spirit-Man, Life-Spirit and Spirit-Self) become an "imperishable star."

It is one of the laws of occultism that all manifestation comes about through vortical or spiraling activity. This spiral movement, which arises through the activity of the Dynamis or Spirits of Movement, is reflected in the spiraling blood within the heart and blood vessels; which, in turn, reflects the spiraling "dance of the Cherubim", or Spirits of Harmony.

The ancient Egyptian's depict the ram-headed god Khnum with his spiraling horns molding the Ka or Etheric-Body, and the Physical-Body on a potter's wheel. This is an image of the formative activity of the Spirits of Form, the Biblical Elohim, or in the Greek of Dionysus the Areopagite, the Exusiai. The ram of the constellation of Aries is the sacrificial ram of Abraham; and, as the ram or "Lamb of God", is connected with the Adam Kadmon, the archetypal human-being that is said to be created from the primal sounding of the letters of the Hebrew alphabet. In fact the various shapes from which the letters of the Hebrew alphabet are composed can be derived from viewing a spiraling ram's horn from different angles.

In light of this, in the Kabbalah it is said that if one could properly pronounce the Hebrew alphabet in one sounding you would manifest the human form. This finds a parallel in Spiritual Science. For, in the distant future, speech will begin to become a more true expression of the Christ-Logos, "the Living-Word", with speech becoming the creative force in mankind which will, in the distant future, replace the procreative function. The human form will actually arise out of the cosmic-speech of the metamorphosed larynx, this will be the true working of the Sun-language of the Logos in mankind. For the counterpart of the heart in the region of the head is the tongue, which shapes the breath from within while the heart shapes the blood from without.

The prototype of this future development within the realm of speech is found expressed in the *genuine* speaking in tongues, which was the result of the descent of the Holy Spirit in "tongues of flame" upon the heads of the Apostles at Pentecost, and which brought about a "birth" of the Spirit of the Cosmos (the Macrocosm) as Cosmic Love within the Souls of the Apostles (the Microcosm). Rudolf Steiner describes this mystery, from his clairvoyant perception of the Akashic Records, in the second lecture of the lecture cycle entitled, *The Fifth Gospel*:

> *We can be led to these events only when, as seers, we find the way to them as I have indicated, when we sink in deepest contemplation into the soul of Peter or of one of the other apostles; who, at the time of Pentecost, felt themselves quickened by the all-prevailing Cosmic Love. Only when we contemplate the souls of these men, and discern the nature of their experiences, is it possible in this indirect way to gaze at the Cross raised on Golgotha . . . For in the consciousness of Peter, what I have now described was, in very truth, an experience that crystallized out of a 'long sleep.' Among the manifold pictures crossing Peter's consciousness, those of the cross raised on Golgotha, the darkening and the earthquake, for example, stood out in vivid relief. These experiences were for Peter the first result of the quickening by the Cosmic Love at Pentecost. And he now knew something he had not really known before: that the event of Golgotha had taken place, and that the body on the Cross was the same body he had often accompanied in life. Now he knew that Jesus had died on the Cross, and that this dying was in reality a birth: the birth of that Spirit outpoured as the all-prevailing Cosmic Love into*

the souls of the disciples assembled at Pentecost. Peter felt it as a ray of the primordial, aeonic Love . . . born when Jesus died on the Cross. And this stupendous truth sank down into Peter's soul: 'It is only illusion that on the Cross a death took place.' This death, preceded as it had been by infinite suffering, was in truth the birth of the ray now penetrating his soul. The all-prevailing Cosmic Love, which had previously been present everywhere outside and around the Earth, had, with the death of Jesus, been born into the Earth.

This image of Pentecostal speech arising through Cosmic Love is a powerful example of the renewal by Christ of the mysterious power which was called in ancient Sanskrit, "mantrika sakti" (the occult potency of speech). In the Vedic lore of ancient India, the sacred language is called "Vach" which is Sanskrit for "speech." H. P. Blavatsky describes the occult significance of this ancient idea in her *Theosophical Glossary*:

To call Vach 'speech' simply, is deficient in clearness. Vach is the mystic personification of speech, and the female Logos, being one with Brahma, who created her out of one-half of his body, which he divided into two portions; she is also one with Viraj (called the 'female' Viraj) who was created in her by Brahma. In one sense Vach is 'speech' by which knowledge was taught to man; in another she is the 'mystic, secret speech' which descends upon and enters into the primeval Rishis, as the 'tongues of fire' are said to have 'sat upon' the apostles. For, she is called 'the female creator', the 'mother of the Vedas', etc., etc. Esoterically, she is the subjective Creative Force which, emanating from the Creative Deity (the subjective Universe, its 'privation', or 'ideation') becomes the manifested 'world of speech', i.e., the concrete expression of ideation, hence the 'Word' or Logos. Vach is 'the male and female' Adam of the first chapter of 'Genesis', and thus called 'Vach-Viraj' by the sages. (See; 'Atharva Veda') She is also 'the celestial Saraswati produced from the heavens', a 'voice derived from speechless Brahma' (Mahabharata): the goddess of wisdom and eloquence. She is called Sata-rupa, the goddess of 'a hundred forms.'

Vach, as seen above, is a name that refers to the Logos, although technically the above compound idea of "Vach-Viraj" relates to the connection between the 3rd Logos (the Holy Spirit) and the 2nd Logos (the Son) as it pertains to the Resurrection, through the power of Cosmic Love, of the Sophia forces that have "fallen" from the Edenic state. These forces of Cosmic Love, which in the future will manifest through Cosmic Speech, are an aspect of the redemption process by which the 2nd Logos, the Christ - as the "new Lord of Karma" - is working into mankind. The initial manifestation of this in mankind is the development of warmth of speech. For, esoterically speaking, in speech you have that which rises up as warmth, and that which descends as fallen substance or "ash." In Cosmic Speech there is present that which arises out of the higher-moral forces of the Spirit. For, as Rudolf Steiner tells us, speech and the breath originate from a realm that is essentially divine, in that they are not completely integrated into the workings of the individual ego; but rather, are manifestations of the activity of higher beings. From this understanding it can be seen that the fruits of the "fallen" nature are, so to speak, unconnected to these higher-moral impulses. This comes about through the privation which results from the unconsciousness of mankind to the spiritual reality of these higher-moral impulses. And so, the process of redemption of these "fallen" forces must now be achieved through the awakening of the heart to the workings of the Spirit. This awakening of the heart can be seen as an awakening to the wisdom-forces that are working within the Cosmos (**XIII-XIV**). These sophianic wisdom-forces nurture the spiritual redemption of mankind through fostering the unfoldment of the Christ-forces that now, since the Mystery of Golgotha, dwell as Cosmic Love within the "cave of the heart."

In ancient Sanskrit, Vach is connected to the sacred speech of Devanagari, the "language or letters of the Devas" or Angelic Beings, the Brahma-Bhashya, or Deva-Bhashya. Bhashya is Sanskrit for speaking, while Deva means "Shining One" or Angelic Being; so that, Deva-Bhashya is the "language of the Shining Ones", and is the primeval language that was brought about through the inspiration of the realm of the Archangels. The devic origins of this primeval language is referred to by H. P. Blavatsky (*The Secret Doctrine, volume 1*, page xliii) in reference to the *Stanzas of Dzyan*, the "very old Book" on which her book, *The Secret Doctrine* is meant to be a commentary. The *Stanzas of Dzyan* were said to be written in the Senzar characters, in ancient times by the initiates of Central Asia, on palm leaves "rendered impervious to the elements by some unknown process."

> The 'very old Book' is the original work from which the many volumes of 'Kiu-ti' [the Tibetan canon] were compiled. Not only this latter and the 'Siphrah Dzeniouta' but even the 'Sepher Jezirah', the work attributed by the Hebrew Kabbalists to their Patriarch Abraham (!), the book of 'Shu-King', China's primitive Bible, the sacred volumes of the Egyptian Thoth-Hermes, the 'Puranas' in India, and the 'Chaldean Book of Numbers' and the 'Pentateuch' [the five Books of Moses] itself, are all derived from [or rather, later expressions of the primordial truths expressed in] that one small parent volume. Tradition says, that it was taken down in 'Senzar', the secret sacerdotal tongue, from the words of Divine Beings, who dictated it to the sons of Light, in Central Asia, at the very beginning of the 5th (our) race; for there was a time when its language (the Senzar) was known to the Initiates of every nation, when the forefathers of the Toltec understood it as easily as the inhabitants of the lost Atlantis, who inherited it, in their turn, from the sages of the 3rd Race, the 'Manushis', who learnt it direct from the Devas of the 2nd and 1st Races.

The origin of this primeval language of the Adepts is to be found in the "night of time", and is traced from ancient Atlantis as the proto-Sanskrit language *Senzar* by H. P. Blavatsky; which is characterized by her as, ". . . a tongue absent from the nomenclature of languages and dialects with which philology is acquainted." (*The Secret Doctrine, volume 1*, page xxxvii). Elsewhere she describes it as; "The mystic name for the secret sacerdotal language or the 'Mystery speech' of the initiated adepts, all over the world."

Although Senzar is unknown to philologists, its character is akin to the descriptions of the "primeval Mother tongue" given by Rudolf Steiner. This ancient "Mother tongue" was the first language, and it developed through the natural response of the soul to the inner and outer worlds. The experience of the outer world was conveyed through the consonants; while the experience of the inner world was expressed through the vowels, from which the languages received their inner-moral impulses. According to H. P. Blavatsky, this "Mother tongue" eventually came to be written in the symbolical language known to occultists as Senzar.

In ancient times, the development of language came about through the activity of Archangelic beings working into the souls of mankind.

Eventually, through the unfoldment of the forces of the Ego, speech came to be experienced as a separate and increasingly human realm. The biblical story of the "Tower of Babel" and the "division of tongues" is an imaginative picture of the transition from this ancient "primeval Mother-tongue" to the various languages of the many peoples of Earth.

The memory of the archaic speech remains in the alchemical "language of the birds", the "green language" of the troubadours, the "signature of all things" of Jacob Boehme, the poet's "language of the heart", and most of all within the "language of the dead"; the understanding of which depends upon the heart's developed powers of cognition - for it is actually an experience that is perceived within the heart.

In the Eastern esoteric schools they speak of two teachings: the "doctrine of the eye" and the "doctrine of the heart", which can be interpreted to mean - the doctrine of the head and the doctrine of the heart. The doctrine of the head is related to the written teachings, while the doctrine of the heart is encompassed within the oral tradition. The doctrine of the head relates to thinking and will, while the doctrine of the heart relates to feeling and will. Both play an important role within the totality of the human being. For without the heart, one's thoughts can be likened to a barren desert devoid of warmth, on the other hand, without the head you don't have clarity of thought. Although the feeling here referred to is not any vague-sentimental state, but rather is the manifestation of the Cosmic Feeling realm; which is the realm of spiritual light itself, and so, is at the actual core of the spiritual evolution of humanity - the development of which brings about a state of "heart thinking" that takes place within the Etheric-Body of formative-forces.

What is needed for the future evolution of humanity is "heart thinking"; that is, a living thinking that is centered in the light processes of Cosmic Feeling that are to be found working as "Sun-laws" within the spiritual center of the heart. This is the true goal of the Grail path outlined in Rudolf Steiner's work. This is achieved, as Wolfram von Eschenbach tells us in *Parzival*, by passing "from dullness, through doubt to saelde" (saelde = blessedness). Viewed from the standpoint of the spiritual scientific understanding of the organ systems, this saelde is achieved by moving from the dullness and fear of the Venus-kidney processes to the "saelde" of the Jupiter-liver process as a transition to the Sun-heart center (**XVI**).

When the dome of the cosmos, which is reflected in the dome of the head by the brain's twelve pairs of cranial nerves, manifests the clarity of its twelve-fold nature through the development of the heart chakra, then one can act out of the free mobility of Cosmic Thought, and thereby redeem the "fallen" nervous system. Some of the details of the nature of this microcosmic mirroring of the Cosmos in mankind are further explained by Rudolf Steiner in the eighth lecture of the lecture cycle entitled, *Macrocosm and Microcosm*.

If it is so that the World of Spirit works at the forming of our nervous system, then it follows that underlying our nervous system there must be a certain law and order corresponding to that of the solar system. Our nervous system must be an inner solar system - for it is organized from the Heaven World.

We will now ask ourselves whether this nervous system really functions as if it were a mirror-image of the solar system out yonder in the Macrocosm. As you know, our measurement of time is governed by the relation of the planets to the Sun; and also, in the yearly cycle of the passage of the Sun through the twelve constellations of the Zodiac. This is an arrangement of time that is based upon the law contained in the number twelve - as a number which expresses the movements taking place in the solar system. There are also twelve months in the year, and in the longest months there are thirty-one days. That again is based upon the mutual relations of the heavenly bodies, and is connected with our time-system. There is a certain irregularity for which there is a good reason, but we cannot go into it now.

Let us try to picture this remarkable time-system within the universe and ask ourselves how these cosmic processes would be reflected in our nervous system. If the forces underlying the Macrocosm are also the forces which have formed our nervous system, we shall certainly find a reflection of them in ourselves; and, in fact, we have twelve cerebral nerves and thirty-one pairs of spinal nerves. The cosmic laws are actually reflected in these spinal nerves and cerebral nerves. The existence of a certain irregularity is explained by the fact that man is destined to be a being who is independent of what is going on outside him.

Just as the Sun's passage through the constellations of the Zodiac takes place in twelve months (and this is reflected in the twelve cerebral nerves), so the days of the month are regulated in accordance with the circuit of the Moon (twenty-eight days). How is the connection of the thirty-one days in the month with the human nervous system to be explained? We have three additional pairs of nerves, i.e. thirty-one in all, which makes us independent beings; otherwise here too we should be governed by the number twenty-eight. Here you can glimpse a deep mystery, a wonderful connection between our nervous system and what is expressed in the great symbols of space - symbols which in themselves are mirrorings of spiritual Beings and activities.

In an old Persian legend Christ says; "Be ye as the wind in the trees experiencing all but attached to none." Through the development of sense-free thought, you gain a once removed vantage-point from the realms of feeling and willing. This does not mean that one shuts off their feelings; but rather, that by becoming more aware of the distinction between one's thinking, feeling, and willing - one is able to develop a more conscious relationship to these three realms. By this path of development there is a gradual increase in one's sensitivity to these three realms - with the possibility of one ultimately arriving at an experience, in the core of one's being within the heart-sun center, as to how the Microcosm is a reflection of the Macrocosm.

Furthermore, from the development that results from this freeing up of the thinking processes, one acquires the capacity to embrace in one's thinking both the seven soul-moods, and the twelve fundamental cosmic view-points (**XVIII, XXI-XXIII**). Thereby, through the workings of the Christ Impulse as we move into the future, there will come about a harmonizing of the realm of the inner being of man with the "Lower Gods"; and consequently, this will result in a harmonization with outer nature and the realm of the "Upper Gods" (**XIX**). Or as it is written; "On Earth as it is in Heaven . . ."

This wholesome development of the supersensible nature of man can eventually lead to an experience that was called in the Ancient Mysteries "seeing the Sun at midnight" (**XI**). Rudolf Steiner discussed this profound initiation experience in the third lecture of the lecture cycle which he gave in Vienna in March of 1910 entitled, *Macrocosm and Microcosm*:

Having undergone such training, the pupils who had thus intensified their inner experiences found themselves possessed of a particular faculty - however strange this may sound - the faculty of seeing through matter, just as the mystic is able to penetrate into his own inner self. They were able to see not merely surfaces of objects but they were able to see through the objects, and above all, through the Earth.

This experience was called in the Ancient Mysteries: 'seeing the Sun at midnight.' The Sun could be seen in its greatest splendor and glory only at the time of the winter solstice, when the whole external sense-world had, so to speak, died away. The pupils of the Mysteries had developed the faculty of seeing the Sun no longer as the dazzling power it is by day, but with all its dazzling brilliance eliminated. They saw the Sun, not as a physical but as a spiritual reality, and they beheld the Sun Spirit. The physical effect of dazzling was extinguished by the Earth's substance, for this had become transparent and allowed only the Sun's spiritual forces to pass through. But something else of great significance was connected with this beholding of the Sun... namely, that there is a living interplay between the planets and the Sun inasmuch as streams flow continually to and fro - from the planets to the Sun and from the Sun to the planets. Something was revealed spiritually that may be compared with the circulation of the blood in the human body. As the blood flows in living circulation from the heart to the organs and from the organs back again to the heart, so did the Sun reveal itself as the center of living spiritual streams flowing to and fro between the Sun and the planets. The solar system revealed itself as a spiritual system of living realities, the external manifestation of which is no more than a symbol. Everything manifested by the individual planets pointed to the great spiritual experience just described.

And so, through the principles of Initiation embodied in Spiritual Science, as spiritual successors to the initiates of the Ancient Mysteries, eventually the Grail seekers will begin to actualize humanity's cosmic destiny as beings of light - as "Spirits of Freedom and Love" - and achieve fulfillment through the path of loving service to others in the newly arising

"Cosmos of Love"; which will come about through the awakening of the Sun-center within the heart as a microcosmic counterpart to the Spiritual Sun - an supersensible fact which has only become possible through the courageous sacrificial deed of Christ the "Great Sun-Being"(**XXV**).

XX

Judgement

Alchemical Salt - the Raven (carbon) is Transformed into the Philosophers' Stone (diamond), or Resurrection Body

Christ said; "Ye shall know them by their deeds." Through attunement with the Divine Plan of the Christ-Logos, the Physical-Body (that would have been no denser than the fragrance of a flower, had it not "fallen" into matter as a consequence of of the "War in Heaven") gradually becomes transformed. This is brought about, in part, by the action of the Holy Spirit upon the rhythm of the heart and lungs - bringing them into harmony with the divine intentions of the Holy Trinity. For, through this attunement with the Divine Plan, the nature of the carbon processes in the Physical-Body of an Initiate become transformed; resulting in the spiritualized essence of the Physical-Body - that part that has been worked into by the Ego - becoming transformed into the Resurrection-Body.

With the "deed of Christ" upon the hill of Golgotha, mankind passed the "Turning-Point of Time" and began their ascent towards becoming "Spirits of Freedom and Love." As a result of the Mystery of Golgotha, Christ entered into Earth evolution in the most intimate way possible. Did he not say; "I shall be with you always"? In the lecture cycle entitled, *The Search for the New Isis - The Divine Sophia*, Rudolf Steiner said; "It's not the Christ that we lack, it's the Sophia of Christ, the Wisdom of Christ that we lack . . ."

That which is brought into being within humanity is derived from the sacrifice of the Spiritual Hierarchies - who have literally donated from their very substance in order to bring humankind into being. By taking up these donated principles, and making them our own, we will evolve through the ranks of the Spiritual Hierarchies. The next stage of evolution will come about when the Spirit-Self has become a fully individuated principle; then, as St. Paul said; "Ye Shall be as the Angels."

Likewise, in the "Apocalypse", St. John the Divine spoke of the "New Jerusalem"; which, according to Esoteric Christianity, represents the etheric globe that will follow the Earth evolution, when evolving humanity will graduate to the angelic kingdom. The great "Masters of Wisdom and of the Harmony of Feeling" such as Christian Rosenkreutz, have already made this transition, and beyond. For, by their having completed the development of both the Spirit-Self and the Life-Spirit, they are actually two stages of evolution beyond humanity. They are beings that have attained "pan-aeonic immortality" - and will not have a single lapse of waking consciousness from now until the end of the Earth evolution. Beyond them is the great Manu who has a fully developed Spirit-Man.

The Rosicrucian image of the discovery of the uncorrupted body of Christian Rosenkreutz in the tomb with the ever-burning lamp, points towards his attainment of the Resurrection-Body. This is one of the keys to the tomb of Christian Rosenkreutz, which has seven sides, representing the seven planetary Archangel's recognition of Christian Rosenkreutz's Archangelic completion of the Spirit-Self and the Life-Spirit.

Through their attainment of "the mastery of wisdom and the harmonization of sensations and feeling", the great "Leaders of Mankind" have become conscious in realms of being in which the ordinary individual is unconscious. In the ordinary human being, the functions of the Physical-Body and the other vehicles of soul and spirit are being maintained by the Angelic Hierarchies that are working under the inspiration of the Divine Plan of the Trinity.

Jesus said; "Know ye not that it is written; 'Ye are gods'?" This statement is a challenge for humanity to strive to make it become a reality. For with the recognition of the true stature of mankind comes humility - as, even the Angels, the lowest rank of the nine orders of Celestial Hierarchies, are far beyond even the most gifted *ordinary human*. For, were you to see a higher being, such as an Archangel, you would think you had seen God. These spiritual facts can only produce in one the experience of the greatest awe and reverence before the absolute, almighty Godhead of the Holy Trinity; and also, awaken the possibility of comprehending love through the recognition of the magnitude of the "deed of Christ" at the Crucifixion - a debt which we can never repay.

The highest example of the Grail path of forgiveness is shown by Christ who was able to say of those who were crucifying Him; "Forgive them for they know not what they do." Also, the highest example of patience is shown by Christ who guides mankind *without compulsion,* thereby giving humanity the freedom to come to Him out of their own free-will, as an act of love.

Through the action of the Holy Spirit awakening the "Christ in you", spiritual transformation gradually takes place. Jesus said; "If, therefore, thine eyes be single thy body shall be filled with God's light." This light is not the self-contained, cold, effulgent light of Lucifer, but the warm, radiant, sophianic light of the Holy Spirit that is an expression of Christ's infinite love and compassion towards all of His creation - and which light is one with the goodness of the Father - "Only My Father in Heaven is good" (**XIV**).

In the years between 1938 and 1943, an Italian nun who is known as Sister L. L. had a series of Christ revelations in which she recorded an experience she had concerning the workings of Christ within the human heart (Sister L. L., in the *Supremo Appello* which is the first of three volumes of revelations of Christ Jesus. As given by Robert Powell in, *Hermetic Astrology, volume 1*, (pages 48-49):

> *Hearts are my kingdom. I came to the Earth to conquer the hearts of men . . . I am your first Friend, he who listens to the beating of your heart and answers all your needs. I am the Faithful One, the True One, the Eternal One . . . I defend my hearts, those living parts of me, who allow me to go into them. In the same way that they represent my interests, their interests become mine. We belong to one another, each to the other . . .*

As one evolves in one's capacity to be a Grail server, it brings about the unfoldment of the supersensible organs of perception which will enable one to "be filled with God's light", and to perceive the worlds of Spirit. Through pursuing the path of the Grail one brings about a crystal clarity in one's thinking, and an awaking within the realm of feeling that expresses itself in the warmth of speech.

The way in which this quickening comes about is that gradually the heart-warmth of speech brings about a stream that bathes the pineal and pituitary centers in the head. It is the development of this frontal etheric stream that will, ultimately in the future, transform the breath from exhaling *unredeemed* carbonic gases that carry forces of death - to the exhaling of *redeemed* forces of life. This *redeemed* carbon is the "phantom carbon" which is the true "stone of the wise" - the "Philosophers' Stone."

Rudolf Steiner once described the "philosophical death" of the adepts who have achieved the "Philosophers' Stone", which is quoted by Rudolf Grosse in chapter nine of his book entitled, *The Christmas Foundation - Beginning of a New Cosmic Age*:

> *The Philosophers' Stone serves a certain purpose . . . and we are not concerned here with physical death but with the following: For one who has come to understand the Philosophers' Stone . . . physical death is only a semblance. For other people it is a real event signifying a tremendous step in life. But for one who, as Cagliostro attempted with his pupils, has done this work on himself and has achieved its purpose, death is only a seeming event. It does not even signify a particularly important step into a new phase. It is real enough for those who are maybe able to observe the adept. They say that he dies. But he himself does not die at all in reality. He has learned to cause all the processes to take place in his physical body which actually do take place in the physical body at the moment of death. Gradually throughout his life, one by one, he causes the processes to take place which occur in the physical body at the moment of death. Everything that normally occurs at death has already taken place in the body of the adept. So now death is no longer possible. He has learned in advance how to live without a physical body which he now takes off as though it were a raincoat . . . This is the Philosophers' Stone which reduces death to insignificance.*

In this quotation, Rudolf Steiner is describing a process that only the higher adepts will attain, and as H. P. Blavatsky once said; "If thou can'st be the noonday sun then satisfy yourself to be a lowly planet." And yet, even though he is describing a stage of development that is far in advance of us ordinary humans, it is very relevant to the spiritual path as a whole - which is similar in nature, but different in degree. For the path of Initiation gradually redeems those "fallen" macrocosmic-zodiacal forces of the nerve-sense system that find their point of origin in the twelve-fold processes which were already established in the Old Saturn incarnation of the Earth (**IV**). "In him was life; and the life was the light of men. And the light shineth in darkness; and the darkness comprehended it not." (John 1:4-5) Likewise, the path of Initiation gradually enlivens the mineral nature of the blood (which is a recent addition to human evolution, since mankind's descent into physical Earth existence).

Through the mastery of the macrocosmic-moral forces of wisdom, and the harmonization of sensations and feelings (**XIII**), we become responsive to the subtle impulses of the spiritual world and grow in a wholesome way towards the future Jupiter evolution; when the Earth will transcend physical existence through its transformation into an ethereal globe.

This spiritual transformation begins within the human heart through the etheric nature of the blood uniting with the "etheric blood" of Christ (which is an expression of His Life-Spirit that has permeated the spiritual atmosphere of the Earth since the Mystery of Golgotha). Through this process of uniting with the "etheric blood" of Christ, the human heart develops toward becoming a microcosmic "Sun" - radiating light, life and love. For as Christ said; "I have come to give you more life, and that abundantly." This mingling of the human and divine brings about a process of "etherization" within the blood, so that minute portions of the blood become rarefied through the influence of the Christ impulse; thereby resulting in a natural harmonization of the rhythm of heart and lung. The blood literally becomes metamorphosed within the hollow spaces created by the vortexing blood within the heart; and thereby, transubstantiates minute amounts of the physical substance of the blood into warm, etheric radiance.

Around the year 1629, a book was produced in the circle of the Rosicrucian author Robert Fludd which spoke of those solitary few who have attained the stage of "Adept", far in advance of ordinary mankind, in book iv of the work, *Summum Bonum* (*The Highest Good*):

> *The Scriptures teach us that no age has existed, exists, or will exist, in which single individuals, experienced in the world and its darknesses, have not been able to retain knowledge of the holy light, counting themselves among the sons of God. Thus in each century and epoch were some, however small in number, who passed through the narrow portal, while the larger part of mankind trod the broader and more conspicuous way. For we read that in each epoch of the Church, some were found who were given the 'victory, the Tree of Life which is in the midst of the Paradise of God' (Revelation, 2:7), the 'hidden manna and the white stone' (Revelation, 2:17), the 'morning star' (Revelation, 2:28), or 'clothed in white raiment' (Revelation, 3:5). They shall receive their heritage and their name shall not be blotted from the Book of Life, and they will be 'pillars in the temple' and will receive 'the new name of the Lamb.'*

XXI

The World

Saturn - Archangel Oriphiel - Memory - 8 Petaled Lotus

Oriphiel is the Archangel of the sphere of Saturn (**V**). The Saturn sphere is the "ring-pass-not" of Earth evolution, it circumscribes the arena of our destiny, and is the gateway to the stars that envelop the reincarnating Ego at the turning-point between incarnations - the "Cosmic-Midnight" - that is in the region of Leo, and from where we begin our descent into rebirth (**XIII**). For after earthly, physical death the soul divests itself of all the astral-etheric substance, which remains from our previous life, that is not worthy to be carried forward with us in our evolution as it rises and expands into the planetary spheres. After the reincarnating monad reaches "Cosmic-Midnight" (at the proper time and with the appropriate stellar and planetary configuration), it starts its descent towards a new earth-life. Then with the help of the divine-spiritual hierarchies, the reincarnating monad will re-clothe itself in astral-etheric substance before coming to its earthly, physical birth.

As mentioned in the chapter on the Fool arcanum, the corresponding center to the sphere of Saturn in a human being is the crown chakra of eight petals which is located above the head, and is often described as the thousand-petalled lotus, due to its shimmering appearance. According to the yogis, the combined petals of the other chakras total fifty, and the crown chakra is the convergence of twenty groupings which each contain fifty streams that proceed from the fifty petals of the six other chakras. These streams are arrayed in an eight-fold manner at the crown chakra.

This is reminiscent of the fifty gates of Binah (or Understanding), in the Kabbalah, of which Moses was said to have opened forty-nine. Binah is the sefirah, or sphere, of Saturn (**VII**). The word sefirah itself is a feminine term which refers to "counting or number." One of the titles of Binah is "Supernal Mother" (Ama = Hebrew, or Aima = Chaldean). In the Ancient Mysteries, one who had attained the crown chakra was called "Father" or "Mother." H. P. Blavatsky in *The Secret Doctrine, volume 1* (pages 290-291), quotes extracts from a private commentary of an Eastern esoteric school regarding the nature of the "Great Mother":

... *'The Initial existence - which may be called while in this state of being the One Life, is as explained, a film for creative or formative purposes. It manifests in seven states, which, with their septenary sub-divisions, are the Forty-nine Fires mentioned in sacred books (in the Vishnu and other Puranas [of ancient India]) ... The first is the ... "Mother" (prima Materia). Separating itself into its primary seven states, it proceeds down cyclically; when having consolidated itself in its last principle as gross matter it revolves around itself and informs, with the seventh emanation of the last, the first and the lowest element (the Serpent biting its own tale).' And later it says 'to man, it gives all that it bestows on all the rest of the manifested units in nature; but develops, furthermore, the reflection of all its Forty-Nine Fires in him. Each of his seven principles is an heir in full to, and a partaker of, the seven principles of the "great Mother." The breath of her first principle is his spirit (Atma) [Spirit-Man]. Her second principle is Budhi (soul) [Life-Spirit] ... The third furnishes him with ... Mind' (Manas) [or Spirit-Self].*

The Seven Year Cycles of Human Life and Historical Evolution

Early Pre-Embryonic - Polarian - 1st Period
Late Pre-Embryonic - Hyperborean - 2nd Period
Embryonic - Lemurian - 3rd Period
0-7 = **Physical-Body** - Atlantean - 4th Period - ended in Leo
   (the years 7-56 relate to the present Post-Atlantean or 5th Period)
7-14 = **Etheric-Body** - 1st Epoch - Old Indian - Cancer
14-21 = **Astral-Body** - 2nd Epoch - Old Persian - Gemini
21-28 = **Sentient-Soul** - 3rd Epoch - Egypto-Chaldean - Taurus
28-35 = **Intellectual-Soul** - 4th Epoch - Graeco-Roman - Aries
35-42 = **Consciousness-Soul** - 5th Epoch - Western European - Pisces
   (the years 42+ are related to the future development of mankind)
42-49 = **Spirit-Self** - 6th Epoch - Eastern European - Aquarius
49-56 = **Life-Spirit** - 7th Epoch - American - Capricorn
56-63 = **Spirit-Man** - 6th Period - will begin in Sagittarius
63-70 = **Extra-Saturnian Zodiacal Mysteries** - 7th Period

From the preceding diagram it can been seen how a human life mirrors evolution microcosmically within the flow of time. This relates to the mystery of seven times seven, or forty-nine years of age within an individual lifetime. For, at forty-nine years of age one has experienced seven, seven-year cycles, completing the cycle of the development of the sixth principle of the Spirit-Self (or in the Eastern terminology Manas; which, in the Western Hermetic Kabbalah, corresponds to the development of "the knowledge and conversation of one's Holy Guardian Angel"). In terms of historical evolution, the Spirit-Self will be developed in the future sixth post-Atlantean epoch of Aquarius (**XXV**) (which sign, according to Ptolemy, is "ruled" by Saturn and is opposite Leo, while Capricorn is also "ruled" by Saturn and is opposite Cancer).

Rudolf Steiner once pointed out that one could come to a meaningful picture of the activity of their Guardian Angel by thinking of all the people that they have encountered during the course of the year. One can also develop sensitivity to their Guardian Angel by spending time with one who has attained a self-realized state, which in the teachings of Yoga is called "darshan"; that is, keeping the company of a self-realized individual.

In the preceding diagram, I also refer to periods which are called in theosophical literature root-races, although this can be very misleading as the periods refer to the principles that are developed and not what we normally think of as the races of mankind. In the past, the introduction and development of new principles was entrusted to particular Folk-Souls with their respective nations. As we move towards the future, this will be increasingly less so because of the change in human evolution that has come about since the beginning of the Michaelic age in 1879 A.D. For, blood ties will gradually lose their significance, and in addition, no new Folk-Soul groups will be formed. Now, as regards to the human embodiment of the higher evolutionary impulses, the emphasis has shifted increasingly towards dependence on the level of development of each individual Ego, as to how far they evolve within a particular cycle.

In the ancient Lemurian period, mankind received from Christ the ability to stand upright, but were incapable of acting out of an inner sense of self; for, mankind was still entirely dependent on the workings of the beings of the higher worlds. In the following Atlantean period, mankind received from Christ the initial tendency to experience an inward sense of self and speak, and think - although they were still prompted in their activities by higher beings. At the beginning of the post-Atlantean period, around four or five thousand years B.C., the Divine-Spiritual Beings began gradually diminishing their intimate connection with the consciousness of "infant-humanity", so that mankind could integrate the Ego as an individuated entity that acted out of freedom instead of necessity - as do the beings that have not achieved the sense of individuality that the Ego brings.

As mankind progressed through the post-Atlantean epochs, they were gradually approached from outside by the Christ Being, the Logos, or "Word" - from the periphery of the Zodiac - and then, through the "heart" of the Sun. The Christ Being approached the Earth as the "Cosmic Ego" who would eventually enter the body of Jesus to become - "the Word made flesh" - or, what Rudolf Steiner referred to as "the Representative of Mankind" (**XXV**). This "most momentous event in Earth evolution" was reflected in the deepest inner workings of the hearts of mankind, so that they would awaken through the forces of the "True-Ego", the "Christ in you", and become the "Spirits of Freedom and Love" - a process which necessarily must happen gradually.

During the Atlantean period, Christ brought about the donation of the Ego by the Exusiai as a latent "seed", although it would only be gradually integrated into mankind over thousands of years. After which, in the post-Atlantean period, came the "division of tongues", for the karmic needs of mankind were becoming more varied; and as a result, the different nations came about in order to accommodate the great karmic variety of the various groups of humankind which subsequently adapted to the geographical conditions and observed the guidance of the initiates of their respective mystery schools.

These diverse paths of evolution were a further consequence of the "fall", and through the intervention of retarded Luciferic spirits, ultimately great strife resulted from mankind's differences due to the actions of the unripe Ego forces that had not yet developed to a harmonious state of being. And yet, precious gifts did result from the great variety of cultures that came about through the development of the various Folk-Souls. This development of the numerous nations and tongues was brought about through the activity of Archangelic beings, operating as Folk-Souls, who are the beings behind the formation of the languages.

With the coming of the modern world, we find the scientists using the modern, universal "language" of mathematics. But the language of mathematics is actually beyond the Archangelic sphere of Mercury, and the realm of earthly language (**V**). Mathematics, on one level, is akin to the realm of what are called in Greek, the Exusiai, or as they are called by Rudolf Steiner - the Spirits of Form. The Exusiai are the same beings that are called Elohim in the Hebrew of the *Old Testament*. Mathematics provides a key to the mystery of the forming of substances (such as; the action of the number ether and its influence upon valence within the scheme of atomic structure). Mathematics also provides a key to understand the mystery of the human form, which is the domain of the Elohim, or Spirits of Form. Although mathematics in its decadent fallen state is under the inspiration of retarded Moon, Mercury, and Mars beings (and other retarded beings).

The number Pi (Π = 3.1415...) is approximated with the fraction 22/7. H. P. Blavatsky speaks of the value of Pi in relationship to the Elohim, or Alhim - the Spirits of Form. Through a process of kabbalistic permutation that is called "gematria", in which each letter has a number value, H. P. B. connects the numbers 3.1415 to the letters of the name Elohim (Alhim) by their Hebrew letter-number value. For, the name Alhim (A = 1, L = 30, H = 5, I = 10, M = 40) has the same numbers present as in the Pi sequence (if you take into account the standard kabbalistic practice of dropping the 0), although they are present in a different sequence. The name Alhim, is found in the *Old Testament* in the opening verse of "Genesis"; "In the beginning God (Alhim) created the Heaven and Earth, and the Earth was without form and void..." In addition to this, H. P. B. in *The Secret Doctrine, volume 1* (page 434), gives an extract from the ancient oriental Senzar texts which conveys in geometrical symbols the number series of the value of Pi (Π = 3.1415); although in this creation account, the numbers are present in the same order as they are in Π.

> 'The Great mother lay with ▲, and the **I**, and the ■, the second **I** and the ★ in her bosom, ready to bring them forth, the valiant sons of the ■ ▲ **I** **I** (or 4,320,000, the Cycle) whose two elders are the ● and the • (Point).'

The Elohim, or Exusiai are two stages of evolution beyond the Archangels, so that their natural dwelling is the Sphere of the Sun. While, Jehovah Elohim has worked from the sphere of the Moon - as a sacrifice - to counteract the effect of the Luciferic forces upon mankind since the Lemurian period, when the Moon separated from the Earth. In "Genesis", the "rib" of Adam was taken to form Eve. Poetically speaking, this reminds one of the Moon in the Eve-ning sky above the Adamic-Earth.

The Elohim, or Exusiai mediate forces that proceed from the region of the constellation of Scorpio the Eagle, or Scorpion; which relates to the Spirit-Self, the Higher-Self in man (IX), and to our connection with the moral-spiritual forces that proceed from our Guardian Angels, as individual representatives of the Holy Spirit, mediating forces that proceed from the region of Taurus; which is the constellation opposite Scorpio (forming part of the Cosmic Cross of the Holy Spirit, **X, XIII-XIV**). Furthermore, in this way of looking at the seven principles, our fifth principle of Spirit-Self corresponds to the fourth principle of the Angels, for they are one stage beyond mankind (**IX**).

The Exusiai, on the other hand, have their lowest vehicle on the Manasic plane, the level of the Spirit-Self which is inspired through the macrocosmic forces of Scorpio. The Exusiai are two stages beyond the Archangels, who have as their lowest vehicle an Astral-Body. The Archangels are working with the macrocosmic forces of Capricorn, the Sea-Goat, that relate to the Astral-Body in mankind. The old Masonic expression of "riding the goat" refers to the regulation, through inner development, of the compulsion of the instinctive animal nature of the untamed Astral-Body.

The Exusiai mediate between the Thrones, or Spirits of Will and the Dynamis, or Spirits of Movement. The Thrones are inspired from out of the region of the constellation of Leo the Lion, and work with Saturn forces from the center of the Earth. While the Dynamis, work from the periphery through the Sphere of Mars in response to the region of the Scales of Libra, the region of Cosmic Budhi, the higher counterpart to the etheric world of life, and the region that relates to the "True-Self" of man, the Life-Spirit, or "Christ in you."

The Higher Members of the Being of Man

Spirit-Man, Atma - the "Divine Spark", the Sophia - Virgo - Kyriotetes
Life-Spirit, Budhi - the True-Self, the "Christ in you" - Libra - Dynamis
Spirit-Self, Manas - the Higher Self - Scorpio - Exusiai
Ego - the Ordinary Self - Sagittarius - Archai

The Higher Members as They are Developed in the Beings of the Third Hierarchy

The Archai possess a fully developed Spirit-Man
The Archangels possess a fully developed Life-Spirit
The Angels possess a fully developed Spirit-Self

This stage of Cosmic Budhi is the level that Gautama Buddha was able to reach - out of his own forces - through his enlightenment under the Bodhi tree, (this is not to say that he could not reach even higher through the grace of higher beings). It is also further noted by Rudolf Steiner, that we must not think of Gautama Buddha's development as stopping at the level that he had reached a few hundred years before Christ. For Buddha is one of the greatest Christian Masters, and has played a vital role in the spread of the Christ impulse even though he does not reincarnate in a human Physical-Body; but rather, the Buddha works for mankind from within a nirmanakaya or spiritual form.

The Buddha, Zarathustra, and Skythianos are the central spiritual Masters, who along with Christian Rosenkreutz, have guided the Rosicrucian stream under the direction of Mani, who is an initiate that has fully attained the Spirit-Man - out of his own forces - and is an embodiment of what is referred to in the *Bible* as the "Paraclete." This relationship of Mani to the biblical idea of the "Paraclete" points to the mission of the Grail impulse - which proceeds from the "Mother Lodge" of humanity - and nurtures the development of the higher spiritual principles as we move towards the future "New Jerusalem" (**XXV**). This point is clarified by Rudolf Steiner in the lecture entitled "Manichaeism", which is included in the lecture cycle published as, *The Temple Legend*.

> *Mani is called the 'Son of the Widow', and his followers are called the 'Sons of the Widow.' However, Mani described himself as the 'Paraclete', the Holy Spirit promised to mankind by Christ. We should understand by this that he saw himself as one incarnation of the Holy Spirit; he did not mean that he was the only one. He explained that the Holy Spirit reincarnated, and that he was one such incarnation.*

Through his awakening by the Holy Spirit - in the service of Christ - Mani has become an embodiment of the "Paraclete" principle, and is a true representative of the Sophia for mankind - a "Grail Angel" that incarnated as the "Grail-King" Parzival in the 9th century. Mani and Manichaeism have a particular task concerning the redemption of evil through the development of appropriate social forms, in order to manifest the impulses of the rightful Archai (or ruling Time Spirit) and counteract the impulses of the retarded Archai, which is a central mission of the true

Templar stream (**XXIV**). The inspiration of this mission of "overcoming evil through goodness" is embodied in one of the battle cries of the Knights Templars - "Vive Dieu Saint Amour" ("Long Live God's Holy Love").

The true mission of Mani is none other than the mission of love as a cosmopolitan, healing impulse; or, to use other words, the Christ-impulse as a social impulse - for the Budhic principle, or Life-Spirit can only manifest (to use the words of Christ) "whenever two or more are gathered in My Name then I shall be in the midst of them." This mission of the Christ impulse as a social impulse will only begin to come to fruition once mankind overcomes thinking of the heart as a "pump", and realizes the heart's true nature as an organ of spiritual cognition for perceiving and radiating light, warmth, wisdom, and love. The manifestation of the Christ impulse within the social realm will be a special task of the sixth epoch - when the principles of Initiation will once again regain their central role within the culture of mankind.

The Harmony of the Spheres and the Chorus of Hearts

If we examine the processes of mathematics in astronomy, we find they are keys to understanding the activity of the Dynamis, the Spirits of Movement (called "Virtues" in the *Bible*) and the mysterious way they give expression to the "Harmony of the Spheres", and the planetary movements that are its fruit. The Dynamis are inspired by the Sophia forces of Wisdom, that proceed through the Kyriotetes, or Spirits of Wisdom, via the sphere of Jupiter (**V**) from the region of Virgo the Virgin (**IX**), which is in the direction of the Super-Galactic Center, and is the center that our Galaxy revolves around. The movements of the Dynamis are in harmony with the spiral "Dance of the Cherubim", the Spirits of Harmony - working from the periphery of the Zodiac - mediating forces from the region of the Cancer the Crab, which the ancients symbolized by two spirals (with a gap between them representing the state of rest or emptiness from which new impulses can arise). The Cherubim act out of the joy of the contemplation of the Seraphim, or Spirits of Love, who are filled with the outpouring of the Holy Trinity. This great symphony of beings enfolds the ordinary Egos of mankind; which in the "Zodiac of the Lamb of God", are related to the Archai, the Spirits of Personality. The Archai presently work through the sphere of Venus (**V**), mediating the forces of the Archer, the constellation of Sagittarius (**IX**), which is symbolized by the Centaur (which is half-man and half-horse, indicating the meeting of the horizontal-astral principle of the animal kingdom, with the upright human Ego). The constellation of Sagittarius is located towards the center of our Galaxy - the Milky Way.

There is a great mystery surrounding the relationship of the Spiritual Hierarchies to the Zodiac, Sun, and Earth, and also to the human heart. The beginning of evolution for mankind was when the Thrones, or Spirits of Will, donated the primal warmth at the beginning of the Old Saturn period from the region of the Lion-Leo (**IV**). The inspiration of the Cherubim had so moved the Thrones that they offered up as substance the primal warmth that is the root of our creation, and that continues on in the warmth of the blood which carries the Ego. Leo relates to the Sun in the Solar System, and the heart in the Zodiacal Man - the Adam Kadmon.

In the Macrocosm, the Thrones work through the Sphere of Saturn from the periphery within the sphere of the Zodiac (**V**), but with a special relationship to the constellation of Leo, through it being the region of space that was the focal point of the Zodiac in the Old Saturn Period (**XIV**). The present-day orbit of the planet Saturn (**V**) performs its circuit at the outermost limit of the Globe of the Old Saturn incarnation of the Earth (**IV**). Also, as regards to the forming of the microcosmic human being, the planet Saturn is also the limit of our "true" Solar System.

Regarding the planets Uranus, Neptune and Pluto: they are not truly members of the Solar System, as Uranus separated off during the Old Saturn period and Neptune and Pluto are, so to speak, visitors from space. Though they have astrological influence, they are not a part of the macrocosmic-microcosmic plan in the same way; for, at the rest, or pralaya - after the Old Saturn, Old Sun and Old Moon evolutions (**IV**), all the planets of the Solar System were rejoined together, with the exception of the three outer planets; Uranus, Neptune, and Pluto.

In the microcosmic human, the Thrones, or Spirits of Will, find their relationship to the warmth at the core of man's being, and also through the Sphere of Saturn, to the spleen and the skeleton - both of which are the birthplaces for the blood cells which are offered up as a continual sacrifice. One is reminded of the Rosicrucian image of the Pelican feeding its young from its own breast.

The working of the heart warmth at the center of man - the "Sun" in man - is similar to the activity of the Thrones when they work from the center of the Earth - the future Sun - both of which in the future will be akin to the nature of the Sun through their radiance of light and warmth; though the Earth has already begun to give off its radiance - which Rudolf Steiner tells us is perceptible to clairvoyant observation as golden light.

With His entry into human evolution, through His dwelling within the hearts of mankind - in the "True-Self" of man - Christ has begun a transformation. By the working of the Christened-Ego forces, mankind and the Earth will gradually begin to radiate light and warmth. By undergoing this metamorphosis, mankind will begin to realize their evolutionary goal as Spirits of Freedom and Love; and as a result, the Earth will slowly come to birth as a star - thereby beginning the fulfillment of the saying of Christ; "Know ye not that it is written; 'Ye are Gods'?".

Rudolf Steiner once shared that to clairvoyant perception, one can see golden streams of light raying out from the center of the earth - for the center of the Earth has become radiant from its golden Sun-nature. This golden light from the center of the Earth streams out to the etheric ring that surrounds the periphery of the Earth. This warm, golden, radiant light is the result of the activity of the Life-Spirit of Christ working within the etheric realm which manifests - for the benefit of all mankind - a realm of pure Wisdom-Love, or Atma-Budhi. This golden Sun-nature is the manifestation of the harmony of the Sophia and Christ natures, and is a culmination of the "Sun laws" that were established by the activity of the Kyriotetes during the Old Sun incarnation of the Earth (**IV**). It is this etheric ring around the Earth, this realm of activity that takes place between the golden "Sun" center of the Earth and its corresponding peripheral Life-Spirit etheric ring, which preserves the perfected astral and etheric vehicles of the Saints and Initiates - that have achieved the highest human expressions; and so, are preserved for the enrichment of the continuing development of mankind. This region is the true "Temple of the Grail", the realm of "Shamballa" which is watched over by Melchizedek, the Manu-Noah, the Initiate of Initiates, who was the leader of the Sun oracle in Atlantis, and led the migration to central Asia at the end of the Atlantean period (**XXV**).

In the realm of the spiritual hierarchies, the combined working of the Spirit-Man, or Atma, and the Life-Spirit, or Budhi, relates respectively to the activities of the the Kyriotetes, or Spirits of Wisdom, and to the Dynamis or Spirits of Movement (**IX**). The Dynamis, through their relationship to the Life-Spirit, or Budhic principle, in man are regents of the principle of love, compassion, and forgiveness towards all sentient beings.

In the "Zodiac of the Lamb of God" (**IX**), the Life-Spirit relates to the constellation of Libra, the Scales. The Life-Spirit is a higher counterpart to the etheric world, which is the highest expression within the vegetable kingdom. One "signature" of the activity of the Dynamis in nature can be seen in the growth of plants that spiral out of the Earth with the distribution of branches, leaves, and petals in mathematical-geometric ratios that are expressions of the harmonies of the planetary spheres. The word planet comes from the Greek word for "wanderer", implying movement in space. The word plant comes from this same word-root and shows the ancient's understanding of the planetary "signatures" in plants. In ancient times, this knowledge was achieved through atavistic clairvoyance guided by what might be called instinctive wisdom; which was similar, in a way, to the abilities of certain animals to avoid poisoned water or plants. In the present age, we can use mathematics to work out these harmonic relationships. In the future (or by those who develop in advance of mankind) it will be seen clairvoyantly. Another related phenomena of responsiveness to the heavens is obvious in certain plants that follow the Sun (heliotropic), or Moon (selenetropic) across the sky.

The Kyriotetes relate to the Spirit-Man, the Atma or "divine spark" in man, which in turn, is reflected in nature by the mineral kingdom. In the "Zodiac of the Lamb of God" (IX), the Kyriotetes relate to the constellation of Virgo, the Virgin Isis-Sophia. This occult fact, leads us to a deeper understanding of the place of Michael, the Archangel of the Sun; for Michael as the leader of the Archangels, has a strong connection to the Sun-Spirit of Wisdom who is the leader of the Kyriotetes that work in service to the Christ. This Sun-leader of the Kyriotetes is a regent of the Cosmic-Sophia forces of Wisdom that stream from the region of the Virgin as Cosmic Intelligence, as a living manifestation of the "Sun laws" from the Old Sun incarnation of the Earth (IV). Michael is the guardian of this Cosmic Intelligence that "fell" to Earth in order to begin working from within mankind, rather than from outside. Michael awaits the fruits of the working of this Cosmic Intelligence in humanity to manifest as loving-wisdom, which will be revealed through the thoughts and deeds of mankind that are enacted in freedom.

When one considers the significance of warmth to the Old Saturn incarnation of the earth (IV), it again leads us to the present Sun; which is thought of as the focal point of the light and warmth in our Solar System. Although the highest regent of the Isis-Sophia forces of Cosmic Light and Cosmic Warmth, is the Cosmic Thought of the Christ-Logos (Osiris) Himself who has been present on Earth - since the Mystery of Golgotha - with the exception of His Spirit-Man principle that remained behind on the Sun.

The solar-wind, which is a plasma wave that flows outward from the Sun to the orbit of Saturn, and then returns to the Sun; can be seen as the "blood" of the Sun. The solar-wind shows the limit of a particular level of activity of the Sun. In light of this, we are actually contained within the Sun and its circulating perimeter, which extends to the orbit of the present planet Saturn, making us, so to speak, "corpuscles in the body of Christ." This analogically corresponds to why the planet Saturn was related by the ancients to the skin; for the skin is the physical outer *limit* of a human being, just as the orbit of Saturn is the *limit*, or "ring-pass-not", of our Solar System, as regards to certain levels of being and activity in space (**V**). On the other hand, the present planet Saturn as Chronos, or "Father Time", is the image of the *limit* in time of human life and the aging process. Also, the planet Saturn is related to the chakra, or astral center, that crowns the head, the *limit* of man.

In the Cosmos, the planet Saturn is the gateway to the beings and forces of the Zodiac, beyond the planetary nature of our Solar System - to the Cherubim, or Spirits of Harmony, and the Seraphim, or Spirits of Universal Love - and above them to the Holy Trinity of the Father, the Son and the Holy Spirit. It is the sum of the activity of all of these beings and forces that finds its center within the heart of man, and is the place within the "Saturn man" of warmth that is the focal-point of the karmic "Saturn laws", from which the spiritual evolution of mankind developed. As a result of Christ's entry into Earth evolution, the karmic laws governing mankind have been transformed from the "Saturn laws" of Cosmic Necessity to the "Sun laws" of Cosmic Love; and which are under the direction of the love of Christ as the "new Lord of Karma" (**XIV**).

The Transformation of the Heart From the "Saturn laws" of Cosmic Necessity to the "Sun laws" of Cosmic Love

Leo is ruled by the Sun and relates to the heart. The warmth of the blood leads back to the donation of the primal warmth by the Thrones, or Spirits of Will, at the beginning of the Old Saturn period; which is three stages of cosmic evolution in the past, as our present physical Earth is the fourth stage of cosmic evolution (**IV**). The Old Saturn period was oriented towards the region of the constellation of Leo, the Lion (**XIV**).

The Archai stage of development, which mankind will attain in the seventh stage of cosmic evolution or Vulcan period, is the culmination of the 3rd Hierarchy or Spirits of Soul (see pages, 117-8), and is the last stage in our *first* seven-fold chain of evolution. Like the Old Saturn period, which began our chain of evolution, the seventh stage or Vulcan period will also be oriented towards Leo. So in essence, it is the warmth of the blood - which is centered within the heart - that makes the complete seven-fold journey from Old Saturn to Vulcan.

Though there are other higher stages beyond the seven-fold chain, the stages are perceived and described according to the law of seven; which is an expression of the seven-fold nature of perception that creates a horizon, or "ring-pass-not" in the perception of Cosmic Time, so that through spiritual development one perceives clairvoyantly three preceding and three following stages from our vantage point on Earth, the fourth.

At this point it would be useful to remember that the primal source of the warmth at the core of our being - the Thrones, or Spirits of Will relate to the sphere of Saturn (**V**); which, according to Ptolemy, "rules" both Capricorn and Aquarius. Furthermore, in the "Zodiac of the Lamb of God" (**IX**), Capricorn relates to the Archangels, and to the Astral-Body; while Aquarius relates to the Angels and to the Etheric-Body. For the Angels are etheric beings whose densest manifestation would be like a fine vapor; the Archangels, on the other hand, are astral beings that dwell on the other side of light.

This relationship of the Archangels to light is a key to a very profound mystery - for the realm of Cosmic Light, that is centered within the heart, is the realm of Cosmic Feeling; and it was through their relationship to the Cosmic Feeling realm that the Archangels influenced the development of language; and furthermore, in the past, it was largely through the realm of the feelings - through the feelings of fear and guilt - that the Hebrews adhered to the laws that are codified in the *Old Testament* as expressions of the Cosmic Will of the Father. Now, through the descent of Cosmic Intelligence to the human realm, mankind has taken upon itself the challenge of mediating between Cosmic Feeling and Cosmic Will with the *free* human expression of the Cosmic Intelligence of the Son - striving to manifest as a principle of Cosmic Love - without compulsion from outside influencing the realm of the feelings and manifesting as fear, guilt, and anger, and other *unfree* lower emotions that can dominate human behavior. This challenge of manifesting Cosmic Intelligence is especially significant since the beginning of the Archangelic period of Michael in 1879 - for Michael is the custodian of Cosmic Intelligence.

Oriphiel, the Archangel of Saturn (**XVIII**), has a singular place within the group of seven planetary Archangels; for, as shown above, Saturn relates to Capricorn which is the region of the Archangels in the "Zodiac of the Lamb of God" (**IX**); and of the seven planetary Archangels, through his Saturnian nature, Oriphiel is most akin to the forces of Capricorn. One could say that, through his Saturnian nature, Oriphiel carries the memory of the Old Saturn period that immediately preceded what was the equivalent of human evolution for the Archangels in the Old Sun period **(IV)**, for the Archangels are two stages beyond mankind; which can be seen by the following chart which demonstrates the evolutionary overlap.

The Globe at which the Angelic Hierarchies and Mankind went through the Fourth, or human equivalent stage of evolution.

Old Saturn - Archai - Primordial Physical Warmth
Old Sun - Archangels - Primordial Etheric
Old Moon - Angels - Primordial Astral
Earth - Mankind - The Ego is added to the Physical, Etheric, and Astral and is carried in the warmth of the blood

The Archangel Oriphiel is the leader of the Archangels who doubt the ability of mankind to evolve in freedom; and, as mentioned above, is inspired by the memory of the Old Saturn state of being immediately preceding the Archangel's equivalent human stage during the Old Sun evolution **(IV)**. The Archangels, through passing their fourth, or equivalent human stage on Old Sun have a special relationship to the Sphere of the Sun, and so, the Sun Archangel Michael has a leadership role in the plan of Christ; for during the Old Sun period, Michael had a singular mission as a vehicle of the Christ Impulse.

The rightful leader of the Archangels, on behalf of Christ, is Michael - the Sun Archangel, who has never lost faith in mankind's ability to attain the stage of the tenth hierarchy, the Spirits of Freedom and Love; and thereby, pass to the rank of the Angels with the gifts of freedom and love. And so, Michael refrains from interfering in mankind's freedom to develop love on their own. The Archangel Michael is looking towards the future goal of the evolution of mankind, the Vulcan Period.

Oriphiel, the Archangel of Saturn, as I have mentioned, is the leader of the Archangels who have their doubts as to mankind's ability to attain an Angelic state *without compulsion.* Oriphiel is the voice of iron necessity, of "the inexorable law of karma", the *Old Testament* law of "an eye for an eye, a tooth for a tooth." This saturnian tendency is shown by the last Archangelic period of Oriphiel - which was during the Roman Empire, the age of absolute external authority - in contrast with the present age of Michael, the age of striving for the individual freedom of the sovereign Ego. The last Archangelic period of Michael was during the approximately 350 year period that ended around 200 B.C., the age of the ancient Greeks - who through Plato, Aristotle, and others - developed the type of thinking that would, one day through its further development, lead mankind to the possibility of individual spiritual freedom (a path that is shown by Rudolf Steiner in his book, *The Philosophy of Freedom*).

As mentioned earlier, the primal warmth globe of the Old Saturn period extended out to the present orbit of the planet Saturn, with the formation of our present planet Saturn taking place at the "ring-pass-not" of the Old Saturn period (**IV**). This is indicative of the central concern of Oriphiel, the Saturn Archangel, for the warmth process of the heart and blood that is centered in the heart.

Oriphiel looks *back* upon the constellation of Leo, the Lion and sees the past of our Cosmos (**XIII**), the Old Saturn period (**IV**). On the other hand, the Archangel Michael (who has recently attained the rank of Archai) looks *forward* towards the region of the Lion (**XIV**), to the Vulcan period (**IV**), which will hold in store a decidedly different outcome for mankind as a result of the greater human freedom that has become possible through the divine intervention of Christ.

The Archangel Michael has a special mission regarding the nature of the development of the human heart, as to how it bears its warmth into future evolution. Michael envisions this warmth of humanity being metamorphosed by the "Sun laws" that are expressed in the light and love of Christ, which has already brought about the seed of a future Sun within the center of the Earth; and likewise, is creating a new Sun-nature within the human heart. In fact, the proper transformation of the Earth into a future Sun depends upon the proper cultivation by mankind, through the Christ impulse, of this Sun-nature within the human heart; a process which leads back to the Cosmic Light relationship that developed in the Old Sun Period (**IV**) between the Kyriotetes (working from the center) and the Archangels (who responded by radiating light from the periphery), and which process was related to the formation of what would later become the human Etheric-Body on Earth; and therefore, because of the central role of the Etheric-Body in human thinking, these "Sun laws" are vital to the wholesome integration of the principle of Cosmic Intelligence within mankind.

As mentioned on numerous occasions, this "Sun" transformation takes place through what Rudolf Steiner called, the "etherization of the blood"; whereby, the etheric nature of the blood of an individual is united with the etheric nature of the blood of Christ and the inspiration that radiates from the Life-Spirit of Christ (**XIV**). This process leads to a transformation of the quality of the warmth of the blood, and establishes an etheric stream that rises up and bathes the pineal and pituitary glands in the center of the head. The "etherization of the blood" leads to the development of the higher spiritual centers in man and ultimately results in a radiant halo that surrounds the periphery of the head.

The Archangel Oriphiel also has a mission concerning the warmth of the heart, and its transformation; but he, along with other Archangels, would prefer to influence mankind from outside, rather than take the risk of giving mankind freedom. Oriphiel would rather take the approach of external authority under the "iron rule of necessity", instead of giving mankind the risky challenge of Michaelic inner-freedom; for if mankind is to realize this challenge - it must be through their own individual effort.

The *Old Testament* is an expression of Cosmic Law (karma = Saturn) and Eugenics (hereditary forces = Moon). On the other hand, the *New Testament* is an expression of Cosmic Thought (Christ the Solar Logos), Cosmic Love ("God is love.") and healing (Mercury = Budhi, or Life-Spirit) - "love hath healing on its wings." For the "Turning Point of Time", which is the Mystery of Golgotha, is the seed for the transition from the Mars half (*Old Testament*, "bones and law") to the Mercury half (*New Testament*, "blood and love") of Earth evolution (**IV**).

The character of the *Old Testament* is very serious, or saturnian in tone with its unquestioned reliance on external laws written on stone tablets. Even in the story of Moses' experience on Mt. Sinai where he hears the words "I Am the I Am", and sees the Lord appear to him in the lightning and in the burning bush - these things are experienced as being outside of him, and are sensed by Him as though reflected within, as the Moon reflects the Sun (or the brain reflects the heart).

In the time of Moses, Michael had a central role concerning the Hebrew people, although mankind was not yet ripe enough for the "Golden Rule", the inner heart-Sun rule of; "Do onto others as you would have them do onto you." (or perhaps, more appropriately; "Do onto others as they would have you do onto them.") For the "Golden Rule" radiates from within as an act of joy, rather than being reflected from outside and followed out of fear of the law.

In *Old Testament* times, Christ had not yet intervened by entering directly into human evolution, and so Michael, (whose name means, "like unto God"), was seen as the "Countenance of Jehovah", arbitrating the "iron rule of necessity." After the coming of Christ, Michael would become the "Countenance of Christ", most especially since the descent of Cosmic Intelligence to the earthly human realm in the 8th century, in preparation for the uniting of the Grail and Arthurian streams in the 9th century; which happened as an earthly reflection of the uniting of the Spirit-Self of Christ with the Life-Spirit of Christ within the spiritual atmosphere of the Earth. For Michael, as the "Countenance of Christ", endeavors to lead mankind in the spirit of the "Golden Rule" along the path of freedom.

The World-Soul

In mankind, the Ego resides in the warmth of the blood and although one might not think of it - due to its relationship to the blood - this warmth is in the shape of the human form. And in addition to this, according to Rudolf Steiner, the inside of the heart is a mathematical inversion of the human form; which in turn, is an image of the circling stars.

As mentioned previously, the movement of the heart and lungs is a microcosmic reflection of the precession of the equinox of 25,920 years. For the astronomical cycle of the precession of the equinox moves at a rate of around 1 degree every 72 years; thereby completing a cycle in about 25,920 years. In the human body this rhythm equals 25,920 breaths in a day, and the pulse of 72 beats per minute. This transformative earthly mystery of the precession of the equinox is the mystery of the archetypal human, which is represented in the image of the World arcanum as the upright androgyne "World-Soul", with its legs forming a cross (which, like the Hanged Man arcanum, is also reminiscent of the crossed legs of the tomb-carvings of the Knights Templars). Furthermore, on the World arcanum, the image of the "World-Soul" is holding a wand in each hand, tilted to represent the axis of the Earth, which brings about the four seasons (**XIV**) and is the hub of the precession of the equinox - a primary cycle of human development (**XXVI**).

In the image that is shown on the World arcanum, the position of the arms of the "World-Soul" form an upward pointing triangle - symbolizing that which ascends through the Resurrection. The "World-Soul" is also surrounded by a wreath that symbolizes the conquest of life over death; and beyond this are the symbols of the four Evangelists: St. Mark - the Lion, St. Luke - the Bull, St. Matthew - the Angel, St. John - the Eagle; which form the cross of the four fixed signs of the Zodiac: Leo, Taurus, Aquarius and Scorpio. On one level of meaning this can be seen as the Macrocosmic Cross of the Holy Spirit (**XIII**); and, on another level of meaning, as representing the Cross of the four Cherubim who governed in the Old Sun period (**XIV**), and the "Sun laws" that were established at that time. In third lecture of the lecture cycle entitled, *The East in the Light of the West*, Rudolf Steiner clarifies a great mystery of the "World-Soul."

> *When a spiritual seer looks back to the time preceding the Christ event, a striking vision comes before him. The external form of the earth, confronting the physical senses as Maya [illusion], vanishes and something comparable to the human form appears, but only as a form, or figure. To spiritual vision, the outer Mayavic earth (and I say the 'earth' deliberately) changed into the form of a man with arms outstretched in the shape of a cross, a male-female [androgyne] form. This reminds us of the wonderful words of Plato, words which he drew from the Mysteries, that the world-soul is crucified on the cross of the world's body. This is exactly the image which presents itself to the eye of the spiritual seer: The Christ died on the cross, and thereupon the earth, which had been a mere form and figure, became filled with life. The coming of the Christ principle into the earth had something in common with the withdrawal of the moon [from the earth in the Lemurian period]; for life was poured into what otherwise would have remained as a mere form.*
>
> *To understand ancient times properly is to realize that they all lead up to the Christ event. Just as men of today look back to the Christ event as a being Who at a certain point of time entered into human evolution; so, pre-Christian initiates all pointed to the coming of the Christ as foreshown by events. Nothing could have been a surer herald of the Christ than the mighty phenomenon, that was visible under certain conditions to spiritual sight, of the disappearance of the physical form of the earth and the vision of the world-soul crucified on the world's body. In dim Indian antiquity it was said by the sages that when their spiritual vision arose, they saw, deep down under the mountains of the earth, near its central point, a cross, and upon it a male-female human being, having on its right side the symbol of the sun and upon its left side the symbol of the moon, and over the rest of the body the various land and sea formations of the earth. This was the clairvoyant vision*

which the sages of ancient India had of the form that was waiting until our earth could be brought to life by the Christ principle. And inasmuch as those ancient sages pointed to the most important prophecy of the Christ event, they were justified, when they looked still more deeply into existence, in saying: the Christ will come because that which points to Him is in existence.

Ancient wisdom at its highest level becomes prophetic; it looks towards that which will come to pass in the future. What the future holds is entirely the result of the present; and so, in the present, spiritual vision can receive intimations of a spiritual event which is to take place in the future. These indications of the Christ event were not given in any outward abstract way, but were revealed to spiritual sight by the phenomenon of the world-soul crucified on the cross of the world's body, waiting to receive the life of the Christ when He would unite Himself with the earth.

The World is a Grail that was anointed, at the Mystery of Golgotha, by receiving the "Sangreal", the "Blood Royal" that is the Sacred Blood of Christ; and thereafter, the World was redeemed through His Resurrection. Through this mystery of mysteries, the World has received the vital renewal of life that will enable evolution to unfold toward its fulfillment in harmony with the Divine Plan. For the World-Soul had, as it were, received a new heart - an etheric heart to circulate the principle of life and regenerate all living things - the Sacred Heart of Christ . . . the true Grail of all Grails.

Incombustible stands the cross, triumphant sign of our kind. I journey beneath it - and each pain, once a thorn, becomes delight.
Novalis

Part 2

The Archangelic Periods

"I have lived, sir, a long time. And the longer I live, the more convincing proofs I see of this truth - that God governs in the affairs of men. And if a sparrow cannot fall on the ground without his notice, is it probable that an empire can rise without his aid?"

Benjamin Franklin, 1706-1790

The Archangelic Periods

The Seven-Fold Mystery of Time-Memory

In the writings of the German abbot Trithemius von Sponheim (1462-1516) are contained a key to the mystery of the guiding historical impulses that proceed from the realm of the Archangels. This information had only been known by Initiates, until it was published by Trithemius. This sequence proceeds in periods Trithemius indicates as being 354 years and 4 months in length. By utilizing the methods of spiritual-scientific, clairvoyant investigation of the Akashic Record, Rudolf Steiner was able to pinpoint the actual transitions between the Archangelic periods. He indicated their length as being "about 350 years on the average" in reference to the overall scheme, and gave specific dates for each individual transition.

The sequence of Archangelic periods follows the days of the week, with their individual planetary rulerships, in a reversed order. These planetary rulerships, in turn, refer to the Archangels of the seven planets, each of whom are considered to be presiding over the leading impulses of a specific period.

The Planets and the Days of the Week

Saturn - Saturday

Venus - Friday

Jupiter - Thursday

Mercury - Wednesday

Mars - Tuesday

Moon - Monday

Sun - Sunday

The Archangelic Periods

	Trithemius	Rudolf Steiner
Saturn - Oriphiel	246 B.C. - 109 A.D.	200 B.C. - 150 A.D.
Venus - Anael	109 - 463	150 - 500
Jupiter - Zachariel	463 - 817	500 - 850
Mercury - Raphael	817 - 1171	850 - 1190
Mars - Samael	1171 - 1525	1190 - 1510
Moon - Gabriel	1525 - 1879	1510 - 1879
Sun - Michael	1879 - 2233	1879 - 2229

The rulerships of the Archangelic periods, and the dates as given by both Trithemius and Rudolf Steiner are shown above. The last date given by Rudolf Steiner for the end of the Age of Michael is approximate, as it has not happened yet; for these are cycles of the historical activities of living beings, and so are not to be understood as being merely, so to speak, mechanistically-astronomical in nature.

The Planetary Spheres, the Archangels, and the Tarot Arcana

Saturn - Oriphiel - The World

Venus - Anael - The Empress

Jupiter - Zachariel - The Wheel of Fortune

Mercury - Raphael - The Magician

Mars - Samael - The Tower

Moon - Gabriel - The High Priestess

Sun - Michael - The Sun

The sequence of the Archangelic periods provides a key by which we can approach our understanding of the Tarot Arcana in a new way. By taking the rulerships that are assigned between the planets and the Archangels and relating them to the Major Arcana, we have a series of pictorial-historical images to work with to deepen our view (I).

In the following sections, a brief overview of certain historic events is given to help bring more understanding of the significance of the Archangelic influences in these periods; especially as they relate to the Grail impulse, in light of Anthroposophical Spiritual Science.

Partial histories are completely impossible. Each history must be a world history; for, only through its relationship to all of history is the historical treatment of an individual situation possible.

Novalis

The Archangelic Period of Oriphiel

Saturn - The World: 200 B.C. - 150 A.D.

During the period of the Archangel Oriphiel (or Ophiel), the Roman Empire was ruling most of the known world with a firm *saturnian* grip. The building of roads, whereby "all roads lead to Rome", created social order, but the order was of an external nature. It was in the midst of this legalistic time that the incarnation of Christ took place. And it was through the hardened legalism of both the scribes and pharisees, and the Roman law, that He was condemned and crucified.

In this period we also find, within certain forms of Gnosticism, highly developed attempts to interpret the meaning of the Christ Mystery, in the light of the Ancient Mysteries, by utilizing the concepts of the Intellectual-Soul. But after a few centuries, the spiritual beings that had inspired certain Gnostic teachers within the realm of thinking, withdrew into the spiritual world where later - beginning in the 8th and 9th centuries - they were to inspire the Grail Mysteries within the realm of feeling and soul-mood.

In the Grail legends, it is told how the Angels took the Grail chalice into the spiritual world and waited for the time when a knight would appear who was worthy to become the Grail King. This is an image of the withdrawal of certain inspirational forces, originating from the beings of the spiritual world, that had to wait until the proper time came in the evolution of mankind, when they could then nurture the necessary forces that would allow the unfoldment of the "I Am", or individual Ego nature, in a way that was appropriate for that time. This mystery came about through the intentions of the higher spiritual beings in the service of Christ.

The Grail legends tell of how, at the Mystery of Golgotha, the side of Christ was pierced by the Roman Centurion Gaius Cassius, who came to be known as Longinus (the Spearman), and that the blood was captured in the Grail chalice by Joseph of Arimathea (or in some accounts by a Roman soldier). This is an interesting picture - in light of the significance of Rome in the spread of *exoteric* Christianity through the Roman Catholic Church.

The next mention that we hear of the Grail, it is in the possession of Joseph of Arimathea; in fact, the Grail chalice possibly originally belonged to him. Joseph of Arimathea had successfully pleaded with Pilate for the body of Christ Jesus after the Crucifixion, and put Christ's body in the tomb that he had originally created for himself. This makes Joseph of Arimathea the actual recipient of both the body and blood of Christ. In consideration of all of this, Joseph of Arimathea along with Mother Mary, Mary Magdalene, Nicodemus, Lazarus-John and the Youth of Nain, among others, can be seen as the sources of the historical, *esoteric* Resurrection Mysteries.

In the German legend entitled, *Sangerkrieg auf der Wartburg*, it says that the crown of Lucifer consisted of 60,000 angels. In one legend it says that the Archangel Michael struck the crown of Lucifer and a stone fell to Earth in the place where the Phoenician city of Tyre was founded (the city of Hiram Abiff). This meteoric stone was made into the chalice of the Holy Grail. The Queen of Sheba is said to have owned it, and from her it passed to King Solomon; from King Solomon it passed to Hiram Abiff, the master-builder of the Temple of Jerusalem. Eventually this meteoric stone chalice is said to have passed into the hands of Joseph of Arimathea and was used at the Last Supper, and is said to be the chalice that received the blood of Christ upon Golgotha.

In the cosmological fragments extracted from the Phoenician temple of Baal-Amon by Sanchuniathon (c. 14th-13th century B.C.?), that were translated into Greek by Philo Byblos (c. 100 A.D.) and preserved by Eusebius (c. 260-340 A.D.) the bishop of Caesarea, is a legendary account of a meteor that is connected with the city of Tyre which parallels the preceding account of the meteoric origin of the Holy Grail. This account, which demonstrates the veneration that was bestowed upon meteors in the ancient world, is given by Isaac Preston Cory in his *Ancient Fragments*:

> *But Astarte called the greatest, and Demarous named Zeus, and Adodus who is entitled the king of the gods, reigned over the country by the consent of Cronus: and Astarte put upon her head, as the mark of her sovereignty, a bull's head: and travelling about the habitable world, she found a star falling through the air, which she took up and consecrated in the holy island of Tyre: and the Phoenicians say that Astarte is the same as Aphrodite [Venus].*

As far as the possible origin of the object known as the Holy Grail, little more can be said; but nonetheless, at the very least, it shows the efforts made by the authors of the Grail legends to connect the mystery of the shedding of the blood of Christ to the redemption of certain pre-Christian mystery streams. Regarding the mystery of the shedding of the blood of Christ and its connection to Hebrew prophecy, St. John says in "The Gospel of St. John" (19:31-37) (Wuest translation):

> *Then the Jews, since it was a day of preparation, in order that the bodies might not remain on the cross on the sabbath, for it was an important sabbath, that sabbath, asked Pilate that their legs might be broken and that they might be carried away. Therefore the soldiers went and broke the legs of the first one and of the other one who was crucified with Him. But upon coming to Jesus, when they saw He was already dead, they did not break his legs. But one of the soldiers with the head of a spear pierced His side, and there came out immediately blood and water. And he who has with discernment seen, and at present has that which he has seen in his mind's eye, has borne testimony, and his testimony is at present on record. And his testimony is genuine, and that one knows positively that he is speaking true things, in order that also you might be believing, for these things took place in order that the scripture might be fulfilled; 'A bone belonging to Him shall not be broken'. And again, another scripture says: 'They shall look on Him whom they pierced.'*

The manner in which the blood flowed out of Christ Jesus on the cross is vividly shown in certain paintings of the Middle Ages as a powerful, spiraling stream that issues from the side of Christ, and in some cases the blood can be seen anointing the heads of one or more persons at the foot of the cross. An interesting fact that was pointed out to me by Ralph Marinelli regarding this scriptural account is that - the blood does not flow once a person has passed away, but instead, slowly oozes in a thick, gelatinous manner; and yet, St. John puts great emphasis on the immediate flow of blood and water as if it were a dynamic event. It is clear that the Romans would have seen that Christ was not breathing and had passed away; for in death by crucifixion, once the person can no longer bear the weight of the body suspending from the arms of the cross, the compression of the chest brings about suffocation. And yet, in spite of all this, St. John tells us of the flowing blood and water. For the life that dwelt within the blood was so vibrantly alive, that one can picture it streaming out of Christ's side and entering into the very life of the Earth.

In the Old French story, *The Grand Saint Graal*, we are given an account of Joseph of Arimathea, which admittedly is a later 13th century version of the Grail story; but nonetheless, it provides us with thought provoking images surrounding the story of Joseph, for it has numerous details that point towards an earlier source deriving from Coptic Egypt. The *Grand Saint Graal* gives important clues in place names and liturgical details that find their parallel in Coptic Egypt; as pointed out by Margaret Murray (the associate of the founder of modern British Egyptology W. M. Flinders Petrie) in her article entitled, "Egyptian Elements in the Grail Romance."

According to Murray, *The Grand Saint Graal* begins with the arrival of Joseph of Arimathea and his family and friends in Babylon, which is not the famous Babylon of history; but rather, Babylon was the name of the fort of Old Cairo in the Egyptian delta region. This fact and others, have obscured the understanding of this story and prevented scholars from properly interpreting the *Grand Saint Graal*. One of the most telling details in this account is where Joseph is given a divine command to make an ark of wood to hold the holy vessel which would, later in the Middle Ages, come to be known as the Holy Grail. In Western Christianity, this type of wooden ark is nowhere to be found; but if we turn to the Coptic Church we find that the ark is a sort of wooden cabinet used to contain the sacramental chalice for the ritual of the Eucharist, and is still in use today. A description of this ark is given in volume 2 of *The Ancient Coptic Churches of Egypt*, by Alfred J. Butler (pages 42-43):

> *Every Coptic altar is furnished with a wooden ark or tabernacle . . . It is a regular instrument in the service of the mass, and at other times lies idle upon the altar. It consists of a cubical box, eight or nine inches high, the top of which is pierced with a circular opening just large enough to admit the chalice. At the consecration the chalice is placed within the tabernacle, and the rim when it is thus enclosed is about flush with the top, so that the paten rests as much on the tabernacle as on the chalice. The four walls of the tabernacle are covered with sacred paintings - our Lord and St. John being the most frequent figures.*

In *The Grand Saint Graal* we are told of how Evalach (Latin, ex = out + valere; to find worthy), the king of Sarras (Greek, sarx = flesh), and his brother in-law Seraphe (like the name of the ancient Egyptian god Serapis, a name which represents the combination of Osiris with the Apis bull; also, Seraphim), the duke of Orbery, are at war with Tholome (which is pronounced like the name Ptolemy, which was the name of numerous Macedonian rulers of Egypt after Alexander the Great). Tholome was the "king of Babylon" (which means the fort of Old Cairo). Joseph of Arimathea prophecies to King Evalach, that he shall be victorious only if he becomes a Christian. Joseph of Arimathea then takes two strips of red cloth and makes a cross on King Evalach's white shield (this is reminiscent of the Templar uniform of a red cross on a white cloak, and of the Rose Cross of Ormus, the disciple of St. Mark, the Apostle of Egypt). Unknown to King Evalach, his wife Queen Sarracynte (like Saracen - a medieval name for the Arabs) is already secretly a Christian who was converted by Salustes, the hermit who had miraculously healed her mother. In the midst of battle, King Evalach is taken prisoner and led to the nearby woods to be executed. King Evalach looks down on his shield and upon seeing the red cross, thinks of Joseph of Arimathea's prophecy and begins to pray for help. Suddenly, a White Knight with a red cross shield around his neck charges out of the forest on a horse "as white as the lily flower" and defeats King Tholome. King Evalach then takes King Tholome prisoner, while his soldiers defeat and capture the soldiers of King Tholome. The White Knight then takes up the banner of King Evalach and, fighting by the side of Duke Seraphe, together they lead the army of King Evalach to victory. And as the text says, "And thus the Egypcien, be goddis myht, at theke tyme weren distroyed be fyht."

As the story continues, a wounded knight is healed by touching the cross on Evalach's shield. Upon seeing this, Duke Seraphe is converted and is baptized under the name Nasciens (Latin, nasci = be born). Nasciens then converts King Evalach, who is baptized with the name Mordrayns (Latin, mors = death + Old English, dragan = to draw; dray - a cart, or, dreynt = overwhelmed). The healed knight is baptized as Clamacides (Latin, clamare = cry out). After the war is over, by the will of God, King Tholome dies. Now with great joy Queen Sarracynte admits her faith, which she has kept secret for twenty seven years (which is approximately one orbit of the planet Saturn), and the people of the kingdom of Sarras are baptized into the Christian faith.

After a long series of events, Joseph of Arimathea shows the Grail, that is resting in the ark, to King Mordrayns (Evalach) and Duke Nasciens

(Seraphe). Duke Nasciens lifts up the "plateyne" that is covering the Grail and is struck blind; but later, he is miraculously healed by the grace that radiates from the Grail. Joseph then proceeds to tell them of the mysteries of the Holy Grail before leaving the country. The narrative continues without Joseph, until later when he is about to cross the sea to Britain.

The Coptic Church traces its foundation back to St. Mark, whom according to the Rosicrucian tradition, initiated Ormus who then founded a secret order of the Rose Cross for the preservation of the esoteric Christian mysteries. Interestingly enough, there is in the possession of the Cairo museum a Coptic grave stele for a man named Dionysius that depicts an ankh cross, or crux ansata (a circle surmounting a Tau or T) and in the center of the circle is a rose - the rose-tau - which coincidentally happens to be an ancient Egyptian name for the area surrounding the Pyramids, Rosetau.

In 451 A.D., due to a controversy over the nature of the divinity of Christ, as to how Christ's divinity relates to His human nature - the Coptic Church, along with four others: the Ethiopian Church, the Syrian Church, the Armenian Church, and the Malabar Church (Syrian Church of India) parted company with Western Christendom.

In the Grail legends it tells of how Joseph of Arimathea went from the Holy Land, after the Mystery of Golgotha, to Britain (the "tin islands") in the West, where he united with the Celtic-Druid stream at Glastonbury. A carry-over of this Druid impulse can be seen in the practice of the monks of the Celtic Church wearing their hair long, with the front shaved back to a line that went across the top from ear to ear - like the Druids before them.

The Celtic Church also calculated Easter like the Eastern Church, according to what is considered the "Johannine" reckoning; for it was a method that was traditionally attributed to St. John the Divine. According to the "Johannine" reckoning, Easter fell *on the day* of the first full Moon after the Spring equinox, instead of the first *Sunday* after the first full Moon of Spring (which is the Roman method in the tradition of St. Augustine). This "Johannine" rule, regarding the determining of the festival of Easter in the Celtic Christian tradition, shows a flexibility that is characteristic of the Celtic peoples. This flexibility of the dates that resulted from the "Johannine" rule allowed the festival to move as it does in nature, in tune with the *etheric* nature forces that were revealed in the solar and lunar agricultural mysteries of the Celts.

By looking at it in this manner we can see that the Roman rule of determining Easter is more *astral* in nature and is connected with the

Mystery of the Sabbath. The Roman rule relates to the development of a social order that is based on a six day work-week with Sunday being a day of rest. This has the added secular, side-benefit of not having the Easter festival disrupt the work week. This way of organizing time within the social order is representative of the formal, saturnian Roman impulse that worked towards the external rule of law from a central authority. The organization of the Celtic Church, on the other hand, was decentralized with the leaders of the different monasteries functioning as autonomous Christians, whose only authority was due to the depth of their spirituality.

The distinction between the Celtic *esoteric* stream and the Roman *exoteric* stream gives one a picture of the nature of the Age of Oriphiel; an age of Roman rule that was a hostile environment to the development of Christianity. And yet, the Roman Empire through its road building, commerce, and social order ultimately resulted in facilitating the spread of Christianity. This centralized authority of the Roman Empire carried over into the Roman Catholic Church, beginning in the period of the Archangel Anael, with the conversion of the Roman Emperor Constantine I "the Great"(c. 285-337 A.D.).

After centuries of independent vitality, the Celtic Christian churches and monasteries would eventually be subjected to the yoke of Rome. For, beginning in England during the period of the Archangel Zachariel, the centralized external authority of Rome would prevail over the Celtic Church at the Synod of Whitby, a debate which was presided over by the Northumbrian King Oswiu in the year 664.

This advance of Roman Christianity would eventually cause the Celtic Christian stream to go underground as an esoteric stream that would secretly flourish in the period of the Archangel Raphael, when the Arthurian Mysteries of the West would unite with the Grail Mysteries of the East during the 9th century. For, Celtic Christianity was by nature more attuned to the "Life" of Christ as experienced within the etheric world of life, which came about through the activity of the Life-Spirit of Christ in the present - *"the spirit of the law."*

The Roman Church, on the other hand, was focused on the law as learned in scripture, a legalistic external authority transmitted from the past - *"the letter of the law."* Nonetheless, despite the opposition from Rome, the spirit of Celtic Christianity continued on, deriving its strength from the spontaneous inspiration that resulted through one's inner spiritual transformation, which is the essence of the path of the Grail.

The Archangelic Period of Anael

Venus - The Empress: 150 - 500 A.D.

In the period of the Archangel Anael (or Hanael), we see a polarization that is expressed in the extremes of love and hate that were displayed in the age of the Christian martyrs. One of the greatest of the Christian martyrs was the initiate Mani, who is also the greatest of the Gnostic teachers and the founder of Manichaeism, "the Religion of Divine Light." Mani was born into the Arsacid Parthian royal line that ruled Persia from 250 B.C. until 226 A.D. He was said to have been born on the 7th or the 25th of April 216 A.D (although some sources say 215 A.D.) in the village of Baromia, just south of Baghdad in Persia (the region of present-day Iraq). Rudolf Steiner says that Mani was the reincarnation of the "youth of Nain", who was raised from the dead by Christ as told in the *Bible*. After his martyrdom in the year 276 A.D., Mani became an even more potent spiritualizing influence in his after-death state as a "Grail Angel" in service to the living Christ.

The spiritual beings who had once inspired what was taught in Gnostic *thought* in the first, second, and third centuries retreated to the spiritual world, and made the transition from inspiring the realm of ideas to inspiring the realm of *feeling* later in the Middle Ages. It was this feeling for the Grail that inspired the Grail seekers from the Dark Ages on into the Middle Ages.

Rudolf Steiner once said to the effect that, those who were living during the time of Christ did not truly understand the significance of the incarnation of Christ until well after their death. For, the understanding by the early Christians of the deeper significance of the "deed of Christ" resulted from their after-death experiences in the spiritual world. These souls, specifically the souls of the Apostles, were able to be a source of spiritual inspiration to those living on Earth, especially to the Church Fathers.

The inspirations that were received from these departed souls became an especially significant spiritualizing influence starting from around the second or third century. Rudolf Steiner speaks of this spiritualizing influence in the second lecture of the lecture cycle entitled, *Three Streams in the Evolution of Mankind - The Connection of the Luciferic-Ahrimanic Impulses with the Christ-Jahve Impulse*.

There were contemporaries of Christ, His disciples that went about with Him, and through the traditional primeval wisdom they could acquire so much wisdom about Him that later they were able to produce the Gospels . . . but they could not really understand Him. Right up to their deaths they certainly never reached a true understanding of the Christ Impulse. When was it, then, that they could achieve this? After their death, in the time after death. Given that Peter or James, let us say, were contemporaries of Christ, when were they ready to understand Christ? Only in the third century after the Mystery of Golgotha . . . for up to their deaths they were not sufficiently mature; they became mature only in the third century.

We are touching here on a very important secret which we must bring with all exactitude before our souls. The contemporaries of Christ had to first go through death, had to live in the spiritual world until the second or third century; and then, in the life after death, knowledge of Christ could dawn upon them, and they could inspire those who, towards the end of the second century, or from the third century on, wrote about the Christ Impulse. Hence the writings about the Christ Impulse from the third century onwards take on a special character; for, through the Church Fathers they received inspiration, more or less clear or more or less clouded. Thus Augustine, whose authority prevailed throughout the Middle Ages, falls into this period. Hence we can see how the only way in which people could be given an understanding of the Christ Impulse was to be inspired on Earth by the Venus wisdom, if I may so call it, which at present man will experience only after death or later in subsequent centuries. And it was a piece of good fortune - a foolish expression but there is no better one - that in the second and third centuries this inspiration could begin. For had men been obliged to wait longer, beyond the year 333 [the mid-point of Earth evolution], they would have become increasingly hardened towards the spiritual world and would have been incapable of receiving any kind of inspiration.

You see, the working of the Christ Impulse into mankind during the centuries of Christian development was bound up with numerous mysteries. And anyone wishing to seek for it again today finds the most important elements in knowledge about the Christ Impulse only by achieving supersensible cognition. For the actual teachers of mankind concerning the Christ Impulse were really the dead, as you have been able to see from what I have now been saying - persons who were contemporaries of Christ, that only in the third century became mature enough to gain a full understanding. This understanding was able to grow during the fourth century, but at the same time the difficulty of inspiring men increased. In the sixth century this difficulty went on increasing, until finally the time came when the inspiring of men through spiritual mysteries concerning the Christ Mystery, and the opposition to it caused by the hardening of mankind, were brought under regulation by Rome. This was done by Rome in the ninth century, in 869, at the Council of Constantinople, where the spirit was finally done away with. This whole matter of inspiration became too far-fetched for Rome, and the dogma was laid down that man possesses in his soul something of the nature of spirit, but that to believe in the spirit [being a part of a human being] is heresy. Men had to be enticed away from the spirit. This in essentials is what is connected with the Eighth Oecumenical Council held in Constantinople in 869, to which I have often referred. It is merely a consequence of this abolition of the spirit when Jesuits today - I have mentioned this recently - say: 'In earlier times there was indeed such a thing as inspiration, but today inspiration is devilish; we may not venture to strive for supersensible knowledge, for then the devil comes in.'

These things, however, are connected with the deepest matters which must interest us if we wish truly to enter into Spiritual Science. They are connected particularly with a certain recognition of the character of wisdom which many so-called spiritual scientists, especially those that gather in so-called secret societies, do not recognize. A certain deception, one might say, is constantly spread abroad among men - spread abroad by those who know spiritual secrets. This deception is veiled by a false contrast, a false polarity. Have you not heard people saying: 'There is Lucifer and his opponent is Christ?' - and thereby setting up Christ and Lucifer as an opposite polarity? I have shown you that even Goethe's Faust-concept suffers from a confusion between Ahriman and Lucifer; from Goethe's inability to distinguish between the Ahrimanic and the Luciferic. The second part of my little book, 'Goethe's Geistesart' [which was published in English as: 'Goethe's Standard of the Soul - As Illustrated in Faust and in the Fairy Story of "The Green Snake and the Beautiful Lily"'] treats of this.

But behind this there is something that is extraordinarily significant. The real contrast, imparted by those who wish to speak the truth out of the spiritual world, is between Ahriman and Lucifer, and the Christ Impulse brings in something different. It has nothing to do with the Ahriman-Lucifer polarity, for it works in equilibrium . . .

In addition to the gradual loss of the understanding of the three-fold nature of the human being as body, soul, and spirit, the teachings of Manichaeism were declared a dualistic heresy. Persian dualism, which left the third element unspoken as it was presented in most of the extant Manichaean writings, became anathema to the Roman Catholic Church. The three-fold wisdom of the true living stream of Manichaeism continues even today (a remnant is found in the three degrees of Freemasonry), and is referred to by the Comte St. Germain as, *La Tres Sainte Trinosophia*, or *The Most Holy Trinosophia* (trino = three-fold, sophia = wisdom); and is the title of one of the two known Hermetic-Alchemical manuscripts that he left to posterity. This three-fold mystery usually escapes the understanding of scholars as they are generally not so concerned with the actual principles of spiritual initiation; but rather, with the history of writings, and that without the benefit of Spiritual Science.

The history of Manichaean studies is admittedly tainted with hostility by being rooted in the writings of its opponents, specifically St. Augustine of Hippo. The approach of St. Augustine was to find an abstract, conceptual way of understanding Christianity through the forces of the Intellectual-Soul that was expressed within the saturnian, legalistic mind-set of Roman jurisprudence, which was very different from the more pictorial-symbolic and ritualistic Sentient-Soul approach of the Manichaeans, which necessarily became supplanted. Nonetheless, the fluid, pictorial-symbolic Manichaean element resurfaced in later times with the youthful spontaneity of the "saelde" principle in the Grail legends. While the abstract-conceptual element rightfully became the dominant cultural impulse, it gradually lost touch with its spiritual foundations. More and more over time, the abstract-conceptual element became brittle like the birch tree, and through its decline became what might be called "hardened (Saturn) kidney (Venus) thinking." Later, by the 18th century, we find these two dispositions of thought metamorphosed into: Jesuitism (Augustine) and Goetheanism (Manichaeism).

A modern example of abstract thinking carried to the extreme is semiotics, such as found in the works of Umberto Eco. Semiotics is a academic system of knowledge that extends beyond linguistics and semantics, which attempts to interpret the meaning of symbols by the abstract synthesis of concepts. Semiotics is not without a certain value, but due to its cold-abstract, one-sided dependence on sense-bound ideas is insufficient to penetrate the realm of esoteric symbolism; and in fact, semiotics should really be considered an exoteric, or perhaps more accurately, in the case of Umberto Eco, an anti-esoteric stream; as can be seen in his bestselling novel *Foucault's Pendulum*.

Abstract thinking is best suited for analyzing mechanical processes. On the other hand, with his Goethean beholding-thinking, Goethe was able to develop his ideas about metamorphoses within the forms of nature. In the opening sentence of *Goethe's Standard of the Soul*, Rudolf Steiner characterized Goethe's opinion of abstract thought as follows: "It is Goethe's conviction that man can never solve the riddle of existence within the limits of a synthetic conception of the world." Goethe, in fact, alludes to the Manichaean stream himself in his epic play *Faust*, for the Manichaean teacher that St. Augustine contended with was named Faustus. In a conversation with his secretary Eckermann on January 18, 1927 Goethe makes reference to the underlying initiation knowledge of *Faust*.

> ... yet everything is of a sense nature, and on the stage it will be quite evident to the eye I have no other wish. If it should come about that the general audience finds pleasure in the representation, that is well - the higher significance will not escape the initiate.

In the early Christian era, the clairvoyant beholding of the spiritual processes behind the sense-world was being replaced by the abstract reflection on physical sense impressions. As the old atavistic clairvoyance of the Sentient-Soul was fading away, it was being replaced by the abstract thoughts of the Intellectual-Soul which brought about a sort of darkening of the inner soul-life, that gradually made spiritual understanding more and more difficult. In chapter one of her book *From Round Table to Grail Castle*, Isabel Wyatt summarizes some of the ideas of Rudolf Steiner regarding this transition in human consciousness:

> *In the fourth century A.D. men carried the cosmic intelligence a first step in the direction of the modern intellect - the old clairvoyant picture-consciousness began to grow shadowy.*
>
> *Till that century, also, the last of the old pre-Christian Mysteries declined, and at the same time the esoteric significance of the new Christian Mystery began to be largely lost. Julian the Apostate, the last human being who would have led the former Sun Mysteries over into the latter, was murdered in 363 A.D.*
>
> *Further, from the beginning of that century, there began to fade that tableau of the life of Christ on Earth which till then had remained visible in the supersensible worlds and out of the perception of which the Gospels had been written. Men had a sense of being left lonely and bereft.*
>
> *With the Arthurian knights this supersensible vision lasted longer; but after the first five centuries of our era, their powers also began gradually to diminish . . .*

In our present epoch, we must find the path to the spirit again - though not by returning to the methods of the past epochs. Instead we should strive to take our modern, developed thinking with us into a new waking-clairvoyant thinking which is fortified by the understandings that arise through Spiritual Science. The source of inspiration of this new healthy soul-development, leads us back to supersensible events that happened in the early Christian era - as a result of the Mystery of Golgotha. Isabel Wyatt further clarifies some of the supersensible realities that work from beyond the threshold of the Spiritual World (ibid):

> *We learn from Rudolf Steiner's spiritual researches that from the fourth and fifth centuries onward, new elementary Spiritual Beings have been descending from other spheres to*

help men on earth. From that period when the lower portion of man's astral body began to preponderate perilously in power, these new Earth-Spirits have so worked on men who had strong moral ideas as to build these moral ideas into their very being and blood, thus uniting a man's individual moral quality with his new and increasing individual freedom . . . These new Earth-Spirits find a path to man through ritual. Rudolf Steiner tells us that 'in the cults of the Churches, those who have vision of realities can often dispense with the person who stands in the flesh before the altar, because - apart altogether from the officiating priests - they are able to perceive the presence of these Spiritual Beings in the ceremonies.'

So we find that in the period of the Archangel Anael, in the early Christian centuries, there were great contributions in Christian thought, specifically from the Church Fathers and the Gnostic teachers. In addition to this, within the pagan world we find the great Neoplatonic teachers: Plotinus (205-270 A.D.), Porphyry (232-304 A.D.), Iamblicus (c. 270-330 A.D.), Proclus (411-485 A.D.), and others who helped provide the philosophical basis, developed out of the works of Plato and Aristotle, for the future understanding of the Christ Mystery in the Middle Ages.

From the beings that inspired the development of *thinking* in the period of the Archangel Anael there was later to arise in Europe, between the eighth and fourteenth centuries, the "imaginative-pictorial" and poetic impulses of the stories surrounding the mystery of the Holy Grail; which, through inspiring the feeling realm, brought about an alignment with the moral forces of the spiritual world and the possibility for receiving wholesome inspirations of the realm of the dead. Later still, these "imaginative-pictorial" impulses would unfold in the symbols of initiation that are to be found in The Chymical Wedding of Christian Rosenkreutz and other Rosicrucian writings - many of which were illustrated with engravings that expressed the principles of Christian initiation and the mystery of the Macrocosm and Microcosm.

In the present epoch of the Consciousness-Soul, we can derive great benefit by drawing spiritual nourishment from these inspired sources which have been given new life through the depth of spiritual scientific understanding that is to be found in the Anthroposophical teachings of Rudolf Steiner. This "imaginative-pictorial" Venus element found its home in the artistic expressions that proceed from the Goetheanum. In the artistic impulses of Rudolf Steiner: the Mystery Dramas, Eurythmy, Sculpture, and Painting, to name a few, this *pictorial* Grail element found an appropriate manifestation for modern humanity. The Grail *ritual* element flourishes in the rites of the Christian Community and the Camphill Movement, both of which were founded under the inspiration of Rudolf Steiner. These ritualistic and pictorial elements have created a sacred context for the awareness to blossom forth of the realms of the after-life; and also, to foster the impulses of the "new Earth-Spirits" that serve the Divine-Ideas of Christ which have been nurtured by the light and wisdom of the Heavenly Sophia - "The Woman Clothed with the Sun."

The Archangelic Period of Zachariel

Jupiter - The Wheel of Fortune: 500 - 850 A.D.

In the period of the Archangel Zachariel we see the struggle between "order and chaos" exemplified by the great migrations of peoples that led to the forming of the nations of Europe. Also, we find the development of the ordered life of the monasteries, which in turn became cultural centers. This struggle between "order and chaos" is depicted in the stories of King Arthur and his twelve Knights of the Round Table - who fought the "dragons" of chaos, and brought order to society by expressing the twelve-fold mysteries of Cosmic Christianity. A remnant of this Celtic-Arthurian stream was discovered in England by Katharine Maltwood, which consists of earthworks formed in a giant representation of the twelve-fold Zodiac, that can be seen in aerial photographs of the island of Glastonbury where legends say King Arthur was buried. In the first chapter of her book entitled, *From Round Table to Grail Castle*, Isabel Wyatt says:

> At the turning point of time, Christ descended from the Sun. But the Round Table still continued to experience Him in Nature. 'After the Mystery of Golgotha,' Rudolf Steiner tells us, 'the Earth was swathed by the Life-Spirit of the Christ. This was perceived in the Irish Mysteries, but above all by the Knights of King Arthur's Round Table, who lived within this Life-Spirit which encircled the Earth and in which there was this constant interplay of the Spirits of the Elements from about and from below . . . The Mystery of Golgotha, legible in the Book of Nature, represented the science of the higher graduates of King Arthur's Round Table.' Thus the pre-Christian Christ-stream of the Arthur Mysteries was metamorphosed by the Mystery of Golgotha into a stream within Celtic Christianity; both were still cosmic.
>
> With Christ had descended that cosmic intelligence which, administered by Michael, had hitherto inspired men in the sun-rays, but which had now to fall from his hands and become an earthly attribute. But the Round Table, itself a picture of the cosmos, an earthly reflection of the heavenly

Zodiac, still clung to the cosmic intelligence, working longer than any other Michael-community to keep it still in Michael's hands.

The Norman tympanum at Parwich in Derbyshire, framed in its arch's chevron-portrayal of the light-ether, is like a soul picture of the Arthur stream now that Christ had come to Earth. The Lamb of God has succeeded Cernussos as woodward [Cernunnos the Celtic Stag-god, the keeper of the woods, who represented an aspect of the pre-Christian experience of the workings of Christ in nature]; the bird of thought hovers above Him; the stag, His forerunner, stands in homage before Him, his antlers metamorphosed into great deep-ribbed leaves. The day-serpent and the night-serpent begin to intertwine man's sleeping and his waking into the healing caduceus of the second half of the Earth's evolution and to breath forth ur-plant forms pointing to that Mercury dissolution which will release the archetypes frozen into matter by Mars in the earlier half. As, with the Persians, new life in the form of the bull when the sun-hero Mithras (their reflection of Michael) bestrode him, so here too the wild beast's tail breaks into leaf, into quicksilver-shaped leaf. But the cross the Lamb carries is still circled with the Celtic sun-torc; it is still the cross of the Cosmic Christ.

Rudolf Steiner had on many occasions spoken of the importance of the Arthurian Mysteries to the development of Esoteric Christianity. One of the most comprehensive views Rudolf Steiner gave was in the final series of lectures on karma and reincarnation he gave in England in August of 1924, before his illness in September of that year. This series was part of a group of over eighty lectures that are published in eight volumes under the title: Karmic Relationships - Esoteric Studies. The following excerpt can be found in volume 8, in the sixth lecture which was given in London on the 27th of August, 1924.

Christian piety is not the same as pagan piety; which means, inner surrender to the gods of nature working and weaving everywhere in the play of nature.

Those who lived around King Arthur absorbed this play

of weaving, working nature in into their very being. And most significant of all was what they were able to receive in the first centuries after the Mystery of Golgotha.

A remarkable phenomena . . . occurred in the world-historic sense when the Mystery of Golgotha took place . . . Up to that time Christ had been a Sun Being, had belonged to the Sun. Before the Mystery of Golgotha had come to pass, the Knights of King Arthur's Round Table stood on these rocks [at the cliffs of Tintagel Castle in Cornwall, England], gazed at the interplay between the Sun-born spirits and the Earth-born spirits, and felt that the forces living in this interplay of nature-spirits poured into their hearts and above all through their etheric bodies. Therewith they received into themselves the Christ Impulse which was then streaming away from the Sun and was living in everything that is brought into being by the Sun-forces.

And so, before the Mystery of Golgotha, the Knights of King Arthur received into themselves the Sun-Spirit, that is to say, the Christ as He was in pre-Christian times. And they sent their messengers out into all of Europe to subdue the wild savagery of the astral bodies of the peoples of Europe, to purify and to civilize, for such was their mission. We see such men as these Knights of King Arthur's Round Table starting, from this point in the West of England, to bear to the peoples of Europe as they were at that time, what they had received from the Sun. Thereby, purifying the astral forces of the then barbarous European population - barbarous at all events in Central and Northern Europe.

Then came the Mystery of Golgotha. What had happened in Asia, over yonder in Asia? The sublime Sun Being, Who was later known as the Christ, left the Sun. This betokened a kind of death for the Christ Being. He went forth from the Sun as we human beings go forth from the Earth when we die. And as a man who dies leaves his physical body behind on the Earth and his etheric body is laid aside, and after three days is visible to the seer, so Christ left behind Him in the Sun that which in my book 'Theosophy' is called the 'Spirit-Man', the seventh member of the human being.

Christ died to the Sun. He died cosmically, from the Sun to the Earth. He came down to the Earth. From the moment of

Golgotha onwards his Life-Spirit was to be seen around the Earth. We ourselves leave behind at death the life-ether, the etheric body, the life-body. After this cosmic death, Christ left his Spirit-Man on the Sun, and His Life-Spirit around the Earth. So that after the Mystery of Golgotha the Earth was swathed, as it were, by the Life-Spirit of the Christ.

Now, the connections between places are not the same in the spiritual life as they are in the physical life. The Life-Spirit of the Christ was perceived in the Irish Mysteries, in the Mysteries of Hibernia - and above all by the Knights of King Arthur's Round Table. And so, up to the time of the Mystery of Golgotha, the Christ Impulse (that belonged to the Sun) actually went out from this place where impulses were received from the Sun. And afterwards [after the Mystery of Golgotha], although the power of the Knights diminished, they lived at the time within this Life-Spirit which encircled the earth and in which there was this constant interplay of light and air, of the Spirits in the elements from above and from below.

Try to picture for yourselves, the cliff with King Arthur's castle upon it and from above the Sun-forces playing down in the light and air, and pouring upwards from below the elementary beings of the earth. There is a living interplay between Sun and earth.

In the centuries which followed the Mystery of Golgotha this all took place within the Life-Spirit of the Christ. So that within the interplay of nature - between sea and rock, air and light - there was revealed, as it were in spiritual light, the Deed at Golgotha.

Understand me rightly, my dear friends. If in the first five centuries of our era men looked out over the sea (and had been prepared by the exercises that were practiced by the twelve who were around King Arthur and who were concerned above all with the Mysteries of the Zodiac), and if they looked out over the sea they could see not merely the play of nature but they could begin to read a meaning in it - just as one reads a book instead of merely staring at it. And as they looked and saw, here a gleam of light, there a curling wave, here the sun mirrored on a rocky cliff, there the sea dashing against the rocks, it all became a flowing, weaving picture - a truth whose *meaning could be deciphered. And when they deciphered it they knew of the spiritual fact of the Mystery of Golgotha. The Mystery of Golgotha was revealed to them because the picture was all irradiated by the Life-Spirit of Christ that had been presented to them within nature.*

Yonder in Asia the Mystery of Golgotha had taken place, and its impulses had penetrated deeply into the hearts and souls of men. We need only think of those who became the first Christians to realize what a change had come about in their souls. While all that I have been telling you was happening in the West, the Christ Himself, (the Christ Who had come down to Earth leaving His Spirit-Man on the Sun and his Life-Spirit within the atmosphere around the earth, bringing down His Ego and His Spirit-Self to the Earth), the Christ was moving from East to West within the hearts of men, through Greece, Northern Africa, Italy, Spain, and across Europe. The Christ worked here within the hearts of men, while over in the West He was working through nature.

And so, on the one hand, we have the story of the Mystery of Golgotha, legible in the Book of Nature for those who were able to read it - working from West to East. It represented, as it were, the science of the higher graduates of King Arthur's Round Table. And, on the other hand, we have a stream flowing from East to West - not in wind and wave, nor air and water, not over hills, nor in the rays of the Sun - but flowing through the blood, and laying hold of the hearts of men on its course from Palestine through Greece and into Italy and Spain.

The one stream flows through nature; the other through the blood and the hearts of men. These two streams flow to meet one another. This pagan stream is still working - even today. It bears the pre-Christian Christ, the Christ Who was proclaimed as a Sun Being by those who were Knights of the Round Table, and also by many others before the Mystery of Golgotha actually took place. The pre-Christian Christ was carried through the world by this stream - even in the age of the Mystery of Golgotha. And a great deal of this wisdom was carried forth into the world by the stream that was known as King Arthur and the Knights of the Round Table.

It is possible, even today, to discover these things. For, there is a pagan Christianity, a Christianity that is not directly bound up with the actual historical Event of Golgotha. And coming upwards to meet this stream there is the form of Christianity that is connected directly with the Mystery of Golgotha, flowing through the blood, through the hearts and souls of men. These two streams come to meet one another - the pre-Christian Christ stream, etherealized as it were, and the Christian Christ stream. The one is known, subsequently, as the Arthur stream - the other as the Grail stream. Later on they came together; they came together in Europe, above all within the spiritual world.

How can we describe this movement? The Christ Who descended through the Mystery of Golgotha - drew into the hearts of men. In these hearts He passed from East to West, from Palestine, through Greece, and across Italy and Spain. For the Christianity of the Grail spread through the blood and the hearts of men. The Christ made his way from East to West.

And meeting Him from the West there came the spiritual etheric Image of the Christ - the Image evoked by the Mystery of Golgotha, but still in the Image of the Christ of the Sun Mysteries.

Behind the scenes of world-history, sublime and wonderful events were taking place. From the West came pagan Christianity, the Arthur-Christianity, also under other names and in other forms. From the East came the Christ in the hearts of men. And then the meeting took place - the meeting between the Christ Who had Himself come down to Earth with His own Image which was brought to Him from West to East. This meeting took place in the year 869 A.D. Up to that year we have two streams, clearly distinct from one another. The one stream, more in the North, passed across Central Europe and bore the Christ as a 'Sun Hero' - whether the name was Baldur or some other. And under the banner of Christ, the 'Sun Hero', the Knights of Arthur spread their culture abroad.

The other stream, inwardly rooted within the hearts of men, which later on became the Grail stream, is to be perceived more in the South, coming from the East. It bears the real Christ, Christ Himself. The other stream brings a Cosmic Image of the Christ to meet it from the West. This meeting of Christ with Himself, of Christ the 'Brother of Humanity' with

Christ the 'Sun Hero' - Who is there only, as it were, in an Image - this meeting of Christ with His own Image took place in the 9th century.

When we consider this significant Arthur stream from West to East, it appears to us as the stream which brings the impulse of the Sun into earthly civilization. In this Arthur stream is working and weaving the Michael stream as we may call it in Christian terminology, the stream in the spiritual life of humanity in which we have been living since the end of the seventies of the last century (1879). The Ruling Power, known by the name of Gabriel, who had held sway for three or four centuries in European civilization, was succeeded at the end of the seventies of the last century by Michael. And the Rulership of Michael will last for three to four centuries, weaving and working within the spiritual life of mankind. And so we have good cause at the present time to speak of the Michael streams, for we ourselves are living once again in an Age of Michael.

We find one of these Michael streams if we look back to the period immediately preceding that of the Mystery of Golgotha, to the Arthur Impulse going out from the West, from England, an Impulse which was kindled originally by the Hibernian Mysteries [in Ireland].

And we find a still more ancient form of this Michael stream if we look back to what happened centuries before the Mystery of Golgotha; when, taking its start from Northern Greece, in Macedonia, the international, cosmopolitan stream connected with the name of Alexander the Great arose under the influence of the conception of the world that is known as Aristotelian. What was achieved through Aristotle and Alexander in that pre Christian age took place under the rulership of Michael, just as now once again we are living under his rulership. The Michael Impulse was there in the spiritual life at the time of Alexander the Great, just as it is there now in our own time. Whenever a Michael Impulse is at work upon the Earth within humanity - it is always a time when that which has been founded in a center of spiritual culture spreads abroad amongst many peoples of the Earth and is carried into many regions, wherever it is possible to carry it.

These twelve-fold zodiacal mysteries of the twelve Knights of the Round Table find their parallel in the twelve tribes of Israel, the twelve Apostles, the twelve Paladins of Charlemagne, and the twelve-fold nature of the Grail Mysteries (along with numerous other examples; such as, the twelve edges of a cube which is a traditional symbol of the Philosophers' Stone). For the twelve-fold themes which are found occurring in so many traditions, are a sign-post pointing to their occultly significant relationship to the twelve-fold mysteries of the Zodiac. Sergei O. Prokofieff gives us the essence of Rudolf Steiner's description of the twelve-fold form of the inner-circle of the Brotherhood of the Holy Grail, in chapter twelve of his book entitled, *The Spiritual Origins of Eastern Europe and the Future Mysteries of the Holy Grail.*

> *In the Grail Mysteries in the spiritual worlds there are three circles to be distinguished: an outer, a middle and an inner. The inner consists of twelve members, who form the esoteric core of the Grail Mysteries and are in direct spiritual communion with the Spirit-Self of Christ. The middle circle consists of thirty-six members. As with the inner circle, to it belong the souls of those people who were already while on Earth associated with the esoteric stream of the Grail and now continue in its service also after death. Thus the physically incarnated Lohengrin belonged to the middle circle, and his supersensible inspirer to the inner circle . . . [certain others] only entered the outer circle of the guardians of the Grail, a circle which consisted of a fairly large number of souls whose stay there usually lasted a comparatively short time.*

It was in the year 769 A.D. that Charibert von Laon, the father of Bertha who was the mother of Charlemagne, founded the Brotherhood of the Holy Grail. Dr. Elisabeth Vreede (who was appointed by Rudolf Steiner to be the head of the Mathematical-Astronomical Section of the School of Spiritual Sciences at the Goetheanum, Dornach, Switzerland, from 1924-1935, and whom Walter J. Stein considered to be a reincarnated leader of the Templar stream), indicated in her researches that the year 828 A.D. was the date of Parzival's achievement of the Grail kingship, an institution that was founded, as we have said, in 769 A.D. After which, a momentous event happened in Earth evolution - the initiate, "Grail King"

Parzival, through his human wisdom, united the Grail stream with the Arthurian stream in 869 A.D. This was an earthly event that signified the uniting of the Life-Spirit of Christ, moving from the East *in the hearts of men*, with the Spirit-Self of Christ moving from the West *in the spiritual atmosphere of the Earth*. For this was also the time when, under the behest of Michael, the Cosmic Intelligence began to descend to Earth and transform from Cosmic Wisdom - that rayed into man from outside - into human wisdom that was achieved through individual striving. In response to this change in the nature of wisdom, Parzival became the initial representative of the attainment the full manifestation of the "I" within the Consciousness-Soul.

The Brotherhood of the Holy Grail are the guardians of the esoteric teachings concerning the stages of human development that come about through the unfolding of the Christ principle within the human soul. In the eighth chapter of the above mentioned book by Isabel Wyatt, she quotes an indication by Rudolf Steiner as to how the Christ principle worked its way into human culture, through the principles of "Spiritual Economy", during the transition from the ancient world to the Middle Ages.

> *On a small scale it is the same in the spiritual worlds as when we sow a grain of corn in the earth; it germinates, and blade and ear spring from it, bearing innumerable grains which are replicas of the one grain of corn we had laid into the earth. In this multiplication of the grain of corn we can perceive an image.*
>
> *When the Mystery of Golgotha was accomplished, through the power of the indwelling Christ - the etheric body and astral body of Jesus of Nazareth were multiplied; ever since that time, many, many replicas have been present in the spiritual world.*
>
> *Such an etheric body was woven into great bearers of Christianity in the 4th, 5th, 6th, to 10th centuries - for example, Augustine.*
>
> *Such an astral body was woven in the 11th to the 14th centuries into Francis of Assisi, Elizabeth of Thuringen, etc.*
>
> *Replicas of the 'I' of Jesus of Nazareth, multiplied many times, are present now in the spiritual worlds.*
>
> *The outer, physical expression for the 'I' is the blood. There have always been men whose task it was, through the*

centuries since the Event of Golgotha, to ensure in secret that humanity gradually matures, so that there may be human beings who are fit to receive the replicas of the 'I' of Christ-Jesus of Nazareth.

To this end it was necessary to discover the secret of how, in the quietude of a profound mystery, this 'I' might be preserved until the appropriate moment in the evolution of the Earth and of humanity. With this aim a Brotherhood of Initiates who preserved the secret was founded: the Brotherhood of the Holy Grail.

This Fellowship has always existed [although it reconstellated at the Mystery of Golgotha]. It is said that its originator [that is, Joseph of Arimathea, who was a central figure of this new stage of development of the Grail stream] took the chalice used by Christ-Jesus at the Last Supper, and in it caught the blood flowing from the wounds of the Redeemer on the Cross. He gathered the blood, the expression of the 'I', in this chalice; the Holy Grail.

And the chalice of the blood of the Redeemer, with the secret of the replica of the 'I' of Christ-Jesus, was preserved in a holy place, in the Brotherhood of those who, through their attainments and their Initiation, are the Brothers of the Holy Grail.

Although little is known about Charibert von Laon (Count Heribert of Laon), the eighth century founder of the Brotherhood of the Holy Grail as a continuation of the Grail stream, in the first section of part two, of the book by Pierre Riche entitled, *The Carolingians - A Family Who Forged Europe*, some interesting details are given about the family of Charibert von Laon:

In 744, Pippin [the Short d. 768, the father of Charlemagne] himself had married the Hugobertian Bertrada [Bertha]. Her father was Count Heribert of Laon, a nephew of Pippin's step-grandmother, Plectrude [the daughter of Hugobert count of the palace, who held lands in the regions of Cologne and Trier, and Irmina who after the death of Hugobert became the second abbess of Oeren near Trier]. The wealthy Hugobertian clan owned lands in the Eifel region, and they had established monasteries at Oeren and Pfalzel and also contributed to the foundation of Echternach. One sister of Plectrude, Adela of Pfalzel, was grandmother of Gregory, the disciple of Boniface and future Bishop of Utrecht, while Count Theuderic of Macon - an ancestor of the Wilhelmine clan - descended from yet another sister, named Chrodelind.

Regarding the ancestors of Charlemagne, Sir Iain Moncreiffe, "Her Majesty's Albany Herald of Arms" has this to say:

In the days when the legions still tramped singing behind their imperial eagles down the paved roads that all led to Rome; at the very time when the province of Gaul became Christian with the rest of the Roman empire; one of the mightiest Gallo-Roman families was that of the Syagrii, and indeed Afranius Syagrius was Consul of Rome in 382. In the following century his descendants, cut off from Rome by barbarian invaders, 'maintained what became in effect a powerful kingdom in the valley of the Seine and central Gaul', and the last of them was described locally as King of the Romans. It has been reasonably suggested that the future Emperor Charlemagne descended in the female line from Afranius Syagrius's maternal grandson Tonantius Ferreolus, Consul in 453 . . . The Syagrii were overthrown in 486 by Clovis (Chlodovech), the Merovingian King of the Franks, who gave their name to France. King Clovis, who caused his rival Frankish Kings to be assassinated (encouraging one to commit parricide and then murdering him) and set up his capital at Paris, was grandson of Merovech, sacral Woden-born King of the Salian Franks from the northern forests beyond the Rhine; and compiled their famous Salic Law.

If this is true, that Charlemagne descended in the female line from Tonantius Ferreolus, which would be from Bertha's side of the family tree, this would actually give the Carolingians historical precedence, from the maternal line, as rulers of Gaul predating the claims of the Merovingian dynasty. Occultly speaking, this would be particularly significant as the Grail bloodline was carried through the female bloodline, which actually is the bloodline that frees the human spirit from the atavistic blood-forces through counteracting the forces of heredity. This Roman bloodline would also be significant in the Christian sense; since the Franks, and subsequently the early Merovingians, were adherents of the decadent Wotan (or Mercury - Odin) mysteries until after the marriage of Clovis to the Burgundian princess Clotilde. For in the year 496, according to tradition, through the promptings of Clotilde and her Roman Catholic confessor Saint Remy, Clovis prayed before going into battle, and upon winning embraced the Roman Catholic Church and caused 3,000 Franks to be baptized in the river near Reims. Clovis was given the title "Novus Constantinus" (the New Constantine); and thereafter, the Merovingian kings proclaimed themselves the "elect of God." Although I must add that the Merovingians, along with many of the Christian princes of Europe at that time, were advocates of the heretical Arian form of Christianity which developed from the teachings of the Alexandrian theologian Arius (d. 335); and which doctrine ironically, the Merovingians were sworn to eliminate through their pact with the Catholic Church.

Arius declared that since God the Son, was begotten by the Father, the Son must have an origin in time and so was not "consubstantial" with the Father; and therefore, was a lesser divinity than the Father. According to esoteric Christianity, this is a doctrine which is insufficient to receive with understanding the true power of the Mystery of Golgotha. The Arian doctrine was condemned at the Council of Nicaea in 325 A.D.

In 810 A.D., Charlemagne attempted to further distance the church from the Arian tendency, with his request to Pope Leo III (pope from December 26th, 795 to June 12th, 816) for the addition of the clause "and from the Son" to the Nicean Creed. Although Pope Leo agreed as to the doctrine implied, he resisted changing the Nicean Creed. This addition, known as the "Filioque clause", which was already the practice of the Frankish church, added the statement "and from the Son" to the line in the Nicean Creed that referred to the Holy Spirit proceeding from the Father.

This subtle doctrinal distinction would ultimately create a dispute between the Catholic Church of Rome in the West and the Byzantine Orthodox Church in the East - as to whether the Holy Spirit could proceed from the Son as well as the Father; and could be interpreted to indicate the nature and extent of the divinity of Christ. Walter Johannes Stein summarizes Rudolf Steiner's views of the "Filioque" dispute in chapter six of *The Ninth Century*:

The West, says Dr. Steiner, must by its very nature accept the additional 'filioque', and the East reject it. For the West is more oriented to the event of Whitsuntide and therewith to the problem of the individual spirit-penetration of each single human being by the Holy Spirit, whereby the Holy Spirit proceeds from the Son. The East is more orientated to the John Baptism at which the Holy Spirit brooded over the waters as once the spirit of God [did] at the beginning of Creation. Then the Spirit came down from the Creator, the Father God, even as at the John Baptism it proceeded from the Father God, who there spoke out of the heights about the Son. The 'filioque' conflict thus shows the difference between the psychological constitution of humanity in East and West. The task assigned to the Middle region is to arrive at such action out of its understanding of the differentiation of humanity over the earth as shall enable the whole of humanity to attain its goal according to its differentiations. The task assigned to Pope Nicholas [Nicholas I, Pope from April 24th, 858 to November 13th, 867] was that of rightly guiding the Middle. In this task he was confronted with a time in which the first doubts were being expressed with regard to the Trinity. . . The doubt here relates to the fate of mankind. For in human fate rules the necessity of the World of the Father - and - the freedom of the World of the Son, inasmuch as in destiny necessity and freedom are in a wonderful way mingled. The Spirit which proceeds from the Father - and - from the Son, from the divinely ordained regulating powers, and from humanly-willed purposings, it is this that rules in destiny. Thus in the problem of human fate is demonstrated the problem of the all-ruling Spirit in its twofold relation to Father and Son.

The official view of the Holy Roman Empire on the "Filioque" was that the Holy Spirit proceeded from the Son as well as the Father; literally, "Qui ex Patre *Filioque* procedit" ("Who from the Father *and the Son* proceeds"); rather than, "*and through the Son.*" This is also the view which is shared by the esoteric teachings of the Grail Mysteries concerning the nature of the Holy Trinity as a three-fold unity.

The dispute over the "Filioque" doctrine, which is largely based on Augustinian theology, further separated the Holy Roman Empire and the church of Rome in the West from the Christian churches of East and the Byzantine Empire. Although in the church of Rome the "Filioque" doctrine remained a controversial point because of its alienation of the Eastern churches. Consequently, the official alteration by Rome of the Nicean Creed to include the "Filioque" did not come about until a couple hundred years later in the time of Pope Benedict VIII (pope from 1012 to 1024), as a result of the promptings of Henry II (973-1024) the German king and emperor of the West.

Through the workings of destiny, the Carolingians found themselves placed politically in the middle of this controversy. The Carolingians embraced not only the full divinity of Christ but also the unofficial "Filioque" doctrine, while maintaining a reluctant relationship with the powers of the church of Rome. This reluctance on the part of Charlemagne was demonstrated by his consternation on being tricked by Pope Leo III into being crowned Holy Roman Emperor in the year 800; about which Einhard, the biographer of Charlemagne writes: "He asserted that he would never have entered the church that day, even though it was a high feast, if he could ever have learned the pontiff's intentions beforehand." For when Charlemagne was not expecting it, the pope put the crown on his head and proclaimed him "Holy Roman Emperor."

This reestablishment in the West of the title of emperor, with its investiture being determined by papal authority, was a political move by the church to obscure the separation of the powers of church and state; and thereby, achieve dominance over the crown. Nonetheless, Charlemagne was able to temporarily counter this power-play by the church in 813. Charlemagne's attempt to overcome this dilemma is described by Bernhard Schimmelpfennig in chapter IV of his book, *The Papacy*:

> And in 813, Charlemagne, after successful negotiations with the envoy of [the Byzantine emperor] Michael I, crowned his son Louis as co-emperor in the Byzantine tradition, without any papal involvement. In so doing, he denied any claims of the pope or Rome to the bestowing of the imperial crown. Louis the Pious acted likewise when a few years later, in 817, he crowned his oldest son Lothair I as co-emperor.
>
> But already during Louis' reign the development had begun that eventually led to the pope having the exclusive right to confer the imperial crown. In 823, [Pope] Paschal I crowned Lothair emperor once again, this time in Rome. His son, Louis

II, by that time king of Italy, received the crown in 850 from [Pope] Leo IV. After Louis' death in 875, [Pope] John VIII showed, by preferring Charles the Bald in 875 and Charles III in 881 over other candidates, that it was the pope who was empowered to bestow the imperial title. . .

This state of affairs, led to an entanglement of the powers of church and state that would not begin to be officially unraveled until after the American Revolution in 1776. Consequently, the burgeoning power of the papal authority in the 9th century caused the Grail mysteries to go underground so as to preserve the purity of the true esoteric stream, and maintain its independence from the church of Rome.

It is in the symbolic alchemical legend of Fleur and Blanchefleur, that was written down by Conrad Fleck in 1220, where we are told that Fleur (Charibert) is the son of King Phenix (Fenis) of Spain and his Queen, both of whom were "heathens." According to Laurence Gardiner, the "Jacobite historiographer royal", the Carolingians also carried Merovingian blood through the line of Bertha. He records that Bertha, the mother of Charlemagne, was descended from a certain Flora of Hungary and the princess Blanche Fleur, the daughter of the Merovingian king Dagobert III (d. 715) and an unnamed Saxon princess. Whether or not Flora (Charibert) is descended from a Spanish king, as mentioned in the legend by Conrad Fleck, Laurence Gardiner does not say and documentation from this early period is very sketchy and at times contradictory. The fourteenth century official history of the crown of Aragon (one of the kingdoms in Spain) *The Chronicle of San Juan de la Pena*, makes no mention of this subject. Although in the legend *Fleur and Blanchefleur*, Conrad Fleck tells of how Fleur inherits the Spanish crown from his father and the kingdom of Hungary from his uncle. It is difficult, in this early period, to separate legend from history regarding all of these details, but the legend nonetheless states that Fleur (Charibert) and Blanchefleur are the parents of Bertha, the bride of Pippin the Short and the mother of Charlemagne. Fortunately we have been given indications, from the spiritual-scientific investigations of Rudolf Steiner, regarding Charibert von Laon - the little known yet legendary Christian initiate who founded the Brotherhood of the Holy Grail in 769 A.D.

It was this esoteric Grail Christianity - expressing the Spirit-Self of Christ working within human hearts - that was destined to unite in the year 869 with the Cosmic Christianity of the Arthurian stream - with its inspiration derived from the Life-Spirit of Christ that was working in the spiritual atmosphere of the Earth. The meeting of these two streams was a healing antidote to the loss of the three-fold teaching of St. Paul - that the spirit dwelt in man along with the soul and body - a teaching that was removed from Christian dogma at the eighth Oecumenical council of 869. This meeting of the Grail and Arthur streams in 869 resulted in the emergence of a revitalized underground esoteric stream dedicated to this central esoteric teaching of St. Paul - that the spirit dwelt in man.

Furthermore, this meeting of the Grail and Arthur streams in the 9th century A.D., with the revitalizing nourishment that is represented by the Grail, stands as a mirror image, as it were, to events surrounding the prophet Elijah in the 9th century B.C.; whereby, during the drought of three and one-half years, that is described in "1 Kings" chapter 17, Elijah was fed by the ravens, and subsequently raised the son of the widow from the dead. These events, in turn, served as a preparation for the later incarnation of Elijah as John the Baptist, as recorded in the account of the transfiguration in "The Gospel of St. Matthew" (17:10-13); and also, as described by Rudolf Steiner, his uniting after death with the spirit-soul nature of the twelve Apostles - most specifically at the raising of Lazarus - with whom he united his being as far as the Consciousness-Soul; with Lazarus thereafter being referred to as John "the disciple whom Jesus loved." And so, if we examine this sequence of events in the spiritual history of mankind, we find that they are critical stages in human evolution which led to the wholesome relation of Cosmic Intelligence to the development of the Consciousness-Soul within the spirit-soul nature of Parzival in the 9th century A.D.

It is perhaps important at this time to point out a supersensible event in the history of mankind that is described by Rudolf Steiner regarding the mission of the Archangel Michael in the preparation of the spiritual impulses that worked behind esoteric Christianity in a particular way starting in the eighth century.

> *What Michael desires is to keep the intelligence, which is developing within humanity, permanently in connection with the Divine-Spiritual Beings.*
>
> *But in this he is meeting with opposition. What the Gods accomplish in their evolution, in that they release the cosmic intellectuality so that it may become part of human nature, stands revealed as a fact within the world. If there are beings*

with the power to perceive this fact, then they can take advantage of it. And such beings do exist. They are the Ahrimanic beings. It is their nature to absorb into themselves all that comes forth from the Gods as intelligence. They have the capacity to unite with their own being the sum-total of all intellectuality, and thus they become the greatest, the most comprehensive and penetrating intelligences in the Cosmos.

Michael foresees how man, in progressing more and more towards his own individual use of intelligence, must meet with these Ahrimanic beings, and how by uniting with them he may succumb to them. For this reason Michael brings the Ahrimanic Powers under his feet; he continually thrusts them into a deeper region than the one in which he is evolving. Michael, thrusting the dragon at his feet into the abyss: that is the mighty picture which lives in human consciousness of the supersensible facts here described.

Evolution progresses. The intellectuality which was at first entirely in the sphere of divine spirituality, detaches itself so far that it becomes the element which ensouls the Cosmos. That which previously had only radiated from the Gods themselves now shines as the manifestation of the Divine from the world of the stars. Formerly the world had been guided by the Divine Being himself: it is now guided by the Divine manifestation which has become objective, and behind this manifestation the Divine Being passes through the next stage of his own development.

Michael is again the ruler of the cosmic intelligence, in so far as this streams through the manifestations of the Cosmos in the order of ideas.

The third phase of evolution is a further separation of the cosmic intelligence from its origin. In the world of the stars, the present order of ideas no longer holds sway as the Divine manifestation; for the stars move and are regulated according to the order of ideas implanted in them in the past. Michael sees how the cosmic intellectuality, which he has hitherto ruled in the Cosmos, proceeds on its way to earthly humanity.

But Michael also sees how the danger of humanity succumbing to the Ahrimanic Powers grows greater and greater. He knows that - as regards himself - he will always have Ahriman under his feet; but will it also be the case with man?

Michael sees the greatest event in the Earth's history taking place. From the kingdom served by Michael himself Christ descends to the sphere of the Earth, so as to be there when the intelligence is wholly within the human individuality. For man will then feel most strongly the impulse to devote himself to the power which has made itself fully and completely into the vehicle of intellectuality. But Christ will be there; through His great sacrifice He will live in the same sphere in which Ahriman also lives. Man will be able to choose between Christ and Ahriman. The world will be able to find the Christ-way in the evolution of humanity.

That is Michael's cosmic experience with that which he has to govern in the Cosmos. In order to remain with that which he has to govern, he enters upon the path that leads from the Cosmos to humanity. He has been on this path since the eighth century A.D., but he really only took up his earthly office, into which his cosmic office has been changed, in the last third of the nineteenth century [in 1879 the beginning of the Age of Michael].

Michael cannot force human beings to do anything. For it is just through intelligence having come entirely into the sphere of the human individuality that compulsion has ceased. But in the supersensible world first bordering on this visible world, Michael can unfold as a majestic, exemplary action that which he wishes to display. He can show himself there with an aura of light, with the gesture of a Spirit-Being, in which all the splendor and glory of the past intelligence of the Gods is revealed. He can show how the intelligence of the past is more true, more beautiful and more virtuous in the present than all that is contained in the immediate intelligence of the present day, which streams to us from Ahriman in deceptive, misleading splendor. He can point out how for him Ahriman will always be the lower spirit, under his feet.

Those persons who can see the supersensible world bordering next upon the visible world, perceive Michael and those belonging to him in the manner here described, engaged in what they would like to do for humanity. Such persons see how - through the picture of Michael in Ahriman's sphere - man is to be led in freedom away from Ahriman to Christ.

> *When through their vision such persons also succeed in opening hearts and minds of others, so that there is a circle of people who know how Michael is now living among men, humanity will begin to celebrate Festivals of Michael which will possess the right contents, and at which souls will allow the power of Michael to revive in them. Michael will then work as a real power among men. Man will be free and yet proceed along his spiritual path of life through the Cosmos - in intimate companionship with Christ.*

In the preceding excerpt from, *Anthroposophical Leading Thoughts - Anthroposophy as a Path of Knowledge - The Michael Mystery*, by Rudolf Steiner (pages 77-79), it is possible to develop a clearer picture of the significance of Grail Christianity as a vehicle of the purest Christ impulses that were nurtured by Michael, in preparation for their coming to fruition within mankind in our present-day Michaelic Age. One cannot help being deeply moved and inspired by those few brave souls who carried this purest Christian impulse through the darker periods of human history, frequently at the risk of death from their *exoteric* Christian "brothers" - yet such is the price of freedom.

One Grail story relates that the cup which has come to be called the Holy Grail of St. Lawrence was at one time in the possession of St. Lawrence, who was one of the seven deacons of Rome in the 3rd century. St. Lawrence was martyred for refusing to give the Romans the sacred cup that was entrusted to his safekeeping by the martyr Pope Sixtus II (Xystus), whose short reign as pope only lasted from August of 257, until he was beheaded a year later on the sixth of August 258. St. Lawrence, who was roasted alive four days after the martyrdom of Pope Sixtus, is reported to have said: "See, the one side is roasted enough; turn me now upon the other side and eat." This cup of St. Lawrence came to be known as the cup of Valencia, for it now rests in Valencia cathedral. In the Middle Ages, this sacred cup was believed to be the cup of the Last Supper. According to legend, it was kept for three hundred years at the monastery of San Juan de la Pena before being removed at the request of Papa Luna, the "antipope" of Peniscola. The cup of St. Lawrence eventually was taken to Valencia cathedral by King Martin "the Humane" of Spain (c. 1399), where it remains to this day.

San Juan de la Pena is located in northern Spain, south of the central Pyrenees mountains in what was once the Kingdom of Aragon. San Juan de la Pena is on the pilgrimage route to Santiago de Compostella, which is the great church dedicated to St. James (Santiago = St. James), the brother of Jesus, who was considered to be the patron saint of all travelers (all of the pilgrimage routes during the Middle Ages were dedicated to St. James). San Juan de la Pena served as a stronghold for the Christian knights of the kingdom of Aragon during the Moorish occupation of Spain and became the burial place for the Kings of Aragon. The significance of San Juan de la Pena is further emphasized by the naming of an official history of the Crown of Aragon, *Cronica de San Juan de la Pena*, or, *The Chronicle of San Juan de la Pena*, which was written around 1370.

As recounted in the book by Ean and Deike Begg entitled, *In Search of the Holy Grail and the Precious Blood - A Traveller's Guide*, there is a curious legend, that seems to be cloaked in alchemical symbolism, which is told regarding the mysterious founding of San Juan de la Pena. It is said that in the 8th century there were two brothers named Voto and Felix, who were hunters. Once when Voto was on horseback in pursuit of a Stag, he chased it high up onto a rocky crag from which it was too dangerous to get back down. Uncertain of what to do, but trusting completely in God, Voto prayed to St. John. The prayer was answered immediately, for Voto and his horse were swept up into the air and floated down, landing safely at the foot of the precipice. He was then led by the Stag to a hidden cave entrance, where nearby lay the uncorrupted body of an ancient hermit by the mouth of a flowing spring.

According to the legend, it was at this site that the monastery of San Juan de la Pena was founded and dedicated to St. John (San Juan). Carved on the capitals of the cloister at San Juan de la Pena are depicted arcane scenes such as: the Last Supper, Cain and Abel, Christ pouring the water that he had transformed into wine at the wedding at Cana, and also a mysterious image showing the head and feet of a man peeking around a corner with his left hand covering his mouth, indicative of secret esoteric teachings.

This region around the Pyrenees mountains, and the neighboring areas north into southern France, and across the alps into Hungary, became connected to the lives of a succession of leading individualities from the time of the legendary Flore (sometimes spelled Flos, or, Fleur) who is celebrated in the medieval story of, *Fleur and Blanchfleur* (Blanscheflur). As I have mentioned earlier, we know from Rudolf Steiner that this Flore is an imaginative picture of Charibert von Laon, the maternal grandfather of Charlemagne who founded the Fellowship of the Holy Grail in 769 A.D. This led to the events in the 9th century that surround the Grail King Parzival who united the Grail Mysteries with the Arthurian Mysteries in the year 869 A.D. Walter Johannes Stein in his book *The Ninth Century*, shows the similarities between the knight Parzival as told by Wolfram von Eschenbach, and the historical personage Luitward, who was "the lord high chancellor" to the Holy Roman Emperor Charles III - but on this historical detail Rudolf Steiner apparently is silent.

After the 8th and 9th centuries, the Grail initiates went underground until the end of the 12th century when they caused the Grail Mysteries to be symbolically portrayed in poetic form, beginning perhaps with *Percival, or The Story of the Grail,* by Chretien de Troyes, which he wrote sometime between 1178 and 1183. These Grail stories were written down in symbolical "sub rosa" or "under the rose" language, the "langue vert" or "green language" of "cant", by troubadours and minnesingers who had received the original stories from emissaries of the Brotherhood of the Holy Grail. This was done in order to preserve and disseminate the esoteric Christian Grail Mysteries, at the transition from the 12th to the 13th century, as mankind moved to the point of spiritual darkness in the year 1250; when, according to Rudolf Steiner, for a brief period of time as a necessary stage in the development of the independent Ego, mankind would lose the ancient faculties of clairvoyance and feel as if orphaned from the world of spirit.

The Archangelic Period of Raphael

Mercury - The Magician: 850 - 1190 A.D.

In the period between 850 and 1190 A.D., the healing impulses of the Archangel Raphael are revealed - through the spiritual forces that worked in the lives of certain key individuals - as a force of healing and community life. Perhaps the clearest example of the Mercury-healing aspect of this time period is St. Francis of Assisi (c. 1182-1226) who was born at the end of the period of Archangel Raphael. St. Francis performed many miracles of healing, such as healing the lepers. If one checks the historical record, one discovers that the leprosy that was plaguing Europe in the time of St. Francis disappeared starting from the moment that St. Francis healed a leper with a kiss. In order to understand this healing miracle esoterically, you have to understand the fruits of the spiritual discipline of a great being such as St. Francis, who was gifted with a Christened Astral-Body that had been transformed through the Christ impulses indwelling it, and was thereby ennobled to the highest levels of intentionality and sacrifice. St. Francis was such a pure embodiment of Christ-Love, which in its very nature is the ultimate healing force, that healing miracles happened wherever he went. We hear in his life story about many of these miracles, but what is not so obvious about these can perhaps be understood with more depth if you consider the esoteric viewpoint. For, to be in the presence of a spiritual being such as St. Francis, would cause healings to spontaneously arise, and harmonious inspirations to work into human relationships as a whole - to the extent that the persons affected were capable of receiving the influx of the radiant love of Christ.

It is one of the ironies of the history of the Catholic Church, that the rules of the Franciscan Order were changed from the purity of the path of their founder St. Francis - against his will - even before he died. But the Church felt that the path of catharsis, or purification taken by St. Francis was too strict of a discipline for other monks, and perhaps that is so. But then what would the Church have done if other monks were to approach the stature of a St. Francis? Perhaps their independent spiritual authority would have threatened the monolithic centralized authority of the Church, which one can imagine the Church leaders would not have wanted.

History tells of the fate of a spiritual movement that based its authority entirely on the purity of its teachers - the Cathars (the pure) or

Albigensians (after the town of Albi in the South of France). This purity came about by means of strict disciplines that resulted in the catharsis of the Astral-Body. The Cathar movement developed out of the Manichaean teachings that were transmitted, between the 3rd century and the Middle Ages, by the trade routes that led from the east to the south of Europe. The Cathars were almost entirely exterminated by the Catholic Church during the Albigensian Crusade which took place in southern France. This European crusade was the result of a decision made at the Eleventh Oecumenical, or Third Lateran Council of 1179 whereby the Church had declared that the Cathars were heretics, making the pronouncement that: "Whosoever shall, according to the council of the Bishops, take up arms against these heretics shall earn two years remission of penance, and shall be placed under the Church's protection." This decision by the council of Bishops ultimately resulted in the death of thousands of men, women, and children. This tragic inquisition was waged against the very same Cathars about whom St. Bernard had said in 1145: "No sermons are more Christian than theirs, and their morals are pure."

Perhaps it would be fitting at this point to comment that the Cathar stream is frequently mistaken by modern authors to be the "true" Grail stream. Although it occurred in the midst of the same milieu within a mood of mutual tolerance, the Cathar movement that flowed from Bulgaria and the East of Europe was a distinct stream from that of the Grail Brotherhood; which streamed into the Carolingian royal court from Spain, and was mingled with influences from the West of Europe and Ireland - for it was this Grail stream which became the esoteric impulse behind the founding of the Order of the Knights Templars. Actually, there are those that feel that it was partly due to the karma created by the involvement of some of the Knights Templars, who under papal orders participated in the Albigensian Crusade, that later led to the downfall of the Templars in 1312.

St. Francis of Assisi and St. Bernard of Clairvaux are two of the finest examples of the spiritual life that the Catholic Church had to offer in the Middle Ages; for the powers of the spirit are able to overcome the human weaknesses that are to be found within man-made bureaucratic institutions like the Church - with its reliance on external authority and primarily exoteric methods of development. Although, the very existence of these and other Saints during the Middle Ages demonstrates the existence of certain unique, inner-esoteric impulses within the Roman Catholic tradition.

In addition to the exoteric Roman Catholic Church, with its hidden esoterism, there were other sources of spiritual inspiration of an esoteric Christian nature that were independent of the Church. These esoteric Christian impulses developed under their own leadership; such as, within Celtic Christianity in the West of Europe, and most especially in the civilizing impulses of the Arthurian "Cosmic Christianity." The esoteric Christian mysteries had also been preserved in a different form by the Magian-Johannine Grail Christianity in the East, among others. In the sixth lecture of the lecture cycle entitled *Supersensible Influences in the History of Mankind*, Rudolf Steiner characterizes this division of the Christian impulses which happened in the beginning of the period of the Archangel Raphael:

> *These impulses can only be rightly understood if we trace their development back through the centuries. A pivotal point in history and one which throws a flood of light upon subsequent happenings of incisive importance in Europe, is the reign of Pope Nicholas I, approximately in the middle of the ninth century, between the years 858 and 867. Before his inner eye, Nicholas I perceived three streams of spiritual life - three streams confronting him like great question-marks (if I may use the term) of civilization.*
>
> *He saw the one stream moving as it were in spiritual heights, across from Asia into Europe. In this stream certain conceptions innate in oriental religion are making their way, in a much modified and changed form, across Southern Europe and Northern Africa, to Spain, France, the British Isles and especially to Ireland. In view of what will presently be said, I will call this the first stream. Springing from the Arabian regions of Asia, it flows across Greece and Italy but also across Africa into Spain and then upwards through the West. But its influence also rays out, in different forms, towards other parts of Europe.*
>
> *Little is said of this stream in the tale told to us as history. We will speak today only of two characteristic features of this stream - which was immeasurably deep in content. One of these is what may be called the esoteric conception of the Mystery of Golgotha. I have often spoken to you of the conception of the Mystery of Golgotha held by those in whom vestiges of the ancient, pre-Christian Initiation-knowledge*

survived. There is an indication of this in the Bible itself - in the coming of the three Magi the Kings from the East. With their knowledge of the secrets of the stars they foresee the approaching Christ Event and set out in search of it.

Preeminently, therefore, the three Magi are examples of men concerned less with the earthly personality of Jesus of Nazareth than with the all-important fact that - a Spiritual Being had descended from the worlds of spirit and soul, and that Christ had come to dwell in the body of Jesus of Nazareth and would impart a mighty impulse to the further evolution of the earth. For these men viewed the Event of Golgotha from a wholly supersensible standpoint.

Vision of the supersensible truth was possible to men in whom the ancient principles of initiation had been kept alive. For the comprehension of this supersensible Event, that was unintelligible within the natural and historical life of the earth, could be achieved with the help of this ancient Initiation-knowledge. But it became more and more difficult to keep alive these ancient principles of Initiation; and therefore, more and more impossible to find appropriate language in which to convey how Christ had come down from supersensible worlds, and had passed through the Mystery of Golgotha; and also, how His Power continues to work through all the subsequent evolution of the earth. Men simply had no means of so shaping their concepts and ideas so that they could find words to convey what had actually come to pass through Christ and through the Mystery of Golgotha.

And so, in order to clothe this Mystery in words, men were forced more and more to pictorial forms of presentation. One such is the story of the Holy Grail, of the precious Cup; said on the one hand, to be the Cup in which Christ Jesus had partaken of the Last Supper with His Apostles; and on the other, to be the Cup in which the Roman soldier [or in other accounts Joseph of Arimathea] at the foot of the Cross caught the blood flowing from the Redeemer. This Cup was then carried by Angels . . . and here is the touch of the supersensible, tendered in faltering words - for what the old Initiates could have conveyed in clear concepts could now only be conveyed by pictures . . . this Cup was carried by Angels to Mont Salvat in Spain and received there by the noble King Titurel. He built a

Temple for the Chalice and there dwelt the Knights of the Holy Grail, keeping watch and ward over the treasure that shields the impulse flowing onwards from the Mystery of Golgotha.

And so we have there a deeply esoteric stream, passing over into a mystery. On the one side we perceive the influence of this deeply esoteric stream in the founding of the academies in Asia, where men studied the ancient Greek philosopher Aristotle, endeavoring to understand the Event of Golgotha with the aid of Aristotelian concepts. Later on, in European civilization, we see attempts made in such a poem as 'Parzival' to convey the living content of this esoteric stream in pictures. We see this same living content shimmering through the teachings that arose especially in the Schools of Ireland. We see too how the best elements of Arabian wisdom flowed into this stream; but how, at the same time, Arabian thought had introduced an alien element, coarsened and corrupted over in Asia through Turkish influence.

Although the esoteric streams of Christianity (and certain selected individuals within the Church) continued to receive the direct inspiration of the Spiritual World; within the Church, the acceptance of the possibility of direct inspiration from the spiritual world was cut off dogmatically and pronounced heresy. For, as just mentioned, in the year 869 the Roman Catholic Church denied the existence of the spirit in man by decreeing that man was a being of body and soul only, and that while man was capable of having certain spiritual qualities - he did not have a spirit. This is in direct contradiction with the teachings of St. Paul who said that man was a three-fold being of body, soul, and spirit. In spite of this teaching of St. Paul, at the Eighth Oecumenical Council in 869, the Church eliminated the teaching that the spirit dwelt in man, which had been a central teaching of Christianity from the very beginning. This doctrine resulted in a loss of spirituality, and an increase in materialism within the Church as a whole. As a result, only certain individuals were able to rise above this dogma and receive the pure influx of the spirit. The separation between spirit and matter was widened even further - one thousand years later - at the Vatican I Council of Rome, that resulted in Pope Pius IX proclaiming, on July 18th, 1870, the "dogma of papal infallibility." Which stated that pronouncements by the pope that were made "ex cathedra" were infallible. ("Ex cathedra" is the ecclesiastical term for official statements by the pope that were considered in Church law to be under the direct inspiration of the Holy Spirit.)

In the book by Johannes Tautz entitled, *Walter Johannes Stein - A Biography*, (page 91) W. J. Stein is quoted regarding these events in the 9th century as they relate to the spiritual quest of modern times:

> *What was still cultivated during the eighth and ninth centuries, that Spirit which lives on in the legend of the Holy Grail, which the world started to deny and which was eradicated from history by the Council of 869 - that spirit is seeking out the hearts of all who would search for it today, the spirit which heals, the spirit which restores to health because it is the unifying spirit of universal humanity.*

On account of the Eight Oecumenical Council, and other changes that happened in the 8th and 9th centuries A.D. (such as the founding of the Holy Roman Empire), the Grail initiates felt it necessary to preserve the inner esoteric teachings outside of the Church - within the circles of knighthood. Also, at the same time, there was an influx of the esoteric tradition into the Latin stream of the Roman Catholic Church through the teachings of St. Dionysius the Areopagite, the first bishop of Athens, that had been committed to writing by a later head of that school known by the same name Dionysius (for it was a common practice, out of respect, for the name of the founder of a school to pass on to the later leaders of the school, as a form of title).

The writings of St. Dionysius were transmitted from the esoteric school of Athens which had been originally founded by Dionysius the Areopagite under the guidance of St. Paul. Although these writings of St. Dionysius focus primarily on the workings of spiritual beings in nature outside of man, the school of Athens also had a definite teaching of the spirit that dwells in man derived from the teachings of St. Paul himself. The departure of the Church in 869 A.D. from the doctrine of St. Paul made it difficult, especially for the lay-person, to come to an experience of the spirit. The central significance of the school of Dionysius for the esoteric impulse within all of Christianity is made clear by Rudolf Steiner, in the fourteenth lecture of the lecture cycle entitled, *Theosophy of the Rosicrucian*.

This path (the Rosicrucian) had been partially prepared long before the time of Christianity. It took on a special form through that great initiate, Dionysius the Areopagite, who in the esoteric school of Paul at Athens inaugurated the training from which all later [Christian] esoteric wisdom and training have been derived.

As the Catholic Church developed as an institution, modeling itself on the Roman Empire, it wished to have sole possession and control of all knowledge; and so, proclaimed that Latin would be the only language of Scripture, thereby making the *Bible* the private domain of those who could read Latin - namely, the priesthood. It eventually was proclaimed to be against the laws of the Catholic Church for anyone to possess a *Bible* that was not in Latin. The clergy were to be the only intermediaries for the people of the "official" scriptural interpretation; and thereby, serve as the "sole" intermediaries to God Himself. In contrast to this tendency, the esoteric Grail stream quietly worked its way through the activities of certain families within the courts of Europe.

In the court of Charlemagne we find representatives of the esoteric Grail stream; such as, Waldo of Reichenau - who wished to represent the teachings of Christ in German (which was his native tongue), just as earlier Ulfilas the bishop of the Goths (310-383) had translated the *Bible* into Gothic (although Ulfilas left out certain parts that he felt were too violent). Waldo was the abbot of the monastery of Reichenau, and held the bishoprics of Pavia and Basle. He was also the rector of the monastery of St. Denys near Paris. (Denys is the French translation of the name Dionysius. This St. Dionysius was a martyr who was the patron saint of France, but in the minds of the people he came to be merged with the Dionysius "the Areopagite" that is mentioned above.)

In the *Translatio Sanguinis*, which was written in 950 A.D., is given the story of Waldo of Reichenau. Walter Johannes Stein in his book *The Ninth Century - World History in the Light of the Holy Grail*, shows how Waldo was an important figure in the Grail tradition through his part in Charlemagne's receipt of the "Praeputium Domini", which is the relic believed to contain the first blood shed by Jesus at his circumcision.

In regard to sacred relics, and whether or not they really are the things that the stories about them say that they are - it is evident that some are and some are not. The significance of these objects is that they became magnets, as it were, of genuine reverence. The genuine reverence of the people which is focused towards these objects doesn't fail to attract the attention of the spiritual world and its manifold spiritual beings - which can bring about healing and blessing as a result.

In *The Ninth Century*, Walter J. Stein also reveals to us the history of the knight Hugo von Turon, or Hugo count of Tours and duke of Burgundy, telling of his relationship to certain Grail relics and to the esoteric, angelical Christianity of St. Dionysius the Areopagite. For it was Hugo von Turon that was sent to Byzantium in the year 811 A.D. to be received by the emperor of the East as an ambassador of Charlemagne, the newly crowned emperor of the West.

Later, in the year 827 A.D., the Byzantine Emperor Michael "the Stammerer" sent the writings of Dionysius the Areopagite to the son of Charlemagne, King St. Louis "the Pious" (d. 840), who gave them to the successor of Waldo at St. Denys - Abbot Hilduin. Apparently the actual text sent from Byzantium is believed to be the copy that currently resides in Paris at the Bibliotheque Nationale (Departement des Manuscrits, Grec 437, fols. 123v-124). These writings were first introduced by Pope Paul I into the court of Pippin III (d. 768), the father of Charlemagne. This earlier copy was translated, albeit rather poorly, into Latin. This inferior copy was replaced with the excellent Latin translation which was made from the superior Greek copy that had been received from Byzantium. This new translation was done in 858 by another key figure of the time who represented the stream of Celtic Christianity, John Scotus Erigena; who, in turn, was influenced in his translation by Anastasius Bibliothecarius.

This Anastasius (who was pope for three days) is the one who was sent to Constantinople to attempt to negotiate a marriage for King Louis II (d. 875) because the Emperor Basilius of Constantinople wished to have his son Constantine marry Ermengarde, the daughter of King Louis II and the namesake of her grandmother Ermengarde, who was the daughter of Hugo von Turon and Bava. This marriage, which would have profoundly effected European history, never occurred.

As a spiritual antidote to the loss of the spirit that occurred in the doctrine of the Church at the council of 869 A.D., we find the "Knights of the Word" of the Grail stream joining to the "Knights of the Sword" of the Arthurian Stream in the year 869 as a renewed esoteric Christian stream that carried the inner spiritual content of Christianity that was guided under the inspiration of the Celtic folk-soul - as an underground secret school - teaching the healing forces of spiritual initiation. This healing force is represented by the healing powers of the Grail, which is the embodiment of the powers of the living "Christ in you."

The Grail initiation does not depend upon membership in any particular church; but rather, it depends upon one's individual spiritual development. This is portrayed by Parzival taking his heathen half-brother with him to the Grail. In fact, it is by doing this that Parzival finally achieves the Grail. This brother of Parzival is named Feirefis, and is the son of Gahmuret (who was the father of Parzival by a different mother named, Herzeloyde), and the heathen Belakane (which means Pelican, and is a traditional symbol of Christian sacrifice). Feirefis, in turn, was said to be the father of the legendary Prester John. It was in search of the legendary kingdom of Prester John that the great explorers went to the East. Rudolf Steiner once spoke to Walter Johannes Stein about the significance of Prester John, regarding which I quote from the book by Johannes Tautz entitled, *W. J. Stein: a Biography* (page 259):

> *Prester John is the leader of a brotherhood which has a special Christian tradition in the East which is much more profound than that of Rome. This brotherhood worked through [Johannes] Scotus Erigena.*

Prester John was the Grail representative in the East; while Parzival and his lineage, through the "Swan Knight" Lohengrin, were the Grail representatives in the West. According to Rudolf Steiner's spiritual scientific teachings, which are elaborated by Walter Johannes Stein in his book *The Ninth Century*, the events in the story of Parzival specifically relate to the 9th century; although they were not written down until the end of the 12th century by Chretien de Troyes in *Perceval*, or as it is also known, *Li Contes del Graal* (*The Story of the Grail*).

It appears from what little we know of Chretien de Troyes, that he wrote the story of the Grail somewhere between the years of 1178 and 1191, making it possibly the earliest written version known. It was shortly after this that Wolfram von Eschenbach wrote *Parzival*. The time frame that extends from the actual events of the story, to their written form coincides with the Archangelic period of Raphael (c. 850 to 1190 A.D.).

In *Parzival*, Wolfram tells of how he received the story of the Grail from a man he refers to as Kyot. According to the Anthroposophist and Grail researcher Werner Greub, the name Kyot is connected to an actual historical figure by the name of Count Guillaume de Toulouse (d. 812), who was a member of the court of Charlemagne and a grandson of

Charles Martel (c. 688-741), the "mayor of the palace" for the late Merovingian kings. Count Guillaume ruled over lands that ran from northern Spain across the Pyrenees into southern France, and were the last bastion against the Saracens, a people that he understood and respected. As St. Guillaume he was canonized in 1035 by the Catholic Church, and he also founded a great school and library which later became the famous monastery which is named after him, Saint-Guilhem-du-Desert (some of its architectural elements were removed and can be seen on display at the Cloisters museum in New York). This monastery is where St. Guillaume eventually retreated from the world at the end of his life.

Guillaume was called by various names and titles in the numerous legends and historical references that refer to him. Some of the names and titles of this important figure given in various sources are: Prince Guillem de Gellone comte de Razes, Duke William of Toulouse, Guilhem au Court-Nez duke or marchiones (or marquises) of Aquitaine, count of Barcelona, count of Auvergne, duke of Narbonne. Guillaume, as William of Orange, is a hero in the old French epic tales about the knights of Charlemagne that were known as the *Chansons de Geste*. Guillaume was a cousin of Charlemagne, and when Charlemagne's son Louis "the Pious" was crowned emperor it was Guillaume who placed the crown on his head; at which time Louis said: "Lord Guillaume . . . it is your lineage that has raised mine up." Guillaume is also one of the most revered figures in Dante's *Divine Comedy*, where he is depicted as William dwelling within the heaven of Mars, with his name flashing upon the arms of a cross alongside the other illustrious warriors that were immortalized by Dante. This same Count Guillaume was also called Willehalm, and was the key figure in Wolfram von Eschenbach's other major epic poem, *Willehalm*.

It is said that Willehalm, who could read both Arabic and Hebrew, was learned in the Star-Wisdom of the Grail that he received from the Arab Flegetanis; which points to the school of Th'abit ben Karaja, who was a teacher of the Sabian star-cult at Harran (the city of Abraham). Th'abit ben Karaja was professor of mathematics, medicine, astronomy, and astrology at the University in Baghdad during the time of the caliphate of Harun al-Rashid; which is the same Harun al-Rashid that came to be immortalized in the Arabic stories known as *The Thousand and One Arabian Nights*, that were translated into English by the famous explorer Sir Richard Burton.

(Incidentally, Sir Richard Burton, through his endorsement of the works of H. P. Blavatsky, by his membership in the Theosophical Society, speaks volumes in light of the severe criticism that was levied against H. P.

B.'s works by European scholars, concerning her esoteric interpretation of Oriental teachings. As H. P. Blavatsky's personal experiences in Eastern Occultism were only paralleled, in the West, by Burton's and very few other brave souls at that time, I think it safe to say that the European "experts" missed their opportunity to learn from someone who actually knew. Although I must add, that as far as Christian esotericism is concerned H. P. B. did not penetrate very far; and so, is unreliable on a great many points - most especially concerning the significance of Christ.)

The above mentioned Harun al-Rashid also figures prominently in Rudolf Steiner's *Karmic Relationships* lecture cycles, and in many other lectures, as a key individual that fostered the unwholesome tendencies of scientific materialism. Harun al-Rashid later incarnated in Elizabethan times as Francis Bacon, viscount of St. Albans (1561-1626), who furthered his pursuit of scientific materialism through his desire to, as he put it, "torture the secrets out of Mother Nature." Francis Bacon's most famous works; *The Advancement of Learning* (1605), and his *Novum Organum* (1620) are credited with the innovation of a program of universal knowledge. Although in retrospect, it is clear that his works were actually a program for inductive experimental science that was built upon the foundation that was laid for the applied mathematical sciences in the *Mathematical Praeface to Euclid* (1570) by John Dee, the author of *Monas Hieroglyphica* (1564).

The Sabian star-wisdom mentioned above in relation to the school of Th'abit ben Karaja, was tolerated in the court of the Caliph Harun al-Rashid, even though it was not Islamic; for, Islam has always recognized the Zoroastrians and the adherents of the Magian stream as being "People of the Book" along with Judaism and Christianity. The content of this Magian stream was transmitted through Willehalm who, by being the recipient of this Grail star-wisdom, was a precursor to the Knights Templars; for in *Parzival*, Wolfram was careful to name the Templars as the guardians of the Grail.

It was the Knights Templars that, along with the school of Chartres Cathedral - among others - were custodians of the development of the spiritual-human through the mysteries of the Temple "not made with hands", and the mysteries of the "Divine Feminine" that embodied the being that is known as Isis-Sophia. The school of Notre Dame de Chartres was dedicated to the "Notre Dame" - the "Blessed Virgin" - and was first headed by Fulbertus (c. 960-1028), who knew several European languages in addition to Latin, and was also learned in mathematics, geometry, astronomy, and theology.

From the great school of Chartres, we also have Bernardus Silvestris (c. 1147) who wrote the remarkable source book of medieval cosmology, *Cosmographia*, which was one of the most influential works of the Middle Ages. Rene Querido speaks of Bernardus Silvestris in his book entitled *The Golden Age of Chartres - The Teachings of a Mystery School and the Eternal Feminine*.

> *No medieval precedent existed for the ambitious theme and form of the 'Cosmographia' of Bernardus Silvestris. Called by present-day scholars a landmark of twelfth-century writing, it describes the creation of the world and of man while offering a brilliant distillation of the development of the Platonic tradition up to its time, showing an informed awareness of the emerging Arabic scientific attitude and incorporating the major motifs of thought of the School of Chartres. Indicating a familiarity with the works of John Scotus Erigena and Dionysius the Areopagite, the 'Cosmographia' today is considered the main inspiration for the world veiw in Chretien de Troyes' romances and for the themes and structures in Dante's 'Divine Comedy.'*

Bernardus Silvestris was continuing in a tradition which included the Roman author Ambrosius Theodosius Macrobius (c. 400 A.D.); but who, by his own account, was not born a Roman. Macrobius once stated, in regard to the mysteries of the Macrocosm and the Microcosm: "The world is man writ large and man is the world writ small." A passage in Bernardus' writings shows the breadth of his learning regarding the precursors of the Christian mysteries of the Macrocosm and the Microcosm.

> *Persia charts the heavenly bodies, Egypt gives birth to the arts, learned Greece reads, Rome wages war. Plato intuits the principles of existence, Achilles fights, and the bountiful hand of Titus pours out riches. A tender virgin gives birth to Christ, at once the idea and the embodiment of God, and earthly existence realizes true divinity.*

The last, and perhaps greatest, of the masters of Chartres was Alanus ab Insulis (c. 1128-1203) who was called "Doctor Universalis." His nine works collectively refer, in the words of Alanus, to "The Saga of the Creation of the New Man and the Redemption of the Earth." Most of the masters of Chartres were of the Cistercian Order, which was the first monastic order to admit lay-brothers. This departure from tradition was followed by the Knights Templars who also admitted lay-brothers. The time had come for a wider reach of the spiritual life - for spiritual impulses to be taken up by individuals outside of the monasteries and the secret brotherhoods. It was the fulfillment of this need that prompted the Christian initiates to make some of the Grail teachings available to the masses through the Grail legends that were first written down by Chrestien de Troyes, Wolfram von Eschenbach, and others.

In looking to find some of the influences of the school of Chartres upon Chrestien de Troyes, the modern medieval scholar T. E. Hart in his article, "Chrestien, Macrobius, and Chartrean Science: The Allegorical Robe as Symbol of Textual Design in the Old French Erec" (*Mediæval Studies, volume XLIII*, 1981), concludes that:

> *Macrobius' 'Commentary [on the Dream of Scipio'], in fact, was one of the three major vehicles through which Platonic and Pythagorean thinking was rediscovered in twelfth-century France, and thus played a prominent role in the remarkable Neoplatonist renascence associated with the Cathedral School at Chartres (the other vehicles being Chalcidius' fragmentary translation of and commentary on the only Platonic dialogue then widely known, the 'Timaeus', and Boethius' 'Consolation of Philosophy.'*

It is sources such as these that provided the mathematical and philosophical framework that was the backbone of the Grail cosmology, and of the "canon of proportion" utilized by the mostly anonymous builders of the gothic cathedrals; those "bibles in stone" that proclaim, along with St. Paul, the divinity that is encountered when you find the "Christ in you"; and, that the true "temple" is the human body, which is a microcosmic reflection of the macrocosmic harmony of the spheres.

This "canon of proportion" was also present in the numerical-initiatic structure of the the Grail stories. In fact, Chrestien even mentions

Macrobius in his earlier work "Erec." This point is discussed by T. E. Hart (ibid); although Hart, while thinking that Chrestien embraces the Neoplatonic-Pythagorean world-view, is very cautious to not present this fact as proven.

> *None of this, of course, constitutes conclusive proof that Chrestien's citation of Macrobius as a source for his digression on the mathematical sciences also implies an allusion to Macrobius' Neoplatonic and Pythagorean world-veiw, with its mystical theology of the sacred decad, its science of the celestial order and of the proportions binding the elements, its knowledge of the numerical ratios of musical consonance, and its belief in the harmony of the spheres.*

Nonetheless, familiarity with the Grail tradition shows that this is no doubt the case. William Harris Stahl, in the introduction to his translation of, *Macrobius' "Commentary on the Dream of Scipio"* says:

> *To the medievalist, Macrobius' 'Commentary' is an intensely interesting document because it was . . . one of the basic source books of the scholastic movement and of medieval science. Next to Chalcidius' commentary, it was the most important source of Platonism in the Latin West in the Middle Ages . . . Adelard of Bath borrowed heavily from the Commentary . . . It was also the main source of the Neoplatonic doctrines of . . . Bernard Silvester of Tours . . . Traces of Macrobian influence are to be found in almost all the writings of Alanus de Insulis. . .*

It was this same cosmological stream that inspired Brunetto Latini, the teacher of Dante; who, in turn, gave out the teachings of the "White Rose of Heaven", and the doctrine of the planetary spheres and their relation to the after-death state in his greatest work the *Divina Comedia*, or *Divine Comedy*. In light of this, it is interesting to note that in Dante's *Divine Comedy*, the individual that Dante encountered when he reached the "White Rose" - which is the highest level of the heavenly firmament, the "Empyrean", or "Paradise of light" - was St. Bernard of Clairvaux.

The Abbey of Clairvaux was the guiding light of the Middle Ages, as its name suggests, Clairvaux - "the valley of light." Saint Bernard was the abbot of the Cistercian abbey of Clairvaux, which he built upon land given to him by the count of Champagne. It was from Clairvaux that St. Bernard inspired and directed the growth of the Cistercian monasteries, that paralleled the growth and development of the Knights Templars, and which had originated from the same circle of people.

St. Bernard was the leading spokesman for Christianity in the early twelfth century, he "counseled kings and rebuked popes." His most famous sermons are commentaries upon King Solomon's "Song of Songs." St. Bernard's kind and gentle nature was demonstrated by his wish for the Crusaders to use the power of persuasion, rather than force, when dealing with the Moors. His open mindedness was shown by his recognition of the heretical Cathars Christian virtues. St. Bernard was the official sponsor of the Knights Templars, and he wrote the rules for the order of "warrior-monks." For his uncle was Andre de Montbard, one of the original nine founders of the Order of the Knights Templars.

The Champagne region of France was the center from which radiated the Knights Templars and the Cistercian impulses of St. Bernard; and also, one of the earliest known written Grail legends in Christendom. The first Grand Master of the Order of Knights Templars was Hugues de Payen, a nobleman from Champagne, who although a vassal of the count of Champagne became his superior when the count joined the Templar order soon after its founding.

It was from the court of Marie de Champagne that Chretien de Troyes wrote the Grail cycle, the *Conte du Graal*, at the request of Philippe d'Alsace. Chretien says that he learned the story from Philippe and wrote it down. Philippe d'Alsace was the son of Dietrich d'Alsace who, when he returned home from the Second Crusade, received a blood relic from Baldwin III, King of Jerusalem (1129-1162) who was the son of Fulk d'Anjou (1095-1143) the ancestor of the Angevin line; which according to various scholars is the Anschau (Anjou) line which Wolfram von Eschenbach refers to as his source for the Grail legend.

This blood relic was said to be part of the blood that Joseph of Arimathea received in the Grail cup during the crucifixion of Christ. Dietrich d'Alsace presented this relic to the town of Bruges where it was preserved in the Chapel of the Sacred Blood. The line of the Angevin was later, in the fifteenth century, to produce "Good King" Rene d'Anjou who rode into battle next to Joan of Arc, thereby bringing about the destined separation of the French and English folk-souls. (I further discuss Rene d'Anjou in the chapter on the Archangelic period of Samael.)

Another important figure, whose life spans the end of the period of Archangel Raphael, is Eleanor of Aquitaine or Alienor d'Aquitaine (c. 1122-1204); and whom, perhaps more than Queen Victoria, deserves to be called the "grandmother of Europe", as pointed out by Desmond Seward in his biography of Eleanor entitled, *Eleanor of Aquitaine - The Mother Queen*.

> *Her daughters were the queens of Castile and Sicily, and the consorts of the counts of Blois, Champagne, and Toulouse and the duke of Saxony. Two grandsons were Holy Roman Emperors and another three were kings of England, Castile and Jerusalem. Her grand-daughters sat on the thrones of France, Portugal, and Scotland, and an illegitimate one was princess of Wales. Louis IX, "Saint Louis", who was to be the most venerated of all French kings, was one of her great-grandsons. Furthermore, her son John's descendants in the direct male line were to rule England until 1485.*

Queen Eleanor was first married to King Louis VII of France (1137-1152). After the annulment of this marriage, she married the future king of England Henry II (1154-1189), producing two sons who both became kings of England: the legendary Richard I Cœur de Lion (the "Lion-hearted") in 1189, and the infamous "John Lackland" in 1199 (and whom, due to his failings as a king, was forced to sign the Magna Carta in June of 1215).

Queen Eleanor, no doubt, was a mass of contradictions in the complex makeup of her temperament and personality. Unusual for a women at that time, she was well educated and knew Latin, French, and English. She also could read and write Provencal, or Langue d'Oc, which was her native tongue, and the language of the troubadours. It is also known that she had highly developed knowledge of the *gai saber* (joyful art) of the troubadours. In fact, the earliest troubadour for which we have a name is her grandfather William IX or Guilhem lo trobador, duc d'Aquitaine and Poitou. Her biography is a pageant of intrigue that must be understood against the backdrop of an oft times cruel male-dominated society. Sentenced to fifteen years in prison for plotting against her husband King Henry II, she emerged from her incarceration at his death with an unbroken spirit and took over the rulership of England. One of the first royal decisions she made was to order the release of prisoners from all over England with the statement: "By my own experience prisons are hateful to men and to be released from them is a most delightful refreshment to the spirit." Queen Eleanor is also noteworthy for winning greater social freedom for women, and creating the first sanctuary for battered women at Fontevrault.

Queen Eleanor also presided over the "Courts of Love"; which were panels, composed mostly of women, that settled "affairs of the heart" according to the codes of chivalry. Due to her expert knowledge of the *gai saber*, Queen Eleanor was the royal patroness of the troubadours. A notable recipient of Queen Eleanor's patronage was Marie de France, who was the abbess of Shaftsbury. Marie de France was quite possibly the illegitimate daughter of Geoffrey Plantagenet; which would have made her the half-sister of Henry II, the husband of Eleanor. She wrote narrative poems called "lais" on Arthurian themes that also included a version of the love story of *Tristan and Iseult*. Eleanor's official court reader was Wace of Jersey who wrote the *Roman de Brut*; which was a poem about King Arthur based on Geoffrey of Monmouth's *History of the Kings of Britain*. And, in addition to these recipients of Queen Eleanor's patronage, we may add the troubadour Chretien de Troyes. In fact, some scholars believe Chretien's earliest romance *Erec et Enide*, to be inspired in part by the life of Queen Eleanor. Although for our purposes it is most notable that it was out of this milieu, specifically under the patronage of Queen Eleanor's eldest daughter Countess Marie de Champagne, that Chretien de Troyes wrote the Grail story, *Le Conte du Graal*, or *Percival*.

"The stone that was struck from the crown of Lucifer..."

Regarding the occult significance of the Grail chalice within the teachings of Spiritual Science, there is a deeper esoteric meaning behind the legend of "the stone that was struck from the crown of Lucifer." For Rudolf Steiner tells us that, "the stone that was struck from the crown of Lucifer by the Archangel Michael" refers to a particular angelic being who did not side with Lucifer in the great "War in Heaven"; but, nonetheless, followed the Luciferic hosts when they "fell" to Earth. The "Angel of the Grail" did this in service to Christ as a sacrifice towards the redemption of humanity. This "Angel of the Grail" was visible to initiates within the Christ stream before and after the time of Christ. In the 9th century, the "Grail Angel" was eventually incarnated as the initiate "Grail King" Parzival, the "pure fool" - for as it says in the *Bible*: "The wisdom of God is folly with men." Bernard C. J. Lievegoed, in the sixth chapter of his book entitled *The Battle for the Soul - The Working Together of Three Great Leaders of Humanity*, characterizes how this great "Leader of Mankind" pioneered the attainment of the spirit in a purely human way within the Consciousness-Soul:

> *Manu's next great incarnation was that of Parzival. He was the first human being to experience a complete Consciousness-Soul development. You can see that especially well when you consider the difference between Mani and Parzival. As Mani, this individuality developed an inconceivable wisdom, while as Parzival he appears as a pure fool. Parzival is born without knowledge. He has to start from scratch and learn through bitter experience. That is an important characteristic of the Consciousness-Soul. We know it in our own lives: nothing is given us in advance, we all have to start from the base-line of the reality of life. Learning through bitter experience . . . We are all Parzivals. We are fools, we don't know our incarnations, our goals in life, we don't know what we are supposed to do, how we should do it . . . We don't know who we are, we walk around and just do something here and there.*

Although he had possessed great cosmic wisdom in other incarnations; Parzival, as a sacrifice to humanity - separated himself from his past spiritual achievements by only partially incorporating his Spirit-Soul being; thereby, leaving behind the exalted capacities developed in his previous incarnations. For, as Wolfram says, he was a "bumpkin."

Starting out from the humblest of beginnings, within a very short time, Parzival had gained sufficient self-mastery to become the "Grail King", and serve as an example of all that is noblest within mankind - through overcoming the luciferic and ahrimanic forces in a purely human way. That this heroic deed would come about through purely human forces, was the highest example of the shift in the relationship of Cosmic Intelligence to mankind. For, in the preceding century, the forces of Cosmic Intelligence had "fallen" to Earth from the realm of Michael in order to become earthly-human intelligence through the principles of "Spiritual Economy" (see: page 439). This came about through Parzival taking-up this Cosmic Intelligence, in a purely human way; and, as a "representative of mankind", being the very first individual to attain a modern "Christ-filled" Consciousness-Soul as a prototype for the future evolution of the human soul.

This Consciousness-Soul initiation of Parzival, in the 9th century, would begin to bear fruit for humanity as a whole in the epoch of the Consciousness-Soul, which would begin in 1414. This new evolutionary theme, that was nurtured by the Christ impulse within the Grail Mysteries, was one of non-interference by the spiritual powers in human affairs - "a mood of waiting", waiting for mankind to develop out of their own forces an inner initiative for the things of the spirit - a truly Michaelic path. What the Michaelic stream wished to bring about was a purely human-wisdom developed through human experience, rather than being handed down from "on high."

In the midst of the struggle with our humanity we can, if we so choose, apply the spiritual-scientific principles of initiation as presented within Anthroposophy. By starting from our ordinary, healthy, human judgment, we can begin to move toward the realm of higher knowledge. As a fruit of this spiritual-scientific Michaelic path, which is the true successor to the Grail Mysteries, we receive the opportunity to pass on to higher realms of being - without the sacrifice of our individual freedom. This is a truly *new spiritual path* for mankind, for it incorporates the gift of the individuated human element that was developed through the experience of separation from the worlds of spirit. This experience of separation from the worlds of spirit is characterized in the Grail stories by Parzival's wanderings in the "wasteland."

The seeds were planted by the "Grail Angel" for the development of this truly *new spiritual path* under the inspiration and guidance of the Christ, with the assistance of the Archangel Michael, and the Archangelic Folk-Soul of the Celtic people (who, as a sacrifice, had become the guiding spirit of Esoteric Christianity). This "Grail Angel" still works upon the development of mankind in the spiritual world between death and rebirth, and during sleep, to insure that mankind maintains a connection to the true worlds of spirit and its multitude of spiritual beings. A key area of the "Grail Angel's" activity is characterized by Bernard Lievegoed in chapter two of his book entitled, *Mystery Streams in Europe and the New Mysteries*:

The angelic being works, as will be explained in the mystery of the etherization of the blood, where the human being, from pure heart forces, becomes enthusiastic for the spirit. He was a Michaelic angelic being and, at the same time, as [a] " thing," an image of the chalice that contained the etherized blood of Christ that renewed the whole earth.

In *The History of the Holy Grail*, by Robert de Boron, the Grail is called a "token"; thereby alluding to the inner-esoteric significance of that which is represented by the Holy Grail. In *Parzival*, Wolfram von Eschenbach called the Grail a "thing" - again referring to something very mysterious. For the underlying theme of the Grail Mystery can be seen as the living relationship that connects parts and wholes - which comes about when the individual beings truly connect to that which is of God. In light of this, the Grail Mystery can be seen as a great cosmic-drama in which the biblical prophecy of the "Paraclete" is unfolded - through the principles of "Spiritual Economy"; whereby, the "Father Ground of Being" is one with the "Christ in you"; and, in turn, are both one with the healing forces of the Holy Spirit.

For this cause I bow my knees unto the Father of our Lord Jesus Christ, of whom the whole family in Heaven and Earth is named, that He would grant you, according to the riches of His glory, to be strengthened with might by His Spirit in the inner man; that Christ may dwell in your hearts by faith; that ye, being rooted and grounded in love, may be able to comprehend with all the saints what is the breadth, and length, and depth, and height; and to know the love of Christ, which passeth knowledge, that ye might be filled with all the fullness of God.
"Ephesians" (3:14-19)

The Archangelic Period of Samael

Mars - The Tower: 1190 -1510 A.D.

In the period of the Archangel Samael, we find a great deal of activity directed toward town-founding; also, during this period, there occurred the martial exploits of the 3rd (1189-1192), 4th (1202-1204), and later Crusades. The Grail impulse is to be found wherever cosmopolitan "universally-human" impulses are at work, building bridges between different peoples. It was through the intermarriage of the "great houses of Europe" that European culture developed, and through these dynastic alliances the peoples of Europe gradually began to develop beyond purely tribal and national interests. For, according to Rudolf Steiner, it was through the mixing of blood by the intermarriage of unrelated people that the old powers of atavistic, or "blood clairvoyance", which had sustained the tribal impulses, were replaced by the developing intellect.

In the medieval saga of *Lohengrin*, it is related how the "Swan Knight" Lohengrin delivered the daughters of the king of England to the various rulers of Europe to be their brides. Through the intermarriage of the ruling houses, the cosmopolitan impulses of the Grail worked toward the development of social stability amongst the nations of Europe by creating a context for social interaction, and was a major step towards town-founding and peaceful commerce between the nations of Europe. Walter J. Stein characterizes the significance of the town-founding impulse in his essay entitled, *England and the Foundation of Commercial Towns - The Origin of the Lohengrin Saga Traced According to English History.*

> *The period in the Middle Ages at which, at first in England and then extending from there over the whole of Europe, towns sprung up as centers of a new economic order, corresponds actually to the time at which humanity passed from the dream world into the modern economic order.*
>
> *Towns serve not only as protective means against attacks by wild neighbors who, devastating the land, terrify the population so that the latter are driven to seek refuge behind strong ramparts, but are also centers of commerce and industry.*

At this time, out of a small group of people, came powerful impulses of the spirit that continue to inspire and bear fruit even to this day. It is said in the legend of the first European king of Jerusalem, Godfrey de Bouillon (c. 1061-1100), that he is descended from the Swan Knight. The swan is a bird that gracefully floats upon the waters, this is a wonderfully symbolic alchemystical picture of the exalted state of the etheric world.

The saga of the Swan Knight Lohengrin is a mythic image of the way in which the cosmopolitan Grail impulses were transmitted *openly* by the *daughters* of the Grail families through marriage, which led to the establishment of family relations between the noble houses of Europe. On the other hand, the *sons* of the Grail families served the Grail *secretly* through esoteric associations, that worked from behind the scenes, striving to bring about new developments within the social-cultural sphere. As pointed out by Walter J. Stein, the existence of these two Grail impulses are revealed in the scene from Wolfram von Eschenbach's *Parzival* where Trevrizent explains the Grail family:

> *Wherever a land is left lordless, if the people pray for a lord to be sent to them from the Grail, that prayer is granted. God sends the men forth secretly; but the maids are openly bestowed in marriage, that their fruit may be gathered back into the Grail's service.*

According to the researches of Walter Johannes Stein, the story of Lohengrin points to the events surrounding the marriage of the five daughters of the "Bretwalda", or the "king of kings of all Britain", King Edward the Elder, "the town-founder" (d. 925) who was the son of Alfred the Great (849-899).

King Alfred the Great was descended in the male line from Anglo-Saxon "Woden-born" (incarnate storm-spirit), Scylding kings of Wessex, that were skioldungs from the Danish sacred pagan city of Lethra on the island of Sjaelland, and claimed descent from Skioldr or Scyld, son of the god Woden (Old Norse, Odinn; Anglo-Saxon, Woden; Old Franconian, Wodan; Old High German, Wutan, Wuotan).

This indicates the tradition of the kings of the Anglo-Saxons who ritually embodied the storm-spirit Woden (the Nordic Mercury). According to Norse mythology, Woden was the "father of the gods" which was indicated by his name, Alfodr "All-Father", and was the king of the

Aesir (the gods who live in Asgard). He was the god of poetry, the god of war, the god of the dead, of magic, of ecstasy, and the creator of the runes.

One of the symbols of Woden is the raven, which can be seen on some of their coins, perched on a cross. "This is why he is called Hrafnagud 'the raven-god'" (Prose Edda). This refers to his two ravens, Huginn and Muninn, that fly over the whole Earth and bring news of many things to Woden before breakfast.

There is a tradition in England, that as long as the ravens continue to live in the Tower of London, England will remain free of foreign invaders. The respect the British have for this curious piece of folklore is shown by the fact that Winston Churchill had men stationed at the Tower of London, during World War II, that were ordered to feed and guard the ravens for the duration of the war.

In the *Snorra Edda*, which was written down by Snorri Sturlson (1179-1241 A.D.), Teutonic mythology was presented in a somewhat systematic way so as to preserve the Old Norse traditions. According to the indications of Rudolf Steiner, in this work are to be found imaginative stories regarding the beings of the spiritual world, that are a remnant of the Teutonic Mysteries of Northern Europe. The Vanir that are described in the Eddas refer to the Archai that guided mankind in the Atlantean period; and likewise, the Aesir are of two generations: the elder Aesir, which are Archangelic beings; and their offspring, which are Angelic beings (also, we must include: Freya and Frey, who though they are offspring of the Vanir are also of Angelic rank).

This Teutonic mystery wisdom leads back to the Scythian Prince Odin who traveled to the north of Europe from the mystery center that had been established by Skythianos in the region of the Black Sea, and founded the Mercury mysteries among the Teutonic people; teaching them the runes and initiating other important cultural impulses. Prince Odin was an incarnation of the great being that would later, in the 6th century B.C. incarnate as the Buddha. This initiate Odin was able to bring the art of writing to the Teutonic people because he was able to receive the inspirations of an exalted Archangelic being into his soul. This exalted Archangelic Odin being was the supersensible bearer of the Mercury-Odin impulse, and had actually attained the development of an Archai but worked as a sacrifice within the ranks of the Archangels to guide the Teutonic people to their future destiny as bearers of the Ego impulse.

This Prince Odin, who was able to receive the inspiration of this Archangelic Odin-being, was one of the twelve Bodhisattvas that are spoken of in the traditions of the East; and so, was among those advanced beings that had left the Earth when the Sun separated from the Earth, later inhabiting the spiritual realm of the *planet* Venus. Through their sojourn in the Sun realm, the Bodhisattvas were able to develop a direct relationship with Christ long before He came to Earth by entering into Jesus of Nazareth. This is also true of the Guardian Angels that had originally guided the Bodhisattvas, first to the Sun realm, then to Venus, and finally to Earth; so as to be exalted leaders of the Christ Mysteries during the post-Atlantean period. The Guardian Angel of this Prince Odin came to be known in the Teutonic Mysteries as Vidar "the silent one." In the story of "Ragnarokr" ("The twilight of the gods", the variant spelling "Ragnarok" which is commonly used is from the Old Norse, and translates as "final destiny of the gods."), it was Vidar who defeated the Fenris wolf (Ahriman) and was included amongst the gods who would continue to live in the new world that came into being after Ragnarokr.

In light of all of this, Alfred the Great was said to be a direct descendant in the male line from a 4th or 5th century King Woden, about whom it says in *The Anglo-Saxon Chronicles*: "From Woden came all our kin and also the Southumbrian's." Although the extant records can only give us a reliable picture of the genealogy leading back to perhaps the 1st or 2nd century A.D., this King Woden could very well have been not only a namesake, but an actual blood descendant of the aforementioned Prince Odin of pre-Christian times.

King Alfred's maternal grandfather was Oslac, the Jutish thegn or chieftain. Alfred the Great, in turn, was descended in the female line, through his mother Judith, from the Frankish Emperor Charlemagne. In our present Grail study, the key line of descent is from Charlemagne, who was descended through his mother, Bertha, from Charibert von Laon, the legendary "Fleur", who had instituted the Fellowship of the Holy Grail in 769 A.D., which merged with the Arthurian stream one hundred years later in 869 A.D. This Grail stream, which worked from East to West, received its spiritual inspiration from the Spirit-Self of Christ that had entered Earth evolution through the mystery of the "Holy-Blood" at Golgotha. This initiatic Grail impulse had worked through Charibert von Laon in the 8th century, and was continued by certain families, central to which were the descendants of Charibert von Laon. And so, with the escorting of the five daughters of King Edward the Elder to their noble spouses by his nephew Turketal, we see an important branch of the Grail family spreading itself into the royal courts of Europe. Once again in this account, we find a matrilineal line of descent, which draws together the ruling houses of Europe and is mysteriously guided by a knight of the male line. In the saga of *Lohengrin*, by Wolfram von Eschenbach, this is imaginatively eluded to (although the historical details are obscured), for the Swan Knight says:

> 'The Grail it was that sent me here to you. Its knight am I; my name is Lohengrin. And now I have unveiled my mystery, to the Grail I must return' . . . He left three tokens behind him, a sword, a horn and a ring, then sailed away. Back over the sea and land he passed to whence he came, to the land of his father Parzival, where the Grail held sway.

The 12th century, *Chronicle of the Kings of England*, which was written by William of Malmesbury, gives further details regarding the children of King Edward "the Elder":

> He brought up his daughters in such wise that in childhood they gave their whole attention to literature, and afterwards employed themselves in the labours of the distaff [spinning] and the needle . . . His sons were so educated that afterwards they might succeed to govern the state, not like rustics but philosophers.

The historical truths that are hidden behind the saga of *Lohengrin* were first brought to light, from the indications of Rudolf Steiner, by Walter Johannes Stein. For, according to Walter Johannes Stein, the saga of *Lohengrin* refers to Turketal, who was the nephew and chancellor of King Edward "the Elder" "the town founder", who is considered by scholars to be the first real king of England, and was son of King Alfred "the Great" of Wessex and the father of King Athelstan "rex totius Britanniae", "king of all Britain" (c. 895-939); whom, according to Masonic legend, is considered to be the original patron of the York Rite of Freemasonry. Turketal is also mentioned in Wolfram von Eschenbach's *Parzival* (III, 364) as a knight of the Holy Grail named Turkentals. It was Turketal who escorted the daughters of King Edward to be married; and thereby, form dynastic alliances with the ruling houses of Europe.

According to the historical records, the marriages of King Edward's daughters are as follows: Eadgitha (d. 946) became the first wife (she was preceded by a concubine) of the Holy Roman Emperor Otto I "the Great" of Germany (912-973); while Elfgifa married Duke Alberich of Burgundy (or Duke Conrad of Burgundy, although Duke Alberich is favored by Georg Waitz in his study entitled, *Jahrbucher der Deutschen Geschichte, Koenig Heinrich I*, Leipzig 1885); Eadgyifu was the second wife of Charles III "the Simplex" ("without guile") king of the West Franks (d. 929), their son was Louis IV "d'Outremer" ("from overseas" in reference to his period of exile under the protection of Athelstan), he was king of France from 936 until his death in 954; Elgive married Ludwig of Aquitania, and Eadhilda (d. 973) married Hugh "the Great" l'Abbe, duke of the Franks and count of Paris; he is the progenitor of the Capet line of kings that ruled France from 987 until 1328. Upon the death of Eadhilda in 937, Hugh married Hadwig, the daughter of King Henry I "the Fowler" of Germany and sister of the aforementioned Holy Roman Emperor Otto I "the Great."

The marriages of the daughters of King Edward the Elder were patronized by his son King Athelstan, this is discussed by Ralph Whitlock in his book entitled, *The Warrior Kings of Saxon England*:

> *Overseas he [Athelstan] was regarded as one of the leading monarchs of Europe. He married one of his sisters to Hugh [Capet], duke of the Franks, who was the effective ruler of Frankland. Henry the Fowler, the German king who was welding together the scattered fragments of the eastern half of Charlemagne's empire, sent an embassy to ask for another of Athelstan's sisters for his son Otto. Athelstan obligingly sent two of them to Otto from which to choose. The young man selected Edith, the elder; and the surplus younger sister was married off to 'a certain duke, near the Alps', probably Conrad of Burgundy. A third sister was given to Louis, prince of Aquitaine. Athelstan's family connections with the ruling-houses of Europe were hence unsurpassed.*

It was the family connections that were built in this way that led to the gradual development of important spiritual and cultural impulses within Europe. This led to a taming of the wild uncivilized astral forces, and created a town-culture that could serve as a foundation for the future development of the Consciousness-Soul epoch; which would begin in 1414, towards the end of the Archangelic period of Samael. A primary role in these cosmopolitan developments was played by the Order of the Knights Templars, who drew their membership from all of the nations of Europe.

The esoteric impulses of the Grail cosmology can be seen within the Knights Templars, whom Wolfram von Eschenbach referred to as "the guardians of the Grail", for the Knights Templars were carriers of the real "treasure" of the Temple of Solomon - the initiatic teachings. The social-cultural developments arising from the Grail impulse were also guarded by the Knights Templar order. It was the Templars who were responsible for the building of fortifications, or hostels, all across Europe that were a day's journey from each other, so as to provide protection to travelers and pilgrims. The Knights Templars were also the founders of banking in Europe, making it possible to write checks so that one could transfer funds without having to make a dangerous journey with the money in hand.

Due to the extensive contributions of money and property that were bestowed on the Templars, they became possessors of immense wealth. Because of their immunity from all secular authority, the Templars were invested with tremendous power and influence, for they only had to answer to their grand master; and he, in turn, only had to answer to the direct authority of the pope.

The extreme power and influence possessed by the Knights Templar order naturally incurred jealousy and greed, most especially from the king of France, Philippe IV (1268-1314), who is known to history as Philippe "le Bel" ("the fair"). Philippe "le Bel" had already demonstrated his greed through his attempts to tax the clergy without papal consent, a practice forbidden by church law. This led to a great struggle with Pope Boniface VIII (c. 1235-1303), who boasted that not only was he pope but also he was the emperor. Philippe tried to have the pope kidnapped by Guillaume de Nogaret (c. 1260-1313) on September 8th, 1303, but the attempt failed, and the pope died the following month on the 12th of October. The next pope was Benedict XI, who only held office from October 22nd, 1303 until July 7th, 1304. After eleven months of hostile debate and political intrigue, on June 5th, 1305, Philippe "le Bel" succeeded in placing his "puppet", Bertrand de Got, on the papal throne as Clement V. On October 13th, 1307, Philippe "le Bel" had all of the Templars in France arrested and subjected to torture in an attempt to get them to confess to a series of fabricated charges. The "confessions", that were extracted by the cruelest forms of torture, were then handed over to Pope Clement with the demand to condemn the Templar order. Arrests soon followed in the other nations of Europe with varying degrees of compliance.

In the midst of all of this, in order to consolidate his control of the papacy, Philippe "le Bel" managed to have the papacy moved to the city of Avignon, France in March of 1309, where the papacy was to reside for 70 years; a period known to historians as the "Babylonish captivity." Succumbing to the demands of Philippe "le Bel", Clement eventually hesitatingly agreed to a hearing which was convened in Vienna, and lasted from October 1311 to May 1312. The general mood of the council was to absolve the Templars from their guilt. Nonetheless, feeling the pressure of Philippe "le Bel", Clement officially dissolved the Templar order by the papal edict *Vox clamantis* on March 22nd, 1312; and later, before an astonished council on the 3rd of April, the edict was read and accordingly all the holdings of the Templars in France were to be transferred to the Knights of St. John of Jerusalem, known as the Hospitallers. Actually, in France the possessions of the Knights Templars passed into the control of Philippe "le Bel", until his death under unknown, mysterious circumstances on November 29th, 1314.

The Knights Templars, who were officially known as "The Poor Knights of Christ and of the Temple of Solomon", possessed the largest fleet in the world. At the time of their suppression, none of the ships of the Templars were captured, they instead continued to sail as ships of the Order of the Temple which had taken on different names in its continued existence from the Holy Land, Scotland, Portugal, and elsewhere.

In Portugal, they merely shortened their name to the Knights of Christ. And as we approach the end of the period of the Archangel Samael, the great explorers began crossing the oceans guided by the impulses of the Knights of Christ under the patronage of Prince Henry "the Navigator" (1394-1460) the third son of King John I of Portugal, and Philippa (daughter of John of Gaunt, duke of Lancaster).

In *Parzival*, Wolfram von Eschenbach refers to the house of Anschau as the source of the original Grail stories. This is a thinly veiled reference to the lineage of the house of Anjou, which is also known as the line of the Angevin. The Angevin played a central role in the founding of the Knights Templars, and was later to produce the enigmatic "Good King" Rene d'Anjou, who rode into battle next to Jeanne d'Arc (Joan of Arc); thereby fulfilling the separation of the French and English folk-souls, with their unique destinies, in the 15th century. Jeanne d'Arc was a subject of Rene d'Anjou, for her home town of Domremy was in the valley of Bar, which was within his domains. When Jeanne d'Arc requested an audience with the duke of Lorraine, he asked her what she wanted and she said; "Your son, a horse and some good men to take me into France." This is a telling remark, for at that time, the only son the duke of Lorraine had was his son in-law, Rene d'Anjou. This fact is rather mysterious when you consider that it appears that Rene's association with Jeanne d'Arc was obscured by writers in the following centuries.

(These events and others surrounding Rene d'Anjou are expanded on in the book entitled, *Holy Blood, Holy Grail,* by M. Baigent, Richard Leigh, and Henry Lincoln; which, is a bestselling work dealing with the Knights Templars and the Holy Grail. Although in recent years more information has come to light that has totally exposed the fraudulent claims set forth in this book that were perpetrated on an unsuspecting public by the members of a group calling itself the Prieure de Sion. This group falsely dates its origin in 1090 or 1099; and furthermore, claims to be the secret core-group behind the founding of the Knights Templars and the Rosicrucian Order, among others. In actuality, the Prieure de Sion is a right-wing order of French Catholics that vainly attempted to reestablish a monarchy in France by fabricating documents supporting the wild illusion that the Merovingian royal line were actually "blood-descendants" of a "secret marriage" between Christ Jesus and Mary Magdalene. This falsehood and others within their forged "Prieure documents", in turn, were used to support the false claims of one Pierre Plantard to be of Merovingian descent. Although in all fairness to the authors of *Holy Blood, Holy Grail,* they were not privy to this deception, and in researching this book they did manage to find other important historical details from *genuine* sources.)

Returning to our subject, Rene d'Anjou was born in the year 1408. Being highly educated, he mastered five languages, and was an artist, a poet, and a champion of chivalric ideals. Traditional sources say that he was inducted into the order of the White Greyhound, or l'Ordre du Levrier Blanc in 1418. Rene d'Anjou was also known to have entered another order of chivalry, l'Ordre de la Fidelite, in the early 1420's, as one of its original members. In 1448, he started his own Order of the Crescent, which he said was based on the earlier Order of the Ship and the Double Crescent that was created by St. Louis IX, the king of France who had died while on crusade at Carthage in 1270, and was said to be "every inch a king." The Order of the Crescent included among its membership, Duke Francesco Sforza of Milan, who was the father of the patron of Leonardo da Vinci, Ludovico Sforza. The famous Visconti-Sforza tarot deck, which is one of the earliest known tarot decks, came out of the circle around the Sforza family.

During his lifetime, Rene d'Anjou held many titles: count of Bar, count of Provence, count of Piedmont, count of Guise, duke of Calabria, duke of Anjou, duke of Lorraine, king of Hungary, king of Naples and Sicily, king of Aragon, Valencia, Majorca, and Sardinia. In addition to these many titles he also held another that is perhaps the most significant in terms of our present study, king of Jerusalem. This latter status was, of course, purely titular as the Holy Land was no longer under European control. Nevertheless, it invoked a continuity extending back to Godfroi de Bouillon; and therefore, was acknowledged by all the European rulers. One of Rene's daughters Marguerite d'Anjou married King Henry VI of England in 1445 and became a prominent figure in the War of the Roses.

During the Crusades, the Knights Templars had received initiatic teachings; for, in the Holy Land, a cross-pollination had occurred between various esoteric streams. Reghellina da Schio, a leading Italian Masonic authority, gives an interesting account of this "mingling of streams" which is quoted by Isabel Cooper-Oakley in chapter two of her book entitled, *Masonry and Medieval Mysticism - Traces of a Hidden Tradition*:

> *. . . in the lifetime of Manes his pupil, Herman, had spread his teaching in Egypt, where the Coptic priests and other Christians mingled it with the mysteries adopted from the Jews. . .*
>
> *It was through these same Coptic priests and the Eastern Christians that both the mysteries of the Children of the Widow, and the cult of the Great Architect, came to us in consequence of apparently unforeseen events, and it will be seen that it was principally by means of the Crusades that they obtained a secure footing in the West. The mysteries maintained their existence under the name of the cult of the Great Architect of the Universe, a name that has its origin in the allegory of Hiram, which represented in the Mysteries "the unknown God", the Eternal, and sole creator of all things and the Regenerator of all beings. . .*
>
> *. . . these doctrines existed during the time of the Crusades, . . . the long time that elapsed during the wars of the Crusades gave them the opportunity of being admitted into all the mysteries of the Children of the Widow, of the Great Architect of the world, and of both principles . . . the Crusaders who had been admitted to the mysteries of the Children of the Widow and initiated therein, imparted them, on their return home, to their pupils in Europe.*

Another account of the continuation of the Manichaean Mysteries within Freemasonry is given by the Masonic writer Bernard H. Springett in his book entitled, *Secret Sects of Syria and the Lebanon*:

> German Masonic writers trace the connection of the Manichaeans with the Western Brotherhood of St. John, relying on what is known as the "Cologne Record", whose authenticity is, as would be expected, rejected by materialistic Masons, but usually accepted as genuine by the more enlightened and broad-minded Mystics. This record, which is dated 1535, states that a secret society under the name of the Brotherhood of St. John existed before 1440, and since then, and up to 1535, under the title of St. John's Order of Freemasonry, or Masonic Brotherhood. This record contains the following passage:
>
>> 'The Brotherhood, or the Order of Freemason Brothers, bound together according to St. John's holy rules traces its origin neither from the Templars, nor from any other spiritual or temporal Knightly Order, but it is older than all similar Orders, and has existed in Palestine and Greece, as well as in various parts of the Roman Empire. Before the Crusades our Brotherhood arose, at a time when, in consequence of the strife between the sects teaching Christian morals, a small number of the initiated, entrusted with the true teaching of virtue, and the sensible exposition of the secret teaching - separated themselves from the mass.'

The historical link connecting the Freemasonic Brotherhood to the Knights Templars is commented on by the eminent German Masonic scholar J. G. Findel in his *History of Freemasonry*:

The Grand Lodge of Germany further assumes that, in the Building Fraternities of the Middle Ages, besides their art, a secret science was carried on, the substratum of which was a real Christian Mystery, serving as a preparatory or elementary school and stepping-stone to that and the St. John's Masonry which latter was not a mere system of moral philosophy, but closely allied and connected with this Mystery. It was conceded that the Freemasonry of our days (St. John's Freemasonry), sprang from the Building Fraternities of the Middle Ages, but at the same time asserted that in the early ages there existed a secret society which strove to compass the perfecting of the human race, precisely in the same manner, and employing similar means, as did the Swedish [Masonic] system, which in fact only followed in the wake of its predecessor, being concealed in the Building Fraternities, so that our society did not arise from them, but made its way through them. The secret science, the Mystery, was very ancient indeed. This Mystery formed the secret of the Higher Degrees of the Rite, which were not merely kept hidden from the rest of the confederation, but also from the members of the inferior degrees of the system itself. This Mystery was fully confirmed by documents which the Grand Lodge of Germany had in its keeping. This secret legend is the same as the Carpocratians, which is that Jesus chose some of the Apostles, and confided to them a secret science, which was transmitted afterwords to the priests of the Order of Knights Templars, and through them to the Building Fraternities, down to the present Freemasons of the Swedish Rite. The Swedish system teaches that there have been men of all nations who have worshipped God in spirit and truth, and, surrounded by idolatry and superstition, have yet preserved their purer faith. Separate from the world, and unknown to it, this Wisdom has been preserved by them and handed down as a Mystery

. . . Having been instructed by Him in a more perfect knowledge of Holy Things, they had, amid persecution, taught in silence that which was committed to their keeping. At the period of the Saracens and the Crusades, they were so greatly oppressed that they must ultimately have sought for protection from without. As fate, however, would have it, seven of them, Syriac Christians, pursued by unbelievers, near Bastrum, were rescued by Knights Templars, and afterwords taken for their protection. When they had lived there for a certain time they begged for permission to dwell with the Canons or

Prebendaries of Jerusalem, as the life there agreed better with their own inclinations and habits. This was accorded them, and Andreas Montebarrensis effected a union of these Syrians with the Canons, to whom, out of gratitude, they imparted all their science, and so completely did they make the priests of the Order the depositories of their secrets that they kept and handed them over to others under certain conditions. Thus, the secret knowledge lived on in the very heart of the Order of Knights Templars until its abolition. The clergy were dispersed with the persecution that ensued, but as the secular arm did not touch them, as it did the knights, they managed to rescue many of their secret writings, and when the knights sought refuge in Scotland, they founded a Chapter at Aberdeen, the first prior of which was Petrus de Bononia. The science was disseminated from this place, but very cautiously . . .

This account tells of the Knights Templars continuing to exist in Scotland where the papal order to suppress the Templars had met with little success, as only two Scottish Templars were ever arrested and this was two years after the first arrests in France. This gave the Templars time to rally their considerable resources and men behind the cause of the Scottish War of Independence which was led by Robert Bruce, the earl of Carrick (1274-1329), who was crowned king of the Scots in 1306. The victory of Robert Bruce at the decisive Battle of Bannockburn - which occurred around St. John's Day, June 24th, 1314 - was just three months after the death of the Templar Grand Master Jacques de Molay. With the final victory of Robert Bruce, at the treaty of Northampton in 1328, began the independence of Scotland from England which lasted 289 years.

With the considerable numbers of Templars that escaped elsewhere in England and Europe it is easy to comprehend that many would have taken to sea in the uncaptured Templar fleet and found refuge in Scotland. In Scotland, Robert Bruce had already been excommunicated from the Catholic Church, so there was no fear of him complying with the papal order of suppression. The Scottish Templars were to continue to play a primary role in Scotland, leading eventually to the development of the Freemasonic Order and the legendary Scots Guard.

The hereditary leadership of the Freemasons was entrusted to the Saint Clair, or Sinclair family of Rosslyn who were the official patrons of the order in Scotland since the days of William Sinclair the jarl, or earl of

Orkney (1406-1496). The famous unfinished chapel of Rosslyn was built by William Sinclair, and was one of the principle pilgrimage points during the late Middle Ages. Rosslyn Chapel is a masterpiece of Gothic architecture. William Sinclair and his masons worked on it for fifty years, until his death in the year 1496 at the ripe old age of ninety. An intriguing aspect to this year, 1496, is that it is only four years after Christopher Columbus "discovered" America; nonetheless, in Rosslyn Chapel are carved varieties of corn cobs and aloe cacti that were only to be found in the New World. In the Sinclair family tradition, they tell of the grandfather of William Sinclair, Prince Henry Sinclair (1345-1400) who traveled to the New World over ninety years before Columbus. The story of Prince Henry Sinclair is also told in the stories and songs of the Micmac Indians from Nova Scotia. Prince Henry came to the Indians in peace, according to a legend written down by the Reverend Silas Rand, who was the first man to record the stories of the Micmac Indians about the man they called Glooscap. The legend, as written by Silas Rand, is to be found in chapter eleven of the book by Andrew Sinclair entitled, *The Sword and the Grail*.

> *The tradition respecting Glooscap is that he came to this country from the East - far across the great sea; that he was a divine being, though in the form of a man. He was not far from any of the Indians . . . Glooscap was the friend and teacher of the Indians. All they knew of the arts he taught them. He taught them the name of the constellations and stars; he taught them how to hunt and fish, and cure what they took; how to cultivate the ground. He was always sober, grave and good. All that the Indians knew of what was wise and good he taught them. His canoe was a granite rock.*

Der Gottesfreund vom Oberland

During the Middle Ages, from small circles of individuals came powerful impulses of the spirit that helped to tame the unruly Mars forces, and established a cultural setting that enabled mankind to progress. One of the greatest spiritual impulses of the Middle Ages was the quiet circle of the "Friends of God" who thrived under the protection of the Knights of St. John of Jerusalem, receiving in letters the spiritual guidance of "a simple layman" known as, "Der Gottesfreund vom Oberland" - "The

Friend of God from the High Lands."

The Friend of God from the High Lands was a layman who, through the prompting of his dreams, approached Johannes Tauler "the Master of Holy Writ", in the year 1346. This layman told Tauler: "The single letters of the Holy Writ are killing your soul . . ." Furthermore he said: "You must know that when the Supreme Master speaks to me, he teaches me more in one hour than you and all the other teachers of our times could teach me to the end of my days." And the Friend of God added: "You yourself know that in the Holy Writ it is said that the letter kills, but that the Spirit gives new life. Now this is the point: the very same letter which is killing you now could also give you new life - if you yourself wanted it."

Upon hearing this, and other wonders, Tauler realized the intimate relationship to Christ that the simple man before him had, and begged to be his student. The Friend of God (for his name is unknown to this day) accepted and gave Tauler an alphabet of rules for his guidance and asked Tauler to refrain from his teaching activities for a time. The Friend of God then said: "When the time comes, which God knows well, He will accept you and make you into a new human being. Then you will become a man 'born anew in God.'"

When Tauler returned to teaching, it was said that whole groups of people would faint upon hearing him speak of things divine. The Friend of God subsequently retreated into the solitude of the mountains and maintained correspondence with a lay-group who called themselves the "Friends of God." Under the guidance of the Friend of God, these disciples followed a nine-fold path of Christian initiation. The central figure of this group was Rulman Merswin (d. 1382), who embodied these nine stages of Christian initiation in his book entitled, *The Little Book of the Nine Rocks.*

The circle of the Friends of God took refuge (with complete and independent freedom) under the protection of the Knights of St. John of Jerusalem within the Hospice on the "Green Island" in the river Ill in Strassbourg, Germany. It is further related that, in an effort to bring the true spirit of Christ back to the Catholic Church, the Friend of God went with a friend to talk to Pope Gregory XI (Pierre Roger de Beaufort, who was pope from 1370-1378). This is apparently the last great effort by the "Masters of Wisdom and of the Harmony of Feeling" to work directly within the Catholic Church; for the methods of spiritual development which are taught in the Catholic Church, were developed to meet the needs of the epoch of the Intellectual-Soul which would soon end in 1414.

Below I give the translation of the alphabet of rules that were given to Tauler by the Friend of God, and which can be found in the excellent book on this "simple lay-person" that I have consulted for this presentation, *The Friend of God From the High Lands,* by Wilhelm Rath. This book by Wilhelm Rath is based upon the writings that were found among the papers of the Hospice of St. John during the middle of the 19th century. Wilhelm Rath was one of the earliest students of Rudolf Steiner. These rules, as they were presented in the original Old German, began each sentence with one of the twenty-three letters of the Old German alphabet, although in the English translation which follows this is not apparent.

The ABC's of the Master's Book

Sir Master,
Since I am to teach you by divine guidance, I should like to make use of the alphabet which children are taught at school. I should like to teach you the letters of the alphabet as one does to children at the beginning of their schooling - all twenty-three of them.

A: *Attempt to live a good and godly life.*
B: *Beware of evil and only do what is good.*
C: *Commence by living modestly and avoiding extremes.*
D: *Learn to live with devotion for all things inner and outer.*
E: *Learn to hand over to God all self-will*
F: *Remain firmly and with earnest faithfulness with and in God.*
G: *Be obedient and willing in all matters divine.*
H: *Do not turn back to worldly matters and to nature (to outer sense appearances and sensuousness).*
I: *Learn in your heart to consider and ponder all good and divine things.*
K: *Be keen and strong in your resisting the temptations of the flesh and of the devil.*
L: *Learn strongly to overcome any lewdness.*
M: *Learn to preserve the love of God and love of man.*
N: *Covet nothing belonging to someone else, whatever it may be.*
O: *Keep order and turn everything to the best.*
P: *Accept punishment, be it God's or other people's, as if you*

had willed it yourself.
Q: Forgive anyone who may have done you a wrong.
R: Learn to cultivate purity of body and soul.
S: Learn to preserve gentleness in all good things.
T: Show trust and truthfulness to all human beings.
U: Avoid excesses of any kind.
X: Always live according to the life and teaching of Christ and arrange your life accordingly.
Y: Ask our dear Lady to help you to learn these lessons well.
Z: Tame your lower nature so that it may learn to keep peace in all things which God may bring you.

This impulse of the spirit, which proceeded from the "Friends of God" in the 14th Century under the patronage of the Knights of St. John of Jerusalem, the Knights Hospitallers, is very different from the present continuation of the Hospitaller order now known as, the Knights of Malta. For the Knights of Malta, along with the secret order known as the Opus Dei, have performed special activities, as a sort of secret diplomatic service for the Vatican, since the removal of the generalissimo of the Jesuits, who was also known as the "Black Pope."

Rudolf Steiner has told us that the Friend of God was an incarnation of Zaratas, or Zarathustra the spiritual leader of the Old Persian epoch. In ancient Atlantis, Zaratas was a leading initiate at the Sun Oracle under the guidance of the Manu, the leader of the Sun Mysteries. This Zaratas, after his incarnation as Zarathustra, had his Astral-Body donated to Hermes (who was a leader of the southern stream of the Mercury Mysteries which were established in Egypt in Lemurian times and which continued through the Atlantean period); while Moses was the recipient of Zaratas' Etheric-Body. The depth of content of these astral and etheric vehicles then came together with the Ego of Zaratas, in the Solomon Jesus of the Gospel of Matthew. Upon the death of the Solomon Jesus, at around age twelve, the spirit of Zaratas incarnated in the pure Nathan Jesus of the Gospel of St. Luke, who was the Adam Kadmon which had never fully entered into a human Physical-Body before that time. This is the real origin of the story of Jesus confounding the Elders at the Temple; for the once simple Nathan Jesus was now embodying the wisdom filled spirit of Zarathustra - one of the greatest "leaders of mankind." This Nathan being, with the radiance of the Christ working through Him as the archetypal human, was the Adam Kadmon that overlighted Krishna as he spoke to Arjuna on the battlefield of Kurukshetra, as told in the *Bhagavad Gita*. After dwelling in the Nathan Jesus until age thirty, the soul of Zaratas departed and the Christ descended into the prepared vehicles of Jesus, at the Baptism by John in the River Jordan, for a period of around three years.

Throughout the centuries, the great being Zaratas (who is also known as the Master Jesus) has incarnated in almost every century; although Rudolf Steiner has not given many names of these incarnations, as they are mostly as an unknown initiate working behind the scenes, so as to avoid suffering martyrdom at the hands of the ignorant multitude. One incarnation of the Master Jesus that Rudolf Steiner spoke of was in the United States, during the Civil War, that was concerned with the freeing of the slaves. One can only guess who this might be, the obvious choices being perhaps Lincoln or his mentor, or Harriet Beecher Stowe; but it's very easy to mistake a student for the teacher, or even a student of a student of a teacher - one cannot guess in such matters. These mysteries are reserved for higher initiates, as the incarnations of great initiates are even more difficult to trace than those of ordinary individuals. This is due to the highly developed purity of self that is possessed by the higher initiates, which makes a more refined impression upon the Akashic Record; and so, is not as easy to perceive clairvoyantly. The Master Jesus works particularly close with St. John the Divine, the only one of the twelve disciples who witnessed of the Mystery of Golgotha, and who is also known from his later incarnation as Christian Rosenkreutz, the leader of the Rosicrucian mysteries.

Christian Rosenkreutz and the Rosicrucian Mysteries

During the epoch of Aries, before the Mystery of Golgotha, in the mysteries of ancient Greece they spoke of Apollo when they referred to the activities of Christ which they perceived working into outer nature out of the Cosmos, from within the Sun sphere. Apollo was not the Christ, but represented the Sun Mysteries as they could be understood at that time by the ancient Greeks. These mysteries were originally an impulse that was brought into Greece from the Hyperborean Mysteries of the far North of Europe, and were mysteries that were concerned with the workings of the "Upper Gods" within the outer Cosmos. They were mysteries of the open sky and outer nature, and through their cosmic character were akin to the Jupiter Mysteries of the Celtic peoples. For there had always been the closest of ties between the Jupiter Mysteries and the Sun Mysteries since the time of ancient Atlantis. In ancient Greece, in addition to the Apollonian Mysteries, they also had other mysteries of the opposite character that dealt with the secrets of the inner-nature of man, and which were known as the Dionysian Mysteries. They represented the mystery wisdom of the South that had entered into Greece from ancient Egypt.

We find the Northern mysteries to be of a more outward turning character, observing the workings of the spirit in nature; such as, the mysteries that were taught by the original Zarathustra back in the epoch of Gemini regarding the "Upper Gods" and his clairvoyant experience of Christ as Ahura Mazda approaching the Earth from the aura of the Sun.

On the other hand, the Southern mysteries had more of an inward-turning character, that was more inclined to look within the soul to find the workings of the Spirit. Like the ancient Egyptians, for example, with their profound inner wisdom of the human body, soul, and spirit that was developed within the Mercury Mysteries, under the guidance of Hermes, during the epoch of Taurus. But, nonetheless, these mysteries were *necessarily* affected by the workings of the Luciferic spirits within the souls of mankind; for, Christ had not yet entered into human evolution and begun to work from inside the souls of mankind. We find these two tendencies expressed in the ancient Greek culture as the Apollonian (outer) mysteries, and the Dionysian (inner) mysteries.

As humanity approached the Mystery of Golgotha, they gradually lost the faculties of atavistic clairvoyance that are associated with the ancient *inward* luciferic forms of consciousness, for Lucifer was receding from the souls of mankind; while Christ, through the Mystery of Golgotha, began to enter the hearts and souls of mankind, literally entering into the blood of humanity, and becoming the essence of God dwelling within the Life-Spirit or True-Self of man - the "not I, but Christ in me" of St. Paul.

As history passed and humanity developed further, the Rosicrucians, under the guidance of Christian Rosenkreutz (or C.R.C. as he is sometimes known) were able to find their way into this inner world strengthened by the Christ Impulse that had entered Earth evolution at Golgotha. While traveling in the East, Christian Rosenkreutz had an experience of Christ which was similar to St. Paul's blinding experience of Christ on the road to Damascus. In addition to this Christ experience, Christian Rosenkreutz received, from the current incarnation of Mani-Parzival, the inner esoteric teachings that had been preserved by Christian initiates since the time of the Apostles in the secret Christian brotherhoods in the East; and which had the result of awakening in his soul and Etheric-Body the synthesis of all twelve fundamental mystery impulses which had been achieved through his transformation that occurred in his previous incarnation in the 13th century, when he lived in seclusion under the guidance of the twelve; a group that consisted of the seven Rishis, and four representative initiates of the first four post-Atlantean epochs, joined by a fifth who encompassed the state of current intellectual culture at that time.

Certain of these mysteries from the East had been transmitted earlier to the West - for these Rosicrucian mysteries can be traced back to the Knights Templars who were the custodians of the impulses which they received from the Grail Brotherhood that was founded by Charibert von Laon (who was the 8th century incarnation of Christian Rosenkreutz). The Grail Mysteries were then led by Parzival in the 9th century when in 869 A.D. the Grail Mysteries of the East and South merged with the Arthurian Mysteries of the West and North. The Grail Mysteries, in turn, found their precursors in the mysteries of the Coptic Christians of Jerusalem and Egypt who had been preparing an inner path to the Christ - which received its inwardness from the natural tendency of the Egyptian soul to want to find a way to the understanding of the workings of the spirit within the human soul through the path of meditation and prayer.

The most well known manifestation of this inward tendency of Egyptian Christianity can be found in the writings of the Desert Fathers, who were the original inspiration for the monastic impulse that spread over Europe in the Middle Ages. This came about, in part, because the monastic impulse was transmitted to the Celts in Ireland by their contact with the Egyptian Christians. These Irish monks were a profound blend of the inward mysteries of Coptic monasticism combined with the pre-Christian Christ impulses that were to be found in their native Druidism; which had preserved elements of the outward mysteries of the Cosmic Christianity of the Arthurian stream, and also certain elements of the inward mysteries of the earlier Hibernian stream. It was these Irish monks who had eventually converted many areas of Europe to Christianity.

These two fundamental tendencies, of the inward and the outward mysteries, came to be united in the Grail stream through the deeds of Parzival. And afterwards, through the development of Rosicrucianism, the foundation was laid for a modern path of Christian development. Had this spiritual synthesis not come about, humanity would have gradually been divided into two groups: first, those that followed a purely monastic impulse divorced from worldly pursuits; and secondly, those that were worldly - but separated from the possibility of developing a deeper understanding of the Christian Mysteries.

Had mankind not been given the possibility of developing a spiritual life, while remaining in the world, then they would have succumbed to the influences of the retarded Angels that inspired the materialistic impulses that were born out of the decadent Egyptian Mysteries. For these retarded Angels are once again active in the world, serving the ends of Ahriman through inspiring materialistic thoughts that only seek for answers from the world of matter, and dreams of world domination.

On the other hand, if mankind only had the option of approaching the spiritual world by the monastic path of development, then this would have been a victory for the Luciferic hosts. For the luciferic tendency is to lose interest in one's fellow man through the selfish striving for the spirit at the expense of worldly pursuits; and thereby, resign oneself to a habitual form of "automatic goodness" that is devoid of the stamp of individuality and Michaelic freedom.

For these two tendencies to be avoided, it was necessary that a path of development arise that was capable, on the one hand, of working through the methods of science into the world of matter and perceiving its true relationship to the spiritual world - thereby thwarting the goals of Ahriman; and, on the other hand, to overcome the Luciferic hosts by approaching the spiritual world without losing touch with the material world and one's individual nature. This was achieved by the Rosicrucians through penetrating into the realm of the Luciferic beings - with soul forces that were so strongly permeated by the Christ impulse - that the negative influences of the Luciferic beings became neutralized. In this way, the luciferic wisdom was, so to speak, captured and rendered into a tool for the service of Christ as embodied in His saying; "Be ye wise as serpents and harmless as doves." The deeper significance of this profound mystery of Rosicrucianism is clarified by Rudolf Steiner in the sixth lecture of the lecture cycle entitled, *East in the Light of the West*.

> As soon as the Christ has worked in the soul for a while, the soul, permeated by the Christ substance, becomes mature enough to penetrate again into the realm of the Luciferic beings. The Rosicrucian initiates were the first to be able to do this. They strove to understand and see the Christ in such a form so that as the mystical Christ He permeated their souls, and lived within them, and that this Christ substance in their inner being became a bulwark of strength against all attacks. It

became a new light within them, an inner, astral light. Historical experience of the Christ in his true being illuminates the soul to such an extent that men again become able to penetrate into the realm of Lucifer; at first only the Rosicrucian initiates were capable of this, and they will gradually carry out into the world what they have been able to experience with regard to the luciferic principle, and will pour out over the world that mighty spiritual union which consists in the fact that the Christ - Who has poured Himself as substance into the human soul - is understood henceforth by means of the spiritual faculties that mature in the spirit of individual men through a new influx of the luciferic principle. Let us consider an initiate of the Rose Cross. He first prepares Himself by the continual direction of the feeling, conceptions and thoughts within his soul to the great central figure of the Christ, by allowing the mighty figure of the Christ, as depicted in the Gospel of St. John, to work upon him, and in this way he purifies and ennobles himself. For our souls change fundamentally when we gaze in reverence upon the figure depicted by the Gospel of St. John. If we receive within us what streams forth from this figure, as described by St. John, the mystical Christ comes to life within us. And if we further this process by the study of other Christian documents, the soul is gradually permeated by the spiritual substance of the Christ, is cleansed and purified and reaches higher worlds. Feelings more especially are purified this way. We either, like Meister Eckhart and Tauler, learn to conceive of the Christ in an universal sense, or else to experience Him with the tenderness of Suso and others; we feel united with that which streamed to the Earth from the wide expanse of the heavenly worlds through the Christ event. Thereby a man makes himself ready to be led as a Rosicrucian initiate consciously into those [inner] regions which in [Greece in] ancient times were called the Dionysian worlds and may now be called Luciferic worlds.

What is the effect upon modern Rosicrucian initiates of this introduction into the Luciferic worlds? If their feelings glow with enthusiasm for the divine as soon as they are permeated with the Christ substance, then the other faculties through which we understand the world are illuminated and strengthened by the luciferic principle.

> *In this way the Rosicrucian initiate ascends to the luciferic principle. His spiritual faculties are intensified and elaborated through initiation, so that he not merely feels the Christ mystically within his soul, but can also describe Him, can speak of Him and picture Him in spiritual images or thought pictures; so the Christ is not merely dimly felt and experienced but stands before him in concrete outlines, as a figure of the outer sense world. It is possible for man to experience the Christ as soul substance when he directs his gaze to that figure of the Christ which meets him in the Gospels. But to describe and understand Him in the way that other phenomena and events in the world are understood; and thereby, to gain an insight into His greatness, His significance and His causative connection with world evolution, is only possible when the Christian initiate advances to knowledge of the Luciferic realms.*
>
> *Thus in Rosicrucian science it is Lucifer who gives us the faculty for describing and understanding the Christ...*

The mysteries of Rosicrucianism are symbolized by the roses which surround the cross, which represents how new life can arise through death - by the power of the eternal spirit - which overcomes the forces of materialism, and the ahrimanic world of death. Likewise, in his epic poem *The Divine Comedy*, Dante described in vivid poetic imagery the ethereal connectedness of all the living, manifested beings as the "Rose of Heaven."

The image of the rose has been associated throughout the centuries with the stream of Esoteric Christianity since the times of Ormus, the founder of an esoteric school under the sign of the Rose Cross, and the Egyptian disciple of St. Mark; who, in turn, received instruction from St. Paul. Within this mystery-name Ormus, is very possibly concealed a veiled reference to the Persian Sun-God, Ormuzd, or Ormazd (Zend, Ahura-Mazda) that Zarathustra, the ancient teacher of the Persians, proclaimed could be perceived in the aura of the Sun; and is the "Great Sun-Being", spoken of by Rudolf Steiner, that incarnated into Jesus at the Baptism. The Persian derivation of the name Ormus is further supported through the origin of the rose itself; for Rudolf Steiner said that Zarathustra was also responsible for the development of the fruit trees through cross-breeding with the rose plant; and likewise, various grains were also cross-bred by Zarathustra from the grasses of the lily family.

The Lily   **The Rose**

Hexagram   Pentagram
Lunar   Solar

The formative relationship of the Persian rose, and the lily to the fruits and grains, can be observed in the geometrical forms that are revealed through cross-section. For the *solar* Persian rose and the apple are both pentagonal in structure; while the *lunar* lily and the grains are both hexagonal in structure:

These geometrical relationships have yet other *microcosmic*, occult meanings; whereby, the hexagram (as a symbol of the penetration of matter by spirit) relates to its *solar* meaning, as the Mogen David, or "Shield of David" in reference to the Solar Logos penetrating into human, physical form - as Christ the "Messiah", the "Lion of the tribe of Judah." Likewise, the pentagram relates to the Holy Spirit; which, according to Rudolf Steiner, was carved over the entrance to the Temple of Solomon.

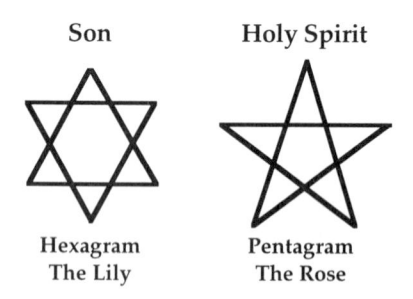

Son   **Holy Spirit**

Hexagram   Pentagram
The Lily   The Rose

Greater light is shed on the esoteric significance of the pentagram through its meaning as a symbol of the planet Venus "the bright Morning Star" ("... we must speak of [the sphere of] Mercury as the Morning Star" Rudolf Steiner); for the pentagonal form of the rose reveals the cosmic "signature" of the *microcosmic,* formative, etheric forces that are mirrored in the *macrocosmic* cycle of the rotating Venus pentagram; which I have discussed in the chapter on the Magician arcanum, and elsewhere (**III**).

In occult literature, the pentagram (which occultly represents - the thinking principle - as the *fifth* principle in man is Manas, or the Spirit-Self) is often thought to symbolize Lucifer the "light-bringer"; that, like Prometheus, "stole the fire of the gods and brought it to Earth." For Lucifer, through working within the souls of mankind since ancient times, had thereby brought the possibility of freedom to the human realm. But the time had come for Lucifer to retreat from the souls of mankind - for Christ was to be that which now worked within the human soul. This transition in human evolution had to come about gradually - like all stages of wholesome development; and so, as individuals freely align themselves with the Christ-forces that now work within the human heart - Lucifer is overcome through the power of the Holy Spirit; and thereby, the luciferic inner-realms are reclaimed by Christ from the "fallen hosts." This mystery is referred to by Rudolf Steiner when he relates that the Rosicrucians - as bearers of the Christ principle - were the first to become "mature enough to penetrate again into the realm of the luciferic beings"; and in so doing - reclaim these realms through the power of the Holy Spirit.

In light of the preceding concepts, we must not consider the Holy Spirit as representing the thinking principle; for, as discussed elsewhere, the Holy Spirit is related to Cosmic Feeling - the realm of Cosmic Light - that is the realm in contention between the Holy Spirit and the "unholy spirit" Lucifer. This redemption takes place through the equilibrium of Cosmic Thinking (Christ overcoming Ahriman), mediating between the realms of Cosmic Feeling (the Holy Spirit, opposed by Lucifer) and Cosmic Will (the Father, opposed by the Asuras). Through the redemption, which takes place in the realm of Cosmic Feeling and manifests within the human heart, Lucifer is subordinated to the Cosmic Will of the Father - and what was once the domain of luciferic wisdom and enthusiasm becomes transformed by the power of the Holy Spirit, through the wisdom of the Sophia, into a worthy "Grail" to receive the "Christ in you."

This redemption, furthermore, overcomes the hosts of Ahriman by forging the "sword" of Michael from the very iron; that, in the past, was a bearer of the involutionary crystallizing impulses of Mars. For this redemption comes about through the healing forces of Mercury dissolving the overly crystallized forms of the past - that create strife between men - in order to fulfill the transition from the Mars half to the Mercury half of Earth evolution, and plant the seeds for the future unfoldment of a true Grail culture during the sixth post-Atlantean period.

The Archangelic Period of Gabriel

Moon - The High Priestess: 1510 - 1879 A.D.

In the period of the Archangel Gabriel, the significance of the forces of heredity within the social-cultural sphere were formalized to the greatest degree, with the division of the races and nations becoming a dominant theme in the course of human evolution. When the period of the Archangel Gabriel is viewed from the perspective of the rightful Michaelic consciousness of the present period, the Gabrielic period appears to be excessively caught up in the forces of heredity, race, and nation.

In light of this, it must be understood that this was the natural expression of the stage of development that was reached by humanity in the Gabrielic time period. For, we are presently only gradually overcoming our dependence upon the lunar forces of heredity and replacing them with the solar forces that radiate from the sovereign individuality of the Ego, or "I Am." This "solarization" process, that takes place through the forces of the Ego, is realized to the extent that we become integrated with the living Christ impulse which works from within the etheric world of life that borders the physical world.

If an impulse arises, in the present Michaelic period, which is attempting to put a central significance on that which is received through the forces of heredity, then that impulse is out of step with the developing wholesome evolution. For those impulses that put undo emphasis on heredity are serving forces of decline that are a carry-over from what was once a necessary and healthy impulse in the period of the Archangel Gabriel.

The same is true regarding the overemphasis of the issues of race and nation, along with heredity. While we, of course, should not abandon these important aspects of our personal karma, we must begin to see these issues in a new way from the perspective of a more cosmopolitan, and planetary consciousness - for the failure to do so drives away the new Vulcan beings that have descended since 1879 in order to enliven the thinking of mankind.

The failure of mankind to embrace a more planetary consciousness will also drive away the new Earth Spirits that entered into relationship with human evolution in the 4th and 5th centuries, and are concerned with the forming of the Jupiter incarnation of the Earth out of the freely developed morality that streams from mankind. To these two groups of wholesome beings, that are concerned with our future evolution, we must also consider the new kingdom of Nature-Beings; that, according to Rudolf Steiner, appeared "in order that our life of soul may be quickened by what it draws from nature" - in order to bring about harmony between our thinking and the moral forces of the Cosmos - through revitalizing our Etheric-Bodies in the period between the Fall and Spring. These beings can also be thwarted in their efforts if mankind does not strive for a new "universally-human" planetary consciousness.

This new "universally-human" planetary consciousness will come about through a shift of emphasis toward the fostering of the individual as a sovereign being - above and beyond the considerations of heredity, race, and nation. We must go beyond seeing the individual as being merely the product of a particular family, race, or nation. We must begin to see each individual human being as a nation unto themselves; or rather, as if they were an individual species unto themselves. This is so because the human individual will increasingly begin to transcend the limited ties of the blood through the impulses that have entered evolution since the beginning of the period of the Archangel Michael in 1879 A.D. This new development will result in what could be described as an individuated, cosmopolitan, Michaelic consciousness - which has been rendered permeable to the spiritualizing Grail forces that entered human evolution through the spilling of the blood of Christ on Golgotha. For, it is the striving of this Grail impulse that we may become free and sovereign individuals who are united as corpuscles in the "Mystical Body of Christ."

Christ entered human evolution from outside of the Earth, from that region of Cosmic Space within the circling Zodiac known in occultism as the "Gate of the Ram", and entered into the stream of time at the Mystery of Golgotha. The resulting shift of the consciousness of humanity will bring about an awakening of mankind from the stream of heredity and time-memory, through the forces of space-consciousness. This will have the further result of mankind coming to an awareness of karma as a process of Cosmic Love. This awakening will develop through the experience of the forces of cosmic-renewal that proceed from the Christ as the "new Lord of Karma."

The Christ-forces of cosmic-renewal that have proceeded from the world of space will become a means of awakening the consciousness of humanity to what can be called the "World of Duration", in which dwell the Angelical beings of the higher spiritual world. This change became possible by the entry of the "Lamb of God" from the world of Cosmic

Space into the earthly stream of time at the Mystery of Golgotha. By integrating the Resurrection forces of life that proceed from the Christ, we transform that which has "fallen" in man and has become a source of suffering. Rudolf Steiner elaborates on this mystery in the ninth lecture of the lecture cycle entitled, *East in the Light of the West.*

> *But the Christ comes under a different category altogether [from all the spiritual impulses that came before Him]. The Christ did not descend to Earth by the path of time. The Christ came to Earth at a certain point of time - but from outside, from space. Zarathustra saw Him when he directed his gaze to the Sun, and spoke of Him as Ahura Mazdao. To the spiritual vision of man in space Ahura Mazdao came nearer and nearer until he descended and became Man. Here, therefore, the interest lies in the approach through space, and not in the time sequence.*
>
> *The approach through space, this advent of the Christ - from out of the infinitude of space and down to our Earth - has an eternal and not a temporary value. With this is connected the fact that Christ's work upon Earth is not carried on only under conditions of time. He does not bring to the Earth anything corresponding to the relationships between father and child, or mother and child, which exist under time conditions - but He brings into the world something which goes on side by side, which co-exists. Brothers live side by side, they co-exist. Parents, children, and grandchildren live one after another in time, and the conditions of time express their individual relation to each other. But the Christ as the Spirit of Space brings a spatial element into the civilization of the Earth. What Christ brings is the co-existence of men in space, a condition of increasing community of soul, regardless of time conditions.*
>
> *The mission of the Earth planet in our cosmic system is to bring love into the world. In olden days, the task of the Earth was to bring in love with the help of time. Inasmuch as through the conditions of ancestry and descent, the blood poured itself from generation to generation, from father to child and grand-children, those who were connected through time were 'ipso facto' those who loved each other. Family*

connections, blood relationships, the descending stream of blood through the generations following each other in time, provided the foundation of love in the olden times. And the cases where love took on more of a moral character, were also rooted in the conditions of time. Men loved their ancestors, those who had preceded them in time.

Through Christ there came the love of soul to soul, so that that which is side by side, which co-exists in space enters a relationship which was at first represented by brothers and sisters living side by side and at the same time - the relationship of brotherly love which one human soul is intended to bear towards another in space. Here the condition of co-existent life in space begins to acquire its special significance.

In the above quotation, Rudolf Steiner has expressed the deeper, occult meaning of the cosmopolitan impulses of the Grail mystery that are summarized in the Johannine saying: "Love ye one another." For this cosmopolitan impulse is destined to become the central theme of the wholesome evolution of mankind as we move into the future.

The Transition from the Mysteries of Heredity to the Mysteries of Cosmic Thought

In the ancient world, the *Old Testament* was the "Book of the Law" and was intended exclusively for the guidance of the mission of the Hebrew people. This particular mission was received by Moses directly through Jehovah Elohim on Mount Sinai and was concerned with creating, through the eugenic mysteries, or mysteries of heredity, Astral, Etheric and Physical-Bodies which would be developed, through strict adherence to the "Book of the Law", in such a manner that it would bring about vehicles worthy of receiving the incarnation of the Messiah - Christ the "Great Sun-Being." This ultimately had to come about through the Essene community, for they had maintained these mysteries of heredity in their purest form. The initiates of the Essene community were the recipients of those Hebrew Mysteries which had secretly maintained the preservation of the Etheric-Body of Shem from ancient times as a means of bringing about the unique hereditary development of the human form within the Hebrew people; which had as its highest mission, the creation of suitable Astral, Etheric, and Physical-Bodies for the incarnation of the "Great Sun-Being" Christ.

The *Old Testament* code of external Law was also directed at the development of a sense of self that was freed from the old form of atavistic clairvoyance. The laws of Moses were effective to the extent that the Hebrews followed them; but as mankind progressed beyond the Mystery of Golgotha - the *New Testament* became the new "Book of the Law." Although the *New Testament* is a "Book of the Law" for all mankind and not just for the Hebrew people, it is the "universally-human" inner law - the law of love, which is embodied in the "Golden Rule."

In *Old Testament* times, the Archangel Michael (whose name means "like unto God") was the central representative of Jehovah Elohim to such a degree that he could be described as the "Countenance of Jehovah." In the years preceeding 869 A.D., the year in which the "Grail King" Parzival united the Arthurian and Grail Mysteries, the Archangel Michael, who is the guardian of Cosmic Intelligence, had changed the manner in which he guided the evolution of mankind. This resulted in the descent of Cosmic Intelligence to Earth so that it could begin to work from within the hearts of mankind beginning in the 9th century. Through this change in the Archangel Michael's manner of working he achieved a new stage in his guidance of the evolution of humanity, and literally was transformed from the "Countenance of Jehovah" to the "Countenance of Christ"; thereby fully accomplishing his integration with the intentions of Christ as regards to the development of Cosmic Intelligence from within mankind.

Near the end of the period of the Archangel Gabriel, in the 1850's, the consciousness of mankind had become so darkened through the lower materialistic forces of the intellect, that the resulting estrangement from the forces of the spiritual world put Earth evolution into jeopardy. This spiritual dilemma did not pass without a response from the spiritual forces which are in service to Christ; but rather, received a resounding victory over the ahrimanic forces of materialism through the defeat of the "Spirits of Darkness" by the Archangel Michael in 1879, the year of the beginning of the Michaelic Age.

This critical turning-point of human evolution, if viewed in the light of the mission of Jehovah, can bring understanding. For the *Old Testament* Jehovah impulse worked through the mysteries of heredity, and was an appropriate and necessary impulse which had served to protect mankind's evolution up to the year 1879. But in 1879, the Michaelic Age brought about a shift in the path of human evolution that led to a greater freedom of consciousness from the forces of the hereditary time-stream through the working of the forces of Cosmic Thought - which had descended to Earth, under the direction of the Archangel Michael, during the 8th century A.D. For at last, the Archangel Michael could take up the rulership of mankind for the first time since his transformation from the "Countenance of Jehovah" into the "Countenance of Christ"; and so, the new Christian path of love within the context of space-consciousness could now fully replace the *Old Testament* law of love as the fruit of the workings of the hereditary time-stream.

Through this change in the evolution of human consciousness, giving undo emphasis to the forces of heredity has become a retarded impulse. This change has also rendered the protection received from Jehovah, through the hereditary forces, increasingly ineffective. The outward symptoms of this change are the widespread breakdown of the nuclear family unit, which could be relied upon for loving support in the past; and, on the other hand, the tendency of individuals today to turn to others of like mind for the type of familial support that in the past would be received, as a matter of course, through the blood ties of the family. These tendencies are symptomatic of the birth within mankind of forces that transcend one's relationship to a particular family, race, or nation - forces of a "universally-human" character which proceed from the individualized manifestation of Cosmic Thought, and are the special gift from Michael as the "Countenance of Christ."

For now, the protection of mankind depends - not on hereditary forces; but rather, on the conscious development of individuals towards becoming "Spirits of Freedom and Love", through the Cosmic Intelligence that is the "sword of Michael"; and thereby, uniting the forces of the blood with the impulses that proceed from the Life-Spirit of Christ which has permeated the spiritual atmosphere of the Earth since the Mystery of Golgotha. These impulses which proceed from the Life-Spirit of Christ have become increasingly accessible since the "Second-Coming of Christ within the etheric world of life"; that began, according to Rudolf Steiner, around 1909. It is the spiritual enthusiasm that arises from these very forces which brings about the "etherization of the blood", and upon which depends our future evolution.

In the future, as we are gradually freed from the forces of heredity, the appearance of mankind will increasingly become an expression of their inner-soul nature. The more highly developed souls will take upon themselves, more and more, the beautiful angelic appearance that is the fruit of the self-sacrificing Cosmic Intelligence - for, "beauty is the fruit of suffering." Those souls who have not overcome their selfish animality will manifest this animality in their appearance, this is the true "Mark of the Beast" - although they will revel in their animality and derive pleasure from evil - and think that it is beautiful. This will be the effect of the unpurified astrality acting upon the Etheric-Body, and will bring about distortions in the manifestation of life, form, and consciousness within the animalistic humans.

These two possible paths for the development of the Ego are represented in the "Zodiac of the Lamb of God" (**IX**) by Sagittarius, the constellation of the Ego; which is a centaur, with the upper body of a human, and the lower body of a horse. This separation of mankind will be determined by whether or not individuals rise to the challenge of true individuality that is represented by the Ego. "By their fruits shall they be known." The two types of "fruits" that result will be: in the first group - those who manifest true individuality and proceed in their evolution towards their destiny as "Spirits of Freedom and Love"; and, in the second group - those who fail to manifest their true individuality by succumbing to a group identity; and thereby - retard their evolution through the resulting enhancement of sub-human forces of animality which impair their capacity to incorporate the Ego into the human form in a wholesome way.

In light of this, Spiritual Science is meant to be a Christ-centered world-veiw through which the cultivation of a "seed" group can begin, in the present fifth cultural epoch, that will actually receive the "fruits" of their strivings in future incarnations in the sixth cultural epoch through their participation in the establishment of a new, free, wholesome, and spiritually redeemed Christ-centered "I Am", or Grail culture that is based upon the principles of Initiation and is under the compassionate guidance of the leader of the "Mother Lodge of Humanity" - Mani/Parzival.

The final "ring-pass-not" for the redemption of mankind is the sixth sub-race, of the sixth root-race, of the sixth or Venus incarnation of the Earth (**IV**). This is one meaning of the "number of the Beast" 666 which is mentioned in "The Revelation of St. John the Divine." We have until then to evolve towards the higher intentions of evolution and to strive toward the redemption of humanity - without interfering in their freedom. For, by the fifth, or Jupiter incarnation of the Earth, there will be groups of lost-souls suffering in the state *that they created for themselves* through their unwillingness to assimilate into their hearts the "law" of love, and so become individuated, radiant beings. The greatest suffering that will be experienced in the future by the souls striving for goodness, will be from the frustration of the desire to redeem the suffering lost-souls into "Spirits of Freedom and Love."

The Archangelic Period of Michael

Sun - The Sun: 1879 - 2229 A.D.

Since 1879 we have experienced the unfoldment of the cosmopolitan impulses of the Archangel Michael as the new Time-Spirit. In the present age of Michael we will see come into being a world economy. The way in which this comes about depends upon the manner in which we rise to the challenge of our development as sovereign-individuals. Ideally, for the fostering of the wholesome unfoldment of this individual sovereignty, the nations of the world should strive to be organized in a three-fold manner - which gives autonomy to the sphere of culture, the sphere of rights, and the sphere of economics; thereby bringing about, not only a separation of church and state, but also making the economic life an independent sphere of activity - freed likewise from the machinations of special interests.

The Michaelic age also brings with it the potential for freeing the thinking from earthbound forms and thereby manifesting true freedom. The means of achieving this is shown by Rudolf Steiner in his book entitled, *The Philosophy of Freedom* (or, *The Philosophy of Spiritual Activity*).

In making this transition, mankind has moved from the influence of the period of the Archangel Gabriel, which lasted from 1510 A.D. to 1879 A.D. During the period of the rulership of the Archangel Gabriel, the forces of heredity were the dominant aspect of human culture, with the different groups of people having a much greater tendency to act out of a response to their ancestral ties.

The period of the Archangel Michael, on the other hand, is an age that is set aside for the cultivation of a more global consciousness, in which mankind comes to realize that "we are all corpuscles in the body of Christ"; and thereby, feel a sense of responsibility to all mankind and not merely our own limited groups. This is the natural result of the free-spiritual impulses that are developing within mankind through the unfoldment in human evolution of the "I Am", or "Christ in you." Of course, if you read the newspaper headlines today you might not think that mankind as a whole is embracing these ideals; for we have only just begun the Michaelic Age, and so in time these impulses will begin to gradually unfold in the minds and hearts of greater and greater numbers.

You only need to look at the historical developments since 1879 to see that there are powerful unredeemed forces working within the political, cultural, and economic spheres. The unleashing of these undeveloped forces has led us to two world wars and countless other conflicts. The greatest antidote to these challenges is to develop freedom in one's thinking. It is not enough to just say you are free, you must have developed the inner forces of sense-free thinking as explained by Rudolf Steiner in *The Philosophy of Freedom*.

By overcoming sense-bound thinking, you empower yourself to experience true freedom in your thinking, which is a bridge to true spiritual understanding. This sense-bound thinking, which can only perceive thoughts as they are reflected on the nervous system, is an important stage in the unfoldment of the human Ego, and is responsible for the development of clarity in mankind's thoughts about the outer world; which, in turn, has also developed in mankind a greater sense of individuality. Although it must be stressed that this stage in the evolution of consciousness, the stage of sense-bound thinking, brings with it powerful negative potentials, especially if this stage of consciousness does not develop properly into the next stage of sense-free thinking. For then there can develop a sort of crystallization, or "mummification" of one's thinking which does not have the mobility of thought such as is present within sense-free thinking, and that is necessary in order to experience a true spiritualization of consciousness.

Rudolf Steiner tells us of how in ancient Egypt, the mummification practices of the Egyptian priests enabled them in later incarnations to gain an enhanced understanding of the material world which contributed to the development of modern science. In light of this, occultly speaking, the modern world-view of scientific materialism can be seen as a direct result of the continued working of these impulses which arose through the ancient Egyptian mummification practices. This evolutionary impulse, which developed out of ancient Egypt, is the formative impulse behind the soul disposition of abstract, scientific-materialism.

This abstract, scientific modality of thought has led to the achievement of great discoveries within the realms of materialistic science, but is fettered by its sense-bound manner of working - so that it can only comprehend the world in a mechanical way. This, in turn, has led to crucial misunderstandings about the true nature of living things through seeing them in an abstract-mechanical way; such as, seeing the human body as a sort of machine, or biochemical combustion unit which is governed by blind forces of nature.

Historically speaking, abstract-thinking actually began with the development of mathematics, astrology, and astronomy in Egypt during the Graeco-Roman epoch, and was later introduced into the conceptual realm, in a new way, by St. Augustine (354-430 A.D.), who was the bishop of the city of Hippo in North Africa. It was St. Augustine who strived for a level of certainty regarding the Christian doctrine of the unseen realms by utilizing the concepts of abstract-reasoning.

This faculty of abstract-reasoning was an important step in the evolution of thinking, but when it was later combined with the "dead" concepts of certain materialistic scientists, it became a great stumbling block to the understanding of nature, life, and consciousness. For, through the sequencing of abstract ideas, which are not derived from observations, certain theories came to be accepted as if they were self-evident truths. Through this methodology, further ideas were developed through the compounding of these unproven theories which resulted in a sort of "scientific" caricature of life. For, the true scientific powers of observation can be eclipsed by the tendency to see the world through the theoretical "filter" of unproven theories, which through time became accepted as "truths", or "laws of nature." It was this tendency to see the world through a theoretical "filter", that Goethe was striving to overcome through his methodology of pure observation, or "beholding." Rudolf Steiner once described Goethe as, ". . . a representative of an epoch of world conceptions, which felt the compulsion to pass over from mere thinking to beholding."

One of the "pillars" of modern physics is Louis de Broglie, who is credited with the formulation of the theories of "wave mechanics", and "undulatory mechanics." Louis de Broglie's work was considered by Albert Einstein to be so significant as to be something that "happens only in large intervals of history." De Broglie had this to say regarding the "tyrannical influences" of dogmatic principles on scientific understanding.

> *History shows clearly that the advances of science have always been frustrated by the tyrannical influences of certain preconceived notions that were turned into unassailable dogmas. For that reason alone, every scientist should periodically make a profound re-examination of his basic principles.*

The theories of de Broglie were considered by many to be as significant to the understanding of physics as the theories of Albert

Einstein, or Max Planck. De Broglie considered photons to be particulars of light while he considered electrons to be particulars of matter; through this he was able to develop a theory of relativist mechanics that was based on Einstein's theory of relativity. De Broglie's theory is a sort of pinnacle of the atomistic tendencies of abstract-materialistic science.

According to Rudolf Steiner, these atomistic tendencies in modern scientific thought arise through the globular structure of the nervous system which brings about a tendency to perceive matter as composed of minute particles. A related concept has even come to be recognized somewhat in modern physics; for now physicists say that atoms appear to be particles *only when they are observed*, but function as waves *when they are not observed*. This atomistic tendency is also reinforced through thinking that thoughts originate within the nervous system in a sort of mysterious electro-chemical way. When, in fact, according to Spiritual Science we perceive thoughts as they are reflected on the nervous system from the etheric world.

In a quote brought to my attention by Rick Knutson, the physicist Max Planck goes a step further than de Broglie's sincere questioning of authority and speaks of the rational necessity of unseen influences within the world of quantum physics (*Lebendige Erde*, No. 3/84, page 133).

Gentlemen! As a physicist - that is someone, who has his lifelong served a sober and objective science - I may surely not be suspected of mere flighty enthusiasm. And so, out of my researches into the atom, I will say the following: There is no such thing as matter on its own. All matter comes about and persists only through a force, which brings the particles into vibration and holds them together in the tiny sun-system of the atom. But as in the whole universe there is neither an intelligent nor eternal (abstract) force - humanity has never been able to achieve the much desired 'perpetuum mobile' - so we must assume that behind this force there is a conscious, intelligent Spirit. This Spirit is the basis of all matter. It is not the visible, though perishable matter, which is the reality, the truth, (for matter, as we have seen, would not exist without this Spirit!), but it is the invisible and immortal Spirit, which is the truth. But as Spirit cannot exist for itself alone, and to every Spirit there belongs a Being, so we are forced to assume Spirit-Being. But as Spirit-Being also cannot exist out of itself alone, and must have been created, so I am not shy in naming this mysterious creator, as have all peoples of all the ancient cultures . . . God.

The inability of certain scientists to conceive of the supersensible realities of the spiritual world as the foundation of existence has led many materialistic scientists to develop a world-view that can only be described as scientific-atheism. By only taking into account, in their world-view, the grossest levels of manifestation they exclude the life which is a manifestation of the unseen worlds of spirit, and substitute instead a "dead" universe of seething chemical-atomic forces. These physicists consider the universe to be based on natural laws, as they understand them, and that the universe conforms to these same chemical-atomic laws throughout eternity. And furthermore, that all that can be known about the origin of the universe can be figured out through the mathematical extrapolation of these laws - as they understand them.

We know from the indications of Rudolf Steiner, that the present state of equilibrium of natural laws only maintains its stability for around ten or fifteen thousand years, and that we are already past the half-way point of this period. After this time of stability, starting from the 6th Period (which begins to unfold around 6695 A.D., in the astronomical age of Sagittarius, **XXVI**), the Spiritual Powers that now work unseen behind the manifested universe will bring about a metamorphoses of Earth evolution into a new state of being which will establish the necessary environment for our further evolution - a state of being which cannot be calculated with the current understandings of materialistic science. In keeping with this concept, Rudolf Steiner once remarked that the physicist's attempts to calculate the origin of the universe mathematically, are like trying to calculate what an infant's stomach was like hundreds of years ago, when in fact the infant did not even exist.

The methods of abstract, scientific-materialistic concepts are very effective within the mineral realm and in dealing with machines. But abstract, scientific-materialistic concepts cannot by themselves lead us to a true understanding of living things. One must not see this as an attack on science, for the methods of science rightfully applied are a path of true understanding. To the scientific-materialist, the stars are merely atomic-chemical events that came into manifestation through the blind forces of gravity acting upon the remnants of a great cosmic explosion or some other inanimate scenario; on the other hand, to the spiritual-scientist, the stars are colonies of beings that were created through the activity of the Spiritual Hierarchies. While the materialistic physicist's attempt to calculate the life of the universe as if it were a great machine that is slowly winding down.

This thermodynamic clock model of the universe has been put into a tail-spin through the recent discovery by the scientist's using the Hubble telescope. For, due to the Hubble telescope's position in space they are now, for the first time, able to observe the movements of far more distant galaxies; which, according to the "Big Bang" theory, should be expanding away from the center of the primeval "explosion" at a speed that is stabilized by the gravitational attraction between the galaxies. But if these initial observations are correct, contrary to their theories they discovered that the expansion of the universe is accelerating rather than remaining constant, or even "winding down." What the discovery of this meta-galactic acceleration has done is to force the scientist's to postulate a force that is counter to gravity; that is, so to speak, a force of levity like the quintessence or fifth element of Aristotle, which is accelerating the rate of meta-galactic expansion (II).

In any event, we known from Anthroposophy that the ethers are living forces of levity which are counter to gravity, that exist in counter-space that is in the physical sense "emptier than empty." All one has to do is see how the plants grow upward from this living activity of the ethers. Perhaps science is now at the threshold of understanding the ethers, and consequently the basis of all life. For, according to Spiritual Science, the universe is not the end result of an evolution that has resulted by *chance* from inanimate chemical activities responding to forces of gravity; but rather, the ethers are seen as a manifestation of the activity of the beings of the spiritual world, which have *intentionally* evolved the universe through a living metamorphosis that proceeds in stages of manifestation.

The Stages of the Planetary Chain of Evolution

1. Old Saturn - 1st Proto-Human Stage
2. Old Sun - 2nd Proto-Human Stage
3. Old Moon - 3rd Proto-human Stage
4. Present Earth - Human Stage
5. Future Jupiter - Angels - 1st Post-Human Stage
6. Future Venus - Archangels - 2nd Post-Human Stage
7. Future Vulcan - Archai - 3rd Post-Human Stage

In *An Outline of Occult Science*, Rudolf Steiner describes the seven stages of our evolution which are the result of a process of metamorphoses through four levels of being (**IV**). Stages one through four brought mankind to the physical-human stage of manifestation, and are followed by three stages of development leading back into the higher worlds - but with a metamorphoses of life, form, and consciousness. Before the fourth stage, which is our present Earth evolution, humanity evolved through three pre-human stages. Likewise after the fourth, or earthly-human stage of evolution, there will follow three stages of ascent within the Spiritual Hierarchies: the Angelic in the fifth or Jupiter evolution, Archangelic in the sixth or Venus evolution, and in the seventh or Vulcan evolution we will reach the stage of development corresponding to our present Archai, or Spirits of Time.

In selfless service to Christ, the Archangel Michael has guided humanity since ancient times. During this extended period of time, Michael has periodically (roughly every 2,400 years) taken his place as a temporary Time-Spirit for a period of around 350 years within the sequence of the seven Archangelic periods. It is through this cyclical, temporary taking on of cosmic responsibility that the group of seven planetary Archangels bring about their evolution to the next stage of existence as Archai. For after the Archangels have acquired the necessary development, which in the case of the seven planetary Archangels comes about, in part, through their experience as the temporary rulers of their respective Archangelic periods, they metamorphose fully into the Archai stage of being (which corresponds to our future Vulcan evolution) by completing the embodiment of the Atma, or Spirit-Man principle.

It is in reference to these facts of Spiritual Science that Rudolf Steiner has indicated that the rank of Archai is Michael's present stage of development. Which means that Michael, rather than merely functioning through the sphere of the Archai for the duration of the Archangelic Period, has actually fully graduated to the rank of Archai or Time Spirit. Through his "graduation" to the rank of Archai, Michael's position in the company of Archangelic hosts was taken over by the Guardian Angel of Gautama Buddha, who was freed from his duties as a Guardian Angel, through the spiritual liberation of the Buddha in the 6th century B.C. And, although the Buddha's Guardian Angel had, by the 6th century B.C., attained the development which was necessary to pass to the rank of Archangel, he had elected to remain in the sphere of the Angels as a sacrifice for mankind in the service of Christ.

The quiescent nature of this "new" Archangel acts out of a spiritual mood which is in keeping with the character of Michael - who patiently awaits the unfoldment of mankind to arise in freedom. This spiritual mood of non-interference in the unfoldment of mankind is represented by this "new" Archangel's name that was carried over from his past mission as an Angel amongst the Teutonic peoples of Northern Europe. For, according to Rudolf Steiner, in Teutonic mythology this Angelic being was known as "the silent one" Vidar (from the Old Norse Vidarr "the wide ruling one" pronounced: Veedar). And also, due to the ascension of Michael to the rank of Archai, this "new" Archangel Vidar is now entrusted with the guardianship, in the spiritual world, of the Adam Kadmon, the archetypal human being that is referred to in Spiritual Science as the Nathan Soul. With his attainment of the rank of Archangel it is perhaps appropriate now to refer to Vidar with a name that is in keeping with his Archangelic character namely - Vidariel.

The hierarchy of the Archai are directly related to the unfoldment of the Ego in man which resides in the warmth of the blood. This is so because the lowest principle of the Archai is on the same plane of being as the primeval substance of the Ego that was donated by the Exusiai (**IX**). It is due to this spiritual-scientific fact, that Rudolf Steiner sometimes refers to the Archai as the Spirits of Personality. The Archai have a further significance for the Ego through the principle of warmth, for they passed through their human equivalent, or fourth stage of development on the first stage of our chain, which was the warmth globe of the Old Saturn incarnation of the Earth (**IV**). The nature of the existence of the Archai on Old Saturn was described further by Rudolf Steiner in a lecture he gave on April 4th, 1909 that is included in the lecture cycle entitled, *The Spiritual Hierarchies and their Reflection in the Physical World*.

> *What really, is the force that worked in the Spirits of Personality on Old Saturn? It is none other than that which we know in man as the power of thinking. For the work of the Spirits of Personality on Old Saturn was, indeed, to exercise the power of their thoughts.*

Michael is from the ranks of the Archangels, and so has passed through the human equivalent, or fourth stage, on the second stage of mankind's evolutionary chain. Michael, through ascending to the ranks of the Archai, has achieved a higher stage of operation from which to serve the Christ in human evolution. For not only is mankind evolving, but so are all of the beings in the universe growing and experiencing their own evolutionary development. This great being Michael, whose name means "like unto God" has, since the 8th to 9th centuries A.D., served as the "Countenance of Christ", as a development beyond his service in the *Old Testament* times as the "Countenance of Jehovah."

Through his passing to the rank of the Archai, Michael can now fully work within the realm from which is derived the very substance of the Ego. This is an inconceivable benefit for mankind, for Michael can now serve as a pure representative of Christ on the most intimate level of the being of man - the Ego. And this he does without attempting to interfere in the course of events. Instead, Michael stands as a silent representative allowing the Egos of mankind to grow with complete freedom into a more mature spiritual understanding.

Human evolution gradually came into being through the warmth in the first period of manifestation - Old Saturn (**IV**), and was then followed by the three stages, or embodiments, that it took to arrive at the human-stage of the physical Earth; but nonetheless, the Earth contains elements that are connected in very intimate and living ways with the preceding stages of being. Rudolf Steiner clarifies what this mystery implies in the fourth lecture of the lecture cycle entitled, *East in the Light of the West*.

> *Those of my readers who have studied earlier lectures on these subjects, will realize that a host of spiritual beings, at different stages of evolution, have been involved in what has come to pass in the human, animal, vegetable and mineral kingdoms during the course of our Earth evolution. All such beings intervene in some way or other in the evolutionary texture of the Earth and of the kingdoms belonging to it. Behind the phenomena surrounding us is a richly constituted spiritual world, just as there was during the periods of Old Saturn, Old Sun, and Old Moon. We must not attempt to understand these spiritual kingdoms by inventing permanent names for these spiritual beings. The names used are not, for the most part, intended to designate individualities, but offices or spheres of duties. So if a particular name is used in connection with a being active during the Old Sun period, it cannot be applied in the same sense to that being as regards its work or function in the Earth evolution; for it has progressed*

by that time. It is necessary to speak of these matters with great accuracy and precision.

The Earth period was not only preceded by three embodiments of the Earth globe, but by three mighty spiritual kingdoms, essentially different from one another when examined by supersensible consciousness. Investigation of the Old Saturn, Old Sun, and Old Moon periods reveals many things which cannot be compared with anything we can name on the Earth, and of which one can only speak by analogy.

It will be remembered that I have spoken of the Old Saturn period as being essentially one of warmth, or of fire; on Old Sun this warmth condensed to air; on Old Moon the air condensed to water, and on Earth the earth element appeared for the first time. But the application of our concept of fire or warmth directly to the evolution of Old Saturn would result in an incorrect picture; for the fire of Saturn differed essentially from the fire of our Earth. There is only one phenomenon which can legitimately be compared to the Saturn fire, and that is the fire which permeates the blood as warmth. This vital warmth, or life principle, is more or less comparable to the substance of which Old Saturn was entirely composed, and the physical fire of today is a descendant, a later product of the Saturn fire; for in its external form - as perceived in space - it has appeared for the first time on the Earth. The warmth of the blood, therefore, is the only thing which can be compared to what was present during the physical evolutionary period of Old Saturn. There is very little indeed in the realm of our present day experience which can be compared in any way with the qualities of these earlier evolutionary periods, all of which were very different from our present Earth existence.

It must be understood, however, that everything in the Old Saturn, Old Sun, and Old Moon periods is comprised within Earth evolution, only it has changed in character. What was laid as a seed on Old Saturn and evolved through the Sun and Moon periods, is to be found in the Earth evolution, although in a changed condition . . .

With the coming of the Michaelic Age, mankind is called upon to develop their connection with the Divine-Spiritual Beings out of their own nature - *in complete freedom*. What is at stake is the possible outcome of human evolution that will come into play if mankind fails to take upon themselves the responsibilities of freedom. For if mankind is to accomplish this task, they must begin to unite the forces of the Ego with the Cosmic Intelligence that is under the guardianship of Michael. Through accomplishing this in the right way, a new possibility of freedom unfolds through the manner in which the human expressions of Cosmic Feeling and Cosmic Willing are equilibrated by this manifestation of Cosmic Intelligence within the human realm. This new development is a direct result of the entry of Christ into human evolution.

The proper unfoldment of this evolutionary process depends upon individuals achieving a balance between the forces of the head and the forces of the heart, equilibrium between that which is above and below, to the right and to the left, and that which is behind and before one in space, as well as time. It is essentially a question of balance, which takes place as a conscious process moment by moment. It is not enough to merely follow "the letter of the law", as an external prompting; but rather, one must embody "the spirit of the law" within the core of one's being - within the mind, heart, and will. One must become capable of moral spontaneity, because what is needed to achieve harmony is in a continual state of flux.

A good example is a musician in a symphony, who as long as he follows the sheet music he will do the right thing - this describes the past path of external law. As we move into the future, it is more like being a musician in a group that is playing improvisational music; and so, finding a harmonious blend depends upon listening to what the others are playing - since a note that is good at one moment will be out of place in another. For there is no sheet music to guide one, but only one's spontaneous understanding of melody, rhythm, and harmony; and so, by integrating one's past experience with needs of the present, one achieves a harmonious result. In light of this, it is important to consider that the members of the improvisational musical group depend on each other to achieve their goal - for if one of them fails, it will affect the overall outcome.

Fortunately, Earth evolution does not depend on great masses of people coming to these understandings. If it can at least begin with a few individuals, it will help counteract unnecessary suffering, and continue to grow as a healing "leaven" over time.

In the essay entitled, "The Activity of Michael and the Future of Mankind", that is included in the collection of brief paragraphs and essays which were published under the title *Anthroposophical Leading Thoughts: Anthroposophy as a Path of Knowledge - The Michael Mystery*, Rudolf

Steiner summarizes the essence of the mission of Michael regarding his custodianship of Cosmic Intelligence. For the Cosmic Intelligence had descended from the rulership of the Exusiai to the rulership of the Archai in the 4th century A.D.; and subsequently, beginning in the 8th and 9th centuries A.D., had further descended to Earth so as to begin working from within the consciousness of mankind. Michael, who has now graduated to the ranks of the Archai, can now serve the development within humanity of this Cosmic Intelligence in a way that was never before possible. For now Michael, as an Archai, exists on the very plane of being in which this Cosmic Intelligence and the human Ego dwell.

How does man stand today in his present stage of evolution with respect to Michael and his hosts?

Man is surrounded today by a world which was once of a wholly divine-spiritual nature - divine-spiritual being of which he also was a member. Thus at that time the world belonging to man was a world of divine-spiritual being. But this was no longer so in a later stage of development. The world had then become a cosmic manifestation of the Divine-Spiritual; the Divine Being hovered behind the manifestation. Nevertheless, the Divine-Spiritual lived and moved in all that was thus manifested. A world of stars was already there, in the light and movement of which the Divine-Spiritual lived and moved and manifested itself. One may say that at that time, in the position or movement of a star, the activity of the Divine and Spiritual was directly evident.

And in all this - in the working of the Divine Spirit in the Cosmos, and in the life of man resulting from this divine activity - Michael was as yet in his own element - unhindered, unrestricted. The adjustment of the relation between the Divine and the Human was in his hands.

But other ages dawned. The world of the stars ceased to be a direct and present manifestation of Divine-Spiritual activity. The constellations lived and moved, maintaining what the Divine activity had been in them in the past. The Divine-Spiritual dwelt in the Cosmos in manifestation no longer, but in the manner of its working only. There was now a certain distinct separation between the Divine-Spiritual and the Cosmic World. Michael, by virtue of his own nature, adhered to the Divine-Spiritual, and endeavored to keep mankind as closely as possible in touch with it.

This he continued to do, more and more. His will was to preserve man from living too intensely in a world which represents only the working of the Divine and Spiritual - which is not the real Being, nor its Manifestation.

It is a deep source of satisfaction to Michael that through man himself he has succeeded in keeping the world of the stars in direct union with the Divine and Spiritual. For when man, having fulfilled his life between death and a new birth, enters on the way to a new Earth-life, in his descent he seeks to establish a harmony between the course of the stars and his coming to life on Earth. In olden times this harmony existed as a matter of course, because the Divine-Spiritual was active in the stars, where human life too had its source. But today, when the course of the stars is only a continuing of the manner in which the Divine-Spiritual worked in the past, this harmony could not exist unless man sought it. Man brings his divine-spiritual portion - which he has preserved from the past - into relation with the stars; which now only bear their divine-spiritual nature within them as an after-working from an earlier time.

In this way there comes into man's relation to the world something of the Divine, which corresponds to former ages and yet appears in these later times. That this is so is the deed of Michael. And this deed gives him such deep satisfaction that in it he finds a portion of his very life, a portion of his sun-like, living energy.

But at the present time, when Michael directs his spiritual eyes to the Earth, he sees another fact as well - very different from the above. During his physical life, between birth and death, man has a world around him in which even the Working of the Divine-Spiritual no longer appears directly, but only something which has remained over as its result; we may describe it by saying it is only the accomplished Work of the Divine-Spiritual. This accomplished Work, in all its forms, is essentially of a Divine-Spiritual kind. To human vision the Divine is manifested in the forms and in the processes of Nature; but it is no longer indwelling as a living principle. Nature is this divinely accomplished work of God; Nature everywhere around us is an image of the Divine Working.

In this world of sun-like Divine glory, but no longer livingly Divine, man dwells. Yet as a result of Michael's working upon him man has maintained his connection with the essential Being of the Divine and Spiritual. He lives as a being permeated by God in a world that is no longer permeated by God.

Into this world that has become empty of God, man will carry what is in him - what his being has become in this present age.

Humanity will evolve into a new world-evolution. The Divine and Spiritual from which man originates can become the cosmically expanding Human Being, radiating with a new light through the Cosmos which now exists only as an image of the Divine and Spiritual...

To understand the meaning of Michael's mission in the Cosmos is to be able to speak in this way. In the present time we must be able to speak of Nature in the way demanded by the evolutionary stage of the Consciousness-Soul or Spiritual-Soul. We must be able to receive into ourselves the purely natural-scientific way of thinking. But we should also learn to feel and speak about Nature in a way that is according to Christ. We ought to learn the Christ-Language - not only about redemption from Nature, about the soul and things Divine - but also about the things of the Cosmos.

When with inward, heartfelt feeling we realize the mission and the deeds of Michael and those belonging to him, when we enter into all that they are in our midst, then we shall be able to maintain our human connection with the Divine and Spiritual origin, and understand how to cultivate the Christ-Language about the Cosmos. For to understand Michael is to find the way in our time to the Logos, as lived by Christ here on Earth and among mankind.

For through the development of this Cosmic Intelligence mankind will, more and more as they move into the future, develop within them the capacity to understand how the visible world has arisen from the supersensible realms of spirit. And through this cosmic understanding, of the reality of the supersensible, will arise an etheric clairvoyance that is capable of perceiving Christ as a spiritual being within the etheric world, such as happened to St. Paul on the road to Damascus.

In the eleventh lecture of the lecture cycle entitled *The Mission of the Individual Folk Souls - in Relation to Teutonic Mythology*, Rudolf Steiner points toward the arising destiny of mankind's development of this Pauline etheric clairvoyance, which will serve as a means of building a bridge to the spiritual reality of the living, risen Christ.

> *Those who are open to the stimulus of Spiritual Science will, from the middle of the twentieth century on, gradually experience a renewal of that which St. Paul saw in etheric clairvoyance as a mystery to come - the 'Mystery of the Living Christ.' There will be a new manifestation of Christ, a manifestation which must come - when human capacities develop naturally to the point when the Christ can be seen in the world in which He has always been present since the Mystery of Golgotha - and in which He can also be experienced by the Initiate. Mankind is gradually growing into that world in order to be able to perceive from the physical plane that which formerly could be perceived only in the Mystery Schools from the perspective of the higher planes.*

It is the spread of true Spiritual Science, which will come about during the Michaelic Age, that will serve as a foundation for the future spiritual evolution of mankind. And through the democratization of this spiritual wisdom, which in the past was only known to initiates, will eventually develop the Grail culture of the future epoch of the Spirit-Self; thereby fulfilling the mission that was prepared through the efforts of the Grail Brotherhood in the 8th and 9th centuries A.D.

> *The root of all eternal interconnectedness is an absolute omnidirectional tendency. In this dwells the power of the hierarchy, the true Freemasonry, and the invisible bond of true thinkers - herein resides the potential for a universal republic.*
>
> Novalis

Part 3

The Seven Post-Atlantean Cultural Epochs

"God is not existent in any ordinary sense, but in a simple and undefinable manner embraces and anticipates all existence in Himself. Hence He is called the 'King of the Ages.'"

Dionysius the Areopagite

The Seven Post-Atlantean Cultural Epochs

I. The Age of Cancer

Astronomical Age of Cancer - 8426 B.C. to 6266 B.C.

Cultural Epoch of Cancer - 7227 B.C. to 5067 B.C.

The Old Indian Cultural Epoch

The Etheric-Body

II. The Age of Gemini

Astronomical Age of Gemini - 6266 B.C. to 4106 B.C.

Cultural Epoch of Gemini - 5067 B.C. to 2907 B.C.

The Old Persian Cultural Epoch

The Astral-Body

III. The Age of Taurus

Astronomical Age of Taurus - 4106 B.C. to 1946 B.C.

Cultural Epoch of Taurus - 2907 B.C. to 747 B.C.

The Egypto-Chaldean Cultural Epoch

The Sentient-Soul

IV. The Age of Aries

Astronomical Age of Aries - 1946 B.C. to 215 A.D.

Cultural Epoch of Aries - 747 B.C. to 1414 A.D.

The Graeco-Roman Cultural Epoch

The Intellectual-Soul

V. The Age of Pisces

Astronomical Age of Pisces - 215 A.D. to 2375 A.D.

Cultural Epoch of Pisces - 1414 A.D. to 3574 A.D.

The Western European Cultural Epoch

The Consciousness-Soul

VI. The Age of Aquarius

Astronomical Age of Aquarius - 2375 A.D. to 4535 A.D.

Cultural Epoch of Aquarius - 3574 A.D. to 5734 A.D.

The Eastern European Cultural Epoch

The Spirit-Self

VII. The Age of Capricorn

Astronomical Age of Capricorn - 4535 A.D. to 6695 A.D.

Cultural Epoch of Capricorn - 5734 A.D. to 7894 A.D.

The American Cultural Epoch

The Life-Spirit

Part 4

Bibliography

"The Word of God is not a sounding but a piercing Word, not pronounceable by the tongue but efficacious in the mind, not sensible to the ear but fascinating to the affection. His face is not an object possessing beauty of form but rather it is the source of all beauty and all form. It is not visible to the bodily eyes, but rejoices the eyes of the heart. And it is pleasing not because of the harmony of its color but by reason of the ardor of the love it excites."

St. Bernard of Clairvaux, 1091-1153

Selected individual lectures of Rudolf Steiner consulted:

Lecture delivered in Vienna, November 8th, 1888 entitled, *Goethe as the Founder of a New Science of Aesthetics.* translated by G. Metaxa, edited by H. Collison. London: Rudolf Steiner Publishing Company, n.d.

Lecture delivered in Berlin, March 17th, 1906 entitled, "Signs and Symbols of the Christmas Festival." translated by D. S. Osmond. (in: *The Festivals and Their Meaning.*)

Lecture delivered on October 20th, 1906 entitled, *The Path of Knowledge and its Stages.* (Typescript Z 275)

Lecture delivered in Berlin, October 25th, 1906 entitled, *The Occult Significance of Blood.* London: Rudolf Steiner Publishing Co., 1926

Lecture delivered in Cologne, December 25th, 1907 entitled, *Goethe - The Mysteries (Die Geheimnisse) - A Christmas and Easter Poem by Goethe.* Spring Valley: Mercury Press, n.d.

Lecture delivered in Berlin, November 13th, 1908 entitled, *The Formation of Concepts and Hegels Theory of Categories.* (in: GA 108, also in manuscript: Z 421)

Lecture delivered in Carlsruhe, January 18th, 1909 entitled, *Practical Training in Thought.* translated by Henry B. Monges, revised by Gilbert Church. New York: The Anthroposophic Press Inc., 1968

Lecture delivered in Berlin, February 15th, 1909 entitled, *Christianity in Human Evolution.* translated by Alan P. Cottrell, Ph.D., edited by Gilbert Church, Ph.D. Spring Valley: The Anthroposophic Press, 1979 (in: GA 109)

Lecture delivered in Berlin, April 29th, 1909 entitled, *Isis and Madonna.* Spring Valley: Mercury Press, 1987 (in: GA 57)

Lecture delivered in Berlin, May 6th, 1909 entitled, "On the History of Christian Rosenkreutz." (see: Paul M. Allen and Carlo Pietzner)

Lecture delivered on May 15th, 1909

Lecture delivered in Munich, March 15th, 1910 entitled, "The Sermon on the Mount - The Land Shamballa." in: The Anthroposophical News Sheet, Volume 8. Dornach: 1940

Lecture delivered in Bielefeld, March 15th, 1910 entitled, *The Significance of Spiritual Research for Moral Action.* translated by Alan P. Cottrell, Ph.D. Spring Valley: The Anthroposophic Press, 1981 (in: GA 127)

Lecture delivered in Berlin, December 12th, 1911 entitled, *And the Temple Becomes Man.* translated by D. S. Osmond. London: Rudolf Steiner Press, 1979

Lecture delivered in Berlin, February 3rd, 1913 entitled, *The Being of Anthroposophy.*

Lecture delivered in Hamburg, November 15th, 1913 entitled, *Jesus and Christ.* translation revised by John Bledsoe. Spring Valley: The Anthroposophic Press, 1976

Lecture delivered in Pforzheim, March 7th, 1914 entitled, *The Pre-Earthly Deeds of Christ*. North Vancouver: Steiner Book Centre Inc., 1976 (in: GA 152)

Lecture delivered in Berlin, December 12th, 1915 entitled, *The Spirit of Fichte in our Midst*. translated by Beresford Kemmis. London: Rudolf Steiner Publishing Company, n.d.

Lecture delivered in Munich, March 18th, 1916 entitled, "Central Europe Between East and West." translated by Anna Meuss and Johanna Collis. in: The Golden Blade, No. 43. Sussex: Imprint, 1991 (in: GA 174a)

Lecture delivered in Dornach, August 12th, 1916 entitled, "The Twelve Senses and the Seven Processes in Man." in: The Golden Blade, No. 27. London: Rudolf Steiner Press, 1975

Lecture delivered in Dornach, August 12th, 1916 entitled, "The Sense Organs and Aesthetic Experience." in: The Golden Blade, No. 27. London: Rudolf Steiner Press, 1975

Lecture delivered in Dornach, December 24th, 1916 entitled, *The Northern Mysteries and the Baldur Myth*. (in: GA 173) (In English in manuscript: Z 276)

Lecture delivered in Zurich, October 9th, 1918 entitled, *The Work of the Angels in Man's Astral Body*. translated by D. S. Osmond with the assistance of Owen Barfield. London: Anthroposophical Publishing Company, 1960

Lecture delivered in Dornach, June 2nd, 1921 entitled, *John Scotus Erigena*. (in: GA 204) (In English in manuscript: EN 3)

Lecture delivered in Dornach, November 6th, 1921 entitled, *The Sun-Mystery in the Course of Human History*. translated by D. S. Osmond London: Rudolf Steiner Press, 1978 (in: GA 208)

Lecture delivered in Oslo (Christiana), November 26th, 1921 entitled, *Paths to Knowledge of Higher Worlds*. Toronto: Steiner Book Centre, 1970 (in: GA 79)

Lecture delivered in Dornach, November 6th, 1921 entitled, *The Alphabet - An Expression of the Mystery of Man*. extensively revised from the translation of V. E. Watkin. Spring Valley: Mercury Press, 1982 (in: GA 209)

Lecture delivered in Dornach, May 26th, 1922 entitled, "The Human Heart." (Also called: "The Development of the Human Etheric and Astral Bodies - the Formation of an Etheric and Astral Heart - the Heart as an Organ of Karma Formation.") (Published in: *The Spirit of Childhood*, by Douglas Gabriel)

Lecture delivered in Dornach, October 22, 1922 entitled, "Pope Nicholas I and the Spiritual Life of Europe." in: Anthroposophical Quarterly, Vol. 23, No. 2, Summer 1978.

Lecture delivered in Dornach, October 22, 1922 entitled, *Spiritual Relations in the Configuration of the Human Organism*.

Lecture delivered in Stuttgart, December 22, 1922 entitled, "The Ear." in: The Golden Blade, No. 22. London: Rudolf Steiner Press, 1970

Lecture delivered in Arnheim, July 19th, 1924

Selected writings and lecture cycles of Rudolf Steiner consulted:

Ancient Myths and The New Isis Mystery. translated by M. Cotterell, translation revised by Mado Spiegler, and the lecture on Isis-Sophia was translated by James H. Hindes. Hudson: The Anthroposophic Press, 1994 (GA 180, and lecture 14 of GA 202)

An Esoteric Cosmology. Spring Valley: St. George Publications, 1978 (in: GA 94) (This early lecture cycle was given in Paris between May 25th and June 14, 1906 the transcript consists of notes by Edouard Schure, lecture 16 was translated by R. M. Querido. "The report does not give a verbally accurate rendering of the text of the lectures." Paul M. Allen)

An Occult Physiology. London: Rudolf Steiner Press, 1983 (GA 128)

An Outline of Occult Science. translated by Maud and Henry B. Monges, revised by Lisa D. Monges. Spring Valley: Anthroposophic Press Inc., 1972 (GA 13)

Anthroposophical Ethics - With an Account of Francis of Assisi. revised by M. Cotterell. London: Anthroposophical Publishing Company, 1955 (S-2600, S-2601, S-2602)

Anthroposophical Leading Thoughts - Anthroposophy as a Path of Knowledge - The Michael Mystery. translated by George and Mary Adams. London: Rudolf Steiner Press, 1973 (GA 26)

The Apocalypse of Saint John. edition revised by M. Cotterell. London: Anthroposophical Publishing Co., 1958 (GA 104)

A Road to Self-Knowledge and The Threshold of the Spiritual World. translated by H. Collison and revised by M. Cotterell. London: Rudolf Steiner Press, 1975 (GA 16 and 17)

Aspects of Human Evolution. translated by Rita Stebbing. Hudson: The Anthroposophic Press, 1987 (GA 176)

A Theory of Knowledge Implicit in Goethe's World Conception. translated by Olin D. Wannamaker. Spring Valley: The Anthroposophic Press Inc., 1978 (GA 2)

Background to the Gospel of St. Mark. translated by E. H. Goddard and D. S. Osmond. London: Rudolf Steiner Press, 1968 (GA 124)

The Balance in the World and Man - Lucifer and Ahriman. translated by D. S. Osmond and M. Adams. North Vancouver: Steiner Book Centre Inc., 1977 (three lectures given in Dornach on Nov. 20th, 21st and 22nd, 1914, in: GA 175)

The Bhagavad Gita and the Epistles of Paul translated by Lisa D. Monges and Doris M. Bugbey. New York: The Anthroposophic Press Inc., 1971 (GA 142)

The Being of Man and His Future Evolution. translated by Pauline Wehrle. London: Rudolf Steiner Press, 1981 (GA 107)

Between Death and Rebirth. translated by E. H. Goddard and D. S. Osmond. London: Rudolf Steiner Press, 1975 (GA 141)

The Bridge Between Universal Spirituality and the Physical Constitution of Man. translated by Dorothy S. Osmond. Spring Valley: The Anthroposophic Press Inc., 1958 (three lectures given on Dec. 17th, 18th and 19th, 1920, from: GA 202)

Building Stones for an Understanding of the Mystery of Golgotha. translated by A. H. Parker. London: Rudolf Steiner Press, 1972 (GA 175)

Christ and the Spiritual World - The Search for the Holy Grail. translation by Charles Davy and D. S. Osmond. London: Rudolf Steiner Press, 1963 (GA 149)

Christianity as a Mystical Fact and the Mysteries of Antiquity. translation and notes by E. A. Frommer, Gabrielle Hess and Peter Kandler, introduction by Rev, Alfred Heidenreich, Ph.D. West Nyack: Rudolf Steiner Publications Inc., 1961 (GA 8)

The Chymical Wedding of Christian Rosenkreutz. (A translation by Carlo Pietzner of the essay, *Die Chymische Hochzeit des Christian Rosenkreutz*, that was originally published in 1917, and is now available in: *A Christian Rosenkreutz Anthology* by Paul M. Allen and Carlo Pietzner)

Cosmic and Human Metamorphoses. London: Anthroposophical Publishing Co., 1926 (GA 175)

Cosmic Memory - Prehistory of Earth and Man. translated by Karl E. Zimmer. Blauvelt: Steinerbooks, 1990 (GA 11)

The Deed of Christ and the Opposing Spiritual Powers - Lucifer, Ahriman, Mephistopheles, Asuras. translation by D. S. Osmond North Vancouver: Steiner Book Centre Inc., 1976 (two lectures given in Berlin on Jan. 1st and Mar. 22nd, 1909, in: GA 107)

Deeper Secrets of Human History in the Light of the Gospel of St. Matthew. translated by D. S. Osmond and A. P. Shepherd. London: Anthroposophical Publishing Company, 1957 (GA 117)

The Driving Force of Spiritual Powers in World History. translated by Dorothy Osmond and Johanna Collis. Toronto: Steiner Book Centre, 1972 (GA 222)

Earthly and Cosmic Man. foreword by Marie Steiner. translated by Dorothy Osmond. London: Rudolf Steiner Publishing Co., 1948 (GA 133)

Earthly Death & Cosmic Life. revised translation by C. D. and D. S. O. London: Rudolf Steiner Press, 1964 (GA 181)

Earthly Knowledge and Heavenly Wisdom. translated by Sabine H. Seiler. Hudson: The Anthroposophic Press, 1991 (GA 221)

The Easter Festival in Relation to the Mysteries. translated by George Adams. London: Rudolf Steiner Press, 1968 (GA 233) (The last lecture discusses the Mysteries of Ephesus, and the Aristotelian categories.)

East in the Light of the West. London: The Rudolf Steiner Publishing Company, 1940 (GA 113)

The Effects of Spiritual Development. translated by A. H. Parker. London: Rudolf Steiner Press, 1978 (GA 145)

Egyptian Myths and Mysteries. translated by Norman Macbeth. New York: The Anthroposophic Press Inc., 1971(GA 106)

Eighteen Monographs by Rudolf Steiner on Astronomy. translated by Rick Mansell. <u>Windows to</u>

the Spiritual - Series One. Redondo Beach: The Rudolf Steiner Research Foundation, 1989 (A translation of the "3rd Science Course", a lecture cycle entitled *The Relationship of the Diverse Branches of Natural Science to Astronomy*, that was given in Stuttgart between January 1st and 18th, 1921.)

Eleven European Mystics. translated by Karl E. Zimmer, introduction by Paul M. Allen. Blauvelt: Rudolf Steiner Publications, 1971 (GA 7)

Esoteric Christianity and the Mission of Christian Rosenkreutz. translated by Pauline Wehrle. London: Rudolf Steiner Press, 1984 (in: GA 130)

Esoteric Development - Selected Lectures and Writings From the Work of Rudolf Steiner. edited by Alice Wulsin, introduction by Alan Howard. Spring Valley: The Anthroposophic Press Inc., 1982 (Includes the lectures: Dec. 7th, 1905 - GA 54; Apr. 8th, 1911 - GA 35; Sept. 26th, 1923 - GA 84; Sept. 20th, 1922 - GA 305; Mar. 16th, 1905 - GA 53; Oct. 20th, 1906 - GA 96; Oct. 21st, 1906 - GA 96; Mar. 2nd, 1915 - GA 157, and the Essay "General Demands Which Every Aspirant for Occult Development Must Put to Himself" - GA 245.)

The Etherisation of the Blood - The Entry of the Etheric Christ into the Evolution of the Earth. translated by Arnold Freeman and D. S. Osmond. London: Rudolf Steiner Press, 1971 (in: GA 130)

The Evolution of Consciousness as revealed through Initiation-Knowledge. translation by V. E. W. and C. D. London: Rudolf Steiner Press, 1966 (GA 227)

The Evolution of the Earth and Man and the Influence of the Stars. translated by Gladys Hahn. Hudson: The Anthroposophic Press, 1987 (GA 354)

The Fall of the Spirits of Darkness. translated by Anna Meuss. Bristol: Rudolf Steiner Press, 1993 (GA 177)

The Festivals and Their Meaning - Christmas, Easter, Ascension and Pentecost, Michaelmas. translation revised by C. D. and D. S. O. London: Rudolf Steiner Press, 1981 (Includes numerous lectures pertaining to the Festivals that were given at various times and places.)

The Fifth Gospel. revised translation by C. D. and D. S. O. London: Rudolf Steiner Press, 1968 (GA 148)

Foundations of Esotericism. translated by Vera and Judith Compton-Burnett. London: Rudolf Steiner Press, 1983 (GA 93a)

The Four Seasons and the Archangels. translation revised by C. D. and D. S. O. London: Rudolf Steiner Press, 1968 (GA 229)

Friedrich Nietzsche - Fighter for Freedom. translated by Margaret Ingram de Ris. Englewood: Rudolf Steiner Publications Inc., 1960

From Buddha to Christ. revised and edited by Gilbert Church, Ph.D. Spring Valley: The Anthroposophic Press, 1978 (5 lectures from: GA 109/58/60/130)

From Jesus to Christ. revised translation by C. D. London: Rudolf Steiner Press, 1973 (GA 131)

From Symptom to Reality in Modern History. translated by A.H. Parker. London: Rudolf Steiner

Press, 1976 (GA 185)

Fruits of Anthroposophy. translated by Anna R. Meuss. London: Rudolf Steiner Press, 1981 (GA 78)

Fundamentals of Anthroposophical Medicine. revised translation by Alice Wulsin. Spring Valley: Mercury Press, 1986

Fundamentals of Therapy - An Extension of the Art of Healing through Spiritual Knowledge. by Rudolf Steiner, Ph.D. and Ita Wegman, M.D. translated by George Adams, M.A. London: Rudolf Steiner Press, 1967 (GA 27) (This is the only book that Rudolf Steiner co-authored. His work with Dr. Ita Wegman led to the founding of the Clinical and Therapeutic Institute in Arlesheim Switzerland.)

Genesis - Secrets of the Bible Story of Creation. translated by Dorothy Lenn, with the assistance of Owen Barfield. London: Anthroposophical Publishing Company, 1959 (GA 122)

Geographic Medicine. revised and emended by Gerald Karnow. Spring Valley: Mercury Press, 1979 (Two lectures given in St. Gallen on Nov. 15th and 16th, 1917)

Das Goetheanum als Gesamtkunstwerk: Rudolf Steiner - Der Baugedanke des Goetheanum. Einleitender Vortrag mit Erklärungen zu den Lichtbildern des Goetheanum-Baues gehalten in Bern am 29. Juni 1921. Zum Bildband erweitert und gestaltet von Walter Roggenkamp. Dornach: Philosophisch-Anthroposophischer Verlag am Goetheanum, 1986 (This is an extensive photographic study of the artwork of the first and second Goetheanum's and also Rudolf Steiner's sculptural works. Although the text is in German, the main body of the work is 259 pages of photographs.)

Die Goetheanum-Fenster - Sprache des Lichtes, Entwurfe und Studien, 2 Banden. Mit Wortlauten Rudolf Steiners, Berichten uber die Arbeit an den Fenstern und Radierungen von Assja Turgenieff sowie einer Bilddockumentation uber die Enstehung der Fenster im ersten und zweiten Goetheanum. Dornach: Rudolf Steiner Verlag, 1996 (This is an extensive photographic study of the stained glass of the first and second Goetheanum's. The text is in German, but the whole second volume consists of 143 pages of photographs and reproductions [many in color] of the stained glass and the original drawings.)

Goethe's Conception of the World. New York: Anthroposophic Press, 1962 (GA 6)

Goethe's Standard of the Soul - As illustrated in Faust and in the Fairy Story of "The Green Snake and the Beautiful Lily." translated by D. S. Osmond, revised by H. Collison. London: Anthroposophical Publishing Company, 1925 (GA 22) (This edition includes an English translation of Goethe's fairy tale "The Green Snake and the Beautiful Lily.")

Goethe's Secret Revelation and The Riddle in Faust. preface by Marie Steiner. Ferndale: Trismegistus Press, 1980 (The companion volume to *Goethe's Standard of the Soul* .)

Goethe the Scientist. translated by Olin D. Wannamaker. New York: The Anthroposophic Press, 1950 (GA 1)

The Gospel of St. John. translated by Maud B. Monges, introduction by Marie Steiner. Spring Valley: The Anthroposophic Press Inc., 1984 (GA 103)

The Gospel of St. John in Its Relation to the Other Three Gospels, Particularly to the Gospel of St. Luke.

translated by Samuel and Loni Lockwood. New York: The Anthroposophic Press, 1948 (GA 112)

The Gospel of St. Luke. revised translation by D. S. Osmond with the assistance of Owen Barfield. London: Rudolf Steiner Press, 1964 (GA 114)

The Gospel of St. Mark. translated by Erna McArthur, Ph.D. New York: Anthroposophic Press Inc., 1950 (GA 139)

The Gospel of St. Matthew. translated by Dorothy Osmond and Mildred Kirkcaldy. London: Rudolf Steiner Press, 1965 (GA 123)

The Guardian of the Threshold. translated by H. Collison. <u>Four Mystery Plays, Volume II.</u> London: Anthroposophical Publishing Company, 1925 (in: GA 14) (The Third Mystery Drama)

Guidance in Esoteric Training. translation revised by Charles Davy and Owen Barfield. London: Rudolf Steiner Press, 1977 (GA 245)

Health and Illness - Lectures to the Workmen, 2 Volumes. introduction by Marie Steiner, translated by Maria St Goar. Spring Valley: Anthroposophic Press, 1981 (GA 348)

How Can Mankind Find the Christ Again? The Threefold Shadow Existence of our Time and the New Light of Christ. translated by Olin D. Wannamaker, Francis E. Dawson and Gladys Hahn, edited by Gladys Hahn. Spring Valley: The Anthroposophic Press, 1984 (GA 187)

Human and Cosmic Thought. translation revised by Charles Davy. London: Rudolf Steiner Press, n.d. (GA 151)

The Human Soul in Relation to World Evolution. translated by Rita Stebbing, foreword by Alan Howard. Spring Valley: The Anthroposophic Press, 1984 (GA 212)

Ideas for a New Europe - Crisis and Opportunity for the West. translated by Johanna Collis, abridged by Richard G. Seddon. Sussex: Rudolf Steiner Press, 1992 (Contains lectures 9-12 from GA 194, and lectures 16-18 from GA 196.)

The Influence of Lucifer and Ahriman - Man's Responsibility for the Earth. London: Rudolf Steiner Press, 1954 (in: GA 193)

Initiate Consciousness - Truth and Error in Spiritual Research. with a foreword and digest of contents by Marie Steiner, translated by Olin D. Wannamaker. New York: The Anthroposophic Press, 1928 (GA 243)

Initiation and Its Results. (see: *The Way of Initiation and Its Results.*)

Initiation Eternity and the Passing Moment. revised by Gilbert Church, Ph.D. Spring Valley: The Anthroposophic Press, 1980 (GA 138)

Inner Impulses of Evolution - The Mexican Mysteries and The Knights Templar. revised and edited by Gilbert Church, Frederic Kozlik and Stewart C. Easton, foreword by Stewart C. Easton, introduction by Frederic Kozlik. Spring Valley: The Anthroposophic Press, 1984 (GA 171)

The Inner Nature of Man and the Life Between Death and a New Birth. translated by D. S. Osmond and Charles Davy. London: Anthroposophical Publishing Company, 1959 (GA 153)

The Inner Realities of Evolution. London: Rudolf Steiner Publishing Company, 1953 (GA 132)

The Karma of Materialism. translated by Rita Stebbing, foreword by Owen Barfield. Spring Valley: The Anthroposophic Press, 1985 (GA 176)

The Karma of Untruthfulness, 2 volumes. translated by Johanna Collis. London: Rudolf Steiner Press, 1988-1992 (GA 173, 174)

Karmic Relationships - Esoteric Studies, 8 volumes. translations by George Adams, D. S. Osmond et al. London: Rudolf Steiner Press, 1972-1975 (GA 235, 236, 237, 238, 239, 240)

Knowledge of Higher Worlds and its Attainment. translated by G. Metaxa, edited by H. Collison. New York: The Anthroposophic Press, 1923 (GA 10)

First Scientific Lecture-Course - Light Course, 2 Vols. with a foreword by Dr. Guenther Wachsmuth, translation by George Adams M.A. East Sussex: Steiner Schools Fellowship, 1977

Macrocosm and Microcosm. revised translation by D. S. O. and C. D. London: Rudolf Steiner Press, 1968 (GA 119)

Man and the World of the Stars - The Spiritual Communion of Mankind. translated by D. S. Osmond. New York: The Anthroposophic Press Inc., 1982 (GA 219)

Man as a Being of Sense and Perception. translated by Dorothy Lenn. London: Anthroposophical Publishing Company, 1958 (Three lectures on the twelve senses that were given in Dornach on July 22nd, 23rd and 24th, 1921)

Man as Symphony of the Creative Word. translated by Judith Compton-Burnett. London: Rudolf Steiner Press, 1978 (GA 230)

Man: Hieroglyph of the Universe. translated by George and Mary Adams. London: Rudolf Steiner Press, 1972 (GA 201)

The Manifestations of Karma. London: Rudolf Steiner Press, 1969 (GA 120)

Man in the Light of Occultism, Theosophy and Philosophy. London: Rudolf Steiner Press, 1964 (GA 137)

Man in the Past, the Present and the Future: The Evolution of Consciousness; and, The Sun-Initiation of the Druid Priest and His Moon-Science. London: Rudolf Steiner Press, 1982 (GA 228)

Man's Life on Earth and in the Spiritual Worlds. translated by George and Mary Adams. London: Anthroposophical Publishing Company, 1952 (April 24, 1922 lecture in: GA 211)

Metamorphoses of the Soul - Paths of Experience, 2 Volumes. translated by C. Davy and C. von Arnim. London: Rudolf Steiner Press, 1983 (GA 58, 59)

The Mission of Individual Folk Souls in Relation to Teutonic Mythology. translated by A. H. Parker. London: Rudolf Steiner Press, 1970 (GA 121)

The Mission of the Archangel Michael. translated by Lisa D. Monges. Spring Valley: The Anthroposophic Press Inc., 1961 (Extracts from GA 194 and 174a)

The Mysteries of Light, of Space and of the Earth. New York: Anthroposophic Press, 1945 (lectures 9-12 from GA 194)

Mystery Knowledge and Mystery Centers. translation and revision by E. H. Goddard and D. S. Osmond. London: Rudolf Steiner Press, 1973 (GA 232)

The Mystery of the Trinity and The Mission of the Spirit. translated by James H. Hindes. Hudson: Anthroposophic Press, 1991 (GA 214)

The Mysteries of the East and of Christianity. translation revised by Charles Davy. London: Rudolf Steiner Press, 1972 (GA 144)

Occult History - Historical Personalities and Events in the Light of Spiritual Science. translation and revision by D. S. Osmond and Charles Davy, appendix and notes additional to those in the German text by D. S. Osmond. London: Anthroposophical Publishing Company, 1957 (GA 126)

The Occult Movement in the Nineteenth Century and its Relation to Modern Culture. translated by D. S. Osmond. London: Rudolf Steiner Press, 1973 (GA 254)

Occult Science and Occult Development - Christ at the Time of the Mystery of Golgotha and Christ in the Twentieth Century. revised translation by D. S. O. London: Rudolf Steiner Press, 1966 (Two lectures given in London on May 1st and 2nd, 1913, in: GA 233.)

The Occult Significance of the Bhagavad Gita. translated by George and Mary Adams with further emendations by Doris M. Bugbey. New York: The Anthroposophic Press Inc., 1968 (GA 146)

Occult Signs and Symbols. translated by Sarah Kurland with emendations by Gilbert Church, Ph.D. Spring Valley: The Anthroposophic Press Inc., 1975 (GA 101)

Philosophy, Cosmology and Religion. translated by Lisa D. Monges and Doris M. Bugbey, revised by Maria St. Goar and edited by Stewart C. Easton. Spring Valley: The Anthroposophic Press Inc., 1984 (GA 215)

The Philosophy of Freedom: The Basis for a Modern World Conception - Some Results of Introspective Observation Following the Methods of Natural Science. London: Rudolf Steiner Press, 1979 (GA 4)

The Philosophy of Spiritual Activity: Fundamentals of a Modern View of the World - Results of Introspective Observations According to the Methods of Natural Science; and, Truth and Knowledge - Introduction to "Philosophy of Spiritual Activity". translated by Rita Stebbing., introduction by Hugo S. Bergman, Ph.D., edited with notes by Paul M. Allen. West Nyack: Rudolf Steiner Publications Inc., 1963 (GA 4) (*The Philosophy of Spiritual Activity* is the same book as *The Philosophy of Freedom* Dr. Steiner said that the first title was appropriate for the West where spiritual activity was the issue, while the second title was appropriate for Central Europe where freedom was the issue. In addition, there is now a new translation by Christopher Bamford with yet a third title, *Intuitive Thinking as a Spiritual Path*. New York: The Anthroposophic Press, 1995.)

The Portal of Initiation - A Rosicrucian Mystery Drama. translated by H. Collison. <u>Four Mystery Plays, Volume I</u>. London: Anthroposophical Publishing Company, 1925 (in: GA 14) (The First Mystery Drama)

The Principle of Spiritual Economy in Connection with Questions of Reincarnation - An Aspect of the

Spiritual Guidance of Man. translated and introduced by Peter Mollenhauser. Hudson: The Anthroposophic Press, 1986 (in: GA 109/111)

Psychoanalysis & Spiritual Psychology. translated by May Laird-Brown, translated revised by Sabine H. Seiler, introduction by Robert J. Sardello. Hudson: The Anthroposophic Press, 1990 (Selected lectures: Nov. 10th and 11th, 1917 in: GA 74 - Feb. 25th and 27th, 1912 in: GA 143 - July 2nd, 1921 in: GA 205)

The Reappearance of Christ in The Etheric. editors Gilbert Church and Alice Wulsin. Spring Valley: The Anthroposophic Press Inc., 1983 (Selected lectures from: GA 118, 130, 182, 186)

The Redemption of Thinking - A Study in the Philosophy of Thomas Aquinas. translated and edited with an introduction and epilogue by A. P. Shepherd and Mildred Robertson Nicoll. Spring Valley: The Anthroposophic Press, 1983 (GA 74)

Reincarnation and Immortality. translations by Michael and Elisabeth Trapp, and Adam Bittleston, edited by Paul M. Allen. Blauvelt: Spiritual Science Library, 1970 (Selected lectures from the dates: Apr. 24th and 25th, 1918; Jan. 12th, 1916; Jan. 24th, 1922; Oct. 9th, 1916 and an essay written in 1905 entitled, *The Science of Spirit and the Social Question.*)

The Riddles of Philosophy. introduction by Fritz C. A. Koelln. Spring Valley: The Anthroposophic Press, 1973 (GA 18) (In this work, Rudolf Steiner summarizes the contributions of the Philosophers throughout the ages.)

Rosicrucian Esotericism. translated by D. S. Osmond. Spring Valley: The Anthroposophic Press, 1978 (in: GA 109/111)

Rosicrucianism and Modern Initiation. translated by Mary Adams. London: Rudolf Steiner Press, 1965 (GA 233a)

The Search for the New Isis - the Divine Sophia. Spring Valley: Mercury Press, 1983 (GA 202)

Secrets of the Threshold. translated by Ruth Pusch. Hudson: The Anthroposophic Press, 1987 (GA 147)

The Social Future. translated by Henry B. Monges. Spring Valley: The Anthroposophic Press Inc., 1972 (GA 332a)

The Soul's Awakening. translated by H. Collison. Four Mystery Plays, Volume II. London: Anthroposophical Publishing Company, 1925 (in: GA 14) (The Fourth Mystery Drama)

The Soul's Probation. translated by H. Collison. Four Mystery Plays, Volume I. London: Anthroposophical Publishing Company, 1911 (in: GA 14) (The Second Mystery Drama)

The Spiritual Guidance of Man. edited by Henry B. Monges. Spring Valley: The Anthroposophic Press Inc., 1976 (GA 15)

The Spiritual Hierarchies and Their Reflection in the Physical World. translated by R. M. Querido. New York: The Anthroposophic Press Inc., 1970 (GA 110)

The Spiritual Hierarchies and the Physical World - Reality and Illusion: The Inner Aspects of Evolution. translated by R. M. Querido and Jann Gates, introduction by Christopher Bamford. Hudson: The Anthroposophic Press Inc., 1996 (This edition contains the lecture cycles: *The*

Spiritual Hierarchies and Their Reflection in the Physical World [GA 110]; and, *The Inner Aspects of Evolution* [GA 132] in one volume; included with the essay by Georg Unger entitled, *Concerning the So-called Interchange of Venus and Mercury*; and the lecture by Rudolf Steiner, given in Dornach on January 11th, 1924 entitled, *Humanity's Relation to the Sun*.)

Spiritual Science and Medicine. London: Rudolf Steiner Press, 1975 (GA 312)

The Stages of Higher Knowledge. translated by Lisa D. Monges and Floyd McKnight. Hudson: The Anthroposophic Press Inc., 1967 (GA 12) (Formerly entitled, *The Gates of Knowledge*)

Study of Man - General Education Course. translated by Daphne Harwood and Helen Fox, revised for this edition by A. C. Harwood. London: Rudolf Steiner Press, 1975 (GA 293)

Supersensible Influences in the History of Mankind. translated by D. S. Osmond, assisted by Owen Barfield. London: Rudolf Steiner Publishing Co., 1956 (GA 216)

Supersensible Knowledge. translated by Rita Stebbing. Hudson: The Anthroposophic Press Inc., 1987 (GA 55)

Supersensible Man. London: Anthroposophical Publishing Company, 1961 (GA 231)

The Temple Legend - Freemasonry & Related Occult Movements. translated by John M. Wood, edited by E. M. Lloyd. London: Rudolf Steiner Press, 1985 (GA 93)

Theosophy - An Introduction to the Supersensible Knowledge of the World and the Destination of Man. translated by Henry B. Monges, revised by Gilbert Church, Ph.D. Hudson: The Anthroposophic Press Inc., 1971 (GA 9)

Theosophy of the Rosicrucian. translated by M. Cotterell and D. S. Osmond. London: Rudolf Steiner Press, 1981 (GA 99)

Three Streams in the Evolution of Mankind - The Connection of the Luciferic-Ahrimanic Impulses with the Christ-Jahve Impulse. revised translation by C. D. London: Rudolf Steiner Press, 1965 (GA 184)

Toward Imagination - Culture and the Individual. translated by Sabine H. Seiler. Hudson: The Anthroposophic Press, 1990 (GA 169)

Turning Points in Spiritual History. translated by Walter F. Fox, edited by Harry Collison. Blauvelt: Spiritual Science Library, 1987 (Six lectures given in Berlin on: Jan. 19, 1911 - Feb. 16, 1911 - Mar. 2, 1911 - Dec. 14, 1911 - Jan. 25, 1912)

Universe, Earth and Man in their Relationship to Egyptian Myths and Modern Civilization. London: Rudolf Steiner Press, 1987 (GA 105)

The Warmth Course. translated by George Adams, revised by Alice Barton Wulsin and Gerald F. Karnow, M.D., edited with introduction and notes by G. A. Balaster and A. Dollfus, translated by Gerald F. Karnow. Spring Valley: Mercury Press, 1988 (GA 321) (A translation of the "2nd Science Course")

The Way of Initiation and its Results. translated by Max Gysi and Clifford Bax, with some biographical notes by Edouard Schure. Ferndale: Trismegistus Press, 1980 (This reprint contains the two books: *The Way of Initiation, or How to Attain Knowledge of the Higher Worlds,* and; *Initiation and its Results* reproduced in facsimile. They were the early precursors of Rudolf Steiner's basic book, *Knowledge of Higher Worlds and its Attainment* [GA 10]. Although it is true that later Rudolf Steiner made many changes in the text of this basic material, and the translation perhaps is not the best; nonetheless, it is exceptionally readable.)

Ways to a New Style of Architecture. London: Anthroposophical Publishing Company, 1927 (GA 286)

The Wisdom of Man, of the Soul, and of the Spirit - Anthroposophy, Psychosophy, Pneumatosophy. translated by Samuel and Loni Lockwood, preface by Marie Steiner. New York: The Anthroposophic Press, 1971 (GA 115)

Wonders of the World - Ordeals of the Soul - Revelations of the Spirit. translation by Dorothy Lenn, assisted by Owen Barfield. London: Rudolf Steiner Press, 1963 (GA 129)

World-Economy - The Formation of a Science of World-Economics. translated by A. O. Barfield and T. Gordon-Jones. London: Rudolf Steiner Press, 1972 (GA 340)

World History in the Light of Anthroposophy. London: Rudolf Steiner Press, 1977 (GA 233)

The World of the Senses and the World of the Spirit. North Vancouver: Steiner Book Centre Inc., 1979 (GA 134)

Other Anthroposophical authors consulted:

Adams, George. *Physical and Ethereal Spaces.* London: Rudolf Steiner Press, 1978

Adams, George and Olive Whicher. *The Plant Between the Sun and the Earth.* London: Rudolf Steiner Press, 1980

Allen, Paul M. and Carlo Pietzner. (compilation and editing) *A Christian Rosenkreutz Anthology.* Blauvelt: Spiritual Science Library, 1981

Bennell, Margaret and Isabel Wyatt. *A Commentary on the Chymical Wedding of Christian Rosenkreutz.* Stroud: The Michael Press, n. d.

Barnwell, John. *Anthroposophical Cosmology - Based on the Work of Rudolf Steiner, Ehrenfried Pfeiffer, Walter Johannes Stein & Others.* Birmingham: Ichor Press, 1994

Baur, Alfred. *Healing Sounds: Fundamentals of Chirophonetics.* translated by Barbara Baldwin. Fair Oaks: Rudolf Steiner College Press, 1993

Betti, Mario. *The Sophia Mystery in Our Time.* translated by Pauline Wehrle. London: Temple Lodge Press, 1994

Biesantz, Hagen and Arne Klingborg. *The Goetheanum - Rudolf Steiner's Architectural Impulse.* with contributions by Ake Fant, Rex Raab and Nikolaus Ruff. translated by Jean Schmid. London: Rudolf Steiner Press, 1979

Bittleston, Adam and Jonathan Westphal. (editors) The Golden Blade, No. 33. London: Rudolf Steiner Press, 1981 (contains numerous articles on the Grail theme)

Blattman, George. *The Sun - The Ancient Mysteries and a New Physics.* Edinburgh: Floris Books, 1985

Bock, Emil. *The Apocalypse of Saint John.* Edinburgh: Floris Books, 1993

Bock, Emil. *Kings and Prophets - Saul, David, Solomon, Elijah, Jonah, Isaiah and Jeremiah.* Edinburgh: Floris Books, 1989

Bock, Emil. *Moses - From the Mysteries of Egypt to the Judges of Israel.* Edinburgh: Floris Books, 1986

Bock, Emil. *Saint Paul - Life, Epistles and Teaching.* Edinburgh: Floris Books, 1993

Bock, Emil. *The Three Years.* London: Christian Community Press, 1969

Easton, Stewart C. *Rudolf Steiner: Herald of a New Epoch.* Spring Valley: The Anthroposophic Press, 1980

Emmichoven, F. W. van. *The Reality in Which We Live - An Introduction to Rudolf Steiner's Spiritual Science (Anthroposophy) Describing the Central Position of the Mystery of Golgotha in the Evolution of Mankind.* translated by Rene Querido. East Grinstead: New Knowledge Books, 1964

Falck-Yitter, Harald. *Aurora: The Northern Lights in Mythology - History and Science.* Edinburgh: Floris Books, 1985

Forward, William and Andrew Wolpert. (editors) *Europe.* The Golden Blade, No. 43. Sussex: Imprint, 1991

Forward, William and Andrew Wolpert. (editors) *The Image of the Blood.* The Golden Blade, No. 48. Edinburgh: Floris Books, 1996 (Virtually the entire issue is dedicated to articles on the spiritual significance of the blood.)

Forward, William and Andrew Wolpert. (editors) *The Quest for the Grail.* The Golden Blade, No. 47. Edinburgh: Floris Books, 1994 (the entire issue consists of articles on the Grail theme)

Francke, Sylvia and Thomas Cawthorne. *The Tree of Life and the Holy Grail.* London: Temple Lodge Press, 1996 (A valiant effort at responding, out of Anthroposophy, to the materialistic speculations of *Holy Blood, Holy Grail.*)

Gabriel, Douglas J. *The Spirit of Childhood.* Berkley, MI: Trinosophia Press, 1995

Glas, Werner. *The Waldorf School Approach to History.* foreword by Stewart C. Easton. A Waldorf Institute of Mercy College - Curriculum Study. Detroit: The Waldorf Institute of Mercy College, 1963

Greub, Werner. *Wolfram von Eschenbach und die Wirklichkeit des Grals.* Dornach: Philosophisch-Anthroposophischer Verlag, 1974 (Unfortunately, so far, no English edition of this important seminal work exists.)

Grosse, Rudolf. *The Christmas Foundation; Beginning of a New Cosmic Age.* translated by Johanna Collis. North Vancouver: Steiner Book Centre, 1984

Grosse, Rudolf. *The Living Being Anthroposophia - A Search for the Archetypal Powers Who Guide Mankind.* translated by Johanna Collis. North Vancouver: Steiner Book Centre Inc., 1986

Hartmann, Georg. *The Goetheanum Glass-Windows.* edited by the Goetheanum - School of Spiritual Science. Dornach: Philosophisch-Anthroposophischer Verlag am Goetheanum, 1972

Hauschka, Rudolf. *The Nature of Substance.* translated by Marjorie Spock and Mary T. Richards. London: Rudolf Steiner Press, 1983

Hentschel, Martin, et al. *Rudolf Steiner - Tafelzeichnungen Entwurfte Architektur.* Ostfildern: Edition Tertium, 1994 (Although the text is in German, the first half of the work is a commentary on a series of full color photographic reproductions of Rudolf Steiner's blackboard drawings from his lectures, the second half is a study of Rudolf Steiner's architectural impulse.)

Hiebel, Frederick. *The Gospel of Hellas - The Mission of Ancient Greece and The Advent of Christ.* New York: Anthroposophic Press, 1949

Hiebel, Frederick. *Treasures of Biblical Research and the Conscience of the Times.* translated by Norman Macbeth. New York: The Anthroposophic Press, 1970 (The Author considers the Dead Sea Scrolls and the Essenes, in the light of Anthroposophy.)

Holtzapfel, Walter. *The Human Organs: Their Functional and Psychological Significance - Liver, Lung, Kidney, Heart.* East Grinstead: The Lanthorn Press, 1993

Husemann, Armin. *The Harmony of the Human Body - Musical Principles in Human Physiology.* Edinburgh: Floris Books, 1989

Jones, Michael. *Nuclear Energy - A Spiritual Perspective.* Edinburgh: Floris Books, 1983

Josephson, Jenny. "Breathing and Circulation and the Foundation Stone Meditation." in: The Golden Blade, No. 44. Sussex: Imprint, 1992

Josephson, Jenny. "The Heart and Lungs." in: The Golden Blade, No. 43. Sussex: Imprint, 1991

Kilner, Philip. "Our Heart - Sounding, Serving, Unifying." in: The Golden Blade, No. 46. Edinburgh: Floris Books, 1993 (important article on the heart and blood flow)

Kipfer, Paul and Evelyn F. Capel. *Deutsch-Englishes Worterverzeichnis aus der Anthroposophischen Literatur - Glossary for German and English Terms in Anthroposophy.* Studienmaterial der Freien Hochschule for Geisteswissenschaft Goetheanum. Dornach: Philosophisch-Anthroposophischer Verlag, 1976

Koenig, Karl. *Earth and Man.* Wyoming: Bio-Dynamic Literature, 1982 (These lectures contain important insights into the nature of the "earthly and cosmic nutrition streams.")

Koenig, Karl., M.D. "Embryology and World Evolution." translated by R. E. K. Meuss, F.I.L. in: The British Homeopathic Journal. (In this remarkable series of talks, Dr. Koenig explores the connection between embryology and the scheme of planetary evolution as given by Rudolf Steiner in *An Outline of Occult Science*, and elsewhere. Further bibliographic information is unavailable.)

Koenig, Karl. *The Human Soul.* Spring Valley: The Anthroposophic Press Inc., 1973

Kolisko, Eugen. *The Threefold Human Organism.* Bournemouth: Kolisko Archive, 1979

Lehrs, Ernst. *Man or Matter - Introduction to a Spiritual Understanding of Nature on the Basis of Goethe's Method of Training, Observation and Thought.* 2nd Edition, revised and enlarged. New York: Harper & Brothers Publishers, 1958 ("What Dr. Lehrs did for me was to suggest that Goethe's scientific views somehow fitted in with his imaginative work, that the same insight was struggling for expression in both, and that it is not reasonable to dismiss as utter nonsense in the field of scientific inquiry what we accept as inspired wisdom in poetry." T. S. Eliot)

Lehrs, Ernst, Ph.D. *'Rosicrucian Foundations of the Age of Natural Science' and other Articles.* Spring Valley: St. George Publications, 1976

Lievegoed, Bernard C. J. *The Battle for the Soul - The Working Together of Three Great Leaders of Humanity.* translated by Philip Mees, foreword by Christopher Schaefer. Stroud: Hawthorn Press, 1994

Lievegoed, Bernard C. J. *Mystery Streams in Europe and the New Mysteries.* Spring Valley: The Anthroposophic Press, 1982

Lievegoed, Bernhard J., M. D. *Towards the 21st Century: Doing the Good.* North Vancouver: Steiner Book Centre Inc., 1979

Marinelli, Ralph, Branko Furst, Hoyte van der Zee, Andrew McGinn, and William Marinelli. "The Heart is Not a Pump - A Refutation of the Pressure Propulsion Premise of Heart Function." in: Frontier Perspectives vol. 5, number 1, Fall/Winter. Philadelphia: The Center for Frontier Sciences at Temple University, 1995

Meeks, John. "Cosmic Rhythms and the Course of History." in: The Golden Blade, No. 31. London: Rudolf Steiner Press, 1979

Meeks, John. "Johannes Kepler and the Philosophical Defense of Astrology." in: Mercury Star Journal, Volume III, No. 1. London: The Christian Community - Temple Lodge Press, Easter, 1977

Mees, Dr. L. F. C. *Living Metals - Relationship Between Man and Metals.* London: Regency Press Ltd., 1974 (An excellent study of the occult significance of the metals according to Anthroposophy.)

Merry, Eleanor. *The Flaming Door - A Preliminary Study of the Mission of the Celtic Folk-Soul by means of Legends and Myths.* Introduction by Adam Bittleston. Sussex: New Knowledge Books, 1962

Meyer, T. H. and Elizabeth Vreede. *The Bodhisattva Question.* translated by John M. Wood. London: Temple Lodge Press, 1993

Meyer, T. H. *D. N. Dunlop - A Man of Our Time.* translated by Ian Bass. London: Temple Lodge Press, 1992

Meyer, T. H. (editor) *Light for the New Millennium: Rudolf Steiner's Association with Helmuth and Eliza von Moltke - Letters, Documents and After-Death Communications.* translated by Heidi Herrmann-Davey, William Forward and Martin Askew, London: Rudolf Steiner Press, 1997 (An important and inspiring source for understanding the karmic connections between the events of the 9th century and the 20th century.)

Pelikan, Wilhelm. *The Secrets of Metals.* translated by Charlotte Lebensart. Spring Valley: Anthroposophic Press Inc., 1973 (Still the best study in English of the occult significance of the metals according to Anthroposophy.)

Pfeiffer, Dr. E. E. *The Chymical Wedding of Christian Rosenkreutz - A Commentary.* transcribed by Fred and Alice Heckel. Spring Valley: Mercury Press, n.d.

Pfeiffer, Dr. E. E. *Life's Resources and Esoteric Streams of Christianity.* New York: Anthroposophic Press, 1963

Pfeiffer, Ehrenfried. *Heart Lectures.* Spring Valley: Mercury Press, n.d.

Pfeiffer, Ehrenfried. *Notes and Lectures,* 2 Volumes. introduction by Paul W. Scharff, M.D. Spring Valley n.d.

Pfeiffer, Ehrenfried E. *The Spiritual Leadership of Mankind.* Spring Valley: Mercury Press, 1985

Pfeiffer, Dr. Ehrenfried. *Sub-nature and Super-nature in the Physiology of Plant and Man - The True Foundations of Nutrition.* Spring Valley: Mercury Press, 1981

Powell, Robert. "Astronomia Nova: I - Julian the Apostate and the Birth of Cosmic Christianity." in: Mercury Star Journal, Volume III, No. 1. London: The Christian Community - Temple Lodge Press, Easter, 1977

Powell, Robert. "Grail Excursus - Essay Review." in: Mercury Star Journal, Volume III, No. 3. London: The Christian Community - Temple Lodge Press, Michaelmas, 1977 (A review of Werner Greub's important book, *Wolfram von Eschenbach und die Wirklichkeit des Grals.*)

Powell, Robert. *Hermetic Astrology - Towards a New Wisdom of the Stars, Volume 1 - Astrology and Reincarnation.* Kinsau: Hermetica, 1987

Powell, Robert, Willi Sucher and Richard Zienko. "Astronomia Nova - Christianity and the Holy Grail in the Light of Star Wisdom (continued)." in: Mercury Star Journal, Volume III, No. 3. London: The Christian Community - Temple Lodge Press, Michaelmas, 1977

Prokofieff, Sergei O. *The Cycle of the Seasons and the Seven Liberal Arts.* translated by Richard Michell. London: Temple Lodge Press, 1995

Prokofieff, Sergei O. *The Cycle of the Year as a Path of Initiation - An Esoteric Study of the Festivals.* translated by Simon Blaxland de Lange. London: Temple Lodge Press, 1991

Prokofieff, Sergei O. "The Future of the Slavic Peoples of the East and the Spiritual Tasks of Central Europe." in: The Golden Blade, No. 43. Sussex: Imprint, 1991

Prokofieff, Sergei O. *Eternal Individuality - Towards a Karmic Biography of Novalis.* translated by Simon Blaxland de Lange. London: Temple Lodge Press, 1992

Prokofieff, Sergei O. *The Heavenly Sophia and the Being Anthroposophia.* translated by Simon Blaxland de Lange. London: Temple Lodge Press, 1996

Prokofieff, Sergei O. *The Occult Significance of Forgiveness.* translated by Simon Blaxland de Lange. London: Temple Lodge Press, 1991

Prokofieff, Sergei O. *Rudolf Steiner and the Founding of the New Mysteries.* translated by Paul King, introduction, afterword and author's revisions and additions to the second edition translated by Simon Blaxland de Lange. London: Temple Lodge Press, 1994

Prokofieff, Sergei O. *Rudolf Steiner's Research into Karma and the Mission of the Anthroposophical Society.* translated by Richard Michell. London: Temple Lodge Press, 1995

Prokofieff, Sergei O. *The Spiritual Origins of Eastern Europe and the Future Mysteries of the Holy Grail.* translated by Simon Blaxland de Lange. London: Temple Lodge Press, 1993

Prokofieff, Sergei O. *The Twelve Holy Nights and the Spiritual Hierarchies.* translated by Simon Blaxland de Lange. London: Temple Lodge Press, 1993

Querido, Rene. *The Golden Age of Chartres - The Teachings of a Mystery School and the Eternal Feminine.* Edinburgh: Floris Books, 1987

Rath, Wilhelm. *The Friend of God From the High Lands.* Stroud: Hawthorn Press, 1991

Roboz, Steven. (compilation) *The Holy Grail - From the Works of Rudolf Steiner.* North Vancouver: Steiner Book Centre Inc., 1979

Roboz, Steven. (compilation) *Islam - Study Notes.* North Vancouver: Steiner Book Centre Inc., 1979

Schmidt-Brabant, Manfred. "Central Europe Between East and West - Present Tasks." translated by Anna Meuss and Johanna Collis. in: The Golden Blade, No. 43. Sussex: Imprint, 1991

Schoeffler, Heinz Herbert, M.D. *The Academy of Gondishapur - Aristotle on the Way to the Orient.* translated by Harold Jurgens, foreword by Friedrich Hiebel. Spring Valley: Mercury Press, 1993

Sease, Virginia. "The Spiritual Contribution of the West - Characteristics of America that point to the Future." in: The Golden Blade, No. 44. Sussex: Imprint, 1992

Seddon, Richard. (compilation and editing) *The End of the Millennium and Beyond - From the Work of Rudolf Steiner.* London: Temple Lodge Press, 1993

Seddon, Richard. *Europa - A Spiritual Biography.* London: Temple Lodge Press, 1995

Seddon, Richard. *The Mystery of Arthur at Tintagel.* London: Rudolf Steiner Press, 1990

Selawry, Alla. *Ehrenfried Pfeiffer - Pioneer of Spiritual Research and Practice.* translated by Joe Reuter, edited by Gerald Karnow. Spring Valley: Mercury Press, 1992

Shepherd, A. P. *The Incarnation.* Spring Valley: The Anthroposophic Press, 1976

Steffen, Albert. *The Death Experience of Manes - Drama in Five Acts.* translation by Daisy Aldan, Elly Havas Simons and Virginia Brett. New York: Folder Editions, 1970

Steffen, Albert. *Mystery-Drama - From Ancient to Modern Times.* translated by Virginia Brett. Hillsdale: Adonis Press, 1977

Stegmann, Carl. *The Other America - The Western World in the Light of Spiritual Science*, 2 Volumes. Oakland: Published by the Author, n.d.

Stein, Walter Johannes. *The Death of Merlin - Arthurian Myth and Alchemy.* Edinburgh: Floris Books, 1989

Stein, Walter Johannes. "England and the Foundation of Commercial Towns - The Origin of the Lohengrin Saga Traced According to English History." in: *The Death of Merlin - Arthurian Myth and Alchemy.* Edinburgh: Floris Books, 1989

Stein, Walter Johannes. *The Ninth Century - World History in the Light of the Holy Grail.* translated by Irene Groves, updated and revised by John M. Wood, with an introduction by John Matthews. London: Temple Lodge Press, 1991

Sucher, Willi. "Astronomia Nova: II - Christianity and the Holy Grail in the Light of Star Wisdom." in: Mercury Star Journal, Volume III, No. 2. London: The Christian Community, Temple Lodge Press, Midsummer 1977

Sucher, Willi. *Cosmic Christianity & The Changing Countenance of Cosmology - An Introduction to Astrosophy: A New Wisdom of the Stars.* Hudson: Anthroposophic Press, 1993 (Astrosophy is the branch of Anthroposophy that pertains to the study of Star-Wisdom; for which, Willi Sucher is the fundamental author.)

Sucher, Willi. *The Drama of the Universe - A New Interpretation.* Meadow Vista: Astrosophy Research Center, 1982

Sucher, Willi. *Isis-Sophia - An Outline of a New Star Wisdom,* 4 Parts. Privately Printed, 1951

Tautz, Johannes. *W. J. Stein - A Biography.* translated by John M. Wood, assisted by Marguerite A. Wood. London: Temple Lodge Press, 1990

Thomas, Nick. *The Battle for the Etheric Realm: Moral Technique and Etheric Technology - Apocalyptic Symptoms.* translated by J. Collis. London: Temple Lodge Press, 1995

Vreede, Elisabeth. *Elisabeth Vreede: Esoteric Studies - From Mathematics to Star-lore.* compiled and translated by Crispian Villeneuve. Pioneers of Spiritual Science 3. London: Temple Lodge Press, 1994

Wachsmuth, Dr. Guenther. *The Etheric Formative-Forces in Cosmos, Earth and Man - A Path of Investigation into the World of the Living,* Vol. 1. translated by Olin D. Wannamaker. London: Anthroposophical Publishing Company, 1932

Wachsmuth, Guenther. *The Evolution of Mankind: Cosmic Evolution - Incarnation of the Earth - the Great Migrations, and Spiritual History.* translated by Norman Macbeth. Dornach: Phil.-Anthr. Press, 1961

Wachsmuth, Guenther. *The Life and Work of Rudolf Steiner - From the Turn of the Century to His Death.* translated by Olin D. Wannamaker and Reginald E. Raab. New York: Whittier Books Inc., 1955

Wachsmuth, Guenther, Ph.D. *Reincarnation as a Phenomenon of Metamorphosis.* translated by Olin D. Wannamaker. Dornach: Philosophic-Anthroposophic Press, 1937

Wegman, Ita. *Ita Wegman: Esoteric Studies - The Michael Impulse.* compiled and translated by Crispian Villeneuve. Pioneers of Spiritual Science 1. London: Temple Lodge Press, 1993

Wegman, Ita. *The Mysteries.* compiled and translated by Crispian Villeneuve. London: Temple Lodge Press, 1995

Whicher, Olive. (compilation and biography) *George Adams: Interpreter of Rudolf Steiner - His Life and a Selection of His Essays.* foreword by Owen Barfield. Sussex: Henry Goulden Ltd., 1977

Whicher, Olive. *Sunspace - Science at a Threshold of Spiritual Understanding.* London: Rudolf Steiner Press, 1989

Wolf, Otto, M. D. "The Heart - A Secondary Organ." in: Mercury - Journal of the Anthroposophical Hygiene Association, No. 7. Spring Valley: Mercury Press, 1985

Wyatt, Isabel. *From Round Table to Grail Castle.* East Grinstead: The Lanthorn Press, 1979

Other authors consulted, along with sundry useful works pertaining to the subjects discussed within:

Addison, C. G. *The Knights Templars.* by C. G. Addison enlarged from the researches of numerous authors: de Vertot, Michaud, de Vogue, Taaffe, Proctor, Mackey, Scott, Burke, Burnes, Mills, Pike, James, Morris, Boutell, Creigh, Woof, Gourdin, Gardner, and others in the departments of chivalry, heraldry, and the Crusades, the whole affording a complete history of Masonic knighthood from the origin of the orders to the present time, adapted to the American System by Robert Macoy. New York: Masonic Publishing Company, 1874

Æsch Metzreph or Purifying Fire. A Chymico-Kabalistic treatise collected from the Kabala Denudata of Knorr von Rosenroth, translated by A Lover of Philalethes, 1714. preface, notes and explanations by "Sapere Aude" [W. Wynn Westcott]. Collectanea Hermetica, Volume IV. Kila: Kessinger Publishing Co., n.d. (also see: W. Wynn Westcott, *Collectanea Hermetica.*) (In the preface by W. Wynn Westcott, he comments on the significance of this important Kabalistic text: "The *Æsch Metzreph* is still extant as a separate treatise in what is called the Hebrew language, but which is more properly Aramaic Chaldee: it was a companion volume to the Chaldean *Book of Numbers* so often referred to by H. P. Blavatsky, and which is no longer to be procured, although I have reason to think that copies still exist in concealment.")

Agrippa von Nettesheim, Heinrich Cornelius. *De Occulta Philosophia.* Graz: Akad. Druck- und Verlagsanstalt, 1967 (First Edition, 1533)

Agrippa, Henry Cornelius. *Fourth Book of Occult Philosophy.* Kila: Kessinger Publishing Co., n.d.

Alan of Lille (Alanus ab Insulis). *Anticlaudianus or The Good and Perfect Man.* translation and commentary by James J. Sheridan. Pontifical Institute of Mediæval Studies - Mediæval Sources in Translation, Volume 14. Toronto: Pontifical Institute of Mediæval Studies, 1973

Alan of Lille (Alanus ab Insulis). *The Plaint of Nature.* translation and commentary by James J. Sheridan. Pontifical Institute of Mediæval Studies - Mediæval Sources in Translation, Volume 26. Toronto: Pontifical Institute of Mediæval Studies, 1980

Allen, Thomas George. (translator)*The Book of the Dead or Going Forth by Day - Ideas of the Ancient Egyptians Concerning the Hereafter as Expressed in Their Own Terms.* Studies in Ancient Oriental Civilization vol. 37. Chicago: The Oriental Institute of the University of Chicago, 1974

Allen, Richard Hinckley. *Star Names - Their Lore and Meaning.* New York: Dover Publications, 1963

A Member of the Michigan Bar. *Irish Celts - A Cyclopedia of Race History.* Containing biographical sketches of more than fifteen hundred distinguished Irish Celts, with a chronological index. Detroit: L. F. Kilroy & Co., 1884

Anderson, Daniel E. *The Masks of Dionysus - A Commentary on Plato's Symposium.* SUNY Series in Ancient Greek Philosophy. Albany: State University of New York Press, 1993

(Andreae, Johann Valentin.) *The Hermetick Romance: or The Chymical Wedding - Written in High Dutch by Christian Rosenkreutz.* translated by E. Foxcroft. London: A. Sowle, 1690 (reprinted in: Paul M. Allen and Carlo Pietzner's, *A Christian Rosenkreutz Anthology*)

Andressohn, J. C. *The Ancestry and Life of Godfrey of Bouillon.* Bloomington: Indiana University Press, 1947

The Anglo-Saxon Chronicle. edited and translated by G. N. Garmonsway. New York: Dutton, 1975

The Anglo-Saxon Chronicles - The Authentic Voices of England, From the Time of Julius Caesar to the Coronation of Henry II. translated and collated by Anne Savage. Godalming: CLB International, 1984

Angus, S. *The Religious Quests of the Graeco-Roman World - A Study in the Historical Background of Early Christianity.* New York: Biblio and Tannen, 1967

Anonymous. *St. John's Order of Freemasonry, or Masonic Brotherhood.* (1535)

Archiv fur Freimaurer und Rosenkreuzer, 2 Volumes. Berlin: A. Mylius, 1783

Aristotle. *The Basic Works of Aristotle.* translated by Richard McKeon. New York: Random House, 1941

Aristotle. *The Complete Works of Aristotle*, 2 Volumes. in the Oxford translation, edited by Jonathan Barnes. Bollingen Series, Volume LXXI/2. Princeton: Princeton University Press, 1984

Aristotle. *Metaphysics.* edited by W. D. Ross. Oxford: Oxford University Press, 1924

Aristotle. *Physics.* edited by W. D. Ross. Oxford: Oxford University Press, 1936

Assmann, Jan. *Egyptian Solar Religion in the New Kingdom - Re, Amun and the Crisis of Polytheism.* Studies in Egyptology. London: Kegan Paul International, 1995

St. Augustine. *The Confessions of St. Augustine.* translated by John Kenneth Ryan. Garden City: Image Books, 1958

St. Augustine. *St. Augustine - Selected Letters.* translated by James Houston Baxter. Loeb Classical Library. London: Heinemann, 1930

St. Augustine. *St. Augustine - The City of God.* an abridged version from the translation by Gerald G. Walsh et al., edited by Vernon J. Bourke. Garden City: Image Books, 1958

Bacon, Francis. *The Advancement of Learning.* (1605) (Available in many subsequent editions)

Bacon, Francis. *Novum Organum.* (1620) (Available in many subsequent editions)

Baigent, Michael, Richard Leigh, and Henry Lincoln. *Holy Blood, Holy Grail.* New York: Delacorte Press, 1982 (Impressive amount of research on the Knights Templars and related themes, but the whole second half of the book gets lost in wild speculations about a supposed royal line alleged by the authors to be descended from the child of Christ Jesus and Mary Magdalene; which, as mentioned before, is based on documents now known to be fabricated; and consequently, misses the whole point of the mission of Christ, and distorts its relationship to the mission of the Templar stream, which was to plant the seeds for the Christologically based social order which will come to fruition in the future epoch of the Spirit-Self.)

Baigent, Michael and Richard Leigh. *The Temple and the Lodge.* New York: Arcade Publishing, 1989

Bailey, H. W. *Zoroastrian Problems in the Ninth Century Books.* Oxford: Oxford University Press, 1943

Baines, John and Jaromir Malek. *Atlas of Ancient Egypt.* edited by Graham Speake. New York: Facts on File, 1980 (As the dates for Egyptian chronology are controversial I have, for the most part, used the dates given in this source. The authors explain their approach on page 36: "The dates are computed from ancient lists, especially the Turin royal papyrus, and various other sources, including a few pieces of astronomical evidence. The margin of error rises from about a decade in the New Kingdom and 3rd Intermediate Period to as much as 150 years for the beginning of the 1st Dynasty. Most 12th-Dynasty dates are fixed precisely, and 18th- and 19th-Dynasty ones must fit one of three astronomically determined alternatives; here a combination of the middle and lowest ones is used...")

Barber, Malcolm. *The Trial of the Templars.* Cambridge: Cambridge University Press, 1978

Barborka, Geoffrey A. *The Divine Plan.* written in the form of a commentary on H. P. Blavatsky's *Secret Doctrine* by Geoffrey A. Barborka expressly for the purpose of those who wish to read and gain a deeper understanding of *The Secret Doctrine.* Adyar: The Theosophical Publishing House, 1972 (A very useful systematic study of the Cosmology of H. P. Blavatsky's *Secret Doctrine.*)

Baring-Gould, Sabine. *Curious Myths of the Middle Ages.* edited with an introduction by Edward Hardy. Oxford: Oxford University Press, 1978

de Darneval, L. Tachet. *Legendary History of Ireland.* translated from the French by John Gilmary Shea. Boston: Patrick Donahoe, 1857

Barton, Tamsyn. *Ancient Astrology.* Sciences of Antiquity Series. London: Routledge, 1994

Bedier, Joseph. *Tristan and Iseult.* translated from the French by Hilaire Belloc. New York: Albert & Charles Boni, 1927

Begg, Ean and Deike. *In Search of the Holy Grail and the Precious Blood - A Traveller's Guide.* foreword by Michael Baigent. London: Thorsons, 1995 (A comprehensive guide to many of the historical sites associated with the Grail tradition.)

Berkhout, Carl T. and Jeffrey B. Russell. *Medieval Heresies: A Bibliography 1960-1979.* Pontifical Institute of Mediæval Studies - Subsidia Mediævalia, Volume 11. Toronto: Pontifical Institute of Mediæval Studies, 1981

St. Bernard of Clairvaux. *On the Song of Songs I - Sermons 1-20.* translated by Kilian Walsh O. C. S. O., introduction by M. Corneille Halflants O. C. S. O. Cistercian Fathers Series, No. 4. Kalamazoo: Cistercian Publications Inc., 1981

St. Bernard of Clairvaux. *On the Song of Songs II - Sermons 21-46.* translated by Kilian Walsh O. C. S. O., introduction by Dom Jean Leclercq. Cistercian Fathers Series, No. 7. Kalamazoo: Cistercian Publications Inc., 1976

St. Bernard of Clairvaux. *On the Song of Songs III - Sermons 47-66.* translated by Kilian Walsh O. C. S. O. & Irene M. Edmonds, introduction by Emero Stiegman. Cistercian Fathers Series, No. 31. Kalamazoo: Cistercian Publications Inc., 1979

St. Bernard of Clairvaux. *On the Song of Songs IV - Sermons 67-86.* translated by Irene M. Edmonds, introduction by Dom Jean Leclercq. Cistercian Fathers Series, No. 40. Kalamazoo: Cistercian Publications Inc., 1980

Bernardus Silvestris. *Cosmographia.* translated with an introduction and notes by Winthrop Wetherbee. New York: Columbia University Press, 1973

The Bhagavad Gita: The Book of Devotion - Dialogue Between Krishna, Lord of Devotion, and Arjuna, Prince of India. from the Sanskrit by William Q. Judge. Los Angeles: The Theosophy Company, 1971

The Bhagavad Gita. with an introductory essay, Sanskrit text, English translation and notes by S. Radhakrishnan. New Delhi: Harper Collins Publishers,1996

Blackburn, Paul. (selection and translations) *Proensa - An Anthology of Troubadour Poetry.* edited and introduced by George Economou. Berkeley: University of California Press, 1978

Blavatsky, H. P. *Isis Unveiled - A Master-Key to the Mysteries of Ancient and Modern Science and Theology.* 2 volumes in one. Los Angeles: The Theosophy Company, 1974 (facsimile of the 1877 first edition)

Blavatsky, H. P. *The Secret Doctrine.* 2 volumes in one. Los Angeles: The Theosophy Company, 1974 (facsimile of the 1888 first edition)

Blavatsky, H. P. *The Stanzas of Dzyan.* London: The Theosophical Publishing Society, 1908

Blavatsky, H. P. *The Theosophical Glossary.* Los Angeles: The Theosophy Company, 1973 (facsimile of the 1892 first edition)

Blavatsky, H. P. *Thoughts on Ormuzd and Ahriman.* U. L. T. Pamphlet No. 7. Bombay: The Theosophy Company Ltd., 1930 (reprint of an 1891 article)

Bolshakov, Andrey O. *Man and his Double in Egyptian Ideology of the Old Kingdom.* Ægypten und Altes Testament, Band 37. Wiesbaden: Harrassowitz Verlag, 1997

de Boron, Sire Robert. *The History of the Holy Grail.* translated by H. L. Skynner, edited by F. J. Furnival. Early English Text Society. London: N. Turner, 1861 (Translation of: *Roman l'Estoire dou Saint Graal*.)

The Book of Enoch. together with a reprint of the Greek fragments, translated by R. H. Charles. Kila: Kessinger Publishing Co., n.d.

The Book of Enoch the Prophet. translated by Richard Laurence, LL.D., Archbishop of Cashel, from an Ethiopic ms. in the Bodleian library, the text now corrected from his latest notes, with an introduction by Lyman Abbott (1883). Secret Doctrine Reference Series. San Diego: Wizards Bookshelf, 1973

Budge, E. A. Wallis. (translator) *The Book of the Dead - An English Translation of the Chapters, Hymns, Etc., of the Theban Recension, with Introduction, Notes, Etc.,* 3 Volumes in one. Books on Egypt and Chaldæa. New York: Barnes & Noble Inc., 1951

Budge, E. A. Wallis. *Osiris & The Egyptian Resurrection,* 2 Volumes. New York: Dover Publications, 1973

Budge, E. A. Wallis. *The Queen of Sheba and Her Only Son Menyelek.* London: Medici Society, 1922

Burckhardt, Titus. *Chartres and the Birth of the Cathedral.* translated from the German by William Stoddart, with a foreword by Keith Critchlow. Bloomington: World Wisdom Books, 1996

Burkitt, F. C. *The Religion of the Manichees.* Cambridge: Cambridge University Press, 1925

Burt, Calvin C., 96°. *Egyptian Masonic History of the Original and Unabridged Ancient and Ninety-six (96°) Rite of Memphis.* Kila: Kessinger Publishing Co., n.d.

Burton, Sir Richard. *The Thousand and One Arabian Nights.* (Available in numerous editions.)

Butler, Alfred J. *The Ancient Coptic Churches of Egypt.* 2 Volumes. Oxford: Clarendon Press, 1884

Canney, M. A. "'Heart and Reins' Further Notes on Hebrew Idioms." in: The Journal of the Manchester Oriental Society, Volume 1. Manchester: Manchester University Press, 1911

Capellanus, Andreas. *The Art of Courtly Love.* translated by J. J. Perry. New York: Columbia University Press, 1941

Carroll, Rev. John J. *An Authentic History of Ireland From the Earliest Times Down.* Chicago: Ezra A. Cook, 1910

Carroll, Rev. John S. *In Patria - An Exposition of Dante's Paradiso.* London: Hodder & Stoughton, 1911

Casartelli, L. C., Bishop of Salford. "'Heart and Reins' in Ancient Iran." in: The Journal of the Manchester Oriental Society, Volume 1. Manchester: Manchester University Press, 1911

Cerny, Jaroslav. *Ancient Egyptian Religion.* Hutchinson's University Library: World Religions. New York: Hutchinson House, 1952 (recently reprinted by: Greenwood Press, Westport, CT)

Charpentier, Louis. *The Mystery of Chartres Cathedral.* translated by Sir Ronald Frazer in collaboration with Janette Jackson. London: Research Into Lost Knowledge Organization, 1972

Chretien de Troyes. *Arthurian Romances: Erec and Enide, Cliges, Lancelot, Yvain and Perceval.* translated with an introduction and notes by D.D.R. Owen. Everyman's Library. London: J.M. Dent & Sons Ltd., 1987

Chretien de Troyes. *Perceval, or the Story of the Grail.* translated by Ruth Harwood Cline. Athens: The University of Georgia Press, 1985

Chretien de Troyes. *The Story of the Grail.* translated by R. W. Linker. Chapel Hill: The University of North Carolina Press, 1952

Cicero. *Somnium Scipionis.* Secret Doctrine Reference Series. San Diego: Wizards Bookshelf, n.d.

Clagett, Marshall. *Ancient Egyptian Science - A Source Book, Volume 1 - Knowledge and Order.* Memoirs of the American Philosophical Society, Volume 184. Philadelphia: American Philosophical Society, 1989

Clagett, Marshall. *Ancient Egyptian Science - A Source Book, Volume 2. - Calendars, Clocks, and Astronomy.* Memoirs of the American Philosophical Society, Volume 214. Philadelphia: American Philosophical Society, 1995 (This two volume set contains translations of the fundamental remaining ancient Egyptian sources on cosmogony and cosmology, explored in relationship to the ancient Egyptian concept of Ma`at or Cosmic-Order.)

Clark, R. T. Rundle. *Myth and Symbol in Ancient Egypt.* London: Thames & Hudson, 1959

de Conick, April D. *Seek to See Him - Ascent and Vision Mysticism in the Gospel of Thomas.* Supplements to Vigiliæ Christianæ. Volume XXXIII. Leiden: E. J. Brill, 1996

Cooper-Oakley, Isabel. *The Count of Saint Germain.* introduction by Paul M. Allen. Blauvelt: Rudolf Steiner Publications, 1970

Cooper-Oakley, Isabel. *Masonry & Medieval Mysticism - Traces of a Hidden Tradition.* London: Theosophical Publishing House Ltd., 1977

Cory, Isaac Preston. *Ancient Fragments of the Phœnician, Chaldæn, Egyptian, Tyrian, Carthaginian, Indian, Persian, and other writers in Greek and English: with an introductory dissertation, and an inquiry into the Philosophy and Trinity of the Ancients.* London: Pickering, 1828

la Coudrette. *The Romans of Partenay, or of Lusignen: otherwise known as The Tale of Melusine.* translated from the French of La Coudrette (before 1500 A.D.) formerly edited from a unique manuscript in the library of Trinity College, Cambridge, with an introduction, notes, and glossarial index, and now revised by the Rev. Walter W. Skeat. Early English Text Society, Original Series, No. 22. 1866. London: Kegan Paul, Trench, Trubner & Co., Ltd., 1899

Craven, Rev. Dr. J. B. *Doctor Robert Fludd (Robertus de Fluctibus) The English Rosicrucian, Life and Writings.* Kirkwall, 1902

Craven, Rev. Dr. J. B. *Count Michael Maier Doctor of Philosophy and of Medicine, Alchemist, Rosicrucian, Mystic, A.D. 1568-1622, Life and Writings.* Kirkwall, 1910

Cristiani, Msgr. Leon. *St. Bernard of Clairvaux - 1190-1153.* translated by M. Angeline

Bouchard. Boston: St. Paul Editions, 1983

Crollius, Oswaldus. (see: P. M. Allen and C. Pietzner's, *A Christian Rosenkreutz Anthology*.)

Currer-Briggs, Noel. *The Shroud and the Grail - A Modern Quest for the True Grail.* London: George Weidenfeld and Nicolson Ltd., 1987

The Chronicle of San Juan de la Pena - A Fourteenth Century Official History of the Crown of Aragon. translated with an introduction and notes by Lynn H. Nelson. Middle Ages Series. Philadelphia: University of Pennsylvania Press, 1991

Dan, Joseph. (editor) *The Early Kabbalah.* New York: Paulist Press, 1986

Dante Alighieri. *The Divine Comedy.* (Available in many editions.)

Dante Alighieri. *The Portable Dante.* translations by Laurence Binyon and D. G. Rossetti. edited with an introduction by Paolo Milano.

Davidson, Gustav. *A Dictionary of Angels - Including the Fallen Ones.* New York: Free Press, 1971

(*The Dead Sea Scrolls*). *The Dead Sea Scriptures.* translated with an introduction and notes by Theodor H. Gaster. Garden City: Doubleday Anchor Books, 1957

Dee, John. *The Hieroglyphic Monad.* translated by J. W. Hamilton-Jones. London: 1947 (first published in Latin under the title *Monas Hieroglyphica*, Antwerp: 1564)

Denomy, A. J. *The Heresy of Courtly Love.* New York: Macmillan Company, 1947

Dhammapada. translated into Tibetan from the Pali by dGe-'dun Chos-'phel, translated into English from the Tibetan by Dharma Publishing Staff. Tibetan Translations Series. Berkeley: Dharma Publishing, 1985 (An excellent edition of a fundamental Buddhist text that is composed of sayings of the Buddha.)

Dionysius the Areopagite. *The Complete Works.* translated by Colm Lubheid. Mahwah: Paulist Press, 1987

Dionysius the Areopagite. *Mystical Theology and The Celestial Hierarchies.* translated from the Greek with Commentaries by the Editors of the Shrine of Wisdom. Surrey: The Shrine of Wisdom, 1965

Dionysius the Areopagite. *The Divine Names and The Mystical Theology.* translated by C. E. Rolt. London. The Society for Promoting Christian Knowledge, 1971

Dionysius the Areopagite. *The Theologia Mystica.* Being the treatise of Saint Dionysius pseudo-Areopagite on Mystical Theology, together with the First and Fifth Epistles, translated from the Greek with an Introduction by Alan Watts. Sausalito: The Society for Comparative Philosophy, Inc., 1971

Dorman, Peter F. *The Monuments of Senenmut - Problems in Historical Methodology.* Studies in Egyptology. London: Kegan Paul International, 1988

Dorman, Peter F. *The Tombs of Senenmut - The Architecture and Decoration of Tombs 71 and 353.*

The Metropolitan Museum of Art Egyptian Expedition, Vol. 24. New York: The Metropolitan Museum of Art, 1991

Duby, Georges. *The Age of the Cathedrals - Art and Society, 980-1420.* translated by Eleanor Levieux and Barbara Thompson. Chicago: The University of Chicago Press, 1981

(Eckhart, Meister.) *Meister Eckhart - A Modern Translation.* by Raymond Bernard Blakney. New York: Harper & Row Publishers, 1941

Eckhart, Meister. *The Essential Sermons, Commentaries, Treatises, and Defense.* translated by B. McGinn. Mahwah: Paulist Press, 1981

(Edda Saemundar). *Poems of the Elder Edda.* translated by Patricia Terry, with an introduction by Charles W. Dunn. Philadelphia: University of Pennsylvania Press, 1990

Edwards, I. E. S. "The Air-Channels in Chephren's Pyramid." in: Studies in Ancient Egypt, the Aegean, and the Sudan - Essays in Honor of Dows Dunham. Boston: Museum of Fine Arts, 1981

Einhard. *The Life of Charlemagne.* translated by Samuel Epes Turner, with a foreword by Sidney Painter. Ann Arbor: The University of Michigan Press, 1960

Ellis, Peter Berresford. *The Druids.* Grand Rapids: W. B. Eerdmans Publishing Company, 1995

Etz, Donald V. "A New Look at the Constellation Figures in the Celestial Diagrams." in: Journal of the American Research Center in Egypt, Volume XXXIV. Boston: The American Research Center in Egypt, 1997 (A study of the Astronomical ceiling of the tomb of Senenmut.)

Euclid of Megara. *The Elements of the Geometrie of the most ancient Philosopher Eucilde of Megara.* faithfully (now first) translated into the Englishe toung, by H. Billingsley, Citizen of London . . . With a very fruitfull Praeface made by M. I. Dee [John Dee]. London: Iohn Daye,1570

Evans-Wentz, W. Y. *The Fairy-Faith in Celtic Counties.* Oxford: Oxford University Press, 1911

Faulkner, Raymond O. (translator) *The Ancient Egyptian Coffin Texts*, 3 Volumes. Warminster: Aris and Philipps Ltd., 1973-1978

Faulkner, Raymond O. (translator) *The Ancient Egyptian Pyramid Texts*. Warminster: Aris & Philipps Ltd., 1969

Faulkner, Raymond O. (translator) *The Egyptian Book of the Dead - The Book of Going Forth by Day.* San Francisco: Chronicle Books, 1994

Faulkner, Raymond O. "The King and the Star Religion in the Pyramid Texts.." in: Journal of Near Eastern Studies, Volume XXV. Chicago: University of Chicago Press, 1966

Faivre, Antoine. *Access to Western Esotericism.* SUNY Series in Western Esoteric Traditions. Albany: State University of New York Press, 1994

Faivre, Antoine. *The Golden Fleece and Alchemy.* SUNY Series in Western Esoteric Traditions. Albany: State University of New York Press, 1993

Ferguson, Lady. *The Story of the Irish Before the Conquest - From the Mythical Period to the*

Invasion under Strongbow. Dublin: Sealy, Bryers & Walker, 1903

Findel, J. G. *History of Freemasonry.* translated from the 2nd German edition, with a preface by G. von Dalen. London: 1866

Fitzpatrick, Benedict. *Ireland and the Foundations of Europe.* New York: Funk & Wagnalls Co., 1927 (This is a valuable study of the contributions made to the Christian conversion of Europe by the Irish monks. The author provides a extensive study of the great monastic schools in Ireland, that were founded between the 5th and 7th centuries, which were some of the greatest seats of learning in Europe until they were closed down by the English beginning in the 16th century. It is said that, in the Middle Ages, when most of the European nobility was illiterate, simple Irish farmers could read Latin and Greek in addition to Gaelic. There is also a considerable amount of information on Johannes Scotus Erigena.)

Fleck, Conrad. *The Sweet and Touching Tale of Fleur and Blanchefleur.* translated by Mrs. Leighton. London: Daniel O'Connor, 1922

Fludd, Robert. *Summum Bonum quod est verum Magiae Cabalae Alchymiae Fratrum Crucis verorum...* Frankfurt: Joachimum Frizium, 1629 ("The authorship of this work has been denied by Fludd, but it is very evident that he was largely responsible for its production and certainly approved of it. It is written in defense of the Rosicrucian Fraternity's claims, and contains the views of Fludd and those of his friends." F. Leigh Gardiner quoted from: *A Catalogue Raisonne of the Works on the Occult Sciences - Rosicrucian Books*, by F. Leigh Gardiner. London: Privately Printed, 1923, which is reprinted in: Paul M. Allen and Carlo Pietzner, *A Christian Rosenkreutz Anthology.*)

Frankfort, H. *Kingship and the Gods.* Chicago: University of Chicago Press, 1948

Fulcanelli. *Le Mystere des Cathedrales - Et l'interpretation esoterique des symboles hermetiques du grand œuvre.* Societe Nouvelle des Editions Pauvert: Paris: 1964

Fulcanelli. *Le Mystere des Cathedrales - Esoteric Interpretation of the Hermetic Symbols of the Great Work.* translated from the French by Mary Sworder, with prefaces by Eugene Canseliet F. C. H., and an introduction by Walter Lang. London: Neville Spearman Ltd., 1971

Fulcanelli. *Fulcanelli - Master Alchemist.* translated from the French by Mary Sworder. Albuquerque: Brotherhood of Life 1986 (reprint of above)

Gabriel. *Goddess Meditations - From Isis to Sophia.* Berkley, MI: Trinosophia Press, 1994

Gabrieli, Francesco. *Arab Historians of the Crusades.* selected and translated from Arabic sources by Francesco Gabrieli. translated from the Italian by E. J. Costello. London: Routledge & Kegan Paul Ltd, 1969

Gardiner, Alan H. *Egyptian Grammar.* Oxford: The Griffith Institute, Clarendon Press, 1927

Gardiner, Alan H. "The Secret Chambers of the Sanctuary of Thoth." in: Journal of Egyptian Archaeology, Volume 11. London: Egypt Exploration Society, 1925

Gardiner, Laurence (The Chevalier Labhran de Saint Germain). *Bloodline of the Holy Grail: The Hidden Lineage of Jesus Revealed.* foreword by Prince Michael of Albany. Shaftsbury: Element Books Ltd., 1996 (Although this is an invaluable genealogical reference by an official genealogist - and I mean no disrespect in the following - but sadly the author has been caught up into the wild hoax from the book *Holy Blood, Holy Grail*; i.e., that Jesus and Mary Magdalene are the ancestors of many of the royal houses of Europe. These types of theories help create a mood of receptivity for the illusory longing for a physical Messiah to "put things right", not knowing that the Christ came already 2,000 years ago; and as he said, "I shall be with you always." If Christ needed to take on another physical incarnation, it would imply that the first was a failure. Instead of looking for a physical incarnation, we should instead humbly strive to approach Him in the Spiritual World. It is no wonder that the great Initiates accomplish their work in the world in anonymity, for they would be swept-up in the misplaced devotion of the "cult of personality.")

Gesenius, W. *Gesenius' Hebrew Grammar.* edited and enlarged by E. Kautzsch, 2nd. edition revised by A. E. Cowley. Oxford: Clarendon Press, 1910

Geoffrey of Monmouth. *The History of the Kings of Britain.* translated with an introduction by Lewis Thorpe. London: The Folio Society, 1969

Gikatilla, Rabbi Joseph ben Abraham. *Sha'are Orah - Gates of Light.* translated by Avi Weinstein, with a foreword by Arthur Hertzberg and an historical introduction by Moshe Idel. The Sacred Literature Series. San Francisco: Harper Collins Publishers, 1994 (Written in 13th century Spain and finally translated into English, this is perhaps the clearest exposition of Kabbalistic thought produced in the Middle Ages.)

Godwin, Joscelyn. *The Theosophical Enlightenment.* SUNY Series in Western Esoteric Traditions. Albany: State University of New York Press, 1994

Godwin, Malcolm. *The Holy Grail - Its Origins, Secrets & Meaning Revealed.* New York: Viking Studio Books, 1994

Goethe, Johann Wolfgang von. *Conversations with Eckermann.* compiled by Johann Peter Eckermann. London: M. Walter Dunn, 1901

Goethe, Johann Wolfgang von. *Faust - A Tragedy.* 2 Volumes in one. translated in the original metres by Bayard Taylor. Boston: Houghton Mifflin Co., 1912 (Still considered by many to be the best English translation of *Faust*.)

Goethe, Johann Wolfgang von. *Goethe - Conversations and Encounters.* edited and translated by David Luke and Robert Pick. Chicago: Henry Regnery Company, 1966

Goethe, Johann Wolfgang von. *The Metamorphoses of Plants.* Biodynamic Farmers and Gardeners Association, 1974

Goethe, Johann Wolfgang von. *Theory of Colors.* translated with notes by Charles Lock Eastlake, introduction by Deane B. Judd. Cambridge: The M. I. T. Press, 1970

Goldin, F. (translator) *Lyrics of the Troubadours and Trouveres.* New York: Doubleday, 1973

Gordon, Robert. "The Significance of the Paradise Myth." American Journal of Semitic Languages and Literatures, Volume LII. Chicago: 1935-1936

Green, Alice Stopford. *History of the Irish State to 1014.* London: Macmillan and Co., Ltd., 1925

Greenfield, Allen H., Hon. 33°, 90°, 95°. (editor and introduction) *The Compleat Rite of Memphis.*

Marietta: Luxor Press, 1998 (This remarkable work brings together in one volume some of the most important features of the Ancient and Ninety-six Degree Rite of Memphis that was spoken of so highly by Rudolf Steiner; and also, includes much illuminating commentary by Allen Greenfield on this difficult to research subject.)

Greenhill, Eleanor Simmons. "A Legend of Terrestrial Paradise in Wauchier's Continuation of the Conte du Graal." M.A. thesis, Columbia University, 1945

Greenlees, Duncan. *The Gospel of the Prophet Mani.* edited and almost wholly newly translated from many languages of original Manichean texts and of excerpts by others, for the first time in English, with a life of the Prophet, an outline of Manichean history, and other introductions, explanatory commentary, full annotations and an illuminating index by Duncan Greenlees, M. A. (Oxon.). The World Gospel Series, Volume 12. Adyar: The Theosophical Publishing House, 1956

Gregory of Tours. *The History of the Franks*, 2 Volumes. translated by O. M. Dalton. Oxford: Clarendon Press, 1927

Griffiths, J. Gwyn. (translation and commentary) *Apuleius of Madauros: The Isis Book (Metamorphoses, Book XI)*. Etudes Preliminaires aux Religions Orientales dans l'Empire Romain publiees par M. J. Vermaseren, Tome 29. Leiden: E. J. Brill, 1975

Griffiths, J. Gwyn. *The Origins of Osiris and his Cult*. Studies in the History of Religions (Supplements to Numen), Volume XL. Leiden: E. J. Brill, 1980

Guenon, Rene. *Fundamental Symbols - The Universal Language of Sacred Science.* compiled and edited by Michel Valsan, translated by Alvin Moore, Jr., revised and edited by Martin Lings. Cambridge: Quinta Essentia, 1995

"*Guillaume d'Orange*" *- Four Twelfth-Century Epics.* introduction and translation by Joan M. Ferrante. New York: 1974

Guilliame de Tyre. *A History of Deeds Done Beyond the Sea.* (c. 1180) translated by E. A. Babcock and A. C. Krey. New York: Columbia University Press, 1943

Hale, Reginald B. *The Magnificent Gael.* Ottawa: MOM Printing, Ltd., 1976

Hall, Manly P. *Americas Assignment with Destiny.* The Adepts in the Western Tradition. Los Angeles: The Philosophical Research Society, 1976

Hall, Manly P. *An Encyclopedic Outline of Masonic, Hermetic, Qabbalistic and Rosicrucian Symbolical Philosophy - The Secret Teachings of all Ages.* Los Angeles: The Philosophical Research Society, 1959

Hall, Manly P. *Man the Grand Symbol of the Mysteries - Essays in Occult Anatomy.* Los Angeles: The Philosophical Research Society, 1932

Hall, Manly P. *Masonic Orders of Fraternity.* The Adepts in the Western Tradition. Los Angeles: The Philosophical Research Society, 1976

Hall, Manly P. *Orders of the Great Work - Alchemy.* The Adepts in the Western Tradition. Los Angeles: The Philosophical Research Society, 1976

Hall, Manly P. *Orders of the Quest - The Holy Grail.* The Adepts in the Western Tradition. Los Angeles: The Philosophical Research Society, 1962

Hall, Manly P. *Orders of the Universal Reformation - Utopias.* The Adepts in the Western Tradition. Los Angeles: The Philosophical Research Society, 1976

Hancock, Graham. *The Sign and the Seal.* New York: Simon & Schuster Inc., 1993 (see: Kebra Negast)

Harrison, C. G. *The Transcendental Universe - Six Lectures on Occult Science, Theosophy, and the Catholic Faith, Delivered before the Berean Society.* London: George Redway, 1896

Harrison, C. G. *The Transcendental Universe - Six Lectures on Occult Science, Theosophy, and the Catholic Faith, Delivered before the Berean Society.* introduction and notes by Christopher Bamford. Hudson: Lindisfarne Press, 1993

Harrison, C. G. *"The Fourth Mystery" Birth and Death.* London: Rider, n.d. [1929]

Hart, T. E. "Chrestien, Macrobius, and Chartrean Science: The Allegorical Robe as Symbol of Textual Design in the Old French Erec." in: Mediæval Studies, Volume XLIII. Toronto: Pontifical Institute of Mediæval Studies, 1981

Heckethorn, Charles W. *Secret Societies of All Ages and Countries,* 2 Volumes. London: George Redway, 1897

Heinrich von dem Turlin. *Diu Crone (The Crown).* translated by J. W. Thomas. Lincoln: University of Nebraska Press, 1989

Hermes Trismegistus. *Tabula Smaragdina,* or *The Emerald Tablet.* (see: Manly P. Hall, *An Encyclopedic Outline of Masonic, Hermetic, Qabbalistic and Rosicrucian Symbolical Philosophy - The Secret Teachings of all Ages,* or, Allen, Paul M. and Carlo Pietzner.)

Higgins, Frank C. *Hermetic Masonry.* Ferndale: Trismegistus Press, 1980 (facsimile edition of: *The Beginning of Masonry - A Collection of Forty Papers on the Hidden Mysteries of Freemasonry,* 1916; and, *A. U. M. "The Lost Word",* 1914)

Hillgarth, J. N. (editor) *Christianity and Paganism, 350-750 - The Conversion of Western Europe.* Middle Ages Series. Philadelphia: University of Pennsylvania Press, 1986

Hogg, Hope W. "'Heart and Reins' in the Ancient Literatures of the Nearer East." in: The Journal of the Manchester Oriental Society. Volume 1. Manchester: Manchester University Press, 1911

Holmes, Urban T. and Amelia Klenke. *Chretien de Troyes and the Grail.* Chapel Hill: University of North Carolina Press, 1959

The Holy Bible. Containing the Old and New Testaments. translated out of the Original Tongues and with the Former Translations diligently compared and revised; commonly known as the authorized (King James) Version. Nashville: A. J. Holman, 1975

Howarth, Stephen. *The Knights Templar - Christian Chivalry and the Crusades, 1095-1314.* New York: Atheneum, 1982

Huckel, Oliver. *Parsifal - A Mystical Drama by Richard Wagner Retold in the Spirit of the Bayreuth Interpretation.* New York: Thomas Y. Crowell & Co., 1903

Hurry, Jamieson B. *Imhotep - The Egyptian God of Medicine.* Oxford: Oxford University Press, 1926

Iamblicus. *The Egyptian Mysteries.* translated by Alexander Wilder. New York: 1911

Iamblicus. *On the Mysteries of the Egyptians.* translated by Thomas Taylor. London: Bertram Dobell, 1895

Inge, W. R. *The Philosophy of Plotinus*, 2 Volumes. London: George Redway, 1923

Ingham, M. F. "The Length of the Sothic Cycle." in: Journal of Egyptian Archaeology, Volume 55. London: Egypt Exploration Society, 1969

Jaeger, C. Stephen. *The Origins of Courtliness - Civilizing Trends and the Formation of Courtly Ideals, 939-1210.* Middle Ages Series. Philadelphia: University of Pennsylvania Press, 1985

James, Edward. *The Origins of France - From Clovis to the Capetians 500-1000.* New Studies in Medieval History. New York: Macmillan Publishing Co., Inc., 1982

John the Scot (Johannes Scotus Erigena). *Periphyseon - On the Division of Nature.* translated by Myra L. Uhlfelder, with summaries by Jean A Potter. The Library of Liberal Arts. Indianapolis: The Bobbs-Merrill Co., Inc., 1976

de Joinville, Sire J. *Chronicles of the Crusades.* translated by M. Shaw. Harmondsworth: Penguin Books, 1976

Judge, William Q. *Instructions to the Esoteric Section of the Theosophical Society.* contained in: H. P. Blavatsky Collected Writings, Volume XII - 1889-1890. Wheaton: Theosophical Publishing House, 1980 (These once secret papers provide detailed information on the path of discipleship according to the Oriental teachings of the E. S. The fact that text of these instructions were actually written by William Q. Judge is indicated by his own words: ". . . I wrote the rules of the E. S. T. myself in London in 1888 at H. P. B.'s request and under the direction of the Master . . ." Although it is a different school of esotericism from Anthroposophy, within these papers are contained a wealth of instruction; for, we must not forget that in the early days Rudolf Steiner lectured to the E. S. T. This material was well understood by many of Rudolf Steiner's early students, and provided a point of departure for the cycle of 31 lectures that were given in Berlin between September 26th, and November 5th of 1905, and were published under the title *Foundations of Esotericism*; thereby, providing a reliable bridge to the works of H. P. B.)

Kebra Nagast (The Glory of Kings). compiled, edited and translated by Miguel F. Brooks. Lawrenceville: The Red Sea Press, 1996 (Translated from the ancient Ethiopic "Geez" language, the *Kebra Nagast* is the official account of the Ethiopian Jews (Falasha) and Christians concerning King Solomon and Queen Makeda of Saba, and how their son Menyelek (Menelik) brought the Ark of the Covenant to Ethiopia (Saba). Whether this was the original Ark or a copy made by King Solomon continues to be a matter of dispute. Apparently, according to Graham Hancock's book *The Sign and the Seal*, the Ethiopian's still possess this Ark in Axum and have used it in their rituals since the times of King Menyelek.)

Kakosy, Laszlo. "Ideas About the Fallen State of the World in Egyptian Religion - Decline of the Golden Age." in: Acta Orientalia Academiæ Scientiæ Hungaricæ, Volume 17. Budapest: 1964

Kakosy, Laszlo. "The Plundering of the Pyramid of Cheops." in: Studien zur Altægyptischen Kultur, Band 16. Hamburg: Helmut Buske Verlag, 1989

Kelly, J. N. D. *The Oxford Dictionary of Popes.* Oxford: Oxford University Press, 1986

King, E. J. *The Grand Priory of The Order of the Hospital of St. John of Jerusalem in England - A Short History.* with a foreword by Major-General The Earl of Scarbrough, G. B. E., K. C. B., A. D. C., F. S. A. Sub-Prior of the Order. London: St. John's Gate, 1924

King, Leonard W. "'Heart and Reins' in Relation to Babylonian Liver Divination." in: The Journal of the Manchester Oriental Society, Volume 1. Manchester: Manchester University Press, 1911

Klimkeit, Hans Joachim. *Gnosis on the Silk Road - Gnostic Parables, Hymns and Prayers from Central Asia.* San Francisco: Harper Collins, 1993

Kreutz, Barbara M. *Before the Normans - Southern Italy in the Ninth & Tenth Centuries.* Philadelphia: University of Pennsylvania Press, 1991

Lancelot of the Lake. translated by C. Corley. Oxford: Oxford University Press, 1989

Lamberton, Robert. *Porphyry On the Cave of the Nymphs.* translator and introductory essay by Robert Lamberton. Barrytown: Station Hill Press, 1983

Langermann, Y. Tzvi. (translator and editor) *Yemenite Midrash - Philosophical Commentaries on the Torah.* San Francisco: Harper Collins Publishers, 1996

Layamon. *Arthurian Chronicles.* translated by E. Mason. London: J. M. Dent & Sons Ltd., 1972

Linker, R. W. (translator) *The Story of the Grail (Li Contes del Graal).* Chapel Hill: University of North Carolina Press, 1952

Loomis, L. *The Grail.* Princeton: Princeton University Press, 1991

Loomis, Roger Sherman. *Arthurian Literature in the Middle Ages.* Oxford: Oxford University Press, 1969

Loomis, Roger Sherman. *Celtic Myth and Arthurian Romance.* New York: Columbia University Press, 1926

Loomis, Roger Sherman. *The Grail - From Celtic Myth to Christian Symbol.* New York: Columbia University Press, 1963

Lomax, Derek W. and David Mackenzie. (editors) *God and Man in Medieval Spain - Essays in Honour of J. R. L. Highfield.* Warminster: Aris & Philipps Ltd., 1989

Lord, Edith. *Cultural Patterns of Ethiopia - Queen of Sheba's Heirs.* Africana Culture and History Series, Volume 1. Washington D.C.: Acropolis Books, 1970 (A fascinating book by the former Advisor on Education to the late Emperor of Ethiopia; whom, according to the ancient Ethiopic text the *Kebra Nagast*, was descended from King Solomon and Queen Makeda of Saba [Sheba].)

Lost Books of the Bible and the Forgotten Books of Eden. Cleveland: The World Publishing Company, 1963 (Contains apocryphal material on Joseph of Arimathea, Nicodemus and other related Grail themes.)

Llull, Ramon. *Doctor Illuminatus - A Ramon Llull Reader.* edited and translated by Anthony Bonner, with a new translation of The Book of the Lover and the Beloved, by Eva Bonner. The Mythos Series. Princeton: Princeton University Press, 1993

Lovelich, Henry. (translator) *History of the Holy Grail (Grand-Saint-Graal).* edited by Frederick J. Furnivall. London: 1925

MacGregor Mathers, S. L. *The Kabbalah Unveiled.* translated into English from the Latin version of Knorr von Rosenroth, and collated with the original Chaldee and Hebrew text by S. L. MacGregor Mathers. London: Routledge, Kegan & Paul, 1926 (Contains selections from the Kabbalistic work the: *Mishnat ha-Zohar*, or: *The Book of Splendour.*)

Mackey, Sampson Arnold. *The Mythological Astronomy of the Ancients Demonstrated...* (1822) Minneapolis: Wizards Bookshelf, 1973

MacManus, Seumas. *The Story of the Irish Race - A Popular History of Ireland.* New York: The Irish Publishing Co., 1922

Macrobius, Ambrosius Theodosius. *Macrobius' "Commentary on the Dream of Scipio."* translated with introduction, notes, and commentary by William Harris Stahl. New York: Columbia University Press, 1952

Malory, Sir Thomas. *Le Morte D'Arthur.* Everyman's Library. London: J. M. Dent & Sons Ltd., 1961

(Maltwood, Katherine E.) *A Guide to Glastonbury's Temple of the Stars.* London: John M. Watkins, 1935

Marks, Claude. *Pilgrims, Heretics, and Lovers - A Medieval Journey.* New York: Macmillan Publishing Co, Inc., 1975

Matarasso, Pauline M. (translator) *The Quest of the Holy Grail (Queste del San Graal).* Harmondsworth: Penguin Books, 1969

Mead, G. R. S. *Apollonius of Tyana - The Philosopher-Reformer of the First Century A.D.* foreword by Leslie Shepard. New Hyde Park: University Books, 1966

Mead, G. R. S. *Fragments of a Faith Forgotten: Some Short Sketches Among the Gnostics Mainly of the First Two Centuries - A Contribution to the Study of Christian Origins Based on the Most Recently Discovered Materials.* London: The Theosophical Publishing Society, 1906

Mead, G. R. S. *Orpheus.* London: John M. Watkins, 1965

Mead, G. R. S. *Thrice Greatest Hermes - Studies in Hellenistic Theosophy and Gnosis*, 3 Volumes. Ferndale: Hermes Press Inc., 1978

Melville, C. C. *Christians and Moors in Spain*, Volume I (711-1150). Warminster: Aris and Philipps Ltd., 1989

Melville, C. C. *Christians and Moors in Spain*, Volume II (1195-1614). Warminster: Aris and Philipps Ltd., 1989

Melville, Charles and Ahmad Ubaydli. *Christians and Moors in Spain*, Volume III: Arabic Sources (711-1501). Warminster: Aris and Philipps Ltd., 1992

Merswin, Rulman. *The Little Book of the Nine Rocks*. (Available in numerous editions.)

Millican, Charles Bowie. *Spenser and the Table Round - A Study in the Contemporaneous Background for Spencer's Use of the Arthurian Legend.* Harvard Studies in Comparative Literature, Volume VIII. Cambridge: Harvard University Press, 1932

Moncreiffe, Sir Iain. *Royal Highness - Ancestry of the Royal Child.* London: Hamish Hamilton, 1982

de Montalembert, Count Charles Forbes Rene de Tryon. *The Monks of the West, From St. Benedict to St. Bernard*, 2 Volumes. Boston: Thomas B. Noonan & Co. (1863)

Munitz, Milton K. (editor) *Theories of the Universe - From Babylonian Myth to Modern Science.* The Library of Scientific Thought. New York: The Free Press, 1965

Murray. Margaret. "Egyptian Elements in the Grail Romance." in: Ancient Egypt, 1916. London: British School of Archaeology in Egypt, 1916

Neugebauer, Otto and Richard Parker. *Egyptian Astronomical Texts*, 3 Volumes. Brown Egyptological Studies, Vols. 3, 5 & 6. Providence: Brown University Press, 1964 (A primary source of Egyptian astronomical texts.)

Neugebauer, Otto. *Exact Sciences in Antiquity.* Providence: Brown University Press, 1957

Neugebauer, Otto. *A History of Ancient Mathematical Astronomy*, 3 Volumes. Studies in the History of Mathematics and Physical Sciences, 1. Berlin: Springer-Verlag, 1975

Nordh, Katarina. *Aspects of Ancient Egyptian Curses and Blessings - Conceptual Background and Transmission.* Boreas - Uppsala Studies in Ancient Mediterranean and Near Eastern Civilizations, Volume 26. Uppsala: Acta Universitatis Upsaliensis, 1996

Norgate, Kate. *England Under the Angevin Kings*, 2 Volumes. London: Macmillan and Co., 1887

Novalis. *Novalis - Pollen and Fragments.* translated and introduced by Arthur Versluis. Grand Rapids: Phanes Press, 1989

Nutt, Alfred. *Studies on the Legend of the Holy Grail.* London: David Nutt, 1888

O'Brien, D. *Theories of Weight in the Ancient World: Four Essays on Democritus, Plato and Aristotle - A Study in the Development of Ideas, Volume 2 - Plato: Weight and Sensation - The Two Theories of the 'Timaeus.'* Philosophia Antiqua, Volume XLI. Leiden: E.J. Brill, 1984 (While a difficult work, it is an excellent presentation of Aristotle's interpretation of Plato regarding what is essentially the fundamental nature of the four elements in terms of the relationship between the 'centre and circumference', and levity and gravity. In addition, the author attempts to bring further clarification through the "exegesis and criticism" of Theophrastus, the student of Aristotle who became the executor of his writings. While the Author is not an esotericist, with this approach he presents these and other fundamental questions concerning the *Timaeus* according to various interpretations of modern scholars. The other volumes in the series are: *Volume 1. Democritus: Weight and Size - An Exercise in the Reconstruction of Early Greek Philosophy; Volume 2. Aristotle: Weight and Movement - 'De caelo' Book Four: A Reconstruction of Aristotle's Theory; Volume 4. Aristotle: Weight and Movement - 'De caelo' Book Four: An Interpretation of Aristotle's Theory.*)

Oldenbourg, Zoe. *Massacre at Montsegur - A History of the Albigensian Crusade.* translated from the French by Peter Green. New York: Dorset Books, 1990

Oosten, Jarich G. *The War of the Gods - The Social Code of Indo-European Mythology.* International Library of Anthropology. London: Routledge & Kegan Paul Ltd., 1985

Oosterhout, G. W. "The Heliacal Rising of Sirius." in: Discussions in Egyptology, Vol. 24. Oxford: D. E. Publications, 1992

Pahlavi Texts. translated by E. W. West. Sacred Books of the East, Volumes V, XVIII, XXIV, XXXVII, XLVII. (Zoroastrian scriptures)

Painter, Sydney. *French Chivalry - Chivalric Ideas and Practices in Mediaeval France.* Great Seal Books. Ithaca: Cornell University Press, 1961

Paracelsus von Hohenheim, Theophrastus. *Hermetic and Alchemical writings of Paracelsus*, 2 Volumes. edited by A. E. Waite. (Several editions)

Paracelsus von Hohenheim, Theophrastus. *Paracelsus - Selected Writings.* edited by J. Jacobi, translated by Norbert Guterman, foreword by C. G. Jung. Bollingen Series, Volume XXVIII. Princeton: Princeton University Press, 1951

Parker, Richard A. "Sothic Dates and Calendar 'Adjustment.'" in: Revue d'Egyptologie, Tome 9. Paris: Imprimerie Nationale, 1952

Partner, Peter. *The Murdered Magicians - The Templars and Their Myth.* New York: Barnes & Noble, 1993

Paul the Deacon. *History of the Lombards (by) Paul the Deacon.* translated by William Dudley Foulke. Sources of Medieval History. Philadelphia: University of Pennsylvania Press, 1974

Peake, Elizabeth. *History of the German Emperors and Their Contemporaries.* translated from the German and compiled from authentic sources. Philadelphia: J. B. Lippencott & Co., 1874

Peebles, Rose Jeffries. "The Legend of Longinus in Ecclesiastical Tradition and in English Literature and its Connection with the Grail." in: Bryn Mawr College Monographs, Volume IX. Baltimore: Bryn Mawr College Press, 1911

"Peredur" in: *The Mabinogion.* translated by Lady Charlotte Guest. Cardiff: John Jones Cardiff Ltd., 1977

Perlesvaus. translated by N. Bryant. Cambridge: D. S. Brewer, 1978

(*Perlesvaus*). *The High History of the Holy Grail.* translated by Sebastian Evans. Everyman's Library. London: J. M. Dent & Sons Ltd., 1912

Petrement, Simone. *A Separate God - The Origins and Teachings of Gnosticism.* translated by Carol Harrison. San Francisco: Harper Collins Publishers, 1990

Philalethes, Eugenius (Thomas Vaughan). (translator and editor) *The Fame and Confession of the Fraternity R: C: Commonly, of the Rosie Cross.* with a praeface annexed thereto, and a short Declaration of their Physicall Work by Eugenius Philalethes. London: Printed by J. M. for Giles Calvert, 1652 (reprinted in: Paul M. Allen and Carlo Pietzner's, *A Christian Rosenkreutz Anthology.*)

Philostratus. *The Life of Apollonius of Tyana.* (see: translation by G. R. S Mead.)

Pistis Sophia. literally translated from the Coptic by George Horner, with an introduction by F. Legge. London: Society for the Promotion of Christian Knowledge, 1924

Pistis Sophia. A Gnostic Gospel (with extracts from the books of the Savior appended) originally translated from Greek into Coptic and now for the first time Englished from Schwartze's Latin version of the only known Coptic ms. and checked by Amelineau's French version, with an introduction by G. R. S. Mead. London: The Theosophical Publishing Society, 1896 (The *Pistis Sophia* is the most complete remaining example of the Valentinian Gnosis.)

Pistis Sophia, (the text from) the Coptic Gnostic Library. edited by C. Schmidt, translation and notes by V. MacDermot. Nag Hammadi Studies, Volume 9. Leiden: E. J. Brill, 1978

Plato. *The Collected Dialogues of Plato.* edited by Edith Hamilton and Huntington Cairns. Bollingen Series, Volume LXXI/1. Princeton: Princeton University Press, 1961

Plato. *The Cratylus, Phaedo, Parmenides, Timaeus and Critias of Plato.* translated by Thomas Taylor, with notes on the Cratylus and an explanatory introduction to each dialogue. Secret Doctrine Reference Series. Minneapolis: Wizards Bookshelf, 1975

Plato. *The Timaeus and the Critias.* translated with an introduction and an appendix on Atlantis by Desmond Lee. Harmondsworth: Penguin Books Ltd., 1977

Plato. *The Timaeus and the Critias.* translated by Thomas Taylor, introduction by R. C. Taliaferro. Bollingen Series, Volume III. Princeton: Princeton University Press, 1944

Plato. *The Dialogues of Plato.* translated by Benjamin Jowett. New York: Random House, 1937

Plato. *The Works of Plato,* 5 Volumes. translated by Thomas Taylor and F. Sydenham.

Plotinus. *Collected Writings of Plotinus.* translated by Thomas Taylor. The Thomas Taylor Series, Volume III. Somerset: The Prometheus Trust, 1994

Plotinus. *The Enneads.* translated by Stephen MacKenna, revised by B. S. Page. London: Faber & Faber, 1962

Porphyry. *Porphyry's Letter to his Wife Marcella - Concerning the Life of Philosophy and the Ascent to the Gods.* translated by Alice Zimmern, introduction by David Fideler. Grand Rapids: Phanes Press, 1986

Porphyry. *On the Caves of the Nymphs in the Thirteenth Book of the Odyssey.* translated by Thomas Taylor. London: John M. Watkins, 1917

Porphyry. *Porphyry's Launching-Points to the Realm of Mind - An Introduction to the Neoplatonic Philosophy of Plotinus.* translated by Kenneth Guthrie, introduction by Michael Hornum. Grand Rapids: Phanes Press, 1988

Proclus. *A Commentary on the First Book of Euclid's Elements.* translated with introduction and notes by Glenn R. Morrow, with a new foreword by Ian Mueller. Princeton: Princeton University Press, 1992

Proclus. *The Elements of Theology.* translation and commentary by E. R. Dodds. Oxford: Oxford University Press, 1963

Proclus. *Proclus the Neoplatonic Philosopher: Ten Doubts Concerning Providence and a Solution of those Doubts and On the Subsistence of Evil.* translated by Thomas Taylor into English from the Latin version by William of Moerbeke. Chicago: Ares Publishers Inc., 1980

Proclus. *The Six Books of Proclus the Platonic Successor, On the Theology of Plato.* translated from the Greek; to which a seventh book is added, in order to supply the deficiency of another book on this subject, which was written by Proclus, but since lost. Also, a translation from the Greek of Proclus' *Elements of Theology*, to which is added, a translation of the treatise of Proclus, *On Providence and Fate*; a translation of extracts from his treatise, entitled, *Ten Doubts Concerning Providence*; and a translation of extracts from his treatise *On the Subsistence of Evil*; as preserved in the *Bibliotheca Gr.* of Fabricius. translated into English from the Greek by Thomas Taylor, 2 Volumes. London: Printed for the Author, 1816

Ptolemy. *The Tetrabiblos; or, Quadripartite of Ptolemy, translated from the copy of Leo Allatus.* with critical and explanatory notes by James Wilson. London: Wm. Hughes, n.d.

Pythagoras. *The Golden Verses of the Pythagoreans.* Fintry: The Shrine of Wisdom, n.d.

Quinn, Esther Casier. *The Quest of Seth - For the Oil of Life.* Chicago: The University of Chicago Press, 1962

Randers-Pehrson, Justine Davis. *Barbarians and Romans - The Birth Struggle of Europe, A.D. 400-700.* Norman: University of Oklahoma Press, 1983

Regardie, Israel. *The Golden Dawn.* St. Paul: Llewellyn Publications, 1993 (. . . one should beware of all secret societies administered by so-called higher grades. . . Rudolf Steiner on January 20th, 1917 in: *The Karma of Untruthfulness*, Vol. 2)

Rene d'Anjou. *King Rene's Book of Love (Le Cueur d'Amours Espris)* reproduced from the illuminated manuscript belonging to the Austrian National Library in Vienna (Cod. Vind. 2597) introduction and commentaries by F. Unterkircher. New York: George Braziller, 1975

Reymond, E. A. E. *The Mythical Origin of the Egyptian Temple.* New York: Barnes & Noble, Inc., 1969

Rhys Davids, T. W. "'Heart and Reins' in India." in: <u>The Journal of the Manchester Oriental Society, Volume 1</u>. Manchester: Manchester University Press, 1911

Richardson, L., Jr. *A New Topographical Dictionary of Ancient Rome.* Baltimore: The Johns Hopkins University Press, 1992 (Contains information on the Temple of Venus Verticordia.)

Riche, Pierre. *The Carolingians - A Family Who Forged Europe.* translated by Michael Idomir

Allen. Middle Ages Series. Philadelphia: University of Pennsylvania Press, 1993

Riche, Pierre. *Daily Life in the World of Charlemagne.* translated, with an introduction by Jo Ann MacNamara. Middle Ages Series. Philadelphia: University of Pennsylvania Press, 1992

Rig-Veda Samhita, 4 Volumes. edited by F. Max Muller. London: 1890-1896

Rist, J. M. *Plotinus - The Road to Reality.* Cambridge: Cambridge University Press, 1967

Roberts, A. and J. Donaldson. (editors) *The Anti-Nicene Fathers.* Grand Rapids: W. B. Eerdmans Publishing Company, 1990

Robinson, James M. (editor) *The Nag Hammadi Library.* translated by members of the Coptic Gnostic Library Project of the Institute for Antiquity and Christianity. San Francisco: Harper & Row Publishers, 1977

Robinson, John J. *Born in Blood - The Lost Secrets of Freemasonry.* New York: M. Evans & Co., 1989

Robinson, John J. *Dungeon, Fire and Sword - The Knights Templar in the Crusades.* New York: M. Evans & Co., 1991

Row, T. Subba. "The Constitution of the Macrocosm." in: The Theosophist, May 1887. London: The Theosophical Publishing Society, 1887

Runciman, Sir Steven. *A History of the Crusades,* 3 Volumes. Cambridge: Cambridge University Press, 1951-1954

Runciman, Sir Steven. *The Medieval Manichee - A Study of the Christian Dualist Heresy.* Cambridge: Cambridge University Press, 1982

Rutherford, John. *The Troubadours - Their Loves and their Lyrics; With Remarks on their Influence, Social and Literary.* London: Smith, Elder, & Co., 1873

Sangerkrieg auf der Wartburg.

Scott, W. (translator) *Hermetica - The Ancient Greek and Latin Writings.* Boston: Shambala, 1985

Scott, W. S. *The Trial of Joan of Arc - Being the Verbatim Report of the Proceedings from the Orleans Manuscript.* translated with an introduction and notes by W. S. Scott. London: The Folio Society, 1956

Scharfenberg, Albrecht von. *Der Jungere Titurel.* edited by Werner Wolf. Bern: 1952

Schimmelpfennig, Bernhard. *The Papacy:* translated by James Sievert. New York: Columbia University Press, 1992

Scholem, Gershom. *Kabbalah.* New York: Dorset Press, 1974

Scholem, Gershom. *Kabbalah and its Symbolism.* New York: 1977

Secret Symbols of the Rosicrucians of the 16th & 17th Centuries. (Originally published in German in three parts in Altona by J. D. A. Eckhardt in 1785-1788, under the title *Geheime Figuren der Rosenkreuzer aus dem 16 und 17 Jahrhundert*. This important work is presently available in an English translation along with many other seminal Rosicrucian works in Paul M. Allen and Carlo Pietzner's *A Christian Rosenkreutz Anthology*. The *Geheime Figuren* was considered by Rudolf Steiner to be an important late Rosicrucian work, and he acknowledged its association with Hinricus Madathanus which is a pseudonym of Count Adrianus a Mynsicht).

Sepher Yetzirah - The Book of Creation - In Theory and Practice. revised by Aryeh Kaplan. York Beach: Samuel Weiser Inc., 1997 (A comprehensive study of the c. 4th century A.D. Kabbalistic work the *Sefer Yesirah*.)

Sepher Yetzirah. (see: W. Wynn Westcott, *Collectanea Hermetica*.)

Sethe, Kurt. *Thebanische Tempelinschriften aus der Griechisch-Romischen Zeit*, Volume 1. Urkunden des Ægyptischen Altertums, begr. von Georg Steindorff, Abt. VIII, Heft. 1. Berlin: Akademie Verlag, 1957

Seward, Desmond. *Eleanor of Aquitaine - The Mother Queen*. New York: Dorset Press, 1978

Simek, Rudolf. *Dictionary of Northern Mythology.* translated from the German by Angela Hall. Cambridge: D. S. Brewer, 1993

Simpson, Otto von. *The Gothic Cathedral*. Bollingen Series, Volume XLVIII. Princeton: Princeton University Press, 1956

Sinclair, Andrew. *The Sword and the Grail - Of the Grail and the Templars and a True Discovery of America*. New York: Crown Publishers, 1992

Sismonde, J. C. L. Simonde. *Historical View of the Literature of the South of Europe*, 2 Volumes. translated with notes, and a life of the author, by Thomas Roscoe. London: George Bell & Sons, 1880-1881

Skeels, Dell. *The Romance of Percival in Prose - A Translation of the E Manuscript of the Didot Perceval*. Seattle: University of Washington Press, 1966

Smith, Sir William. *Everyman's Smaller Classical Dictionary*. revised from Sir William Smith by E. H. Blakeney and J. Warrington. Everyman's Reference Library. London: J. M. Dent & Sons Ltd., 1952 (contains information on the Temple of Venus Verticordia)

Smith, George Eliot. "'Heart and Reins' in Mummification." in: The Journal of the Manchester Oriental Society, Volume 1. Manchester: Manchester University Press, 1911

Smith, Justin H. *The Troubadours at Home - Their Lives and Personalities, Their Songs and Their World*, 2 Volumes. New York: G. P. Putnam's Sons, 1899

Solmsen, Friedrich. *Isis among the Greeks and Romans*. Martin Classical Lectures, Volume XXV. Harvard University Press, 1979

Spence, Lewis. *The Origins and History of Druidism*. London: Rider & Co., 1949

Springett, Bernard H. *Secret Sects of Syria and the Lebanon - A Consideration of Their Origin, Creeds, and Religious Ceremonies, and Their Influence upon Modern Freemasonry*. London: George Allen & Unwin Ltd., 1922

Squire, Charles. *Celtic Myths and Legends.* London: Gresham Publishing, 1912

Stephen, Sir James. *Lectures on the History of France.* New York: Harper & Brothers Publishers, 1851

Stevenson, David. *The Origins of Freemasonry - Scotland's Century, 1590-1710.* Cambridge: Cambridge University Press, 1988

Stewart, H. M. "Some Pre-`Amarnah Sun-Hymns." in: Journal of Egyptian Archaeology, Volume 46. London: Egypt Exploration Society, 1960

St. Germain, Comte. *The Most Holy Trinosophia of the Comte St. Germain.* with introductory material and commentary by Manly P. Hall, illustrated with a complete photostatic facsimile of the original manuscript in the Bibliotheque de Troyes. Los Angeles: The Philosophical Research Society, 1962

Stolcius, Daniel. *Viridarium Chymicum* [*The Pleasure Garden of Chymistry*]. Frankfort am Main: Lucas Jennis, 1624 (contains: *The Twelve Keys of Basilius Valentinius.* reprinted in: Paul M. Allen and Carlo Pietzner's, *A Christian Rosenkreutz Anthology.*)

Sturlson, Snorri. *The Prose Edda.* translated by Jean I. Young. Berkeley: University of California Press, 1964 (*Snorra Edda*)

Sugar, Peter F. (editor) *A History of Hungary.* Bloomington: Indiana University Press, 1990

(Sulpicius Severus). *The Western Fathers: Being the Lives of SS. Martin of Tours, Ambrose, Augustine of Hippo, Honoratus of Arles, and Germanus of Auxerre - The Makers of Christendom.* translated by Frederick Russell Hoare. New York: Sheed and Ward, 1954

The System Bible Study: Being an Effort to Give the Most Complete, the Most Concise and the Most Useful Book of Classified Bible Helps - the Gems - the Masterpieces - the Crown-Jewels - the Heart of the Bible, by Many of the World's Greatest Bible Scholars. revised and enlarged edition. Chicago: The System Bible Company, 1927

Tauler, Johannes. *Sermons.* translated by M. Schrader. New York: Paulist Press, 1985

Taylor, Thomas. *The Eleusinian and Bacchic Mysteries.* a dissertation. with introduction, notes emendations, and glossary by Alexander Wilder M.D. Secret Doctrine Reference Series. San Diego: Wizards Bookshelf, 1987

Taylor, Thomas. *Two Orations of the Emperor Julian one to the sovereign Sun and the other to the Mother of the Gods.* translated from the Greek with notes, and a copious introduction, in which some of the greatest arcana of the Grecian theology are unfolded. London: Printed for Edward Jeffrey, 1793

Theologia Germanica. translated by Susanna Winkworth. London: Stuart & Watkins, 1966 (A classic work of Christian mysticism produced out of the mileau of the Friends of God.)

Thierry of Chartres, et al. *Commentaries on Boethius by Thierry of Chartres and His School.* edited by Nikolaus M. Haring. Pontifical Institute of Mediæval Studies - Studies and Texts, Volume 20. Toronto: Pontifical Institute of Mediæval Studies, 1971

Thomas a Kempis. *Imitatio Christi (The Imitation of Christ).* (This classic work has been reprinted in over six thousand different editions since it was first printed in 1471, see below: *The Treasury of Christian Spiritual Classics.*)

Tolkien, John Ronald Renel. (translator) *Sir Gawain and the Green Knight.* Oxford: Oxford University Press, 1968

The Treasury of Christian Spiritual Classics. complete and unabridged, with introductions by Timothy P. Weber. Nashville: Thomas Nelson Publishers, 1994 (This collection includes: *The Confessions of St. Augustine*, by St. Augustine; *The Practice of the Presence of God*, by Brother Lawrence; *Revelations of Divine Love*, by Julian of Norwich; *The Imitation of Christ*, by Thomas a Kempis; and, *Selections of Sermons on the Song of Songs*, by St. Bernard of Clairvaux.)

Treharne, R. F. *The Glastonbury Legends.* London: Cresset Press, Ltd., 1967

Trimble, Virginia. "Astronomical Investigations concerning the so-called Air-shafts of Cheops' Pyramid." in: Mitteilungen des Instituts fur Orientforschung Akademie der Wissenschaften zu Berlin, Band 10, Heft 2/3. Berlin: Akademie der Wissenschaften, 1964

Trithemius von Sponheim, Johannes. *Von den Siben Geysten oder Engeln.* Nurnberg: Holtzel, 1522 (The earliest known source for the Archangelic Periods.)

Tupper, Henry Allen, et al. *The System Bible Study.* Chicago: The System Bible Company, 1927

(*Upanishads*). *Sixty Upanishads of the Veda.* translated by V. M. Bedekar and G. B. Palsule from the German translations of Paul Deussen [1897], 2 Volumes. Delhi: Motilal Banarsidass, 1987

(*Upanishads*). *The Principle Upanishads.* translated by S. Radhakrishnan. New Delhi: Harper Collins Publishers,1996

(*Upanishads*). *The Ten Principle Upanishads.* translated by Shree Purohit Swami and W. B. Yeats. New York: MacMillan Publishing Co., Inc., 1975

(*Urkunden VIII.* see: Kurt Sethe)

Valentinius, Basilius. *The Triumphal Chariot of Antimony.* with the commentary of Theodore Kerckringus, a Doctor of Medicine. translated with a biographical preface by A. E. Waite, and edited with additional corrections by Joseph Bouleur. Edmonds: The Alchemical Press, 1992 (For *The Twelve Keys of Basilius Valentinius* see: Daniel Stolcius.)

VandenBroeck, Andre. *Al-kemi - A Memoir - Hermetic, Occult, Political, and Private Aspects of R. A. Schwaller de Lubicz.* with a comment by Saul Bellow. Hudson: Lindisfarne Press, 1987

(*Vedas*). *Rg-Veda Samhita - The Sacred Hymns of the Brahmins*, 6 Volumes. translated by F. Max Muller. London: William H. Allen, 1849-74

(*Vedas*). *Rg-Veda Samhita - Together with the Commentary of Sayana Acharya.* edited by F. Max Muller. Varanasi: Chowkhamba Sanskrit Series, 1966

Versluis, Arthur. *TheoSophia - Hidden Dimensions of Christianity.* Hudson: Lindisfarne Press, 1994

Vinaver, Eugene. *The Rise of Romance.* Oxford: Oxford University Press, 1971 de Vore, Nicholas. *Encyclopedia of Astrology.* with special articles by Charles A. Jayne and Frederic van Norstrand. A Littlefield, Adams Quality Paperback, No. 323. Totowa: Littlefield, Adams & Co., 1976

Vossler, Karl. *Mediaeval Culture - An Introduction to Dante and His Times,* 2 Volumes. translated by William Cranston Lawton. New York: Harcourt, Brace and Company, 1929

Wace, R. Arthurian Chronicles. translated by E. Mason. London: J. M. Dent & Sons Ltd., 1972

Waddell, Helen. *The Desert Fathers - Translations from the Latin.* Ann Arbor: University of Michigan Press, 1972

Waite, Arthur Edward. *The Brotherhood of the Rosy Cross - Being Records of the House of the Holy Spirit in its Inward and Outward History.* Secaucus: University Books, 1973

Waite, Arthur Edward. *The Hidden Church of the Holy Grail.* London: Rebman, 1909

Waite, Arthur Edward. *The Real History of the Rosicrucians.* Mokelumne Hill: Health Research, 1960

Waitz, Georg. *Jahrbucher der Deutschen Geschichte - Koenig Heinrich I.* Leipzig: 1885

Wallis, Richard T. and Jay Bregman. (editor and associate editor) *Neoplatonism and Gnosticism.* Papers presented at the International Conference on Neoplatonism and Gnosticism, University of Oklahoma, March 18-21, 1984. International Society for Neoplatonic Studies. Studies in Neoplatonism: Ancient and Modern, Volume 6. Albany: State University of New York Press, 1992

Walsh, Michael. *Opus Dei - An Investigation into the Secret Society Struggling for Power within the Roman Catholic Church.* San Francisco: Harper Collins Publishers, 1992

Ward, J. S. M. *Freemasonry and the Ancient Gods.* London: Baskerville Press, 1926

Ward, J. S. M. *Who Was Hiram Abiff?* London: Baskerville Press, 1925

Weisheipl, James A. (editor) *Albertus Magnus and the Sciences - Commemorative Essays.* Pontifical Institute of Mediæval Studies - Studies and Texts, Volume 49. Toronto: Pontifical Institute of Mediæval Studies, 1980

Weisse, John A., M.D. *The Obelisk and Freemasonry.* New York: J. W. Bouton, 1880

Westcott, W. Wynn. (editor) *Collectanea Hermetica,* 10 Volumes in one. York Beach: Samuel Weiser Inc., 1998

Weston, Jesse Laidlaw. *From Ritual to Romance.* Cambridge: Cambridge University Press, 1957

Weston, Jesse Laidlaw. *The Legend of Sir Lancelot du Lac.* London: 1920

Weston, Jesse Laidlaw. *The Legend of Sir Perceval - Studies upon its Origin, Development, and Position in the Arthurian Cycle,* 2 Volumes. London: 1906-1909

Whitby, Charles J. *The Wisdom of Plotinus - A Metaphysical Study.* London: William Rider and

Sons Ltd., 1909

Whitlock, Ralph. *The Warrior Kings of Saxon England.* New York: Barnes & Noble Books, 1993

William of Malmesbury. *History of the Kings of England.* translated by Sebastian Evans, revised by Charles W. Dunn. New York: Dutton, 1958

Williamson, J. Bruce. *The History of the Temple, London - From the Institution of the Order of the Knights of the Temple to the Close of the Stuart Period.* compiled from the Original Records of the Two Learned and Honorable Societies of the Temple by J. Bruce Williamson of the Middle Temple. London: John Murray, 1924

Wolfram von Eschenbach. *Parzival.* translated by A. T. Hatto. London: Penguin Books, 1980

Wolfram von Eschenbach. *Parzival.* translated by Helen M. Mustard and Charles E. Passage. New York: Vintage Books, 1961

Wolfram von Eschenbach. *Parzival.* edited by H. D. Sacker. Cambridge: Cambridge University Press, 1980

Wolfram von Eschenbach. *Parzival.* translated by Jesse Laidlaw Weston. London: 1894

Wolfram von Eschenbach. *Titurel.* translation and studies by Charles E. Passage. New York: 1984

Wolfram von Eschenbach. *The Middle High German Poem of Willehalm.* translated by, Charles E. Passage. New York: Frederick Ungar Publishing Co., 1977

Wolfson, Elliot R. *Circle in the Square - Studies in the Use of Gender in Kabbalistic Symbolism.* Albany: State University of New York Press, 1995

Wolfson, Harry Austryn. *Philo - Foundations of Religious Philosophy in Judaism, Christianity and Islam, 2 Volumes.* Cambridge: Harvard University Press, 1947

Wuest, Kenneth S. (translator) *The New Testament - An Expanded Translation.* Grand Rapids: W. B. Eerdmans Publishing Company, 1961

Yagley, Robert. (editor) *The Book of Courtly Love - Medieval Stories and Songs.* New York: Barnes & Noble Books, 1997

Yarker, John. *Notes on the Scientific and Religious Mysteries of Antiquity; the Gnosis and Secret Schools of the Middle Ages; Modern Rosicrucianism; and the Various Rites and Degrees of Free and Accepted Masonry.* London: John Hogg et al., 1872

Yarker, John. *The Secret High Degree Rituals of the Masonic Rite of Memphis.* Kila: Kessinger Publishing Co., n.d.

Yates, Francis A. *The Art of Memory.* London: Routledge and Kegan Paul Ltd., 1966

Yates, Francis A. *Giordano Bruno and the Hermetic Tradition.* Chicago: The University of Chicago, 1964

Yates, Francis A. *The Occult Philosophy in the Elizabethan Age.* London: Routledge and Kegan

Paul Ltd., 1979

Yates, Francis A. *The Rosicrucian Enlightenment.* London: Routledge and Kegan Paul Ltd., 1972

Zaehner, R. C. *Zurvan - A Zoroastrian Dilemma.* New York: Biblio and Tannen, 1972

Zatzikhoven, Ulrich von. *Lanzelet.* translated by Kenneth G. T. Webster. New York: Columbia University Press, 1951

The Zend Avesta. translated by J. Darmesteter. Sacred Books of the East, Volumes IV & XXIII. (The principle Zoroastrian scripture)

(*Zohar.*) *The Wisdom of the Zohar - An Anthology of Texts*, 3 Volumes. arranged by Fischel Lachower and Isaiah Tishby, with extensive introductions and explanations by Isaiah Tishby, translated from the Hebrew by David Goldstein. London: The Littman Library of Jewish Civilization, 1994 (An extensive traditional study of a principle Kabbalistic text. According to W. Wynn Westcott; "Tradition assigns its authorship to Rabbi Simeon ben Jochai, A.D. 80, but modern criticism is inclined to believe that a very large portion of it is no older than 1280, when it was certainly edited and published by Rabbi Moses de Leon, of Guadalaxara in Spain. . . There are portions of the doctrines of the *Zohar* which bear the impress of Chaldee thought and civilization, to which the Jewish race had been exposed in the Babylonish captivity." This comment by Westcott supports the statement by Rudolf Steiner that the Jews were exposed to the Chaldean-Babylonian teachings of the contemporary incarnation of Zaratas during their "Babylonian captivity", c. 586-538 B.C.)

Zohar: The Book of Splendor - Basic Readings from the Kabbalah. selected and edited by Gershom Scholem. New York: Schocken Books, 1977

Quotation Acknowledgments

In the following, I wish to gratefully acknowledge the permissions which were so graciously extended, by the following authors and publishers, to use the quotations that are included in this book. As to the omissions in this list, I have made numerous attempts to contact the individuals concerning the many quotations I have used in this book, and did not receive a response from several of them. But since all of the remaining quotations are either public domain, or well within the guidelines of "fair-use" according to the copyright statutes, I do not foresee any problems; and so, nonetheless, I must extend my gratitude to these individuals, in absentia, even though it may pass unnoticed.

The works of Rudolf Steiner, and also the works of the numerous anthroposophical authors, that are listed in the bibliography, and are quoted in this work are "used by permission of Anthroposophic Press, Hudson, N.Y. 12534."

Aris & Philipps Ltd., Warminster: *The Ancient Egyptian Pyramid Texts*, translated by Raymond O. Faulkner. ©1969 "Used by permission of Aris & Philipps Ltd., Warminster."

Brotherhood of Life, Albuquerque: *Fulcanelli - Master Alchemist*, translated by Mary Sworder, from the French edition of Fulcanelli's work: *Le Mystere des Cathedrales - Et l'interpretation esoterique des symboles hermetiques du grand œuvre*, Societe Nouvelle des Editions Pauvert, Paris © 1964. English translation © 1986 by the Brotherhood of Life, Albuquerque. "Used by permission of Richard E. Buhler: Brotherhood of Life, 110 Dartmouth SE, Albuquerque, NM, 87106."

Helmut Buske Verlag, Hamburg: "The Plundering of the Pyramid of Cheops", by Laszlo Kakosy, in: Studien zur Altægyptischen Kultur, Band 16. © 1989 "Used by permission of Helmut Buske Verlag GmbH, Hamburg."

Columbia University Press, New York: *Cosmographia*, by Bernardus Silvestris, translated with an introduction and notes by Winthrop Wetherbee. © 1973 "Used by permission of the Rights & Permissions Dept., Columbia University Press, New York."

Columbia University Press, New York: *Macrobius' "Commentary on the Dream of Scipio"*, by Ambrosius Theodosius Macrobius, translated with introduction, notes, and commentary by William Harris Stahl. © 1952 "Used by permission of the Rights & Permissions Dept., Columbia University Press, New York."

Columbia University Press, New York: *The Papacy*, by Bernhard Schimmelpfennig, translated by James Sievert. © 1992 "Used by permission of the Rights & Permissions Dept., Columbia University Press, New York."

Crown Publishers, New York: *The Sword and the Grail - Of the Grail and the Templars and a True Discovery of America*, by Andrew Sinclair. © 1992 by Timon Films Ltd. & Orcadian Trust. "Used by permission of the Copyright & Permissions Dept., Crown Publishers, New York."

Dorset Press, New York: *Eleanor of Aquitaine - The Mother Queen*, by Desmond Seward. © 1978 "Used by permission of David & Charles Publishers, Devon U.K."

W. B. Eerdmans Publishing Company, Grand Rapids: *The New Testament - An Expanded Translation*, by Kenneth S. Wuest. © 1961 "Used by permission of the Rights & Permissions Dept., W. B. Eerdmans Publishing Company."

Egypt Exploration Society, London: "Some Pre-`Amarnah Sun-Hymns", by H. M. Stewart, in: Journal of Egyptian Archaeology, Volume 46. © 1960 "Used by permission of the Committee of the Egypt Exploration Society, London."

Eotvos Loraad Universitat, Budapest: "Ideas About the Fallen State of the World in Egyptian Religion - Decline of the Golden Age", by Laszlo Kakosy, in: Acta Orientalia Academiæ Scientiæ Hungaricæ, Volume 17. © 1964 "Used by permission of Laszlo Kakosy, Budapest."

Kegan Paul International, London: *Egyptian Solar Religion in the New Kingdom - Re, Amun and the Crisis of Polytheism*, by Jan Assmann. Studies in Egyptology. © 1995 "Used by permission of Kegan Paul International, London, WC 1B 3SW."

Lindisfarne Press, Hudson: *TheoSophia - Hidden Dimensions of Christianity*, by Arthur Versluis. © 1994 "Used by permission of Anthroposophic Press, Hudson, N.Y. 12534."

Luxor Press, Marietta: *The Compleat Rite of Memphis*, edited and introduced by Allen H. Greenfield, Hon. 33°, 90°, 95°. © 1998 "Used by permission of Luxor Press, Marietta, GA 30065."

Manchester University Press, Manchester: "'Heart and Reins' in the Ancient Literatures of the Nearer East", by Hope W. Hogg, in: The Journal of the Manchester Oriental Society. Volume 1. © 1911 "Used by permission of the Permissions Dept., Manchester University Press, Manchester."

Oxford University Press, Oxford: *The Ancient Coptic Churches of Egypt*, 2 Volumes, by Alfred J. Butler. © 1884 "Used by permission of Oxford University Press, Oxford."

Oxford University Press, Oxford: *Imhotep - The Egyptian God of Medicine*, by Jamieson B. Hurry. © 1926 "Used by permission of Oxford University Press, Oxford."

Paulist Press, New York: *The Early Kabbalah*, edited and introduced by Joseph Dan, texts translated by Ronald C. Kiener, preface by Moshe Idel. The Classics of Western Spirituality Series. © 1986 by Joseph Dan & Ronald C. Kiener. The quotation from the introduction by Joseph Dan is "used by permission of the Paulist Press, New York."

University of Pennsylvania Press, Philadelphia: *The Carolingians - A Family Who Forged Europe*, by Pierre Riche, translated by Michael Idomir Allen. Middle Ages Series. English translation © 1993 by the University of Pennsylvania Press. Translated from the French edition of, *Les Caroliengiens: une famille qui fit l'Europe*, by Pierre Riche © 1983 by Hachette. "Used by permission of University of Pennsylvania Press."

Phanes Press, Grand Rapids: *Novalis - Pollen and Fragments*. by Novalis (Friedrich von Hardenberg), translated and introduced by Arthur Versluis. © 1989 The translations from the German that are quoted on pages 405 & 411 are "used by permission of Phanes Press, Grand Rapids."

Pontifical Institute of Mediæval Studies, Toronto: "Chrestien, Macrobius, and Chartrean Science: The Allegorical Robe as Symbol of Textual Design in the Old French Erec", by T. E. Hart, in: Mediæval Studies, Volume XLIII. © 1981 "Used by permission of the Pontifical Institute of Mediæval Studies, Toronto."

Princeton University Press, Princeton: *Doctor Illuminatus - A Ramon Llull Reader*, by Ramon Llull, edited and translated by Anthony Bonner; with a new translation of *The Book of the Lover and the Beloved*, by Eva Bonner. The Mythos Series. © 1993 "Used by permission of the Princeton University Press, Princeton."

Quinta Essentia, Cambridge: *Fundamental Symbols - The Universal Language of Sacred Science.* by Rene Guenon, compiled and edited by Michel Valsan, translated by Alvin Moore, Jr., revised and edited by Martin Lings. This revised English edition © 1995 Quinta Essentia. "Used by permission of The Islamic Texts Society, Cambridge, U.K."

Random House, Inc. - Vintage Books, New York: *Parzival*, by Wolfram von Eschenbach, translated by Helen M. Mustard and Charles E. Passage. © 1961 "Used by permission of Random House, Inc., New York."

Thanks to Cornelius Pietzner for permission to quote extracts from his father Carlo Pietzner's translation of the essay by Rudolf Steiner, *Die Chymische Hochzeit des Christian Rosenkreutz*, © 1968, 1981 by Rudolf Steiner Publications, a division of Garber Communications, Inc., Blauvelt, New York.

State University of New York Press, Albany: *Circle in the Square - Studies in the Use of Gender in Kabbalistic Symbolism*, by Elliot R. Wolfson. © 1995 "Used by permission of the State University of New York Press, Albany."

Part 5

Grail Diagrams

"We affirm a crowd of angels and ministers, whom God, the maker and creator of the world, designated to their numerous tasks through his Word. He gave them responsibility over the good order of the universe, over the elements, the heavens, the world, and all it contains."

Athenagoras

(Athenagoras was an Athenian Platonic philosopher who wrote an apology, addressed to the Roman Emperor Marcus Aurelius, on behalf of the Christians, in 177 A.D.)

I

The Major Arcana and the Macrocosm and Microcosm

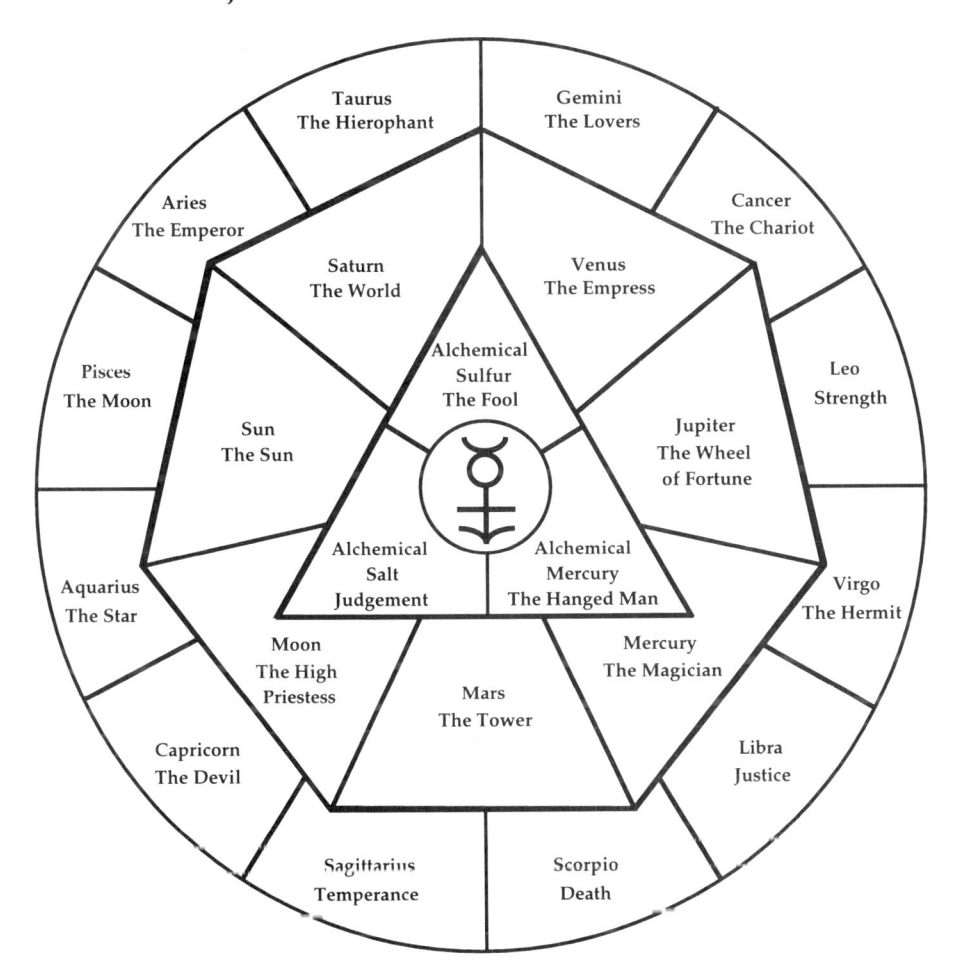

Above we see the Major Arcana of the Tarot with their correspondences pertaining to the mysteries of the Macrocosm and Microcosm. These relationships are: in the outer circle - to the constellations of the Zodiac, in the septagon - to the Sun, Moon and planets, in the triangle - to the three alchemical principles. In the center is the Hieroglyphic Monad of John Dee (1527-1607), from his book *Monas Hieroglyphica*, that was published at Antwerp in 1564. This symbol is composed of the joining together of the astrological glyphs of the Sun, Moon, Mercury, Venus, Mars, Jupiter, Saturn and the Earth, along with the glyph for Aries, the Ram or "Lamb of God." The Hieroglyphic Monad, which represents the microcosmic human being, is also present on the "invitation" in *The Chymical Wedding of Christian Rosenkreutz*, by Johann Valentin Andreae (1616).

II

The Rosicrucian Symbols of the Quintessence and the Four Elements, and the Corresponding Ethers

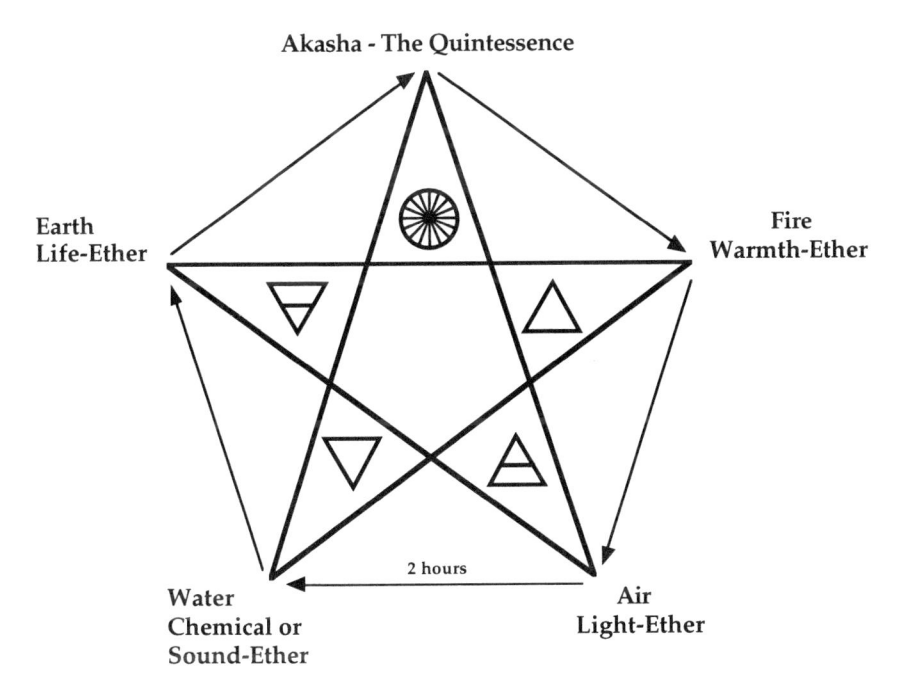

Akasha - The Quintessence

Earth
Life-Ether

Fire
Warmth-Ether

2 hours

Water
Chemical or
Sound-Ether

Air
Light-Ether

"Out of the Four Elements Come All Things"

"In the beginning all things
Consist of the four elements,
Even those which you surmise
Are but pure elements."

"Nothing pure is found.
The Creator of the world
Mixes all elements
With his dexterous hands."

"Therefore our moon and sun
Shine with great pleasure;
And our daughter
Has received the life."

from: The Pleasure Garden of Chymistry, by Daniel Stolcius, 1624

The Rosicrucian Symbols of the Seven-Fold Human Being

The triangle is an alchemical symbol for the Three-Fold Spirit of Man:
Spirit-Self (Sulfur), Life-Spirit (Mercury), and Spirit-Man (Salt).

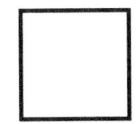

The square is an alchemical symbol for the Four-Fold being of Man:
Ego (Fire), Astral-Body (Air) Ether-Body (Water), and Physical-Body (Earth).

III

Venus Pentagram

Superior Conjunction

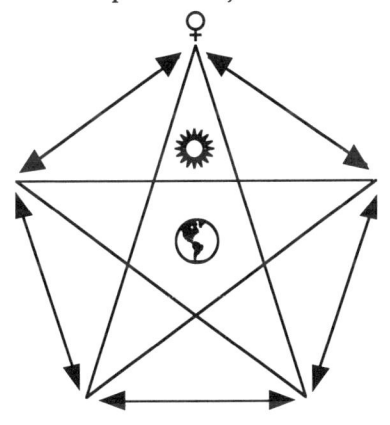

Inferior Conjunction

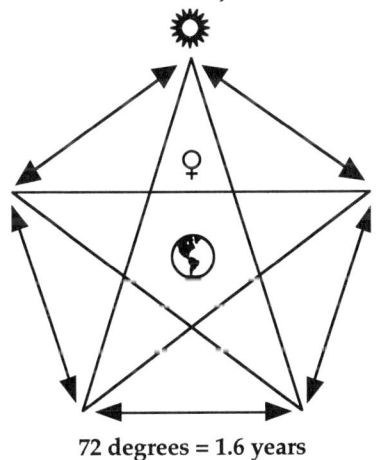

72 degrees = 1.6 years

Sun = ☀ Venus = ♀ Earth = 🜨

360 ÷ 2.4 = 150 x 8 = 1,200 (1,199)

"Five is not only an odd, but also a spherical number: for all its multiplications into itself terminate in five; and therefore they end where they begin." Thomas Taylor (1758-1835 A.D.)

IV

The Seven Globes and the Law of Seven

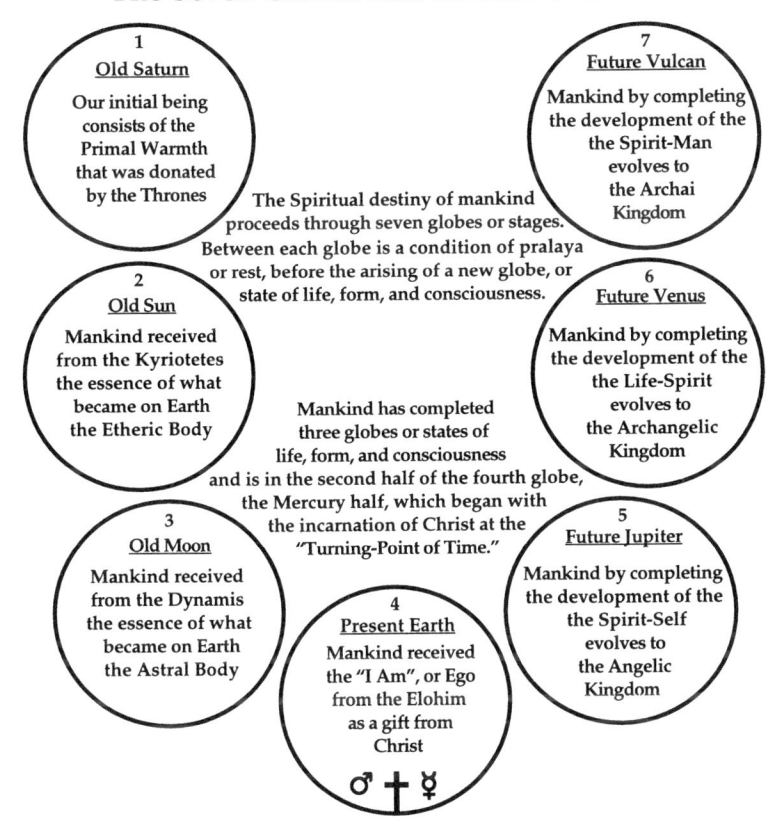

1 Old Saturn
Our initial being consists of the Primal Warmth that was donated by the Thrones

7 Future Vulcan
Mankind by completing the development of the the Spirit-Man evolves to the Archai Kingdom

The Spiritual destiny of mankind proceeds through seven globes or stages. Between each globe is a condition of pralaya or rest, before the arising of a new globe, or state of life, form, and consciousness.

2 Old Sun
Mankind received from the Kyriotetes the essence of what became on Earth the Etheric Body

6 Future Venus
Mankind by completing the development of the the Life-Spirit evolves to the Archangelic Kingdom

Mankind has completed three globes or states of life, form, and consciousness and is in the second half of the fourth globe, the Mercury half, which began with the incarnation of Christ at the "Turning-Point of Time."

3 Old Moon
Mankind received from the Dynamis the essence of what became on Earth the Astral Body

5 Future Jupiter
Mankind by completing the development of the the Spirit-Self evolves to the Angelic Kingdom

4 Present Earth
Mankind received the "I Am", or Ego from the Elohim as a gift from Christ

♂ ☩ ☿

The 7x7x7 Stages of World Evolution

The Seven Stages of Consciousness (Planetary Evolutions)   **The Seven Conditions of Form (Globes)**

1) Trance Consciousness, Universal Consciousness (Old Saturn).............Arupa (formless)
2) Deep Sleep Consciousness, Dreamless Consciousness (Old Sun)...........Rupa (form)
3) Dream Consciousness, Picture Consciousness (Old Moon)....................Astral
4) Waking Consciousness, Awareness of Objects (Earth)..........................Physical
5) Psychic or Conscious Picture Consciousness (Future Jupiter).................Plastic-Astral
6) Super-Psychic or Conscious Sleep-Consciousness (Future Venus)..........Intellectual
7) Spiritual or Conscious Universal Consciousness (Future Vulcan).........Archetypal or Primal-Pictorial

"Every Condition of Form again goes through 7x7 stages of development; for instance our present Fourth Condition of Form (of the Mineral Kingdom, within the Fourth Planet, the Earth) goes through the so-called 7 Root-Races (ages or main periods of time) and again through the Cultural Epochs of our present Fifth Root-Race (post-Atlantean period)."   Rudolf Steiner, Foundations of Esotericism, pages 264-265

V

The Spiritual Beings and the Spheres of the Planets and Zodiac

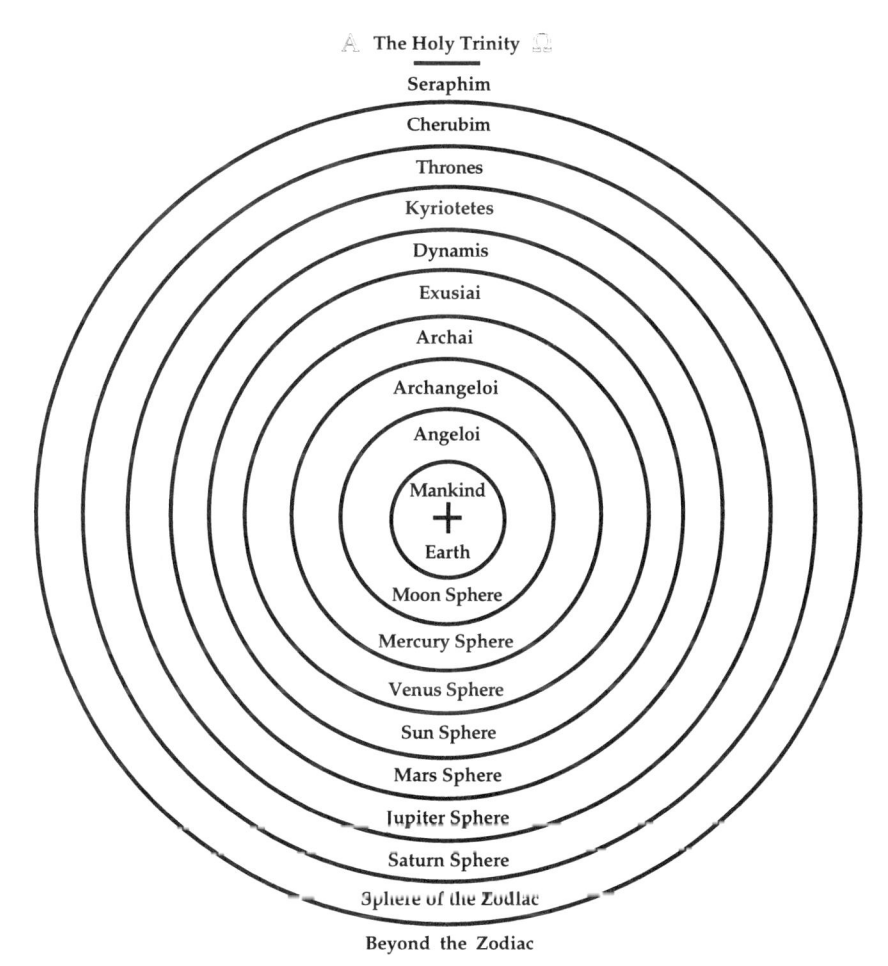

A. The Holy Trinity Ω

Seraphim
Cherubim
Thrones
Kyriotetes
Dynamis
Exusiai
Archai
Archangeloi
Angeloi
Mankind
✢
Earth
Moon Sphere
Mercury Sphere
Venus Sphere
Sun Sphere
Mars Sphere
Jupiter Sphere
Saturn Sphere
Sphere of the Zodiac

Beyond the Zodiac

"If I have told you earthly things, and ye believe not,
how shall ye believe, if I tell you of heavenly things?"
St. John 3:12

Humanity dwells within the spheres of the planetary system as viewed from the Earth. These spheres indicate the "ring-pass-not" of the activities of the numerous Spiritual Beings that are concerned with our evolution, and also circumscribe the spheres of the related higher planes of being that are reflected within the macrocosmic human being. It can be seen that, the names of Mercury and Venus are reversed from their current astronomical names. This provides a key to understanding the occult teachings that refer to the ascending planes of being, and the Angelic Beings which inhabit them.

VI

The Ancient Chaldean Names for the Planets

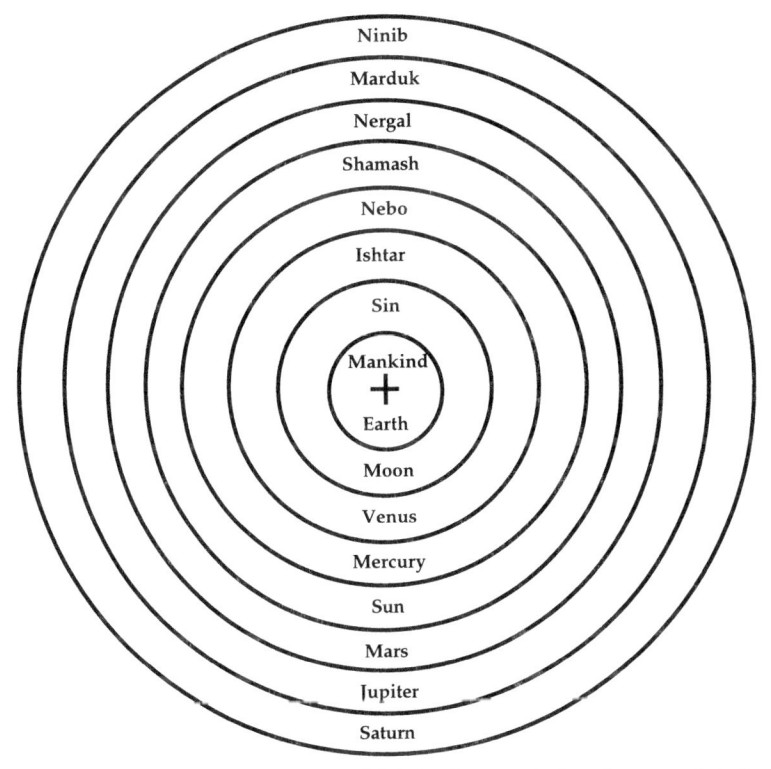

```
Ninib
Marduk
Nergal
Shamash
Nebo
Ishtar
Sin
Mankind
   +
Earth
Moon
Venus
Mercury
Sun
Mars
Jupiter
Saturn
```

"The Aristotelian's assert that some of their books are esoteric and some exoteric."
Clement of Alexandria (c. 150-215 A.D.)

The ancient Chaldean names for the planets are shown above related to their current astronomical names. According to H. P. Blavatsky, much of the content of the Hebrew Kabbalah is derived from the earlier Chaldean *Book of Numbers*; which is said to be written in a form of Chaldean Aramaic. There are only two or three known copies of the Chaldean *Book of Numbers* said to exist, and the whereabouts of these are unknown. This connection is intriguing when one considers that, according to Rudolf Steiner, the Hebrews were taught by Zaratas during the period of the Babylonian Captivity (c. 586-538 B.C.). But other remains of the ancient Chaldean secret doctrine do exist, this is partly due to the writings of Berossus, a priest of Bel Marduk at Babylon. At the request of Alexander the Great, Berossus committed to writing certain teachings from the chronological and astronomical temple-records. Of these writings, we only have fragments that remain from a lost work of Eusebius of Caesarea (c. 260-340 A.D.). Fortunately for posterity, much has come to light from the cuneiform clay tablets on the doctrines of ancient Mesopotamia. In the 4th century B.C., Alexander the Great created schools to transmit the ancient mystery wisdom, cast in the form of the nature wisdom of Aristotle. Due to its esoteric character, this nature wisdom was left out of the written works of Aristotle that were codified by Theophrastus. This Aristotelian nature wisdom continued as a tradition nonetheless, and influenced the development of the Kabbalah, Alchemy, and Rosicrucianism; with the names Mercury and Venus reversed so as to veil the esoteric meaning from the eyes of the profane.

VII

The Planetary Spheres, the Kabbalistic Sefirot, and the Esoteric Christian Angelical Hierarchies

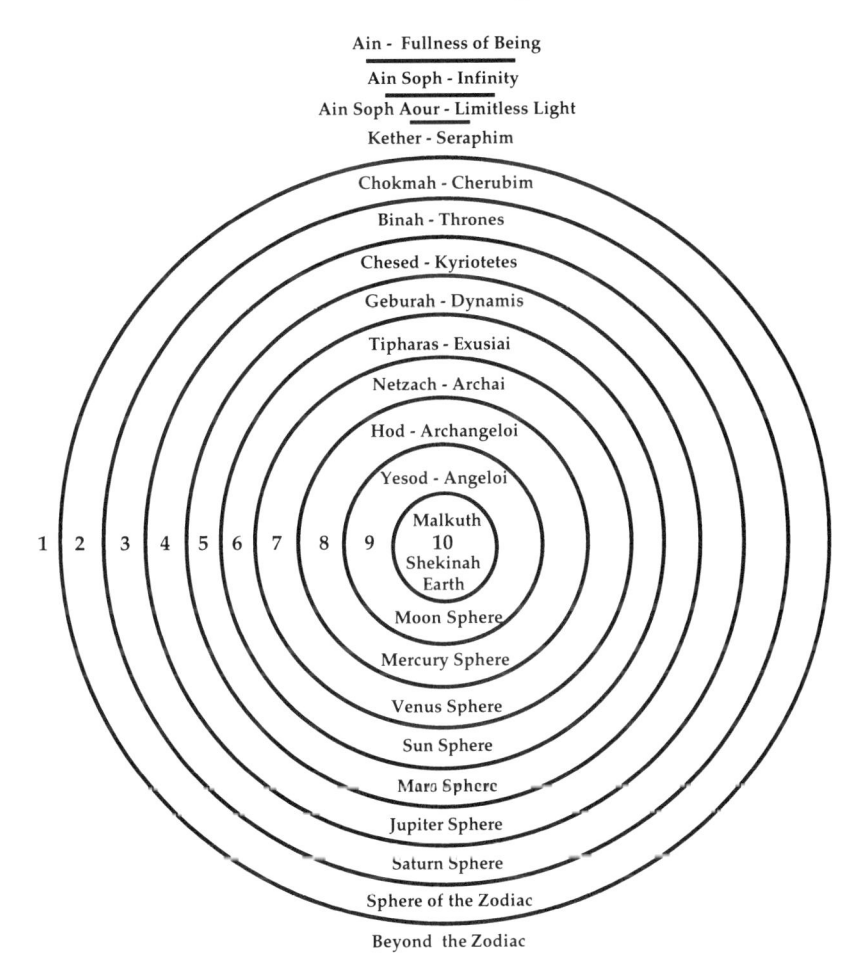

Ain - Fullness of Being
Ain Soph - Infinity
Ain Soph Aour - Limitless Light
Kether - Seraphim
Chokmah - Cherubim
Binah - Thrones
Chesed - Kyriotetes
Geburah - Dynamis
Tipharas - Exusiai
Netzach - Archai
Hod - Archangeloi
Yesod - Angeloi
Malkuth 10 Shekinah Earth
Moon Sphere
Mercury Sphere
Venus Sphere
Sun Sphere
Mars Sphere
Jupiter Sphere
Saturn Sphere
Sphere of the Zodiac
Beyond the Zodiac

1 2 3 4 5 6 7 8 9

"See, saith He, that thou make all things according to the pattern shown to you on the mountain."
Hebrews 8:5

The Hebrew Kabbalah, like various other esoteric traditions in the West, was affected by the reversal of the names of Mercury and Venus. This can be seen in the number sequence of the Tree of Life that extends from Kether "the Crown" (1), to Malkuth "the Kingdom" (10). Netzach is assigned to Venus and the number 7, which is the number after 6 the number of the Sun; therefore, Netzach would refer to the planet Mercury and the sphere of Venus. Likewise, Hod which is assigned to Mercury, by being the 8th Sefirah between the 7th and 9th, refers to the planet Venus and the sphere of Mercury.

VIII

The Two Sophias and the Seven Sacred Planets of Gnosticism

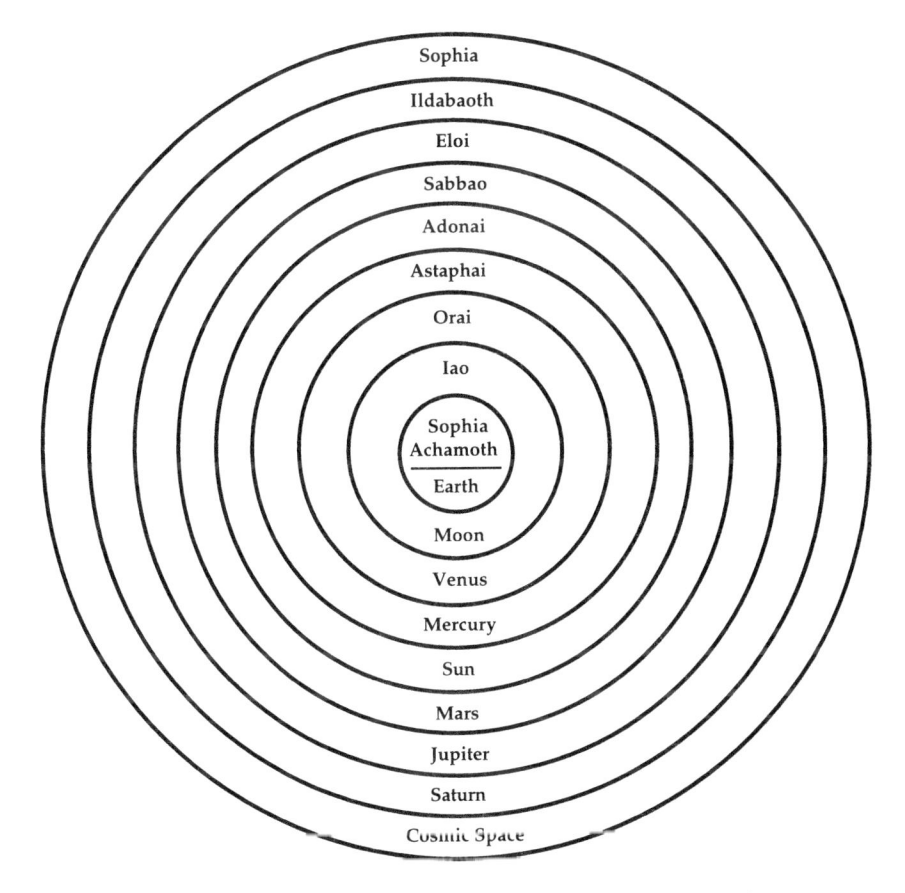

Sophia
Ildabaoth
Eloi
Sabbao
Adonai
Astaphai
Orai
Iao
Sophia Achamoth
Earth
Moon
Venus
Mercury
Sun
Mars
Jupiter
Saturn
Cosmic Space

"Jesus said. 'I tell my mysteries to those who are worthy of my mysteries.'"
The Gospel according to Thomas, verse 62

The Gnostics were teachers in the early Christian era, who attempted to understand the significance of the Christ event through the impulses that remained from the Ancient Mysteries. After a few centuries, this Gnostic wisdom gradually declined as the Angelic Beings that had inspired it, within the realm of thought, retreated into the Spiritual World. In the 8th and 9th centuries, these Angelic Beings returned to inspire the Brotherhood of the Holy Grail, although in a new way - from within the realm of feeling. This "Grail mood" of independent spiritual striving continued on into the Middle Ages, culminating with the transmission of the Grail impulse in the Grail legends. This is what is meant when the Grail stories speak of how the Holy Grail was taken by the Angels - and held for a time above the Earth - awaiting the proper time for the Grail to be returned to mankind.

IX

The Zodiac of the Lamb of God

"Ex Deo Nascimur - In Christo Morimur - Per Spiritum Sanctum Reviviscimus."
"Out of God We are Born - In Christ We Die - Through the Holy Spirit We are Resurrected."

The Father Ground of Being beyond the Zodiac

Diagram sectors (clockwise from top):

- Holy Spirit / 3rd Member of the Trinity
- Seraphim / 1st Hierarchy / Gemini / Archai's 7th Principle
- Cherubim / 2nd Hierarchy / Cancer / Archangel's 7th Principle
- Thrones / 3rd Hierarchy / Leo / Angel's 7th Principle
- Kyriotetes / 4th Hierarchy / Virgo / Spirit-Man / Man's 7th Principle
- Dynamis / 5th Hierarchy / Libra / Life-Spirit / Man's 6th Principle
- Exusiai / 6th Hierarchy / Scorpio / Spirit-Self / Man's 5th Principle
- Archai / 7th Hierarchy / Sagittarius / Ego / Man's 4th Principle
- Archangeloi / 8th Hierarchy / Capricorn / Astral-Body / Man's 3rd Principle
- Angeloi / 9th Hierarchy / Aquarius / Etheric-Body / Man's 2nd Principle
- Human / 10th Hierarchy / Pisces / the Physical Body / Man's 1st Principle
- Son / 2nd Member of the Trinity / Aries "Lamb of God" / Dynamis' 7th Principle
- Taurus / Exusiai's 7th Principle

Center: A / Ω / M / E / C / N / I / D / PSSR

"Everything that is in the great world, is in man too, for he is created out of it therefore he is the small world and his heart is his center."
Hinricus Madathanus Theosophus
(c. 1590-1638)

"... Then the King will come forth without a blemish, clean, He will stand before you. He can decorate you with his blood and renovate you."   The First Key of Basilius Valentinus

In this diagram, we find Rudolf Steiner's indications regarding the "Zodiac of the Lamb of God." This shows the hierarchies under the guidance of Christ, as they relate to the seven-fold microcosmic-human in time, and the twelve-fold macrocosmic-human in space, within the context of the Zodiac.

X

The Zodiacal Cosmic Crosses of the Holy Trinity

"Do not Christians and Heathens, Jews and Gentiles, poets and philosophers, unite in allowing the starry influences?"   Sir Walter Scott (1771-1832 A.D.)

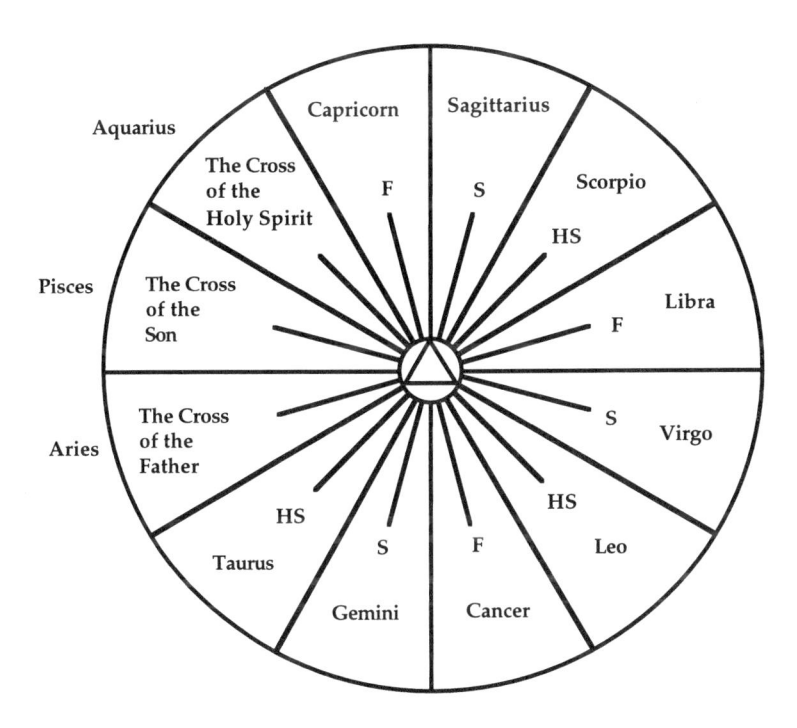

"That which is called the Christian religion existed among the ancients, and never did not exist, from the beginning of the human race until Christ came in the flesh, at which time the true religion which already existed began to be called Christianity."
St. Augustine of Hippo (354-430 A.D.)

Here we see Rudolf Steiner's indications regarding a fundamental way of relating the Zodiac to the Holy Trinity. This is useful for understanding the historical stream of time. It can be seen that in the next epoch, the 6th epoch, which will occur under the influence of the constellation of Aquarius, mankind will be brought into a more intimate relationship to the Mystery of Pentecost, or the manifestation of the divine workings of the Holy Spirit. In the preceding epoch, the 4th, which was under the influence of the constellation of Aries, mankind was primarily guided by the Abrahamic Father God impulse. In the present Piscean 5th epoch, Christ is revealed as the living manifestation of the "Word" or Logos, from within the etheric world of life.

XI

The Macrocosmic Cross of the Father

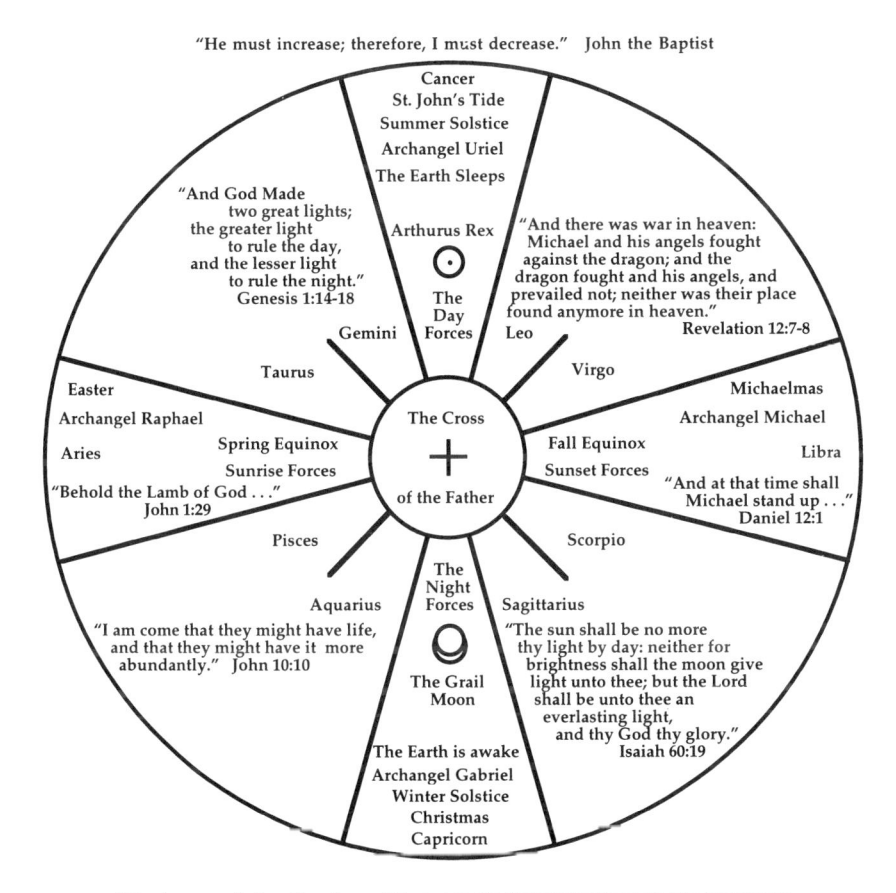

"He must increase; therefore, I must decrease." John the Baptist

```
                         Cancer
                         St. John's Tide
                         Summer Solstice
                         Archangel Uriel
                         The Earth Sleeps
    "And God Made
    two great lights;
    the greater light    Arthurus Rex    "And there was war in heaven:
    to rule the day,                      Michael and his angels fought
    and the lesser light       ☉          against the dragon; and the
    to rule the night."                   dragon fought and his angels, and
    Genesis 1:14-18       The             prevailed not; neither was their place
                          Day             found anymore in heaven."
              Gemini      Forces   Leo            Revelation 12:7-8

              Taurus                      Virgo
Easter                                                    Michaelmas
Archangel Raphael          The Cross              Archangel Michael
         Spring Equinox                Fall Equinox           Libra
Aries                         ✛                       
         Sunrise Forces                Sunset Forces      "And at that time shall
"Behold the Lamb of God..."  of the Father             Michael stand up..."
         John 1:29                                         Daniel 12:1
              Pisces                      Scorpio
                          The
                          Night
              Aquarius    Forces   Sagittarius
"I am come that they might have life,     "The sun shall be no more
and that they might have it more           thy light by day: neither for
abundantly."  John 10:10     ☾             brightness shall the moon give
                                           light unto thee; but the Lord
                          The Grail        shall be unto thee an
                          Moon             everlasting light,
                                           and thy God thy glory."
                         The Earth is awake        Isaiah 60:19
                         Archangel Gabriel
                         Winter Solstice
                         Christmas
                         Capricorn
```

"The heavens declare the glory of God, and the firmament showeth His handiwork. Day unto day uttereth speech, and night unto night showeth knowledge."
Psalms 19:1-6

In the lecture cycle entitled *The Four Seasons and the Archangels*, Rudolf Steiner gave us a path whereby we might experience the Christ Impulse working within the cycle of the seasons of the year, and the festivals of the Christian calendar. By observing the changing forces of nature during the course of the year, one's understanding of the workings of the Life-Spirit of Christ can grow through its revelation from within the etheric world of life. The Life-Spirit of Christ has a particular relationship to the constellation of the Scales of Libra in the "Zodiac of the Lamb of God", and also to the Fall festival of Michaelmas. By embracing a more Michaelic living-etheric thinking we create the proper mood of soul to facilitate the etherization of the blood. This comes about through the impulses that have entered human evolution through the Life-Spirit of Christ, and is the beginning of the Resurrection process.

XII

The Macrocosmic Cross of the Son

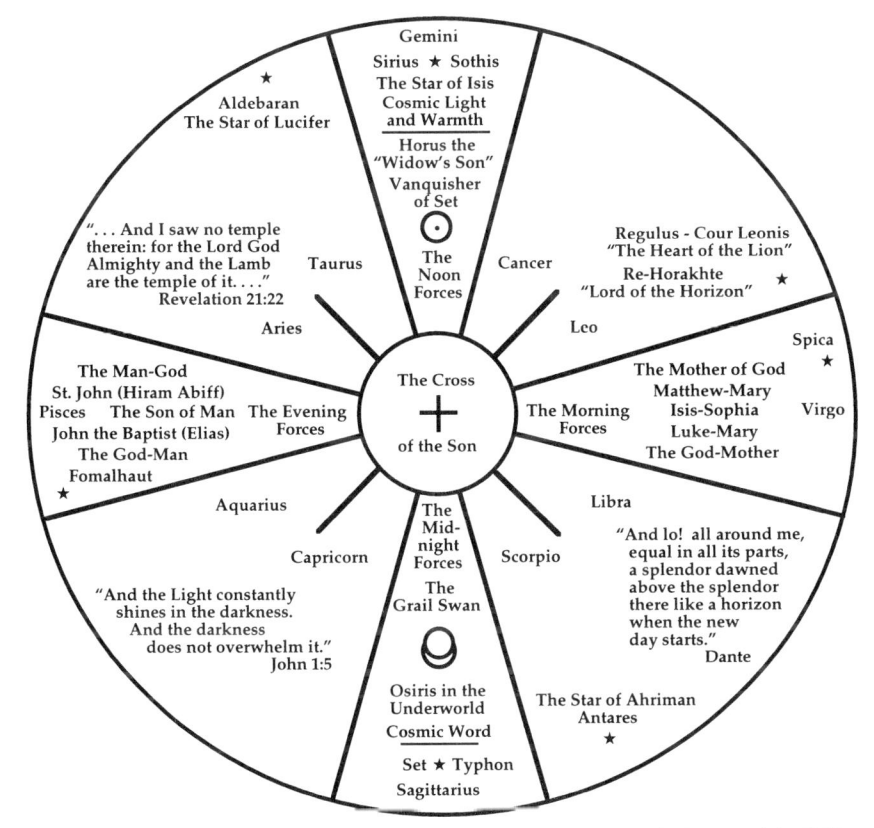

```
                        Gemini
                        Sirius ★ Sothis
              ★         The Star of Isis
         Aldebaran      Cosmic Light
    The Star of Lucifer and Warmth
                        Horus the
                        "Widow's Son"
                        Vanquisher
                        of Set
    "...And I saw no temple              Regulus - Cour Leonis
    therein: for the Lord God            "The Heart of the Lion"
    Almighty and the Lamb    Taurus  The   Cancer   Re-Horakhte
    are the temple of it...."           Noon         "Lord of the Horizon"  ★
    Revelation 21:22                    Forces
                        Aries                    Leo
                                                              Spica
    The Man-God                          The Mother of God   ★
    St. John (Hiram Abiff)               Matthew-Mary
    Pisces  The Son of Man  The Evening  The Morning  Isis-Sophia
    John the Baptist (Elias) Forces     Forces    Luke-Mary     Virgo
    The God-Man                          The God-Mother
    Fomalhaut       The Cross
    ★                of the Son
         Aquarius                     Libra
                                              "And lo! all around me,
                 Capricorn                     equal in all its parts,
                            The Mid-           a splendor dawned
    "And the Light constantly  night   Scorpio above the splendor
    shines in the darkness.   Forces           there like a horizon
    And the darkness          The              when the new
    does not overwhelm it."   Grail Swan        day starts."
    John 1:5                                           Dante

                        Osiris in the
                        Underworld     The Star of Ahriman
                        Cosmic Word    Antares
                                       ★
                        Set ★ Typhon
                        Sagittarius
```

"I am that living and fiery essence of the divine substance that glows in the beauty of the fields. I shine in the water, I burn in the sun, and the moon, and the stars." St. Hildegard of Bingen

In *Parzival* it says: "Learn to read the starry script . . ." The Knights Templars were the recipients of the star-wisdom of the East; this pure Persian-Magian stream, that understood the cosmic significance of the Christ event, had become all but lost with the suppression of the Manichaeans. It was the "Sons of the Widow", the Manichaeans, who possessed an esoteric Christian synthesis of the Ancient Mysteries, and an understanding of how Osiris (the Cosmic Word), for whom the "Widow" Isis (the human soul) mourned, was to be found in a transformed manner as Christ - the "Word made flesh." The mysteries of the "Sons of the Widow" along with the Rose Cross mysteries of Ormus, were transmitted to the Knights Templars, and to the cathedral builders, and from there to the Rosicrucians. With the exception of Chartres which was oriented North-East, the Notre Dame cathedrals were oriented towards the East, towards the morning forces of the Virgin, to whom they were dedicated, and they were laid out geographically so as to represent the stars of the constellation of Virgo. To come to an understanding of the Christ through the Isis-Sophia forces, this is what the Templars wished to do, to accomplish this they would concentrate on the experience of the Christ within, and dedicate themselves to the Virgin Mary - Mary-Sophia.

XIII

The Macrocosmic Cross of the Holy Spirit

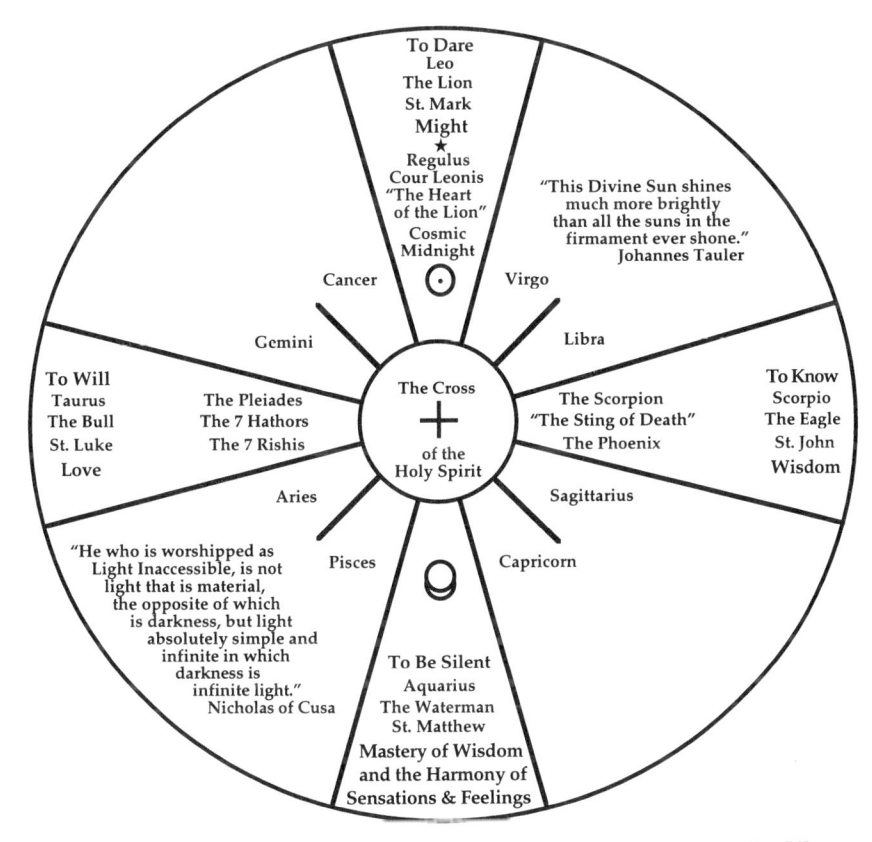

Diagram of a circular wheel divided into twelve zodiacal segments with the following text:

- **To Dare** — Leo, The Lion, St. Mark, Might ★ Regulus, Cour Leonis "The Heart of the Lion", Cosmic Midnight
- "This Divine Sun shines much more brightly than all the suns in the firmament ever shone." — Johannes Tauler
- Cancer
- Virgo
- Gemini
- Libra
- **To Will** — Taurus, The Bull, St. Luke, Love
- The Pleiades, The 7 Hathors, The 7 Rishis
- **The Cross † of the Holy Spirit**
- The Scorpion, "The Sting of Death", The Phoenix
- **To Know** — Scorpio, The Eagle, St. John, Wisdom
- Aries
- Sagittarius
- "He who is worshipped as Light Inaccessible, is not light that is material, the opposite of which is darkness, but light absolutely simple and infinite in which darkness is infinite light." — Nicholas of Cusa
- Pisces
- Capricorn
- **To Be Silent** — Aquarius, The Waterman, St. Matthew, Mastery of Wisdom and the Harmony of Sensations & Feelings

The Four Powers of the Sphinx: To Know - To Will - To Dare - To Be Silent

"The Gospel of St. John reveals to us the magnitude of the wisdom of Christ Jesus; the Gospel of Luke, the power of his love. When we study the Gospel of St. Mark, the picture will primarily be one of might, of the creative powers permeating the universe in all their glory. In that Gospel there is something overwhelming in the intensity with which the cosmic forces come to expression: when we really begin to understand the content of the Gospel of St. Mark, it is as though these forces were surging towards us from all directions of space. While the Gospel of St. Luke brings inner warmth into the soul and the Gospel of St. John fills it with hope, the Gospel of St. Mark makes us aware of the overwhelming power and splendor of the cosmic forces - so overwhelming that the soul feels wellnigh shattered. The Gospel of St. Matthew is different. All three elements are present here: the warmth of feeling and love, the knowledge full of hope and promise, the majesty of the universe. These elements are present in the Gospel of St. Matthew in a modified form, and for this reason, seem to be more humanly akin to us than in the other Gospels. Whereas the wisdom, the love and the splendor depicted in the other three Gospels might overwhelm us almost to the point of collapse, we feel able to stand erect before the picture presented in the Gospel of St. Matthew..." Rudolf Steiner 9/1/1910

XIV

The Order of the Four Gospel Initiations

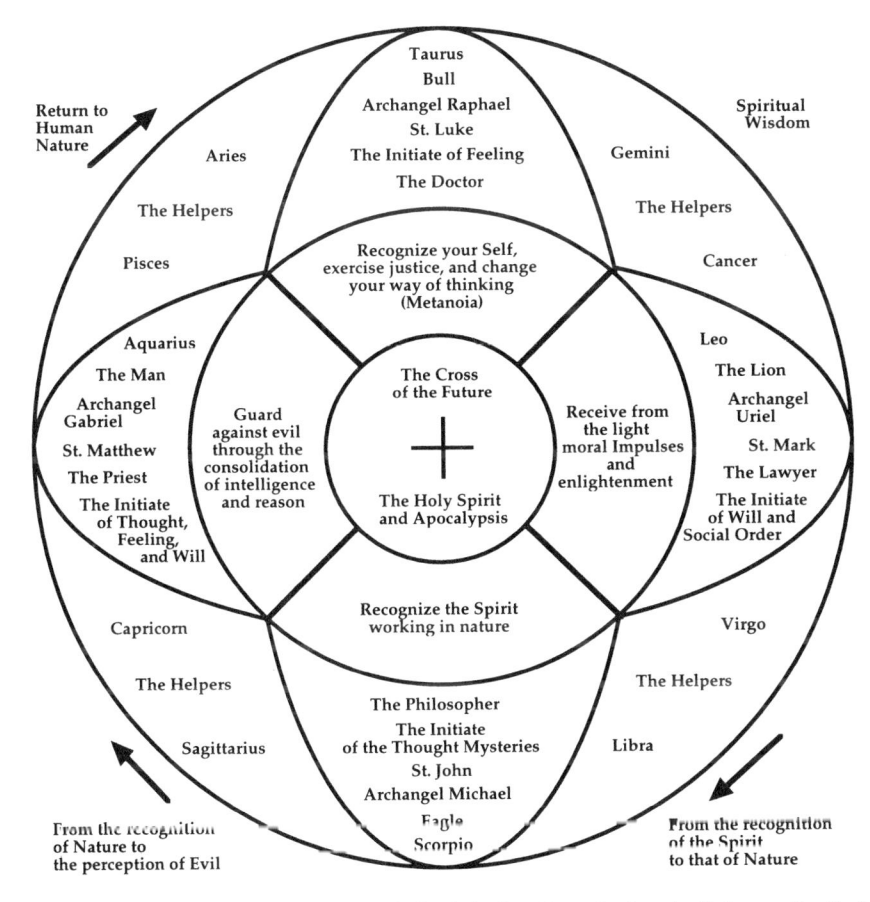

```
                          Taurus
                           Bull
   Return to         Archangel Raphael        Spiritual
   Human                St. Luke              Wisdom
   Nature     Aries  The Initiate of Feeling  Gemini
                         The Doctor
         The Helpers                      The Helpers

         Pisces    Recognize your Self,     Cancer
                 exercise justice, and change
                      your way of thinking
                         (Metanoia)

         Aquarius                             Leo
         The Man                          The Lion
         Archangel    Guard      The Cross  Receive from   Archangel
         Gabriel    against evil of the Future the light   Uriel
         St. Matthew through the            moral Impulses St. Mark
         The Priest  consolidation    +        and         The Lawyer
                    of intelligence        enlightenment
         The Initiate  and reason  The Holy Spirit         The Initiate
         of Thought,             and Apocalypsis           of Will and
         Feeling,                                          Social Order
         and Will

                          Recognize the Spirit
         Capricorn        working in nature      Virgo

              The Helpers                  The Helpers
                         The Philosopher
                         The Initiate
                   Sagittarius of the Thought Mysteries  Libra
                              St. John
                         Archangel Michael
                              Eagle
   From the recognition      Scorpio          From the recognition
   of Nature to                                of the Spirit
   the perception of Evil                      to that of Nature
```

The Order of Four, reveals the zodiacal symbols of the four Gospels given by Polycarp, the disciple of St. John. The Lion, Eagle, Bull, and Man represent the four approaches of the Gospels, and the four realms of Initiation. Esoterically as a group (together with the pairs of helpers) they represent the harmonization of the impulses of the four Cherubim who created and governed in the Sun-State. The Four Beasts in the vision of Ezekiel are the four Archangels in the Earth-State, which relate to the four seasons (time) and the four directions (space). The second ring, gives meditations for the seasons and the Archangels. In the center ring, the Cross of the Holy Spirit indicates the state which will be reached in the 6th epoch. The four beasts in the Revelation of St. John represent the challenge of future powers connected with the four realms of Initiation. The positions of the Archangels in the constellations point to the the sequence of planetary conditions, and their directions of occurrence in space: Old Saturn-Leo, Old Sun-Scorpio, Old Moon-Aquarius, Earth-Taurus (which is divided into a Mars half and a Mercury half). The Earth has passed the "Turning-Point of Time", shifting from the involutionary spiral, to the spiral of unfoldment initiated by Christ (which is why the Zodiac in some of the diagrams is reversed): Future Jupiter-Aquarius, Future Venus-Scorpio, Future Vulcan-Leo.

XV

The Seven Metals and the Seven Planets Geometrically Arranged According to their Atomic Weights

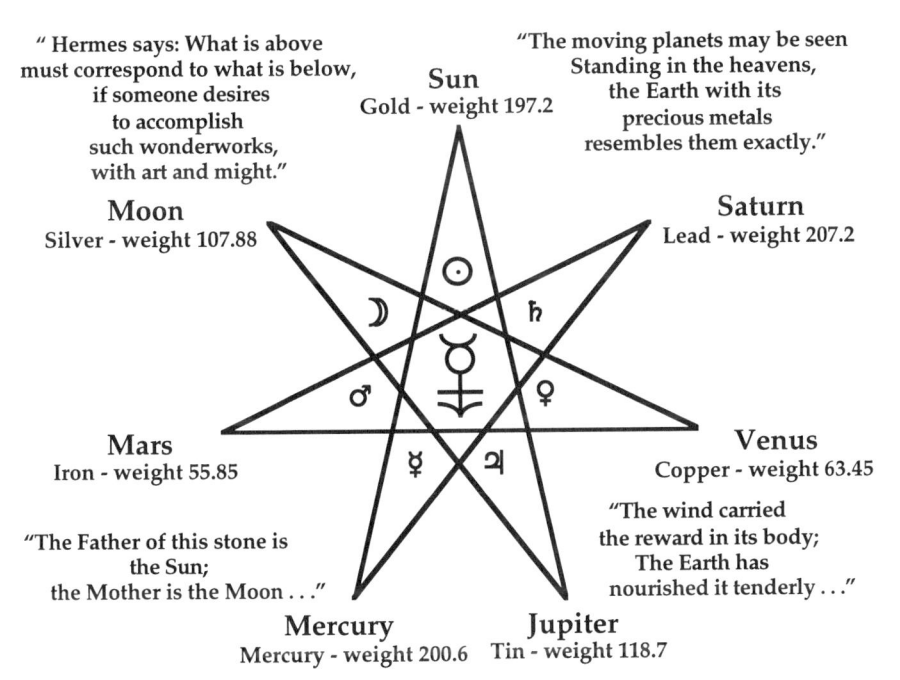

"Hermes says: What is above must correspond to what is below, if someone desires to accomplish such wonderworks, with art and might."

Sun
Gold - weight 197.2

"The moving planets may be seen Standing in the heavens, the Earth with its precious metals resembles them exactly."

Moon
Silver - weight 107.88

Saturn
Lead - weight 207.2

Mars
Iron - weight 55.85

Venus
Copper - weight 63.45

"The Father of this stone is the Sun; the Mother is the Moon..."

"The wind carried the reward in its body; The Earth has nourished it tenderly..."

Mercury
Mercury - weight 200.6

Jupiter
Tin - weight 118.7

"Here are portrayed the hidden treasures of the Earth And how the stars of the heavens are locked up deep in the mountains. The Earth contains its own planets, to which the elements give their qualities and powers. If you doubt who they are you must look closely at all metals. Heaven will help you to understand..."

"See you here nothing, then there is nothing. Why do you ask for more? In the midst of the clear light you will be stone blind..."

Quotations from: *The Pleasure Garden of Chymistry*, by Daniel Stolcius 1624, in which is contained: "The Twelve Keys of Basilius Valentinus"

The seven metals are substances that came about on Earth from the separation of the Sun, Moon and planets from the primal globe; with each metal being an expression of the essential nature of one of the "seven wanderers." As shown above, if you arrange the metals and the Sun, Moon and planets in a circle, according to the sequence of the days of the week, you will find that by connecting the metals in the sequence of their atomic weights it forms a seven-pointed star. This is a beautiful example of the musical laws of creation that are expressed through the harmonies of the "Music of the Spheres."

XVI

The Seven Planets and the Seven Organs

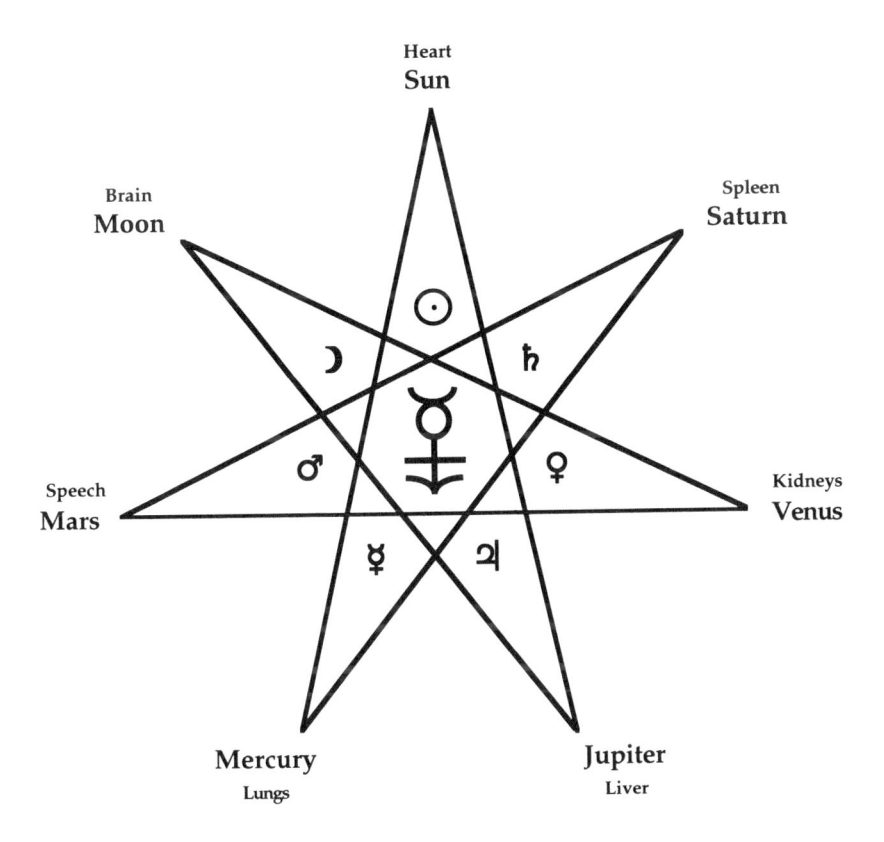

```
           Heart
            Sun

Brain                        Spleen
Moon                          Saturn



Speech                        Kidneys
Mars                           Venus



      Mercury      Jupiter
       Lungs        Liver
```

"An unfailing experience of mundane events in harmony with the changes occurring in the Heavens, has instructed and compelled my unwilling belief." Johannes Kepler (1571-1630 A.D.)

The seven organs are an expression of activities that are related to the beings of the planets. The present nature and form of the organs - is a metamorphosis of processes that are related to the separation of each of the respective planets from the primal globe - of what eventually became our present Earth. In addition to this, the organs of the human body are developed by the individual, with the help of the Spiritual Beings that are encountered during the descent through the planetary spheres before birth. This comes about through the individual's experiences, as they contract into their earthly existence, of the Sun, Moon, and planets.

XVII

The Seven Planetary Spheres and the Physiological Motions

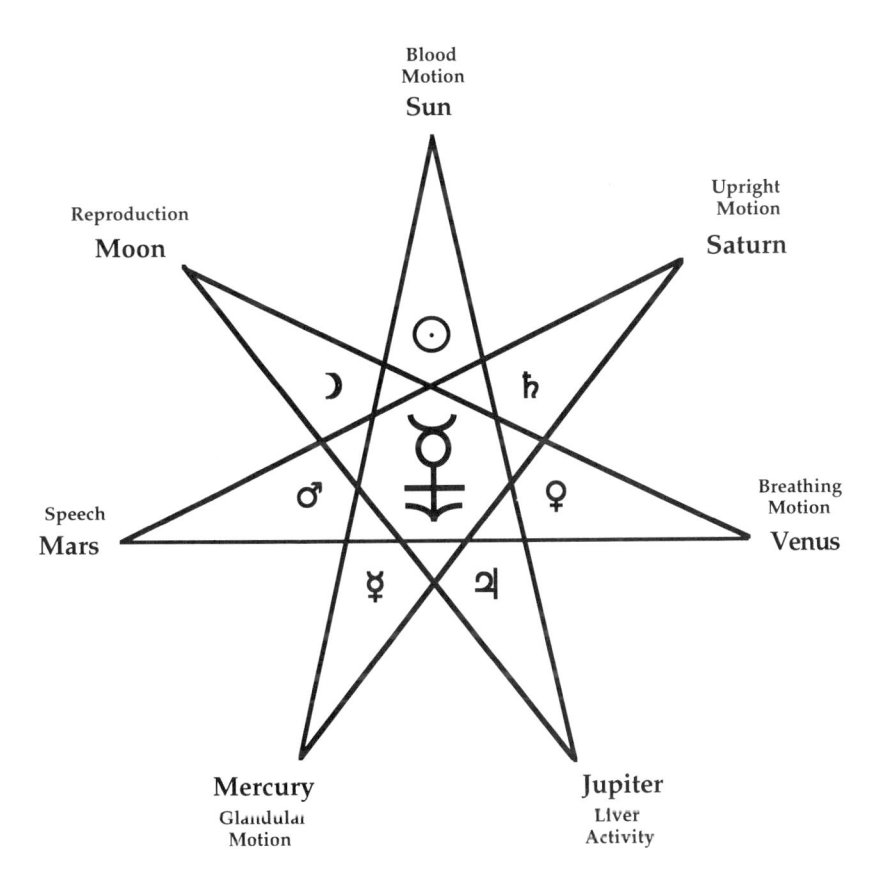

Blood
Motion
Sun

Upright
Motion
Saturn

Reproduction
Moon

Breathing
Motion
Venus

Speech
Mars

Mercury
Glandular
Motion

Jupiter
Liver
Activity

"The celestial bodies are the cause of all that takes place in the sub-lunar world."
St. Thomas Aquinas (1225-1274 A.D.)

The seven physiological motions of the human body are an expression of the activities of particular Spiritual Hierarchies, whose activities are related to the planetary spheres. The names Mercury and Venus, refer to Occult Mercury and Occult Venus, which are reversed from the current astronomical usage of these names.

XVIII

The Seven Planetary Spheres and the Seven Soul Moods

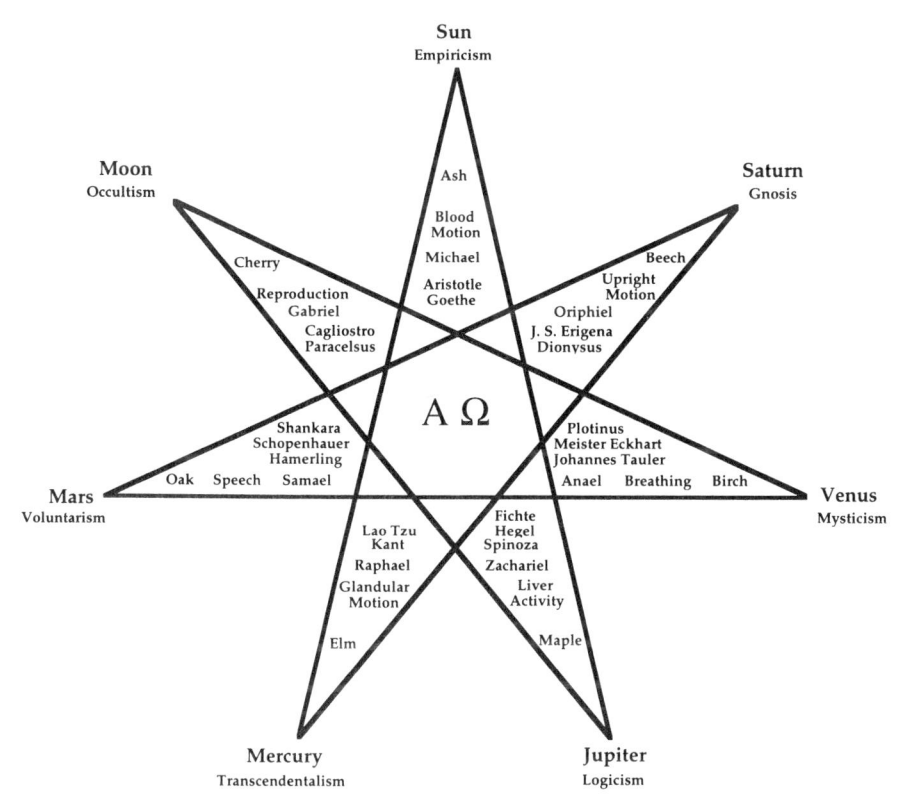

```
                        Sun
                    Empiricism

                         Ash
                         Blood
                         Motion
                    Michael          Beech
        Cherry      Aristotle   Upright
                    Goethe      Motion
   Reproduction              Oriphiel
   Gabriel       Cagliostro   J. S. Erigena
                 Paracelsus   Dionysus

                      A Ω

          Shankara              Plotinus
          Schopenhauer          Meister Eckhart
          Hamerling             Johannes Tauler
     Oak  Speech  Samael    Anael  Breathing  Birch
Mars                                              Venus
Voluntarism                                    Mysticism
                  Lao Tzu   Fichte
                  Kant      Hegel
                            Spinoza
                  Raphael   Zachariel
                  Glandular Liver
                  Motion    Activity

              Elm              Maple

            Mercury          Jupiter
       Transcendentalism     Logicism
```

Saturn - Gnosticism: "A man is a Gnostic when his disposition is such that he gets to know the things of the world not through the senses, but through certain cognitional forces in the soul itself."

Jupiter - Logicism: "The special mark of Logicism consists in its enabling the soul to connect thoughts, concepts and ideas with one another."

Mars - Voluntarism: This soul mood is described by Rudolf Steiner, to the effect that, one has the soul disposition to perceive all of reality as a manifestation of will.

Sun - Empiricism: ". . . signifies a soul mood which simply accepts whatever experience may offer."

Venus - Mysticism: ". . . the soul has become quiet and seeks inwardly for divine light."

Mercury - Transcendentalism: "When I perceive things, their nature approaches me; but I do not perceive it. It hides behind, but it approaches me . . . this world everywhere proclaims its essential being."

Moon - Occultism: "The essential nature of things is beyond the range of ordinary human knowledge . . . one must seek the inner being of things by another way than through external sense-perception and the ordinary means of cognition."

XIX

The Seven Planets and the Seven Liberal Arts

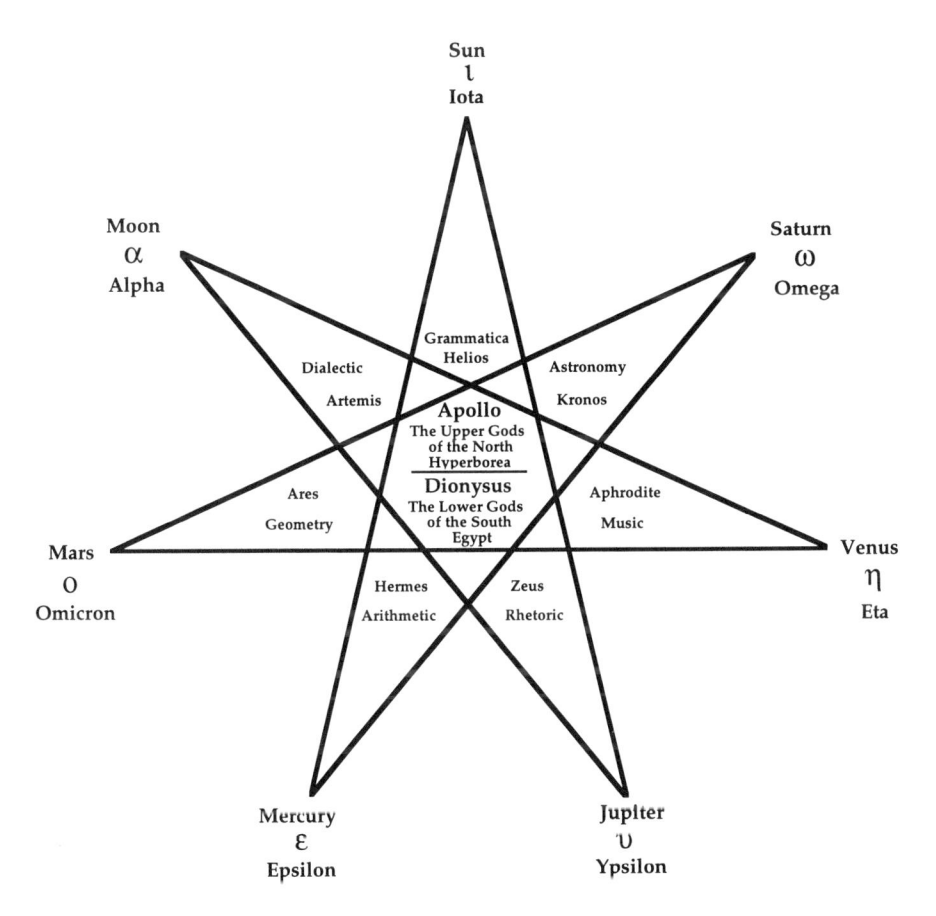

```
                    Sun
                     ι
                    Iota

    Moon                              Saturn
     α                                  ω
   Alpha                              Omega

              Grammatica
              Helios
      Dialectic        Astronomy
      Artemis          Kronos
                Apollo
                The Upper Gods
                of the North
                Hyperborea
                Dionysus
        Ares    The Lower Gods   Aphrodite
      Geometry  of the South     Music
                Egypt
  Mars ──────────────────────────────── Venus
   O                                     η
  Omicron    Hermes    Zeus             Eta
           Arithmetic  Rhetoric


         Mercury            Jupiter
            ε                  υ
         Epsilon            Ypsilon
```

"A physician without a knowledge of Astrology has no right to call himself a physician."
Hippocrates (d. 361 B.C.)

Ancient Greece was the meeting place of the Hyperborean Apollo Mysteries of the North, with the Dionysian Mysteries that were received from Egypt in the South. The Northern mysteries, were primarily concerned with the outer-mysteries of nature, and of the periphery of the Cosmos. The Southern mysteries, on the other hand, were primarily concerned with the inner-mysteries of the human body. Here you see the seven planets as they are related to the vowels, liberal arts, and Greek gods.

XX

The Three-Fold Soul Forces as they are Related to the Planets during Sleep and in the Waking State

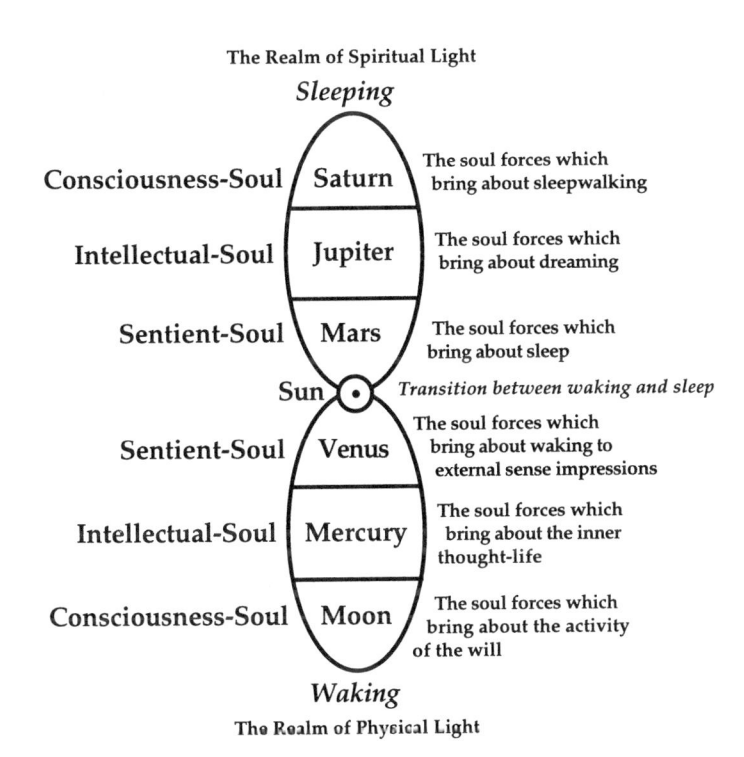

The Realm of Spiritual Light
Sleeping

Consciousness-Soul	Saturn	The soul forces which bring about sleepwalking
Intellectual-Soul	Jupiter	The soul forces which bring about dreaming
Sentient-Soul	Mars	The soul forces which bring about sleep
	Sun ⊙	*Transition between waking and sleep*
Sentient-Soul	Venus	The soul forces which bring about waking to external sense impressions
Intellectual-Soul	Mercury	The soul forces which bring about the inner thought-life
Consciousness-Soul	Moon	The soul forces which bring about the activity of the will

Waking
The Realm of Physical Light

In the lecture cycle: *Macrocosm and Microcosm*, given in Vienna during March of 1910, Rudolf Steiner explained the way in which the soul forces are active in waking, and in sleep, by relating them to the planets; however, this should be understood to mean Occult Venus and Mercury, and so, the names are reversed from those of current astronomy.

XXI

The Zodiacal Order of the 12 Senses and the 12 Philosophic Viewpoints

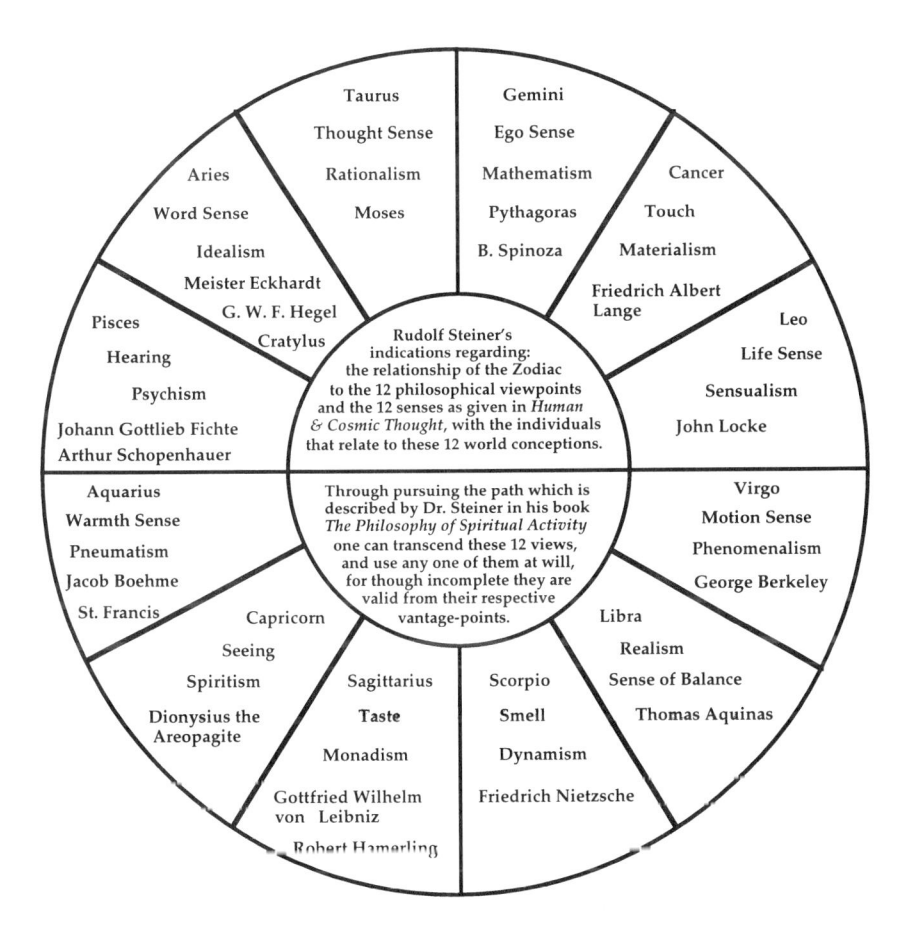

Aries — Word Sense — Idealism — Meister Eckhardt, G. W. F. Hegel, Cratylus

Taurus — Thought Sense — Rationalism — Moses

Gemini — Ego Sense — Mathematism — Pythagoras, B. Spinoza

Cancer — Touch — Materialism — Friedrich Albert Lange

Leo — Life Sense — Sensualism — John Locke

Virgo — Motion Sense — Phenomenalism — George Berkeley

Libra — Sense of Balance — Realism — Thomas Aquinas

Scorpio — Smell — Dynamism — Friedrich Nietzsche

Sagittarius — Taste — Monadism — Gottfried Wilhelm von Leibniz, Robert Hamerling

Capricorn — Seeing — Spiritism — Dionysius the Areopagite

Aquarius — Warmth Sense — Pneumatism — Jacob Boehme, St. Francis

Pisces — Hearing — Psychism — Johann Gottlieb Fichte, Arthur Schopenhauer

Rudolf Steiner's indications regarding: the relationship of the Zodiac to the 12 philosophical viewpoints and the 12 senses as given in *Human & Cosmic Thought*, with the individuals that relate to these 12 world conceptions.

Through pursuing the path which is described by Dr. Steiner in his book *The Philosophy of Spiritual Activity* one can transcend these 12 views, and use any one of them at will, for though incomplete they are valid from their respective vantage-points.

"Anthroposophy is the philosophy of love. Anyone who sees it as one view of the world among many knows nothing of its true nature. Like love it is all-embracing. It results from reading in the stars and it subsumes all possible conceptions of the world of which each legitimate one is accorded its sphere of influence. Thus the fixed stars will themselves bring us the wisdom which has passed through love. Essentially, there are twelve philosophies. Any others are intermediate stages as the compass has only a specific number of designated points in space because the others are found between them. Together, twelve ways of looking at the world provide a comprehensive view. Each is an individual perspective. Each is legitimate but also incomplete and needs to be supplemented by the others. They represent twelve stages of selflessness, twelve philosophies. . . The final highest stage is the sense which perceives another 'I'. This intuitive cognition allows us to look back at our own being as if it were a number, to embrace the other lovingly." Walter Johannes Stein

XXII

The Aristotelian Categories and the Zodiacal Order of the 12 Senses and the 12 Philosophic Viewpoints

Taurus
Thought Sense
Rationalism
Action

Gemini
Ego Sense
Mathematism
Relationship

Aries
Word Sense
Idealism
Quality

Cancer
Touch
Materialism
Space

Pisces
Hearing
Psychism
Suffering

Leo
Life Sense
Sensualism
Time

Aquarius
Warmth Sense
Pneumatism
Behavior / Attitude

Virgo
Motion Sense
Phenomenalism
Appearance

Capricorn
Seeing
Spiritism
Position

Libra
Sense of Balance
Realism
Being

Sagittarius
Taste
Monadism
Quantity

Scorpio
Smell
Dynamism
Creative / Substance

Here in Italics I have included Rudolf Steiner's indications regarding one way of relating the *Aristotelian Categories* to the 12 zodiacal constellations, the 12 fundamental philosophical viewpoints, and the 12 senses.

The Principles as seen by Aristotle and Rudolf Steiner, according to Heinz H. Schoeffler, M.D., can be seen on the bottom-left; on the bottom-right is the dichotomy, or two aspects of the Spirit or Nous

Aristotle

Dianoetikon
Kinetikon
Orektikon
Aisthetikon
Threptike - Psyche Phytike
Soma

Rudolf Steiner

Consciousness-Soul
Intellectual-Soul
Sentient-Soul
Sentient-Body
Etheric-Body
Physical-Body

Aristotle's Dichotomy of Spirit

Nous Poietikos - Active Formative Spirit
Apathes - Incapable of Suffering
Aparthos - Incorruptable and Immortal
Nous Pathetikos - Passive Moldable Spirit
Suffering Intellect
Phthartos - Impermanent

XXIII

Another Perspective on the Zodiacal Order of the 12 Senses and the 12 Philosophic Viewpoints

Taurus
Warmth Sense
Rationalism
Imagination Influenced by Soul
Forward-Backward

Gemini
Hearing
Mathematism
Symmetry Inspiration
Music
Gift of the Cherubim

Aries
Seeing
Idealism
Imagination Poetry Inspired by Thrones

Cancer
Word Sense
Materialism
Inspiration Influenced by Inner Experience

Pisces
Taste
Psychism
Imagination Influenced by Matter

Leo
Thought Sense
Sensualism
Intuition
Painting Inspired by Seraphim

Ehrenfried Pfeiffer's indications regarding another way of looking at the relationship of the Zodiac to the 12 philosophical viewpoints and the 12 senses.

Aquarius
Smell
Pneumatism
Mystical Union with God

Virgo
Ego Sense
Phenomenalism
Intuition Influenced by Being

Capricorn
Sense of Balance
Spiritism
Inner Calm
Feeling oneself as a Spiritual Being
Dance Inspired by the Dynamis

Libra
Touch
Realism
Penetration by the Feeling of God

Sagittarius
Motion Sense
Monadism
The Sensation of one's own Free Soul
Mimic Art Inspired by Archangels

Scorpio
Life Sense
Dynamism
Satisfaction
Sculpture Inspired by Archai

Thinking is a spiritual process which is inspired by the beings of the spiritual world. How we think determines what beings are working behind the scenes. At the present stage of evolution, the Angels "... form pictures in man's Astral-Body under the guidance of the the Spirits of Form (Exusiai, or Elohim)." This is revealed in the ability to imagine a geometric form with the mind's eye; if we introduce movement into this form (for example, through having it rotate, or metamorphose into other geometric forms) then we involve beings higher than the Spirits of Form - we involve the Dynamis, the Spirits of Movement. The inability to imagine moving forms is the fruit of crystallized thinking, this crystallization can also be present within the realm of concepts. To overcome this we should strive to understand the way others think, as if it were our own, then we are moving towards Intuition, and a free Christ-filled Michaelic thinking. Rudolf Steiner elsewhere gives yet another 12 fold scheme different from the two shown in this book. If one wishes to understand Spiritual Science, then flexibility of thought is required, so as to develop - a truly living thinking.

XXIV

The Temple of Man and the Seven Cultural Epochs

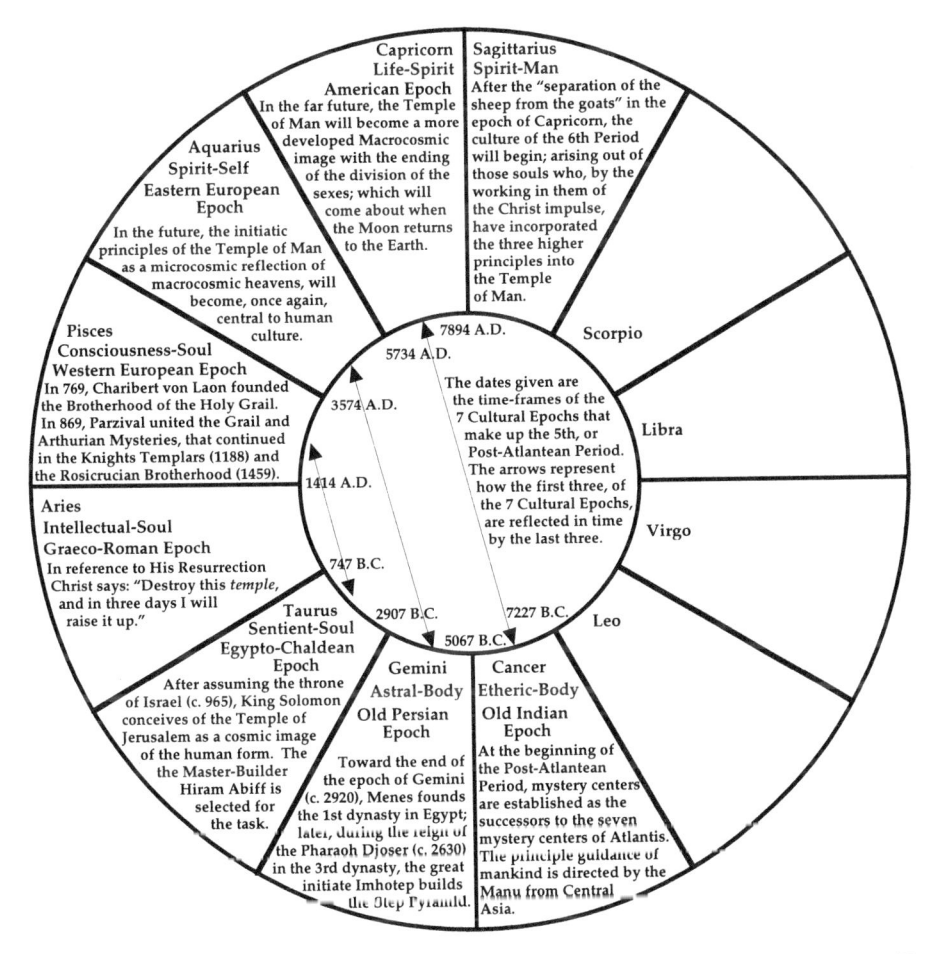

Capricorn / Life-Spirit / American Epoch
In the far future, the Temple of Man will become a more developed Macrocosmic image with the ending of the division of the sexes; which will come about when the Moon returns to the Earth.

Sagittarius / Spirit-Man
After the "separation of the sheep from the goats" in the epoch of Capricorn, the culture of the 6th Period will begin; arising out of those souls who, by the working in them of the Christ impulse, have incorporated the three higher principles into the Temple of Man.

Aquarius / Spirit-Self / Eastern European Epoch
In the future, the initiatic principles of the Temple of Man as a microcosmic reflection of macrocosmic heavens, will become, once again, central to human culture.

Pisces / Consciousness-Soul / Western European Epoch
In 769, Charibert von Laon founded the Brotherhood of the Holy Grail. In 869, Parzival united the Grail and Arthurian Mysteries, that continued in the Knights Templars (1188) and the Rosicrucian Brotherhood (1459).

Aries / Intellectual-Soul / Graeco-Roman Epoch
In reference to His Resurrection Christ says: "Destroy this *temple*, and in three days I will raise it up."

Taurus / Sentient-Soul / Egypto-Chaldean Epoch
After assuming the throne of Israel (c. 965), King Solomon conceives of the Temple of Jerusalem as a cosmic image of the human form. The Master-Builder Hiram Abiff is selected for the task.

Gemini / Astral-Body / Old Persian Epoch
Toward the end of the epoch of Gemini (c. 2920), Menes founds the 1st dynasty in Egypt; later, during the reign of the Pharaoh Djoser (c. 2630) in the 3rd dynasty, the great initiate Imhotep builds the Step Pyramid.

Cancer / Etheric-Body / Old Indian Epoch
At the beginning of the Post-Atlantean Period, mystery centers are established as the successors to the seven mystery centers of Atlantis. The principle guidance of mankind is directed by the Manu from Central Asia.

The dates given are the time-frames of the 7 Cultural Epochs that make up the 5th, or Post-Atlantean Period. The arrows represent how the first three, of the 7 Cultural Epochs, are reflected in time by the last three.

7894 A.D.
5734 A.D.
3574 A.D.
1414 A.D.
747 B.C.
2907 B.C.
5067 B.C.
7227 B.C.

Scorpio
Libra
Virgo
Leo

The central task of human evolution is to foster the development of the human form as a worthy dwelling-place for the "I Am" or True-Ego. In the words of St. Paul; ". . . ye are the temple of the living God . . ." II Corinthians (6:16). This work of the building of the "Temple of Man" has been under the guidance of the "Masters of Wisdom and of the Harmony of Sensations and Feelings" throughout human history. For the last two millennia, this task has been directed secretly from behind the scenes. In the not too distant future, this work concerning the "Temple of Man" will be directed openly - when mankind evolves to the point where they recognize that the Esoteric-Christian mysteries of initiation are the central guiding impulse of humanity. This secret wisdom of the "Temple of Man" was safeguarded by the Knights Templars and the builders of the Gothic cathedrals in the Middle Ages; from there it passed on to the Rosicrucians. With the coming of the Michaelic age in 1879, this wisdom could now be freely given to the world by Rudolf Steiner from the modern "Temple of Man" - the Goetheanum.

XXV

The Sun Mystery and the Seven Cultural Epochs

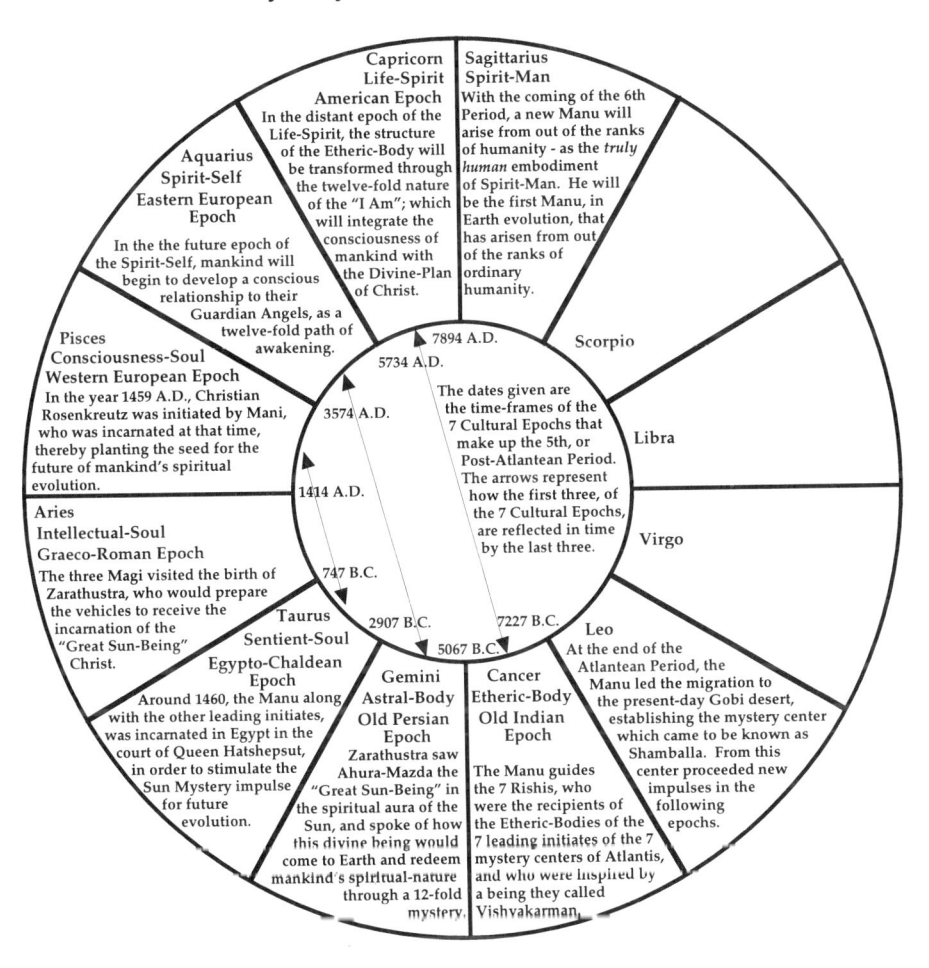

Capricorn / Life-Spirit / American Epoch
In the distant epoch of the Life-Spirit, the structure of the Etheric-Body will be transformed through the twelve-fold nature of the "I Am"; which will integrate the consciousness of mankind with the Divine-Plan of Christ.

Sagittarius / Spirit-Man
With the coming of the 6th Period, a new Manu will arise from out of the ranks of humanity - as the *truly human* embodiment of Spirit-Man. He will be the first Manu, in Earth evolution, that has arisen from out of the ranks of ordinary humanity.

Aquarius / Spirit-Self / Eastern European Epoch
In the the future epoch of the Spirit-Self, mankind will begin to develop a conscious relationship to their Guardian Angels, as a twelve-fold path of awakening.

Pisces / Consciousness-Soul / Western European Epoch
In the year 1459 A.D., Christian Rosenkreutz was initiated by Mani, who was incarnated at that time, thereby planting the seed for the future of mankind's spiritual evolution.

Aries / Intellectual-Soul / Graeco-Roman Epoch
The three Magi visited the birth of Zarathustra, who would prepare the vehicles to receive the incarnation of the "Great Sun-Being" Christ.

Taurus / Sentient-Soul / Egypto-Chaldean Epoch
Around 1460, the Manu along with the other leading initiates, was incarnated in Egypt in the court of Queen Hatshepsut, in order to stimulate the Sun Mystery impulse for future evolution.

Gemini / Astral-Body / Old Persian Epoch
Zarathustra saw Ahura-Mazda the "Great Sun-Being" in the spiritual aura of the Sun, and spoke of how this divine being would come to Earth and redeem mankind's spiritual-nature through a 12-fold mystery.

Cancer / Etheric-Body / Old Indian Epoch
The Manu guides the 7 Rishis, who were the recipients of the Etheric-Bodies of the 7 leading initiates of Atlantis, and who were inspired by a being they called Vishvakarman.

Leo
At the end of the Atlantean Period, the Manu led the migration to the present-day Gobi desert, establishing the mystery center which came to be known as Shamballa. From this center proceeded new impulses in the following epochs.

Scorpio

Libra

Virgo

Dates in circle: 7894 A.D., 5734 A.D., 3574 A.D., 1414 A.D., 747 B.C., 2907 B.C., 5067 B.C., 7227 B.C.

The dates given are the time-frames of the 7 Cultural Epochs that make up the 5th, or Post-Atlantean Period. The arrows represent how the first three, of the 7 Cultural Epochs, are reflected in time by the last three.

The Sun mystery center was the central mystery center in ancient Atlantis, and was under the direction of the Manu. This Sun mystery center maintained an exalted form of wisdom which included the content of the other planetary mystery centers. Near the end of the Atlantean Period, Manu-Noah directed the migration to Central Asia in order to found a civilization center. From this civilization center, which came to be known as Shamballa, proceeded impulses during the succeeding post-Atlantean epochs which contributed to the further development of humanity according to the intentions of the Divine Plan of Christ. The brotherhood that developed through Shamballa (which has since retreated from the physical world) is known as the "Mother Lodge of Humanity." The great "Leaders of Mankind", which brought about the leading impulses of the post-Atlantean epochs, were incarnations of emissaries of this "Mother Lodge of Humanity." It was these "Leaders of Mankind" that prepared humanity for the incarnation of the "Great Sun-Being" Christ.

XXVI

The Spiritual Hierarchies and the Seven Cultural Epochs

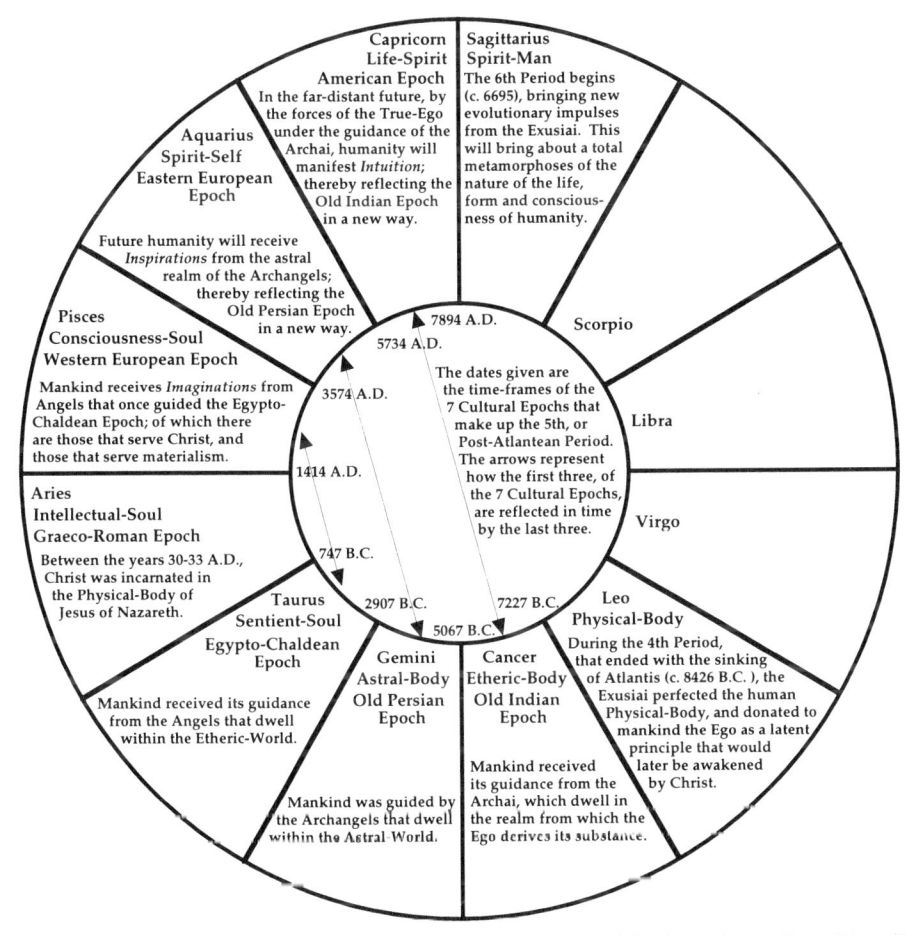

Capricorn
Life-Spirit
American Epoch
In the far-distant future, by the forces of the True-Ego under the guidance of the Archai, humanity will manifest *Intuition*; thereby reflecting the Old Indian Epoch in a new way.

Sagittarius
Spirit-Man
The 6th Period begins (c. 6695), bringing new evolutionary impulses from the Exusiai. This will bring about a total metamorphoses of the nature of the life, form and consciousness of humanity.

Aquarius
Spirit-Self
Eastern European Epoch
Future humanity will receive *Inspirations* from the astral realm of the Archangels; thereby reflecting the Old Persian Epoch in a new way.

Pisces
Consciousness-Soul
Western European Epoch
Mankind receives *Imaginations* from Angels that once guided the Egypto-Chaldean Epoch; of which there are those that serve Christ, and those that serve materialism.

Aries
Intellectual-Soul
Graeco-Roman Epoch
Between the years 30-33 A.D., Christ was incarnated in the Physical-Body of Jesus of Nazareth.

Taurus
Sentient-Soul
Egypto-Chaldean Epoch
Mankind received its guidance from the Angels that dwell within the Etheric-World.

Gemini
Astral-Body
Old Persian Epoch
Mankind was guided by the Archangels that dwell within the Astral-World.

Cancer
Etheric-Body
Old Indian Epoch
Mankind received its guidance from the Archai, which dwell in the realm from which the Ego derives its substance.

Leo
Physical-Body
During the 4th Period, that ended with the sinking of Atlantis (c. 8426 B.C.), the Exusiai perfected the human Physical-Body, and donated to mankind the Ego as a latent principle that would later be awakened by Christ.

Virgo

Libra

Scorpio

Dates within circle: 7894 A.D., 5734 A.D., 3574 A.D., 1414 A.D., 747 B.C., 2907 B.C., 5067 B.C., 7227 B.C.

The dates given are the time-frames of the 7 Cultural Epochs that make up the 5th, or Post-Atlantean Period. The arrows represent how the first three, of the 7 Cultural Epochs, are reflected in time by the last three.

Throughout the course of human evolution, mankind has been nurtured by the various orders of Angelical Hierarchies. As to which stage of the Angelical Hierarchies have played the central role in the developing consciousness of mankind, this has changed in each of the post-Atlantean epochs. Beginning with the inspiration of the Archai in the Old Indian Epoch, the spiritual guidance of mankind descended through the orders of Angelical Hierarchies until, in the Graeco-Roman Epoch, mankind received their guidance primarily from the human realm. It was in this epoch of human guidance that Christ "the Great Sun-Being" - "the leader of all of the Angelical Hierarchies" - incarnated in human form for around three years in the prepared vehicles of Jesus of Nazareth, culminating in the "Mystery of Golgotha" at the "Turning-Point of Time." As a result of this intervention by Christ in human evolution, mankind will experience progressively higher levels of consciousness, which will come about through the development of the human-spiritual principles that correspond to the levels of being where these various orders of Angelical Hierarchies dwell.

Part 6

Appendix:

From the history lecture of the Rose-Croix Degree,
the 18° of the Ancient and 96° Rite of Memphis
as presented by,
John Yarker 97°, Grand Hierophant, Hon. Member of Egypt
1833-1913 A.D.

"Now I must mention the various branches of Freemasonry and their tendencies, even if I am only to indicate something briefly. First of all, it is to be borne in mind that the whole of the masonic higher degrees trace back to a personality often spoken about but equally very much misunderstood. He was particularly misunderstood by nineteenth century historians, who have no idea of the difficult situations an occultist can meet in life. This personality is the ill-famed and little understood [disciple of the Count St. Germain] Cagliostro. The so-called Count Cagliostro, in whom an individuality concealed itself which was recognized in its true nature only by the highest initiates ..."

Rudolf Steiner 12/16/1904

"I have now to inform you, my brethren, that the Order of the Rose-Croix is of the highest antiquity, and has a double origin assigned to it, the one historic and the other philosophic. It was founded by Ormus, who was a Serapian Priest at Memphis [in Egypt], and a friend of the Christian Apostles. Converted by St. Mark in the year 46, he reformed the doctrines and ceremonies of the Egyptians by the recognition of the law of the Apostles. His disciples united with the Essenes, who had founded Lodges or Schools of Solomonic science, and traveled from the East to propagate their secret doctrines in the West, where they instructed their pupils in the mysteries of religion and philosophy. The Society, thus became divided into two sects, or orders, known as conservators of the Mosaic secrets, and conservators of the Hermetic secrets, or the doctrines of the Egyptian Thoth [Hermes]. The Rosicrucians of the twelfth century were Hermetic philosophers, who derived from an anterior association which came from the East, with the mission of propagating the secret sciences in the West. Three of them founded in Britain a philosophical seminary, where they taught the sublime sciences. Of these some joined the Crusaders to fight in Palestine, side by side, with those valiant Maccabees, and because known as Knights of Palestine and Knights of the Rose-Croix, forming themselves into armed associations for the protection of pilgrims who visited the Holy City; there they cultivated our mysteries and entrusted them to Garimont, Patriarch of Jerusalem, and Hugh de Payens in the year 1118.

In Germany, it is related that one Christian Rosy Cross was born in 1387, and making a voyage to the Holy Land he had at Damascus some conferences with wise Chaldeans from whom he learned the occult sciences; after which he perfected himself in the Lodges of Egypt, Libya and Constantinople. Returning to Germany, he established an order, of which the substance descended to the Freemasons of Britain and Germany by different channels.

The Rosicrucian branch of the Masonic tree consisted primarily of three classes; and promotion from one class to another was only accorded to merit. Candidates for the first class were required to possess a veritable knowledge and approved morality, and to have rendered services to humanity.

The aim of the sublime institution was to place enlightened men under shelter from vulgar error during their philosophical studies, and to inspire them with strong desires for their moral perfection, for benevolence, love of labour, and the practice of all those virtues which give to man, delicate and generous sentiments and the love of humanity. The Neophyte was admitted to the second class when he possessed that happy disposition which warms the soul with enthusiasm; a true Knight in defense of the weak and oppressed, and comprehending that ardent philosophy which has produced those revered men, whose passage on earth was marked by great benefits. The entry into the third class was accorded only to those few, who, to wisdom of spirit, added morality of heart, nobility of soul, constancy and firmness of character, which are virtues worthy of heaven and the love and admiration of the brethren..."

✡ Egyptian Rite of Memphis ✡

✮ Rose-Croix Ode No. 1 ✮

"Darkest shades of night dispelling,
Light effulgent fills the mind;
Holy love within us dwelling,
Boundless love for all mankind."

†

✠ I.N.R.I. ✠

In light of the preceding excerpt, from the Rose-Croix degree of the Egyptian Rite of Memphis, it is perhaps appropriate to comment upon its substance as it has such a key relationship to our present exposition. The above mentioned individuals, Garimont, Patriarch of Jerusalem and Hugh de Payens, the first Grand Master of the Knights Templars, are said to have received the secrets of the Egyptian Ormus stream along with other mysteries in Jerusalem in 1118; this, in turn, led to the foundation of the Knights Templars as a repository for this *Disciplina Arcani*, and the establishment of Jerusalem as a center from which would radiate the revivifying forces of Esoteric Christianity. The Patriarch Garimont, that is mentioned above, refers to none other than Gormond of Picquigny, a Picardy priest who rose out of obscurity, and whose election to the Patriarchate was successfully supported by Baldwin II a month after his coronation as king of Jerusalem in 1118. Elsewhere, we find more information concerning the foundation of the Knights Templars in the "Instructions of the Chevalier d'Orient" wherein is said (for a more complete quotation see above, pg. 65):

> *Eighty-one Masons under the leadership of Garimonts, the Patriarch of Jerusalem, went in the year 1150, to Europe and betook themselves to the Bishop of Upsala who received them in very friendly fashion and was consequently initiated into the mysteries of the Copts which the Masons had brought with them; later he was entrusted with the deposit of the collection of those teachings, rites and mysteries. The Bishop took pains to enclose and conceal them in the subterranean vault of the tower of the "Four Crowns" which at that time, was the crown treasure chamber of the King of Sweden. Nine of these Masons, amongst them Hugo de Paganis [Payens], founded in Europe the Order of the Knights Templars; later on they received from the Bishop the dogmas, mysteries and teachings of the Coptic Priests, confided to him. . .*

This quotation demonstrates the tenuous state of the historical details passed on through the centuries within the various systems of Masonry and the chivalric orders. For in the above excerpt, "Garimonts, the Patriarch of Jerusalem" is credited with leading "eighty-one Masons" to Upsala Sweden in the year 1150. When in fact the Patriarch Gormond died in 1128, and furthermore, Hugh de Payens died on May 24th 1136. Could it be the record gives the wrong date, or involves the wrong characters; or, as in the eyes of so many modern scholars, that it serves as evidence that it never happened? This leads us to a very puzzling end for our quest - which only leaves us with many unanswered questions. For if one examines the sources of the esoteric stream one finds that, for the most part, they are fabulous legendary accounts involving events that are difficult to treat in a purely historical manner. One may see from this that, like the life of Christ, it is difficult to prove from other written sources that these historical events ever actually occurred - or even if many of these individuals ever lived; i.e., Hermes, Moses, King Solomon, Hiram Abiff, Ormus, Fleur and Blanchfleur, Parzival, King Arthur, Prester John, the "Child of Montsegur", Christian Rosenkreutz, Comte St. Germain, among others - for the list goes on and on. It is if they were events that were "concealed from the eyes of the profane" so as to pass unnoticed until someone would come along with the ability to set the record straight from the primary source of all knowledge of human history - the Akashic Records. It is a tremendous gift that has been given to mankind through the works of Rudolf Steiner - a gift that allows the understanding of the drama of human history to unfold through the revelations of the Akashic Records that were received directly under the inspiration of the Living Christ by Rudolf Steiner, under the guidance of the "Masters of Wisdom and of the Harmonization of Sensations and Feelings."

Yes Rudolf Steiner has given us many pieces to the puzzle of our destiny; and yet, as far as many details are concerned, many pieces remain to be discovered. And so, in closing, I must end upon a note which was struck previously in reference to the Fool arcanum - at the beginning of our journey. For it must remain for future generations of "Noble Travelers" to continue this spiritual quest - the answers to which will only be vouchsafed to them if they do not forget to ask the healing Grail question: "Whom does the Grail serve?" - when they arrive at the "Castle of the Grail."